Handbook of Forensic Mental Health

Edited by

**Keith Soothill, Paul Rogers
and Mairead Dolan**

Routledge
Taylor & Francis Group

LONDON AND NEW YORK

First Published in 2008 by Willan Publishing

This edition published in 2012 by Routledge
2 Park Square, Milton Park, Abingdon, Oxon, OX14 4RN
711 Third Avenue, New York, NY 10017

Routledge is an imprint of the Taylor & Francis Group, an informa business

First published 2008

ISBN 978-1-84392-262-9 hardback
      978-1-84392-261-2 paperback

British Library Cataloguing-in-Publication Data

A catalogue record for this book is available from the British Library

Project managed by Deer Park Productions, Tavistock, Devon
Typeset by Pantek Arts Ltd, Maidstone, Kent

Contents

Part 1: Setting the Scene – The Administrative and Social Framework

Part 2: Understanding the Forensic Mental Health Process and Systems

Part 4: Skills for Forensic Mental Health Practitioners

List of figures and tables

Figures

Tables

List of abbreviations

ABCS	Abel and Becker Cognition Scale
AC	approved clinician
ACCT	Assessment, Care in Custody and Teamwork
ACF	Assessment and Classification of Function
ACR	automatic conditional release
ADHD	attention deficit hyperactivity disorder
AMHP	approved mental health professional
APA	American Psychiatric Association
APD/ASPD	antisocial personality disorder
ASBO	antisocial behaviour order
ASMRO	Addressing Substance Misuse Related Offending (alcohol and drugs programme)
ASW	approved social worker
AUR	automatic unconditional release
BMA	British Medical Association
BME	black and minority ethnicity
BPRS	Brief Psychiatric Rating Scale
CALM	Controlling Anger and Learning to Manage it (anger management programme)
CAMHS	Child and Adolescent Mental Health Services
CAST-MR	Competence Assessment to Stand Trial – Mental Retardation
CBT	cognitive-behavioural therapy
CCTV	closed-circuit television
CD	conduct disorder
CDSR	Cochrane Database of Systematic Reviews
CDVP	Community Domestic Violence Programme
CFMHT	community forensic mental health team
CI	co-investigator
CJA	Criminal Justice Act
CJS	criminal justice system

CMHT	community mental health team
CPA	Care Programme Approach
CPS	Crown Prosecution Service
CRD	NHS Centre for Reviews and Dissemination
CSC	Cognitive Self Change Programme
CSIP	Care Services Improvement Partnership
CTO	compulsory treatment order
CV	curriculum vitae
DARE	Database of Abstracts of Reviews of Effectiveness
DBT	dialectical behaviour therapy
DCR	discretionary conditional release
DfES	Department for Education and Skills
DoH	Department of Health
DPSPD	dangerous people with severe personality disorder
DRAMS	Dynamic Risk Assessment and Management System
DRR	drug rehabilitation requirement
DSM	Diagnostic and Statistical Manual of Mental Disorder
DSPD	dangerous and severe personality disorder
ECHR	European Convention on Human Rights
ECT	electro-convulsive therapy
EPP	extended sentence for public protection
EPS	Emotional Problem Scale
FACTS	Forensic Adolescent Consultation and Treatment Service
FMH	forensic mental health
GAM	General Aggression Model
GAP	Group for the Advancement of Psychiatry
GEE	Generalised Estimating Equations
GOBP	General Offending Behaviour Programme
GP	general practitioner
HAC	Health Advisory Committee [for the Prison Service]
HAC	Home Affairs Committee
HASI	Hayes Ability Screening Index
HCR-20	Historical Clinical and Risk – 20 Items Violence Risk Assessment Scheme

HDC	home detention curfew
HMCIP	HM Chief Inspector of Prisons
HMPS	HM Prison Service
HO	Home Office
ICAP	Integrated Cognitive Antisocial Personality theory
ICD	International Classification of Diseases
ID	intellectual disability
IDAP	Integrated Domestic Abuse Programme
IMR	inmate medical record
IPCUs	intensive psychiatric care units
IPDE	International Personality Disorder Examination
IPP	imprisonment for public protection
IPT	Imaginal Provocation Test
IQ	intelligence quotient
LASCH	local authority secure children's home
MacVRAS	MacArthur Violence Risk Assessment Study
MAPPA	multi-agency public protection arrangements
MAPPP	multi-agency public protection panel
MASRAM	multi-agency sex offender risk assessment and management
MCMI	Millon Clinical Multi-Axial Inventory
MDO	mentally disordered offender
MDT	mode deactivation therapy
MHA 1983	Mental Health Act 1983
MHAC	Mental Health Act Commission
MHRT	Mental Health Review Tribunal
MHTR	mental health treatment requirement
MMPI	Minnesota Multiphasic Personality Inventory
MSEI	Multi-Dimensional Self-Esteem Inventory
MSI	Multiphasic Sex Inventory
MSP	Member of the Scottish Parliament
MTFC	multidimensional treatment foster care
Nacro	National Association for the Care and Resettlement of Offenders
NAO	National Audit Office
NAS	Novaco Anger Scale
NAW	National Assembly of Wales

NHS SMS	NHS Security Management Service
NHS	National Health Service
NICE	National Institute of Clinical Excellence
NIMHE	National Institute for Mental Health England
NMC	Nursing and Midwifery Council
NOMS	National Offender Management Service
NPD	National Probation Directorate
NPS	National Probation Service
NPSA	National Patient Safety Agency
NSCAG	National Specialist Commissioning Advisory Group
NSF	National Service Framework
NSIC	National Statistics Information Centre
NSPCC	National Society for the Prevention of Cruelty to Children
NTA	National Treatment Agency
OASys	Offender Assessment System
OBP	offender behaviour programme
ODEAT	OASys development, evaluation and analysis team
OGRS	Offender Group Reconviction Scale
OLR	order for life-long restriction
ONS	Office for National Statistics
OPD	operational psychodynamic diagnostics
OSAP	Offender Substance Abuse Programme
PACE	Police and Criminal Evidence Act 1984
PAI	Personality Assessment Inventory
PANSS	Positive and Negative Syndrome Scale
PCC	Powers of Criminal Courts (Sentencing) Act 2000
PCL	(Hare) Psychopathy Checklist
PCL-R	(Hare) Psychopathy Checklist – Revised
PCL:SV	(Hare) Psychopathy Checklist: Screening Version
PCT	primary care trust
PD	personality disorder
PDNOS	personality disorder not otherwise specified
PERI	psychiatric epidemiology research interview
PI	principal investigator
PICU	psychiatric intensive care unit
PPG	Penile Plethysmograph
PRISM	Programme for Individual Substance Misusers

PSA	Public service agreement
PSE	present state examination
PSR	pre-sentence report
PTSD	posttraumatic stress disorder
QACSO	questionnaire on attitudes consistent with sexual offences
RAO	risk assessment order
RAP	Resettlement and Aftercare Provision
RC	responsible clinician
RCP	Royal College of Psychiatrists
RCT	randomised controlled trial
REBT	Rational Emotive Behaviour Therapy
RM2000	Risk Matrix 2000
RMA	Risk Management Authority
RMO	responsible medical officer
RNR	Risk/Needs/Responsivity approach
RRASOR	Rapid Risk Assessment for Sex Offender Recidivism
RSO	registered sex offender
RSVP	Risk for Sexual Violence Protocol
SARA	Spousal Abuse Risk Assessment
SCAN	Schedule for Clinical Assessment in Neuropsychiatry
SCID	Structured Clinical Interview for DSM
SCT	Supervised Community Treatment
SGC	Sentencing Guidelines Council
SIDP	Structured Interview for DSM-IV (Personality)
SMI	severe mental illness
SMS	short message service
SNAP	Security Needs Assessment Profile
SOAD	second opinion appointed doctor
SOAP	Sex Offender Assessment Pack
SOGP	Sex Offender Group Programme
SORAG	Sex Offence Risk Appraisal Guide
SOTP	Sex Offender Treatment Programme
SPSI	Social Problem Solving Inventory
STC	secure training colleges
STEP	Sex Offender Treatment Evaluation Project
SUD	substance use disorder

SVR-20	Sexual Violence Risk-20
SWAP-200	Shedler-Westen Assessment Procedure-200
TASC	treatment for appropriate social control
TBS	Terbeschikkingstelling (Dutch system)
TC	therapeutic community
TCO	threat/control-override symptoms
TTD	transfer for treatment direction
UK	United Kingdom
UKCC	United Kingdom Central Council for Nursing, Midwifery and Health Visiting
VES	Victim Empathy Distortion Scale
ViSOR	Violent and Sex Offender Register
VRAG	Violence Risk Appraisal Guide
VRS	Violence Risk Scale
WAG	Welsh Assembly Government
WAO	Wales Audit Office
WARS	Ward Anger Rating Scale
WHO	World Health Organisation
YJB	Youth Justice Board
YJS	youth justice system
YOT	youth offending team

Notes on contributors

Bettadapura Ashim is a Consultant Forensic Psychiatrist in the North West of England. Having recently completed a qualifying law degree, he is interested in the interface between psychiatry and the law. He has recently published two articles in peer-reviewed journals and contributed a chapter in a Gaskell publication, *Computers in Psychiatry*.

Susan Bailey OBE is Professor of Child and Adolescent Forensic Mental Health, University of Central Lancashire. Her clinical work has centred on the development of specialist services for young offenders with mental health needs. In research she has brought together a nationally and internationally collaborative programme of practice-centred, user-informed research on pathways into screening of needs and risk assessment and interventions with and outcomes on young offenders and complex need children. She has actively worked to reduce the stigma still associated with mental illness, especially in vulnerable groups.

Anthony Beech is a Professor of Criminological Psychology at the University of Birmingham, and a Fellow of the British Psychological Society. Over the last 15 years he has been involved in treatment evaluation and the development of systems to look at treatment need and treatment change in sex offenders. He has produced over 140 papers, chapters and other professional publications mainly on these topics and other related subjects.

Richard Benson is a Senior Lecturer in Forensic Health at the University of Glamorgan. He has experience of working in senior clinical/managerial roles within a range of forensic and prison settings. He has recently enrolled to commence his PhD examining the effectiveness of training and obtained his MSc in Forensic Behavioural Science in 1995. He is currently the lead for a range of forensic-related modules at the University of Glamorgan.

Danny Clark OBE is Head of the Attitudes, Thinking and Behaviour Interventions Unit of the National Offender Management Service, in the Ministry for Justice. He was previously employed as a forensic psychologist working in both the Prison and Probation Services. He was responsible for the research on and development of OASys. He has made a significant contribution to the implementation of accredited cognitive-behavioural programmes for offenders in custodial and community settings. His other interests include psychopathy, violent offending and therapeutic communities, all subjects on which he has publications. He is a member of the Canadian Correctional Services Programmes Accreditation panel.

Michael Daffern is a clinical psychologist by training. He has worked in prisons and in general and forensic mental health services. Currently, he is Principal Psychologist with Forensicare, the Victorian Institute of Forensic Mental Health in Melbourne, Australia. He is also Lecturer with the Centre for Forensic Behavioural Science, Monash University, and Special Lecturer within the Division of Psychiatry at The University of Nottingham. Dr Daffern's research has primarily focused on aggression and violence. His research interests include behavioural assessment methods, offence paralleling behaviour, risk assessment and aggression within institutions.

Andrew Day is an Associate Research Professor in Forensic Psychology with the School of Psychology at the University of South Australia. He has practised as a clinical and forensic psychologist both the UK and Australia. He is currently involved in a range of research activities relating to the rehabilitation of offenders, and has a particular interest in the treatment of anger-related problems in violent offenders.

Mairead Dolan is Professor of Forensic Psychiatry, and Neuroscience at the University of Manchester. She is Associate Medical R&D Director at Bolton Salford Trafford NHS Trust. Professor Dolan's research interests include personality disorder and risk assessment in mentally disordered offenders. She has supervised Mike Doyle's work on risk assessment and has published extensively on the validation of North American risk assessment tools in UK samples. She is currently principal investigator on two randomised controlled treatment trials in incarcerated personality disordered patients. She also has a themed programme of research on the neurobiological basis of anti-social behaviour across the lifespan. More recently she has been involved in pioneering research looking at objective methods of detecting description in forensic samples. She is working collaboratively with Professor Thapar at Cardiff University on an imaging study of behavioural inhibition and emotional information processing in adolescents with attention deficit hyperacticity disorder. She is the co-editor (with Professor S. Bailey) and contributor to the first textbook on adolescent forensic psychiatry.

Mike Doyle is Forensic Nurse Consultant at the Adult Forensic Directorate at the Edenfield Centre Manchester and Honorary Research Fellow at the Department of Psychiatry University of Manchester. Currently conducting research evaluating risk assessment, funded by the National Forensic R&D Programme. Accredited by the British Association of Behavioural & Cognitive Psychotherapies as a Behavioural and Cognitive Psychotherapist. Published widely on risk assessment and management and he is also a Director of the International Association of Forensic Mental Health Services and the nursing representative in the International Association of Forensic mental health.

Conor Duggan is Professor of Forensic Mental Health at the University of Nottingham and Honorary Consultant Psychiatrist at a Medium Secure Unit. His research interests are treatment needs in personality disordered offenders, their long-term course and the neuropsychological basis of psychopathy. He is especially interested in (a) how routine clinical services can directly inform the research agenda and (b) how forensic mental health relates to its satellite disciplines. He is Editor of the *Journal of Forensic Psychiatry and Psychology* and currently chairs a NICE Guideline Committee on the treatment of Antisocial Personality Disorder.

Philip Fennell is a Professor of Law in Cardiff Law School, College of Cardiff, University of Wales, where he teaches Medical Law, Public Law and Human Rights. He has published many articles on law and psychiatry. His book entitled *Treatment Without Consent: Law, Psychiatry and the Treatment of Mental Disorder since 1845*, was published by Routledge in 1996. He is a member of the Law Society's Mental Health and Disability Committee and was a member of the Mental Health Act Commission from 1983 to 1989. In 2000 Philip lectured to the judiciary as part of the judicial training for the implementation of the Human Rights Act 1998. From November 2004 to March 2005 he served as specialist legal adviser to the Joint Parliamentary Scrutiny Committee on the Draft Mental Health Bill 2004. In November 2006 he was appointed specialist legal adviser to the Parliamentary Joint Committee on Human Rights for the Committee's scrutiny of the Mental Health Bill 2006.

Dawn Fisher, Consultant Clinical and Forensic Psychologist, is Head of Psychology at Llanarth Court Hospital in Wales. She is also an Honorary Senior Research Fellow at the University of Birmingham. She was a member of the Correctional Services Accreditation Panel between 1999 and 2002. She has been extensively involved in sexual offender assessment and treatment for around 20 years and has recently co-written one of three probation-based sex offender treatment programmes running in the UK. She has also written extensively on the assessment and treatment of sexual offenders. Since 1990 she has been involved in research into the effectiveness of sex offender treatment programmes. She was a founder member of NOTA, the national organisation for the treatment of sex offenders and regularly presents at conferences both in the UK and abroad.

David Forshaw is a Consultant in Forensic Psychiatry at Thornford Park Independent Hospital, which is part of Priory Secure Services. He has published in several fields including medical ethics, addictions, history of psychiatry and forensic psychiatry. He co-edited the postgraduate textbook *Postgraduate Psychiatry: Clinical and Scientific Foundations*. He is a founding director and proprietor of a group of companies, Psycare, which specialise in the provision of care facilities in the community for people with long-standing mental health problems including forensic mental health issues.

Kevin Gournay CBE recently retired from the Institute of Psychiatry (King's College, University of London) where he held a chair for 11 years. He is a Chartered Psychologist and a Registered Nurse. He has carried out research on areas as diverse as CBT, violence, suicide, schizophrenia, medication, epidemiology and primary care and supervised several MRC research training fellows.

He is the author of 300 books, monographs, papers, chapters and major conference papers. His diverse interests include policy work for the Department of Health, chairing a NICE panel on the management of violence and being a member of the DSPD and mental health in prison expert groups. He has worked for the Joint Parliamentary Committee on Human Rights which examined deaths in custody. In retirement he continues in clinical practice as a CBT therapist and as an expert witness.

Nicola Gray holds a joint clinical-academic appointment at the School of Psychology, Cardiff University and the South Wales Forensic Mental Health Service at Caswell Clinic, where she works as a Professor in Psychology and a Consultant Clinical and Forensic Psychologist. Professor Gray has focused her research efforts on the field of risk assessment, and is currently investigating the effectiveness of risk assessment tools, such as the HCR-20, in specific clinical populations (such as people with personality disorder or learning disability). She is also pioneering research on measuring implicit attitudes and intentions to offence-related behaviours, using the Implicit Association Test (IAT).

John Gunn CBE is Emeritus Professor of Forensic Psychiatry at the Institute of Psychiatry, King's College London. He is the past chairman of the Faculty of Forensic Psychiatry in the Royal College of Psychiatrists, and is currently a member of the Parole Board for England and Wales. At the Institute of Psychiatry he developed a large postgraduate teaching centre for forensic psychiatry and together with Professor Pamela Taylor he edited a textbook of forensic psychiatry. His research has been concerned with prisons and special hospitals, epidemiology and the therapeutic community at Grendon prison. He co-edits *Criminal Behaviour and Mental Health*.

Sheilagh Hodgins is Professor of the Department of Forensic Mental Health Science at the Institute of Psychiatry, King's College London. She has authored numerous papers, book chapters, and books focusing on antisocial, violent, and criminal behaviours among persons with mental disorders. Currently, she is conducting investigations that aim to identify the causal mechanisms leading to early-onset antisocial behaviour that remains stable over the lifespan among persons who develop schizophrenia, studies of factors that maintain these unwanted behaviours, and treatments to reduce violent behaviour. In addition, she is undertaking studies of the neurobiological abnormalities associated with persistent violent offending.

Kevin Howells is Professor of Forensic Clinical Psychology at the University of Nottingham and Head of the Peaks Academic and Research Unit at Rampton Hospital. The Peaks is a high secure facility for DSPD (Dangerous and Severe Personality Disorder) patients. He has worked as a clinician and academic in the UK and in Australia and is a visiting Professor at the Centre for Applied Psychological Research at the University of South Australia. He has research interests in anger and its links to violence, readiness for treatment and in cognitive-behavioural interventions for offenders.

Bill Kerslake has been Head of Policy for Health and Substance Misuse at the Youth Justice Board for England and Wales since 2003. He leads on the YJB's Health Partnership work with national and regional stakeholders to improve access to services for young people in the youth justice system. Previously he worked as a social work practitioner in New Zealand and London for 10 years in hospital, local authority and adult community mental health teams, and has practised as an approved social worker managing assessments under the Mental Health Act. He spent two years as a research associate with the Sainsbury Centre for Mental Health before joining the Audit Commission as a Value for Money auditor of local authority and health services, from which he was seconded to the YJB in 2002.

William R. Lindsay is a Consultant Forensic Clinical Psychologist at the State Hospital and NHS Tayside and is Chair of Learning Disabilities and Forensic Psychology at the University of Abertay, Dundee. He is a leading research and clinical authority on offenders with intellectual disability and publishes widely in the field. He also has major clinical and research interests in cognitive therapy with people with developmental disabilities.

Madelaine Lockmuller is a Consultant Clinical and Forensic Psychologist and is the Head of Forensic Clinical Psychology for the West of England Forensic Mental Health Service, based at Fromeside medium secure unit in Bristol. Her career in forensic mental health has included clinical and research work at three medium secure units, a special hospital and residential project for adolescent sexual offenders. She has been involved in the assessment and treatment of sexual offenders within the forensic mental health system throughout her career and has a specific interest in sexual offending by individuals suffering from mental illness. She has conducted research in this area that is due for publication.

Mary McMurran is Professor in the Section of Forensic Mental Health, Division of Psychiatry, University of Nottingham. Her research interests include: social problem solving as a model of understanding and treating people with personality disorders; the assessment and treatment of alcohol-related aggression and violence; and understanding and enhancing offenders' motivation to engage in therapy. She has written over 100 articles and book chapters. She is a Fellow of the British Psychological Society and recipient of the BPS Division of Forensic Psychology's Lifetime Achievement Award in 2005.

Tony Maden is Professor of Forensic Psychiatry at Imperial College London and Clinical Director of the dangerous and severe personality disorder service at West London Mental Health NHS Trust. His main research interests are in needs assessment in forensic mental health, and violence risk management. He is the author of *Treating Violence: A Guide to Risk Management in Mental Health* (Oxford University Press 2007).

Paul Mullen holds the Foundation Chair of Forensic Psychiatry at Monash University and Clinical Director of the Victorian Institute of Forensic Mental Health, having previously been Professor of Psychological Medicine at the

University of Otago, New Zealand and Consultant Psychiatrist to the Bethlem Royal and Maudsley Hospitals. His current interests include: the schizophrenic syndrome and offending behaviours; stalkers and their victims; the querulous; the impact of child sexual abuse; threats and threateners, and phenomenology.

Paul Rogers became the first university appointed Professor in Forensic Nursing in 2004. Prior to that he worked in medium security in a range of roles, the last being Clinical Nurse Specialist in CBT, before embarking on his research career. He was the recipient of a Welsh Assembly PhD Fellowship in 1999 and an MRC post doctoral Fellowship in 2002. His research interests involve: symptoms and violence, risk assessment and prediction, CBT and posttraumatic stress disorder. He has published approximately 100 peer-reviewed professional papers and holds a range of advisory positions in England and Wales.

Jane Senior qualified as a mental health nurse in 1990 and has since worked in a variety of in-patient, community and high and medium secure services. She worked for the Prison Service in a young offenders' institution for four years during which time she completed a Master's degree in criminology. She has worked as a researcher full-time since 2000, completing a PhD examining the development of comprehensive mental healthcare systems in prisons. She currently works for the University of Manchester, managing both the Prison Health Research Network and the North West Forensic Academic Network.

Jenny Shaw is Professor of Forensic Psychiatry, University of Manchester and consultant forensic psychiatrist at Guild Lodge secure unit, Preston. She is assistant director of the National Confidential Inquiry into Suicide and Homicide by People with Mental Illness and her research interests include homicide, prison mental health and suicide in the criminal justice system.

Pete Snowden is a Consultant Forensic Psychiatrist in the North West of England. He is currently Clinical Director of the Personality Disorder Service at Ashworth High Security Hospital. He has published widely in journals, and has authored a number of chapters in textbooks on forensic mental health. He led the Department of Health project on services for those with personality disorder, *Personality disorder: no longer a diagnosis of exclusion*.

Keith Soothill is Emeritus Professor of Social Research in the Department of Applied Social Science, Lancaster University, UK and is now based in the Centre for Applied Statistics at Lancaster. He has recently been Chair of the Department of Health advisory committee for the Research and Development programme on Forensic Mental Health. His publications span the areas of crime and health. He has co-authored the book, *Making Sense of Criminology* (Polity Press) and the monograph, *Murder and serious sexual assault: What criminal histories can reveal about future serious offending* (Home Office), and co-edited, *Questioning Crime and Criminology* (Willan Publishing). His current research interests are in the areas of homicide, sex offending, and criminal careers.

John L. Taylor is Professor of Developmental Disability Psychology at Northumbria University and Head of Psychological Therapies and Research with Northumberland, Tyne and Wear NHS Trust. Until recently he was Chair of the British Psychological Society's Faculty for Forensic Clinical Psychology and the Learning Disability Steering Group of the NHS Forensic Mental Health Research and Development Programme. He has published work related to his clinical research interests in assessment and treatment of offenders with developmental disabilities in a range of research and professional journals and recently co-authored the book, *Anger Treatment for People with Developmental Disabilities* (Wiley).

Pamela J. Taylor is Professor of Forensic Psychiatry, Cardiff University, and Visiting Professor, Institute of Psychiatry, King's College, London. She is forensic psychiatry adviser to the Welsh Assembly Government, and chairman of the Royal College of Psychiatrists' Welsh Forensic Psychiatry Faculty. Previous posts include Professor of Special Hospital Psychiatry, Institute of Psychiatry, and Medical Director, Special Hospitals' Service Authority. With John Gunn she has edited a forensic psychiatry textbook. She researches into psychosis and violence and mental disorder in prisoners, and is currently leading a multi-national study. Editorial work includes *Criminal Behaviour and Mental Health* and *Behavioural Sciences and the Law*.

Lindsay Thomson is Medical Director of the State Hospitals Board for Scotland and the Forensic Mental Health Services Managed Care Network and Reader in Forensic Psychiatry at the University of Edinburgh. Her research interests include outcomes in mentally disordered offenders; risk assessment and management of harm to others; the impact of legislative change; and service design for mentally disordered offenders. She co-authored the first textbook on psychiatry and the Scottish legal system and legislation: *Mental Health and Scots Law in Practice*.

Tegwyn Williams is Consultant Psychiatrist and Clinical Director of Mental Health, Bro Morgannwg NHS Trust, Bridgend, Wales. He trained in medicine at St George's and Guy's Hospitals in London and returned to Wales and started working as a Consultant Forensic Psychiatrist at the Caswell Clinic in 1992. He has special interest in women patients and patients who commit homicide. He has represented Forensic Psychiatry in Wales on various international professional and government bodies. He was the medical lead in the Caswell Clinic from 1992 and the Clinical Director of the Caswell Clinic from October 2003 until he became the Director of Mental Health in the Bro Morgannwg NHS Trust in June 2005.

Preface and acknowledgements

Much has happened within the fields of forensic mental health and forensic psychiatry in recent years. While probing origins is rarely straightforward, there seems little doubt that the focus on forensic mental health in the United Kingdom has changed markedly over the past decade and a half. The killing of Jonathan Zito by Christopher Clunis – a patient with schizophrenia who had been discharged from hospital and who stabbed and killed Zito at a London Underground station on 17 December 1992 – symbolises part of that change.

The tragic event of Zito's killing became a signal crime[1] that helped to highlight similar incidents. These tragic and high-profile killings by people with mental illness were used to suggest that the community care model for mental health services had failed. Certainly there was a concern felt more centrally at governmental level whether the professionals involved with forensic mental health – in terms of both theory and practice – could adequately meet the challenge that the public was implicitly demanding: that of public protection.

There was, in fact, the launch of two trajectories. One, which is the main focus of this book, is the development of a knowledge base for forensic mental health. The other, which became a more explosive issue, was managing the moral panic that was developing around the topic of mentally ill persons being in the community. To some extent, the latter view was partially defused when Taylor and Gunn (1999) considered whether homicides by people with mental illness had, indeed, become more frequent as psychiatric services had changed. They persuasively argued that there was little fluctuation in the numbers of people with a mental illness committing criminal homicide over the 38 years studied and, in fact, noted a 3 per cent annual decline in their contribution to the official statistics. While they suggested that 'there appears to be some case for specially focused improvement of services for people with a personality disorder and/or substance misuse', their main conclusion was that 'there is no evidence that it is anything but stigmatising to claim that their living in the community is a dangerous experiment that should be reversed'. While this message proved reassuring for professionals actively involved in forensic mental health, the politicians, who were, in turn, heavily influenced by the media, would not be so readily persuaded by rational argument. The counter argument was that you are much more likely to be killed while crossing a road by a speeding motorist than by a lion roaming the streets, but if you had a choice which would you prefer to meet on your next shopping trip! Whatever one's views of the contentious programme developed by the Home Office around the neologism, DSPD (dangerous and severe personality disorder), one can see its introduction as another staging post in managing the political and moral panic that both developed and was partly orchestrated by the media and campaigners following the killing of Jonathan Zito.

In contrast, the 'knowledge' trajectory has had a less public journey. It is not totally distinct from the other more public trajectory – so, for instance, the DSPD programme is underpinned by a million pound evaluation study which should eventually add to the growing knowledge base on this rare but most dangerous of society's deviants. Another manifestation of this new thirst for knowledge was the establishment of the National Programme on Forensic Mental Health R&D. Following David Farrington, one of the editors (Keith Soothill) became Chair of the Advisory Committee in 2003. In the course of its 'life', the National Programme has funded 79 projects, numerous research fellowships, sponsored conferences and commissioned expert papers. Additionally there were unmeasured processes which are hard to capture, but include assisting researchers and clinicians to advertise events and offering ethical and methodological advice on an as needed basis. The funding from the R&D Forensic Mental Health initiative provided a form of 'protected status' that everyone knew would end at some point. However, when the new Department of Health strategy *Best Research for Best Health* was issued in 2006, it was decided without consultation that the Programme would cease commissioning with immediate effect and close in March 2007. In the event the administration of the programme finally ended in June 2007 which coincided with the end of the lease to house the administrative office in Liverpool. Sadly, the future of this very important area of research activity is still not clear now that forensic mental health researchers have to compete with the more publicly attractive health areas such as childcare and cancer services.

As editors, we are immensely grateful to the contributors to this book, and we are delighted that such an array of talent agreed to come on board. They have accepted with apparent good humour our various chivvying for chapters. They accepted the suggestions – not sure about the humour as we were not there when they received the e-mails! – for changes and revisions. Anyway, it all came good in the end. But many of the contributors have done much more. They have agreed to comment on other chapters providing helpful and supportive messages. There have also been others and we wish to thank Ian Baguley, Clair Chilvers, Derek Perkins and Joanne Wood in particular.

Finally, our thanks to Brian Willan and his colleagues at Willan Publishing. They must be the best publishers to work with, knowing how to support and what to advise. It is important to note that as much as we have tried to cover all that is relevant to England, Scotland, Wales and Northern Ireland, there will be times where this cannot be possible. To compare and contrast each policy, legal system and healthcare system and then apply this to local practices would have been an impossible task. Nonetheless, we hope that the crux of the messages contained within each chapter are more than generalisable to all. Hopefully, we will have readers who will think the project was all worthwhile.

The Editors
March 2008

Note

1 Innes (2004: 17) argues that 'the concept of signal crimes focuses upon the processes of social reaction through which a criminal event comes to be defined as a problem and is thereby imbued with meaning for a public audience'.

References

Innes, M. (2004) 'Crime as a signal, crime as a memory', *Journal for Crime, Conflict and the Media*, 1 (2): 15–22.

Taylor, P. and Gunn, J. (1999) 'Homicides by people with mental illness: myth and reality', *British Journal of Psychiatry*, January, 174: 9–14.

Part I

Setting the Scene – The Administrative and Social Framework

Keith Soothill

Understanding forensic mental health is a complex task. Indeed, what is forensic mental health is contentious. In Chapter 1 Paul Rogers and Keith Soothill insist on the need to recognise and embrace the fact that the boundaries of the subject area are 'fuzzy'. Furthermore, what complicates the picture is that the area is dynamic. Certainly there have been massive changes over the past decade and a half. Soothill and Rogers capture part of this in recognising that there are now a variety of professional voices involved. No longer is it the preserve of the discipline of forensic psychiatry. Forensic psychology, mental health nursing, social work and occupational therapy are professions that have become more closely involved in the forensic field. Now interdisciplinary working is a critical issue. Also, users are increasingly attempting to have a more credible voice. There has been a greater investment in research in recent years, but Soothill and Rogers are cautious about the current situation. They suggest that there is a dearth of thinking about this very important area of research activity. The very maintenance and development of forensic mental health is at risk.

In Chapter 2 Lindsay Thomson makes a very important contribution in reminding us that in the United Kingdom there is not one forensic mental health system, but four. The four systems reflect the countries that make up the UK – England, Northern Ireland, Scotland and Wales. Rarely have the intricacies of the similarities and the differences between the four systems been so carefully detailed. Practitioners need to know the administrative and legal frameworks within which they are working. Thomson points out that we are at a very interesting stage in the development of forensic mental health services in the UK. Will the effects of devolved power lead to more differences in the care and management of mentally disordered offenders? Astutely, Thomson notes that this could create an opportunity for naturalistic experiments comparing system effects for the issues posed by mentally disordered offenders are similar throughout the UK, assuming that our populations are the same.

In Chapter 3 David Forshaw provides a very readable account of the origins and early development of forensic mental health. Here he captures how closely the development of the field has been entwined with the development of the discipline of psychiatry. He captures its origins within the broader historical context. However, while there are underlying historical forces at play, it is fascinating how the growth of mental health legislation is so often the response to very dramatic and unusual events. Moral outcries and moral panics are not phenomena unique to the late twentieth and early twenty-first centuries. How does all this relate to the present? The present is often shaped by being trapped by the past and trying to overthrow those trappings. Without historical knowledge it is impossible to know what is new. After all, Clement Attlee, the British Prime Minster after the Second World War, maintained in a speech in 1950 that 'I think the British have the distinction above all other nations of being able to put new wine into old bottles without bursting them'. Of course, there is never a definitive history and the way that other disciplines have become increasingly embroiled in forensic work is perhaps another history that still needs to be told.

Reference

Attlee, C. (1950) Speech, *Hansard*, 24 October 1950, col. 2705.

Chapter 1

Understanding forensic mental health and the variety of professional voices

Paul Rogers and Keith Soothill

Introduction

The aim of this chapter is not to rehearse or summarise all the issues that will be presented in this book, but to try to set the scene by painting with a broad brush. What is forensic mental health? Where is it 'done'? When is it done? By whom is it done and onto whom? And finally, and most crucially, how can we develop an understanding of the issues?

What is forensic mental health?

Semantics is often an appropriate start to a project. But probing the meaning of words can also be offputting. Establishing precise definitions can be tedious and, like medieval philosophers seeking the 'philosopher's stone' by which they could turn base metal into gold, the task may be impossible to accomplish. Interestingly when one of us went to a meeting recently, the person chairing the group started with the line 'We really don't want to be too definitive about this definition lark!' Our aim is a rather different one. From the outset we are trying to establish the boundaries of the domain of forensic mental health. Again there are difficulties, for the boundaries are not clear. However, our message is a clear one. We need both to recognise and embrace the fact that the boundaries of our subject area are 'fuzzy'.

Recognising 'fuzziness' takes the pressure off. What is regarded as the domain of forensic mental health in one historical era may be different from that of another era. There will also be differences between individual professions, different services and different countries in terms of what they see as the boundaries of forensic mental health. In short, there are no absolutes that we must seek.

'Forensic mental health' would not be a term in general use 40 years ago and there are still those around who are reluctant to embrace it. Up until recently, forensic psychiatry was the dominant term with multi-professional staff working in forensic psychiatric units or services. The term, forensic mental health, reflects the movement away from services which are determined by a medical/illness model and towards a health/prevention model.

Mullen (2000: 307) defines forensic mental health as:

> ... an area of specialisation that, in the criminal sphere, involves the assessment and treatment of those who are both mentally disordered and whose behaviour has led, or could lead, to offending.

We would like to extend this to also include offenders who are not currently mentally disordered but have the propensity to be so. Thus forensic mental health takes a preventative approach to both offending and mental ill health.

Where is forensic mental health done?

Forensic mental health can occur anywhere within health and is not the sole bastion of what we would traditionally consider forensic mental health clinicians. If we concentrate on offenders, then mental health issues are abundant in police stations, prisons, probation services, psychiatric hospitals and back in the community. Patients who offend and who have mental health problems come into contact with all aspects of health and public service. The police custody sergeant is as concerned with deaths in custody as the ward manager in a high-security hospital. The probation officer is just as concerned with understanding how a person's mental disorder is linked to their offending as a social worker who is working with a family where domestic violence occurs, initiated by someone with mental health problems. The simple answer to 'where' does forensic mental health occur is that it is everywhere. Furthermore, the greater the understanding that non-forensic mental health clinicians have about the potential for offending among those with mental disorder, the greater the possibility of early detection where problems may be developing. This is crucial and a consideration for the future if we wish to try and divert people from the laborious and lengthy 'offender pathways' that currently exist. Investment in prevention and diversion at the earliest possible point must be the goals of all health and public service employees and organisations. Why wait until sentencing to determine if a person is mentally ill when it can be done at the point of arrest? Why wait to intervene after an offence has occurred, when crisis resolution and home treatment could have stopped the offending in the first place? Put simply, the need for forensic mental health and the fact that it is becoming a growth industry must be viewed as a failure in the other sections of health. Surely the goal of health services should be to prevent offending at all costs?

Who does forensic mental health?

Forensic mental health covers a wide plethora of professions if we agree that the focus of such work is the reduction of offending in those with mental health problems or mental health problems in those who have offended. This forensic mental health industry is ever-expanding. Generally speaking, there are the five main professions: forensic psychiatry, forensic psychology, mental health nursing, social work and occupational therapy. It is questionable as to whether mental health nursing, social work and occupational therapy have a claim to a 'forensic' label.

Forensic psychiatry

Forensic psychiatry is 'that part of psychiatry which deals with patients and problems at the interface of the legal and psychiatric systems' (Gunn 2004: S1). Furthermore, Gunn argued that 'such a definition implies a speciality that does not travel easily, and the practice of forensic psychiatry does vary considerably from one country to another'. Gunn (2004: S1) also defined forensic psychiatry in this paper as 'the prevention, amelioration, and treatment of victimization that is associated with mental disease'. Here lies the problem: many people can have differing views about what forensic psychiatry is or isn't. Put simply, forensic means legal and therefore forensic psychiatry can cover a plethora of people who have come into contact with the legal system and have a mental disorder.

Mullen (2000) argues that simplistic definitions of forensic psychiatry based upon literal meanings to acting exclusively as handmaidens to the court are constraining. Mullen suggests that defining forensic psychiatry in terms of the assessment and treatment of the mentally abnormal offender delineates an area of concern that could potentially engulf much of mental health.

Forensic psychology

Forensic psychology is defined as being:

> ... devoted to psychological aspects of legal processes in courts. The term is also often used to refer to investigative and criminological psychology: applying psychological theory to criminal investigation, understanding psychological problems associated with criminal behaviour, and the treatment of criminals. (British Psychological Society 2007)

Both forensic psychiatry and forensic psychology have one unique aspect which helps with the forensic 'identity' that the other professions of nursing, social work and occupational therapy do not: that of specialised and recognised training.

Forensic mental health nursing

It has been argued that there is no such thing as a forensic mental health nurse. Whyte (1997, 2000) has consistently argued that forensic mental health nursing is exactly the same as mental health nursing. Quite simply, Whyte has a very strong case as there is no separate forensic training, and all nurses working in forensic mental health are mental health nurses working with a population that is 'forensic'. Collins (2000: 39) states that:

> There has always been substantial debate surrounding the 'forensic nurse' ever since the term came into regular use ... criticisms of the role range from 'glorified custodians' to a homogeneous group who strut around swinging a capacious bunch of keys, in a quest for domination of those under their care.

Many dispute these arguments and desperately try to make a case that forensic mental health nursing is a separate discrete branch of mental health nursing (Kettles and Woods 2006; Kettles and Robinson 2000). However, the evidence for a forensic nursing as a separate specialism is currently a weak one. There is a lack of high quality and meaningful studies which demonstrate what it is that 'forensic' mental health nurses do. Undoubtedly, the debate will surely go on for a long time and it is appropriate that the topic should remain on the agenda.

Forensic social work

Forensic social work has the same 'problem' as nursing when attempting to identify itself as a discrete speciality: there is no 'forensic training' or forensic registration. Thus definition proves difficult. Interestingly, the British Association of Social Workers has a 'Forensic Social Work' special interest group. Consequently, the role is an extension of the general social work role, only again with a forensic population.

Forensic occupational therapists

Again forensic occupational therapy has no direct forensic route or registration. Little is known about the role, although recently a book by Couldrick and Alred (2003) entitled *Forensic Occupational Therapy* has been published.

Service users

Service user involvement has slowly gathered pace in forensic mental health (Faulkner and Morris 2003), though, much slower than in non-forensic mental health settings. But this is not all. Over the past 20 years, there has been an increasing insistence that service users should have a voice about mental health services. The barrier of recognising that the service user has a role to play has probably been broken, but the nature and the strength of that particular voice is still being questioned and negotiated. Some units insist on having a service user on interview panels for new staff while others will not hear of it. The challenge when recognising the contributions that service users can make is to ensure that tokenism isn't at play. Coffey (2006: 82) conducted a literature review of research into service users' views in forensic mental health and noted many problems with the quality of the research to date.

> Studies focussing upon diagnostic groups (Ryan *et al.* 2002; Sainsbury *et al.* 2004) or location, for instance medium secure services (Morrison *et al.* 1996) and community (Gerber *et al.* 2003), did not present sufficient detail to determine similarities and differences between groups and settings. Given the particular needs of women (Byrt, Lomas, Gardiner and Lewis 2001) and the over-representation and treatment of black and ethnic minority groups (Bennett Inquiry, 2003; Lelliot, Audini and Duffett 2001) it is noteworthy that few studies have investigated these experiences.

Clearly, forensic mental health has a long way to go before truly understanding and incorporating the service user's experiences and insights into ensuring high-quality service delivery. Coffey (2006) concluded in his review that:

Forensic mental health researchers have not yet accessed views of services in a sustained, systematic, and critical fashion or in a way that represents the multiple perspectives of service users.

Interdisciplinary working

The killing of Jonathan Zito by Christopher Clunis has gone a long way to focus the mind on some of the problems within forensic mental health. The later inquiry team indicated that the case was a 'catalogue of failure and missed opportunity', finding that 'the more disturbed Christopher Clunis became, the less effective was the care he received'. The inquiry team expressed concern at the lack of the prompt response by the police, but also criticised doctors, psychiatric nurses and social workers for failing to assess Christopher Clunis's history of violence and for failing to work closely together (Court 1994).

The Clunis case highlighted what many in forensic mental health already knew. New territorial battles surrounding professional power were emerging in the forensic mental health field. One scratch under the surface and the true interprofessional problems floated to the top. The problem has been eased somewhat through *Agenda for Change*, where all professions except psychiatry have been rewarded on the same salary scheme based upon the importance of their work and not their professional tribe; however, it must be said that, despite this rather expensive governmental reform of pay scales, it is probably only time until the new, forced larger and 'non-psychiatry tribe' begin asking why psychiatry is allowed to be paid upon professional status when everyone else has given up their roots. Soothill *et al.* (1995: 3) proclaimed that 'how they all work together – or fail to do so – will be one of the critical questions in the coming decade or so.' It is not an exaggeration to say that the issue remains a central question of healthcare generally and no doubt will continue to ebb or even eat away within forensic mental health.

Why do we have forensic mental health?

Writing a quarter of a century ago, Soothill *et al.* (1981: 33) note that 'some of the greatest dilemmas in the management of deviants have recently been raised at the interface of the two control systems – issues of liberty and confinement, ethics and efficacy of the psychiatric treatment of offenders and so on.' The picture remains the same and perhaps will always be so.

The devil is in the detail! And the 'why' is the $64,000 question. Scott (1975) suggested that 'detaining custodial institutions have two aims: one therapeutic; and the other custodial'. Forensic mental health has two obvious roles: the need to treat people who are mentally unwell and the need to protect society. Undoubtedly this is a balancing act where these two roles can conflict with each other causing forensic mental health clinicians and services to come into conflict with politicians who then intervene. However, politicians cannot get this balance right either. This is evidenced by the political pendulum surrounding two inquiries into Ashworth Hospital in the 1990s. The first Ashworth Hospital inquiry (Blom-Cooper *et al.* 1992) considered the hospital as being an abusive, authoritarian institution (Beales 2004: 270) resulting in a politically driven, vast liberalisation of the hospital regime. However, did the liberalisation go too far? Only seven years later a second Ashworth Hospital inquiry occurred (Fallon *et al.* 1999). Fallon investigated and confirmed complaints of patients trading in pornographic material, a young child visiting convicted dangerous paedophiles and being 'groomed' for abuse, patients running ward businesses, misuse of drugs and alcohol and gross lapses in security. This led to the Tilt Report (Tilt *et al.* 2000) which investigated all three English Special Hospitals and recommended greater levels of security, calling for patients' telephone calls to be recorded, random searches of patient quarters and improvements to perimeter and internal security systems. Thus, since 1992, we have come full circle, where the emphasis is now back on security. It could be argued that we are so focused on getting the balance right between a secure environment with a caring environment that the primary issue of how we get people better through an effective environment gets lost in the fallout.

Forensic mental health is undoubtedly a political imperative. Nothing causes a press and societal outcry quite as much as a stranger-homicide committed by a 'madman', as rare as these are. However, the role of social policeman does not sit easy with clinicians, who at the end of the day are primarily concerned with the care and treatment of those who are not well. The question as to what responsibility forensic mental health should take in managing societal dangerousness is one that will continue. The dispute between the Home Secretary and the then President of the Royal College of Psychiatrists about whether psychiatrists should be preventively detaining untreatable psychopaths under the Mental Health Act clearly illustrates the problem when a Home Office Minister said: 'Don't expect the public to pay your salary if you don't protect the public' (Sen *et al.* 2007: 340).

Political influence over or interference with forensic mental health will cause concern to many clinicians, especially when it is related to issues of dangerousness. Exworthy and Gunn (2003) observed this when commenting on the Tilt Report (Tilt *et al.* 2000: 470):

> The emphasis throughout the report on the more tangible aspects of security such as high walls and better locks, and the virtual absence of consideration of the less overt contribution of relational security, fits in with the official preoccupation with 'dangerousness' in recent years.

Exworthy and Gunn (2003: 470) go on to state that:

> ... recent evidence of the greater prominence of public protection within the mental health service provision is seen in initiatives such as the creation of a new 'condition' – dangerous severe personality disorder (DSPD) – which requires a new form of service provision and could permit preventive detention.

The tension between public protection and the treatment of mentally disordered offenders is pivotal. Certainly one of the reasons why we have forensic mental health is to balance the needs of treating those with mental disorder who have offended in as humane a manner as possible, while at the same time meeting society's need for safety. The problem of the processes by which this is achieved is one that will probably never be resolved for all patients, in all environments at all times.

However, as discussed in Chapter 21, the tendency to separate the functions of patient care and society's need for safety as two separate processes suggests that these processes are not related. However, they are: in fact, the more intensive the care and treatment of a patient, the more secure a person becomes.

Clearly the issue of why we do what we do is an important one concerning medical ethics, underpinned by human rights. Adherence to medical ethics is of great concern to all forensic mental health clinicians. Sen and colleagues (2007: 340) provide a very good illustration of the problems of applying the 'four principles plus scope' approach which should underpin medical ethics. This approach provides clinicians with what is stated as a 'simple, accessible and culturally neutral framework for dealing with this difficult and confusing area of medicine' (Sen *et al.* 2007: 340). These 'four principles plus scope' approach are: respect for autonomy, beneficence, non-maleficence and justice, coupled with their scope of application. Sen and colleagues (2007: 340) report that:

> The practice of forensic psychiatry illustrates some of these difficulties. It includes all aspects of the care and treatment of offenders with mental disorders or patients posing similar problems of antisocial behaviour. Because the patients are offenders and are in hospital for treatment, both for their own benefit and to reduce risk to society, the forensic psychiatrist thus has an ethical obligation towards both the patient and to the wider society. This would also include addressing the interests of the patients on the same ward and staff working on the ward, who might be at risk from the patient.

Sen and colleagues (2007: 341) conclude that the two cases that they present:

> … highlight some ethical dilemmas common in forensic clinical practice. We would also argue that, although the four-principles approach may work well in the context of traditional dyadic doctor–patient relationships, it has limitations in the forensic domain: firstly, because the principles are often in conflict with one another; secondly, because the forensic psychiatrist may have duties to third parties other than the patient, which are not covered by the four-principles approach; and, lastly, because forensic practice requires special attention to justice.

Research in forensic mental health

The foregoing has to a large degree emphasised that working in forensic mental health is in many ways different. Within the house of academia this difference is appreciated insofar that forensic work in psychiatry and psychology demands specialised and recognised training. Other disciplines involved in forensic work also recognise difference but one of degree rather than of kind. Their emphasis is more in pointing to similarities and continuities between the demands of forensic work and the application of their skills in other contexts. The tension between what is different about forensic mental health and what is similar to other areas needs to be confronted in understanding the one remaining voice which is often neglected – namely the voice of the researcher into forensic mental health.

Constructing a knowledge base is the prerequisite to establishing a discipline or even a subdiscipline. The same questions posed at the beginning of this chapter – namely, what is forensic mental health, where is it 'done', when is it done, by whom is it done and, most crucially, why do we have it? – can again be posed in relation to research into forensic mental health.

Again the boundaries are elastic, for forensic mental health research can cover everything which is embraced by the term, 'forensic mental health'. We have already stressed that the practice of forensic work can vary in terms of both time and place. However, similar research questions tend to emerge and these can be posed as questions about *process* and questions about *outcome*. 'Process' essentially refers to the practice of forensic mental health – how do practitioners go about their work, what are the decision points in the process and questions of fairness and justice need to be addressed. 'Outcome', in contrast, is concerned with results and whether an intervention, for example, makes a difference. 'Outcome' is much more about effectiveness, while 'process' is much more about equity. But these, of course, are not the only types of questions that need to be addressed. There are also very basic issues, such as a description of the type of persons who enter the system. What are their characteristics and so on? Epidemiologists have the skills to design this kind of research and to interpret the results.

Research in its various guises should feature in all the diverse activities which comprise the field of forensic mental health. While all activity can be usefully monitored to ensure that standards are being maintained, research has a different purpose. Its task is to aid understanding.

Sadly, when entrenched views are resistant to challenge, research is regarded as a dangerous interloper. Sometimes research is only embraced if it comes up with treasured preconceptions and is quickly dismissed if its insights are unexpected or unwanted. However, ultimately, researchers are essentially the custodians and arbiters of the knowledge base. So who are they?

Pinning down who the researchers are is more hazardous than it may at first appear. In the forensic mental health field there are those who do nothing else but engage in research. But, in a comparatively small subdiscipline, such persons are few and far between. Mostly, researchers are practitioners and/or teachers who seem to find it increasingly difficult to fit in the demands of research with all their other commitments, usually declaring 'the beast of bureaucracy' as the main enemy. Further, different funding models within the field can sometimes disadvantage the furtherance of research. And yet, interestingly, research in forensic mental health has increased hugely over the past 30 or so years. There are now specialist journals, such as the *Journal of Forensic Psychiatry and Psychology*, *Criminal Behaviour and Mental Health* and *Personality and Mental Health*, where research findings can be published.

In the 1960s there were just three or four talented male psychiatrists who represented the research interest of what was then the narrower field of forensic psychiatry. This has markedly changed. Different disciplines have declared an interest and the gender balance of the researchers has dramatically shifted.

A recent study (Soothill *et al.* submitted) has probed the gender, ages and professional groupings of this emerging research community. Curiously, the killing of Jonathan Zito mentioned earlier can be regarded as the catalyst for this recent development in forensic mental health research. The public outcry orchestrated by the media and a public campaign by his widow, Jayne Zito, helped to maintain interest in the case. The tragic event was not a solitary incident, but became a signal crime that helped to highlight similar incidents (see this volume, Preface note 1). These tragic and high-profile killings by people with mental illness were used to suggest that the community care model for mental health services had failed. This concern developed into something of a moral panic about the safety of the community. In fact, Taylor and Gunn (1999) considered whether such homicides had, indeed, become more frequent as psychiatric services had changed. Extracting data from the Criminal Statistics for England and Wales between 1957 and 1995 and subjecting the material to trend analysis, they argued that there was little fluctuation in the numbers of people with a mental illness committing criminal homicide over the 38 years studied and, in fact, noted a 3 per cent annual decline in their contribution to the official statistics. While they suggested that 'there appears to be some case for specially focused improvement of services for people with a personality disorder and/or substance misuse', their main conclusion was that 'there is no evidence that it is anything but stigmatising to claim that their living in the community is a dangerous experiment that should be reversed'. Nevertheless, despite this robust defence of the community care model, the public mood had certainly shifted. The corollary was a concern felt more centrally at governmental level whether the professionals involved with forensic mental health could adequately meet the challenge that the public was implicitly demanding. Hence, the moral panic was also accompanied by a more measured concern about the validity of the knowledge base that underpinned the professional response.

The NHS Forensic Mental Health Programme over a twelve-year period (1996–2007 inclusive) had as its aim the development of the research base of forensic mental health. The programme essentially had two phases. The first phase (1996–99) of the national programme was originally formed under the auspices of the High Secure Psychiatric Services Commissioning Board and was operating in a context whereby the need for an improved academic base in the special hospitals was explicitly recognised. This interim period ended as planned after three years when the Programme became one of the NHS National Research Programmes in April 1999 within the remit of the R&D Board. A new advisory committee was established revisiting the objectives. The stated objectives of the new Programme closely mirrored the original objectives: dealing with potential or actual mentally disordered offenders, looking at the life course of these individuals, dealing with a range of settings in the NHS and CJS, service-led research, development of an evidence base for NHS and CJS services, development of research and a research culture, and influencing other funding bodies.

A substantial priority-setting exercise was undertaken with a wide range of stakeholders; expert papers were commissioned to provide overviews of key research areas and identify key research gaps and these, together with consideration of national priorities, played a stronger role in embedding forensic mental health research in the priorities and practice of the wider NHS. However, there was recognition that there should in addition be a role for responsive or investigator-led research in this area. In short, the research opportunities were opened to a much wider pool of potential researchers – but the situation whereby all the academics except one were funded by the NHS at the local level remained. Nevertheless, the development of research capacity remained a key priority.

The funding from the R&D forensic mental health initiative provided a form of 'protected status' that everyone knew would end at some point. However, when the new Department of Health strategy, *Best Research for Best Health*, was issued in 2006, it was decided without consultation that the Programme would cease commissioning with immediate effect and close in March 2007. In the event the administration of the Programme finally ended in June 2007.

While the Programme had many initiatives, including the commissioning of expert papers and appointing research fellowships, an analysis of the principal investigators (PIs) and the co-investigators (CIs) of the 79 projects commissioned by the Programme provides a useful profile of the persons who have been recently contributing to the knowledge base of forensic mental health. Certainly, of course, there will be others who are involved in forensic mental health research who did not apply for funding from this programme; they may have secured funding elsewhere or the focus of the programme may not have attracted them. Nevertheless, there were 213 different persons (127 males and 86 females) who were involved as either PIs or CIs (or both) and these investigators must be regarded as pivotal to the continued development of FMH research in the UK. Of these, there were 20 persons involved in the 12-year 'life' of the Programme as either a PI or a CI (or both), while 37 were involved as PIs only and the remaining 156 as CIs only. In short, these are the ones who have had a successful experience in applying for funding and who, thus, can be considered as providing the backbone of an active research community.

Table 1.1 shows the age and gender profile – as at 31 December 2007 – of all those who have been successful applicants in the search for project funding from this source. Of course, not all those who have had interests in the past will continue to have the same interests. Some may have moved from a research interest to a more mainstream teaching role or have become engrossed in practice that does not leave time for research. Others may have retired while, sadly, some will have died. Nevertheless, for any active research community, the remaining persons are likely to be pivotal players. These are the ones who have had a successful experience in applying for funding; in brief, these are the ones that might perhaps be regarded as the backbone of a research community in forensic mental health.

Table 1.1 The ages of all those who have been successfully involved as applicants in the FMH programme as principal investigators or co-investigators (or both) – a 'virtual research community' on 31 December 2007

Age	Male		Female		Total	
	No.	%	No.	%	No.	%
25–29	3	2.4	6	7.0	9	4.2
30–34	1	0.8	8	9.3	9	4.2
35–39	9	7.1	9	10.5	18	8.5
40–44	18	14.2	21	24.4	39	18.3
45–49	26	20.5	17	19.8	43	20.2
50–54	27	21.3	7	8.1	34	16.0
55–59	22	17.3	12	14.0	34	16.0
60–64	9	7.1	4	4.7	13	6.1
65+	6	4.7	–	–	6	2.8
No information	6	4.7	2	2.3	8	3.8
Total	127	100.0	86	100.0	213	100.0

Table 1.1 indicates that these 'players' are quite evenly divided in the four age groups between 40 and 59 years. The females, on average, are younger than the males with the peak age group for the males being 50–54 years (21.3 per cent) and for the females being 40–44 years (20.2 per cent). This difference will largely reflect the greater preponderance of females among co-investigators while the more responsible position of principal investigator will tend to be held by older persons and these older persons are more likely to be males. Whether this is a generational effect – that is, whether there will be a higher proportion of older females becoming PIs in the next decade or so – is a moot point and cannot be answered by this data.

Moving on to the professional groupings of these successful applicants, Table 1.2 highlights how psychiatrists in general – and male psychiatrists in particular – dominate as recipients of the awards for project grants. Just over one-third of the grants were awarded to psychiatrists (in fact, one-quarter of the grants were awarded to *male* psychiatrists), while psychologists secured one-quarter of the grants with female psychologists outperforming their male counterparts.

Among the other professional groupings around one in ten grants were awarded to nurses with a similar proportion to social scientists. Male nurses seem to be considerably more successful than female nurses (but this may simply reflect that more male nurses apply than female ones), while among the other professional groupings of the 'Other' category, the gender balance is more evenly divided.

Table 1.2 Professional backgrounds of all those who have been successfully involved as applicants in the FMH programme as principal investigators or co-investigators (or both)

Professional background	Male		Female		Total	
	No.	%	No.	%	No.	%
Psychiatrist	56	44.1	21	24.4	77	36.2
Psychologist	25	19.7	28	32.6	53	24.9
Other:						
Nurse	15	11.8	5	5.8	20	9.4
Social scientist	12	9.4	13	15.1	25	11.7
Health research	7	5.5	8	9.3	15	7.0
Medical/geneticist	4	3.1	4	4.7	8	3.8
Statistician	3	2.4	5	5.8	8	3.8
User	1	0.8	–	–	1	0.5
No information	4	3.1	2	2.3	6	2.8
Total	127	100.0	86	100.0	213	100.0

So what do the two tables really mean? We can perhaps say with some confidence that the forensic mental health research community is looking more buoyant than it has done so for decades. Instead of perhaps three or four figures that dominated the meagre field of forensic mental health research in the 1960s, there are now many 'players' in the field. Instead of just a few male psychiatrists, females and other professional groupings now play a very significant part. Also the age distribution looks healthy and there is no imminent 'retirement problem' with a particular peak in an older age group. There is much that is very encouraging. However, there are also issues to confront.

Seen from the various standpoints of the interest groups involved in forensic mental health research, there are a variety of perspectives to consider. Certainly psychiatry no longer has an almost monopolistic position in pursuing research in this area. There are several other professional groups involved. Nevertheless, with the funding emerging from the FMH R&D initiative, psychiatrists retain a somewhat dominant position. Psychiatrists are more likely to get awards and very much more likely to be given further awards than the other professional groupings. In contrast, psychologists, the next major group involved in forensic research, while nowadays having a massive presence in this area, seem to do less well proportionately in obtaining grants than psychiatrists. Perhaps psychiatrists do, indeed, produce better proposals and focus on topics that are more likely to be welcomed by the advisory committee of the Programme or perhaps the committee is, albeit unconsciously, biased towards accepting proposals from psychiatrists. This study certainly does not reveal the answers but raises the questions. One possibility is that nursing tends to focus on trying to understand the patient experience through qualitative methodologies, while psychiatry and psychology are more experienced through their training programmes in measuring outcomes. In a forensic world where we don't really have a strong evidence base as to what works, then the latter will probably always take precedence.

Additionally, the success of psychiatrists compared with psychologists can be linked with the gender issue. Females have a presence in the forensic field which would have been quite unimaginable even a couple of decades ago and yet some familiar patterns seem to continue. Females still tend to do less well proportionately and are more likely to be in the role of co-investigators rather than principal investigators. In terms of females being more likely to be co-investigators than principal investigators, there is an age question also to consider. Females involved in research in this study tend to be younger than the males, so perhaps it is a generational issue. Thus, perhaps the next generation of females will produce more principal investigators as the females gain more experience. Females are probably emerging more slowly from the handmaiden or deferential role than some might expect. However, it will also probably remain the case that females are more likely to move out of research and into caring roles to a much greater extent than males, and so it remains another moot point whether the next generation of females in their 40s will be sufficiently evident to produce research proposals as principal investigators.

The other professional groupings categorised as 'Other' in this study are too different to be considered as a coherent group. There is little doubt that their presence is nowadays evident in ways that – like females – would have been unimaginable even a decade ago. However, again like females, it is not too clear how the research base of these disparate professional groups will grow; there are, indeed, dangers that their research bases will wither rather than grow if there are inclement conditions. Now we must consider the more structural issues that are likely to affect all members of the forensic mental health community, although the issues will affect some more than others. Structurally there are issues that may produce a troubling tension and indicate the fragility of the FMH research community.

Firstly, there is the inexorable move in most areas of research to a concentration of resources to fewer locations. The work of the FMH initiative has demonstrated that the developing talent is widely distributed. While there has been some concentration of resources in places such as the Institute of Psychiatry, London and the University of Manchester, the diversity of the successful applications is what has been most noteworthy. If there is an attempt to concentrate resources, then this diversity – which can be regarded as a strength – will be lost.

The link between practice and research needs to be considered. In brief, while a concentration of resources may be commendable in theoretical subjects that are divorced from practice or where there is very expensive apparatus to purchase, it has much less rationale when research is trying to inform practice and to maintain high standards within practice. It may be trite to say that a greater concentration of resources within, say, London and Manchester may not help the maintenance and development of national standards, but there are other structural issues at stake.

Once one takes forensic work as covering activity beyond the special hospitals where there is a concentration of personnel, then the issue of numbers becomes much more paramount. Thankfully, in dealing with mentally disordered offenders, the numbers are comparatively few in relation to the general population. The large samples beloved of many funding bodies are simply not available to the forensic researcher. Of course, to build up numbers, cooperation between institutions who house researchers will become increasingly important. However, this requirement needs a national network rather than a concentration of researchers within just a few institutions. However, it is not the experience of this R&D programme that institutions, mostly universities, have been particularly helpful in attempting to nurture the long-term future of forensic work. The resources provided by the programme have rarely been integrated into a long-term plan for research at the local or regional level.

There are certainly some very highly committed, overworked but very focused individuals whom this recent programme of research has clearly identified. The hinterland is also much richer with talent than perhaps many might have expected. However, the verdict must be that the forensic mental health research community is currently very fragile. The Department of Health R&D FMH initiative certainly provided scope for research which seems to have been used fruitfully, but could also have provided a basis for thinking about the future development of forensic mental health research. Sadly, it is thinking about the future of this very important area of research activity which currently seems remarkably lacking. Constructive thinking about what is required is certainly needed. However, the aim of this book is more modest. It is to review the knowledge base of this fuzzy area called 'forensic mental health', to explain the administrative contours and the legal framework. Without an understanding of the issues and an appreciation of the variety of professional voices involved, the maintenance and development of forensic mental health will not happen.

References

Beales, D. (2004) 'Pendulum management in secure services'. *British Journal of Psychiatry*, 184: 270–1.

Bennett Inquiry (2003) *The Independent Inquiry into the Death of David Bennett (Chaired by Sir John Blofeld)*. Cambridge: Norfolk, Suffolk and Cambridgeshire Strategic Health Authority.

Blom-Cooper, L. (1992) *Report of the Committee of Inquiry into Complaints about Ashworth Hospital*. London: HMSO.

British Psychological Society (2007) *Forensic Psychology*. Available to download from: http://www.bps.org.uk/careers/society_qual/forensic_qual.cfm (last accessed 1 July 2007).

Byrt, R., Lomas, C., Gardiner, G. and Lewis, D. (2001) 'Working with women in secure environments', *Journal of Psychosocial Nursing and Mental Health Services*, 39: 42–50, 58–9.

Coffey, M. (2006) 'Researching service user views in forensic mental health: a literature review', *Journal of Forensic Psychiatry and Psychology*, 17 (1): 73–107.

Collins, M. (2000) 'The practitioner new to the role of forensic psychiatric nurse', in D. Robinson and A. Kettles (eds), *Forensic Nursing and Multidisciplinary Care of the Mentally Disordered Offender*. London: Jessica Kingsley.

Couldrick, L. and Alred, D. (2003) *Forensic Occupational Therapy*. London: Whurr.

Court, C. (1994) 'Clunis inquiry cites "catalogue of failure"', *British Medical Journal*, 5 March, 308: 613. See: http://www.bmj.com/cgi/content/full/308/6929/613 (last accessed 13 July 2007).

Department of Health (2006) *Best Research for Best Health: A New National Health Research Strategy. The NHS Contribution to Health Research in England*. Available from http://www.dh.gov.uk/en/Publicationsandstatistics/Publications/Publications PolicyAndGuidance/DH_412712 (accessed 17 September 2007).

Exworthy, T. and Gunn, J. (2003) 'Taking another tilt at high secure hospitals – the Tilt Report and its consequences for secure psychiatric services'. *British Journal of Psychiatry*, 182: 469–71.

Fallon, P., Bluglass, R. and Edwards, B. (1999) *Report of the Committee of Inquiry into the Personality Disorder Unit, Ashworth Special Hospital*. London: Stationery Office.

Faulkner, A. and Morris, B. (2003) *User Involvement in Forensic Mental Health Research and Development*. Liverpool: NHS National Programme on Forensic Mental Health Research and Development.

Gerber, G. J., Prince, P. N., Duffy, S., McDougall, L., Cooper, J. and Dowler, S. (2003) 'Adjustment, integration, and quality of life among forensic patients receiving community outreach services'. *International Journal of Forensic Mental Health*, 2: 129–36.

Gunn, J. (2004) 'What is forensic psychiatry?', *Criminal Behaviour and Mental Health*, 14: S1–S5.

Kettles, A. and Robinson, D. (2000) 'Overview and contemporary issues in the role of the forensic nurse in the UK', in D. Robinson and A. Kettles (eds), *Forensic Nursing and Multidisciplinary Care of the Mentally Disordered Offender*. London: Jessica Kingsley, pp. 25–38.

Kettles, A. and Woods, P. (2006) 'A concept analysis of "forensic" nursing', *British Journal of Forensic Practice*, September. Available to download from: http://findarticles.com/p/articles/mi_qa4121/is_200609/ai_n17192936

Lelliot, P., Audini, B. and Duffett, R. (2001) 'Survey of patients from an inner-London health authority in medium secure psychiatric care', *British Journal of Psychiatry*, 178: 62–6.

Morrison, P., Burnard, P. and Philips, C. (1996) 'Patient satisfaction in a forensic unit', *Journal of Mental Health*, 5: 369–77.

Mullen, P. (2000) 'Forensic mental health'. *British Journal of Psychiatry*, 176: 307–11.

Ryan, S., Moore, E., Taylor, P. J., Wilkinson, E., Lingiah, T. and Christmas, M. (2002) 'The voice of detainees in a high security setting on services for people with personality disorder', *Criminal Behaviour and Mental Health*, 12: 254–68.

Sainsbury, L., Krishnan, G. and Evans, C. (2004) 'Motivating factors for male forensic patients with personality disorder', *Criminal Behaviour and Mental Health*, 14: 29–38.

Scott, P. D. (1975) *Has Psychiatry Failed in the Treatment of Offenders?* (The Fifth Denis Carroll Memorial Lecture). London: Institute for the Study and Treatment of Delinquency.

Sen, P., Gordon, H., Adshead, G. and Irons, A. (2007) 'Ethical dilemmas in forensic psychiatry: two illustrative cases', *Journal of Medical Ethics*, 33: 337–41.

Soothill, K., Harney, K., Maggs, A. and Chilvers, C. (submitted) 'The forensic mental health tribes: identifying a research community'.

Soothill, K., Adserballe, H., Bernheim, J., Dasamanjali, T., Harding, T. W., Ribeiro, R. P., Reinhold, F. and Soueif, M. I. (1981) 'Social control of deviants in six countries', *Medicine, Science and the Law*, 21 (1): 31–40.

Taylor, P. and Gunn, J. (1999) 'Homicides by people with mental illness: myth and reality', *British Journal of Psychiatry*. January, 174: 9–14.

Tilt, R., Perry, B. and Martin, C. (2000) *Report of the Review of Security at the High Security Hospitals*. London: Department of Health.

Whyte, L. (1997) 'Forensic nursing: a review of concepts and definitions'. *Nursing Standard*, 11 (23): 46–7.

Whyte, L. (2000) 'Educational aspects of forensic nursing', in D. Robinson and A. Kettles (eds), *Forensic Nursing and Multidisciplinary Care of the Mentally Disordered Offender*. London: Jessica Kingsley.

Chapter 2

The forensic mental health system in the United Kingdom

Lindsay Thomson

Introduction

Contrary to the title of this chapter, there is not one system of forensic mental health within the United Kingdom, rather there are four reflecting the countries that make up the UK – England, Northern Ireland, Scotland and Wales. To understand these systems it is necessary to have some knowledge of the geographical, socio-economic and political landscape of each country. Having set the scene, this chapter describes the system within each in terms of mental health policy, legislation, forensic mental health services within the National Health Service and the criminal justice system, and mechanisms to ensure public safety. Tables are used throughout to provide an at-a-glance comparison of the four systems. Detailed descriptions of specific components can be found in later chapters.

Setting the scene

Socio-economic background

The geographical and socio-demographic characteristics of each country within the United Kingdom are described in Table 2.1 with basic data on rates of mental disorder and crime. While the latter uses a similar methodology for data collection in each country, there may still be cultural variations in the reporting of crime to the police. This may be particularly true in Northern Ireland where the police have traditionally been associated with one side of the religious–political divide. Caution must be exercised in comparing rates of mental disorder between Northern Ireland and the rest of the UK. The Northern Ireland study employed a different methodology with different time periods and created a prevalence hierarchy using primary diagnosis alone. Rates of psychoses were, however, similar throughout the UK.

Table 2.1 The United Kingdom

Country	England	Wales	Northern Ireland	Scotland
Geographical area	130,395 km^2	20,600 km^2	14,139 km^2	49,000 km^2
Population[a]	49,138,831	2,903,085	1,685,267	5,062,011
Ethnicity[a] – white	87%	96%	> 99%	98%
Unemployment rates (2002)	5.1%	6%	6.3%	6.8%
Rates of mental disorder/ 1000 adults[b] (16–74 years) Probable psychoses* Neuroses** Alcohol dependence*** Drug dependence*	5 165 72 36	5 190 93 23	> 14 years[c] 6 97* 14* 3	5 141 84 60
Legal system	Common law	Common law	Common law	Common and civil law
Age of criminal responsibility (years)	10	10	10	8
Recorded crime rates/ 10,000 (2005–06)	1040[d]	870[d]	731[e]	1,964[f]
Prison population/ 100,000 (2002)[g]	139 with Wales	139 with England	62	126

* in past year   ** in past week   *** in past 6 months
[a] Office for National Statistics (2002)
[b] Office for National Statistics (2001)
[c] McConnell *et al.* (2002)
[d] Walker *et al.* (2006)
[e] Police Service of Northern Ireland (2006)
[f] Scottish Executive (2006a)
[g] Home Office (2003a)

Political systems

The UK is a political union of four countries with a constitutional monarchy. The House of Commons is the supreme legislative body consisting of 646 elected members of the Westminster Parliament. Its second chamber, the House of Lords, has a review and amendment function for proposed legislation and is made up of non-elected members. All legislation relevant to England is made at Westminster. A proposal to create regional government in England is no longer active following an unsuccessful referendum in the North East in 2004 although there is an elected mayor and assembly in London. Devolved government exists in varying forms in Northern Ireland, Scotland and Wales.

The Northern Ireland Assembly provides devolved government for that country under the terms of the Good Friday Agreement 1998. It has 108 members and powers to legislate on transferred matters such as education, health or transport. Areas such as criminal justice are reserved to the Westminster Parliament or exempted, for example defence. Acts of the Assembly are subject to judicial review if they exceed the competencies of the Assembly, discriminate on religious or political grounds, or violate European law or the European Convention on Human Rights. The Assembly sat between December 1999 and October 2002 when the Ulster Unionist Party walked out after an investigation into an alleged IRA spy ring led to no convictions. The Assembly recommenced in May 2007.

The Act of Union 1707 united Scotland with England and Wales. The Scotland Act 1998 established a Scottish Parliament and a Scottish Executive which has both governmental and civil service functions. The Act followed a referendum of the Scottish people in 1997. The Scottish, or Holyrood, Parliament has 129 Members of the Scottish Parliament (MSPs). It can legislate on all matters such as health, criminal justice or education, except for those powers specifically reserved to the Westminster Parliament, such as defence, energy or social security. It has tax-raising powers.

The National Assembly for Wales was set up following a referendum of the people of Wales in 1997 and the Government of Wales Act 1998. It has 60 Assembly Members and has powers to create secondary legislation to amend primary legislation passed by Westminster. The Government of Wales Act 2006 gave powers to legislate in devolved fields but members of the Westminster Parliament have powers to veto Assembly laws or measures. It is important to note that matters relating to health have been devolved to the Welsh Assembly but the criminal justice system in Wales remains the responsibility of the United Kingdom Parliament through the Home Office and the new Ministry of Justice. This can cause logistical difficulties when England launches a joint Department of Health/Home Office or Ministry of Justice initiative (e.g. devolving the delivery of prisoner healthcare from the Prison estate to the NHS). Wales is bound by the criminal justice aspect of the Home Office's remit but not bound by the Department of Health's remit. Attempting to disentangle which part of an initiative or guidance belongs to which body is difficult and, generally speaking, uncertainty prevails. This means that much of the criminal justice data relevant to Wales are published as joint English and Welsh statistics.

Legal systems

There are three distinct legal systems within the UK and the court structure of each is set out in Figures 2.1–2.3. English law is relevant to both England and Wales and is based on common-law principles as is the law of Northern Ireland; in contrast, Scots law is a system based on both common law and civil-law principles. Common-law draws from precedents set by previous judgments whereas civil law interprets legal principles.

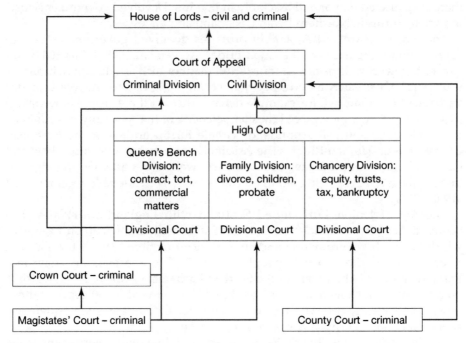

Figure 2.1   Court structure: England and Wales

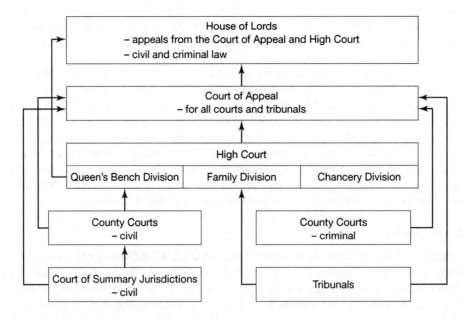

Figure 2.2   Court structure: Northern Ireland

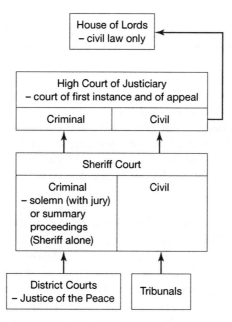

Figure 2.3 Court structure: Scotland

Components of forensic mental health systems

Policy framework

England

The Department of Health published the *Review of Health and Social Services for Mentally Disordered Offenders and Others Requiring Similar Services* in 1992 (Department of Health and Home Office 1992 – Reed Report). It set out five guiding principles for the care and treatment of mentally disordered offenders:

- with regard to quality of care and proper attention to the needs of individuals;
- as far as possible in the community rather than institutional settings;
- under conditions of no greater security than is justified by the degree of danger they present to themselves or to others;
- in such a way as to maximise rehabilitation and their chances of sustaining an independent life;
- as near as possible to their own homes or families if they have them.

The National Framework for Mental Health (Department of Health 1999) defined national standards and service models for promoting mental health and treating mental illness, put in place underpinning programmes to support local delivery and established milestones and a specific group of high-level performance indicators against which progress within agreed timescales would be measured.

Wales

The *Welsh Revised Adult Mental Health National Service Framework* (Welsh Assembly Government 2005) sets out eight key actions involving:

- social inclusion, health promotion and tackling stigma; service user and carer empowerment; promotion of opportunities for a normal pattern of daily life;
- providing equitable and accessible services;
- commissioning effective, comprehensive and responsive services;
- delivering effective, comprehensive and responsive services;
- effective client assessment and care pathways; and
- ensuring a well staffed, skilled and supported workforce.

Northern Ireland

Since 2003 Northern Ireland has been engaged in the Bamford Review of Mental Health and Disability. Its report on forensic services (Bamford Review 2006) makes detailed recommendations for the development of forensic mental health and learning disability services in Northern Ireland. It acknowledges that levels of mental disorder in people subject to the criminal justice system are high, that current services are inadequate and that equivalence of access for this population to services should be a fundamental aim. It recognises that the majority of people with mental disorder pose no increased risk of harm to others but that for those who do, there must be adequate services to identify, assess and manage such individuals in both the health and criminal justice systems.

The principles for forensic services in Northern Ireland are:

- People who are in police stations, on bail, attending court, in prison, on probation or otherwise subject to the criminal justice system must have equity of access to and provision of the full range of statutory mental health and learning disability services (principle of equivalence).
- There should be joint cooperative planning between the criminal justice agencies and the health and personal social services and joint delivery of services in order to best meet the needs of service users and carers.

Mentally disordered offenders and others with similar needs should receive treatment, care and support for their mental disorder that is:

- as far as possible in the community rather than inpatient settings;
- under conditions of security and restriction no greater than as are justified by the degree of danger they present to themselves or others; and
- open, accountable and subject to external review.

Scotland

The primary policy document of the Scottish Executive is *Health, Social Work and Related Services for Mentally Disordered Offenders in Scotland* (The MDO Policy). (Scottish Office 1999). It describes mentally disordered offenders as those who are 'considered to suffer from a mental disorder as defined in [Scottish mental health legislation], whether or not they are, or may be, managed under its provisions and come to the attention of the criminal justice system'. It adopted the Reed guiding principles set out previously for the care and treatment of mentally disordered offenders.

The MDO Policy, which was complementary to the *Framework for Mental Health Services in Scotland* (Scottish Office 1997), tasked Health Boards with the organisation of a range of inpatient facilities and community services. The policy highlighted the concept of the 'managed clinical network' to ensure a formal relationship between the components of a service based on standards of service, quality assurance and seamless provision of care. The Forensic Mental Health Services Managed Care Network was established in 2003 to provide a strategic overview and direction for the planning and development of specialist services. It has produced a number of policy and working documents which resulted in a New National Policy for Forensic Mental Health Services (Scottish Executive 2006b). This provides policy on care standards, resolving clinical conflicts and security liaison and gives guidance on levels of security, services for women and services for people with learning disability. It recognises areas of further work on the development of services for people with personality disorder, risk management strategies and in teaching, training and research.

Mental health legislation

Mental health legislation is a necessary component of all forensic mental health systems to allow the care and treatment of patients unwilling or unable to accept this on a voluntary basis, or to allow diversion from the criminal justice to the mental health system. Tables 2.2–2.5 set out the relevant Acts and basic definitions used within mental health legislation throughout the UK, and the civil provisions for each country. Legislation for mentally disordered offenders is described below under the criminal justice system. The relevant provisions of the Mental Health Act 2007 are described within the text in each section or table and Chapters 11 and 12 contain further information.

Mental Health Act 2007 – England and Wales

The Mental Health Act 2007 received royal assent in July 2007. This was the government's third attempt to revise mental health legislation in England and Wales and it again met with stern opposition. The 2007 Act amends rather than replaces the Mental Health Act 1983. The part of this Act referring specifically to mentally disordered offenders is subject to little change, other than the abolition of time-limited restriction orders, although the broader definition of mental disorder may affect any detention. The Act introduces the concept of treatment availability to replace the concept of 'treatability' – that the detained patient will be stabilised or improved by the treatment. Community treatment orders are introduced and a wider range of professionals are able to undertake specific roles within the Act. For the first time, England and Wales will each have its own Code of Practice to the Act.

Table 2.2 Mental Health Legislation: Definitions and Exclusion Criteria

Definition / Legislation	England and Wales Mental Health Act 1983	Northern Ireland Mental Health (NI) Order 1986	Scotland Mental Health (Care and Treatment) (Scotland) Act 2003
Mental disorder	Mental disorder means mental illness, arrested or incomplete development of mind, psychopathic disorder, and any other disorder or disability of mind	Mental disorder means mental illness, mental handicap and any other disorder or disability of mind	Mental disorder means mental illness, personality disorder or learning disability however caused or manifested
Mental illness	Mental illness is not defined	Mental illness means a state of mind which affects a person's thinking, perceiving, emotion or judgment to the extent that he requires care or medical treatment in his own interests or the interests of other persons	Mental illness is not defined
Mental impairment	Mental impairment means a state of arrested or incomplete development of mind (not amounting to severe mental impairment) which includes significant impairment of intelligence and social functioning and is associated with abnormally aggressive or seriously irresponsible conduct on the part of the person concerned	–	
Severe mental impairment	Severe mental impairment means a state of arrested or incomplete development of mind which includes severe impairment of intelligence and social functioning and is associated with abnormally aggressive or seriously irresponsible conduct on the part of the person concerned	Severe mental impairment means a state of arrested or incomplete development of mind which includes severe impairment of intelligence and social functioning and is associated with abnormally aggressive or seriously irresponsible conduct on the part of the person concerned	–

Table 2.2 (continued)

Definition Legislation	England and Wales Mental Health Act 1983	Northern Ireland Mental Health (NI) Order 1986	Scotland Mental Health (Care and Treatment) (Scotland) Act 2003
Psychopathic disorder	Psychopathic disorder means a persistent disorder or disability of mind (whether or not including significant impairment of intelligence) which results in abnormally aggressive or seriously irresponsible conduct on the part of the person concerned	–	–
Mental handicap	–	Mental handicap means a state of arrested or incomplete development of mind which includes significant impairment of intelligence and social functioning	–
Severe mental handicap	–	Severe mental handicap means a state of arrested or incomplete development of mind which includes severe impairment of intelligence and social functioning	–
Exclusions	Persons suffering from mental disorder by reason only of promiscuity or other immoral conduct, sexual deviancy, or dependence on alcohol or drugs, are excluded	Persons suffering from mental disorder by reason only of personality disorder, promiscuity, or other immoral conduct, sexual deviancy or dependence on alcohol or drugs, are excluded from detention on these grounds alone	A person is not mentally disordered by reason only of any of the following: sexual orientation; sexual deviancy; transsexualism; transvestism; dependence on, or use of, alcohol or drugs; behaviour that causes, or is likely to cause, harassment, alarm or distress to any other person; or acting as no prudent person would act

Interestingly a caveat exists whereby any power of Welsh ministers to make regulations or an order regarding mental health legislation is exercisable by statutory instrument but must be approved by resolution of the National Assembly for Wales. Thus a potential for conflict between England and Wales on legislative powers could arise, thereby causing further confusion relating to the England/Wales relationship.

Under the Mental Health Act 2007 when enacted, mental disorder means 'any disorder or disability of the mind'. A person cannot be treated as mentally disordered by reason of learning disability unless they exhibit abnormally aggressive or seriously irresponsible behaviour. Learning disability is defined as 'a state of arrested or incomplete development of the mind which includes significant impairment of intelligence and social functioning'. Dependence on alcohol or drugs are the only exclusion criteria.

Forensic mental health services

Between the mid-nineteenth century and the late-twentieth century, the high security special hospitals in England and the State Hospital in Scotland were the sole providers of specialist hospital in-patient services for offender patients. It was with the publication of the Glancy (Department of Health and Social Security 1974) and Butler (Department of Health and Social Security 1975) Reports, however, that the basis of our current forensic mental health systems was developed with a system of regional secure units in England and Wales.

There are two essential components to successful forensic mental health services: firstly, there should be a range of services from the community to high security, incorporating services to the criminal justice system; and secondly, there should be strong links between forensic services and general adult psychiatry, learning disability, psychotherapy, and child and adolescent psychiatry. These assist in the identification of patients and their throughput between services and levels of security as appropriate. Security can itself be considered as a therapeutic component and the principles of assessment and management are common to each level.

High-security psychiatric hospitals

There are four high-security psychiatric hospitals in the United Kingdom which care for people with dangerous, violent or criminal propensities under civil mental health legislation or legislation for mentally disordered offenders. Table 2.6 summarises the roles of the four high-security hospitals. Patients from Northern Ireland in need of high security go to the State Hospital in Scotland, and Welsh patients go to English high-security hospitals, particularly Ashworth.

Table 2.3 England and Wales – Mental Health Act 1983: Part II Compulsory Admission and Detention (NB. The Mental Health Act 2007 for England and Wales will introduce a broader definition of mental disorder when enacted.)

Purpose	Section	Grounds for Detention	Duration	Signatories/applicant	Appeal
Admission for assessment	2	Mental disorder Patient's health or safety / protection of others Requires hospitalisation	28 days	Two doctors (one approved)/ nearest relative or approved social worker applies	Mental Health Review Tribunal – application by patient
Admission for treatment	3	Mental illness, (severe) mental impairment and psychopathic disorder makes hospital treatment appropriate – if psychopathic disorder or mental impairment, such treatment is likely to alleviate or prevent deterioration of his condition Necessary for patient's health or safety or for protection of others and it cannot be provided unless detained	6 months	Two doctors (one approved)/nearest relative or approved social worker applies	Mental Health Review Tribunal – application by patient, nearest relative or by hospital managers
Emergency admission	4	Mental disorder Patient's health or safety, or protection of others Requires urgent hospitalisation	72 hours	One doctor/application by nearest relative or approved social worker	None
Emergency detention of patient in hospital	5(2)	Liable to be detained in hospital in pursuance of an application for admission for assessment	72 hours	Doctor in charge or nominated deputy / same	None

Table 2.3 (continued)

Purpose	Section	Grounds for Detention	Duration	Signatories/applicant	Appeal
Nurses' holding power	5(4)	Mental disorder Patient's health or safety / protection of others Requires immediate restraint from leaving hospital Not practicable to obtain doctor immediately for s. 5(2)	6 hours	Nurse of the prescribed class/none	None

Detention can proceed from s. 4 or s. 5(2) → s. 2 → s. 3 or commence with s. 2 or s. 3. Detention can be terminated at any stage by the responsible medical officer or by the Mental Health Review Tribunal.

Note

The Mental Health Act 2007 introduces supervised community treatment (ss. 17A–G). The necessary pre-conditions of making a community treatment order are that:

(a) the patient is suffering from mental disorder (any disorder or disability of mind) of a nature or degree which makes it appropriate for him to receive medical treatment;

(b) it is necessary for his health or safety or for the protection of other persons that he should receive such treatment;

(c) subject to his being liable to be recalled, such treatment can be provided without his continuing to be detained in a hospital;

(d) it is necessary that the responsible clinician should be able to exercise the power to recall the patient to hospital (the Bill said necessary for the patient's health or safety or for the protection of others – the Act simply says necessary).

(e) appropriate medical treatment is available for him.

Source: Thomson (2004).

Table 2.4   Northern Ireland – Mental Health (Northern Ireland) Order 1986: Part II Compulsory Admission

Purpose	Article	Grounds for Detention	Duration	Signatories/applicant	Appeal
Admission for assessment	4	Mental disorder Requires hospitalisation Substantial likelihood of serious physical harm to self or others	7 days with possible extension to 14 days	One doctor/nearest relative or approved social worker	Mental Health Review Tribunal
Assessment of patients already in hospital	7(2)	Mental disorder Requires ongoing hospitalisation Substantial likelihood of serious physical harm to self or others	48 hours	Hospital doctor	None
Nurses' holding power	7(3)	Mental disorder Requires application for assessment Not practicable to secure immediate attendance of doctor	6 hours	Nurse of the prescribed class	None
Detention for treatment	12	Mental illness or severe mental impairment Requires hospitalisation Substantial likelihood of serious physical harm to self or others	6 months, renewable for a further 6 months and subsequently yearly	One doctor approved by the Commission/ nearest relative or approved social worker	Mental Health Review Tribunal

'Detention can proceed from Art. 7(3) if required → Art. 7(2) if required → Art. 4 → Art. 12. Detention can be terminated at any stage by the Responsible Medical Officer, the Responsible Board, the nearest relative (if not opposed by the RMO); or by the Mental Health Review Tribunal following an appeal.'
Source: Thomson (2004).

Table 2.5 Scotland – Mental Health (Care and Treatment) (Scotland) Act 2003

Purpose	Section	Grounds	Duration	Signatories/consent	Revocation/appeal	Treatment
Emergency detention	36(1)	It is likely that the patient has a mental disorder Significantly impaired ability to make decisions about provision of medical treatment because of mental disorder likely Significant risk to patient's health, safety or welfare; or to the safety of others Necessary as a matter of urgency to detain patient in hospital to determine what medical treatment requires to be provided Undesirable delay in making arrangements for a short-term detention certificate	72 hours	One fully registered doctor/mental health officer if practicable	By an approved medical practitioner No appeal	Nil Urgent – section 243
Short-term detention in hospital	44(1)	It is likely that the patient has a mental disorder Patient has significantly impaired ability to make decisions about provision of medical treatment because of mental disorder Necessary to detain the patient in hospital to determine what medical treatment should be given, or to give medical treatment. Significant risk to patient's health, safety or welfare of patient; or to the safety of others The granting of a short-term detention certificate is necessary	28 days	Approved medical practitioner/mental health officer Must consult named person if practicable	The responsible medical officer (RMO) or Mental Welfare Commission can revoke the certificate The patient can appeal to the Mental Health Tribunal for Scotland	Authorised

Table 2.5 (continued)

Purpose	Section	Grounds	Duration	Signatories/consent	Revocation/appeal	Treatment
Short-term detention: extension certificate	47(1)	Patient is detained under short-term detention certificate Patient has a mental disorder Patient has significantly impaired ability to make decisions about provision of medical treatment because of mental disorder Necessary to detain the patient in hospital to determine what medical treatment should be given, or to give medical treatment Significant risk to patient's health, safety or welfare of patient; or to the safety of others An application should be made for a compulsory treatment order because of a change in the patient's mental health Not reasonably practicable to apply for CTO before expiry of short term detention certificate	3 working days from end of short-term detention certificate (excludes Saturday, Sunday or Bank Holidays)	Approved medical practitioner/mental officer if possible	The RMO or Mental Welfare Commission can revoke the certificate The patient can appeal to the Mental Health Tribunal	Authorised
Extension of short-term detention pending determination of application by the Tribunal	68	Patient detained under short-term detention certificate or an extension certificate Application for compulsory treatment order has been made Determination of application is pending	5 working days	Automatic if grounds are satisfied	By RMO No appeal	Authorised

Table 2.5 (continued)

Purpose	Section	Grounds	Duration	Signatories/consent	Revocation/appeal	Treatment
Compulsory Treatment Order (CTO)	64(4)	Patient has a mental disorder Patient has significantly impaired ability to make decisions about provision of medical treatment because of mental disorder Significant risk to patient's health, safety or welfare; or to the safety of others without such medical treatment Medical treatment likely to prevent mental disorder worsening; or alleviate symptoms or effects of disorder; and such treatment is available The making of a compulsory treatment order is necessary	6 months Renewable for a further 6 months and subsequently yearly The care plan measures can be varied by application to the Tribunal	2 doctors (1 approved); application including proposed care plan by mental health officer; Mental Health Tribunal approval	Can be revoked by RMO or the Mental Welfare Commission To Mental Health Tribunal 3 months after making a CTO or once during each period of renewal	Measures authorised by Tribunal
Interim Compulsory Treatment Order	65	As for CTO except the making of an interim CTO is necessary	28 days Maximum of 56 days in total for all interim measures	Determined by the Mental Health Tribunal for Scotland pending its determination of a CTO	Can be revoked by RMO, the Mental Welfare Commission, or automatically on granting of compulsory treatment order	Measures authorised by Tribunal

Table 2.5 (continued)

Purpose	Section	Grounds	Duration	Signatories/consent	Revocation/appeal	Treatment
Nurses power to detain pending medical examination	299	Patient has a mental disorder Necessary for the protection of the patient's health, safety or welfare; or the safety of others that the patient be immediately restrained from leaving the hospital Not practicable to secure immediate medical examination Necessary to carry out a medical examination to determine if an emergency detention or short-term detention certificate is warranted	2 hours and can be extended by 1 hour if the doctor arrives after the expiry of the first hour of the holding period	Nurse of the prescribed class – usually registered mental nurse	No revocation No appeal	Nil

Detention can proceed from an emergency certificate to a short-term certificate to a compulsory treatment order. Alternatively, a short-term detention certificate can be granted immediately by an approved doctor with the consent of an MHO (preferred route). In a non-urgent situation an application can be made directly for a compulsory treatment order. An emergency or short-term detention cannot be reapplied immediately. Tribunal decisions can be appealed to the Sheriff Principal. Appeals against the decisions of the Sheriff Principal are made to the Court of Session.

Table 2.6 High security psychiatric hospitals within the United Kingdom

Hospital (founded)	Ashworth (1990): Moss Side 1913 and Park Lane 1974 combined	Broadmoor (1863)	Rampton (1914)	The State Hospital (1948)
Location	Maghull	Crowthorne	Retford	Lanarkshire
Areas of responsibility	England and Wales Mental illness and personality disorder	England and Wales Mental illness and personality disorder DSPD* unit – The Paddock	England and Wales Mental illness, personality disorder and learning disablility DSPD* unit – the Peaks National Female High Security Service National High Security Service of the Deaf	Scotland and Northern Ireland Mental illness and learning disability
Beds	275	326	370	250
Management	Merseycare NHS Trust	West London Mental Health NHS Trust	Nottinghamshire Healthcare NHS Trust	The State Hospitals Board for Scotland

* DSPD – dangerous and severe personality disorder

Studies of referrals to high-security psychiatric care have shown that patients who were admitted had a more serious mental disorder and index offence than those rejected (Berry *et al.* 2003; Pimm *et al.* 2004). Differences in views between referring and accepting teams were found in less than a tenth of cases (Sayal and Maden 2002).

The population of the high-security hospitals has been extensively described (Maden *et al.* 1993; Thomson *et al.* 1997; Taylor *et al.* 1998). A typical patient is a male in his thirties with schizophrenia and a history of antisocial behaviour and/or substance abuse. Adverse events in childhood and poor physical health are common. A number of major differences were found in a comparison of the English and Scottish high-security hospitals research cohorts (Taylor and Thomson, personal communication): primary diagnosis of schizophrenia 55 per cent v. 70 per cent; primary diagnosis of personality disorder 24 per cent v. 3 per cent; co-morbid schizophrenia and personality disorder 18 per cent v. 33 per cent; ethnicity non-caucasion 26 per cent v. 1 per cent; history of substance abuse 10 per cent v. 41 per cent; and a median length of stay 6 v. 3 years. The proportion of patients in both groups with learning disability (10 per cent v.

9 per cent) was similar as were the histories of violent and sexual offending with over a quarter of patients admitted following a homicide, and the median age of first admission to high-security care 29 and 30 years. There were more women in the English cohort (17 per cent v. 11 per cent). Between 30 to 50 per cent of patients in both settings were said not to require high security psychiatric care. Since these findings were made endeavours have been made to relocate patients in England to lower security by the use of ring-fenced funding and in Scotland there has been the development of some medium-secure provision and the introduction of appeals against excessive security under the Mental Health (Care and Treatment) (Scotland) Act 2003.

In each setting the patient's management is organised by a multidisciplinary team comprising psychiatric, nursing, social work, psychology, occupational therapy and security staff. Regular case conferences are held and reviews of detention carried out or formal reports on restricted patients prepared. Patients receive a restriction order because of the nature of their index offence, previous behaviour and potential risk to the public. The progress of these patients is monitored by governmental departments. Treatment plans are developed at case conferences and aim: to improve the patient's mental state, physical health, social functioning, self-care and self-esteem; to reduce aggressive or challenging behaviour; to promote the use of coping techniques; to encourage community links; and to establish ongoing analysis of risk following each intervention.

Outcome studies of patients transferred from high security found a recidivism rate of 34 per cent and 31 per cent in England/Wales and Scotland respectively, and a violent recidivism rate of 15 per cent and 19 per cent after ten years (Buchanan 1998; Thomson 2005).

Medium-secure psychiatric care

The development of medium-secure psychiatric provision in the UK began in England and Wales following publication of the Butler Report in 1975 (Department of Health and Social Security 1975). It demonstrated the need for step-down secure psychiatric facilities from high security and for regionally based secure provision. Medium-secure units provide more than just an inpatient service for mentally disordered offenders. They are a focal point for the provision of forensic services to the community and to criminal justice services, for the training of forensic mental health staff and for research.

Scotland opened its first medium-secure unit in Edinburgh in 2001 (Nelson 2003). The Orchard Clinic provides treatment for 50 mentally disordered offenders or others requiring similar services. A 74-bed medium-secure unit, Rowanbank, opened in Glasgow in August 2007. A further unit of 30 beds covering the north of Scotland is planned for Tayside. The Shannon Clinic opened in 2005 and is the medium-secure facility for Northern Ireland with 34 beds.

A study of referrals to 34 medium-secure care units found that assessment of need for medium security was associated with symptoms of acute schizophrenia, non-compliance with treatment, a history of sexually inappropriate behaviour, current issues of self-harm, a serious index offence and a history of recent or multiple custodial sentences (Melzer et al. 2004a). Just under a fifth of those assessed in prison were not admitted, and just under a quarter of those admitted needed low-security or open psychiatric care. Examination of the deci-sion-making of assessors found that complex judgments were made and that a basic motivation was clinical benefit to the patient (Grounds *et al.* 2004). Common reasons for referral included aggressive behaviour, deteriorating mental state, need for diagnostic assessment and non-compliance with treat-ment. Forty-two per cent of assessed patients needed medium-secure care, one-third on a long-term basis (Melzer *et el.* 2004b).

Patients from a deprived socio-economic background (Coid *et al.* 2001) or of African-Caribbean origin are over-represented in medium-secure units (Maden *et al.* 1999a; Riordan *et al.* 2004). The latter group has a greater prevalence of psy-chosis and a lower prevalence of personality disorder.

An area of development in recent years has been that of long-term medium secure care (McKenna *et al.* 1999). The estimated need was set at 200 long-term medium-secure beds (Department of Health 2000a) and some £25 million was made available to transfer inappropriately placed patients from high security to other appropriate resources (Department of Health 2000b). The first long-term medium-secure unit with 24 beds was opened in West London for men aged 18 years or over who had spent at least three years in high-security hospital and who were thought would benefit from treatment in medium security for at least two years (Power *et al.* 2006).

Outcome studies of patients from medium-secure settings are relatively con-sistent allowing for different lengths of follow-up. Maden *et al.* (1999b) in a follow-up study over 6.6 years of patients (n = 234) discharged from medium-secure units found that 75 per cent were readmitted, 24 per cent were convicted of further offences, 20 per cent never reached the community and 8 per cent returned to prison although 48 per cent were admitted from that source. No dif-ference was found in the outcome of various ethnic groups. A ten-year follow-up study (n = 63) of patients formerly in medium-secure care found that 92 per cent remained in contact with psychiatric services, 30 per cent had been reconvicted of a violent offence and two had committed suicide (Baxter *et al.* 1999). A study of all people discharged from medium secure units in England and Wales over a twelve-month period found that 16 per cent of men and 9 per cent of women reoffended up to two years after discharge (Maden *et al.* 2006).

Low-secure psychiatric care
Low-secure psychiatric care takes two forms: firstly, the locked ward typically used for the rehabilitation of patients who frequently have controlled access to the community; and secondly, intensive psychiatric care units (IPCUs) which deal with acutely disturbed patients. Such units are not primarily for forensic patients although they may be found in these settings. Low-secure forensic psy-chiatric units have been established in some areas to cater for the needs of minor offenders or for the rehabilitation of mentally disordered offenders from higher security. A comparison of patients within a low-secure setting examined those undergoing rehabilitation from high security and all other patients (Smith *et al.* 2004). The high-security group was more likely to have a diagnosis of schizophrenia, a more serious index offence, more previous convictions and a significantly earlier age of onset of illness. One study showed that one-third of

patients in low-secure care in a region of England did not require that level of security (Beer *et al.* 2005). This group was more likely to be female and not considered to be a risk to others.

Community forensic mental health services

Two models of community forensic mental health services are in operation: the integrated model with forensic practitioners working within community mental health teams (CMHTs); and the parallel model with forensic care provided by a specialist community forensic mental health team (CFMHT). Key characteristics identified in parallel teams include specialist line management and supervision, forensic psychology, good links with criminal justice systems, protected funding and capped caseloads (Mohan *et al.* 2004). As yet, there is no study comparing the outcome of patients referred to CFMHTs and CMHTs but there is a logic that suggests that the former will develop specialist skills to utilise risk assessment and management, and targeted treatment for mentally disordered offenders in the community. Indeed, Vaughan *et al.* (2000) demonstrated that community teams in one area of the UK lacked the required skills in supporting MDOs in the community. They suggested the need to supplement these teams and to provide additional support from CFMH teams.

A study of CFMHTs in England and Wales identified 37 teams and 26 (70 per cent) responded to the survey (Judge *et al.* 2004). Eighty per cent operated on a parallel model and all offered risk assessment and management, whereas half offered anger management and cognitive behavioural therapy. Few offered treatment for personality disorder, substance misuse or sex offending. Access to appropriate accommodation and social services is essential for successful management of forensic patients within the community.

Independent secure psychiatric facilities

It is well recognised that private secure facilities have filled a major gap in the provision of forensic services in England and Wales, particularly for long-term medium-secure psychiatric care (Moss 2000). Approximately 50 per cent of secure psychiatric beds are provided by the independent sector, including specialist provision for women. Patients are sent from Scotland and Northern Ireland to such facilities although there has been some development of the independent sector in Scotland with the opening of a low-secure unit for patients with learning disability and one for patients with mental illness. Interestingly, the recent published agreement between the coalition government of Labour and Plaid Cymru Groups in the National Assembly of Wales on 27 June 2007 entitled *One Wales: A Progressive Agenda for the Government of Wales* states that 'we will eliminate the use of private sector hospitals in Wales by 2011' (National Assembly of Wales 2007: 9). What this actually means, only time will tell but it does set out a model of healthcare which will be watched very carefully across the UK.

Levels of security

Use of the least restrictive alternative for any psychiatric care is contained within each country's forensic mental health policy and is a basic principle of the Mental Health (Care and Treatment) (Scotland) Act 2003. Evidence of patients held in excess security is found in all levels of secure psychiatric care. Given the agreement on this principle, it is important to consider how judgments are made on an appropriate level of security. Structured guidance can be found from two sources: the Security Needs Assessment Profile (SNAP) and the Matrix of Security (Forensic Network 2004).

The Security Needs Assessment Profile was developed as a structured framework to aid decision-making regarding the appropriate level of security for a psychiatric inpatient (Davies *et al.* 2004). It contains 22 security items (see Figure 2.4) split between the three domains of physical and procedural security and relational skills. It was developed by detailed analysis of security practice in high- and medium-secure services and through extensive consultation with clinicians and security staff. It was subsequently validated in a study of 27 medium- and 8 low-secure units. For each item there is a general descriptor and case vignette, and four criteria intended to match levels of need: 3 = high, 2 = medium, 1 = low locked, 0 = open.

The Matrix of Security was developed by the Forensic Network Working Group (2004) and builds on the work of Kennedy (2002). This has not been validated in any setting nor is it available as a manual with operational criteria or case examples. It was designed as an instrument to assist clinical teams in

---

Physical security
1. Perimeter
2. Internal
3. Entry
4. Facilities

Procedural security
5. Patient supervision
6. Treatment environment
7. Searching
8. Access to potential weapons and fire-setting materials
9. Internal movement
10. Leave
11. External communications
12. Visitors
13. Visiting children
14. Media interest
15. Detecting illicit or restricted substances
16. Access to alcohol
17. Access to pornographic materials
18. Access to information technology equipment

Skills
19. Management of violence and aggression
20. Relational skills
21. Response to nursing interventions and treatment programme
22. Security intelligence

Figure 2.4 Items in the Security Needs Assessment Profile (SNAP)

decision-making about levels of security. It sets out a detailed description of environmental and procedural security for open wards, IPCUs, low-, medium- and high-security forensic units. The major components of the matrix are set out in Figure 2.5 but each component consists of a number of delineated factors. For example, design and construction gives expected standards for each level of security for the perimeter, control of access to the site, building design to deter escape, window and door security, and furniture design.

Management of patients within forensic mental health services
The major components of the assessment and management of forensic patients are summarised in Figure 2.6 and the majority of these considerations are common to all levels of security.

Specialist groups
There are a number of specialist groups that require access to forensic mental health services designed for their particular needs including people with learning disability (Hogue et al. 2006; Doody et al. 2000), women (Thomson et al. 2001; Thomas et al. 2005), children and adolescents (Wheatley et al. 2004), the elderly (Coid et al. 2002) and patients with hearing impairment (Young et al. 2000). There has been considerable recent development in forensic services for people with personality disorder in England and Wales since the publication of the 'no longer a diagnosis of exclusion' document (NIMHE 2003). This has led to the development of pilot community forensic services and to the funding of five pilot inpatient forensic secure units for the assessment and treatment of people with a primary diagnosis of personality disorder.

The most contentious development, however, has been the concept of dangerous and severe personality disorder (DSPD) and the creation of four DSPD services with 300 places covering England and Wales, two within the prison service and two within the high-security hospital service (Home Office 2004). For the purpose of DSPD assessments the criteria for severe personality disorder is deemed as met if an individual has a psychopathy checklist (PCL-R) score of 30 or above (or the screening version equivalent), or a PCL-R score of 25–29 plus at least one DSM-IV personality diagnosis other than ASPD, or two or more DSM-IV personality disorder diagnoses.

Environmental security	Procedural security
Design and construction	Visitors
Equipment	Child visitors
Communications	Internal movement between clinical areas
Items – restricted	Patient absence from hospital
Items – daily living equipment	Policies and contingency planning
Items – access to money, valuable and belongings	

Figure 2.5 Matrix of security

Multidisciplinary teamwork	Psychosocial treatment
Care programme approach/	
care plan	● structured – work placements
Risk assessment and management –	day – daily living
structured clinical judgement	activities/skills
Physical healthcare	– recreation
Advocacy	● family intervention
Medication	● education programmes
Management of aggression:	● cognitive behavioural therapy
● environment and activities	● substance misuse awareness and relapse
● prevention	prevention
● control and restraint	● anger management
● seclusion	● anxiety management
● rapid tranquilisation	● social skills training
Restricted patient procedures	● assertiveness training
Social care	● index offence work
● Social services – assessment of need	● sex offender treatment programmes
● Employment schemes	

Figure 2.6 Management of patients within forensic mental health services: components of care

In Scotland a different approach was taken by the MacLean Committee in dealing with serious violent and sexual offenders with personality disorders (Scottish Executive 2000). It 'concluded that a third way approach in Scotland was neither feasible nor advantageous and that if offenders with personality disorders are assessed as high risk they should be managed along the lines recommended for other high-risk offenders'. The emphasis is on offence and risk rather than on a diagnosis such as psychopathy or severe personality disorder. The MacLean recommendations were largely enacted in the Criminal Justice (Scotland) Act 2003 as amendments to the Criminal Procedure (Scotland) Act 1995 and became operational in early 2006. The principal developments are:

- The creation of the Risk Management Authority (RMA) which has responsibility for setting standards, guidelines and guidance for risk assessment and risk management, training and accreditation, and policy and research.
- The introduction of a risk assessment order (RAO) which is a 90 (maximum 180) day period of assessment to allow the preparation of a risk assessment report to assist the court in determining if 'the nature of, or the circumstances of the commission of, the offence of which the convicted person has been found guilty either in themselves or as part of a pattern of behaviour are such as to demonstrate that there is a likelihood that he, if at liberty, will seriously endanger the lives, or physical or psychological well-being, of members of the public at large'. An RAO can be applied by the court to an offender convicted of a serious violent or sexual offence, or an offence that endangers life. The emphasis is on clinical risk assessment.
- The introduction of an order for life-long restriction (OLR) which is a lifelong sentence imposed on the basis of risk if the court believes on a balance of

probabilities that the risk criteria outlined above are met. An OLR is an indeterminate prison sentence although a tariff is set by the court. Release following the set prison period is dependent on an updated risk assessment and a proposed management plan as approved by the RMA. The Parole Board will impose licence conditions in the community. An OLR can be applied to a mentally disordered offender given a hospital direction (an initial period in hospital combined with a prison sentence) who fulfils the risk criteria outlined above. This is not the case for patients given a compulsion order with or without restrictions on discharge. Decisions on recommendations of these various psychiatric disposals should be based on the link between an individual's mental disorder, his index offence and future risk because of that mental disorder.

There are no specific services for forensic patients with personality disorder in Northern Ireland and a diagnosis of personality disorder is an exclusion criterion from use of their mental health legislation. The recent review of forensic services recommended, however, a detailed needs assessment to inform planning of services for people with personality disorder at all levels of security within both health and criminal justice systems including the development of a therapeutic community for those unable to manage within the prison setting (Bamford Review 2006).

Forensic mental health services to the criminal justice system

All three systems have diversion pathways at each stage of the criminal justice process to allow for the assessment and, if necessary, treatment of an individual within a health setting. This does not prevent the justice process from progressing either at the same time or at a later stage. See (see Figure 2.7).

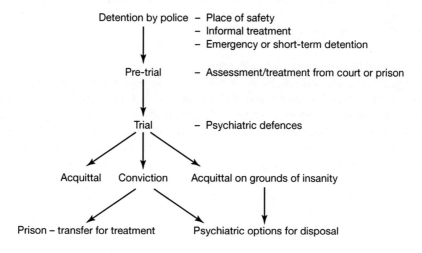

Figure 2.7 Criminal justice and mental health systems: diversion pathway

Forensic mental health services to the police

All forensic mental health systems within the UK offer some form of service to the police. The degree of sophistication of this system varies, not so much on a national basis, but largely on an urban–rural split. The police regularly become involved with members of the public with mental disorders and must consider a number of issues including the use of a place of safety order (see Table 2.7), fitness to remain in custody and medical needs, fitness for interview (Gudjonnson *et al.* 2000) and need for an appropriate adult (Thomson *et al.* 2007). There have been various studies of diversion from the criminal justice system to mental health services at point of arrest in all three countries (e.g. Riordan *et al.* 2000; McGilloway and Donnelly 2004; Graham 2001; Vaughan *et al.* 2001; James 2000). Following assessment, prisoners can be transferred to psychiatric hospital on a voluntary basis or under civil mental health legislation depending on the urgency of transfer and the seriousness of the alleged offence. Alternatively, arrangements can be made at the first court appearance to obtain a psychiatric opinion or to transfer to an appropriate level of security for assessment and/or treatment (see Table 2.8).

Forensic mental health services to courts

In most areas of the UK a mental health service is available to the courts usually in response to requests for psychiatric reports. Prosecutors can then decide whether it is in the public interest to go ahead with prosecution. In some areas specific diversion or court liaison schemes exist (e.g. White *et al.* 2002). A study of a supra-district diversion centre found that 0.46 per cent of all arrests in the central London area were referred to the scheme, with 0.28 per cent being admitted (James and Harlow 2000). This scheme served a population of 500,000 but accounted for 12.8 per cent of all unrestricted hospital orders in England suggesting that there is gross inequity of these schemes across the UK even allowing for increased demands within a capital city. Table 2.8 sets out the legislation available to courts to divert to the psychiatric system for assessment pre-trial or pre-sentencing.

Fitness to plead and psychiatric defences

Throughout the United Kingdom, a conviction is dependent on evidence proving beyond reasonable doubt that the accused carried out the offence (*actus reus*) and deliberately intended or risked a harmful outcome (*mens rea*). It is recognised that mental disorder may interfere with a person's ability to defend him or herself, or reduce or remove responsibility for a crime. Accordingly, each jurisdiction has provisions regarding fitness to plead and for specific psychiatric defences. These are summarised in Table 2.9. Alcohol or drug misuse is seldom accepted as a defence, unless involuntary or causing a secondary disorder such as Korsakoff's psychosis.

Table 2.7 Removal to a place of safety from a public place by police officers

Country	Legislation	Purpose	Conditions	Duration
England and Wales	MHA 1983 s. 136	To obtain examination by doctor and approved social worker	Police officer believes person in a public place appears to be suffering form a mental disorder. In immediate need of care and control	72 hours
Northern Ireland	MH(NI)O 1986 Art. 130	To obtain examination by doctor and approved social worker	Police officer believes person in a public place appears to be suffering form a mental disorder. In immediate need of care and control	48 hours
Scotland	MH(CandT)(S) Act 2003 s. 297	To obtain medical examination	Police officer suspects mental disorder in a person in a public place. In immediate need of care and treatment. In patient's interest, or for the protection of others to remove him to a place of safety	24 hours

Table 2.8 Legislation for diversion of mentally disordered offenders pre-trial or pre-sentencing (NB. The Mental Health Act 2007 for England and Wales will introduce a broader definition of mental disorder when enacted)

Country	Legislation	Purpose	Conditions	Evidence	Duration
England and Wales	MHA 1983 s. 35	Remand to hospital for report	Mental disorder / Bail impracticable / Pre-trial or pre-sentencing / Bed available in 7 days	Written or oral from one approved doctor under s. 12, to Magistrates' or Crown Court	28 days, renewable for 28 days to maximum of 12 weeks
England and Wales	MHA 1983 s. 36	Remand to hospital for treatment	Mental illness or severe mental impairment / Hospital treatment appropriate / Bail impracticable / Pre-trial or pre-sentencing / Bed available in 7 days	Written or oral from two doctors (one approved under s. 12) to Crown Court	28 days, renewable for 28 days to maximum of 12 weeks
Northern Ireland	MH(NI)O 1986 Art. 42	Remand to hospital for report	Suspected of suffering from mental illness or severe mental impairment / Bail impracticable / Crown Court – pre trial / Magistrates court – convicted or satisfied he committed the charge	Oral from one Part II doctor	28 days, renewable for 28 days to maximum of 12 weeks
Northern Ireland	MH(NI)O 1986 Art. 43	Remand to hospital for treatment	Mental illness or severe mental impairment / Pre-trial or pre-sentencing	Oral from one Part II doctor	28 days, renewable for 28 days to maximum of 12 weeks

Table 2.8 (continued)

Country	Legislation	Purpose	Conditions	Evidence	Duration
Scotland	Criminal Procedure (Scotland) Act 1995 Assessment order s. 52D	Assessment in hospital pre-trial or pre-sentencing From court or prison Restricted patient status	Reasonable grounds to believe: • mental disorder • risk to health, welfare or safety, or safety of others • detention in hospital necessary to determine if treatment order criteria met Assessment could not be undertaken if patient not in hospital Bed available in 7 days	Written or oral from one registered doctor to court Or written and submitted to court via Scottish Ministers if remanded prisoner	28 days (7-day extension)
Scotland	Criminal Procedure (Scotland) Act 1995 Treatment order s. 52M	Treatment in hospital pre-trial or sentencing From court or prison Restricted patient status	Mental disorder Available treatment likely to prevent medical disorder from worsening or alleviate symptoms or effects Risk to health, welfare or safety, or safety of others Bed available in 7 days Can be applied for directly or after an assessment order	Written or oral from two registered doctors (1 approved medical practitioner) to court Or written and submitted to court via Scottish Ministers if remanded prisoner	No time limit – as for remand period: 40 days summary or 110–140 days solemn proceedings
Scotland	Criminal Procedure (Scotland) Act 1995 Pre-sentence inquiry into mental or physical condition s. 200	To assess mental or physical condition in community on bail, or in hospital or prison on remand	Convicted of an offence punishable by imprisonment Needs inquiry into mental or physical condition If hospital proposed • suffering from a mental disorder • suitable hospital placement available NB Overlap with s. 52 D and M	Written or oral from one registered doctor to court	3 weeks (extension for 3 weeks)

Table 2.9   Fitness to plead and psychiatric defences

Fitness to plead/psychiatric defence	England and Wales	Northern Ireland	Scotland
Fitness to plead	Criminal Procedure (Insanity Act and Unfitness to Plead) Act 1991, ss. 2–3 and Sch. 1–2 *R v. Pritchard*	MH(NI)O 1986, Arts 49 and 50A *R v. Pritchard*	Criminal Procedure (S) Act 1995, ss. 54–57 *HMA v. Wilson* (1942) *Stewart v. HMA*
Insanity at time of the offence	Criminal Procedure Insanity Act 1964 s. 5, amended by Criminal Procedure (Insanity and Unfitness to Plead) Act 1991, s. 3	Criminal Justice (NI) Order 1986, Art. 50 Criminal Justice Act (NI) 1966 – defines insanity	Criminal Procedure (S) Act 1995, ss. 54 and 57 *HMA v. Kidd* 1960
Automatism: Sane – single events → acquittal Insane – disease of the mind → not guilty by reasons of insanity	*Bratty v. Attorney General for Northern Ireland* (1963)	*Bratty v. Attorney General for Northern Ireland* (1963)	*Simon Fraser* (1878) 4 Couper 70 *HMA v. Ritchie* (1926) JC 45 *Ross v. HMA* (1991) JC 210
Diminished responsibility – reduces a murder charge to manslaughter or culpable homicide	Homicide Act 1957 s. 2	Criminal Justice (NI) Order 1966 – impaired mental responsibility	*Galbraith v. H. M. Advocate* (2001) SCCR 551
Infanticide	Infanticide Act 1938	Criminal Justice (NI) Order 1966	No equivalent

Fitness to plead refers to an individual's mental state at the time of trial and can change. The tests are similar in each jurisdiction: does the individual understand the charge; can s/he distinguish between a plea of guilty and not guilty; can s/he challenge a juror (not applicable in Scotland); can s/he follow proceedings in court; and can s/he instruct a lawyer. Changes in all relevant legislation in the 1990s ensured that any case where an individual was found insane and unfit to plead was subject to a trial of the facts to establish whether the defendant committed the alleged act and brought in a wide range of potential disposals.

The special defence of insanity exists because it is recognised that offences can be committed directly because of psychotic symptoms. It is an individual's mental state at the time of the offence that is relevant. The 1843 McNaghten rules relevant to England and Wales set two criteria by which to judge insanity: firstly that the individual had at the time of the offence a mental disorder, and secondly that this led to the absence of *mens rea* (a guilty mind). In the words of the judgment the 'accused was labouring under such a defect of reason, from disease of the mind, as not to know the nature and quality of the act he was doing, or if he did know it, that he did not know that what he was doing was wrong.' The legal test in Northern Ireland is similar to that in England and Wales. An insane person suffers from an abnormality of mind which prevents him from appreciating what he is doing, or from appreciating that what he is doing is either wrong or contrary to law, or from controlling his own conduct (CJA(NI) 1966). In Scotland the definition is wider with both cognitive and volitional components. In *Lord Advocate* v. *Kidd* (1960) JC 61 it was stated that:

> ... in order to excuse a person from responsibility on the grounds of insanity there must have been an alienation of reason in relation to the act committed. There must have been some mental defect ... by which his reason was overpowered, and he was thereby rendered incapable of exerting his reason to control his conduct and reactions. If his reason was alienated in relation to the act committed, he was not responsible for the act, even although otherwise he may have been apparently quite rational.

The burden of proof in each country lies with the defence and is decided on the balance of probabilities. If the judge legally accepts an insanity plea, the jurors must decide if an individual was insane at the time of the offence. A wide range of options for the disposal of a case is open to the court following an acquittal on the grounds of insanity.

Automatism was defined by the Court of Appeal as 'the state of a person who, though capable of action, is not conscious of what he is doing ... It means unconscious involuntary action, and it is a defence because the mind does not go with what is being done' (*Bratty* v. *Attorney General for Northern Ireland* (1963)). Given that the person is not aware of their actions, s/he cannot have *mens rea*. Automatism has been divided into two types: a sane automatism leads to a full acquittal whereas an insane automatism leads to a verdict of not guilty by reason of insanity and a wide range of disposals. The difference between the two is based on whether the automatism or behaviour leading to the offence is likely to recur. The court's concern is primarily about public safety.

The psychiatric defence of diminished responsibility reduces a murder charge to manslaughter, or culpable homicide in Scotland, and a full range of legal disposals is available to the judge. It is important because a conviction for murder leads to an automatic life sentence. This is currently a topic of debate. Only the defence can raise the issue of diminished responsibility. The criteria for diminished responsibility in England and Wales are set out in s. 2 of the Homicide Act 1957:

> Where a person kills or is party to the killing of another, he shall not be convicted of murder if he was suffering from such an abnormality of mind (whether arising from a condition of arrested or retarded development of mind or any inherent cause or induced by disease or injury) as substantially impaired his mental responsibility for his acts and omissions in doing or being a party to the killing.

Abnormality of mind was defined in *R* v. *Byrne* (1960) as:

> ... a state of mind so different from that of ordinary human beings that the reasonable man would term it abnormal. It appears to us to be wide enough to cover the mind's activities in all its aspects, not only the perception of physical acts and matters and the ability to form a rational judgement as to whether the act is right or wrong, but also the ability to exercise will-power to control physical acts in accordance with that rational judgement.

The grounds for diminished responsibility were widened in Scotland following *Galbraith* v. *HMA* (2001). For full details of psychiatric defences in Scotland see Darjee (2005) and for further information on psychiatric defences elsewhere in the United Kingdom see Chapter 12. There is no psychiatric defence of infanticide in Scotland; the defence of diminished responsibility or insanity would be used instead.

There are a number of options open to the court for the final disposal of mentally disordered offenders. These are summarised in Table 2.10.

Forensic mental health services to prisons

The prison population in the UK is approximately 80,000 (Home Office 2003a – see Table 1) and it is known to have significantly increased rates of psychiatric morbidity (Davidson *et al.* 1995; Singleton *et al.* 1998) compared to the general population. Prisoners are assessed on reception to prison for mental and physical disorders. The sophistication of mental health services varies within different prisons but most have access to a psychiatrist. Suicide in prison is a major concern and is five times higher than the national average for a population of a similar age and gender (Fazel *et al.* 2005). This has resulted in the development of suicide risk management strategies within prison services and listener schemes supervised by the Samaritans. Legislation exists to transfer remanded or sentenced prisoners in need of hospital care because of mental disorder to hospital (see Table 2.11). There is concern about the prolonged delay in transfer that is occurring particularly in England, and about women from Wales being

Table 2.10 Legislation available to courts for final disposal of mentally disordered offenders (NB. The Mental Health Act 2007 for England and Wales will introduce a broader definition of mental disorder when enacted)

Country	Legislation	Purpose	Conditions	Evidence	Duration
England and Wales	MHA 1983, s. 38 Interim hospital order	Inpatient assessment and treatment	Hospital order may be appropriate Convicted Bed available in 28 days	Written or oral from two doctors (one approved doctor under s. 12 and one employed by specified hospital) to Magistrates' or Crown Court	12 weeks, renewable thereafter every every 28 days to a maximum of 6 months
England and Wales	MHA 1983, s. 37 Hospital order or guardianship order	Inpatient treatment	Mental illness or severe mental impairment; or Psychopathic disorder or mental impairment if treatment will alleviate or prevent deterioration Convicted At least 16 for guardianship order	Written or oral from two doctors (one approved under s. 12) to Crown Court	6 months, renewable for 6 months and thereafter annually
England and Wales	MHA 1983 s. 41 Restrictions on discharge	Necessary to protect the public from serious harm	Hospital order Necessary for the protection of the public from serious harm	Oral from one of the two doctors recommending a hospital order	Duration specified by court but often indefinite Always indefinite in 2007 Act
England and Wales	Crime (Sentences) Act 1997, s. 45 A* Hospital and limitation direction	Combines hospital detention and prison sentence	Psychopathic disorder Mental disorder from which the offender is suffering is of a nature or degree which makes it appropriate for him to be detained in a hospital for medical treatment Such treatment is likely to alleviate or prevent a deterioration of his condition	Two doctors, one must give oral evidence	Length of sentence

Table 2.10 (continued)

Country	Legislation	Purpose	Conditions	Evidence	Duration
Northern Ireland	MH(NI)O 1986, Art. 45 Interim hospital order	Inpatient assessment and treatment	Mental illness or severe mental impairment Hospital order may be appropriate Convicted	Oral from a Part II doctor and oral/written from another doctor to Magistrates' or Crown Court	12 weeks, renewable thereafter every 28 days to a maximum of 6 months
Northern Ireland	MH(NI)O 1986, Art. 44 Hospital order or guardianship order	Inpatient treatment	Mental illness or severe mental impairment Convicted or court satisfied committed offence At least 16 for guardianship order	Oral from a Part II doctor and oral/written from another doctor to Magistrates' or Crown Court Written or oral from approved social worker for guardianship order	6 months, renewable for 6 months and thereafter annually
Northern Ireland	MH(NI)O 1986 Art. 47 Restrictions on discharge	Necessary to protect the public from serious harm	Hospital order Necessary for the protection of the public from serious harm	Oral from one of the two doctors recommending a hospital order	Duration specified by court but often indefinite
Scotland	Criminal Procedure (Scotland) Act 1995, s. 53 Interim compulsion order	Inpatient assessment and treatment	Mental disorder Available treatment likely to prevent medical disorder from worsening or alleviate symptoms or effects Risk to health, welfare or safety, or safety of others Bed available in 7 days Likely compulsion and restriction orders or hospital direction (NB Not just relevant to State Hospital)	Written or oral from two doctors (one approved medical practitioner)	3–12 months (12 weekly renewal)

Table 2.10 (continued)

Country	Legislation	Purpose	Conditions	Evidence	Duration
Scotland	Criminal Procedure (Scotland) Act 1995, s. 57A Compulsion order	Treatment in hospital or community with attendance, access and residence requirements	Mental disorder Available treatment likely to prevent medical disorder from worsening or alleviate symptoms or effects Risk to health, welfare or safety, or safety of others Hospital – bed available in 7 days Convicted of an offence punishable by imprisonment	Written or oral from two doctors (one approved medical practitioner)	6 months, renewable for 6 months and thereafter annually
Scotland	Criminal Procedure (Scotland) Act 1995, s. 59 Restriction order	Control of high-risk patients Combined with inpatient compulsion order Leave and transfer decisions with Scottish Ministers	Serious offence Antecedents of individual Risk of further offences as a result of mental disorder if set at large	Oral evidence of one medical practitioner	Without limit of time
Scotland	Criminal Procedure (Scotland) Act 1995, s. 59A Hospital direction	Combines hospital detention and prison sentence	As compulsion order Link between mental disorder, offence +/– risk of future violence is weak	Oral or written from two doctors (one approved medical practitioner) (NB Doctors can recommend a hospital direction)	Length of prison sentence Compulsory treatment order can follow

Table 2.10 (continued)

Country	Legislation	Purpose	Conditions	Evidence	Duration
Scotland	Criminal Procedure (Scotland) Act 1995, ss. 60B/58(1A) Intervention and guardianship orders	Personal welfare decisions or management (not financial) Intervention order authorises single decisions Guardianship order provides continuous management	Found insane or offence punishable by imprisonment Mental disorder Compulsion order not required Incapacity for relevant matters Personal welfare issues	Two medical reports (one approved medical practitioner) MHO or chief social work officer report	One decision 3 years to indefinite

* Under the 2007 Mental Health Act for England and Wales the hospital and restriction direction has been extended to include all forms of mental disorder. The criteria are:

(a) that the offender is suffering from mental disorder;
(b) that the mental disorder from which the offender is suffering is of a nature or degree which makes it appropriate for him to be detained in a hospital for medical treatment; and
(c) that appropriate medical treatment is available for him.

imprisoned in England because of the lack of a Welsh facility. Through care provides a transition from prison to care in the community and is particularly relevant for mentally disordered offenders. A risk and needs assessment is carried out by social services and appropriate community arrangements made, including the use of the care programme approach for those with major mental disorder.

Probation

Psychiatric input to probation services, or criminal justice social work services in Scotland, is required for the purpose of assessment and management, but also for probation orders with a condition of medical treatment (Clark *et al.* 2002) (see Table 2.12).

Parole and life licence

Each country has in place a system for parole and life licence. Typically psychiatric or psychological reports form part of the dossier to be considered for prisoner release. A condition of licence can be attendance for treatment of a mental disorder. The Offender Management Bill for England and Wales is likely to have more far-reaching effects on the Probation Service and the system will be tested severely with the introduction of the new indeterminate sentence of imprisonment (or detention) for public protection which will apply to offenders who are convicted of a serious offence (that is a specified sexual or violent offence carrying a maximum penalty of 10 years' imprisonment or more) and who are considered by the court to pose a 'significant risk to members of the public of serious harm'. It has been estimated that there will be about 25,000 new cases over the next ten years.

Systems

The focus of many systems for the management of mentally disordered offenders is centred around public safety. Within each country there are systems for the management of restricted patients and for scrutiny of adverse events. The newest systematic development in the UK is that of multi-agency public protection arrangements (MAPPA). These were created in England and Wales under the Criminal Justice and Court Services Act 2000 and require police and probation to work together to manage the risks posed by dangerous offenders in the community (Home Office 2003c). This was extended to include the Prison Service and there is a statutory duty for health, housing, social services, education, social security and employment services, youth offending teams and electronic monitoring providers to cooperate with multi-agency public protection panels (MAPPs). These have four core functions:

- identification of MAPPA offenders;
- sharing of relevant information;
- assessment of risk of serious harm;
- management of risk of serious harm.

Table 2.11 Legislation for transfer of remand or sentenced prisoners to psychiatric hospital

Country	Legislation	Purpose	Conditions	Evidence	Duration
England and Wales	Mental Health Act 1983, s. 48*	Transfer to hospital of remanded prisoners	Mental illness or severe mental impairment Of a nature or degree that makes hospital appropriate Treatment is urgently required	Two written medical reports to Secretary of State (Home Office)	Until recovery or trial
Northern Ireland	Mental Health (NI) Order 1986, Art. 54 Transfer direction	Transfer to hospital of remanded prisoners	Mental illness or severe mental impairment Of a nature or degree that makes hospital appropriate Treatment is urgently required	Two written medical reports to Secretary of State	Until recovery or trial
Scotland	Criminal Procedure (Scotland) Act 1995, ss. 52D or 52M Assessment and treatment orders	Assessment or treatment in hospital pre-trial or sentencing From court or prison Restricted patient status	See Table 2.8		
England and Wales	MHA 1983, s. 47 +/− s. 49**	Transfer to hospital of sentenced prisoners	Mental illness or severe mental impairment; or Psychopathic disorder or mental impairment if treatment will alleviate or prevent deterioration	Two written medical reports (one recognised under section 12) to Secretary of State (Home Office)	Section 47 alone – 6 months, renewable for 6 months and thereafter annually Sections 47 and 49 – length of sentence

Table 2.11 (continued)

Country	Legislation	Purpose	Conditions	Evidence	Duration
Northern Ireland	MH(NI)O 1986 Art. 53 +/– Art. 55 – s. 136 Restricted patient status	Transfer to hospital of sentenced prisoners	Mental illness or severe mental impairment Bed available in 14 days	Two written medical reports (one Part II doctor) to Secretary of State (Northern Ireland Office)	Article 53 alone – 6 months, renewable for 6 months and thereafter annually Articles 53 and 55 – length of sentence
Scotland	MH (C and T) (S) Act 2003 Transfer for treatment direction (TTD) Restricted patient status	Treatment in hospital of sentenced prisoners	Mental disorder Available treatment likely to prevent medical disorder from worsening or alleviate symptoms or effects Risk to health, welfare or safety, or safety of others TTD necessary Bed available in 7 days	Two medical reports (one approved medical practitioner) to Scottish Ministers	Length of prison sentence

* Under MHA 2007 for England and Wales for transfer of a prisoner on remand the Home Secretary will have to be satisfied:

(a) that the person is suffering from mental disorder of a nature or degree which makes it appropriate for him to be detained in hospital for medical treatment; and

(b) he is in urgent need of such treatment; and

(c) appropriate medical treatment is available for him.

** Under MHA 2007 for England and Wales for transfer of a sentenced prisoner the Home Secretary will have to be satisfied the individual is:

(a) suffering from mental disorder (any disorder or disability of mind); and

(b) the mental disorder is of a nature or degree which makes it appropriate for him to be detained in hospital for medical treatment; and

(c) that appropriate medical treatment is available for him; and

(d) having regard to the public interest and to all the other circumstances, a transfer is expedient.

Table 2.12 Probation orders with condition of medical treatment

Country	Legislation	Purpose	Conditions	Evidence	Duration
England and Wales	Criminal Justice Act 1991 s. 9(3) and Sch. 1A Probation order	Medical treatment of a mental disorder	Mental condition of the offender: (a) is such as requires and may be susceptible to treatment; but (b) is not such as to warrant the making of a hospital order or guardianship order within the meaning of that Act Patient and probation officer agree	Oral or written by one registered doctor approved under s. 12(2), MHA 1983	6 months – 3 years
Northern Ireland	Criminal Justice (Northern Ireland) Order 1996, Sch. 14 Requirements as to treatment for mental conditions Mental Health (NI) Order 1986 Article Probation order	Medical treatment of a mental disorder	Mental condition of offender: (a) is such as requires and may be susceptible to treatment; but (b) is not such as to warrant his detention in pursuance of a hospital order under Part III of MH(NI)O 1986 Patient and probation officer agree	Oral or written by one registered doctor approved under Part II, MH(NI)O 1986	Maximum 12 months
Scotland	Criminal Procedure (Scotland) Act 1995, s. 23 Probation order	Medical or psychological treatments of a mental condition	Mental condition of offender: Requires and may be susceptible to treatment; but is not such as to warrant a compulsory treatment order or compulsion order Patient and criminal justice social worker agree	Oral or written by one registered doctor approved under s. 22, MH(CandT) Act 2003 or a chartered psychologist	6 months-3 years

Four features of MAPPA good practice have been identified:

- defensible decisions;
- rigorous risk assessment;
- delivery of risk management plans that match identified public protection need;
- evaluation of performance to improve delivery.

The guidance clearly recognises that risk can be reduced and managed but not eliminated. MAPPA offers three levels of input: advice; multiple agency involvment in the coordination of an individual's care; and, for high risk cases, intensive management and shared responsibility.

A multi-agency sex offender risk assessment and management (MASRAM) strategy is in place in Northern Ireland using voluntary agreements between agencies. The need to make this statutory and to extend the scheme to all violent and sexual offenders is currently under review. The Management of Offenders etc. (Scotland) Act 2005 established community justice authorities. Under public protection arrangements the police, local authorities and the Scottish Prison Service must establish joint arrangements to assess and manage the risk posed by sexual and violent offenders. This includes the NHS where the sexual and violent offenders are also mentally disordered offenders. The principles and aims of MAPPA are precisely the same as in England and Wales.

Comment

We are at a very interesting stage in the development of forensic mental health services in the UK. The issues posed by mentally disordered offenders are similar throughout the UK but the effects of devolved power are already leading to differences in their care and management, and create an opportunity for naturalistic experiments. It is crucial that the various similarities and differences between the countries that make up the UK – England, Wales, Scotland and Northern Ireland – are both recognised and understood.

Acknowledgments

The author acknowledges the contribution of the international forensic mental health research collaboration SWANZDSAJCS to the structure of this chapter, and to Dr Fred Browne and Dr Ian Bownes for advice on legislation relevant to Northern Ireland.

References

Bamford Review of Mental Health and Learning Disability (Northern Ireland) (2006) *Forensic Services*. Belfast.

Baxter, R., Rabe-Hesketh, S. and Parrott, J. (1999) 'Characteristics, needs and reoffending in a group of patients with schizophrenia formerly treated in medium security', *Journal of Forensic Psychiatry*, 10: 69–83.

Beer, D., Spiller, M. J., Pickard, M., Graystock, S., McGovan, P., Leese, M., Turk, V., Brooks, D. and Bouras, N. (2005) 'Low secure units: factors predicting delayed discharge', *Journal of Forensic Psychiatry and Psychology*, 16 (44): 621–37.

Berry, A., Larkin, E., Taylor, P., Leese, M., Watson, N. and Duggan, C. (2003) 'Referred to high security care: determinants of a bed offer/admission and placement after one year', *Criminal Behaviour and Mental Health*, 13 (4): 310–20.

Buchanan, A. (1998) 'Criminal conviction after discharge from special (high security) hospital: incidence in the first 10 years', *British Journal of Psychiatry*, 172: 472–6.

Clark, T., Kenny-Herbert, J., Baker, J. and Humphreys, M. (2002) 'Psychiatric probation orders: failed provision or future panacea?', *Medicine, Science and the Law*, 42 (1): 58–63.

Coid, J., Fazel, S. and Kahtan, N. (2002) 'Elderly patients admitted to secure forensic psychiatry services', *Journal of Forensic Psychiatry*, 13 (2): 416–27.

Coid, J., Kahtan, N., Cook, A., Galt, S. and Jarmin, B. (2001) 'Predicting admission rates to secure forensic psychiatry services', *Psychological Medicine*, 31 (3): 531–9.

Darjee, R. (2005) 'Psychiatric defences. Services', in J. McManus and L. D. G. Thomson (eds), *Mental Health and Scots Law in Practice*, Edinburgh: W. Green, pp. 161–82.

Davidson, M., Humphreys, M. S., Johnstone, E. C. and Cunningham Owens, D. G. (1995) 'Prevalence of psychiatric morbidity among remand prisoners in Scotland', *British Journal of Psychiatry*, 167: 545–8.

Davies, S., Collins, M. and Ashwell, C. (2004) *Validation and Calibration of Security Needs Assessment Profile by National Survey of Security Provided by Secure Services in England.* Final Report. Department of Health, National Research and Development Programme on Forensic Mental Health, Liverpool.

Department of Health (1999) *The National Framework for Mental Health: Modern Standards and Service Models.* Liverpool: DoH.

Department of Health (2000a) *The NHS Plan: A Plan for Investment, a Plan for Reform.* London: Department of Health.

Department of Health (2000b) *Report of the Review of Security at the High Secure Hospitals* (Tilt Report). London: Department of Health.

Department of Health and Home Office (1992) *Review of Health and Social Services for Mentally Disordered Offenders and Others Requiring Similar Services* (Reed Report), C 2088. London: HMSO.

Department of Health and Social Security (1974) *Revised Report of the Working Party on Security in NHS Psychiatric Hospitals* (Glancy Report). London: DHSS.

Department of Health and Social Security (1975) *Report of the Committee on Mentally Abnormal Offenders* (Butler Report), Cmmd 624. London. HMSO.

Doody, G. A., Thomson, L. D. G., Miller, P. and Johnstone, E. C. (2000) 'Predictors of admission to a high security hospital for people with intellectual disability with and without schizophrenia', *Journal of Intellectual Disability Research*, 44 (2): 13–137.

Fazel, S., Benning, R. and Danesh, J. (2005) 'Suicides in male prisoners in England and Wales, 1978–2003', *Lancet*, 366 (9493): 1301–2.

Forensic Network (2004) 'Definitions of levels of security in psychiatric inpatient facilities in Scotland'. See: www.forensicnetwork.scot.nhs.uk.

Graham, J. (2001) 'Policing and the mentally disordered', *Scottish Medical Journal*, 46 (2): 38–9.

Grounds, A., Gelsthorpe, L., Howes, M., Meltzer, D., Tom, B., Brugha, T., Fryers, T., Gatward, R. and Meltzer, H. (2004) 'Access to medium secure psychiatric care in England and Wales, no. 2: a qualitative study of admission decision-making', *Journal of Forensic Psychiatry and Psychology*, 15 (1): 32–49.

Gudjonsson, G., Hayes, G. and Rowlands, P. (2000) 'Fitness to be interviewed and psychological vulnerability: the views of doctors, lawyers and police officers', *Journal of Forensic Psychiatry*, 11(1): 75–92.

Hogue, T., Steptoe, L., Taylor, J., Lindsay, W., Mooney, P., Pinkney, L., Johnston, S., Smith, A. and O'Brien, G. (2006) 'A comparison of offenders with intellectual disability across three levels of Security', *Criminal Behaviour and Mental Health*, 16 (1): 13–28.

Home Office (2003a) *World Prison Population Statistics*, 4th edn, Research, Development and Statistics Directorate, Findings 188. London: Home Office.

Home Office (2003b) *Crime in England and Wales 2002/2003*, Home Office Statistical Bulletin, eds J. Simmons and T. Dodd. London: Home Office, Table 3.05.

Home Office (2003c) *Multi-Agency Public Protection Arrangements Guidance* Crown copyright 2004. London: Home Office.

Home Office (2004) *Dangerous and Severe Personality Disorder (DSPD) High Secure Services, Planning and Delivery Guide*. London: Home Office, HM Prison Service and Department of Health.

James, D. (2000) 'Police station diversion schemes: role in efficacy in Central London', *Journal of Forensic Psychiatry*, 11 (3): 532–55.

James, D. V. and Harlow, P. (2000) 'Increasing the power of psychiatric court diversion: a new model of supra-district diversion centre', *Medicine, Science and the Law*, 40 (1): 52–60.

Judge, J., Harty, M.-A. and Fahy, T. (2004) 'Survey of community forensic psychiatry services in England and Wales', *Journal of Forensic Psychiatry and Psychology*, 15 (2): 244–53.

Kennedy, H. G. (2002) 'Therapeutic uses of security: mapping forensic mental health services by stratifying risk', *Advances in Psychiatric Treatment*, 8: 433–43.

McConnell, P., Bebbington, P., McClelland, R., Gillespie, K. and Houghton, F. (2002) 'Prevalence of psychiatric disorder and the need for psychiatric care in Northern Ireland', *British Journal of Psychiatry*, 181: 214–19.

McGilloway, S. and Donnelly, M. (2004) 'Mental illness in the UK criminal justice system: a police liaison scheme for mentally disordered offenders in Belfast', *Journal of Mental Health*, 13 (3): 263–75.

McKenna, J., Shaw, J., Porceddu, K., Ganley, A., Skaife, K., and Avenport, S. (1999) '"Long-stay medium secure" patients in special hospital', *Journal of Forensic Psychiatry*, 10 (2): 333–42.

Maden, A., Curle, C., Meux, C., Burrow, S. and Gunn, J. (1993) 'The treatment and security needs of patients in special hospitals', *Criminal Behaviour and Mental Health*, 3: 290–306.

Maden, A., Friendship, C., McClintock, T. and Rutter, S. (1999a) 'Outcome of admission to a medium secure psychiatric unit 2. Role of ethnic origin', *British Journal of Psychiatry*, 175: 317–21.

Maden, A., Rutter, S., McClintock, T., Friendship, C. and Gunn, J. (1999b) 'Outcome of admission to a medium secure psychiatric unit 1. Short and long-term outcome', *British Journal of Psychiatry*, 175: 313–16.

Maden, A., Skapinakis, P., Lewis, G., Scott, F. and Jamieson, E. (2006) 'Gender differences in re-offending after discharge from medium secure units: national cohort study in England and Wales', *British Journal of Psychiatry*, 189 (August): 168–72.

Melzer, D., Tom, B., Brugha, T., Fryers, T., Gatward, R., Grounds, A., Johnson, T. and Meltzer, H. (2004a) 'Access to medium secure psychiatric care in England and Wales, 1: A national survey of admission assessments', *Journal of Forensic Psychiatry and Psychology*, 15 (1): 7–31.

Melzer, D., Tom, B., Brugha, T., Fryers, T. Gatward, R., Grounds, A., Johnson, T., and Melzer, H. (2004b) 'Access to medium secure psychiatric care in England and Wales 3. The clinical needs of assessed patients', *Journal of Forensic Psychiatry and Psychology*, 15 (1): 50–65.

Mohan, R., Slade, M. and Fahy, T. (2004) 'Clinical characteristics of community forensic mental health services', *Psychiatric Services*, 55 (11): 1294–98.

Moss, K. R. (2000) 'A comparative study of admissions to two public sector regional secure units and one independent medium secure psychiatric hospital', *Medicine, Science and Law*, 40 (3): 216–222.

National Assembly of Wales (2007) *One Wales: A Progressive Agenda for the Government of Wales.* Available from: http://news.bbc.co.uk/1/shared/bsp/hi/pdfs/27_06_07_onewales.pdf (last accessed 15 July 2007).

Nelson, D. (2003) 'Service innovations: the Orchard Clinic, Scotland's first medium secure unit', *Psychiatric Bulletin*, 27 (3): 105–7.

NIMHE (2003) *Personality Disorder: No Longer a Diagnosis of Exclusion. Policy Implementation Guidance for the Development of Services for People with Personality Disorder.* London: National Institute for Mental Health in England, Gateway ref. 1055.

Office for National Statistics (2001) *Psychiatric Morbidity Among Adults Living in Private Households, 2000.* London: Stationery Office.

Office for National Statistics (2002) *2001 United Kingdom Census.* See: www.statistics.gov.uk/census/

Pimm, J., Stewart, M. E., Lawrie, S. M. and Thomson. L. D. G. (2004) 'Detecting the dangerous, violent or criminal patient: an analysis of referrals to maximum security psychiatric care', *Medicine, Science and the Law*, 44 (1): 19–26.

Police Service of Northern Ireland (2006) *Recorded Crime and Clearances 1 April 2005 – 31 March 2006*, Statistical Report No. 1.

Power, N., Harwood, D. and Akinkunmi, A. (2006) 'The first long-term medium secure unit in the NHS in England and Wales', *Psychiatric Bulletin*, 30 (1): 25–8.

Riordan, S., Donaldson, S. and Humphreys, M. (2004) 'The imposition of restricted hospital orders: potential effects of ethnic origin', *International Journal of Law and Psychiatry*, 27 (2): 171–7.

Riordan, S., Wix, S., Kenney-Herbert, J. and Humphreys, M. (2000) 'Diversion at the point of arrest: mentally disordered people and contact with the police', *Journal of Forensic Psychiatry*, 11 (3): 683–90.

Sayal, K. and Maden, A. (2002) 'The treatment and security needs of patients in special hospitals: views of referring and accepting teams', *Criminal Behaviour and Mental Health*, 12 (4): 244–53.

Scottish Executive (2000) *Serious, Violent and Sexual Offenders: The MacLean Committee Report.* Edinburgh.

Scottish Executive (2006a) *Recorded Crime in Scotland 2005/06*, Statistical Bulletin, Criminal Justice Series CrJ/2005/6. Edinburgh.

Scottish Executive (2006b) *Forensic Mental Health Services*, Health Department, Directorate for Service Policy and Planning, NHS HDL (2006) 48. Edinburgh.

Scottish Office (1997) *Framework for Mental Health Services in Scotland.* NHS MEL(1997) 62. Edinburgh.

Scottish Office (1999) *Health and Social Work and Related Services for Mentally Disordered Offenders in Scotland*, Management Executive Letter (1999) 5. Edinburgh.

Singleton, N., Meltzer, H., Gatward, R. (1998) *Psychiatric Morbidity Among Prisoners in England and Wales, The Office for National Statistics.* London: Stationery Office.

Smith, H., White, T. and MacCall, C. (2004) 'A comparison of special hospital patients and other admissions to a regional low security unit', *Journal of Forensic Psychiatry and Psychology*, 15 (4): 660–8.

Taylor, P. J., Leese, M., Williams, D., Butwell, M., Daly, R. and Larkin, E. (1998) 'Mental disorder and violence: a special (high security) hospital study', *British Journal of Psychiatry*, 172: 218–26.

Thomas, F., Dylan, M., Shaw, J., Thomas, S., Thornycoft, G. and Leese, M. (2005) 'Redeveloping secure psychiatric services for women', *Medicine, Science and the Law*, 45 (4): 331–39.

Thomson, L. D. G. (2004) 'Mental health legislation and definitions', *Companion to Psychiatric Studies*, 7th edn. London: Churchill Livingstone, pp. 792–803.

Thomson, L. D. G. (2005) 'Mental disorder and psychiatric services', in J. McManus and L. D. G. Thomson (eds), *Mental Health and Scots Law in Practice*. Edinburgh: W. Green, pp. 1–16.

Thomson, L. D. G., Galt, V. and Darjee, R. (2007) 'Professionalising the role of appropriate adults', *Journal of Forensic Psychiatry and Psychology*, 18 (1): 99–119.

Thomson, L. D. G., Bogue, J. P., Humphreys, M. S. and Johnstone, E. C. (1997) 'The state hospital survey: a description of psychiatric patients in conditions of special security in Scotland', *Journal of Forensic Psychiatry*, 8 (2): 263–84.

Thomson, L. D. G., Bogue, J. P., Humphreys, M. and Johnstone, E.C. (2001) 'A survey of female patients in high security psychiatric care in Scotland', *Criminal Behaviour and Mental Health*, 11 (2): 86–93.

Tomar, R., Treasanden, R. H. and Shah, A. K. (2005) 'Is there a case for a specialist forensic psychiatry service for the elderly?', *International Journal of Geriatric Psychiatry*, 20 (1): 51–6.

Vaughan, P. J., Pullen, N. and Kelly, M. (2000) 'Services for mentally disordered offenders in community psychiatry teams', *Journal of Forensic Psychiatry*, 11 (3): 571–86.

Vaughan, P. J., Kelly, M. and Pullen N. (2001) 'The working practices of the police in relation to mentally disordered offenders and diversion services', *Medicine, Science and the Law*, 41 (4): 13–20.

Walker, A., Kershaw, C. and Nicholas, S. (2006) *Crime in England and Wales 2005/2006*, Research Development Statistics. London: Home Office.

Welsh Assembly Government (2005) *Adult Mental Health Services. Raising the Standard. The Revised Adult Mental Health National Service Framework and Action Plan for Wales*. See: http://www.wales.nhs.uk/

Wheatley, M., Waine, J., Spence, K., Hollin, C. and Hollin, H. (2004) 'The characteristics of 80 adolescents referred for secure in-patient care', *Clinical Psychology and Psychotherapy*, 11 (2): 83–9.

White, T., Ramsay, L., Morrison, R. (2002) 'Audit of the forensic psychiatry liaison service to Glasgow Sheriff Court 1994 to 1998', *Medicine Science and the Law*, 42 (1): 64–70.

Young, A., Monteiro, B. and Ridgeway, S. (2000) 'Deaf people's mental health needs in the criminal justice system: a review of the UK literature', *Journal of Forensic Psychiatry*, 11 (3): 556–70.

Chapter 3

The origins and early development of forensic mental health

David Forshaw

Introduction

The present plethora of organisations and professions involved in the study, care and delivery of services in forensic mental health evolved as a result of various influences over many centuries but particularly over the last two. The origins of the subject can be traced to a range of interdependent fields of scientific knowledge and social endeavour including medicine, nursing, neurosciences, law, psychology, criminology, police, sociology and politics (Forshaw and Rollin 1990). Some of these fields can trace their own origins to antiquity while others are much more recent. Several major contributions were made from some subjects that did not withstand the rigours of scientific progress, for example phrenology (Cooter 1981; Colaizzi 1989), or they led to unacceptable social consequences such as eugenics (Forshaw and Rollin 1990).

Many of the isles and countries that make up the United Kingdom and British Isles have their own domestic jurisdictions. Eire was part of the British Isles during the nineteenth century. Each separate jurisdiction has its own specific history with respect to mental health legislation and services. Developments in England were broadly typical and often set the trend though there were significant exceptions such as the evolution of the diminished responsibility defence in Scottish courts and the establishment of the first special hospital near Dublin in the nineteenth century. This overview of the field will focus on England in order to avoid repetition.

The interests of current-day professionals specialising in forensic mental health differ from their more generalist colleagues in several ways. The most obvious are those arising as a result of the dangerousness of the clients and the consequent need for a close association with the legal system and the use of secure facilities. The core concerns of modern forensic mental health professionals tend to relate to mental health legislation, criminal responsibility and secure psychiatric facilities. This brief overview will highlight some of the principal historical developments in these areas after some background comments which will help place the subject in its overall historical context and relate it to the foundation of general psychiatry.

General historical context

This very brief account of the history of the field focuses on the last two centuries. The nineteenth and twentieth centuries witnessed arguably the most dramatic changes in our social, political, scientific and technological evolution. From the comfort of our modern 'space age' domesticity it is hard to conceptualise everyday life 50 years ago, let alone some two centuries ago.

George III reigned in England during the closing years of the eighteenth century. The United States of America had rebelled against the monarchy and won its independence from Britain. The French people had risen against their king and ruling aristocracy and their bloody revolution had rocked the old order across Europe. Out of its ferment arose a new Republic that led the continent into a period of unrest and war and saw the emergence of a new and militaristic empire. The Napoleonic Wars instigated the social and political processes that were to ultimately culminate in the movement away from small agrarian states to the foundations of larger nation states such as Germany and Italy later in the century. Professional armies protecting nation states and furthering national interests replaced mercenary armies marauding for the gain and advantage of a regional or religious ruler. In parallel with these upheavals the Industrial Revolution was gaining pace with its rapid and progressive urbanisation of the population. In England it drove the rapid change away from an agriculture-based economy to an industrial and commercial-based economy. Small town markets were yielding to prototypal commodity and stock markets increasingly located in the capital. The aristocrat was yielding to the industrialist and banker. The merchant flourished and the tradesman and professional found a growing population able to afford their labours. These advances led to the need to develop centralised controls and administration and the modern civil service started to emerge.

English nineteenth-century philosophy was dominated by utilitarian ethics. Its rule-based nature encouraged the conviction that social reforms could be brought about in an ordered and semi-scientific way. The social reformers would first conduct an empirical study to determine the nature and magnitude of a social problem and identify possible solutions. They would then compare the probable consequences of each possible solution with reference to the guiding rule of 'acting to maximise the greatest happiness for the greatest number'. The chosen option ought to be that which would most likely maximise the overall happiness. The outcome of the chosen option would be checked after implementation and the whole process reviewed again if needed. Jeremy Bentham, often described as the father of utilitarianism, argued for the widespread use of this basic process in the form of the parliamentary process of inquiry, report, debate and subsequent legislation. The legislation would state the rules of conduct expected of the population or delineate the actions to be taken by public or private institutions. They would specify the inducements for compliance and outline the punishments for infringements. Punishment was seen as a necessary evil to deter future infringements and it was not necessarily considered as retribution (Geis 1960).

Legislation proved both an efficient and democratic way of bringing in new law but also provided a basis for a more cost-effective process of enforcement than the often confused, and sometimes contradictory, common law. The early nineteenth century witnessed the shift to increasing reliance on legislation as the main statement of English law (Manchester 1980). Armed with this tool for instigating progressive change, the early social reformers and legislators set about reforms in a range of areas including the abolition of slavery, improvement in the conditions in prisons, limiting the use of capital punishment and improvement of the care of the insane. As the nineteenth century progressed consolidation and codifying acts became essential additional tools for the reformer in order to clarify and simplify the earlier mix of case law and statutes (Baker 1979). The modern legal and parliamentary systems were established and used to demarcate and shape mental health care.

The nineteenth century saw the progressive unfolding of various technological developments. It quickly became the age of steam power. A network of railways displaced the canals for fast transport of goods and people on land. Steam power gradually replaced sail power at sea. The telegraph opened up rapid communication across distances. Events on the other side of a continent, and later ocean, could be reported within hours instead of days or weeks. The advent of photography revolutionised our ability to visualise distant people and places and so ourselves. The scientific discoveries in the basic sciences of physics, chemistry and biology, particularly Darwin's work on evolution, further revolutionised the way man saw himself, his world and his place in the world. Gas and electricity in the streets and home made their first appearance and started to revolutionise domestic life.

Queen Victoria's reign started in 1837 and later coincided with the height of her Empire's international power and wealth with England firmly in the centre of a world on which the sun never set. Her reign witnessed the appearance of state intervention in the care of the mentally ill on an unprecedented scale. This was mediated by legislation during the first decades of her reign that required counties to provide public asylums. The significance of the ensuing asylum era for the history of psychiatry is difficult to over estimate. Andrew Scull (1981: 6) emphasised this when he wrote:

> The Victorian age saw the transformation of the madhouse into the asylum into the mental hospital; of the mad doctor into the alienist into the psychiatrist; and of the madman (and madwoman) into the mental patient.

The outstanding advances in science and technology during the twentieth century saw the practical and widespread application and development of the cinema, telephone, radio, motorcar, aeroplane, television, jet engine, computer, nuclear power, satellite and the World Wide Web. Each major development precipitated a new mini social revolution or new age. However, the twentieth century was characterised by conflict. Dictatorships vied with democracies. Fascism, communism, capitalism, imperialism and socialism, or combinations thereof, fought each other in two devastating world wars and a host of regional conflicts. In some respects, the conflicts hastened technical developments and enhanced expectations of a better world to come. However, cynicism generally replaced any such optimism. The conflicts were often distractions from the process of development of forensic mental health. 'Shell shock' and 'battle fatigue' diverted much attention. In some instances physical resources were transferred away, for example the newly acquired Moss Side Hospital was loaned to the War Office in 1914. However, the widespread acceptance and consolidation of the newly introduced dynamic psychological therapies in the wake of the First World War and group and community therapies following the Second World War greatly facilitated the application of these techniques into forensic settings between the world wars and during the post-war era respectively.

Early foundations of psychiatry

The roots of modern general psychiatry can be traced to the closing years of the eighteenth century and the first half of the nineteenth. Social historians have suggested many possible reasons for this. The Industrial Revolution was driving urbanisation with its concomitant reliance on organised care and support for the infirm from people other than the increasingly distant family. Some historians have noted the apparent prevalence of a sense of optimism among the intelligentsia and leaders of this time and the widespread popular belief that the application of will power and 'scientific method' would solve most, if not all, problems. However, the optimism was fragile and easily undermined by the threat of social unrest as exemplified by the French Revolution. These historians have argued that the fragility of the optimism led to an intolerance of irrationality because it was perceived as contagious and a threat to social order. As a consequence, the response to the insane was to segregate them by incarceration in institutions (Foucault 1967). Society protected itself by the process of stigmatising the mentally disordered as 'deviant', then isolating them and rationalising the process as being for 'their own good' (Szasz 1970).

The highly publicised mental disorder of King George III towards the end of the eighteenth century raised public awareness of mental illness and helped focus attention on the plight of the insane at this time (MacAlpine and Hunter 1969).

Other historians have pointed to the various groups of practitioners who were unifying into an identifiable medical profession and demarcating specific areas of influence. Some of these practitioners saw the possibilities of 'trade' in managing the mentally disordered and so turned their attention to the subject. Medical practitioners in the field organised themselves into an effective economic and political group in order to further their own interests and those of their clients (Parry Jones 1972; Hervey 1985). This claimed 'medical imperialistion of the insane' led to the foundation of psychiatry as a medical speciality at the time. Once established and recognised by the state and delegated the power to protect and care for the insane, psychiatry was inevitably placed in the position of having to balance between 'protection' and 'oppression' with the result that the field was positioned in the public arena (Szasz 1974). Public scrutiny was inevitable. Fears that vulnerable, but sane, individuals were admitted unjustly to asylums by unscrupulous relatives and doctors were often expressed (Jones 1972). From this perspective, it is no coincidence that the first major act solely concerned with the care of the insane was aimed mainly at dealing with preventing improper incarceration.

Medical historians tend to emphasise the role of developing medical concepts and discoveries in shaping the history of medicine. A principal factor contributing to the success of the development of psychiatry at this time was the importation from the European continent of the clinico-pathological approach to the study of illness (Ackerknecht 1959). This consisted of observing symptoms and signs during life and correlating them with pathological findings at post mortem. Initially, the pathological changes studied were gross anatomical abnormalities but, as the nineteenth century progressed, histological changes were evaluated and, later still, biochemical lesions investigated. The correlations often suggested techniques for eliciting physical signs during life such as Auenbrugger's use of percussion, and Laennec's use of the stethoscope, to detect fluid in the lung. The successes of the approach in general medicine were impressive (Ackerknecht 1982). The identification of the underlying pathology for general paresis of the insane by French physicians in the nineteenth century encouraged alienists, and others, to believe that the utilisation of this technique would ultimately yield results in the realm of mental disorder. Implicit was a belief in monism; mental illness was brain illness. This optimistic belief in medicine's ultimate victory provided a rationale for the medical profession's jurisdiction over mental disorder.

An important aspect of the clinico-pathological approach at the time was the large hospital. Such institutions provided sufficient numbers of patients to allow meaningful correlations. Also, they provided opportunities for treatment facilities to be shared. Large mental asylums, in this view, did not just 'lock away the insane' but provided greater opportunities to study the phenomena and concentrated facilities for treatment.

Physicians complemented the insights gained from their clinicopathological studies with an understanding of physiological processes revealed by scientific experiments. Early in the process, the results of careful observations led to the realisation that long cherished treatments were ineffectual and often barbaric. Samuel Tuke (1813) described how the Retreat's physician Thomas Fowler came to this conclusion soon after the opening of the private asylum in York in the late eighteenth century. He recognised that the mentally ill retained some self-control over their behaviour and he aimed to facilitate this by ensuring the asylum provided an atmosphere of retreat and family support. Other physicians and attendants came to similar conclusions and the reliance on restraint, bleeding and purges for treatment waned. 'Moral management' was established. By the middle third of the nineteenth century it had progressed to a 'total nonrestraint movement' under the influence of proponents such as Edward Parker Charlesworth and Robert Gardiner Hill from the Lincoln Asylum, and John Connolly in the Hanwell Asylum (Hunter and MacAlpine 1963). The violent criminally insane patients challenged this progressive movement. Concerns were frequently expressed that the criminally insane presented real dangers to other patients within the asylums (Willis 1843; Hood 1854). Also, asylums were not generally as secure as prisons and many feared that removing restraint would furnish greater opportunities for escapes. Removal of the criminally insane from the general asylums was the obvious solution and calls for separate secure facilities increased as the total non-restraint movement gained in influence. The segregation and concentration of the criminally insane in specialist institutions provided both the academic opportunity and clinical foundation for the development of forensic mental health.

The main contribution of the clinico-pathological approach to psychiatry was the shift of emphasis towards the careful delineation and description of signs and symptoms of mental illnesses. This led to an understanding that the most dominant individual symptom or sign was not as important as recognising the combinations and timings of symptoms and signs in 'syndromes'. This culminated in the late nineteenth century and early twentieth century in Kraepelin's classic descriptions of manic-depressive psychosis and dementia praecox (later relabelled schizophrenia) (Ackerknecht 1982). As psychiatrists focused on more detailed studies of mental states they realised that the range of abnormal mental phenomena extended beyond abnormal moods and delusions and included distorted volitions, hallucinations and automatic behaviours in altered states of consciousness such as those associated with epilepsy.

Physicians came to understand that patients were affected by their illnesses in many ways. For example, Kraepelin (1919) noted how the ability of patients with dementia praecox to make rational judgments was adversely affected by the disease process. As understanding of abnormal mental phenomena grew practitioners concluded that their patient's responsibilities for their actions were undermined by these phenomena. The doctors argued for a broader concept of criminal responsibility and often met public, official and legal disbelief and opposition. The use of capital punishment prior to the abolition of the death penalty for murder in 1965 ensured that the outcomes of such debates in court often meant life or death for the defendant. The highly publicised debates in court in some rare sensational case raised the public profile of the subject and emphasised the need for practitioners to become familiar with various legal practices and concepts. Forensic mental health had some added dimensions.

The most obvious medical contributions to psychiatry during the second half of the twentieth century were pharmaceutical. The introduction of the major tranquillisers, anti-depressants and mood stabilisers revolutionised psychiatric practice and provided the necessary stability for care of the mentally ill to move out of the old, large mental hospitals and into the community.

The growth of mental health legislation

At the end of the sixteenth century the only public asylum for the insane in England was Bethlem in London. By the end of the following century a handful of others had been added. Norwich, Manchester, York and Liverpool had opened their own public lunatic asylums or infirmaries. The Poor Laws had provided the basis for the reception of vagrants and the poor into asylums. However, asylum places were limited and the poor were often incarcerated in gaols or workhouses.

For centuries, relatives, concerned that a mentally ill member of the family was squandering their livelihoods, had been able to approach a court for a declaration of insanity that legally transferred control over the patient's estate to an appointed representative. From the sixteenth century the Court of Wards and Liveries had dealt with this but the procedure was complex and costly. In the nineteenth century the process was simplified and the costs reduced by hearing the cases before special commissioners who, from 1845, were called the Masters in Lunacy. Admission to asylums could follow such a procedure and patients dealt with under this jurisdiction were known as Chancery Lunatics and the hearing in court called an inquisition. However, the mentally disordered relative could also be managed at home with a private attendant.

The growth in public asylums in the seventeenth century was paralleled by an expansion of madhouses owned by private individuals and operated for commercial profit. This increase in the facilities for detaining people was naturally associated with growing public concern about the powers of the managers of these facilities and the potential for unjust admission of sane people by unscrupulous relatives and asylum managers. These anxieties were particularly focused on the private facilities. The first major attempt at formalisation of the legal basis for the reception of the insane emerged late in the eighteenth century. The Act for Regulating Madhouses 1774 (14 Geo III c.9) aimed mainly to counter the concerns about inappropriate detentions. The Act required proprietors of private asylums to submit to licensing, notification of receptions and inspection. The principal purpose of inspection was to ensure that those wrongfully detained were released. Licences could be revoked if inspection was refused but the inspectors, or Commissioners as they were officially known, had few effective means of action or remedies under the Act if they found neglect.

Growing public concern about conditions within private and public asylums led to a series of Parliamentary Select Committees that reported in 1807, 1815–17 and 1828. Their reports shocked the public. Asylum inmates were often subjected to inhumane treatment. Many were restrained in irons for prolonged periods, poorly clothed and kept in cold damp cells with filthy straw mattresses (Sharpe 1815). The committee reporting in 1828 had examined asylums in London and Middlesex. It identified the deficient arrangements for inspection and the inadequate powers of the inspecting Commissioners as the main reasons for the persistence of the problem. It recommended increasing the number of Commissioners and advised extending their role to include inquiry into the behaviour of attendants and the investigation of patient's complaints. These new Commissioners for the Metropolis ought to be given, argued the committee, the power to recommend the revoking of a proprietor's licence if conditions were inadequate. The committee also recommended the appointment of lay members in addition to those who were medically qualified. The Madhouse Act 1828 (9 Geo IV c.41) enacted these suggestions. The new Metropolitan Commissioners in Lunacy consisted of a maximum of 15 lay and five medical members.

The Act for the Care and Treatment of Insane Persons (2 & 3 Will IV c.107) 1832 shifted the balance between lay and professional members more towards professionals and two barristers joined the commission.

In 1842 the number of commissioners was increased again and their jurisdiction extended to inspection of asylums throughout the country for a three-year trial period (5 & 6 Vict c.87). Conditions within asylums between 1828 and 1844 did improve though to what extent the new commissioners were responsible is difficult to determine. However, despite tensions between the medical and lay members (Hervey 1985), it was generally accepted by many contemporary commentators that they had played an important role (Jones 1972).

The Metropolitan Commissioners' Report of 1844 noted few serious abuses in the asylums inspected but the authors were concerned about the lack of consistent standards and the fact that many counties were not meeting the needs of their population by failing to provide a county asylum. The Commissioners noted that the law did not require counties to build asylums. The Commissioners were also concerned about the lack of inspection of the insane detained in places other than asylums such as in workhouses and gaols. The Lunatics Act (8 & 9 Vict c.100) 1845 countered these deficiencies and empowered the Commissioners to inspect asylums throughout the country beyond the three-year trial period instigated in 1842 and extended the inspection rights to include workhouses and gaols. The new commissioners were called the Lunacy Commissioners. Interestingly, the Bethlem Hospital remained exempt from inspection until after the passage of the amendment acts of 1853. The counties were now required to establish an asylum (though some united in joint programmes) and the following years witnessed the building of many new public asylums during the asylum era. The medical profession's responses to the Lunacy Commissioner's greater powers were ambivalent but the practitioners slowly accepted the system (Hervey 1985).

During the 45 years following the 1845 Act Parliament passed several amendments and related acts with the result that mental health law became fragmented and cumbersome. A comprehensive consolidation act was enacted in 1890. Under this Lunacy Act (53 & 54 Vict c.5) the role of the Lunacy Commissioners in inspection and reporting continued. Private asylums were permitted to receive both voluntary and involuntary admissions but the public asylums were limited to admissions under an order of the Act or following inquisition. As with modern mental health legislation, the Act specified the orders for admission. Paupers were admitted under a summary reception order after a police or poor law relieving officer had petitioned a Justice of the Peace with a supporting medical certificate. Non-paupers were admitted under a reception order. This order required two medical certificates and the patient's relative petitioned the Justice of the Peace. In an emergency, private patients could be admitted for up to seven days under an urgency order after petition of the asylum authorities by a relative. A medical certificate was required. Summary reception and reception orders needed renewal after one, two, three and five years and then at five yearly intervals. As with modern Mental Health Act legislation, there were a number of rules relating to the medical certificates. They had to be completed within seven days before the petition and, when two medical certificates were required, the signatories were required to be unrelated to each other by blood or business interests.

The reception and summary reception orders of the 1890 Lunacy Act were for relatively long periods. By the 1920s it was realised that many involuntary patients were likely to benefit from treatment over shorter periods. A temporary admission order, lasting six months, was introduced by the Mental Treatment Act (20 & 21 Geo V c.23) 1930. The Act also allowed voluntary admission to public mental hospitals.

The Ministry of Health had been formed in 1919 and responsibility for control of lunacy transferred from the Home Secretary to the Minister of Health. Hence, by the 1930s the fundamental components of modern mental health legislation were in place though the nineteenth-century requirement to petition a Justice of the Peace for the majority of admission orders might seem unnecessarily bureaucratic today. This was addressed by the Mental Health Act 1959 (7 & 8 Eliz II c.72). Compulsory civil admissions became medical rather than judicial matters (Jones 2006). However, admissions via the criminal courts and transfers from prisons remained the concern of the judiciary and the Home Office.

The law relating to the criminally insane

The first dedicated Act relating specifically to the management of mentally disordered offenders was passed in 1800 following the trial of Hadfield for high treason. He had discharged a pistol in the direction of the Royal Box in the Drury Lane Theatre in London as King George III entered. Hadfield had sustained a serious head wound at the Battle of Lincelles in Flanders in May 1794. Since then he had suffered from violent episodes of madness terrifying his family and friends. He believed that God had decreed that he ought to die to save the world but that he must not die by his own hand. Hadfield's solution was to commit high treason and so arrange his own execution. In fact, Hadfield's diseased state of mind was recognised at the trial and the judge directed the jury to find him 'not guilty: he being under the influence of insanity at the time the act was committed'.

The case highlighted the law's lack of clear instruction on disposal in such circumstances. Technically the defendant had been found not guilty. He had been acquitted and so he should have been released though it was obviously unsafe to do so. True, there were precedents in the past of such individuals being released to the care of their relatives and subsequently being admitted to an asylum or managed at home. There were even examples of individuals, such as Margaret Nicholson who attempted to stab George III in 1786, who were admitted to Bethlem on the legal grounds of archaic crown privileges relating to offences committed within a specified distance, or verge, of a royal residence. In the age of modern legislation, it was argued, a clear statement of the law was needed. The Act for the Safe Custody of Insane Persons Charged with Offences (39 & 40 Geo III c.94) 1800 followed and made provision for the safe detention of individuals found insane and acquitted of treason, murder or felony at His Majesty's Pleasure. Hadfield's case prompted Dr John Johnstone to publish the first specialist medical text on the *Medical Jurisprudence of Insanity* in 1800.

Unfortunately, the Act of 1800 had not stated where or how insane defendants were to be detained other than to note that it should be in a 'place and manner as to His Majesty shall see fit'. The Act made no mention of treatment. The Report from the Select Committee Appointed to Enquire into the State of Lunatics in 1807 recorded that 37 people had been detained by 1807 in gaols under the Act. The committee deplored their detention in gaols and called for provisions to allow admission to asylums. The Act for the Better Care and Maintenance of Pauper and Criminal Lunatics (48 Geo III c.96) followed in 1808. This permitted such insane individuals detained in penal institutions to be admitted to asylums, providing funding from private sources or the parish was agreed, but it did not require such admission. Little changed. The Repeal Act (1 & 2 Vict c.14) 1838 finally specified that, where possible, the place of safety referred to in the 1800 Act was to be considered an asylum. The Act for Making

Further Provisions for the Confinement and Maintenance of Insane Prisoners (3 & 4 Vict c.54) 1840 extended the jurisdiction of the 1800 Act to include similar acquittals in cases of misdemeanour.

The Amendment Act 1816 (56 Geo III c.117) allowed the transfer to asylum of sentenced prisoners who were found to be insane while serving a penal sentence. The Criminal Lunatics Act (30 Vict c.75) 1867 permitted transfer of convicted idiots and imbeciles who were unable to tolerate prison.

The Act of 1840 introduced an interesting legal device that seemed to sidestep the courts by permitting the direct transfer from prison to asylum of defendants awaiting trial under the instructions of a Secretary of State. In 1885, the Home Secretary ordered the admission of Baron Huddleston Marshall to Broadmoor Asylum before his trial for murder of a young girl. The public protest that justice had been set aside by the Home Secretary's action led to recommendations that in future this provision of the 1840 Act should not be used except with extreme caution. Later acts acknowledged this potential problem by giving separate consideration to individuals on remand awaiting trial. The main essentials of the law relating to the criminally insane were established by the time of the consolidation act of 1890.

The evolution of ideas about criminal responsibility

Since antiquity philosophers and theologians have argued that someone ought to be held morally responsible for their actions only if those actions were within his or her control and he or she wanted, or was reckless about, the reasonably anticipated consequences of those actions. People were morally good or bad depending upon their intentions. The law took a practical approach. It made a distinction between the action, the *actus rea*, and the guilty state of mind or *mens rea* (Edwards 1955). The distinction formed the basis for the legal recognition that mental disorder might absolve someone from criminal responsibility. Two early legal tests for criminal responsibility were the 'rightwrong test' and the 'wild beast test' (Radzinowicz 1968). These tests were based upon what the perpetrator knew at the time of committing the offence. In the former, an individual was considered not responsible if the mental disorder was such that the individual 'did not know that what they were doing was wrong'. This was interpreted in the sense of wrong as against the law rather than morally wrong. In the second test, the mental disorder needed to be such that the person did not know what they were doing 'no more than an infant, or than a wild beast'. The mental disorder needed to be extreme.

With growing knowledge about the symptoms of mental illness came a better comprehension of how mental illness might influence a person's intent when committing a crime. By the beginning of the nineteenth century the importance of delusions in mental illness were well appreciated and it was realised that a deluded person was not necessarily a furious manic or a totally withdrawn and stuporous melancholic. The individual's ability to reason and carry on their life in areas other than that covered by the delusion might remain relatively intact. This new understanding challenged the validity of the old tests. At Hadfield's trial for high treason in 1800, his defence counsel, Thomas Erskine, dismissed the wild beast test out of hand in his comment 'no such madman ever existed'. He argued that if a man was deluded at the time of the offence and the act was committed under the influence of the delusion then the man should not be held legally responsible (Ridgeway 1812). Hadfield was found 'not guilty, he being under the influence of insanity'. This was an acquittal though he was ultimately detained in Bethlem.

During the early decades of the nineteenth century there were several high-profile trials in which these more enlightened views held sway. Jonathan Martin was acquitted in 1829 of arson and felony when he set fire to the York Minister under the influence of delusional beliefs about the church. He was sent to an asylum. Interestingly, the jury had initially returned a verdict of 'guilty but consider that he was insane at the time' but the judge recorded the verdict as 'not guilty'. However, Edward Oxford was found 'guilty but insane' at his trial after firing two pistols at Queen Victoria on Constitution Hill in 1840. He appeared to believe that he was an agent of a secret society. The different wording of the verdict in his case was regarded as making more sense to the public because a 'not guilty' verdict implied to the public mind that the individual had not committed the offence at all when patently the defendant had committed the act albeit while labouring under a mental disorder. Though there had been uncertainty about whether the pistols were loaded the discharging of the pistols was still a treasonable act. Notwithstanding the wording of the verdict, with its implication that it was not an acquittal, he was also sent for detention in an asylum.

During the same period there were several cases where less enlightened views held sway. John Bellingham shot Spencer Perceval, then serving as both Chancellor and Prime Minister, inside the entrance to the House of Commons in 1812. The victim died. The public outrage was great. Bellingham was tried and convicted within a week. His defence counsel had unsuccessfully sought a postponement in order to prepare an insanity defence and seek a medical witness. There was a family history of insanity and there were witnesses who would attest that Bellingham was periodically deranged and confused. Bellingham was a merchant from Liverpool who had incurred several debts and served a period of imprisonment in Russia. He blamed the government for his plight and had sought recompense. He said he had assassinated Spencer Perceval because the government had refused to recompense him. Bellingham was hanged seven days later. The trial and execution of Bellingham were to become renowned as one of the greatest injustices carried out by the English legal system.

The conception of partial insanity or monomania, when an individual might be deluded in one area of their mental life but otherwise sane, was popular in the early nineteenth century. The concept of monomania was popularised among English-speaking alienists by Sir Alexander Morison (1840), among others, who drew heavily from the work of French physicians such as Esquirol. Morison was physician to Bethlem when the criminal wings were open. He took the opportunity to study the relationship between mental illness and offending and collected some simple statistics. He noted how illnesses could be associated with crime in different ways. For example, he noted how theft might be committed in dementia and idiocy because of an 'indistinct' notion of property and morality. Of the Bethlem patients, he described how the following diagnoses were associated with homicides: furious maniacs, mischievous idiots, monomaniacs labouring under delusion, monomaniacs overpowered by 'irresistible impulses' and melancholics. Physicians wishing to explain irresistible impulses often likened them to the longings or pica of pregnancy. Feuchtersleben (1847) maintained that these longings were sometimes present to such a degree in pregnancy that it amounted to mania. He cited Reil's example of a woman whose longing was to eat her husband. She had killed him and then salted his flesh. However, many physicians were uneasy at the thought that irresistible impulses or instinctive monomania *per se* should constitute some sort of defence of insanity. Even Morison (1848: 457) expressed his doubts in his lectures:

> There can be no security for life, if the consequences of an act may be evaded by metaphysical conjectures on the strength of morbid impulses, and the impossibility of controlling evil passions. There is not a crime for which, with some show of reason, the excuse might not be made – 'I did it because I could not help it'.

In 1843 a jury found 29-year-old Daniel McNaughton 'not guilty on the ground of insanity' at his trial for murder of the Prime Minster's private secretary, Edward Drummond. The victim died five days after being shot in the back in Parliament Street in London. McNaughton, the son of a Glasgow wood turner, had mistaken Drummond for the Prime Minister, Sir Robert Peel. Evidence was presented in court that McNaughton had been deluded for years. He believed that there was a conspiracy against him led by the Tories. An unprecedented number of physicians gave evidence in the court. They were unanimous in testifying to his insanity. Dr Edward Monro and Sir Alexander Morison from Bethlem appeared for the defence, among others, and Dr Forbes Winslow and Dr Philips gave evidence for the crown (West and Walk 1977).

The public cry of injustice in response to the court's verdict was loud and vehement. Queen Victoria expressed her discontent. The authorities were unable to disregard the public response and the issue was hotly debated in the House of Lords. Lord Lyndhurst (the Lord Chancellor) recommended the use of an archaic constitutional device that permitted the House to ask a panel of judges to clarify the law by responding to a series of questions on the topic. The judges gave their answers to the questions on 19 June 1843 and their replies have been referred to ever since as the 'McNaughton Rules'. One of the judges dissented from the general view and the judges indicated that their replies only applied to 'those persons who labour under such partial delusions only, and are not in other respects insane.' The following quotes contain the essences of the 'rules' (Wallis 1892: 931, 931, 932, 930, 932 and 932 respectively):

- 'Every man is to be presumed to be sane, and to posses a sufficient degree of reason to be responsible for his crimes, until the contrary be proved'.
- 'To establish a defence on the ground of insanity, it must be clearly proved that at the time of the committing of the act the accused party was labouring under such defect of reason, from disease of the mind, as not to know the nature and quality of the act he was doing, or, if he did know it, that he did not know he was doing what was wrong'.

- A defendant labouring under a delusion 'must be considered in the same situation as to responsibility as if the facts with respect to which the delusion exists were real'.
- An insane defendant is 'punishable, according to the nature of the crime committed, if he knew, at the time of committing such crime, that he was acting contrary to law, by which expression we understand your Lordships to mean the law of the land'.
- 'It is for the jury to decide' whether the defendant is insane or not.
- Dr Forbes Winslow had given his opinion in court on the defendant's insanity without having interviewed him. The judges were asked to comment on the legality of this and they replied that physicians in these circumstances 'cannot in strictness be asked' for an opinion.

The 'rules' indicate that McNaughton ought to have been found guilty in the view of the judges. McNaughton knew that it was against the law of the land to kill and his delusion of persecution was such that he was not killing in self-defence but rather to stop constant harassment. From the psychiatric perspective the rules represented a retrogressive step though more defensible than the wild beast test. The alienists expressed two main sets of concerns. First, this view of insanity was oversimplistic. Mental illness often presented with symptoms other than delusions and the expectation that someone with a delusion would be able to act normally in all other respects, just assuming the content of the delusion were true, was misguided and a misunderstanding of the depth and pervasiveness to which delusions and mental illness could influence behaviour.

The second concern focused on the role given to the jury to decide a defendant's sanity. Many physicians believed that injustices were inevitable as a trial was just not long enough to explain the range of issues involved to an untrained audience. To counteract this ignorance James Duncan published a little book in 1853 intended to increase the general knowledge among jurors about insanity. He was particularly keen to educate them about irrational and irresistible propensities and impulses to commit crimes such as occurred in pyromania and kleptomania (Duncan 1853). An alternative solution was proposed by several other leading nineteenth-century alienists, including Charles Bucknill, Forbes Winslow and Harrington Tuke. They were concerned that the adversarial system inherent in English law courts was not conducive to arriving at a well-considered opinion on matters of insanity. They argued that the courts ought to appoint independent medical experts to examine and decide the sanity of defendants. The credibility of their argument was damaged by a number of court cases highlighting the lack of agreement about insanity among physicians and illustrating how incomprehensible the ideas of alienists were to many in the general population. Perhaps, the most infamous of these cases was the trial for murder of George Victor Townley.

In 1864 Townley savagely stabbed his fiancée after she jilted him. Forbes Winslow had argued in court that there was a family history of insanity and that Townley had an 'inherited predisposition to insanity' and that he was 'morally insane' as manifest by his excessive temper and excitability. The defence of insanity failed and he was condemned to death. Townley's family were affluent. They obtained a certificate of insanity signed by two doctors and three Justices of the Peace and the Home Secretary ordered his transfer to Bethlem before the allotted time for the execution. The public response was to accuse everyone concerned of corruption. The psychiatrists were publicly divided on the issue of Townley's insanity with Maudsley and Lockhart Robertson strongly disagreeing with Forbes Winslow. The Home Secretary ordered another examination of Townley by three physicians all of whom pronounced him of sound mind. Townley was promptly returned to prison but his death penalty was commuted to penal servitude for life. Townley committed suicide (Forshaw and Rollin 1990). Maudsley later varied his view.

English physicians continued to express concern about the harsh guidelines contained within the McNaughton rules throughout the remainder of the nineteenth and the first half of the twentieth centuries. Despite the judges' provisory remarks that the answers they had given to their Lordships questions following McNaughton's trial applied only to cases of partial insanity, the rules became the standard test of insanity in English courts.

A review of reported cases suggests that despite various high-profile cases, precedents and rulings in the nineteenth century, there was no dramatic increase in the number of individuals acquitted on the grounds of insanity (Walker 1968).

In 1878 Simon Fraser killed his young son at night. He claimed he was asleep at the time and so he pleaded not guilty at his trial for murder. A doctor tried unsuccessfully to argue that Fraser had been temporarily insane. However, after hearing the evidence, the judge instructed the jury to consider a verdict to the effect that Fraser had killed his son but he had been 'unconscious of the act due to somnambulism'. The jury accepted the judge's suggestion. Fraser was allowed to go free after pledging to sleep alone in future. The defence of automatism had been established and complemented the insanity defence.

A nineteenth-century Scottish case was to ultimately offer a more satisfactory resolution to the debate around the insanity defence. In 1867 Alexander Dingwall was tried in Aberdeen for the murder of his wife on Hogmanay. Before she died from her knife wounds she had insisted that Dingwall had not known what he was doing at the time and that he was only ever violent after he had been drinking. He had been dependent on alcohol for at least a decade as evidenced by his suffering from delirium tremens. He was a middle-aged ex-soldier from a respectable family. He had stabbed his wife in the early hours of the morning sometime after returning from a night's heavy drinking. The judge instructed the jury to consider that though Dingwall was sane they could return a verdict of 'murder with extenuating circumstances' implying manslaughter. The jury complied. This Scottish finding was less controversial to the public than the English verdicts because it was clearly not an acquittal. The plea was to be called diminished responsibility in subsequent years but it would not find its way into English Law for nearly another century (Smith 1981).

Many legal reformers called for the incorporation of the Scottish diminished responsibility plea into English law throughout the closing years of the nineteenth century and into the twentieth. The situation finally changed in response to the recommendations of two influential inquiries into legal reform: the Royal Commission on Capital Punishment 1949–53, chaired by Sir Ernest Gowers, and the Committee of the Inns of Court Conservative and Unionist Society, chaired by Sir Lionel Heald. Both the Gowers and Heald Reports advised the acceptance of diminished responsibility pleas in English courts. The Homicide Act 1957 (5 & 6 Eliz II c.11) introduced the plea into English Law.

The development of secure psychiatric facilities

The arguments for admitting insane offenders into asylums in the nineteenth century were straightforward. Admission permitted the individuals to receive care and treatment. Also, it was felt inappropriate and inhumane to detain someone in prison or gaol, where conditions were generally much worse than in the asylums, particularly if they had been acquitted on the grounds of insanity. However, the admission of insane offenders into asylums raised many concerns, such as the shortage of places.

Hadfield's case quickly highlighted a serious problem. He was admitted to Bethlem after the passing of the Act of 1800. He escaped. After his recapture he was returned to prison. Another obvious concern was for the immediate physical safety of the other patients in the asylum when potentially dangerous mentally disordered offenders were admitted to their company. This issue would have presented a significant difficulty for the total non-restraint movement if separate accommodation had not been arranged. Some relatives expressed a more subtle concern. They were anxious that the presence of criminals in the midst of their loved ones might have some sort of morally corrupting or bad influence. This became a particular concern after the Act of 1816 permitted the transfer from prison of criminals who became insane while serving a sentence. The Metropolitan Commissioners in Lunacy wrote, in their report of 1844, 'Some consideration, moreover, is due to the feelings of the relatives of patients, who have reasonable ground to complain of atrocious criminals being forced into their society'. This led to a natural concern on behalf of asylum managers that an institution admitting insane offenders would have difficulty in attracting private patients of the 'refined classes' (O'Donoghue 1914). The asylum managers were also concerned about the extra cost of providing additional security measures to prevent escapes and ensure the safety of other patients and staff.

The obvious solutions to these problems were the confinement of insane offenders either in separate asylums dedicated to the care of insane offenders or in purpose-built wings within large general asylums. The Select Committee reports of 1807 and 1815–17 had recommended that a separate asylum for the criminally insane should be built (Sharpe 1815). This recommendation was often repeated over the next 40 years. The cost of such a project was considered too high at that time. However, Bethlem in Moorfields was in a dreadful condition in the first decade of the nineteenth century and the asylum managers had decided to build new premises in St George's Fields on the current day site of the Imperial War Museum in London. The government approached the managers and negotiated the building of two criminal blocks on the grounds of the new asylum to the rear of the main building. These opened in 1816. The male wing accommodated 45 patients and the female block was designed to house 15. Each block had a basement and three floors. The passages from the main hospital opened onto galleries that, in the male block, were divided into cages by metal wires and rods and opened into a sleeping room. Hadfield was returned to Bethlem.

The discharge of patients from the criminal blocks was under the jurisdiction of the Home Secretary. Concern that discharged patients might relapse and reoffend ensured that the politicians responsible for making the decisions about a patient's liberty wanted to see a period of stability after the patient's mental state had improved before agreeing to discharge. The period required depended on the seriousness of the offence that the patient had a 'propensity to commit' (Forshaw and Rollin 1990). The effect of this policy was that the blocks filled to capacity. An extension for another 30 patients was completed in 1837 but these were quickly filled. The Metropolitan Commissioners noted in their report of 1844 that though Bethlem housed 85 criminal patients there were another 139 distributed around other private and public asylums. The proprietors of Fisherton House near Salisbury agreed to build a separate criminal ward in 1848 to take patients who were considered less dangerous than those sent to Bethlem. By the fifth annual Report of the new Commissioners in Lunacy in 1851 the number of criminal patients in ordinary private or public asylums had increased to 264 and the Commissioners described the relief offered by Fisherton as inadequate. The Chairman of the Commissioners, the Earl of Shaftesbury, again advocated the building of a separate asylum for insane offenders but to no avail.

Sir William Hood, superintendent of Bethlem for a decade from 1852, managed to free 40 beds in Bethlem's male criminal block by moving the more settled patients to another ward (O'Donoghue 1914). The vacated beds were quickly filled. In 1854, Hood publicly recommended a separate asylum for the criminally insane in his book. By 1856 conditions in the criminal blocks in Bethlem were unacceptable and decried as 'radically bad' in the tenth Report of the Lunacy Commissioners published that year. In contrast, the same report described conditions in Bethlem generally as 'altogether creditable'.

The Act of 1844 had resulted in counties building their own facilities for the insane and pauper patients were being admitted to these asylums rather than to Bethlem, which increasingly found it had to attract private patients. Hood was keen to see the criminal blocks in Bethlem close as he considered that their presence tainted the reputation of Bethlem and discouraged the private patients (O'Donoghue 1914).

The debate in England about the most suitable accommodation for managing the criminally insane was paralleled by a similar debate in Ireland. The Report on the District, Local and Private Lunatic Asylums in Ireland for 1845 recorded that there were 84 criminal lunatics in various asylums around Ireland and a further 21 detained in gaols. The following year's report urged the building of a central criminal asylum. Dundrum Central Criminal Asylum was built in 1850 with 120 places of which 80 were for males. Dundrum had more space for its patients than the cramped criminal wings in Bethlem. Security in Bethlem's blocks needed to be visibly closer to the patients than in the new special hospital with its secure perimeter wall. The space available within Dundrum allowed a less oppressive management. In 1857 it was reported that no mechanical coercion had been used over the preceding two years. The expectation that a separate criminal asylum would be more conducive to moral management and total non-restraint was confirmed.

The continuing inadequate conditions in England for the care of the criminally insane led to renewed calls during the late 1850s for the opening of a separate criminal lunatic asylum in England. The success of Dundrum added extra support to the arguments. In 1860 the Act for the Better Provision for the Custody and Care of Criminal Lunatics (23 & 24 Vict c.75) passed into law and provided the legislative authority to build the Broadmoor Criminal Lunatic Asylum in Berkshire. It was built to accommodate 400 men and 100 women and opened in 1863 (Partridge 1953). It was not long before it was realised that the beds tended to be blocked by convalescent patients whom the Home Secretary was reluctant to release. However, the ending of the transportation of convicts to the colonies in the late 1860s may have contributed a little to the increased demand on asylum places. Certainly, the effect on prisons was considerable (Hughes 1987). Broadmoor started to add extensions to accommodate the growing numbers. In 1867 an extra 50 female places were added and by 1903 the hospital housed nearly 760 patients. However, the Lunacy Commissioners noted that there were 109 criminally insane patients still distributed around the other ordinary asylums in England and Wales in that year. Between 1908 and 1913 a print shop in the grounds of Her Majesty's Prison Parkhurst was temporarily converted to the Parkhurst Criminal Lunatic Asylum for 50 male patients. It closed a year after the opening of the second Criminal Lunatic Asylum, Rampton, in Nottinghamshire.

The learning disabled offender was often described as presenting a different range of clinical and security problems to the mentally ill. The Board of Control was established by the Mental Deficiency Act 1913 (3 & 4 Geo V c23). It was charged with the responsibility of providing and maintaining specialist asylum-based care for 'dangerous mental defectives'. As with the criminal lunatic services, decisions about admission and discharge remained with the Home Secretary. An old inebriate's asylum, Farmfield in Surrey, was converted into the first separate facility for dangerous mental defectives and remained open between 1914 and 1922. It housed 90. The Board of Control obtained the Moss Side site near Liverpool with the intention of opening a larger facility but it was transferred to the War Office after the start of the First World War. It was used as a Military Hospital for Nervous Disorders. After the war it was briefly used as a hospital for the 'dangerous mentally impaired' until 1920. Moss Side was then leased to the Ministry of Pensions as an 'epileptic colony' before being returned, once again, to its originally intended use in 1933.

With the foundation of the National Health Service in the 1940s, the ownership of Rampton, Moss Side and Broadmoor Hospitals passed to the Ministry of Health during the closing years of the decade. The Board of Control took on the responsibility for their management though decisions about admissions and discharges remained with the Home Secretary. The Mental Health Act 1959 (7 & 8 Eliz II c.72) saw the dissolution of the Board of Controls and the handing over of its responsibilities to the Department of Health and Social Security (Parker 1985). Park Lane Special Hospital was built in the 1970s and subsequently merged with Moss Side opposite to form Ashworth Hospital. The management of the special hospitals recently passed to nearby National Health Service Trusts while discharges and leaves of restricted patients fall under the province of the new Ministry for Justice.

From the 1950s onwards the priority for mental health service provision shifted from care in large asylums to care in the community. It quickly became apparent that there was a need for secure beds outside those available within the special hospitals. Individuals who would have been managed in the locked wards of the old asylums still needed to be managed in secure facilities for their own protection and/or the protection of the public. However, they did not need conditions of high security as found in the special hospitals. The Glancy Report (Department of Health and Social Security 1974) on disturbed and dangerous patients and the Butler Report (Home Office and Department of Health and Social Services 1975) on mentally abnormal offenders led to the development of such units. The Butler Report (1975) recommended that each National Health Service Region should have a unit and they were originally called Regional Secure Units. This term is largely redundant now as many regions have more than one Medium Secure Unit. The first Interim Medium Secure Unit was opened in Merseyside in 1980 and the Regional Secure Unit in Norwich was the first purpose-built unit to be opened. The Butler Report (1975) and the more recent Reed Report (1992) set out the core principles of secure provision (Kennedy 2002).

The 1990s and early years of the new millennium witnessed a period of intense political interest in forensic mental health. In 1992 the first of two inquiries into Ashworth Hospital (Blom-Cooper et al. 1992) reported which concluded that the hospital was an abusive, authoritarian institution and, as a result, the practices of the special hospitals were closely scrutinised and modernisation began. For example, patients were still being locked in their bedrooms and dormitories at night, a practice more akin to prisons than hospitals. Seven years later a second inquiry into Ashworth Hospital was commissioned (Fallon et al. 1999). Fallon investigated and confirmed complaints of patients trading in pornographic material, a young child visiting dangerous paedophiles and being 'groomed', patients running ward businesses, misuse of drugs and alcohol, and gross lapses in security. A review of security in all three English Special Hospitals followed. The Tilt Report (Tilt et al. 2000) recommended greater levels of security including the recording of patients' telephone calls, greater use of random searches of patient quarters and improvements to perimeter and internal security systems. However, the issues relating to levels of security are covered elsewhere in this volume.

The penal reforms of the nineteenth century led to the development of physical and mental healthcare services within the prisons. During the twentieth century various therapeutic programmes and units were developed within the prisons including services for personality disordered individuals and addicts. Since the 1990s there has been a determined effort to involve National Health Service providers in the provision of healthcare within the prisons in a variety of areas including mental healthcare units and addiction services. The development of various court diversion schemes and community forensic services in inner-city areas in recent decades ensures that forensic mental health now has a broad base. However, these developments are more properly the concern of other chapters in this volume.

Concluding remarks

Forensic mental health grew out of the asylum era. The structural foundations were laid in the early criminal lunatic wings and asylums. The conceptual frameworks evolved from an amalgam of the clinico-pathological approach, the social and legal reform movements, and the ideas about criminal responsibility debated in the various high-profile trials of the nineteenth century. Since the emergence of effective pharmaceutical and psychological treatments during the twentieth century there has been a growing impetus to manage the mentally ill offender in the lowest possible conditions of security. The influx of practitioners into the expanding medium and lesser secure services has ensured the field has proliferated and reached its present day maturity.

Selected further reading

The classic text by Hunter, R. and MacAlpine, I. (1963) *Three Hundred Years of Psychiatry 1535–1860*, Oxford: Oxford University Press presents the history of psychiatry in a series of commentaries and extracts from historical works arranged in chronological order with comprehensive indices permitting the reader to track the development of various different themes and topics,

The monograph by Smith R. (1981) *Trial by Medicine. Insanity and Responsibility in Victorian Trials*, Edinburgh: Edinburgh University Press explores in depth the evolution of criminal responsbility in the nineteenth century.

The two volumes of Walker, N. (1968) *Crime and Insanity in England*, Edinburgh: Edinburgh University Press provide a readable and comprehensive account of the development of the 'English Approach' to the problem of the mentally disordered offender from the perspective of criminology.

References

Ackerknecht, E. H. (1959) *A Short History of Psychiatry*. New York: Hafner.

Ackerknecht, E. H. (1982) *A Short History of Medicine*, revised edn. Baltimore, MD: John Hopkins University Press.

Baker, J.H. (1979) *Introduction to English Legal History*, 2nd edn. London: Butterworths.

Blom-Cooper, L., Brown, M., and Dolan, R. (1992) *Report of a Committee of Inquiry into Complaints about Ashworth Hospital*. London: HMSO.

Colaizzi, J. (1989) *Homicidal Insanity, 1800–1985*. Tuscaloosa, AL: University of Alabama Press.

Cooter, R. (1981) 'Phrenology and British alienists, ca.1825-1845', in Scull, A. (ed.), *Madhouses, Mad Doctors, and Madmen. The Social History of Psychiatry in the Victorian Era*. London: Athlone Press.

Department of Health and Social Security (1974) *Revised Report of the Working Party on Security in NHS Psychiatric Hospitals* (Glancy Report). London: DHSS.

Duncan, J. F. (1853) *Popular Errors on the Subject of Insanity Examined and Exposed*. London: Churchill.

Edwards, J. (1955) *Mens Rea in Statutory Offences*. London: Macmillan.

Fallon, P., Bluglass, R. Edwards, B. and Daniels, G. (1999) *Report of the Committee of Inquiry into the Personality Disorder Unit, Ashworth Special Hospital*. London: Stationery Office.

Feuchtersleben, E. Von (1847) *The Principles of Medical Psychology*, trans. H. Evans Lloyd and B. G. Babington. London: Sydenham Society.

Forshaw, D. M. and Rollin, H. (1990) 'The history of forensic psychiatry', in Bluglass, R. and Bowden, P. (eds), *Principles and Practice of Forensic Psychiatry*. Edinburgh: Churchill Livingstone.

Foucault, M. (1967) *Madness and Civilization. A History of Insanity in the Age of Reason*, trans. R. Howard. London: Tavistock Publications.

Geis, G. (1960) 'Jeremy Bentham', in Mannheim, H. (ed.), *Pioneers in Criminology*. London: Stevens & Sons.

Hervey, N. (1985) 'A slavish bowing down: the Lunacy Commission and the psychiatric profession 1845–60', in Bynum, W. F., Porter, R. and Shepherd, M. (eds), *The Anatomy of Madness. Essays in the History of Psychiatry*, Vol. II, 'Institutions and Society'. London: Tavistock Publications.

Home Office and Department of Health and Social Services (1975) *Report of the Committee on Mentally Abnormal Offenders* (Butler Report). London: HMSO.

Hood, W. C. (1854) *Suggestions for the Future Provision of Criminal Lunatics*. London: Churchill.

Hughes, R. (1987) *The Fatal Shore. A History of the Transportation of Convicts to Australia, 1787–1868*. London: Collins Harvill.

Hunter, R. and MacAlpine, I. (1963) *Three Hundred Years of Psychiatry 1535–1860*. Oxford: Oxford University Press.

Jones, K. (1972) *A History of the Mental Health Services*. London: Routledge & Kegan Paul.

Jones, R. (2006) *Mental Health Act Manual*, 10th edn. London: Sweet & Maxwell.

Kennedy, H. G. (2002) 'Therapeutic uses of security: mapping forensic mental health services by stratifying risk', *Advances in Psychiatric Treatment*, 8: 433–43.

Kraepelin, E. (1919) *Dementia Praecox and Paraphrenia*, trans. R. M. Barclay. Edinburgh: Livingstone.

MacAlpine, I. and Hunter R. (1969) *George III and the Mad Business*. London: Allen Lane.

Manchester, A. H. (1980) *A Modern Legal History of England and Wales 1750–1950*. London: Butterworths.

Morison, A. (1840) *The Physiognomy of Mental Diseases*, 2nd edn. Published for the Author, London.

Morison, A. (1848) *Outlines of Lectures on the Nature, Causes, and Treatment of Insanity*, 4th edn, ed. T.C. Morison. London: Longmans.

O'Donoghue, E. G. (1914) *The Story of Bethlem Hospital from its Foundation in 1247*. London: Fisher Unwin.

Parker, E. (1985) 'The development of secure provision', in Gostin, L. (ed.), *Secure Provision. A Review of Special Services for the Mentally Ill and Mentally Handicapped in England and Wales*. London: Tavistock.

ParryJones, W. Ll. (1972) *The Trade in Lunacy. A Study of Private Madhouses in England in the Eighteenth and Nineteenth Centuries*. London: Routledge & Kegan Paul.

Partridge, R. (1953) *Broadmoor. A History of Criminal Lunacy and Its Problems*. London: Chatto & Windus.

Radzinowicz, L. (1948–1968) *A History of the English Criminal Law*, Vols 1–4. London: Macmillan.

Reed, J. (1992) *Review of Health and Social Services for Mentally Disordered Offenders and Others Requiring Similar Services: Final Summary Report*, Cm 2088. London: Stationery Office.

Ridgeway, J. (ed.) (1812) *Speeches of Lord Erskine, when at the Bar on Miscellaneous Subjects*. London: Ridgeway.

Scull, A. (1981) 'The social history of psychiatry in the Victorian era, in Scull, A. (ed.), *Madhouses, Mad Doctors, and Madmen. The Social History of Psychiatry in the Victorian Era*. London: Athlone Press.

Sharpe, J. B. (ed.) (1815) *Report, Together with the Minutes of Evidence and an Appendix of Papers from the Committee Appointed to Consider of Provision Being Made for the Better Regulations of Madhouses in England.* London: Baldwin, Cradock & Joy.

Smith, R. (1981) *Trial by Medicine. Insanity and Responsibility in Victorian Trials.* Edinburgh: Edinburgh University Press.

Szasz, T. S. (1970) *The Manufacture of Madness. A Comparative Study of the Inquisition and the Mental Health Movement.* New York. Harper & Row.

Szasz, T. S. (1974) *The Age of Madness. The History of Involuntary Mental Hospitalization Presented in Selected Texts.* New York: Jason Aronson.

Tilt, R., Perry, B. and Martin, C. (2000) *Report of the Review of Security at the High Security Hospitals.* London: Department of Health.

Tuke, S. (1813) *Description of the Retreat, an Institution near York, for Insane Persons of the Society of Friends.* York: Alexander.

Walker, N. (1968) *Crime and Insanity in England. Volume One: The Historical Perspective.* Edinburgh: Edinburgh University Press.

Wallis, J. E. P. (1892) *Reports of State Trials. New Series. 1839 to 1843.* London: HMSO.

West, D. J. and Walk, A. (eds) (1977) *Daniel McNaughton His Trial and the Aftermath.* London: Gaskell.

Willis, F. (1843) *A Treatise on Mental Derangement,* 2nd edn. London: Longman, Brown, Green & Longmans.

Part 2

Understanding the Forensic Mental Health Process and the Systems

Keith Soothill

Very considerable differences can exist between different countries in the processing and management of offenders, for among other things there are different legal arrangements, different services and resources available and, perhaps not least, different cultural settings. The family or immediate social group has always had a role in controlling deviance which is usually referred to as the *informal* social control network, but most interest has centred around the development of more *formal* networks that exist in the community for assessing and controlling deviance.

Interestingly, when formal systems begin to develop, it is usually possible to identify a description of the formal social control network which is remarkably similar in all countries. In short, whatever the procedure, there is potentially a logical progression for the deviant from the time that his/her behaviour first comes to the attention of formal social control agents to the time that he/she is released from official control.

The two major systems of social control are the criminal justice and mental health systems and forensic mental health practitioners work at the interface of these two control systems. In both systems – in most countries – there are two major divides, that is by age and by disposal. In brief, there are systems which deal with juveniles or young persons on the one hand, and systems which deal with adults on the other. However, there are still some stark circumstances where children as young as ten are detained in male adult prisoners (e.g. in the Republic of Georgia (Rogers *et al.* 2006)). Similarly, another great divide is in disposal in both the criminal justice and mental health systems. Within the criminal justice system the distinction between custodial and non-custodial sentences is crucial; the former means a loss of liberty and the latter does not. Within the mental health system, there is a similar distinction between compulsory admission and outpatient treatment where the former again means loss of liberty and the latter does not. Of course, there can be other social and administrative divisions where different procedures may operate. Gender is an obvious one, for there are often different provisions for females in the criminal justice and mental health systems. Ethnicity is another where there may be a concern that different practices develop which may or may not be acceptable. Equity and justice in relation to social divisions are themes which should never be neglected, but age and disposal are more pivotal in understanding the structure of most forensic mental health systems.

Sue Bailey and Bill Kerslake in Chapter 4 explain the systems for juveniles and young persons, recognising that the major challenge of altering the trajectories of persistent young offenders has to be met in the context of satisfying public demands for retribution, together with welfare and civil liberties considerations. The context of the challenge is no different from that faced in dealing with adults, but the stakes are so much higher. Should we intervene earlier and, if so, how? Bailey and Kerslake remind us that over the last 30 years there has been a gradual shift in opinion regarding the effectiveness of intervention with delinquents, from the 'nothing works' approaches to a 'what works' approach. They note that the jury is still out for 'what works' in the long term but the evidence base that can be placed before the jury is growing. This chapter presents much of the evidence available to date. Much more is known than many are willing to acknowledge, but the quick-fix solution beloved of politicians and the media is not available. The volatile mix between the genetic, psychological and social factors needs much greater understanding.

In some respects Tony Maden in Chapter 5 has a less onerous task in focusing on adults, for most of the rest of this volume is implicitly or explicitly considering adult behaviour. Maden outlines the process of assessment and treatment for adults. He notes that, in an ideal world, access to treatment would be determined entirely by clinical need. However, in practice, we fall far short of this ideal. Indeed, we need to recognise that it is a rather arbitrary process of how individuals are selected to enter the system. It depends to a large extent on the mentally disordered offender coming to the notice of police, the courts, lawyers or prison staff. As a result the more florid and obvious forms of mental disorder are more likely to be noticed and to result in psychiatric assessment. The discrepancy between what *ought* to happen and what *does* happen is a feature of much forensic mental health work. Maden reminds us that services face pressures to justify the apparent inefficiencies of the system and points to the need to investigate ways of improving access to services. Yet, as Professor Glyn Lewis, Professor of Psychiatric Epidemiology at Bristol University, frequently points out (personal communication), we must be careful never to forget the quiet ones, who take up little time or attention from staff. The quiet ones' needs are as great as those who cause day-to-day disturbances, yet rarely have the time with staff to discuss what is happening to them.

In Chapter 6 Danny Clark focuses on non-custodial sentences and mentally disordered offenders. He points out that, while the focus is inevitably on the continually rising numbers of persons imprisoned, a much larger group processed by the courts is given a community sentence by the courts when convicted. In fact, mentally disordered offenders (MDOs) serving community services are largely neglected in the literature and yet such offenders represent a major challenge. The chapter outlines the process of supervision in the community, how they are dealt with by the Probation Service and other agencies, and how mental health issues might impinge on other aspects of the sentence. The changes which are currently occurring in the criminal justice system are likely to impact on MDOs in the community in several ways. The introduction of 'end to end' offender management should bring many advantages in terms of consistency and continuity. The NOMS commissioning and contestability agenda will mean that more interventions will be delivered by other organisations. It will provide an opportunity for the voluntary and commercial sectors to develop new treatment approaches for groups like MDOs where gaps in provision exist. Hopes are being raised but, perhaps in this area more than most, one needs to say 'watch this space'. The greatest problem will be ensuring that another tier of services communicates with the existing tiers, something which remains a constant challenge.

Jane Senior and Jenny Shaw identify in Chapter 7 the important recent developments in mental healthcare in prisons. Certainly, as they note, the history of healthcare services in prisons has been hazardous. The social reformer, John Howard, highlighted many of the issues in 1777 in his seminal tome, *The State of the Prisons in England and Wales*. Since then, progress has not been smooth. We nowadays seem to be much more aware of the nature of the problems, but resolution still seems far away in some areas. Senior and Shaw claim that prison health services are currently subject to investment in terms of a number of active work programmes focused on clinical improvements across all types of healthcare services. There certainly has been a move forward in that there has been a recognition that the partnership between the National Health Service and HM Prison Service is vital to ensure the success of current and future development work, with a need to find for the differing cultures of both organisations some kind of middle ground, so that the work of each is complementary, not antagonistic, to the aims of the other. This is an area where one needs to take a long-term view if one is to avoid despondency. The developing partnership between the National Health Service and HM Prison Service is a definite advance to the stand-off between the two institutions 30 years ago.

There are crucial issues to confront when the mentally disordered deviant is released from prison or hospital. It is an important step in the care pathway of mentally disordered offenders. Pete Snowden and Bettadapura Ashim in Chapter 8 explain the procedures and issues that are relevant in the discharge or release of mentally disordered offenders. This is an area where media interest is high when mentally disordered offenders discharged from custody go on to commit serious offences, while media interest is non-existent in recognising the routine successes of the procedures. The serious offences of some high-profile cases which have been widely reported have prompted changes to legislation, some of which are controversial. Snowden and Ashim usefully remind us of some of the ethical problems and the legal rules that apply. There are important dilemmas to confront. After all, the core of the health professional's role is the treatment of patients, while the focus of the Home Office is unequivocally that of public protection. In brief, the mission of forensic mental health should be something more than the simple pursuit of public protection.

References

Rogers, P., Keukens, R. and Van Voren, R. (2006) 'Reforming the delivery of forensic mental health and prison health in the Republic of Georgia', *Mental Health Practice*, 9 (5): 38–40.

Chapter 4

The process and systems for juveniles and young persons

Sue Bailey and Bill Kerslake

Introduction

Both rates of mental disorders and offending are high during adolescence. This chapter reviews the prevalence rates of mental disorders in young offenders, the screening and assessment of juveniles, and the principles of interventions with young offenders. It then goes on to describe the principles of forensic mental health, policy and practice, how mental disorders in adolescence can impact on offending and antisocial behaviour, how policy is shaping practice in this field and how mental health practitioners may be involved in meeting mental health needs and undertaking medico-legal assessments.

Adolescence as a context

The adolescent population in the UK constitutes half of the child population with around 7.5 million young people in the transitional stage between childhood and adulthood (age 10–19) (Coleman and Schofield 2003).

More than at any other time in the life-course, adolescence is the stage of possibility and of the promises and worries that attend this possibility (Oyserman and Martois 1990). Adolescence is a transitional stage of development between childhood and adulthood. The developmental tasks of adolescence centre on autonomy and connection with others, rebellion and the development of independence, the development of identity and distinction from and continuity with others. The physical changes of puberty are generally seen as the starting point of adolescence while the end is less clearly delineated. Adolescence ends with attainment of 'full maturity'. A range of social and cultural influences including the legal age of majority may influence the definition of maturity (Bailey 2006).

Mortality among adolescents, in contrast to almost all other age groups, did not fall during the second half of the twentieth century, the main causes being accidents and self-harm (Coleman and Schofield 2003). Health needs are greater in this age band than in children in middle childhood (5–12 years) or of young adults, and arises mainly out of chronic illness and mental health problems. The main concerns of young people, in relation to health, focus on issues of immediacy that impact on their relations with peers and include problems with skin, weight, appearance, emotions and sexual health including contraception. So, within this context, what are the procedures in dealing with offending behaviour?

Youth Justice Board

The Youth Justice Board for England and Wales is a non-departmental public body created by the Crime and Disorder Act 1998 with responsibility for improving the youth justice system in England and Wales.

In England and Wales the age of criminal responsibility currently stands at 10 (s. 37, Crime and Disorder Act 1998) and the principal aim of any youth justice system (YJS) is to prevent offending by children and young people under 18 years of age in England and Wales. The Youth Justice Board supports the achievement of this aim by:

- advising the Home Secretary for England and Wales on the operation of and standards for the youth justice system;
- monitoring the performance;
- purchasing places for young people remanded in or sentenced to custody;
- identifying and promoting effective practice;
- making grants to local authorities and other bodies;
- commissioning research and publishing effective practice information.

The Youth Justice Board (YJB) and youth offending teams (YOTs) were established following a review by the Audit Commission, *Misspent Youth* (1996), which identified that local services and mainstream departments were failing to meet the complex needs of young people who offend. The requirement for local authorities to establish multidisciplinary, multi-agency youth offending teams with representation from the probation, police, education, health and social services was set out in s. 39 of the Crime and Disorder Act 1998. Section 115 of this Act gave authority for agencies to share personal information where it is necessary or expedient to the successful implementation of the Act.

There are 157 youth offending teams in England and Wales, while the YJB commissions some 3,000 custodial places at any one time for young people under the age of 18 years in 18 Prison Service young offender institutions, 15 local authority secure children's home and four private-sector secure training centres (STCs).

In 2005–06 there were 301,860 recorded offences, the four highest recorded offences being theft and handling (18.5 per cent), violence against the person (18.1 per cent), motoring offences (16.6 per cent) and criminal damage (12.9 per cent). Sixteen and 17-year-olds were responsible for 49.6 per cent of offences with males responsible for 80.6 per cent and females 19.4 per cent of all offences resulting in a disposal. Offences by ethnicity were white (85.2 per cent) and black and minority ethnic (14.8 per cent). Of the 212,242 disposals 80 per cent received pre-court first-tier disposals with a further 17 per cent receiving a community sentence and 3 per cent a custodial sentence (*Youth Justice Annual Statistics 2005/06* – Youth Justice Board 2007).

A key strategy for the Youth Justice Board in reducing offending is targeting the risk factors for offending through partnership work with mainstream agencies including the Home Office, the Department of Health, the Department for Education and Skills, the National Treatment Agency, the Welsh Assembly government and the voluntary sector to ensure young people in the youth justice system have access to the mainstream and specialist services they require.

Mental health needs of young people in the youth justice system

Standard 9 (the Child and Adolescent Mental Health Services (CAMHS) standard) of the *National Service Framework for Children, Young People and Maternity Services* (DoH 2004) in England has set out a vision of a comprehensive child and adolescent mental health service. A young person in contact with the criminal justice system, whether in custody or in the community, should have the same access to this comprehensive service as any other child or young person within the general population. Treatment options should not be affected by a young offender's status within the criminal justice system. This is also consistent with the principles set out in *Every Child Matters: Change for Children.* The Change for Children Programme has the aim of improving outcomes for all children in the following five areas: being healthy, staying safe, enjoying and achieving, making a positive contribution, and achieving economic well-being, and to narrow the gap in outcomes between those who do well and those who do not.

Prevalence rates of mental disorders in adolescents

Decades of scientific research on the phenomenon of adolescent delinquency have resulted in the recognition of a large number of environmental and individual risk factors (Rutter *et al.* 1998). Until recently, research on psychiatric pathology as risk factors for delinquency has not received much attention (Vermeiren 2003). Over the past few years, interest in the subject seems to have grown, because several sound prevalence studies have been conducted on psychiatric disorders in juvenile justice populations (Dixon *et al.* 2004; Gosden *et al.* 2003; Lederman *et al.* 2004; McCabe *et al.* 2002; Ruchkin *et al.* 2003; Teplin *et al.* 2002; Vreugdenhil *et al.* 2004a; Wasserman *et al.* 2002). As current research has consistently shown high rates of disorders, the debate is slowly shifting towards aspects of clinical relevance (i.e. for judicial handling and therapeutic intervention). For specific disorders with overall low prevalence, such as autism spectrum disorders and psychosis, research is still on the epidemiological level.

Recently, Grisso and Zimring (2004) have listed three principal reasons for concern regarding mental disorders in youthful offenders – the custodial treatment obligation (i.e. the obligation to respond to mental health needs), assurance of due process in adjudicative proceedings and public safety (i.e. the extent that there is a relation between an adolescent's mental health status and future violent behaviour, and the obligation to offer specific provisions). Too often, mental health treatment within the juvenile justice system is lacking for those in need. A study by Domalanta and colleagues (Domalanta *et al.* 2003) showed that only about 20 per cent of depressed incarcerated youth and only 10 per cent of adolescents with other disorders were receiving treatment. Fewer than half of incarcerated youth who required treatment because of substance use disorder (SUD) received intervention (Johnson *et al.* 2004).

Although research consistently reveals high levels of psychiatric disorders among detained juveniles, rates vary widely by study, ranging from more than 50 per cent to 100 per cent (Dixon *et al.* 2004; Gosden *et al.* 2003; Lederman *et al.* 2004; McCabe *et al.* 2002; Ruchkin *et al.* 2003; Teplin *et al.* 2002; Vreugdenhil *et al.*

2004a; Wasserman *et al.* 2002; Atkins *et al.* 1999; Shelton 2001; Vermeiren *et al.* 2002). Conduct disorders (CD) and substance use disorders (SUDs) carry the highest prevalence rates, but other mental disorders also present commonly in this population.

Limitations of current research

The variations of rates can be explained. So, for example, the type and nature of psychiatric interviews vary by study. Second, the moment of investigation and the period of diagnostic assessment also differ by study. Some studies focus on youth shortly after detention (Teplin *et al.* 2002), whereas others investigate youth in the post-adjudication phase (Vreugdenhil *et al.* 2004; Wasserman *et al.* 2002). The moment of assessment is relevant because detention itself may influence the psychological condition (e.g. by exacerbating depressive symptoms) (Vermeiren *et al.* 2003).

Third, enormous differences exist among studies on relevant socio-demographic and criminological characteristics, such as age, gender, ethnicity, family structure, socio-economic status and the nature of criminal behaviour.

Fourth, studies were conducted in different countries and, for those in the United States, in different states.

Fifth, some studies investigated antisocial youths referred specifically for psychiatric assessment. Although this population provide evidence of the types of psychopathology typically present in the delinquent youths referred for clinical services, using this information to generalise to the whole delinquent population is unjustified.

Last, because information from parents is largely unavailable, almost all current prevalence studies have relied uniquely on the youths themselves as informants. Although understandable given the difficulties in finding parents willing to be interviewed, this approach may hamper the reliability of findings.

Screening and assessment instruments in clinical (non-forensic) settings

In generic child and adolescent mental health services, checklists, rating scales, questionnaires and (semi)-structured interview schedules have been devised to improve the reliability about internalising disorders, including suicidal thoughts and gestures, whereas parents and caregivers report more reliably about externalising disorders.

In the populations served by the generic child and adolescent mental health services, a youngster's abnormal behaviour can usually be recognised with sufficient accuracy for routine screening purposes by a brief symptom/behavioural checklist such as the Rutter A Scale (Rutter 1967) or the Child Behaviour Checklist (Achenbach and Edeibrock 1983). The Strengths and Difficulties Questionnaire (Goodman 1997; Bourdon *et al.* 2005) is a newer instrument that has the merit of being shorter than the Child Behaviour Checklist. More specific instruments such as the Conners' Parent and Teacher Questionnaires (Conners 1971) have shown particular value in identifying attention deficit hyperactivity disorder (ADHD) and evaluating response to pharmacological treatment of children and young adolescents who have the disorder.

Instruments for clinical diagnostic assessment include a number of highly structured interviews, such as the Diagnostic Interview for Children and Adolescents (Herjanic and Reich 1982) and the Diagnostic Interview Schedule for Children (Costello *et al.* 1985), and semi-structured instruments that require greater clinical interpretation and thus greater training to ensure reliability. The most widely used semi-structured interview is the Schedule for Affective Disorder and Schizophrenia for School Age Children (Orvaschel *et al.* 1982). In addition, assessment of family relationships is important, as is the developmental anamnesis and, when specific dysfunction exists, (neuro)psychological tests. Detailed description of the construction and performance of these instruments is outside the scope of this article. Readers are directed to Gowers (2004).

Screening and assessment in forensic child and adolescent contexts

In the forensic clinical field where written communication between various disciplines is common, a commonly understood language of reliable and valid diagnoses is important. In forensic settings, assessment of adolescents who have mental health problems is beset with obstacles. The fear of being sentenced on the basis of their own information can make adolescents reticent. They may perceive forensic experts as part of the court process rather than as professionals who might be able to provide help. Similarly, they may view professionals in the same way they view other adults (e.g. parents and teachers) with whom they have had difficulty in sustaining positive relationships. In any assessment, the interviewer needs to strike a balance between engagement and the need to elicit information. Another important aspect is the instability of adolescents' emotions from day to day, especially in the context of incarceration (Kroll *et al.* 2002) where emotional reactions may be seen as a real expression of fear and helpfulness.

In the United States and Europe, recent studies of young offenders have used large samples across custody and community settings with clear definitions of mental disorders and reliable measures of adolescent psychopathology (Kroll *et al.* 2002; Kazdin 2000; Harrington *et al.* 2005; Teplin *et al.* 2002; Vermeiren 2003; Vreugdenhil *et al.* 2004b). Developmental psychopathology (Garmezy and Rutter 1983; Cicchetti 1984) has enabled clinicians to understand better how mental disorders in adolescence emerge, evolve and change in a developmental context. Grisso and colleagues (2005) point to four conceptual aspects of mental disorders in the forensic adolescent population that should be taken into account when screening for and assessing disorders (and the subsequent trajectory of the disorders into adulthood, including links with violence, delinquency and early onset psychosis). The concepts are age relativity, discontinuity, comorbidity and demographic differences.

Age relativity
Developmental psychopathologists delineate symptoms of disorder if young offenders deviate from the average behaviours of children and youth at a particular developmental stage and, importantly, if they lead to psychosocial problems in the context of the developmental period (Cicchetti and Rogosch 2002; Mash and Dozois 2003). In juvenile justice, age is a critical factor in establishing criminal responsibility and in the appropriate placement of young persons who are deemed to require incarceration. These factors vary from

jurisdiction to jurisdiction. For example, legal responsibility in the Netherlands starts at twelve years of age and in the United Kingdom at ten years. This variety has implications for the design of instruments, applicability across countries and comparability of samples.

Discontinuity

Cicchetti and Rogosch (2002) use two concepts to iterate complex pathways in the development and remission of disorders during childhood and adolescence that must be considered in every forensic assessment. Equifinality means that disorders of different origins can lead to the same outcomes and is best exemplified in adolescents who have severe depression who may not necessarily have presented with the same problems in childhood but who have similar clinical presentations in their adolescent years. Multifinality refers to clinical presentations with similar starting points leading to different disorders (Coll *et al.* 1984). Because the expression of symptoms and disorders may change over time, repetitive assessment is a requirement.

Comorbidity

Comorbidity means that youngsters meet criteria for more than one disorder. Comorbidity is more common in delinquents than in the general population (Teplin *et al.* 2002; Harrington and Bailey 2004) with some disorders such as conduct disorder, depression and substance misuse frequently co-occurring (Harrington *et al.* 2005).

Demographic differences

A complex range of factors influences the varying rates of mental disorders across communities and settings. Arrest patterns, for instance, vary from city to city, from neighbourhood to neighbourhood and from decade to decade. Mental disorder is more prevalent in children and adolescents who live in poverty (Bailey *et al.* 2004). Differences in responses related to cultural backgrounds (across ethnic backgrounds and also across the diverse range of adolescent subcultures) need much more investigation.

Prevalences of mental disorders among juvenile offenders may differ substantially at the different stages of their involvement with the juvenile justice system. Doreleijers (2005) demonstrated that the rates of mental disorder in youth varied depending on the severity of their involvement with the juvenile justice system: 30 per cent in arrested adolescents, 65 per cent in adolescents brought before the court, 70 per cent in adolescents having an assessment on the request of the court and 90 per cent in those who are sentenced to detention or forced treatment.

Pathways of care and the juvenile justice system

For the benefit of young persons in the juvenile justice system, it is crucial to develop clear pathways of care. Early identification of mental health needs may result in diversion from custody by using community services rather than adjudication and, thus, derive economic benefit from a non-custodial disposal. Nonetheless, a significant number of young persons progress to pre-trial assessment.

Pre-adjudication dispositions should be informed by the best available screening and assessment processes. In this context specific tools may be used to derive markers of psychopathology and of ongoing risk to self and others as well as to address medico-legal questions posed by the criminal justice system, including assessment on disposition, matters of public protection, treatment for mental disorders, the need for security and the likelihood of recidivism.

For those detained in prison, a first-look screen must determine if urgent problems (such as suicidal intent or consequences of substance use) require immediate attention; a detailed diagnostic assessment of the young person may take a longer period of time and continue as the youngster moves from one institution to another. Later critical transitions, for which an additional screening may be useful, include re-entry into the community, assessment of readiness for re-entry, mental health planning for integrated continuing care post-detention as part of a multi-agency re-entry strategy and, where necessary, community residential programmes monitoring emotion or reactions, especially where the young person is returning to stressful conditions such as a troublesome family.

Needs assessment

Needs and risk assessment are two separate but intertwined processes. Assessment of danger to others and the need to address this problem is at the centre of legislative and policy decision-making. The attention of the public and media are focused on this area.

Risk assessment has a theory and methodology separate from needs assessment. It combines statistical data with clinical information in a way that integrates historical variables, current crucial variables and the contextual or environmental factors. Some of these clinical and contextual factors are potential areas of need. Therefore needs assessment may both inform and be a response to the risk assessment process (Bailey 2002a; Bailey and Dolan 2004). The reciprocal process can be termed 'risk management' when accurate information about the risk assessment, combined with recurrent needs assessment, leads to risk management procedures. Core to this assessment are appropriate mental health screening tools and processes that are available to the young person at any point in the system (Bailey and Tarbuck 2006) (see Figure 4.1).

Two recent studies in the United Kingdom have used the Salford Needs Assessment Schedule for Adolescents (Kroll et al. 1999). One study adopted a cross-sectional design investigating 301 young offenders, 151 in custody and 150 in the community, in six geographically representative areas across England and Wales. Each young person was interviewed to obtain demographic information and mental health and social needs. Participants were found to have high levels of need in a number of different areas, including mental health (31 per cent), education/work (48 per cent) and social relationships (36 per cent), but these needs were often unmet because they were not recognised. One in five young offenders was identified as having mental retardation (IQ < 70) (Chitsabesan et al. 2006).

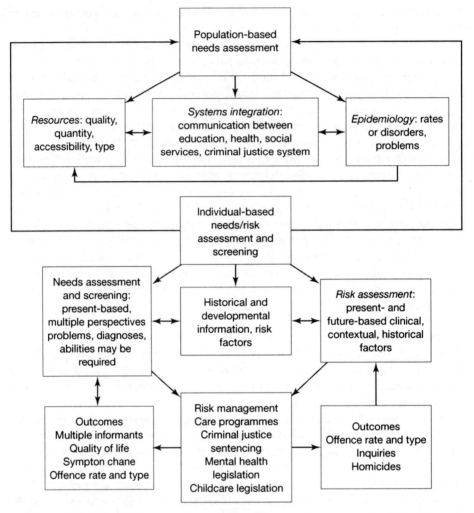

Figure 4.1 Relationship between various screening, need assessment, risk assessment and management approaches in juvenile justice systems
Source: Kroll (2004).

Overarching interventions with juvenile delinquents

A large number of different treatments have been used to try to reduce antisocial behaviour. These include psychotherapy, pharmacotherapy, school interventions, residential programmes and social treatments. Kazdin, in 1993, documented over 230 psychotherapies that were available, the great majority of which had not been systematically studied. In this review focus is on treatments with a testable scientific basis and which have been evaluated in randomised trials (Sukhodolsky and Ruchkin 2006) and applied to populations of young offenders.

Meta-analyses of treatment approaches to juvenile delinquency have produced reasonably consistent findings (Andrews *et al.* 1990; Lipsey 1995; Lipsey and Wilson 1993; Lösel 1995). Lipsey (1995) considered nearly 400 group-comparison studies published since 1950. The main finding was that there was an overall reduction of 10 per cent in reoffending rates in treatment groups as compared to untreated groups. As might be expected, there were of course considerable variations in the results of individual studies. The best results were obtained from cognitive behavioural, skills-orientated and multi-modal methods. The results from deterrent trials were particularly poor, though the numbers in these studies were relatively small. Specifically, treatment approaches that were participatory, collaborative and problem-solving were particularly likely to be beneficial. Family and parenting interventions also seem to reduce the risk of subsequent delinquency among older children and adolescents (Woolfenden *et al.* 2003).

McGuire and Priestley (1995) identified six principles for effective programmes. First, the intensity should match the extent of the risk posed by the offender. Second, there should be a focus on active collaboration, which is not too didactic or unstructured. Third, there should be close integration with the community from which the offender came. Fourth, there should be an emphasis on behavioural or cognitive approaches. Fifth, the programme should be delivered with high quality and the staff should be trained adequately and monitored. Finally, there should be a focus on the proximal causes of offending behaviour rather than distal causes. In other words, the programme should focus on peer groups, promoting current family communication and enhancing self-management and problem-solving skills. There should not be a focus on early childhood or other distal causes of delinquency.

All of these reviews suggest that there are a number of promising targets for treatment programmes, which include antisocial thoughts, antisocial peer associations, promotion of family communication and affection, promotion of family supervision, identification of positive role models, improving problem-solving skills, reducing chemical dependencies, provision of adequate living conditions, and helping the young offender to identify high-risk situations for antisocial behaviours. Conversely, the systematic reviews have also suggested a number of approaches that are unlikely to be promising. For instance, improving self-esteem without reducing antisocial cognitions is unlikely to be of value. Similarly, it is unlikely that a focus on emotional symptoms that is not clearly linked to criminal conduct will be of great benefit.

Research into practice

Only recently in the USA and Europe have studies on delinquents been carried out using larger samples across custody and community with clear definitions of mental disorders and better measures of adolescent psychopathology (Chitsabesan *et al.* 2006; Odgers *et al.* 2005; Kazdin 2000; Kroll *et al.* 2002; Teplin *et al.* 2002; Vermeiren *et al.* 2003). Young offenders under 20 account for more than half of the violent crimes in the UK. Statistics on the onset of serious and violent delinquents show that about half of persistent juvenile offenders are active by 12 to 13-years-old and prevalence peaks between 17 and 18 (Coleman and Schofield 2005). This has major service implications for child and adolescent mental health and multi-agency child services. The real cost of children's needs not being met early are overall:

- the impact of their antisocial behaviour on society;
- their own vulnerability as they drift and/or are captured into juvenile justice systems, with marked communication problems, learning disability and/or mental disorder;
- the challenge of successful diversion from court when already in the juvenile justice system; and
- the provision of out and inreach services to young people in both secure youth justice facilities (those, for example, in the UK who are being dealt with in multi-agency youth offending teams) are key for specialist CAMHS services in keeping a clear focus on the overlapping but different tasks of meeting mental health need and assisting multi-agency teams in offence reduction interventions.

Forensic mental health is an area of specialisation that in the criminal sphere includes the assessment and treatment of those who are both mentally disordered and whose behaviour has led or could lead to offending. Defining forensic psychiatry in terms of the assessment and treatment of the mentally abnormal offender delineates an area of concern that could potentially engulf much of mental health. Public health policy has long recognised the government's obligation to attend to the basic health needs of prisoners and the importance of meeting the health and mental health needs of children. Traditionally, child and adolescent mental health practitioners have continued to work as generalists. Within their specialism they may include forensic work, not only child care proceedings, but also direct forensic medico-legal work where the young children are the alleged perpetrators rather than the victims.

Child psychiatrists need to be closely involved with developing specialist community and inpatient resources, including secure facilities for children and adolescents who may be:

- mentally disordered offenders;
- sex offenders and abusers;
- severely suicidal and self-harming adolescents;
- very severely mentally ill adolescents;
- adolescents who need to begin psychiatric rehabilitation in secure circumstances;
- brain-injured adolescents and those with severe organic disorders.

Weaving together local generic and more regional specialist services allows for multidimensional concepts of problems encountered by these young people to be tackled by the local mental health services in conjunction with other agencies (Bailey 2005). Local specialist child and adolescent mental health services can be augmented by advice and training offered by an identified peripatetic outreach team that is based in and works from specialised centres of expertise in forensic child and mental health. The primary responsibility remains with the staff of local services and the role of the outreach services is supportive and consultative.

There has to be a seamless delivery of service between general child and adolescent services and specialist forensic provision, with solutions tailored to local need. Services delivered directly to patients and their families by centres of specialist expertise in forensic child and adolescent mental health now include specialist community assessment and treatment services providing input not only to other child and mental health services but working with secure social care units, young offender institutions/correctional institutions and juvenile justice services in the community.

Oppositional disorders, conduct disorder and ADHD

Towards a developmental understanding of violence, (Fonagy 2003) distils out historical psychodynamic thinking, now supported by modern developmental data, to remind us that aggression and violence appear to be present from early childhood, toddlerhood and perhaps from birth.

Substantially higher rates of physically aggressive behaviour are found in children and adolescents with attention deficit hyperactivity disorder, with those who meet the criteria for ADHD and conduct disorder having substantially greater risks of delinquent acts in adolescence, harmful acts in later adolescence and continued violence and offending into adulthood (Fischer *et al.* 1993; Frick 1998a). Children with hyperactivity, impulsivity, attention deficits and serious conduct problems may also be at risk for developing psychopathy (Seagrave and Grisso 2002).

Distorted or biased thought processes have over time been implicated in the development of violence (Beck 1999). Psychological treatments aimed at reducing violent behaviour in adolescents and young adults have traditionally centred on violence as learned behaviour and that patterns of violence and criminal behaviour are embedded in habits of thinking (McGuire and Priestly 1995). In juvenile delinquents significant cognitive attributional bias has been shown in aggressive children and youths. They are more likely to perceive neutral acts by others as hostile, and more likely to believe conflicts can be satisfactorily resolved by aggression. In the social context, as the young individual becomes more disliked and rejected by peers, the opportunity for viewing the world this way increases (Dodge and Schwartz 1997). By their late teens they can hold highly suspicious attitudes and be quick to perceive disrespect from others (Scott 2004). In the social context of juvenile incarceration, being 'para' (paranoid) can become in peer group interactions the shared norm (Farrant 2001).

Depression anxiety and PTSD in childhood and adolescence

As well as the recognised feelings of low mood in depression there is also some evidence of irritability, hostility and anger when depression occurs in adolescence. Irritability in adolescence leads to interpreting annoyances by others as direct threats, increasing the risk of defensive aggression (Dubicka and Harrington 2004). Nowhere is this more apparent than in juvenile justice populations (Harrington *et al.* 2005; Kroll *et al.* 2002), which has resonance in the adult paranoid thinking literature (Bentall *et al.* 1994; Martin and Penn 2001). A self-serving bias with a tendency to attribute good outcomes to the self and bad outcomes to external causes observed in ordinary people is usually regarded as a mechanism for maintaining self-esteem in the face of threats to the self.

Posttraumatic stress disorder (PTSD) is related to the conditioning of neuro-biological fear responses underlying tendencies to react aggressively to protect the self when exposed to reminders of earlier trauma (Fletcher 2003). In the recent escalating context of children who have experienced violence in war-torn countries and those who live in a context of 'urban war zones', Garbarino (2001) sets out an ecological framework to explain the process and conditions that transform the 'developmental challenge' of violence into developmental harm in some children – an accumulation of risk models for understanding how and when children suffer the most adverse consequences of exposure to community violence and go beyond their limits of resilience.

The combination of depression, anxiety and severe PTSD is being increasingly recognised in the child literature as being linked to a trajectory into adult antisocial personality disorder (Harrington and Bailey 2004).

Autism spectrum disorders and learning disability

Autism spectrum disorders are being increasingly recognised in adolescent forensic populations. Their identification is critical to the understanding of violent offending. This is particularly so if an offence or assault is bizarre in nature or the degree or nature of aggression is unaccountable. O'Brien (1996) and Howlin (1997) proposed four reasons for offending and aggression in autistic persons:

• Their social naivety may allow them to be led into criminal acts by others.
• Aggression may arise from a disruption of routines.
• Antisocial behaviour may stem from a lack of understanding or misinterpretation of social cues.
• Crimes may reflect obsessions, especially when these involved morbid fascination with violence – there are similarities with the intense and obsessional nature of fantasies described in some adult sadists (Bailey 2002b).

In the extant adult research on paranoid beliefs and autism spectrum disorder, authors such as Craig *et al.* (2004) and Blackshaw *et al.* (2001) conclude utilising measures of theory of mind that 'the paranoia observed in Asperger syndrome therefore does not appear to stem from the same factors as seen in the paranoia observed in people with a diagnosis of schizophrenia' (Blackshaw *et al.* 2001: 158). They postulate the paranoia in the former has a different quality to that observed in the latter. Rather than stemming from a defensive strategy, it may stem from a confusion of not understanding the subtleties of social interaction and social rules.

Early onset psychosis

Non-psychotic behavioural disturbance occurs in about half of the cases of early-onset schizophrenia and can last between one and seven years. It includes externalising behaviours, attention-deficit disorder and conduct disorder. This emphasises the need for mental health assessments repeated over time to include a focus on changes in social functioning (often from an already chaotic baseline level) to a state including perceptual distortion, ideas of reference and delusional mood (Clark 2001; James 2004).

As in adult life (Taylor and Gunn 1999), most young people with schizophrenia are non-delinquent and non-violent. Nevertheless, there may be an increased risk of violence to others when they have active symptoms, especially when there is misuse of drugs or alcohol. The risk of violent acts is related to subjective feelings of tension, ideas of violence, delusional symptoms that incorporate named persons known to the individual, persecutory delusions, fear of imminent attack, feelings of sustained anger and fear, passivity experiences reducing the sense of self-control and command hallucinations. Protective factors include responding to and compliance with physical and psychosocial treatments, good social networks, a valued home environment, no interest in or knowledge of weapons as a means of violence, good insight into the psychiatric illness and any previous violent aggressive behaviour, and a fear of their own potential for violence. These features require particular attention but the best predictors of future violent offending in young people with mental disorder are the same as those in the general adolescent population (Clare *et al.* 2000). In findings from a retrospective study of 39 12–18-year-olds admitted to a specialist national inpatient adolescent medium-secure unit and a regional adolescent inpatient unit, Clare *et al.* (2000) found that the violence was related to developmental and social factors rather than psychopathology, which included persecutory delusions present in 12 of the 14 violent group and 23 of 25 of the non-violent group.

'Psychopathic personality' in young people

A three-factor structure has been proposed (Cooke and Michie 2001), which includes:

- an arrogant, deceitful interpersonal style, involving dishonesty, manipulation, grandiosity and glibness;
- defective emotional experience, involving lack of remorse, poor empathy, shallow emotions and a lack of responsibility for one's own actions;
- behavioural manifestations of impulsiveness, irresponsibility and sensation-seeking.

Conduct disorder, antisocial personality disorder and psychopathy are often seen as developmental disorders that span the life course and the terms are sometimes used interchangeably. Conduct disorder and antisocial personality disorder primarily focus on behavioural problems; psychopathy, as described by Hare (1991), emphasises deficits in affective and interpersonal functioning.

The relationship between callous-unemotional traits and conduct disorder

Frick (2002) and Lynam (2002) argue that, theoretically, personality traits are relatively stable across adolescence into adulthood and that there are remarkable similarities between the literature on psychopathy in adults and that emerging on children and adolescents. Others (e.g. Seagrave and Grisso 2002) suggest that psychopathy as a construct has a high false-positive rate in adolescence, as this is a period of considerable developmental change.

Knowledge about the nature, stability and consequences of juvenile psychopathy, however, is still very limited. There have been no published longitudinal studies of the stability of psychopathy as assessed by any of the current measures and it remains unclear to what degree the antisocial behavioural items that contribute to the psychopathy label change over time, given what we know about adolescent-limited antisocial behaviours. Many researchers in this field suggest that it is premature to assign the psychopathy label to younger cohorts and refer to juveniles with 'psychopathic characteristics' rather than using the term 'psychopathy'.

Nevertheless, delinquent offenders with pronounced psychopathic characteristics have an earlier onset of offending (Brandt et al. 1997; Forth and Burke 1998), commit more crimes and reoffend more often (Forth and Burke 1998; Myers et al. 1995) and more violently (Brandt et al. 1997; Spain et al. 2004) than non-psychopathic criminal youth. Psychopathy scores have also been found to correlate significantly with the severity of conduct problems, antisocial behaviour and delinquency in adolescents (Forth and Burke 1998). Christian et al. (1997) have also demonstrated that children with callous-unemotional traits engage in more persistent antisocial behaviour. In addition, they exhibit insensitivity to punishment cues irrespective of whether or not they have conduct problems (O'Brien and Frick 1996). In fact, it is argued that callous-unemotional traits develop as part of a unique temperamental style, low behavioural inhibition, which makes the child poorly responsive to socialisation (Frick 1998b).

The callous-unemotional and interpersonal aspects of psychopathy share some features with the pervasive developmental disorders. There have been no studies in forensic cohorts to explore the similarities and differences between these disorders or the level of comorbidity between them, despite evidence that autistic-spectrum disorders are prevalent in criminal samples (Soderstrom et al. 2004).

Substance misuse

The relationship between substance misuse, and more specifically cannabis use, and the development of schizophrenia and other psychoses has been well established (Green et al. 2005; Rey and Tennant 2002; Semple et al. 2005), although recent research has implied either a common vulnerability or bi-directional causal relationship between the use of cannabis and psychosis (Ferdinand et al. 2005). In comparing psychiatric outcomes at age 26 with the use of cannabis during adolescence, Arseneault et al. (2002) added to the current evidence base three new findings. The authors found that cannabis use is associated with an increased risk of experiencing symptoms of schizophrenia. After controlling for those symptoms that precede the onset of cannabis use, the onset of cannabis use before the age of 16 increases the risk of such symptoms developing and this risk is specific to cannabis use. In a prospective cohort study (2,437 young people aged 14 to 24 years) of cannabis use, predisposition for psychosis and psychotic symptoms in young people, Henquet et al. (2005) demonstrated that cannabis use moderately increases the risk of psychotic symptoms in young people but has a much stronger effect in those with evidence of predisposition for psychosis.

Policy-makers responding to need

Standard 8 of the English National Service Framework (NSF) (DoH 2004) specifically states that young people with complex needs should have access to services that promote social inclusion. Standard 9 of the English NSF has established a clear responsibility for primary care trusts to ensure that local needs assessments identify young people in special circumstances, including YOIs, and sets out expectations that services are in place to meet their needs. It also states that all young people from birth to their eighteenth birthday should have access to timely, integrated services.

The YJB have in place a performance indicator which seeks to have young people who have been identified with acute mental health needs seen by CAMHS in five working days and those with non-acute needs seen within 15 working days. Positive progress is being made on the performance indicator, with 85 per cent of young people with acute needs and 89 per cent with non-acute needs reported by YOTs as being seen within the target times during 2005–06 (Youth Justice Board 2007).

In addition to the YOTs, people working in the criminal justice system, particularly the court system, need to able to identify where young people have mental health problems. A good understanding of a young person's mental health needs and their influence on offending behaviour can inform the sentencing and placement process and help ensure that young people have access to the mental health services they require as they move through the youth justice system. A key area of concern for the YJB and the courts is the length of time it can take for psychiatric reports to be provided to the courts. Future work is planned by the YJB and DoH to explore possible improvements to the way in which CAMHS can better support the court system.

Improving access to CAMHS

The lack of clarity in the provision of CAMHS for 16–17-year-olds in England has been a particular concern for the YJB, as 45.6 per cent of young people in the youth justice system who received a disposal in 2005/06 fall into this age group. The YJB and DoH CAMHS are working together to implement the agenda set out in the English Children's National Service Framework. Over the ten-year lifetime of the Framework and as CAMHS develop, they will take responsibility for those young people who in some areas fall between services or are seen by adult mental health services

Role of health workers in YOTs

Health workers in YOTs form a significant outreach resource and work directly with some of the most vulnerable and difficult to engage young people, providing assessment, early intervention and appropriate referral into a range of primary and secondary health care services. YOTs, and health workers within these teams, play a vital role in the development of local comprehensive Tiers 1 and 2 CAMHS, with some senior CAMHS YOT workers providing Tier 3 provision with appropriate supervision (see Figure 4.2).

TIER 1

PRIMARY CARE PROFESSIONALS PROVIDING NON-SPECIALIST CAMHS			
Health visitors	GPs	Teachers	Social workers

TIER 2

INDIVIDUAL PROFESSIONALS WHO RELATE TO OTHERS THROUGH A NETWORK				
Clinical nurse specialist	Child and adolescent psychiatrist	Clinical psychologist	Community paediatrician	Hospital paediatrician

TIER 3

SPECIALIST CHILD ADOLESCENT MENTAL HEALTH SERVICES
Specialist multi-disciplinary child and adolescent mental health teams (CAMHS) providing assessment, treatment and consultation to children, their families and carers. Specialist CAMHS usually comprise psychiatrists, clinical nurse specialists, family therapists, psychologists and creatve therapists.

TIER 4

HIGHLY SPECIALISED TERTIARY LEVEL CAMHS			
Secure adolescent forensic units	Impatient child and adolescent units	Eating disorders units	Specialist community: Forensic Adolescent Consultation and Treatment Service (FACTS)

Figure 4.2 A tiered model of CAMHS

As specialist CAMHS develop nationally, the intention is that they will be able to provide an improved level of advice and supervision to workers operating at CAMHS Tiers 1 and 2. Already many health workers – and especially CAMHS workers in YOTs – have developed close links and protocols with CAMH specialist services. In particular, where there are CAMHS workers in YOTs, we would like to see these workers operating as virtual or direct members of local specialist CAMHS, providing an outreach community service to the YOT while receiving clinical supervision from the CAMHS team.

YOT primary healthcare workers also make up a significant percentage of the YOT health workforce. It is important that all health workers receive direct professional supervision from their host agency as expected under secondment arrangements for all YOT staff.

The majority of YOTs have a health worker as part of the team, provided originally by the health authority and now by local primary care trusts (PCTs). Unfortunately, some YOTs are still having difficulty with establishing and maintaining the health worker resource required to be provided under s. 39 of the Crime and Disorder Act 1998. The DoH and YJB need to ensure that the commitment for these workers in YOTs is maintained by PCTs. The recent Health Care Commission report (2006) *A Review of Healthcare in the Community for Young People Who Offend* found that 17 per cent of YOTs do not have a health worker.

Young offenders with health needs in custodial settings

From April 2003, the Department of Health took on responsibility for funding health services within all Prison Service establishments in England and Wales. As part of a rolling programme from 2004 to 2006, primary care trusts that have a prison in their boundary have taken on the commissioning role for health services for their local unit. Additional funds have been provided by the DoH to improve health services in all prisons, of which some funds have benefited units holding young people. The YJB, DoH and Prison Service have a Joint Health Steering Group and Management Board in place to deliver a joint health and well-being development programme to improve access to health services for young people in the youth justice system. As part of this work CAMHS in-reach Commissioning Guidance for PCTs was published by the DoH in March 2007.

Comprehensive health screening tool

The YJB in partnership with the DoH, Prison Service and National Treatment Agency (NTA) is currently piloting a comprehensive health screening tool which includes health, mental health and substance misuse in four establishments. The YJB have commissioned a specialist team to develop a four-part screening tool which assesses high-risk health needs when young people arrive at establishments and then undertakes a detailed health, mental health and substance misuse screen over their first five days in custody. This then forms a single healthcare plan linked to their sentence plan. This tool requires a multi-disciplinary approach to assessment and information sharing and significantly reduces duplication of assessment by staff with young people. The tool will eventually be placed onto an electronic case management system being developed with the youth justice system called E-ASSET. Once the pilots have concluded in 2007 the intention is that this tool will be rolled out across the custodial estate holding young people under 18 years

Transfer to appropriate CAMHS medium-secure provision

There are particular difficulties in finding suitable provision for young people with complex, severe or persistent mental disorders. Over the last five years both the DoH and Home Office have been concerned about the shortage of secure mental health beds for young people. Developments being led by the DoH National Specialist Commissioning Advisory Group (NSCAG) to increase the provision of medium secure CAMHS forensic units will provide a capacity of 88 beds by 2008.

Substance misuse

Research commissioned by the YJB shows that young people in the youth justice system are more likely to use drugs than other groups of young people and are more likely to suffer substance misuse-related problems.

The study *Substance Misuse and the Juvenile Secure Estate* (Galahad SMS Ltd and Youth Justice Board 2004) identified that 90 per cent of young people had taken an illegal drug at some point in their life, 72 per cent used cannabis daily in the 12 months before their arrest, 74 per cent drank alcohol more than once a week with the majority drinking more than six units each time, and 51 per cent were poly-drug users and used two or more substances more than once a week. The same study identified significant levels of dual diagnosis mental health needs and the use of substances to self-medicate with 30 per cent saying they had used a drug not to get high but to feel normal and 38 per cent had taken a drug to 'forget everything' or 'blot everything out'.

The YJB and Home Office, with the support of the DoH, NTA and DfES, have been establishing an end-to-end system to ensure young people's substance misuse needs can be identified and addressed at each stage of the youth justice system. YJB and HO research indicates that young people in the youth justice system are the highest and earliest users of drugs, including Class A drugs (House of Commons and Youth Justice Board 2004).

The YJB contributes directly to *Drug Strategy in England* and *Tackling Substance Misuse in Wales – A Partnership Approach* and the delivery of the Home Office young people's drug PSA target to:

> reduce the use of class A drugs and frequent use of any illicit drug among all young people under the age of 25, especially by the most vulnerable young people.

Substance misuse workers in YOTs

There are over 200 YOT substance misuse worker posts across England and Wales. The YJB works closely with the National Treatment Agency to improve access to services for young people supervised by YOTs in England. This work over the last three years has seen YOTs become responsible for the highest number of referrals to young people treatment services of all services working with young people.

In 2005/6 YOTs in England and Wales screened 79,027 young people for substance misuse; 15,414 required a further assessment and 12,874 received an intervention within 20 working days.

Substance misuse services in custody

The YJB has led the development of improved substance misuse services in the custodial estate. Informed by research into substance misuse needs and provision for young people in custody (Galahad 2004), additional funds from the Drug Strategy have been invested (2003–06) to significantly improve substance misuse services and resettlement for the under 18s in 37 custodial establishments. There are substance misuse teams in all YOIs and provision in secure training colleges (STCs) and local authority secure children's homes (LASCHs) to deliver the YJB *National Specification for Substance Misuse for Juveniles in Custody*.

The National Specification for Substance Misuse has driven change in five key areas of substance misuse intervention which include identification and assessment, detoxification and clinical management, education and prevention, support and programme, throughcare and resettlement. This programme has been delivered in partnership with the NTA, DoH, Home Office and DfES.

Clinical management guidance

The YJB is piloting detoxification and clinical management guidance for young people in five custodial units with a view to publishing this guidance once the pilot work is complete in 2007 for use across the estate. Currently there is no guidance available nationally for under 18s so this will be a significant resource for custodial health units.

Intensive resettlement and aftercare provision schemes

As part of the work to improve substance misuse and dual diagnosis services in custody the YJB has developed an a new intensive throughcare and aftercare scheme called RAP – Resettlement and Aftercare Provision – to ensure achievements made through substance misuse interventions in custody are capitalised on when young people leave custody, which is a critical time with young people being at risk of relapse and overdose.

Fifty-nine YOTs (local authorities) have a RAP scheme in place that provides intensive support to over 1,896 young people leaving custody and on community sentences, who have significant substance misuse and dual diagnosis needs.

RAP teams are attached to YOTs and undertake detailed resettlement planning with young people while in custody, provide up to 25 hours, intensive support during the community element of a custodial detention and training order, and can provide up to six months of ongoing support following the end of the sentence, which gives more time for young people to stabilise and engage with mainstream services.

RAP schemes work to ensure that young people have access to the ongoing specialist and mainsteam services they require including: substance misuse and mental health services; access to education, training, employment and leisure activities; support for parents; and work with their peer group. Many schemes are supported by the voluntary sector and recruit mentors who provide their time to support the young person on a voluntary basis normally at evenings and weekends to provide extended periods of aftercare.

RAP works with some of the most complex young people in the youth justice system and aims to impact on their substance misuse, mental health needs and history of repeat offending. A fundamental element of RAP is that it is individually tailored to a young person's needs and participation is voluntary.

Early monitoring data is showing significantly low reoffending, breach and return to custody rates among young people while on RAP. This scheme also has significant potential to reduce the demand for custody by reducing the number of young people who return to custody. RAP is being evaluated and the research project will report to the YJB in March 2008.

The role of the CAMHS specialist in medico-legal assessment

In *T & V* v. *United Kingdom* (1999) European Centre of Human Rights Judgements, 16 December, it was stated that a child's age, level of maturity and intellectual and emotional capacities must be taken into account when they are charged with a criminal offence and that appropriate steps should be taken in order to promote their ability to understand and participate in the court proceedings. A responsibility therefore falls on the defence lawyer to be aware of the possibility that a young person may not be able to participate effectively in the trial process, particularly if they are under 14 years old or have learning problems or a history of absence from school (Ashford *et al.* 2006). In 1985, the Office of the High Commissioner for Human Rights, in reference to the age of criminal responsibility, stated that there is a close relationship between the notion of responsibility for delinquent or criminal behaviour and other social rights and responsibilities.

In discussing issues of fitness to plead and capacity to participate in legal proceedings, Ashford and Bailey (2004) state that all young defendants, regardless of the offences they are charged with, should be tried in youth courts with permission for adult sanctions for older youths if certain conditions are met. This should enable a mode of trial for young defendants to be subject to safeguards that can enhance understanding and participation. Assessment of cognitive and emotional capacities should occur before any decisions on venue and mode of trial take place.

One fundamental distinction in the criminal law is between conditions that negate criminal liability and those that might mitigate the punishment deserved under particular circumstances. Very young children and the profoundly mentally ill may lack the minimum capacity necessary to justify punishment. Those exhibiting less profound impairments of the same kind may qualify for a lesser level of deserved punishment even though they may meet the minimum conditions for some punishment. Immaturity, like mental disorder, can serve both as an excuse and as mitigation in the determination of just punishment. Capacity is sometimes thought of as a generic skill that a person either has or lacks. However, that is not so. To begin with, it is multifaceted, with four key elements as follows:

- the capacity to understand information relevant to the specific decision at issue (understanding);
- the capacity to appreciate one's situation as the defendant is confronted with a specific legal decision (appreciation);
- the capacity to think rationally about alternative courses of action (reasoning);
- the capacity to express a choice among alternatives (choice).

Any evaluation of competence (Grisso 1997) should include assessment of possibly relevant psychopathology, emotional understanding as well cognitive level, the child's experiences and appreciation of situations comparable to the one relevant to the crime and to the trial, and any particular features that may be pertinent in this individual and this set of circumstances. The general principles to be used in the assessment are broadly comparable to those employed in any clinical evaluation. However, particular attention needs to be paid to developmental background, emotional and cognitive maturity, trauma, exposure and substance misuse. The likely appropriate sources for obtaining clinical data relevant to assessment of a juvenile's competence to stand trial will include a variety of historical records, a range of interviews and other observations, and in some cases, specialised tests. Records of the child's school functioning, past clinical assessment, treatment history and previous legal involvements need to be obtained. In coming to an overall formulation, there should be a particular focus on how both developmental and psychopathological features may be relevant to the forensic issues that have to be addressed.

The main focus is on the youth's ability to understand and cope with the legal process. This comes from three sources: direct questioning of the defendant, inferences from the functioning in other areas and direct observation of the defendant's behaviour and interaction with others. It is useful to inquire about the youth's expectations about what the consequences of the court involvement might prove to be. Because the course of juvenile proceedings can vary so widely, with consequences ranging from the extremely aversive to extremely beneficial, rational understanding will necessarily involve a high degree of uncertainty. Potentially relevant problems include: inattention, depression, disorganisation of thought processes that interfered with the ability to consider alternatives, hopelessness such that the decision is felt not to matter, delusion or other fixed beliefs that distort understanding of options (or their likely outcomes), maturity of judgment and the developmental challenges of adolescence.

In providing information to the court, written reports have the advantage of a standard format that helps the consultant to be sure that s/he has considered all the relevant questions; it also provides a familiar structure for readers. In essence, for the sake of consistency and clarity, competence reports need to cover the following areas:

- identifying information and referral questions;
- the description of the structure of the evaluation including sources and a notation of the confidentiality expectations;
- the provision of clinical and forensic data.

Ashford *et al.* (2006) itemise the issues that a clinical psychologist with experience of assessing adolescents should be asked to address. This includes the young person's understanding of the charges and the possible consequences of guilty and not guilty pleas, and their ability to make rational decisions relevant to the legal process, to remember relevant facts, to communicate in a coherent manner, to understand testimony in court and to behave appropriately in the courtroom. Grisso (2000) outlined a conceptual framework for psychiatric assessment of competence in young people that includes assessment of their understanding of the charges they face and the potential consequences, an understanding of the trial process, the young person's capacity to communicate with their lawyer in their defence and their general ability to participate in the courtroom proceedings.

In court, a child's ability to give an account of events can be impaired by a number of factors, including poor physical health on the day of the trial, overwhelming anxiety or anger about giving evidence, or intimidation by the physical surroundings of the court. From a psychological perspective, however, the basic evidential capacity of the child defendant will depend on two main components:

- the child's mental state – this needs to be stable, therefore any disturbance that might interfere with the child's perception of the world and the ability to understand it will impair evidential capacity;
- the child's cognitive ability – a concept that includes a large number of facets, such as memory, understanding and the ability to communicate. The last includes both verbal (speech) and non-verbal means, as well as the ability

both to comprehend and to express thought. Any psychological assessment therefore has to be across a range of domains.

Discrepancies are particularly likely in the areas of educational achievement, adaptive skills and social and emotional development. A child's ability often is gauged on educational achievement and given as being equivalent to that of a certain age, e.g. a 15-year-old child might have the everyday living skills of a 7-year-old. However, a child who might be unable to cope with monetary change or public transport might well have the emotional and social experiences of an older child and the drives of an adolescent.

When discussing developmental psychology and child development, it is important to bear in mind that none of these processes operates in a vacuum. The child's experience of parenting (important in relation to physical and emotional development), the provision of appropriate role models (moral development and self-control depend heavily on appropriate modelling and social learning) and the learning environment (whether it fostered or hindered intellectual development) all have a vital role. For instance, during adolescence, as young people take on a wider and more social perspective and become integrated within a peer group, they will nevertheless tend to adopt social values and norms (i.e. ideas about 'right and wrong') that are very similar to those of their parents. Hence, despite any demonstrations of teenage rebellion (often short-lived), the majority of adolescents will tend to adopt parental mores, either law-abiding or delinquent.

It should be emphasised that clear-cut ages do not apply to the completion of physical, intellectual, emotional and social development. For most young people, given appropriate parenting, normal biological development and a structured, emotionally supportive and stimulating environment, the bulk of the aforementioned processes should be achieved by late teenage years and a considerable degree of intellectual maturation may have occurred by the age of 14.

When delivering forensic mental health services for children and adolescents it is important that the services are developed in such a way that their needs are met and that the services build on established concepts of service design in line with a strategic framework. Doing so will require long-term planning that actively addresses the requirements of an adequate size and composition of an appropriately trained, supervised and managed workforce. Such services should be developed with an awareness of the scope of existing services and recognition of current demands, analysing gaps in current services. There should also be an awareness of the growth points in professional practice, service development and research (Williams 2005).

Treatment and special crimes

Juvenile homicide

Studies show that children and adolescents who murder share a constellation of psychological, cognitive, neuropsychiatric, educational and family system disturbance (Cornell et al. 1987; Myers et al. 1995; Myers and Scott 1998). In the UK, young people who commit grave sadistic crimes including juvenile homicide are liable to periods of lengthy incarceration. Detention itself can provide time for further neurodevelopmental, cognitive and emotional growth. Irrespective of treatment models, the provisions of education, vocational training, consistent role models and continued family contact are of critical importance.

Youths who have been prosecuted for murder or manslaughter vary only slightly or not at all from other juvenile delinquents on points such as age, gender and ethnic background, and only to a limited extent on risk factors. Murder and manslaughter are committed alone comparatively more often, and on average the perpetrators start their criminal activities at a later age and are much less likely to have previous convictions than (other) minors taken into judicial youth institutions. At the same time, it is clear that while the group of youths involved in murder and manslaughter may be small, it is anything but homogeneous. There is great variety in terms of motives, victims, *modus operandi*, etc. In simple terms each case stands on its own.

Sexually abusive behaviour

Sexually inappropriate behaviour in children and adolescents constitutes a substantial health and social problem (James and Neil 1996). Most, but not all, abusers are male, often come from disadvantaged backgrounds with a history of victimisation, sexual and physical abuse (Skuse *et al.* 1998) and show high rates of psychopathology (Dolan *et al.* 1996; Hummel *et al.* 2000). Of particular concern is a significant subgroup with mild learning disability whose treatment programmes have to be tailored to their level of development and cognitive ability. Young abusers come within the criminal justice system but also should be considered in their own right within the child protection framework. Most adult sexual abusers of children started their abuse when adolescents and yet neither ICD 10 nor DSM IV has a diagnostic category for paedophilia in those under 16. Vizard and colleagues (1996) suggested the creation of a new disorder 'Sexual Arousal Disorder of Childhood' to help identify this vulnerable group who in turn place vulnerable others at risk. Langstrom and colleagues (2000) advocated the development of empirically based typologies for this offender group.

A structured, carefully planned multi-agency approach is required when working with sexually aggressive younger children and sexually abusive adolescents. The three stages to assessment of juvenile sexual offenders (Becker 1998; O'Callaghan and Print 1994; Vizard 2006) are:

1 clarification and rapport building;
2 mapping the abuse: the fantasies, strategies and behaviours; and
3 the future, placement treatment and personal change.

The treatment process occurs in the context of:

1 the crisis of disclosure;
2 family assessment;
3 therapeutic work in a protective context for the victim; and
4 reconstruction and reunification of the family.

The 'family' (Bentovim 1998) in this context may include foster carers or long-term residential carers.

Treatment outcome

The earliest possible interventions with young over-sexualised children, before their patterns of sexually aggressive behaviours become entrenched, are likely to be most effective. However, there is a dearth of longitudinal follow-up studies looking at treatment outcomes with this younger group of children.

New approaches to cognitive-behavioural therapy (CBT) with sexually abusing youth have recently been described within the context of relapse prevention (Steen 2005) and a more complex CBT intervention, mode deactivation therapy (MDT), has been suggested for disturbed, sexually abusive young people with reactive conduct disorders or personality disorders (Apsche and Ward Bailey 2005). CBT group work with sexually abusing children and young people is widely practised in the UK and the principles of this work are described by Print and O'Callaghan (1999).

However, other treatment approaches will take into account the living context of the young person and the need for his or her carers to be provided with support and explanation of the treatment process in order to maximise positive results. For instance, when children and young people who sexually abuse are still living at home or in contact with their parents, family work is usually needed. Hackett *et al.* (2002) describe an approach to group work with parents of children with sexually abusive behaviour.

There are a significant number of mid-adolescent, recidivist, delinquent, sexually abusive youth who are too dangerous to other children and young people to be treated (with any treatment modality) alongside other young people. Many of these young people have been through the court system or are currently facing charges. For these reasons, treatment of the sexually abusive young person needs to be undertaken within a close supervised, intensive, community-based foster placement with specially trained foster carers who are experienced in dealing with young offenders, risk and dangerousness. This type of approach is known by various names such as multidimensional treatment foster care (MTFC) (Chamberlain and Reid 1998) or forensic foster care (Yokely and Boettner 2002). Early results from small-scale studies with this type of intervention are reasonably encouraging.

In summary, the components of effective treatment interventions with children and young people who sexually abuse will include the following:

- A well planned, systemic, child protection orientated, treatment context should be provided in which therapy can occur.
- Treatment should be one of a number of positive interventions into the life of the young person and his or her family.
- All interventions should be part of an agreed inter-agency care plan for the young person.
- Offence-specific interventions, such as CBT, aimed at straightening out the distorted cognitions and self-justifications of sexually abusing young people should be the core of any intervention programme for this client group.
- Treatment programmes which focus solely on the victimisation of the young person are likely to be seriously counterproductive and to miss opportunities to challenge the young person on his or her offending behaviour.

- Interventions should occur at all possible levels including individual work with the young person, family work (where relevant), support for foster carers or for professional care staff and consultation with the professional network.

Firesetting/arson

Arson can have a devastating impact on the victim and the wider society. Juvenile arsonists are not a homogenous group, with a wide range of familial (Fineman 1980), social (Patterson 1982), developmental, interpersonal (Vreeland and Lowin 1980), clinical and 'legal' needs. Kolko and Kazdin (1992) highlighted the importance of attraction to fire, heightened arousal, impulsivity and limited social competence. As with other forms of serious antisocial behaviours, no single standard treatment approach will be appropriate for all individuals (Repo and Virkunnen 1997). In addition to the general assessment of antisocial behaviour the specific domains to be considered include:

- history of fireplay;
- history of hoax telephone calls;
- social context of firesetting (whether alone or with peers);
- where the fires were set;
- previous threats/targets;
- type of fire, single/multiple seats of fire setting;
- motivation(anger resolution, boredom, rejection, cry for help, thrill seeking, firefighting, crime concealment, no motivation, curiosity and peer pressure).

For recidivistic firesetters, therapy may include:

- psychotherapy to increase the understanding of the behaviour, including antecedents defining the problem behaviour, and establishing the behavioural reinforcers;
- skills training to promote adaptive coping mechanisms;
- understanding environmental factors to manage or self-trigger solutions;
- counselling to reduce psychological distress;
- behavioural techniques to extinguish the behaviour;
- education to promote understanding of cause and effect; and
- supervision for the staff caring for the adolescent.

Early modelling experiences and early exposure to related phenomena militate against a good outcome.

Adolescent girls

Longitudinal data demonstrate that girlhood aggression contributes to a cascading set of negative outcomes as young women move into adolescence and adulthood.
    Young girls who engage in disruptive behaviour and fighting are at risk for:

- being rejected by peers
- feeling alienated ...
- and unsupported in their relationships with peers and adults

- struggling academically
- affiliating with other peers prone to deviant behaviour
- becoming involved in more serious antisocial behaviours
- choosing antisocial romantic partners
- initiating and receiving partner violence
- becoming adolescent mothers
- having children with more health problems
- being less sensitive and responsive as parents.

Some are sufficiently antisocial and even violent that they may be incarcerated; if they are also mothers, they may lose custody of their children and opportunities for stable employment and relationships are much diminished.

Given the low base rates of girls engaging in physical aggression and violence, identifying girls at risk is a critically important step for prevention and intervention programmes.

High-risk groups of girls to target include those girls who are temperamentally overactive as toddlers and pre-schoolers (fewer than boys), and also those girls who have early pubertal development (girls report engaging in high levels of bullying as they enter puberty). This group are likely to be victims as well as perpetrators. Sexually abused girls – especially those abused by their biological fathers over a long period of time – are also at risk of becoming perpetrators of aggression, as well sadly as being victims of sexual abuse.

From the available literature interventions to reduce rates of aggression, relational aggression and violence in female children and adolescents should address the following:

- Pre-natal delivery of programmes for high-risk expectant mothers (especially young mothers and those themselves aggressive or disruptive as children).
- Augmenting the parenting skills of at risk young mothers – the evidence shows that children of young mothers with histories of girlhood aggression may themselves be more prone to infection and injuries.
  - This could be done by additional parenting skills around key issues of hygiene, childproofing of homes, good nutrition, meal planning and household management.
  - Given that these at-risk mothers are prone to maternal irritability and harsh parenting they are more likely to understand normal infant behaviour such as a child being irritable during nappy changing as an intentional act on the part of the child. The increased tendency of these mothers to hold hostile attributions about other human beings will include carrying this over into perceptions about the way in which their own child responds to them. Therefore there is a need to help young mothers to respond optimally to the perceived challenging behaviour of their infants and toddlers. The result should be that these young mothers would be less likely to then engage in coercive parenting practice which in turn would avoid a cycle of these children themselves becoming aggressive and antisocial.
- Middle childhood girls, episodes of physical aggression are often preceded by relational aggression. This then means interventions are needed to help these girls in:

- relating to others;
- managing strong emotions, just as with boys;
- understanding the unfolding of their own aggression;
- understanding exactly how 'girl talk' ignites into hurtful indirect social relational aggression;
- understanding how relational aggression leads to physical violence by some girls towards peers, adults and romantic partners;
- in the overall context of intervention programmes, being able to recognise when a girl's aggression is adaptive in the immediate situation as a means of social ascendancy or standing up to abuse.

Conclusions

The major challenge of altering the trajectories of persistent young offenders has to be met in the context of satisfying public demands for retribution, together with welfare and civil liberties considerations. In England and Wales, for example, we lock up more than 3,000 juveniles at any one time.

The treatment of delinquents in institutional settings has to meet the sometimes contradictory need to control young people, to remove their liberty and to maintain good order in the institution, at the same time as offering education and training to foster future prosocial participation in society and meeting their welfare needs. At least in England and Wales, the legislative overhaul of youth justice embodied in the Crime and Disorder Act 1998 has mandated practitioners to bridge the gap between residential and community treatments and to involve families, using youth offending teams (YOTs) to meet this complex mix of needs, but the public demand to remove antisocial youths from the street has led to the implementation of antisocial behaviour orders including children with learning disabilities.

Over the last 30 years there has been a gradual shift in opinion regarding the effectiveness of intervention with delinquents, from the 'nothing works' approach to a 'what works' approach. The jury is still out for 'what works' in the long term but the evidence base that can be placed before the jury is growing. In practice, the pressure from politicians and public will remain for a quick-fix solution to problems that span cultures, countries and generations. The most important childhood predictors of adolescent violence include troublesome and antisocial behaviour, daring and hyperactivity, low IQ and attainment, antisocial parents, poor child rearing, harsh and erratic discipline, poor supervision, parental conflict, broken families, low family income and large family size (Lösel and Bender 2006). Important policy implications are that home visiting programmes, parent training and skills training programmes singly and in combination should be implemented at an early stage to prevent adolescent high-risk behaviour and offending. The best knowledge about risk factors has been obtained in longitudinal studies and the best knowledge of effective programmes has been obtained in randomised experiments.

Provision of appropriately designed programmes can significantly reduce recidivism among persistent offenders. The mode and style of delivery is important: high-quality staff and staff training are required, together with a system for 'monitoring integrity'. Where comparisons are possible, effect sizes are higher for community-based rather than institution-based programmes. In prison settings, the strongest effects are obtained when programmes are integrated into the institutional regimes.

Our knowledge of the true prevalence rates of mental disorders in a young offending population is developing (Kazdin 2000), so that mental health issues (Bailey 2006) can be addressed with a good evidence base. Child and adolescent mental health practitioners have the skills to set the understanding of delinquency in a developmental context and treat those young offenders with mental disorders (Bailey 2006). However, it is a contentious area, and likely to remain so. While, as stated earlier, the jury is still out for 'what works', examining the success of and scope for intervention is increasingly being assisted by an established international research network in Europe and the USA whereby experience can be usefully shared.

Further selected reading

The article by Bailey, S., Doreleijers, T. and Tarbuck, P. (2006) 'Recent developments in mental health screening and assessment in juvenile justice systems', *Child and Adolescent Psychiatric Clinics of North America, 15:* 391–406, describes some general aspects of screening and assessment in forensic populations, followed by a description of four specific instruments.

The article by Chitsabesan, P., Kroll, L., Bailey, S., Kenning, C., Sneider, S., MacDonald, W. and Theodosiou, L. (2006) 'Mental health needs of young offenders in custody and in the community', *British Journal of Psychiatry, 188:* 534–40, evaluates the mental health and psychosocial needs of a nationally representative sample of juvenile offenders in England and Wales.

The book by Bailey, S. and Dolan, M. (2004) *Adolescent Forensic Psychiatry*. London: Arnold, examines a broad range of issues on the psychiatric needs of adolescents related to offending behaviour, including the relationship between adolescents' problems and their state of mental health, giving practical advice on assessment, treatment and outcomes for different disorders.

References

Achenbach, T. M., Edeibrock, C. S. (1983) *Manual for the Child Behaviour Checklist and Revised Child Behaviour Profile*. Burlington, VT: University of Vermont.

Andrews, D., Zinger, I., Hoge, R., Bonta, J., Gendreau, P. and Cullen, F. (1990) 'Does correctional treatment work? A clinically relevant and psychologically informed metaanalysis', *Criminology*, 28: 369–404.

Apsche, J. A. and Ward Bailey, S. R. (2005) 'Mode deactivation therapy: cognitive behavioral therapy for adolescents with reactive conduct disorders and/or personality disorders/ traits', in M. C. Calder (ed.), *Children and Young People Who Sexually Abuse: New Theory, Research, and Practice Developments*. Lyme Regis: Russell House.

Arseneault, L., Cannon, M., Poulton, R., Murray, R., Caspi, A., Moffitt, T. E. (2002) 'Cannabis use in adolescence and risk for adult psychosis: longitudinal prospective study', *British Medical Journal*, 325 (7374): 1213.

Ashford, M. and Bailey, S. (2004) 'The youth justice system in England and Wales', in S. Bailey and M. Dolan (eds), *Adolescent Forensic Psychiatry*. London: Arnold, pp. 409–16.

Ashford, M., Chard, A. and Redhouse, N. (2006) *Defending Young People in the Criminal Justice System*, 3rd edn. Glasgow: Legal Action Groups

Atkins, D., Pumariega, A. J., Rogers, K., Montgomery, L., Nybro, C., Jeffers, G. and Sease, F. (1999) 'Mental health and incarcerated youth. I: Prevalence and nature of psychopathology', *Journal of Child and Family Studies*, 8: 193–204.

Audit Commission (1996) *Misspent Youth: Young People and Crime*. London: Audit Commission.

Bailey, S. (2002a) 'Treatment of delinquents', in M. Rutter and E. Taylor (eds), *Child and Adolescent Psychiatry: Modern Approaches*, 4th edn. Oxford: Blackwell Scientific, pp. 1019–37.

Bailey, S. (2002b) 'Violent children: a framework for assessment', *Advances in Psychiatric Treatment*, 8: 97–106.

Bailey, S. (2005) 'The National Service Framework: children come of age', *Child and Adolescent Mental Health*, 10 (3): 127–30.

Bailey, S. (2006) 'Adolescence and beyond: twelve years onwards', in J. Aldgate, W. Rose, D. Jones and C. Jeffrey (eds), *The Developing World of the Child*. London: Jessica Kingsley, pp. 208–25.

Bailey, S. and Dolan, M. (2004) 'Violence', in S. Bailey and M. Dolan (eds), *Adolescent Forensic Psychiatry*. London: Arnold, pp. 213–27.

Bailey, S. and Tarbuck, P. (2006) 'Recent advances in the development of screening tools for mental health in young offenders', *Current Opinion in Psychiatry*, 19: 373–7.

Bailey, S., Jasper, A., and Ross, K. (2004) 'Social diversity', in S. Bailey and M. Dolan (eds), *Adolescent Forensic Psychiatry*. London: Arnold, pp. 181–201.

Beck, A. T. (1999) *Prisoners of Hate: The Cognitive Basis of Anger, Hostility, and Violence*. New York: HarperCollins.

Becker, J. V. (1998) 'The assessment of adolescent perpetrators of childhood sexual abuse', *Irish Journal of Psychology*, 19 (1): 68–81.

Bentall, R. P., Kinderman, P. and Kaney, S. (1994) 'The self, attributional process and normal beliefs – towards a model of persecutory delusions', *Behaviour Research and Therapy*, 32 (3): 331–41.

Bentovim, A. (1998) 'Family systemic approach to work with young sex offenders', *Irish Journal of Psychology*, 19: 119–35.

Bentovim, A. and Williams, B. (1998) 'Children and adolescents: victims who become perpetrators', *Advances in Psychiatric Treatment*, 4: 101–7.

Blackshaw, A. J., Kinderman, P., Hare, D. J. and Hatton, C. (2001) 'Theory of mind, causal attribution and paranoia in Asperger syndrome', *Autism*, 5 (2): 147–63.

Bourdon, K. H., Goodman, R., Rae, D. S., Simpson, G. and Koretz, D. S. (2005) 'The Strengths and Difficulties Questionnaire: US normative data and psychometric properties', *Journal American Academy of Child and Adolescent Psychiatry*, 44 (6): 557–64.

Brandt, J. R., Kennedy, W. A., Patrick, C. J. and Curtin, J. (1997) 'Assessment of psychopathy in a population of incarcerated adolescent offenders', *Psychological Assessment*, 9: 429–35.

Chamberlain, P. and Reid, P. B. (1998) 'Comparison of two community alternatives to incarceration for chronic juvenile offenders', *Journal of Consulting and Clinical Psychology*, 66 (4): 624–33.

Chitsabesan, P., Kroll, L., Bailey, S., Kenning, C., Sneider, S., Macdonald, W. and Theodosiou, L. (2006) 'Mental health needs of young offenders in custody and in the community', *British Journal of Psychiatry*, 188: 534–40.

Christian, R. E., Frick, P. J., Hill, N. L., Tyler, L. and Frazer, D. R. (1997) 'Psychopathy and conduct problems in children. Implications for subtyping children with conduct problems', *Journal of the American Academy of Child and Adolescent Psychiatry*, 36: 233–41.

Cicchetti, D. (1984) 'The emergence of developmental psychopathology', *Child Development*, 55 (1): 1–7.

Cicchetti, D. and Rogosch, F. A. (2002) 'A developmental psychopathology perspective on adolescence', *Journal Consult Clinical Psychology*, 70 (1): 6–20.

Clare, P., Bailey, S. and Clark, A. (2000) 'Relationship between psychotic disorders in adolescence and criminally violent behaviour', *British Journal of Psychiatry*, 177: 275–9.

Clark, R. E. (2001) 'Family support and substance use outcomes for persons with mental illness and substance use disorders', *Schizophrenia Bulletin*, 27 (1): 93–101.

Coleman, J. and Schofield, J. (2003) *Key Data on Adolescence*. Brighton: Trust for Study of Adolescence.

Coleman, J. and Schofield, J. (2005) *Key Data on Adolescence*, 5th edn. Brighton: Trust for Study of Adolescence.

Coll, G. C., Kagan, J. and Resnick, J. S. (1984) 'Behavioural inhibition in young children', *Child Development*, 55: 1005–19.

Conners, C. K. (1971) 'Recent drug studies with children', *Journal of Learning Disability*, 4: 467–83.

Cooke, D. J. and Michie, C. (2001) 'Refining the construct of psychopathy: towards a hierarchical model', *Psychological Assessment*, 13: 171–88.

Cornell, D. G., Benedek, E. P. and Benedek, B. A. (1987) 'Juvenile homicide. Prior adjustment and a proposed typology', *American Journal of Orthopsychiatry*, 57: 383–93.

Costello, E. J., Edeibrook, C. and Costell, A. J. (1985) 'Validity of the NIMH Diagnostic Interview Schedule for Children: a comparison between psychiatric and paediatric referrals', *Journal of Abnormal Child Psychology*, 13: 579–95.

Craig, J. S., Hatton, C., Craig, F. B. and Bentall, R. P. (2004) 'Persecutory beliefs, attributions and theory of mind: comparison of patients with paranoid delusions, Asperger's syndrome and healthy controls', *Schizophrenia Research*, 69 (1): 29–33.

Department for Education and Skills (2004) *Every Child Matters: Change for Children*. Nottingham: Department for Education and Skills.

Department of Health (2004) *National Service Framework for Children, Young People and Maternity Services*. London: DoH.

Department of Health (2007) *Promoting mental health for children held in secure settings. A framework for commissioning services*. London: DoH.

Dixon, A., Howie, P. and Starling, J. (2004) 'Psychopathology in female offenders', *Journal of Child Psychology and Psychiatry*, 45: 1150–8.

Dodge, K. A. and Schwartz, D. (1997) 'Social information processing mechanisms in aggressive behavior', in D. M. Stoff, J. Breiling and J. D. Maser (eds), *Handbook of Antisocial Behavior*. New York: Wiley.

Dolan, M., Holloway, J., Bailey, S. and Kroll, L. (1996) 'The psychosocial characteristics of juvenile sexual offenders referred to an adolescent forensic service in the UK', *Medicine Science and the Law*, 36 (4): 343–52.

Domalanta, D. D., Risser, W. L., Roberts, R. E. and Risser, J. M. H. (2003) 'Prevalence of depression and other psychiatric disorders among incarcerated youths', *Journal of the American Academy of Child and Adolescent Psychiatry* 42 (4): 477–84.

Doreleijers, T. (2005) '"Justicialising" juvenile offenders to a more evidence based approach', *Dutch Journal of Criminology*, 47: 38–45.

Dubicka, B. and Harrington, R. (2004) 'Affective conduct disorder', in S. Bailey and M. Dolan (eds), *Adolescent Forensic Psychiatry*. London: Arnold, pp. 124–43.

Farrant, F. (2001) *Troubled Inside: Responding to the Mental Health Needs of Children and Young People in Prison*. London: Prison Reform Trust.

Ferdinand, R. F., Sondeijker, F., van der Ende, J., Selten J. P., Huizink, A. and Verhulst, F. C. (2005) 'Cannabis use predicts future psychotic symptoms, and vice versa', *Addiction*, 100 (5): 612–18.

Fineman, K. R. (1980) 'Firesetting in childhood and adolescence', *Psychiatric Clinics of North America*, 3 (3): 483–500.

Fischer, M., Barkley, R. A., Fletcher, K. E. and Smallish, L. (1993) 'The adolescent outcome of hyperactive children – predictors of psychiatric, academic, social and emotional adjustment', *Journal of the American Academy of Child and Adolescent Psychiatry*, 32 (2): 324–32.

Fletcher, K. E. (2003) 'Childhood posttraumatic stress disorder, in E. J. Mash and R. A. Barkley (eds), *Child Psychopathology*, 2nd edn. New York: Guildford Press, pp. 330–71.

Fonagy, P. (2003) 'Towards a developmental understanding of violence', *British Journal of Psychiatry*, 183: 190–2.

Forth, A. E. and Burke H. C. (1998) 'Psychopathy in adolescence: assessment, violence and developmental precursors', in D. Cooke, A. Forth and R. Hare (eds), *Psychopathy: Theory, Research and Implications for Society*. Dordrecht: Kluwer, pp. 205–30.

Frick, P. J. (1998a) *Conduct Disorders and Severe Antisocial Behaviour*. New York: Plenum Press, pp. 9–20.

Frick, P. J. (1998b) 'Callous-unemotional traits and conduct problems: applying the two-factor model of psychopathy to children', in D. Cooke, A. Forth and R. Hare (eds), *Psychopathy: Theory, Research and Implications for Society*. Dordrecht: Kluwer, pp. 161–89.

Frick, P. J. (2002) 'Juvenile psychopathy from a developmental perspective: implications for construct development and use in forensic assessments', *Law and Human Behaviour*, 26: 247–53.

Galahad SMS Ltd and Youth Justice Board (2004) *Substance Misuse and the Juvenile Secure Estate*. London: Youth Justice Board.

Garbarino, J. (2001) 'An ecological perspective on the effects of violence on children', *Journal of Community Psychology*, 29 (3): 361–78.

Garmezy, N. and Rutter, M. (1983) *Stress, Coping and Development in Children*. New York: McGraw-Hill.

Gleeson, C., Robinson, M. and Neal, R. (2002) 'A review of teenagers' perceived needs and access to primary healthcare – implications for school health services', *Primary Health Care Research and Development*, 3: 184–93.

Glover, E. (1960) *The Roots of Crime*. New York: International University Press.

Goodman, R. (1997) 'The Strength and Difficulties Questionnaire: a research note', *Journal of Child Psychology and Psychiatry*, 38: 581–6.

Gosden, N. P., Kramp, P., Gabrielsen, G. and Sestoft, D. (2003) 'Prevalence of mental disorders among 15–17-year-old male adolescent remand prisoners in Denmark', *ACTA Psychiatricia Scandinavica*, 107 (2): 102–10.

Gowers, S. G. (2004) 'Assessing adolescent mental health', in S. Bailey and M. Dolan (eds), *Textbook of Adolescent Forensic Psychiatry*. London: Arnold, pp. 3–13.

Green, B., Young, R. and Kavanagh, D. (2005) 'Cannabis use and misuse prevalence among people with psychosis', *British Journal of Psychiatry*, 187 (4):306–13.

Grisso, T. (1997) 'The competence of adolescents as trial defendants', *Psychology, Public Policy and Law*, 3: 3–32.

Grisso, T. (2000) 'What we know about youths' capacities as trial defendants', in T. Grisso and R. G. Schwartz (eds), *Youth on Trial*. Chicago: University of Chicago Press, pp. 139–71.

Grisso, T. and Zimring, F. E. (2004) *Double Jeopardy: Adolescent Offenders with Mental Disorders*. Chicago: University of Chicago Press.

Grisso, T., Vincent, G. and Seagrave, D. (eds) (2005) *Mental Health Screening and Assessment in Juvenile Justice*. London: Guildford Press.

Hackett, S., Telford, P. and Slack, K. (2002) 'Groupwork with parents of children who sexually harm', in M. C. Calder (ed.), *Young People Who Sexually Abuse: Building the Evidence Base for Your Practice*. Lyme Regis: Russell House.

Hare, R. D. (1991) *The Hare Psychopathy Checklist – Revised*. Toronto: Multi Health Systems.

Harrington, R. C. and Bailey, S. (2004) *The Scope for Preventing Antisocial Personality Disorder by Intervening in Adolescence*. NHS National Programme on Forensic Mental Health Research and Development, Expert Paper.

Harrington, R. C., Kroll, L., Rothwell, J., McCarthy, K., Bradley, D. and Bailey, S. (2005) 'Psychosocial needs of boys in secure care for serious or persistent offending', *Journal of Child Psychology and Psychiatry*, 46 (8): 859–66.

Harrington, R., Bailey, S., Chitsabesan, P., Kroll, L., MacDonald, W., Sneider, S., Kenning, C., Taylor, G., Byford, S. and Barrett, B. (2005) *Mental Health Needs and Effectiveness of Provision for Young Offenders in Custody and in the Community*. London: Youth Justice Board.

Healthcare Commission and Her Majesty's Inspectorate of Probation (2006) *A Review of Healthcare in the Community for Young People Who Offend. Commission for Healthcare Audit and Inspection*, at: http://www.healthcarecommission.org.uk/_db/_documents/YOTs_report.pdf (accessed 11 September 2007).

Henquet, C., Krabbendam, L., Spauwen, J., Kaplan, C., Lieb, R., Wittchen, H.-U. and Van Os, J. (2005) 'Prospective cohort study of cannabis use, predisposition for psychosis, and psychotic symptoms in young people', *British Medical Journal*, 330 (7481): 11–14.

Herjanic, B. and Reich, I. N. (1982) 'Development of a structured diagnostic interview for children: agreement between child and parent on individual symptoms', *Journal of Abnormal Child Psychology*, 10: 307–24.

Home Office (2002) Updated Drug Strategy 2002. London: Home Office.

House of Commons and Youth Justice Board (2004) 'Written Evidence: Memorandum 31 submitted by the Youth Justice Board for England and Wales'. Available online at: http://www.publications.parliament.uk/pa/cm200405/cmselect/cmhaff/193/193w e56.htm (accessed 19 June 2007).

Howlin, P. (1997) *'Autism': Preparing for Adulthood*. London: Routledge.

Hummel, P., Thomke, V., Oldenburger, H. A. and Specht, F. (2000) 'Male adolescent sex offenders against children: similarities and differences between those offenders with and those without a history of sexual abuse', *Journal of Adolescence*, 23: 305–17.

James, A. (2004) 'Schizophrenia', in S. Bailey and M. Dolan (eds), *Adolescent Forensic Psychiatry*. London: Arnold, pp. 152–63.

James, A. C. and Neil, P. (1996) 'Juvenile sexual offending: one-year period prevalence study within Oxfordshire', *Child Abuse and Neglect*, 20 (6): 477–85.

Johnson, T. P., Cho, Y. I., Fendrich, M., Graf, I., Kelly-Wilson, L. and Pickup, L. (2004) 'Treatment need and utilisation among youth entering the juvenile corrections system', *Journal Substance Abuse Treatment*, 26: 117–28.

Kazdin, A. E. (1993) 'Treatment of conduct disorder: progress and directions in psychotherapy research', *Developmental Psychopathology*, 5: 277–310.

Kazdin, A. E. (2000) 'Adolescent development, mental disorders, and decision making of delinquent youths', in T. Grisso and R. G. Schwartz (eds), *Youth on Trial: A Developmental Perspective on Juvenile Justice*. Chicago: University of Chicago Press, pp. 33–65.

Kolko, D. J. and Kazdin, A. E. (1992) 'The emergence and re-occurrence of child firesetting. A one year prospective study', *Journal of Abnormal Child Psychology*, 201: 17–37.

Kroll, L. (2004) 'Needs assessment in adolescent offenders', in S. Bailey and M. Dolan (eds), *Adolescent Forensic Psychiatry*. London: Arnold, pp. 14–26.

Kroll, L., Rothwell, J., Bradley, D., Shah, P., Bailey, S. and Harrington, R. C. (2002) 'Mental health needs of boys in secure care for serious or persistent offending: a prospective, longitudinal study', *Lancet*, 359: 1975–9.

Kroll, L., Woodham, A., Rothwell, J., Bailey, S., Tobias, C., Harrington, R. (1999) 'Reliability of the Salford Needs Assessment Schedule for Adolescents', *Psychological Medicine*, 29: 891–902.

Langstrom, N., Grann, M. and Lindblad, F. (2000) 'A preliminary typology of young sex offenders', *Journal of Adolescence*, 23: 319–29.

Lederman, C. S., Dakof, G. A., Larrea, M. A. and Li, H. (2004) 'Characteristics of adolescent females in juvenile detention', *International Journal of Law and Psychiatry*, 27 (4): 321–37.

Lipsey, M. W. (1995) 'What do we learn from 400 research studies on the effectiveness of treatment with juvenile delinquents?', in J. McGuire (ed.), *What Works: Reducing Offending: Guidelines from Research and Practice*. Chichester: Wiley.

Lipsey, M. W. and Wilson, D. B. (1993) 'The efficacy of psychosocial, educational, and behavioural treatment: confirmation from meta-analysis', *American Psychologist*, 48: 1181–209.

Lösel, F. (1995) 'The efficacy of correctional treatment: a review and synthesis of meta-evaluations', in J. McGuire (ed.), *What Works: Reducing Reoffending: Guidelines from Research and Practice*. Chichester: Wiley, pp. 57–82.

Lösel, F. and Bender, D. (2006) 'Risk factors for serious and violent antisocial behaviour in childhood and youth', in A. Hagell and J. D. Renuka (eds), *Children Who Commit Acts of Serious Interpersonal Violence – Messages for Best Practice*. London and Philadelphia: Jessica Kingsley, pp. 42–72.

Lynam, D. R. (2002) 'Fledgling psychopathy: a view from personality theory', *Law and Human Behaviour*, 26 (2): 255–9.

McCabe, K. M., Lansing, A. E., Garland, A. and Hough, R. (2002) 'Gender differences in psychopathology, functional impairment, and familial risk factors among adjudicated delinquents', *Journal of the American Academy of Child and Adolescent Psychiatry*, 41 (7): 860–7.

McGuire, J. and Priestley, P. (1995) 'Reviewing "what works": past, present and future', in J. McGuire (ed.), *What Works: Reducing Reoffending: Guidelines from Research and Practice*. Chichester: Wiley, pp. 3–34.

Martin, J. A. and Penn, D. L. (2001) 'Social cognition and subclinical paranoid ideation', *British Journal of Clinical Psychology*, 40: 261–5.

Mash, E. J. and Dozois, D. J. A. (2003) 'Child psychopathology: a developmental-systems perspective', in E. J. Mash and R. A. Barkley (eds), *Child Psychopathology*, 2nd edn. New York: Guildford Press, pp. 3–71.

Myers, W. C. and Scott, K. (1998) 'Psychotic and conduct disorder symptoms in juvenile murderers', *Journal of Homicide Studies*, 2 (2): 160–75.

Myers, W. C., Burket, R. C. and Harris, H. E. (1995) 'Adolescent psychopathy in relation to delinquent behaviours, conduct disorder, and personality disorder', *Journal of Forensic Sciences*, 40: 436–40.

O'Brien, B. S. and Frick, P. J. (1996) 'Reward dominance associations with anxiety conduct problems and psychopathy in children', *Journal of Abnormal Child Psychology*, 24: 223–40.

O'Brien, G. (1996) 'The psychiatric management of adult autism', *Advances in Psychiatric Treatment*, 2: 173–7.

O'Callaghan, D. and Print, B. (1994) 'Adolescent sexual abusers research: assessment and treatment', in T. Morrison, M. Erooga and R. C. Beckett (eds), *Sexual Offending Against Children. Assessment and Treatment of Male Abusers*. London: Routledge, pp. 146–77.

Odgers, C. L., Burnette, M. L., Chauhan, P., Moretti, M., Reppucci, M. and Dickon, N. (2005) 'Misdiagnosing the problem: mental health profiles of incarcerated juveniles', *Canadian Child and Adolescent Psychiatry Review*, 14 (1): 26–9.

Orvaschel, H., Pulg-Antich, J. and Chambers, W. (1982) 'Retrospective assessment of prepubertal major depression with the Kiddie-SADS-E', *Journal of the American Academy of Child Psychiatry*, 21: 695–707.

Oyserman, D. and Martois, H. R. (1990) 'Possible selves and delinquency', *Journal of Personality and Social Psychology*, 59: 112–15.

Patterson, G. R. (1982) *Coercive Family Process*. Eugene, OR: Castalia.

Print, B. and O'Callaghan, D. (1999) 'Working with young men who have sexually abused others', in M. Erooga and H. Masson (eds), *Children and Young People Who Sexually Abuse Others*. London: Routledge, pp. 124–45.

Repo, E. and Virkunnen, M. (1997) 'Young arsonists, history of conduct disorder, psychiatric diagnosis, and criminal recidivism', *Journal of Forensic Psychiatry*, 8: 311–20.

Rey, J. M. and Tennant, C. C. (2002) 'Cannabis and mental health – more evidence establishes clear link between use of cannabis and psychiatric illness', *British Medical Journal*, 325 (7374): 1183–4.

Ruchkin, V., Koposov, R., Vermerien, R. and Schwab-Stone, M. (2003) 'Psychopathology and age at onset of conduct problems in juvenile delinquents', *Journal of Clinical Psychology*, 64: 913–20.

Rutter, M. (1967) 'A children's behaviour questionnaire for completion by teachers: preliminary findings', *Journal of Child Psychology and Psychiatry and Allied Disciplines*, 8: 1–11.

Rutter, M., Giller, H. and Hagell, A. (1998) *Antisocial Behaviour by Young People*. New York: Cambridge University Press.

Scott, S. (2004) 'Helping children with aggression and conduct problems: best practices for intervention', *Child and Adolescent Mental Health*, 9: 92.

Seagrave, D. and Grisso, T. (2002) 'Adolescent development and the measurement of juvenile psychopathy', *Law and Human Behavior*, 26: 219–39.

Semple, D. M., McIntosh, A. M. and Lawrie, S. M. (2005) 'Cannabis as a risk factor for psychosis: systematic review', *Journal of Psychopharmacology*, 19 (2): 187–94.

Shelton, D (2001) 'Emotional disorders in young offenders', *Journal of Nurse Scholarship*, 33: 259–63.

Skuse, D., Bentovim, A., Hodges, J., Stevenson, C., Andreou, M., Lanyado, M., New, M., Williams, B. and McMillan, D. (1998) 'Risk factors for development of sexually abusive behaviour in sexually victimised adolescent boys. Cross sectional study', *British Medical Journal*, 317: 175–9.

Soderstrom, H., Sjodin, A.-K. and Carlstedt, A. F. (2004) 'Adult psychopathic personality with childhood-onset hyperactivity and conduct disorder: a central problem constellation in forensic psychiatry', *Psychiatry Research*, 121: 271–80.

Spain, S. E., Douglas, K. S., Poythress, N. G. and Epstein, M. A. (2004) 'The relationship between psychopathic features, violence and treatment outcome: the comparison of three youth measures of psychopathic features', *Behavioural Sciences and the Law*, 22: 85–102.

Steen, C. (2005) 'Cognitive-behavioural treatment under the relapse prevention umbrella', in M. C. Calder (ed.), *Children and Young People Who Sexually Abuse: New Theory, Research and Practice Developments*. Lyme Regis: Russell House, pp. 217–30.

Sukhodolsky, D. G. and Ruchkin, V. (2006) 'Evidence based psychosocial treatments in the juvenile justice system', *Child and Adolescent Clinics of North America*, 15 (2): 501–16.

Taylor, P. J. and Gunn, J. (1999) 'Homicides by people with mental illness: myth and reality', *British Journal of Psychiatry*, 174: 9–14.

Teplin, L. A., Abram, K. M., McClelland, G. M., Dulcan, M. K. and Mericle, A. A. (2002) 'Psychiatric disorders in youth in juvenile detention', *Archives of General Psychiatry*, 59 (12): 1133–43.

The National Assembly for Wales-Cynulliad Cenedlaethol Cymru (2000) *Tackling Substance Misuse in Wales. A partnership approach.*

Vermeiren, R. (2003) 'Psychopathology and delinquency in adolescents: a descriptive and developmental perspective', *Clinical Psychology Review*, 23: 277–318.

Vermeiren, R., Schwab-Stone, M., Deboutte, D., Leckman, P. E. and Ruchkin, V. (2003) 'Violence exposure and substance use in adolescents: findings from three countries', *Pediatrics*, 111 (3): 535–40.

Vermerien, R., Schwab-Stone, M., Ruchkin, V., De Clippele, A. and Deboutte, D. (2002) 'Predicting recidivism in delinquent adolescents from psychological and psychiatric assessment', *Comprehensive Psychiatry*, 43 (2): 142–9.

Vizard, E. (2006) 'Sexually abusive behaviour by children and adolescents', *Child and Adolescent Mental Health*, 11 (1): 2–8.

Vizard, E., Wynick, S., Hawkes, C., Woods, J. and Jenkins, J. (1996) 'Juvenile sexual offenders', *British Journal of Psychiatry*, 168: 259–62.

Vreeland, R. G. and Lowin, B. M. (1980) 'Psychological aspects of firesetting', in D. Canter (ed.), *Fires and Human Behaviour*. New York: Wiley.

Vreugdenhil, C., Doreleijers, T., Vermeiren, R., Wouters, L. and van den Brink, W. (2004a) 'Psychiatric disorders in a representative sample of incarcerated boys in the Netherlands', *Journal of the American Academy of Child and Adolescent Psychiatry*, 43: 97–104.

Vreugdenhil, C., Vermeiren, R., Wouters, L., Doreleijers, T. and van den Brink, W. (2004b) 'Psychotic symptoms among male adolescent detainees in the Netherlands', *Schizophrenia Bulletin*, 30: 73–86.

Wasserman, G. A., McReynolds, L. S., Lucas, C. P., Fisher, P. and Santos, L. (2002) 'The voice DISC-IV with incarcerated male youths: prevalence of disorder', *Journal of the American Academy of Child and Adolescent Psychiatry*, 41 (3): 314–21.

Williams, R. (2005) 'Professional capability: evidence - and values-based frameworks for psychiatrists and mental health services', *Current Opinion in Psychiatry*, 18 (4): 361–9.

Woolfenden, S. R., Williams, K. and Peat, J. (2003) *Family and Parenting Interventions in Children and Adolescents with Conduct Disorder and Delinquency Aged 10–17* (Cochrane Review). Oxford: Cochrane Library, Issue 3.

World Health Organisation. (1992) 'The ICD 10 classification of mental and behavioural disorders', *Clinical Descriptions and Diagnostic Guidelines*. Geneva: World Health Organisation.

Yokely, J. and Boettner, S. (2002) 'Forensic foster care for young people who sexually abuse: lessons from treatment', in M. C. Calder (ed.), *Young People Who Sexually Abuse. Building the Evidence Base for Your Practice*. Lyme Regis: Russell House, pp. 309–32.

Youth Justice Board (2004) *National Specification for Substance Misuse for Juveniles in Custody*. London: Youth Justice Board for England and Wales.

Youth Justice Board (2005) *Risk and Protective Factors*. Research undertaken by Communities that Care on behalf of the Youth Justice Board for England and Wales.

Youth Justice Board (2007) *Youth Justice Annual Statistics 2005/06*. London: Youth Justice Board for England and Wales.

Chapter 5

The process and systems for adults

Tony Maden

Introduction

This chapter describes the interfaces between the criminal justice and mental health systems as they apply to adult offenders. It is concerned with the processes by which behaviour comes first to be identified as an offence, and how the offender may then pass from one system to another.

Much of the chapter consists of a description of the services, but it is important also to bear in mind the underlying assumptions and principles. In many of its operations the system in England and Wales is pragmatic, with the aim of delivering treatment to the mentally disordered offender. Yet, if we consider the rising numbers of prisoners with severe mental health problems, the system is demonstrably failing in this aim most of the time. It is easier to understand some of these problems, and it may also be easier to solve them, if we make explicit some of the guiding forces which operate in the background but are rarely stated.

The main conflicts are between the demands of a health service based on clinical need and those of a criminal justice system designed to deliver 'just deserts' punishment to offenders. Although these systems work according to different rules and could exist in parallel universes, in practice they impinge upon each other's operations in both planned and unintended ways. The criminal justice system makes it more difficult for offenders to access treatment for mental health problems, and our mental health systems sometimes interfere with the process of punishment. Those who work within one or other system sometimes fail to understand the other perspective, and they may resent what they see as unwarranted interference in their work.

At worst, movement from one system to the other may appear to be determined by arbitrary criteria. Prison staff see a quiet inmate transferred to hospital because he has schizophrenia while a threatening, disturbed man is left in their segregation unit because he has a personality disorder. Staff in a medium secure hospital may take a man from the courts because he is mentally ill, treat his mental illness successfully and quickly, then be unable to discharge him because his personality disorder and associated drug or alcohol use mean that he continues to present a high risk of serious offending. As a result the service is unable to admit other offenders who have acute illnesses. In court, two men who have committed similar offences may be treated very differently, with one receiving a hospital order and the other a lengthy prison sentence, because of the perceived nature of their psychological problems.

This conflict is perhaps best illustrated by the debate over the prevalence of mental disorder in prisoners. Figures from the Office of National Statistics (Singleton *et al.* 1998) show high rates of mental disorder in male sentenced prisoners including psychosis (4 per cent), neurosis (40 per cent), personality disorder (64 per cent) and drug problems (43 per cent). These figures have been presented as an indictment of the criminal justice system, as if it is inherently wrong for any mentally disordered person to be in prison. Yet most people would agree that the presence of mild mental illness or an alcohol problem should not interfere with the criminal process, except to place it under an obligation to provide suitable treatment within prison. Yet this view, in which the only concern is clinical need for treatment, is often complicated because mental disorder sometimes affects criminal responsibility in a way that physical illness does not. With more serious illnesses, such as schizophrenia, there is concern not only that it may be difficult to meet treatment needs within prison but also that there may be some injustice in the sufferer having been sentenced to prison in the first place.

There is no simple way to resolve these tensions and this chapter does not claim to provide any panacea. Instead it sets out the most important challenges facing these systems, and identifies those factors that make the problems worse as well as those changes that could help towards a solution.

Informal processing

Mental illness usually comes to notice because of the violation of social expectations and rules and in some cases that violation will also be an offence, at least in a technical sense. But, as we know, most criminal behaviour never results in a prosecution and mentally disordered offenders are certainly no exception to the rule. In fact, their offending behaviour may be less likely to result in a prosecution. The apparent presence of mental disorder often influences the decision as to whether or not an offender should be prosecuted or dealt with informally. We have no way of knowing just how often law-breaking brings the mentally disordered to the attention of services without the need for prosecution, because such cases do not appear in official figures.

As well as the extent of the phenomenon being uncertain, practice varies across the country as well as between countries. There may be widely differing attitudes within neighbouring services. It is easy to imagine that a service operating within an area with high crime rates may be more likely to manage minor offending informally.

Some commentators have questioned whether the opposite principle applies, i.e. that mentally disordered offending is more likely to result in arrest and prosecution. Monahan (1992) referred to the 'turkey effect', according to which principle mentally disordered offenders are more liable to arrest because they are less motivated or able to take evasive action after the event. While there are many examples of such behaviour, even in relation to serious offences, those working in the field will also be familiar with police reluctance to arrest and process offenders they see as obviously mentally disordered. Perhaps the most famous documented example was the case of Christopher Clunis, who killed Jonathan Zito in 1991. The subsequent inquiry (Ritchie *et al.* 1994) was critical of the police for failing to respond to a catalogue of antisocial behaviour, including publicly brandishing a knife, in the years leading up to the offence.

The failure of the criminal justice system to respond adequately to mentally disordered offending is rarely so dramatic as in the Clunis case, but it often causes problems. Prosecution and conviction lead to a record that is accessible, at least in principle, to those looking after the patient at a later date. By contrast, informal records of violent or other offending behaviour often get lost with time or are subject to distortion by 'Chinese whispers'. The process can work both ways, in that trivial misdemeanours come to be presented as evidence of serious antisocial tendencies, or potentially serious violence may be forgotten or trivialised. These problems have been explored in several homicide inquiries (e.g. Blom-Cooper *et al.* 1995; Blom-Cooper *et al.* 1996) where the ambiguity has contributed to later management problems.

A particular problem has arisen in recent years as the health service has become more aware of the problem of violence in all health settings and adopted a policy of zero tolerance. John Denham, the then Minister of State for Health, launching the NHS zero tolerance zone campaign in October 1991, stated, 'Aggression, violence and threatening behaviour will not be tolerated any longer' (NAO 2003: 1).

The underlying principle was that violence within a hospital should be treated in the same way as violence in any other setting, which one would expect to lead to prosecution. It is not clear precisely how this policy was applied to the mentally ill. As a consequence, many hospitals drew up policies for the involvement of police in dealing with violent patients, whether the victim was another patient or a member of staff. However, a dilemma often arose because a rigid application of the zero tolerance principle would criminalise acutely ill patients whose responsibility for their actions was, at the least, grossly impaired. At best there was a waste of time and money through the involvement of the police and a criminal court in reaching that conclusion. Interestingly, the National Audit Office (NAO) (2003) report found that little progress had been made in protecting NHS staff from violence. It found that four-fifths of trusts failed to meet the Department of Health's zero tolerance target of a 20 per cent reduction in violent incidents by April 2002. The work started under 'Zero Tolerance' is now the responsibility of the NHS SMS (Security Management Service) and the failings of the 'zero tolerance' campaign are widely accepted.

More general guidance has also been issued to the police, emphasising that the obvious presence of mental disorder should not automatically mean that the criminal process is abandoned. These developments are an interesting example of our changing attitudes towards crime and violence by the mentally disordered. Most healthcare workers welcome the policy of zero tolerance in principle, while also recognising that there will always be a grey area when the offence is relatively minor and the mental disorder is serious.

Section 136

Section 136 of the Mental Health Act 1983 (MHA 1983) gives the police the power to convey a mentally disordered person from a public place to a place of safety for a mental health assessment as an alternative to arrest and prosecution. The assumption is that the place of safety will usually be a hospital and, ideally, a suite designed for the purpose of safe assessment. Most mental health services have such a facility.

After examination at the place of safety, possible outcomes include admission to hospital (voluntarily or as a detained patient), referral back to the police and prosecution or no action at all, i.e. the person is free to go. The decision to involve the police again assumes there is no mental disorder present, or that the mental disorder is so mild as not to require immediate action or interference with the due process of law. In practice this may be difficult as the police are anxious to hand over the mentally disordered individual to services, and will rarely wait to learn the outcome of the assessment because they have more pressing demands on their time.

The advantage of this system is that it gives priority to the mental health of the individual and, in the case of serious mental illness, can lead to rapid, compulsory admission to hospital without the disadvantage and stigma that would accompany prosecution and conviction.

Diversion from custody

After an offender has been arrested, charged and processed there are still ways of avoiding conviction, chief among which is the system of court diversion. Diversion schemes were set up because numerous research projects showed that the process of remand into custody for psychiatric reports often worked to the detriment of the mentally disordered person (e.g. Coid 1988a, 1988b). The system operated slowly, so a mentally ill offender could spend weeks or even months on remand waiting for the local service to come in and prepare a psychiatric report, only for that report to have no effect on the eventual outcome. In many cases the time spent in custody on remand would exceed the sentence that could have been imposed for the offence, and in many cases the offence itself would not have attracted any custodial penalty.

The court diversion scheme arranges for mental health personnel to be on hand to carry out an initial assessment, usually at the magistrates' court and timed to coincide with the defendant's first appearance. A typical arrangement would be for a community psychiatric nurse to carry out the initial screening, with cases filtered and referred on to a psychiatrist as necessary. Ideally, the seriously mentally ill person charged with a minor offence will be diverted from the criminal justice system at the earliest possible stage. In many cases the prosecution will be dropped because it will not be in the public interest to proceed.

The care options range from outpatient appointments through voluntary treatments of drug and alcohol problems right up to detention in a mental hospital under civil sections of the Mental Health Act, depending on the nature of the mental health problems and the presence of any risks.

Court diversion schemes are now widely accepted, following their first appearance in the late 1980s. They have reduced the length of time spent by the mentally ill on remand awaiting reports. However, concerns remain about their longer-term effectiveness. Many of the patients diverted to hospital remain there for about 28 days, the maximum allowed under s. 2 of the MHA 1983 for assessment and treatment, then take their own discharge as soon as they become voluntary patients (Joseph 1990). Many of their problems, such as homelessness, remain unresolved and within a relatively short time they have lost touch with services, defaulted from treatment, relapsed and committed further offences. Thus the cycle begins again, giving rise to the term 'revolving door patients'.

Such patients raise the question of how diversion schemes should be judged. Many of the patients have chronic (i.e. long-term) illnesses. Is it sufficient to treat the acute episode and allow them to repeat the cycle again? Or should there be longer-term treatment, even if many would resist such treatment and therefore have to be compelled to accept it? The repeated cycle of admission, relapse and readmission is damaging to a person's long-term health and social prospects, but one could argue that so long as the individual has the capacity to exercise his or her judgment at the point of discharge, the state should not intervene. On the other hand, the MHA 1983 allows detention if necessary for the patient's health (including mental health), so the judgment is one of degree. In practice the decision is more likely to be influenced by the possibility of risk to others, so revolving door patients are generally those who commit repeated petty offences rather than anything more serious.

Proposed new mental health legislation would affect the management of this group of patients by allowing for compulsory treatment in the community, often referred to as a community treatment order. The proposal remains contentious and some authors argue that compulsory treatment of the mentally ill can be justified only when there is impaired capacity or judgment – as is the case in physical illness (Dawson and Szmukler 2006).

Remands for reports

The court has the power to remand the defendant to hospital for reports under s. 35 of the MHA 1983. Use of this power has decreased over time for various reasons. It does not allow for treatment, which would necessitate the imposition of an additional civil section (s. 3 of the Act). Second, the order can only be made if a bed is available, and beds are often scarce. Section 36 allows a remand to hospital for treatment, which overcomes the first of these problems but not the second. These sections can be used to remand to an open, locked or medium-secure bed as necessary.

Both powers are relatively cumbersome as they involve the courts in admission and discharge, and for that reason there has been a growth in the use of s. 48 which gives the Home Secretary power to direct the transfer of a remanded prisoner to hospital for urgent treatment. The court is not involved so there is flexibility based primarily on clinical need, although there will sometimes be disagreement between the clinicians and the Home Office over the degree of security required. Also, the power is based on the need for treatment, not assessment. In practice, the power is used to secure both treatment and a definitive assessment and report to the court. Assuming a bed is available, the main problem arises from the efficiency of the procedure; in the case of a moderately serious offence, the mental illness may have been treated by the time the case is tried, so a hospital order is no longer an appropriate disposal even if the patient was acutely ill at the time of the offence.

A far more problematic practice is the remand into custody for medical reports. As noted above, such remands are an expensive and inefficient way of obtaining reports and, for minor offences, often have the effect of prolonging the time spent in custody by a mentally disordered offender and contribute to the high rates of mental disorder invariably seen in the remand population (Birmingham et al. 1996).

The outcome of a remand in custody for medical reports is often unsatisfactory. In a detailed study of a busy remand prison in London, Robertson et al. (1994) showed that even for seriously mentally ill men the process of remanding to custody for reports led to a hospital bed in only a minority. As part of the same study, Dell et al. (1993a, 1993b) showed that psychotic women tended to fare better than psychotic men but also experienced long delays. Non-psychotic prisoners rarely ended up with any form of treatment.

Although remand in custody for reports is generally accepted to be unsatisfactory, it still happens. The diversion schemes described above apply mainly to petty offenders. For more serious offences there have been attempts to create secure wards that can provide an alternative to prison and allow rapid assessment. Specialised medium-secure remand units have had some success but they tend to fill up rapidly with patients who stay a long time, which interferes with the original purpose of rapid admission and turnover (Murray et al. 1996; Weaver et al. 1997a, 1997b). The reasons for this problem can be divided into clinical and administrative. On the clinical side, patients may be slow to respond to treatment or, if they do improve, they may remain liable to relapse if returned to prison. Relapse may occur because of the additional stresses of prison life or, more simply, because prisoners cannot be compelled to take medication. The solution lies in a higher standard of medical care in prison, although there are no plans to extend mental health legislation to allow compulsory treatment in prison.

The administrative problems relate mainly to delays in the criminal justice system. A serious offence may take a year or longer to come to trial, during which the patient's treatment may be held back. As noted above, a return to prison may be problematic, yet even if the patient has responded to treatment it will rarely be possible to move the patient on towards the community or even to a less secure setting. At a lower level of violence risk, such problems deter psychiatric intensive care units (PICUs) from becoming involved in the treatment of remanded prisoners. PICUs take acutely disturbed patients and aim to return them to a less intensive ward as quickly as possible in order to maintain turnover. Remand prisoners are often acutely ill so a PICU is clinically appropriate but a problem arises because the treated prisoner cannot be moved onto a less secure ward without the consent of the court or the Home Office, which will often not be forthcoming. The position often remains unresolved until after the trial, so such patients may end up spending months on a unit whose length of stay is usually measured in days.

The purpose of psychiatric reports:

There are generally three components:

1 fitness to plead and stand trial;
2 detection of psychiatric factors that may provide a defence or mitigation;
3 advice on disposal.

Fitness to plead

In a small number of cases where the defendant is seriously mentally ill, he will be judged by the psychiatrist to be unfit to plead or to stand trial. In the case of minor offences consideration would be given to halting the prosecution on the grounds that it was not in the public interest to proceed, but for more serious offences there is special legislation.

It used to be the case that unfitness to plead halted the trial process. Possibly as a result of this dramatic consequence, the numbers found unfit to plead were very small, approximately 20 per year from 1980 (Grubin 1991a). Before 1982 it was rare for such persons ever to be returned for trial but from 1982 onwards about half came back to court (Grubin 1991b). There was strong pressure to get the person fit because the alternative was indefinite detention in hospital even if the original charge was minor.

This unsatisfactory state of affairs changed with the Criminal Procedure (Insanity and Unfitness to Plead) Act 1991, which specifies two separate court processes when fitness to plead is raised as an issue. The first is to determine whether or not the individual is fit to plead, an issue which has to be decided by a jury although they would invariably be directed by a judge. The second part of the process, assuming the defendant is found unfit to plead, is a trial of the facts to establish whether or not the defendant committed the act with which he is charged. The intention behind this two-stage process was to avoid the injustice of a person who is unfit to plead being liable to prolonged detention in hospital when he may not have committed the offences for which he was charged. The new Act also allows for a much wider range of disposals when the defendant is found to have committed the act with which he was charged. Hence disposal can be tailored to the offence and to the risks and treatment needs of the individual.

Although most psychiatric reports include mention of fitness to plead it is still rare for defendants in England and Wales to be found unfit, so this legislation applies only to a tiny minority of those mentally disordered people who find themselves before the courts. In most cases therefore the report will deal with psychiatric defences, mitigation or disposal.

Trial and sentencing

In offenders who are fit to plead the next stage is the trial. In contrast to legal systems in some countries, the law in England and Wales generally does not involve psychiatrists in the determination of legal responsibility, with the notable exceptions of manslaughter on the grounds of diminished responsibility in the case of a murder charge, and the rare legal finding of insanity. These exceptions are considered in more detail below.

Outside these special groups, offenders are tried or plead guilty and it is only at the sentencing stage that expert evidence concerning their mental health becomes important. Psychiatric reports at the sentencing stage tend to have one of two purposes. The first is mitigation, by which the convicted person will argue that, although he should still be punished, the punishment should be reduced because the degree of his culpability was mitigated by the presence of mental disorder. Examples include alcoholism or minor degrees of depression.

The other purpose of a psychiatric report is to argue for treatment as an alternative to punishment or an adjunct to it. The best example of the former is the use of a hospital order under s. 37 of the MHA 1983. This order requires the mentally disordered person to be detained in hospital for treatment. The initial period of detention is fixed by the Act at six months but the order can be renewed indefinitely on the recommendation of the consultant psychiatrist, who is known for these purposes as the responsible medical officer. After a year the order is renewable every 12 months. There are corresponding rights of appeal to the Mental Health Review Tribunal which has the power to order discharge. The consultant can discharge the order at any time if he/she concludes that the criteria for detention are no longer met.

Although most mentally disordered offenders would regard detention in a hospital as punishment, the law does not recognise it as such and there is no tariff element to sentencing. The decision as to when the offender should be discharged, whether taken by the consultant or the tribunal, is determined solely by health and risk criteria; there is no reference to retribution, tariff or just deserts.

It can be argued that this system is unfair, as it effectively excuses the mentally disordered offender of all responsibility for the offence. In effect, the doctor making the recommendation for detention under s. 37 is being asked to decide whether an offender should be punished or treated. There is no explicit reference to responsibility in the Mental Health Act – beyond the court's determination that the offender committed the offence concerned – yet it is implicit in the treatment option that the offender does not deserve punishment.

It is worth noting in passing that other countries handle this issue differently. In the Netherlands, the court is required to decide on the extent to which a mentally disordered offender is to be held responsible for the crime, and the offender receives a sentence of imprisonment commensurate with the crime and degree of responsibility. For offenders considered to pose a risk, the court will also make a TBS (*terbeschikkingstelling*, which translates loosely as at the disposal of the state) order which mandates indefinite detention for treatment and reduction of risk within the TBS system. Although the order is made at the time of the trial the TBS order does not come into force until the sentence of imprisonment has been served. The only similar option in England and Wales is the hybrid order (see below).

The ethics of the hospital order are confused. Psychiatrists would claim not to address questions of responsibility – most would say they lack the expertise to do so – yet the decision to recommend a hospital order has profound implications for responsibility. The ethics will not be explored further here but the practical implications deserve a mention. In effect, the hospital order creates two categories of mentally disordered offender. One category receives no punishment and is instead treated in hospital for as long as their clinical state dictates it to be necessary. The second category receives a punishment, often a prison sentence, and may receive no treatment or a lower standard of treatment for mental disorder in prison.

In defence of this system, it has been argued for many years that the correct sentence for a seriously mentally ill offender is a hospital order. To the extent that this did not happen, it was an error or failing of the system and ought to be prevented by creating more secure beds and by improving the system of assessment and reporting to the courts. However, it has become apparent in recent years that the number of mentally ill people in prison is increasing, and has reached a level at which many people argue that it will never be possible to meet the demand by creating more secure hospital beds. In these circumstances, it seems unfair to offer excellent treatment to the minority who receive a hospital order while providing inadequate treatment to the seriously mentally ill who end up in prison.

It has been suggested that we should optimise our use of resources by transferring mentally ill prisoners to hospital for treatment as necessary, then moving them back to prison once their acute symptoms are under control. The success of any such system would, of course, depend on also improving services within prisons for treating and maintaining the mentally ill.

Hybrid order

The hybrid order, more correctly known as a hospital and limitation order, was created by the Crime (Sentences) Act 1997 which inserted s. 45a into the MHA 1983. This section allows the court to sentence a mentally disordered offender to custody while ordering his/her immediate transfer to hospital, thus dealing with some of the issues above. The offender remains in hospital for as long as treatment is necessary. The sentencing judge retains the option to give a determinate or a life sentence, depending on the nature of the offence and the likely risks to the public. The advantages of this order are that it allows flexibility, but it is rarely used. It has mainly been used in cases of psychopathic disorder when the response to treatment is in doubt. In such cases the disadvantage of the hospital order is that it allows no way out if the mentally disordered person does not respond to treatment and resents being held in hospital. The hybrid order allows the option in such circumstances of a transfer back to the prison system – with a possibility of a return to hospital for further treatment if the situation changes in the future.

The restriction order

If a mentally disordered offender has committed a serious offence and is thought to represent a danger to the public, an option available to the court is to make a hospital order under s. 37, as above, but also to add a restriction order under s. 41 of the Mental Health Act. The effect of the restriction order is to remove from the consultant the power to discharge the patient, which is instead given to the Home Office or to a Mental Health Review Tribunal. The restriction order may be for a fixed period, although in practice it is usually imposed without limit of time because there is no way of saying with any certainty when the risk to the public will diminish to an acceptable level (see Gunn and Taylor 1993: 167–209 for more details of the law).

The importance of the restriction order is that it introduces a tier of responsibility above and beyond the purely medical. The restriction order recognises the doctor's dual obligation to the patient on the one hand and to protect the public on the other. It amounts to an explicit statement that it should not be for a doctor to decide whether the risks posed by a patient have now been reduced to a level at which it is acceptable to discharge him to the community. Rather, the doctor ought to seek outside, non-medical advice as to whether the residual risk is acceptable (see Maden 2007 for a fuller discussion). In specific terms the advice sought is from the Home Office, whose primary responsibility is public protection, or from the Mental Health Review Tribunal, which functions as a court of law.

For clinicians, one of the most important aspects of the hospital order with restrictions is that it allows for the possibility of conditional discharge, subject to the agreement of the Home Office or the Mental Health Review Tribunal. Conditional discharge is exactly what it says: the patient is discharged from hospital but must abide by certain conditions. Conditions are tailored to the individual case and can be very variable, although they always include an agreement to comply with medical treatment and supervision. The patient remains liable to recall to hospital if he/she fails to comply with these conditions.

The hospital order with restrictions therefore amounts to the only example in England and Wales of a community treatment order. Current government proposals would introduce a community treatment order that would allow mandatory supervision in the community for patients who meet the civil criteria for detention under Part 2 of the Act. The intention is to deal with those patients who present a risk to self or others when they are mentally unwell, who respond well to treatment so are ready to be discharged from hospital to the community, yet remain likely to relapse quickly and present a risk if they default from treatment.

As a proposed community treatment order is not aimed specifically at mentally disordered offenders it is not discussed in detail here. However, it will have implications for mentally disordered offenders. An anomaly of the law at present is that patients detained under s. 37 of the Mental Health Act without a restriction order cannot be compelled to comply with treatment in the community after discharge. There is no legal provision for mandatory supervision and treatment after discharge. Yet, as will be seen below, some of the patients detained under s. 37 of the Act are transferred prisoners who may have committed extremely serious offences but then have been transferred to mental health services because they developed mental illness during their sentence. Their long-term management presents an enormous problem to services because of the lack of any means of mandating compulsory aftercare. The advent of a community treatment order would probably help to speed up discharge in this group.

Diminished responsibility

The defence of not guilty to murder but guilty to manslaughter on the grounds of diminished responsibility applies only to murder. Conviction for murder carries a mandatory life sentence, whereas a conviction for manslaughter leaves open a full range of sentences, including imprisonment or a hospital order.

Transfer of prisoners for treatment

The processes for moving mentally disordered offenders into hospital, as described above, are intimately bound up with the criminal justice process, including arrest, trial and sentencing. But the Mental Health Act also allows for the straightforward transfer of prisoners to hospital for treatment of a mental disorder. The position is exactly analogous to the way in which a prisoner with a serious physical disorder could be moved to hospital for treatment as necessary; there would be no reference to questions of guilt, responsibility or other aspects of the criminal process.

As described above, a remand prisoner can be transferred under s. 48 of the Act if he/she is in need of urgent treatment for a mental disorder. The same applies to a sentenced prisoner. They can be transferred to hospital under s. 47 of the Act if they develop a mental illness that requires such a transfer, subject to the recommendation of two doctors and the approval of the Home Secretary. The Act makes no distinction between mental illness that may have been present at the time of the offence, and mental illness that developed later. The deciding factors are the severity of the illness and the clinical need for hospital treatment.

As there is no reference to a court of law the process is straightforward in principle but it can be much more difficult in practice. The problem is that prisoners serving a sentence are given relatively low priority by hospitals whose primary concern is to admit patients who are in the community and present a risk. Second on the list of priorities are those offenders who are in custody but due to be tried; here the court exerts pressure on the service to provide a rapid response. As a result, there is often a very long waiting list for sentenced prisoners awaiting transfer. The only group to face similar problems are offender-patients awaiting transfer from high security to a lower level of security, and they at least have the advantage of being within the NHS. One part of the health service is likely to be able to exert more pressure on another part than is the case for a prison.

The underlying issue is the separation of prison medical care from the NHS, and the consequent differences in the standard of care. The intention is to move towards closer integration (Department of Health 1999) and most services within prisons will be provided by the NHS under contract.

Treatment and security

When an admission to hospital depends on having the approval of the courts or the Home Secretary, problems can arise if there is disagreement about the level of security required. The usual scenario is that the clinician decides that the patient needs a lower level of security than that requested by the court or the Home Secretary. Conflict may arise because one or other side gets it wrong, or simply because they have different priorities. The Home Office sees its task as one of public protection and is less concerned about scarce NHS resources.

In the case of transferred prisoners the Home Secretary has the power to direct a hospital to take a patient, so there can only be one winner if the dispute cannot be resolved by discussion. In fact, the power to direct is rarely used and tends to be brought into play when clinicians cannot agree among themselves, for example about whether a patient requires high or medium security. There is plenty of scope for disagreement as most decisions rest on clinical opinion. Also, there is no agreed definition of medium security and there is considerable variation between the practices of different units.

Current issues

It is convenient to consider many problems in terms of patient pathways, a frame of reference that focuses on the experience of the individual, and also addresses the long-term nature of many mental disorders. It may be relatively easy to deal with an acute episode, but what about the long-term outcome?

Court diversion schemes have done much to improve the treatment of mentally disordered offenders who have committed relatively minor offences. They will often be moved efficiently into the hospital system but, as noted above, the long-term prognosis may be poor in terms of repeated relapse and remission.

Another major problem is that transfer from prison to hospital often involves long delays. While imprisonment controls many of the risks to the public, it leaves the offender and, to a lesser extent, prison staff exposed to a considerable risk of suicide, self-harm and violence. For this reason the issue has been given greater priority by the Director of Mental Health for England, and there are various proposals for a time limit to be imposed on the length of time allowed in which to arrange the transfer of an acutely mentally ill person from prison to hospital.

The advantage of setting time limits is that they lead inevitably to targets, and the mere process of setting targets tends to direct attention towards a problem and, hopefully, leads to its improvement. The downside would be that it would almost certainly be impossible to meet some of the more stringent targets that have been suggested. One proposal for a seven-day time limit seems particularly unrealistic when current delays run into weeks, months or even years in exceptional cases. Also, as medium-secure psychiatric beds already run at high capacity, it is difficult to see how the more ambitious targets could be met without a major reorganisation of the current system, if one assumes that further, massive expansion of secure beds is not a possibility.

A third major problem concerns the detection of mental disorder in offenders. At all stages the process tends to be rather haphazard. The police may or may not detect a problem; defence solicitors may or may not request reports; a court may notice or overlook mental illness; and the prison may or may not notice the presence of mental illness.

Much attention has centred on the prisons and the mandatory medical screening at reception. Birmingham *et al.* (1997) found that screening missed 30 of the 50 patients they considered to be in need of urgent psychiatric intervention, and argued for a more systematic and effective screening process. On the other hand, screening for major mental illness is not straightforward, nor is it commonly adopted in any other mental health system. It can also be argued that there are priorities other than screening, when the system fails to provide adequate care for so many severely mentally ill prisoners even after they have come to notice.

What should we do about personality disorder?

Most prisoners, and probably most serious offenders, meet the diagnostic criteria for a personality disorder. However, it would be wrong to conclude from that observation that a majority of prisoners are mentally disordered or in need of mental health intervention. Part of the problem is in the unsatisfactory nature of the definition of personality disorder. Early American studies concluded that 90 per cent of prisoners suffered from a personality disorder, largely because the definition of antisocial personality disorder (ASPD) in the American diagnostic system overlapped so substantially with criminality.

Furthermore, if a diagnosis applies to almost everybody it ceases to have much meaning. Surveys of mental disorder in offender or prison populations were originally used to put pressure on mental health services to make better provision for them, but too much emphasis on the figures for personality disorder, along with drug and alcohol problems, risks becoming counterproductive by inducing a form of compassion fatigue. If a problem is presented as so overwhelming that it can never be solved, inaction becomes the obvious response.

The underlying problem is that the implications for the service provision for those with personality disorder by the Health Service are far from clear. The diagnosis itself has virtually no meaning in terms of treatment needs. The label may mean that the offender needs nothing beyond those services which are offered to all offenders within a humane, rehabilitative prison system; it may mean there is a need for help with substance misuse problems; there may be a need for medication; and in rare cases there may be a need for treatment in hospital. The difficulty is that these treatment needs are not determined by the diagnosis alone, but by other aspects of the assessment. This is not a new issue for mental health services because a mental health diagnosis rarely dictates any particular course of treatment, but the problem is much more severe in the case of personality disorder, where the label gives virtually no guidance as to what ought to be provided.

The Mental Health Act allows for the detention in a hospital of patients with a personality disorder who also meet the criteria for psychopathic disorder. The definition includes abnormally aggressive or seriously irresponsible conduct and there is an added stipulation that treatment in hospital should be likely to ameliorate or prevent deterioration in the condition. This is the so called 'treatability' clause, which has provoked much argument, and is responsible for a fair degree of ill-feeling between mental health services on the one hand, and criminal justice services and the government on the other.

In fact, detention in hospital is rarely appropriate for patients suffering from a personality disorder. Such conditions are, by nature, chronic and enduring so their medical management is more a matter of managing the consequences of a disability or handicap rather than curative intervention in a disease process. Admission to hospital may be necessary in a crisis but it is not going to solve the underlying problem.

Unfortunately, because compulsory treatment in hospital is an issue only for an almost infinitesimal proportion of all the offenders with personality disorder, the main impact of the treatability clause has been on other forms of voluntary treatment. An unintended consequence of the 1983 Act was that psychiatric services and individual practitioners gave little thought to the provision of any services for those with personality disorder. Instead, they made use of the treatability criterion to reject patients, even from voluntary services, on the grounds that they were untreatable.

Following a series of high-profile disasters, in which patients rejected from services went on to kill, the government attempted to reverse this trend with the publication of its policy document, *Personality Disorder: No Longer a Diagnosis of Exclusion* (Department of Health 2003). Criminal justice and mental health services are now struggling with the implications of this document.

There are many problems. The principle of social inclusion dictates that it is unacceptable to exclude a whole class of people from access to services, but on the other hand a diagnosis that is so imprecise, and prevalent in so many offenders, demands some way of establishing reasonable expectations. It also requires some form of gatekeeping procedure if mental health services are not to be swamped by an ill-defined demand for services in the absence of any good evidence base on which to plan treatment or, depending on need, long-term management of a chronic condition.

For the time being, the practical implications are as follows. First, most offenders suffer from a personality disorder and its presence should rarely be allowed to dictate management of the case. The vast majority of offenders, irrespective of whether or not they have fulfilled diagnostic criteria for personality disorder, should be offered and may benefit from services such as those for drug and alcohol misuse, or offending behaviour programmes aimed at helping people to break the cycle of offending and imprisonment.

Second, if the offence is serious (which usually implies a violent and/or sexual offence, particularly if there is a predatory element) then there should be an assessment of risk within the criminal justice system. The Probation Service, as part of the National Offender Management Service, has a protocol for assessing risk (the Offender Assessment System or OASys) which includes some measures of personality disorder although it is designed for use by non-clinicians. The courts have available a range of disposals, including indeterminate public protection sentences, many of which will be triggered by the risk assessment process described above.

Most psychiatrists believe that, although the law allows it, there is rarely if ever a case for recommending a hospital order with restrictions in the case of personality disorder alone, i.e. in the absence of mental illnesses such as schizophrenia. After sentencing, offenders with a personality disorder and a fairly high risk of reoffending will almost invariably be directed into offending behaviour programmes, and a lack of progress there may lead to a referral to hospital for transfer if it is thought that they require psychiatric or psychological intervention beyond that which can be provided within the prison system.

Discussions about hospital transfer or treatment, however, concern a tiny minority of all the offenders with personality disorder. The vast majority are looked after within ordinary criminal justice facilities, or are subject to probation orders. Many prisoners given a discretionary life sentence suffer from a severe personality disorder and they are supervised safely in the community within a criminal justice framework rather than within the health service. However, health services should not withdraw entirely from offering any support in such supervision. The probation officer will often need to liaise with mental health services to exclude the possibility that the offender is developing a mental illness or in order to provide a specialised input in cases of severe personality disorder and/or sexual deviation.

It is often difficult for the Probation Service to get help of this kind, and the extent of liaison between health services and probation is immensely variable throughout the country. In an international context, we have particularly low rates of use of medication for the treatment of sex offenders, even though there is good evidence for its use in the right circumstances. This deficiency has probably arisen because doctors have opted out of this type of work.

The role of the health service in dealing with this type of offender ought to have been made easier in recent years by the advent of the multi-agency public protection panels (MAPPPs). These panels see risk as a problem for the whole community. Mental health services can help by providing advice and assessments as required, but it is not their sole responsibility to manage the risk of sexual or violent offending. There have been some teething problems as health services and the MAPPPs establish ground rules for dealing with problems posed by medical confidentiality, but this model offers a promising way out of the dilemma as to how mental health services can become involved in managing the risk posed by personality disordered offenders in the community.

The organisation of forensic mental health services

Most offenders are dealt with by general mental health services because most offences are minor. Forensic services therefore cater for the minority of mentally disordered offenders at the more severe end of the spectrum. Forensic mental health services originally consisted of high and medium security, but the last 20 years has also seen the growth of forensic low-secure and community provision.

High-security provision in England and Wales consists of about 900 beds in England and Wales, at Ashworth, Rampton and Broadmoor, the former 'special' hospitals. All are operated by the NHS but have security commensurate with a category B prison. The number of beds has fallen in recent years as a result of pressure to ensure that security of this level is reserved only for those offenders who really need it. The average length of stay in a high-security hospital is about eight years. The tightening of security following the Tilt Report (2000) in the wake of the second Ashworth Hospital Inquiry (Fallon *et al.* 1999) has meant that there is little or no outside leave from high-security hospitals, so most of the work of reintegration into the community takes place at medium security.

There are approximately 4,000 places in medium-secure units available in England and Wales, with about half in the NHS and half in the independent sector. Medium security is poorly defined but should generally indicate that a patient within the unit has at least two locked doors between him/her and the outside world. Security arrangements at the unit should be such that the keys carried by staff within the unit are not capable of opening the outer one of those two doors. The average length of stay tends to be about two years, and most of the patients suffer from mental illness, usually schizophrenia.

Low-secure services are more difficult to define. The creation of low-secure forensic services came from pressure to bridge the gap between acute psychiatric intensive care units (PICUs) which tended to have a length of stay of only a few days and medium security. Low-secure forensic services tend to take offenders who require prolonged treatment or rehabilitation, yet do not present a level of risk that requires confinement in a more expensive medium-secure setting. Some low-secure units cater for patients who are likely to stay for many years or even indefinitely.

The advent of forensic community services raises questions about the distinction between forensic and general psychiatric services. Forensic services have more staff with lower caseloads and would justify their resources by claiming to deal with patients who present a higher risk of violent or sexual offending than do ordinary psychiatric patients. So far so good, but risk is impossible to define in unidimensional terms, so 'higher risk' is a vague concept. The situation is further complicated because most services in England and Wales do not use structured clinical methods of risk assessment, so any comparison relies on unstructured clinical judgment which is likely to be unreliable. Further exploration of these issues is beyond the scope of this chapter but Buchanan (2002) deals with some of them.

Continuities and change

Forensic mental health services have tended to concentrate on mental illness, mainly schizophrenia. These services, despite the security, have offered a fairly conventional treatment package that in its main principles would resemble that found in the old asylums. Patients were given medication and would be expected to engage in occupational or vocational therapies, along with occasional psychotherapy of a psychoanalytic or behavioural type. Forensic units were slow to embrace the cognitive behavioural offending behaviour programme that developed in the Canadian correctional system (McGuire 1995) and have spread rapidly within the prisons of England and Wales. Even now, provision of specific psychological services for drug and alcohol problems is still patchy within medium-secure units, despite the known importance of these problems in increasing the risks associated with mental illness.

The ambivalence about offending behaviour programmes also extends to the more structured assessment of the risks of violent and sexual offending. It is generally agreed in the international literature that the best way to approach this problem is a structured clinical method of assessing risk, but it is only in recent years that forensic services have started to incorporate such approaches into their assessment procedures which for many years were exclusively clinical.

Risk assessment is often discussed in terms of which instrument is the best predictor of risk but this is a false goal; individual prediction is an impossible task and no instrument is accurate enough to be more than an adjunct to clinical assessment. Nevertheless, there are compelling reasons for introducing a degree of structure into risk assessments because of the need to ensure non-discriminatory practice. Forensic services often have a statistical over-representation of black and minority ethnic patients compared to their representation in the community. Although the reasons for this statistical over-representation are complicated, and it cannot be attributed simply to discrimination, there is an overwhelming need to ensure that risk assessment and other procedures are transparent and, as far as possible, free of bias. It is impossible to do that so long as they are based on clinical discretion alone.

Future directions

In an ideal world, access to treatment would be determined entirely by clinical need. This principle sounds simple enough but it is impossible to achieve in a world of limited resources and, in practice, we fall far short of the ideal. Any attempt at practical application immediately encounters several difficult questions. How are offenders selected for assessment and treatment? How can the system respond to changing clinical need? And how do we achieve an equitable compromise between conflicting demands for treatment?

The process of assessment and treatment has been outlined above but a more complicated issue is that of how individuals are selected to enter the system. It is a rather arbitrary process that depends to a large extent on the mentally disordered offender coming to the notice of police, the courts, lawyers or prison staff. At all stages the more florid and obvious forms of mental disorder are more likely to result in psychiatric assessment. An offender who is behaving bizarrely will be more likely to be taken by the police to a hospital for a s. 136 assessment. Later in the process, the requirements of the Police and Criminal Evidence Act will lead to the involvement of an appropriate adult if there are difficulties in conducting an interview. It is open to the defence lawyer to involve a psychiatrist at any stage of the proceedings but some are more alert to the presence of mental disorder than others.

The court can also request a psychiatric report and is required to do so for certain charges, including murder. In other offences there is wide discretion, and the process is affected by the defendant's attitude. A plea of not guilty may mean that the question of the defendant's mental state is never raised.

These arbitrary features of the selection process become important because the hospital order, made at the time of sentencing, is essentially an all-or-none disposal. The offender chosen for treatment remains in hospital until they are fit to enter the community, which may be many years later. Discharge is often delayed for reasons unconnected to the original mental illness. They include risks associated with the patient's personality, drug use or lifestyle, none of which would justify a hospital order in the first place. By contrast, the offender who is not chosen for treatment may go to prison and find it difficult or impossible to access treatment later, even if they do develop a serious mental illness.

This arrangement is sometimes labelled a 'rescue' model, in which a minority of prisoners are removed from the criminal justice system and do not return, whereas the majority of mentally disordered offenders remain within the criminal justice system and receive less satisfactory treatment. Services face pressure to justify the apparent inefficiencies of this system and to investigate ways of improving access to services.

One of the major changes in the National Health Service over the last decade or so is the increasing recognition of inequalities in access. The problem has been there since the Service was created but the response was a typical British fudge, whereby professionals got together in the elite equivalent of a smoke-filled room to sort out the problem among themselves without ever having to account for their decisions. The dilemma has now been made more explicit, as typified by debates about 'postcode lotteries' or the decisions taken by the National Institute for Clinical Excellence (NICE) to ration expensive treatments.

Forensic mental health is not at the forefront of such debates but neither is it immune to change. The next few years will see increasing pressure on services to justify their practices and, in particular, to show that they represent the most efficient use of scarce resources. It seems unlikely that the 'rescue' model will survive this pressure, and we are likely to see greater freedom of movement between health and criminal justice systems. One aspect of these changes is the more flexible movement of mentally disordered offenders between the institutions of prison and hospital, but the other important dimension is the movement of health services into prisons. Inreach is already established but economic pressures alone are likely to see it expand massively. The benefits are considerable in terms of equality of access, but the challenge for health workers will be to maintain ethical and clinical standards while providing services within a correctional setting.

Selected further reading

Although approaching 20 years old, Sim, J. (1990) *Medical Power in Prisons*. Buckingham: Open University Press, is still considered a key text in prison health. Taken together with Jewkes, Y. and Johnston, H. (eds) (2007) *Prison Readings*. Cullompton: Willan the reader will then have a comprehensive coverage of prison healthcare.

Additionally, Gunn, J.C. and Taylor, P. J. (1993) *Forensic Psychiatry: Clinical Legal and Ethical Issues*. Oxford: Butterworth Heinemann, offers a comprehensive coverage of forensic psychiatric practice, including prison healthcare.

References

Birmingham, L., Mason, D. and Grubin, D. (1996) 'Prevalence of mental disorder in remand prisoners: consecutive case study', *British Medical Journal*, 313: 1521–4.
Birmingham, L., Mason, D. and Grubin, D. (1997) 'Health screening at first reception into prison', *Journal of Forensic Psychiatry*, 8: 435–9.

Blom-Cooper, L., Hally, H. and Murphy, E. (1995) *The Falling Shadow. One Patient's Mental Health Care*. London: Duckworth.

Blom-Cooper, L., Grounds, A., Guinan, P., Parker, A. and Taylor, M. (1996) *The Case of Jason Mitchell: Report of the Independent Panel of Inquiry*. London: Duckworth.

Buchanan, A. (2002) *Care of the Mentally Disordered Offender in the Community*. Oxford: Oxford Medical Publications.

Coid, J. (1988a) 'Mentally abnormal prisoners on remand. I. Accepted or rejected by the NHS?', *British Medical Journal*, 296: 1779–82.

Coid, J. (1988b) 'Mentally abnormal prisoners on remand. II. Services provided by Oxford and Wessex regions', *British Medical Journal*, 296: 1783–8.

Dawson, J. and Szmukler, G. (2006) 'Fusion of mental health and incapacity legislation', *British Journal of Psychiatry*, 188: 504–9.

Dell, S., Robertson, G., James, K. and Grounds, A. (1993a) 'Remands and psychiatric assessments in Holloway prison. I. The psychotic population', *British Journal of Psychiatry*, 163: 634–40.

Dell, S., Robertson, G., James, K. and Grounds, A. (1993b) 'Remands and psychiatric assessments in Holloway prison. II. The non-psychotic population', *British Journal of Psychiatry*, 163: 640–644.

Department of Health (1999) *The Future Organisation of Prison Health Care*, Report by the Joint Prison Service and National Health Service Executive Working Group. London: Department of Health.

Department of Health (2003) *Personality Disorder: No Longer a Diagnosis of Exclusion*. London: Department of Health.

Fallon, P., Bluglass, R., Edwards, B. and Daniels, G. (1999) *Report of the Committee of Inquiry into the Personality Disorder Unit, Ashworth Special Hospital*. London: Stationery Office.

Grubin, D. H. (1991a) 'Unfit to plead in England and Wales 1976–1988: a survey', *British of Journal of Psychiatry*, 158: 540–8.

Grubin, D. H. (1991b) 'Regaining fitness: patients found unfit to plead who return for trial', *Journal of Forensic Psychiatry*, 2: 139–84.

Gunn, J. C. and Taylor, P. J. (1993) *Forensic Psychiatry: Clinical, Legal and Ethical Issues*. Oxford: Butterworth Heinemann.

Joseph, P. L. A. (1990) 'Mentally disordered homeless offenders – diversion from custody', *Health Trends*, 22: 51–3.

McGuire, J. (ed.) (1995) *What Works? Reducing Re-offending*. London: John Wiley & Sons.

Maden, A. (2007) *Treating Violence*. Oxford: Oxford University Press.

Monahan, J. (1992) 'Mental disorder and violent behavior. Perceptions and evidence', *American Psychologist*, 47 (4): 511–21.

Murray, K., Akinkumni, A. and Lock, M. (1996) 'The Bentham Unit: a pilot remand and assessment service for male mentally disordered remand prisoners. I. Clinical activity in the first year and related ethical, practical and funding issues', *British Journal of Psychiatry*, 170: 456–61.

NAO (2003) *A Safer Place to Work: Protecting NHS Hospital and Ambulance Staff from Violence and Aggression*, Report prepared by the Comptroller and Auditor General, HC 527. London: National Audit Office.

Ritchie, J., Dick, D. and Lingham, R. (1994) *The Report of the Inquiry into the Care and Treatment of Christopher Clunis*. London: HMSO.

Robertson, G., Dell, S., James, K. and Grounds, A. (1994) 'Psychotic men remanded in custody to Brixton prison', *British Journal of Psychiatry*, 164: 55–61.

Singleton, N., Meltzer, H., Gatwood, R., Coid, J. and Deasy, D. (1998) *Psychiatric Morbidity among Prisoners in England and Wales*. London: Office for National Statistics.

Tilt Report (2000) *Report of the Review of Security at the High Security Hospitals.* London: Department of Health.

Weaver, T., Taylor, F., Cunningham, B., Maden, A., Rees, S. and Renton, A. (1997a) 'Impact of a dedicated service for male mentally disordered remand prisoners in north west London: retrospective study', *British Medical Journal*, 314: 1244–5.

Weaver, T., Taylor, F., Cunningham, B., Maden, A., Rees, S. and Renton, A. (1997b) 'The Bentham Unit: a pilot remand and assessment service for male mentally disordered offenders. II: Report of an independent evaluation', *British Journal of Psychiatry*, 170: 462–6.

Chapter 6

Non-custodial sentences and mentally disordered offenders

Danny Clark

Introduction

Many MDOs (mentally disordered offenders) processed by the courts receive prison sentences. However, a second much larger group are given a community sentence by the courts when convicted. MDOs serving community sentences are a neglected group in the literature compared with those who are imprisoned. Prisoners are perceived as more serious offenders and considered to have greater needs in terms of resettlement difficulties (e.g. access to accommodation, healthcare, benefits and maintaining relationships, etc.). It is assumed that serving a community sentence does not alter offenders' circumstances because they remain at liberty to receive treatment from mental health service providers. This chapter will try to redress the balance and focus on this group, outlining the process of supervision in the community, how they are dealt with by the Probation Service and other agencies, and describing how mental health issues might impinge on other aspects of the sentence.

The starting point is necessarily a description of the framework within which community sentences operate and how this has been dramatically revised over the last few years by a number of legislative changes and new initiatives which include the implementation of the 2003 Criminal Justice Act, the creation of the NPS (National Probation Service) in 2001, and and the Carter Report and the establishment of NOMS (National Offender Management Service). It is acknowledged that the content of this chapter is relevant only to England and Wales as a different legal framework exists in Scotland and Northern Ireland. In the latter two countries community sentences are managed differently with less separation between the responsibilities of probation and other social work services. The need for brevity means that these differences cannot be discussed in detail.

The Criminal Justice Act 2003

The Criminal Justice Act 2003 made a number of far-reaching changes to the way offenders are dealt with by the courts. The thrust of the Act was to create a clear framework specifying the purposes of sentencing as:

- the punishment of offenders;
- the reduction of crime (including its reduction by deterrence);
- the reform and rehabilitation of offenders;
- the protection of the public;
- the making of reparation by offenders to persons affected by their offence.

Prior to the implementation of the Act, the courts chose from a range of discrete options when sentencing. They could impose a community punishment order, requiring offenders to engage in unpaid work. They could agree a community rehabilitation order, which required offenders to be supervised by the Probation Service for a given period of time, sometimes with additional requirements to attend group work or educational courses. For serious offenders they could combine a punishment and rehabilitation order. In general the input provided was at the discretion of the probation officer. There were a number of other specific sentences, such as drug treatment and testing orders, for those with an established substance misuse need and requirements for persistent offenders which would include a higher level of supervision and attendance along with curfews and close monitoring.

The new Act replaced these different sentences with one community sentence, but within this gave sentencers more discretion to choose from a series of 12 requirements to enable them to tailor the sentence to the individual offender:

- Unpaid work
- Activity requirement
- Accredited programme
- Prohibited activity
- Curfew
- Exclusion
- Residence
- Mental health treatment
- Drug rehabilitation
- Alcohol treatment
- Supervision
- Attendance centre.

The requirements may be combined subject to their being compatible, their suitability for the offender, the offender's religious beliefs or times of work and education not being compromised, and the overall restriction on liberty or punitive content being commensurate with the seriousness of the offending. The Probation Service provides advice on suitable combinations to the courts and the Sentencing Guidelines Council indicates the type of requirements that might be appropriate for the level of seriousness of offending. So, for example, a less serious offence would usually result in a single requirement.

The Criminal Justice Act also made provisions for a change in the way custody could be used. New sentencing arrangements known as custody plus and intermittent custody were created. Custody plus was to provide a flexible sentence of less than 12 months where a short period of custody, possibly only weeks, would be followed by community supervision, but with the possibility of immediate return to prison if the terms and conditions of supervision were not met. In effect a taste of imprisonment would have become a thirteenth punitive option in community sentencing. Intermittent custody allows offenders to serve a custodial sentence in small segments, either weekend or weekday incarceration with the premise that this would assist offenders in maintaining employment, accommodation or family ties. At the time of writing custody plus has not been enacted – the proposals have been a victim of the spiralling prison population and costs. Intermittent custody has been piloted, but become virtually obsolete because of low demand.

Changes in the Probation Service

In 2001 the National Probation Directorate (NPD) was established to set policy and direct and manage the performance of the 42 autonomous probation areas in England and Wales. This was part of an ongoing strategy to revise and improve the way probation worked (Underdown and Ellis 1998). A major theme of this change was to shift the emphasis of probation work from what had originally been a social work perspective of assisting the offender to one in which the chief role of probation was to protect the public by reducing reoffending and managing risk of harm through the close monitoring and supervision of offenders and by providing interventions to address factors associated with reoffending. Key to this change were the introduction of a national assessment system to identify risk and needs, a commitment to evidence practice and the introduction of national standards and performance targets for all areas of work. In practice this has meant a move away from the model of the probation officer working independently, primarily through their own input in one-to-one supervision sessions, to a case management function, in which much of the rehabilitative work was delivered through a series of planned interventions.

NOMS

Stephen Carter was commissioned by the government in 2003 to examine perceived difficulties in the functioning of the correctional services and make recommendations. His report concentrated upon the organisational structures considered necessary for delivering a new approach to 'offender management'. Carter's findings were received by the incumbent Home Secretary but were never published, although a response document, *Reducing Crime: Changing Lives*, was released by the Home Office (2004).

In its response to the Correctional Services Review, the government created NOMS:

> as an overarching structure to deliver the implementation of 'a new approach to offender management'. This single approach had to apply across the wide range of different sentences to which offenders are subject, and had to be flexible enough to respond to the diverse needs, circumstances and motivations of offenders themselves. It needed to embrace the

work of the different providers of an offender's correctional experience. It needed to be 'end-to-end', seamless, and integrated, with a single offender manager responsible for the whole of each single sentence'. (NOMS 2005: 2)

But beyond this specification the detail of its design, and its implementation, was for NOMS to resolve.

The basis of offender management is that a single person, the offender manager, is responsible for an offender throughout their entire sentence, whether the sentence is served in custody, in the community or a mixture of both. The offender manager is responsible for assessing the offender, planning their sentence and ensuring that the plan is carried out. While the offender manager has overall responsibility for the offender, they are supported by other key workers delivering interventions and other interested parties, such as the offender's family and mental health specialists. According to the NOMS model the principles of offender management are as follows:

- *Consistency*. The offender experiences a consistency of message and behaviour, throughout his sentence and by different people working with them at the same time.
- *Commitment*. Research indicates that the prospects for success are greater when an offender develops a sense of reciprocal commitment to the staff working with them (Farrall 2004).
- *Consolidation*. Gains are short-lived if new learning is not turned into routine and instinctive behaviour through a process which reinforces and rewards it (McGuire 1996).
- *Continuity*. There needs to be continuity of care or treatment, but also a high degree of continuity of relationship running through the whole of the period of engagement. This is a prerequisite to achieving the earlier three principles.

However, the creation of NOMS is not just about end-to-end offender management. There is another agenda, which is to increase efficiency and value for money in correctional services through contestability and the introduction of additional providers of services. The correctional services are following the path already trodden by the NHS and other government agencies in introducing commissioning into the delivery of services. This is evidenced by the reorganisation of NOMS in early 2006 into two large directorates: the Commissioning and Partnerships Directorate and the Performance Management Directorate. A further Criminal Justice Bill has been introduced into Parliament which allows probation areas to convert to probation trusts and makes provision for the purchase of services locally by regional offender managers from a variety of sources.

It is too early to know how this will play out. There is some tension between these two drivers of the NOMS agenda: an offender management model with the stated aim of providing consistency, commitment, consolidation and continuity of services, and plans to allow a greater variety of organisations to provide services with greater regional variation in provision. It makes the offender manager role pivotal in ensuring that appropriate services are available and integrated for the individual offender.

The above description of the wide-ranging changes which have occurred over the last eight years provides a flavour of the issues which are currently influencing decision-making. What the repercussions of this upheaval are for services for MDOs remains unanswered. The best way to explore this topic is by examining the various stages in the process of a community sentence with reference to this group.

Assessment and reporting

For most offenders the first contact with the Probation Service is through an assessment process when the court requests additional information to inform their sentencing decisions. Some offenders are not assessed at this stage, but most offenders commencing a community sentence will have an OASys (Offender Assessment System) document completed prior to or at the beginning of the sentence.

OASys (NPD 2002) is a standard means of systematically identifying risks and criminogenic needs for all offenders. It was jointly developed by the prison and probation services from 1998 onwards. Before 1998, a number of different assessment tools were used by probation areas and the Prison Service had no formal process for assessing prisoners other than lifers. OASys was designed as a particularly comprehensive system of assessment. It was based on evidence generated from existing risk assessment instruments and other contemporary research. OASys continues to be researched and developed by ODEAT (the OASys Development, Evaluation and Analysis Team). Findings from the initial pilot studies demonstrated that OASys provided a good actuarial prediction of likelihood of reconviction (Howard *et al.* 2006). OASys provides assessors with a protocol for assessing and evidencing issues relating to risk of serious harm and guidance for recording any risk management strategies. It also generates a profile of the individual offender's criminogenic needs (see Table 6.1) which then forms the basis of a offender management plan, which is an integral part of OASys.

OASys is reassessed at specific points throughout sentence, for example on release from custody or at the end of an intervention. It provides a template in which the needs of each offender, the steps taken to meet these needs and any resultant change in risks, attitudes and behaviour are recorded. OASys is an essential tool in the process of developing end-to-end case management as envisaged by the Carter Report. Over three quarters of a million separate OASys assessments have been recorded and these form a rich database which can be used to further validate and develop the instrument.

However, OASys does have its detractors and the developers of the system are fully aware of some of its limitations. Prominent among these is the generic nature of the assessment. OASys was designed to be used with all offenders – it provides a detailed assessment of all the factors commonly associated with increased likelihood of reoffending, but it cannot assess in detail unusual factors which are only associated with specific groups. Nor can it provide the level of detail required to formulate a treatment plan in some areas. For example, sex offenders require additional assessment because, although OASys will identify some factors which predict their likelihood of future offending, it does not

Table 6.1 The sections of OASys

OASys has 13 sections addressing identifying needs. The first 12 examine factors which research shows are related to risk of reconviction. At the end of each section, links to risk of serious harm, risks to the individual, other risks and offending behaviour are highlighted. An actuarial risk predictor is calculated, based on the score on each of these sections. The sections are weighted in the contribution they make to the risk predictor on the basis of earlier research findings and the OAsys pilot study. Section 13, health and other considerations, is not used in assessing risk of reconviction or serious harm but is useful for considering suitability of interventions.

OASYS section	Description of section	Contribution to risk of reconviction score[*]
1. **Offending information**	Examines current and previous offences. Research studies confirm criminal history as the best predictor of future conviction.	Together these sections contribute 30% of the risk of reconviction score
2. **Analysis of offences**	Helps to identify risk of serious harm, risks to the individual and other risks.	
3. **Accommodation**	Looks at whether accommodation is available, the quality of current accommodation and whether the location encourages reoffending or creates a risk of harm.	7% of reconviction score
4. **Education, training and employability**	Records education levels and any learning difficulties, employment history, vocational qualifications and attitudes towards training and work.	12% of reconviction score score
5. **Financial management and income**	The section deals with income and how it directly relates to reoffending. It looks at resources, how income is managed and pressures on income such as gambling.	7% of reconviction
6. **Relationships**	Assesses whether the offender's satisfaction with their relationships and their stability relate to their offending behaviour. Includes family history, partnerships and any evidence of domestic abuse.	3.5% of reconviction score
7. **Lifestyle and associates**	The section examines aspects of the offender's current lifestyle and offending; peer influences; how offenders spend their time, with whom they mix, whether there are any protective factors in their lifestyle.	9% of reconviction score

Table 6.1 (continued)

OASYS section	Description of section	Contribution to risk of reconviction score *
8. Drug misuse	Identifies the extent and type of drug misuse and its effects on an offender's life. Research consistently links misuse of drugs with reoffending.	9% of reconviction score
9. Alcohol misuse	Examines patterns of alcohol use and links to reoffending, especially in relation to violent offending.	3% of reconviction score
10. Emotional well-being	This section examines the extent to which emotional problems interfere with the offender's functioning or create risk of harm to themselves or others. It records evidence of psychiatric history and treatments and links between mental health problems and offending behaviour.	3.5% of reconviction score
11. Thinking and behaviour	Assesses the offender's application of reasoning, especially to social problems. Research indicates that offenders tend not to think things through, are poor problem-solvers, fail to consider the consequences of their behaviour and do not see things from other people's perspectives. Those with a number of such 'cognitive deficits' will be more likely to reoffend.	7% of reconviction score
12. Attitudes	Examines the offender's attitude towards their offending and towards supervision and society in general. Evidence of antisocial attitudes is linked to likelihood of reconviction.	9% of reconviction score
13. Health and other considerations	The section does not contribute to assessing risk of reconviction or harm. Assessors use this section when considering suitability for community punishments (which may involve physical work), electronic monitoring and programmes. This information will be mainly used by the Probation Service but also assists the Prison Service to determine suitable allocations to work and in sentence planning.	Not applicable

* The reconviction score ranges from 0 to 168 and is divided into three groups: low risk (scores below 50), medium risk (scores of 50 to 100) and high risk (scores above 100). The measure is based on group reconviction rates which means that it reflects the usual likelihood that someone with that score will be reconvicted. Around 50% of the items which contribute to the reconviction score are 'dynamic' meaning that they can change in either direction over time, raising or reducing the risk of reconviction.

assess level of sexual deviancy or examine the cognitions supportive of sexual offending. The OASys manual strongly recommends that where a conviction is for a sexual offence or there appears to be a sexual motivation for offending further specialist assessment should be undertaken

Another limitation is the skills base of assessors. Assessors do need adequate training. The original training package developed to implement OASys made assumptions regarding the level of the existing assessment skills of staff which appear to have been unfounded. The training was revised to eliminate some of these problems, but it is still likely that some assessments will be less reliable than others. Quality is also affected by the time pressures exerted on staff to complete the assessment. This is especially true at the court stage where timeliness targets exist for completing pre-sentence reports (PSRs). Allied with time pressures is the quality of collateral information available to assessors to inform the assessment. One of the most important aspects of the OASys procedure is that it is not just based on an interview with the offender. Assessors must reach their own judgments on scoring each section of OASys using as many sources of evidence as possible to support their views. In many instances there are still difficulties obtaining information, especially when it is held by other agencies outside the criminal justice system.

These limitations have been discussed in some detail because they are highly relevant when assessing offenders who may have mental health problems. The OASys section primarily relating to mental health issues is entitled 'emotional well-being'. It consists of two parts. There is a series of questions relating to current psychological and mental health problems. Two questions ask specifically about current psychiatric or psychological problems and contact, diagnosis or treatment by mental health professionals. Other items relate to coping and vulnerability, social isolation, self-image and evidence of suicidal or self-harming thoughts or behaviour. These items are scored by assessors and require written evidence explaining how the score was derived. The OASys manual gives clear guidance on how to score each individual item including examples to match each gradation on the three-point scale (Home Office 2001). The unscored items in the section are markers for life history events which may have a significant impact on current cognitive and psychological functioning.

The adequacy of section 10 has been questioned by some groups. Kutchinsky (2006) states:

> As this section deals with what is likely to be the most complex and sensitive area for an offender, the extent of accurate self-reporting must be called into question. Equally, probation staff are then relying on a somewhat simplistic scoring system, and minimal training, to make difficult judgments to distinguish between different levels of mental health need.

While accepting that the essence of this statement is factual, this view perhaps expects more of OASys and probation staff than is realistically possible.

Section 10 of OASys was thoroughly overhauled, simplified and the manual guidance rewritten after extensive piloting. The earlier pilot versions of OASys had far more detail regarding different types of mental disorders and their classification. However, feedback from assessors indicated that they were extremely unhappy with making judgments that they considered were beyond their professional competence. The decision was made that this section would focus on two areas. Firstly, it would allow assessors to record mental disorders which were already diagnosed and instances where contact with a mental health services provider was already established. This ensured that the information was captured and could be taken into account in offender management. Secondly, it provides the opportunity for assessors to note behaviours which might be associated with mental disorder without having to formulate any hypothesis about an underlying condition. Each section of OASys has a 'cut-off point' that signifies when a problem might exist. If an offender's aggregated score for a section is greater than this threshold, this should trigger some appropriate action. For section 10 the action which assessors are guided to by the OASys manual is to seek advice from a mental health professional or consider making a referral to mental health services. By this means a properly completed OASys can assist in identifying issues and lead on to a fuller assessment.

It is recognised that having a mental disorder is not necessarily a risk factor for future offending. So, section 10 does not make a large contribution towards the actuarial risk predictor calculated by OASys. This combination of low threshold for further assessment and limited contribution to predicted risk allows section 10 to identify need without signalling the need for restrictions.

Offender management

Supervision

The role of offender management was described earlier in this chapter. Under current legal requirements the Probation Service is responsible for the supervision of all community sentences. Supervision is more than contact to monitor and manage compliance with any other requirements, but can involve:

- undertaking work to promote personal and behavioural change;
- monitoring and reviewing patterns of behaviour and personal activity;
- work to increase motivation;
- practical support to increase compliance with other requirements;
- reinforcement of learning from programmes or activity requirement;
- individual counselling and modelling of pro-social behaviour;
- advocacy on behalf of the offender and arranging contact and support from other agencies.

Orders with a single supervision requirement provide a basic level of support and referral to other agencies for assistance with practical or personal problems related to the person's offending. However, for cases of medium or high seriousness, some combinations of requirements are usefully supported by a supervision requirement.

The level of supervision provided will depend on the needs of the offender and the point in the order. National probation standards provide guidance for how often the offender will be seen.

Mental health treatment requirement

Many community sentenced offenders who have a recognised mental disorder will be subject to an MHTR (mental health treatment requirement). The *Probation Bench Handbook* (NPD 2006: 21) describes a mental health treatment order in the following terms.

> The purpose of such an order is to allow the offender to be dealt with by way of a Community Order and provide access to treatment where issues other than mental disorder contribute to offending but the mental condition does not require a Hospital or Guardianship Order. The Mental Health Treatment Requirement under the direction of a psychiatrist or chartered psychologist, or both, may be for all or any part of the order as specified by the court up to the maximum of three years. Treatment can be as an in-patient or out-patient and this must be stated in the order. No further specific definition of the treatment should appear on the order. The Responsible Medical Officer agreeing to treat the offender should be named on the order.

Probation staff are advised that an MHTR is likely to be appropriate for medium to high seriousness offenders and PSR writers usually recommend its use in conjunction with a supervision requirement.

When an MHTR is imposed the supervision element of the sentence remains the responsibility of the offender manger. The Probation Service National Standards for the supervision of a community order apply and the order must be enforced, including breech proceedings if appropriate. The CPA (Care Programme Approach), which provides the framework for the management of health service users, will also apply during community supervision. CPA is intended to provide a framework for the delivery of care to all adults with mental health problems in contact with mental health services. The CPA ensures the delivery of appropriate levels of care to a patient and aims to minimise the risk that the patient will lose contact with services. The key elements of CPA are: assessment of health and care needs; a care plan; involvement of the individual in producing the plan; regular reviews; and the appointment of mental health work as care coordinator. The CPA is the interface for coordinating input from the Probation Service and mental health services. To work correctly it requires a high level of communication between all parties.

For offenders who are not subject to an MHTR but are receiving mental health treatment, the CPA will still provide a vehicle for communication between the health services and the offender manager. However, because the offender does not have an MHTR, there are no powers for probation to warn or to breech the offender for failure to comply with treatment. Mentally disordered offenders subject to criminal justice orders or licences are subject to MAPPA, depending on the risk they pose, in the same manner as any other offender.

Breach

If an offender fails to abide by the conditions of the community sentence one option open to the court is to revoke the order and deal with the offender in any way which would be available to it if the offender were appearing for sentence for that offence for the first time, including imprisonment or relevant disposals under the Mental Health Act 1983. When considering any breach of a mentally disordered offender subject to community supervision, the vulnerability and any risk posed by offenders to themselves and/or others, together with the impact of breach action on any available or potential treatments, are key considerations, particularly when considering imprisonment. When offenders have refused to undergo treatment they should not be treated as having breached the order simply by virtue of this refusal, if the court considers that refusal is reasonable in the circumstances.

The *Probation Bench Handbook* (NPD 2005) notes that the process of breach can be used positively to divert offenders from the criminal justice process, or at least the penal system. If breach is unavoidable the court can consider what is the least restrictive and damaging outcome to a potentially vulnerable offender consistent with the risk assessment. Possible alternatives to continued criminal justice/penal system involvement are: guardianship or hospital order (s. 37, MHA 1983) or civil admission to hospital (s. 3, MHA 1983). If these are considered the probation officer must have consulted with the Community Mental Health Team and, in the case of a guardianship order, have made the necessary referral to the local authority.

Practice

Arrangements for mentally disordered offenders on community sentences vary enormously from one probation area to another and from one individual offender manger to another. For example, some probation areas will have a specialist team or member of staff who will manage MDOs whereas another area will disperse them among all offender managers. The former is probably the better model, because the specialist has greater knowledge of MDOs, probably has an interest the area and will also have cultivated a network of contacts within the mental health services to assist them. But in some areas size and geography make this unfeasible. One of the adverse side effects of implementing the new Offender Management Model is the abolition of specialist roles in some areas.

There will be great differences in the knowledge and experience of MDOs among probation staff. Many probation staff perceive their role with MDOs as being to refer and defer to the specialist services available. Initial training for probation officers provides little input on MDOs and little in-service training is organised nationally or locally on the subject. The last in-service training produced by the Home Office was eight years ago (Roberts 1999). It is often left to the offender manager to seek out resources and information themselves. Where the formal organisation has left a gap this has been filled to some extent by voluntary organisations. For example, Nacro (2005) and Revolving Door (Kutchinsky 2006) have produced material aimed at educating and informing probation staff about MDOs.

Access to interventions

The community sentence provides a number of options in terms of rehabilitative interventions, most of which cannot be imposed unless the offender manager indicates suitability and the offender is willing to comply.

A DRR (drug rehabilitation requirement) lasts at least six months and provides treatment to reduce dependency on or propensity to misuse drugs and involves regular testing for drug use. The intervention is delivered on a multi-agency basis coordinated by a local drug action team and will include NHS input. The court must be satisfied that: the offender is dependent on, or has a propensity to misuse drugs and that this requires treatment which can be arranged. The alcohol treatment requirement has the same format as the DRR, except for the drug testing element. Similar conditions apply in terms of eligibility and provision. Many MDOs evidence comorbidity and have substance misuse problems so are likely to receive these disposals. Home Office statistics (RDS NOMS 2004) confirm that offenders receiving DRR are often at greater risk of reconviction and have greater needs than any other group of offenders, including those sentenced to imprisonment. Needless to say significant numbers fail to complete treatment. However, there is evidence (Harper and Chitty 2004) to demonstrate that those who remain in treatment for at least a critical 12 weeks are very likely to complete and have reduced reconviction rates.

Accredited programmes

OBPs (offending behaviour programmes) are the main intervention for offenders serving community sentences. The Probation Service has a long history of doing 'group work' with offenders, traditionally unstructured and unevaluated. Only with the reforms to improve effective practice in the late 1990s was a suite of structured programmes grounded in theory and based on evidence launched. The National Probation Directorate (2006) report that over 34,000 offenders were being referred to programmes nationwide with 17,400 successfully completing them in 2005–06.

OBP design is quality assured by the Correctional Services Accreditation Panel, which is an independent body of international experts appointed by the Home Secretary. This panel accredits programmes likely to reduce reconviction on the basis of research evidence and existing knowledge. The panel considers 11 criteria, fully described in the Annual Report of the Correctional Services Accreditation Panel (Home Office 2006) to ensure the interventions:

- are based on a sound theoretical model change;
- have appropriate selection criteria;
- address a range of dynamic risk factors;
- employ effective treatment methods;
- include skills practice;
- are sufficient in terms of intensity and duration; are integrated into overall sentence management and planning;
- describe the measure taken to ensure they are delivered as intended; and
- incorporate an appropriate level of monitoring and ongoing evaluation.

Table 6.2 Probation offending behaviour programmes – general offending programmes

Programme:	Enhanced thinking skills	Think First	One to One	Cognitive skills booster	Women's acquisitive crime
Description of programme	Addresses thinking and behaviour associated with offending Employs a sequenced series of structured exercises designed to teach inter-personal problem-solving skills	An offence-focused programme that addresses thinking and behaviour Phase 1 teaches problem-solving skills, phase 2 applies to offending, phase 3 rehearses self-management and social skills	Teaches a range of problem-solving skills in order to change behaviour and the underpinning thoughts Attitudes and values related to offending	Designed to reinforce learning from general offending programmes through skills rehearsal and relapse prevention	Based on MI techniques – works with women in each stage Emphasis on emotional management and building healthy relationships
Target group	Male and female medium to medium high risk (OGRS 41–100), but where an individual is scoring 75 and over the sentence plan should identify additional work to reflect the higher risk (the equivalent OASys range would be 50–160 with offenders over 100 requiring additional work)	Male and female medium to high risk (OGRS 41–100), but where an individual is scoring 75 and over the sentence plan should identify additional work to reflect the higher risk (the equivalent OASys range would be 50–160 with offenders over 100 requiring additional work)	Male and female medium to medium high risk of reconviction (OGRS 41–100), but where an individual is scoring 75 and over the sentence plan should identify additional work to reflect the higher risk (the equivalent OASys range would be 50–160 with offenders over 100 requiring additional work)	Male and female offenders who have already completed a general offender programme	Female OGRS 31 plus (or OASys 40 plus) override women who have a current conviction of an acquisitive nature or there is a pattern of previous offending or the current offence has an underlying motivation of an acquisitive nature

Programme:	Enhanced thinking skills	Think First	One to One	Cognitive skills booster	Women's acquisitive crime
Selection criteria	Level and range of cognitive skills deficits assessed through OASys scores	Level and range of cognitive skills deficits assessed through general offender matrix	Level and range of cognitive skills deficits assessed through general offender matrix Complex pattern of personal problems, personal characteristics that make group learning difficult	Previous completion of general offender programme and evidence that they have benefited from the original GOBP	Level and range of cognitive skills deficits assessed through OASys
Exclusion criteria	Lacks the offending-related needs, serious mental health problems, inability to learn in a group setting	Lacks the offending-related needs, serious mental health problems, inability to learn in a group setting	Lacks the offending-related needs, serious mental health problems, inability to meet the learning outcomes, e.g. severe drug dependency	Has failed to benefit sufficiently from the original programme	Serious mental health issues, inability to meet the learning outcomes, e.g. severe drug dependency
Programme sessions	20 sessions of 2–2.5 hours	22 sessions of 2–2.5 hours	21 sessions of 1–1.5 hours	10–12 × 2–2.5 hour sessions depending on group size – normally 10	31 sessions of 2 hours each Additional work will be needed for the higher risk women or those with greater need

Table 6.2 (continued)

Programme:	Enhanced thinking skills	Think First	One to One	Cognitive skills booster	Women's acquisitive crime
Pre-programme	None specified	4 pre-programme sessions	1 pre-programme motivational session	1 pre-programme session	1 preparation session held by tutors
Post-programme	None specified	4 sessions + 2 optional sessions	None specified	Relapse prevention work with manager	None specified
Core programme duration (excl. pre and post sessions)	4–10 weeks (40–50 hours total)	6–22 weeks (44–55 hours excluding pre and post sessions)	Up to 11 weeks at two sessions per week (21–32 hours total) Suspension of up to 6 weeks – restart after individual assessment at appropriate point Suspension 6 weeks or longer – restart at beginning	4–10 weeks (20–25 hours in total)	Twice a week for 16 weeks Three times a week for 11 weeks
Group size	Minimum 4, maximum 12, optimum 10	Minimum 4, maximum 12, optimum 10	Individual delivery	Minimum 4, maximum 12, optimum 8	Minimum 3, optimum 8–10

GOBP – General Offending Behaviour Programme(s)
OGRS – Offender Group Reconviction Scale – a statistical predictor of the likelihood of reconviction within two years based on offender's age and previous criminal record

Eighteen programmes are accredited for use in the community and several others are in the process of being piloted. As shown in Table 6.2, these range from general offending programmes which address the cognitive skills deficits common to a large majority of offenders to programmes for specific groups such as sex offenders and domestic violence perpetrators (as shown in Tables 6.3, 6.4 and 6.5).

Attendance at programme sessions is not voluntary and failure to attend can result in breech and resentencing. Programmes are generally delivered by probation staff who have been specially trained as facilitators, supported by a treatment manager who is an experienced facilitator. It is the treatment manager's role to ensure that facilitators maintain programme integrity while being responsive to the needs of participants. All programme sessions are video monitored to ensure quality of delivery and have additional work pre-programme and follow-up for participants to generalise and reinforce learning.

The majority of offending behaviour programmes adopt a cognitive behavioural approach which has been shown to be effective in changing attitudes and behaviour for a wide range of psychological problems with many client groups, including offenders, substance misusers and those with mental health problems. The programmes assume a social learning theory model of criminality which has been most fully expounded by Andrews and Bonta (1998). In this model of criminal behaviour it is assumed that most people learn through childhood and early adulthood the skills required to function in a socially acceptable non-criminal way. However, if individuals are exposed to harsh, abusive or inconsistent parenting, have a negative schooling experience, are exposed mainly to criminal or deviant role models and do not have the opportunity to practise and be reinforced for pro-social behaviour, they are likely to develop deficits in their thinking and behavioural repertoire which affect their ability to act appropriately in later life. These deficits lead to a propensity to antisocial and criminal behaviour, as well as other psychological and social problems.

Bandura (1999) describes how people with such deficits often have a lack of self-efficacy in that they have neither the disposition nor ability to change and take advantage of services offered to them such as educational or job opportunities, unless the ingrained styles of thinking and patterns of behaviour can be changed. The cognitive behavioural approach involves teaching a number of basic thinking and behavioural skills in a very structured way in order to ameliorate some of these deficits. The skills are taught through motivational enhancement, cognitive restructuring, role play and social skills practice and modelling. But it has to be recognised that attempting to teach these skills which are normally acquired over many years is a daunting task, requiring highly committed staff who are well trained and properly supported, a high degree of programme integrity and follow-up to reinforce learning if progress made is to be sustained.

Table 6.3 Probation offending behaviour programmes – aggression programmes

Programme	Aggression replacement training	CALM (managing negative emotions)	CDVP (domestic violence)	IDAP (domestic violence)	Cognitive self-change block 6 (instrumental violence)
Description of programme	Aims to reduce aggressive behaviour through teaching social skills, anger management techniques and improved moral reasoning	Aims to reduce aggressive and offending behaviour which is related to poor emotional management through teaching social skills, emotional management techniques and REBT	CBT domestic violence sequential programme for male perpetrators of medium to high risk of harm Based on CSC and similar to prison domestic violence programme Includes inter-agency risk assessment / information exchange management, victim contact, proactive case management and core group work	CBT offender focused, challenging attitudes and beliefs Teaches non-controlling behaviour strategies and enhanced victim empathy Includes inter-agency risk assessment / information exchange management, victim contact, proactive case management and core group work	An integral part of a programme which starts in prisons and continues in the community Reinforces learning from the prison-based blocks, applies it to the community setting and maintains an up-to-date relapse prevention plan

Programme	Aggression replacement training	CALM (managing negative emotions)	CDVP (domestic violence)	IDAP (domestic violence)	Cognitive self-change block 6 (instrumental violence)
Target group	Male and female offenders, OGRS 41–100, but where an individual is scoring 75 and over the sentence plan should identify additional work to reflect the higher risk (the equivalent OASys range would be 50–160 with offenders over 100 requiring additional work) *And/or* Medium or above risk of harm in the community (OASys) High or very high risk requires further structured work or a sequenced programme to be work) provided	Males only, OGRS 41–100, but where an individual is scoring 75 and over the sentence plan should identify additional work to reflect the higher risk (the equivalent OASys range would be 50–160 with offenders over 100 requiring additional work) *And/or* Medium or above risk of harm in the community (OASys) High or very high risk requires further structured work or a sequenced programme to be provided	Male offenders who were or are in heterosexual relationships with medium and medium/high risk of harm offenders	Male offenders, in/ were in heterosexual relationships, who are of medium to high risk of harm	High-risk seriously violent male offenders who have been released on licence after completing blocks 1–5 in prison

Table 6.3 (continued)

Programme	Aggression replacement training	CALM (managing negative emotions)	CDVP (domestic violence)	IDAP (domestic violence)	Cognitive self-change block 6 (instrumental violence)
Selection criteria	Current aggressive offence and/or established pattern of aggressive behaviour. Deficits measured in OASys in two of the following areas: social skills, emotional management, perspective taking and moral development	Current offence of aggression or loss of emotional control and/or previous pattern of aggression or loss of emotional control. Deficits, measured by OASys in two of the following areas: social skills, emotional management, perspective taking and pro-criminal attitudes	Use of Spousal Abuse Risk Assessment (SARA), male, offence committed in context of domestic violence	Spousal Abuse Risk Assessment tool (SARA) male, offence committed in context of domestic violence	Release from prison having started the programme
Exclusion criteria	Offenders who are primarily instrumentally violent and domestic violence offenders	Primarily instrumentally violent and domestic violence offenders	In denial, severe mental health issues, inability to meet learning outcomes, e.g. severe drug dependency	In denial, serious mental health problems, inability to meet the learning outcomes, e.g. severe drug dependency	Not applicable

Programme	Aggression replacement training	CALM (managing negative emotions)	CDVP (domestic violence)	IDAP (domestic violence)	Cognitive self-change block 6 (instrumental violence)
Programme sessions	18 sessions of 2 hours	24 sessions of 2–2.5 hours	25 group work sessions of 2 hours Sequential but flexible Can be delivered 2/3 times per week 9 individual sessions including pre and post	27 group sessions of 2 hours, delivered weekly Modular rolling programme 13 individual sessions including pre and post	One-to-one sessions in the context of licence appointments
Pre-programme	5 sessions	None specified	3 pre-programme individual sessions plus one pre-group	4 individual sessions plus one group orientation	N/A
Post-programme	5 sessions	None specified	4 relapse prevention sessions	At least four relapse prevention session with case manager	N/A
Core programme duration	6–12 weeks (36 hours total)	8–24 weeks	9–13 weeks	Probably not less than 27 weeks in total plus pre and post sessions	Maximum until the end of the licence or until ended by risk management decision
Group size	Minimum 3, maximum 10	Minimum 3, maximum 10	8–12	8–12	N/A

CALM – Controlling Anger and Learning to Manage it (anger management programme)
CDVP – Community Domestic Violence Programme
CSC – Cognitive Self Change Programme
IDAP – Integrated Domestic Abuse Progamme
REBT – Rational Emotive Behaviour Therapy
SARA – Spousal Abuse Risk Assessment

Overall the evidence that cognitive behavioural programmes effectively reduce reoffending is greater than for other types of interventions, such as basic education, employment and training or other forms of group therapy. However, despite the positive international evidence to be found in virtually all of the published meta-analysis studies and systematic reviews, Harper and Chitty (2004) point out that there are still considerable gaps in the UK evidence base, particularly in relation to delivering programmes on such a large scale, and in relation to what the characteristics of offenders are who benefit from them.

OBPs need to be considered as one aspect of the overall strategy to reduce reoffending. Generally there are several factors linked to an individual's offending, requiring a range of services and interventions. Offending behaviour programmes are often the only component of an offender's sentence which attempts to address their attitude to offending directly. But, because the programmes work by changing attitudes and teaching skills, they can produce beneficial changes in many areas of the offender's life. For example improved problem-solving and interpersonal skills will increase the likelihood of offenders finding and maintaining employment and suitable accommodation and establishing supporting relations. Thus OBPs can enhance the effectiveness of other interventions such as work-related training and strategies to reduce social exclusion. OBPs underpin the probation services, public protection work. Sex offender treatment programmes (SOTPs) and violent offender programmes have a critical role in work to assess, reduce and manage the risk presented by sexual and violent offenders.

One would expect that cognitive behavioural programmes would be beneficial to offenders suffering from mental disorders. After all the cognitive behavioural techniques used were originally developed by clinical psychologists and psychiatrists working with patients suffering from a range of psychological problems and mental illness. Analysis based on OASys shows a high level of correlation between the emotional and psychological problems reported in section 10 of OASys and problems with antisocial attitudes, thinking and behaviour covered in sections 11 and 12, demonstrating that many offenders who are known to have mental health problems (or should have further assessment) meet the criteria to attend offending behaviour programmes.

In practice, though, mentally disordered offenders have been under-represented among programme completers. There are barriers to attendance which are only now being resolved. The barriers begin with the PSR author who must decide to recommend an OBP. To be recommended offenders must be eligible for an OBP in terms of their risk – most OBPs are designed for offenders in the medium to high risk of reoffending bands. It is difficult to know if this disadvantages MDOs. First-time offenders or those without previous convictions because of diversion from the courts, and many female offenders who on average have lower risk scores than males, could be excluded. Next, offenders must evidence the criminogenic needs which are targeted by the programme – this can be a barrier to participation if an offender's attitudes and thinking deficits are masked by the mental disorder. The third stage involves applying a list of exclusion criteria and is the part of the process which most often affects MDOs. Exclusions vary from programme to programme but usually include an IQ threshold, some criteria around learning

Table 6.4 Probation offending behaviour programmes – sex offender programmes

Programme	C-SOGP (West Midlands)	TV-SOGP (Thames Valley Programme)	N-SOGP (Northumbria Programme)	I-SOGP
Description of programme	Aims to reduce offending by adult male sex offenders	Aims to reduce offending by adult male sex offenders and to provide support to partners of perpetrators	Rolling programme which aims to reduce offending by adult male sex offenders	Aim to reduce offending by non-contact Internet sex offenders
Target group	Adult males within normal IQ range who commit any type of sexual offence Also accept voluntary referrals, e.g. from Social Services	Adult males within normal IQ range who commit any type of sexual offence Also accept voluntary referrals, e.g. from Social Services	Adult males within normal IQ range who commit any type of sexual offence Also accept voluntary referrals, e.g. from Social Services	Adult males with normal IQ who commit non-contact Internet related sex offences
Selection criteria	Sexual offence	Sexual offence	Sexual offence	Internet sexual offence
Exclusion criteria	General exclusion criteria apply Some discretion to take total denial of any incident	General exclusion criteria apply plus total denial of any incident	General exclusion criteria apply plus total denial of any incident	High deviancy or contact offence

Table 6.4 (continued)

Programme	C-SOGP (West Midlands)	TV-SOGP (Thames Valley Programme)	N-SOGP (Northumbria Programme)	I-SOGP
Programme sessions	50-hour induction module Low risk/low deviancy men then go directly to 50-hour relapse prevention programme High risk/high deviancy men undertake full programme (250 hours) consisting of 6 modules Men can join in at the beginning of each module Men who have successfully completed prison SOTP can go directly to the relapse prevention programme	10 consecutive day Foundation Block Victim Empathy block twice weekly sessions of 2 hours (60 hours) Life Skills block twice weekly sessions of 2 hours (40 hours) Relapse prevention weekly sessions of 2 hours (44 hours) Partners programme weekly sessions of 2 hours (36 hours) High risk/high deviancy men do whole programme, low risk, low deviancy men can miss out Life Skills block Men who have successfully completed prison SOTP can go directly to the relapse prevention programme	Offenders assessed as high risk/deviance attend Core Programme (144 hours min.) followed by Relapse Prevention (36 hours), giving total programme length of 180 hours Low risk/deviance offenders will normally complete individual work with offender manager followed by relapse prevention module Offenders released from prison will follow similar route depending on assessment Sessions are normally run for 3.5 hours during the day, but can be run as two evening sessions a week The Core Programme is a rolling group and the Relapse Prevention module is closed	70 hours focusing on Internet-related offending Includes core module to challenge offending, impulse control and emotional management skills, victim empathy and awareness Motivational work and relapse prevention tailored to Internet offences
Pre-programme	Flexible sessions included in case manager's pack	Flexible sessions included in case manager's pack	Flexible sessions included in case manager's pack	Flexible package including material specifically developed for this group

Programme	C-SOGP (West Midlands)	TV-SOGP (Thames Valley Programme)	N-SOGP (Northumbria Programme)	I-SOGP
Post-programme	Monitoring risk factors and reinforcement included in case manager's pack	Monitoring risk factors and reinforcement included in case manager's pack	Monitoring risk factors and reinforcement included in case manager's pack	Monitoring risk factors and reinforcement included in case manager's pack
Core programme duration (excl. pre and post sessions)	Either 100 hours or 260 hours depending on risk/deviancy profile	Either 196 hours for high risk/high deviancy men or 156 hours for low risk/low deviancy men	Either 180 hours for high risk/deviance or 36 hours plus individual work for low risk/deviance	70 hours
Group size	Maximum 10, optimum 8	Maximum 10, optimum 8	Maximum 10, optimum 8	1-2-1 or group up to 10, optimum 8

SOGP – Sex Offender Group Programme
SOTP – Sex Offender Treatment Programme

disabilities and something about severe or acute psychiatric or mental disorder. None of these factors are supposed to be an absolute barrier to attendance and each case should be considered on its merits but it does seem to be fairly common practice to operate blanket exclusions even where difficulties are not severe, especially when places are limited.

Once offenders with mental health problems are accepted onto a programme there can be difficulties around compliance. A concern raised by the Revolving Doors Agency (Kutchinsky 2006) is that where MDOs are assessed as having multiple needs, courts may try to simultaneously address a range of needs within a community order, making it increasingly difficult for individuals to keep the numerous conditions of their order. OBPs can be very demanding for offenders – there are strict criteria for attendance and offenders are expected to arrive promptly and attend all sessions. Sessions missed must be made up by attending individual 'catch-ups'. Most OBPs involve assignments or practice to be completed between sessions. For people who are vulnerable or are leading a chaotic lifestyle the demands may be too great and they may well drop out of treatment leading to breech. The average attrition rate from programmes is around a third of starters, rising to over 50 per cent for some programmes targeted at substance misuse. In general it is offenders who present the multiple needs and those diagnosed with personality disorders who are more likely not to complete programmes.

Assuming offenders with mental health problems are referred to OBPs, another barrier to them benefiting from the programmes may well be the responsivity demonstrated by facilitators in making the sessions relevant to individual participants. When accredited programmes were first introduced emphasis was placed on maintaining treatment integrity. Staff were trained and encouraged to stick to the programme and not to deviate or introduce new content. This had the unintended consequence of limiting facilitators, willingness to respond to the diversity of the group despite the clear messages from the research evidence on the importance of responsivity to the needs and learning style of the group (Andrews and Bonta 1998). As facilitators have become more experienced with the material and through revision of training, it has been possible to reposition the concept of responsivity at the heart of programme delivery. However, most programme staff, especially those recruited directly to this role, will not have received much training or have much knowledge of mental health problems and this could limit their ability to deliver responsively to this group with the consequence that some MDOs will disengage and gain little benefit from the programme.

These barriers are not insurmountable and steps can be taken to improve access to OBPs for MDOs. Indeed this is required under equality legislation and is the subject of an internal NOMS review. Much could be achieved through education and training. PSR authors need to change their mindset to see the possible exclusion criteria as issues to be overcome rather than a complete bar to attendance. Facilitators need a greater awareness of mental health issues and how to respond to these. Other areas which might be improved are the support given to offenders attending programmes. Surveys of programme staff and offenders have shown that one of the key factors in ensuring that offenders complete programmes is the support they receive from their offender manager before, during and after the intervention. Positive input by offender managers and the involvement of other agencies dealing with MDOs could greatly assist here.

Table 6.5 Probation offending behaviour programmes – substance misuse programmes

Programme	ASRO	Drink impaired drivers	OSAP	PRISM
Description of programme	Modular group work programme. Aims to teach offenders the skills required to reduce or stop substance misuse	Programme combines cognitive behavioural work and education. Aims to reduce the risk of future drink-related driving offences	Modular group work programme. Aims to teach offenders the skills required to reduce or stop substance misuse	Programme for one-to-one delivery. Aims to teach offenders the skills required to reduce or stop substance misuse
Target group	Male and female medium to high risk (OGRS 50–100 or OASys scores above 64), but where an individual is scoring 75 (OASys 100) and over the sentence plan should identify additional work to reflect the higher risk	Male and female offenders who commit a drink drive-related offence. Priority to be given to those whose offence has an aggravating factor, e.g. high reading, accident or repeat offence	Male and female medium to high risk of offending (OGRS 50–100 or OASys scores above 64), but where an individual is scoring 75 (OASys 100) and over the sentence plan should identify additional work to reflect the higher risk	Male and female medium to high risk of offending (OGRS 50–100 or OASys score above 64), but where an individual is scoring 75 (OASys over 100) and over the sentence plan should identify additional work to reflect the higher risk
Selection criteria	Offending is related to substance misuse. Offenders sufficiently stable and motivated	Drink drive-related offence and relevant skills or knowledge deficits	Offending is related to substance misuse. Offenders sufficiently stable and motivated	Offending is related to substance misuse. Offenders sufficiently stable and motivated
Exclusion criteria	As for general offending behaviour programmes	As for other general offending behaviour programmes. Not suitable for problem drinkers until they are stabilised	As for general offending behaviour programmes	As for general offending behaviour programmes

Table 6.5 (continued)

Programme	ASRO	Drink impaired drivers	OSAP	PRISM
Exclusion criteria		The programme is unlikely to be suitable for offenders with more than four previous convictions who are likely to have a wider range of criminogenic needs which cannot be met by this programme		
Programme sessions	20 sessions of 2.5 hours Programme has modular structure Sessions can be delivered from one to three times per week	14 sessions of 2.5 hours to be delivered weekly	26 sessions of 2.5 hours Programme has modular structure Can be delivered from one to three times per week	20 sessions from between 45 and 120 minutes Sessions recommended twice weekly for sessions 1–4, weekly for sessions 5–12, and two-weekly or weekly for sessions 13–20
Pre-programme	Written guidance re preparatory work for case managers	4 pre-programme sessions	3 pre-programme sessions	Written guidance re-preparatory work for case managers
Core programme duration (excl. pre and post sessions)	10–20 weeks (50 hours in total)	14 weeks (35 hours in total)	12–24 weeks	10–20 sessions (50 hours in total)

Programme	ASRO	Drink impaired drivers	OSAP	PRISM
Post-programme	None specified, other than action post programme report	Written guidance by offender managers which details further optional work in 6 areas depending upon the progress which the offender made in the core programme	Minimum 4 maintenance sessions with case worker	None specified, other than action post programme report
Group size	8–12	Minimum 4, maximum 12, optimum 10	8–12	Not applicable

ASRO – Addressing Substanc Misuse Related Offending (alcohol and drugs programme)
OSAP – Offender Substance Abuse Programme
PRISM – Programme for Individual Substance Misusers

The Probation Service is also exploring the option of providing cognitive behavioural programmes specifically tailored to some offenders with mental health problems. For example, an adapted sex offender programme for those with cognitive impairment and learning disabilities is currently being piloted in the community. The one-to-one programme has the advantage that it can be far more flexible than the group programme – it covers the same ground but is designed so that material can be personalised and adapted to suit a sole participant. Sessions can be rescheduled more easily and the programme can proceed at a pace which is suited to the individual. There are of course drawbacks to using one-to-one, not least the higher costs incurred and the tendency for programme drift unless facilitators are very disciplined.

Conclusions

MDOs serving community sentences present a challenge for the Probation Service. Staff do not always have sufficient training or knowledge or feel competent to assess and supervise them. Consequently they tend rely on referral to other agencies when this is possible. MHTRs provide a mechanism the courts can use to ensure mental health services input is coordinated with probation work, but the number of requirements made remains extremely small because of the need to identify suitable provision prior to sentencing. Where a mental disorder coexists with a substance misuse dependency a DRR can sometimes provide a better route into treatment for both conditions. Many MDOs, especially those with mild psychological dysfunction or personality disorder, can benefit from accredited programmes but it is only recently that some of the issues around selection and responsivity have begun to be addressed.

The shared responsibility for MDOs between probation staff and CFMHTs (community forensic mental health teams) can be problematic. Of course, there are many examples of excellent practice where probation staff work in close liaison with local CFMHTs and the CPA works well, but this is dependent on local arrangements and varies greatly from one probation area to another. There is always a danger that MDOs serving community sentences will slip through the gap with neither group being prepared to take the initiative or make them a priority. There is undoubtedly a major piece of work to be done in here in improving these links. This would require a lead from NOMS at the centre and should include a review of the information-sharing protocols and communications and the current training arrangements for probation staff, especially for offender managers.

The changes which are occurring in the criminal justice system are likely to impact on MDOs in several ways. The introduction of 'end-to-end' offender management should bring many advantages in terms of consistency and continuity, although in some probation areas this has meant that a specialist function which dealt with certain groups of offenders may be lost.

The NOMS commissioning and contestability agenda will mean that more interventions will be delivered by other organisations. Some probation areas already contract provision of more specialist programmes such as sex offender treatment to partnership organisations. At present these bodies deliver exactly the same programmes as probation staff. But in future they might be encouraged to bring forward new innovative interventions. This is an opportunity for the voluntary and commercial sectors to develop new treatment approaches for groups like MDOs where gaps in provision exist. Of course the more organisations involved the greater the need for good communication and the increased importance of the offender managers' coordinating function. At present supervision of offenders serving community sentences is always the role of the Probation Service. But changes to the legal framework due to become law this year will allow NOMS to allocate the work elsewhere. One can surmise this could happen in two ways. One option would be that a whole probation area and its caseload would be contested and given to an alternative provider. The other option would be that services to certain groups of offenders, including offender management, might be handed over to another specialist provider. One could speculate that the mentally disordered offender might benefit from such an approach.

Selected further reading

Andrews, D.A. and Bonta, J. (2003) *The Psychology of Criminal Conduct*, 3rd edn. Cincinati, OH: Anderson provides the most encompassing account of the application of social learning theory to criminal behaviour and interventions to reduce recidivism. Mentally disordered offenders are dealt with specifically in Chapter 9 on 'exceptional offenders'.

Canton, R. (2005) 'Risk assessment and compliance in probation and mental health practice', in B. Littlechild and D. Fearns (eds), *Mental Disorder and Crimnal Justice*. Lyme Regis: Russell House, pp. 139–55, gives an account of probation practice with mentally disordered offenders in terms of assessment, coercion and compliance.

Mackenzie, D.L. (2006) *What Works in Corrections: Reducing the Criminal Activities of Offenders and Delinquents*. Cambridge: Cambridge University Press, is the most recent resumé of the international evidence on what interventions are likely to be successful with groups of offenders, though it is not specific to mentally disordered offenders.

The National Probation Directorate (2005) *OASys Information: Briefing 26*. London Home Office, provides an overview of OASys (the Offender Assessment System), including aims, components of the assessment and implementation.

References

Andrews, D.A. and Bonta, J. (1998) *The Psychology of Criminal Conduct*, 2nd edn. Cincinati, OH: Anderson.

Bandura, A. (1999) *Self-Efficacy: The Exercise of Control*. New York: W. H. Freeman.

Farrall, S. (2004) *Rethinking What Works With Offenders: Probation, Social Context and Desistance from Crime*. Cullompton: Willan.

Harper, G. and Chitty, C. (2004) *The Impact of Corrections on Re-offending: A Review of What Works*, Home Office Research Study No. 291. London: Home Office.

Home Office (2001) *Offender Assessment System Manual*. London: Home Office.

Home Office (2004) *Reducing Crime: Changing Lives*. London: Home Office.

Home Office (2006) *5th Annual Report of the Correctional Services Accreditation Panel*. London: Home Office.

Howard, P., Clark, D.A. and Garnham, N. (2006) *An Evaluation of the Offender Assessment System in Three Pilots 1999–2001*. London: Home Office.

Kutchinsky, N. (2006) *Development Programme for Extending Offender Healthcare Support.* London: Revolving Door Agency.

McGuire, J. (1996) *Cognitive-Behavioural Approaches: An Introductory Course on Theory and Research.* Liverpool: University of Liverpool.

Nacro (2005) *Working with Mentally Disordered Offenders.* London: Nacro Publications.

National Probation Directorate (2002) *NPD Briefing Number 2: Introduction to OASys 2005–2006.* London: Home Office.

National Probation Directorate (2005) *The Probation Bench Handbook: A Guide to the Work of the National Probation Service for Judges,* 1st edn. London: Home Office.

National Probation Directorate, Interventions Unit (2006) *Annual Report for Accredited Programmes 2005–2006.* London: Home Office.

NOMS (National Offender Management System) (2005) *The NOMS Offender Management Model.* London: Home Office.

NOMS (National Offender Management System) (2006) *The Correctional Services Accreditation Panel Report 2005–2006.* London: Home Office.

RDS NOMS (2005) *Offender Management Caseload Statistics 2004.* London: Home Office.

Roberts, S. (1999) *A Learning Development Programme for Work with Mentally Disordered Offenders.* London: Home Office, Probation Unit.

Underdown, A. and Ellis, T. (1998) *Strategies for Effective Offender Supervision: Report of the HIMP What Works Project.* London: Home Office.

Chapter 7

Mental healthcare in prisons

Jane Senior and Jenny Shaw

Introduction

In this chapter we seek to explore issues related to the interface between the criminal justice system and mental health services in relation to the management of prisoners with mental health problems.

Recurrent media headlines highlight the 'scandal' of large numbers of mentally ill people languishing in our jails, without venturing to offer any further critique into the complexities of the problem. And yet the problem is complex. Only a minority of prisoners are experiencing severe and enduring mental illness which warrants detention under mental health legislation; the vast majority of those making up the stark headline statistics have common mental health problems, frequently compounded by substance abuse. These people have always been, and will continue to remain, in our prison system.

This chapter examines the history of healthcare services in prisons, criticisms of healthcare provision past and present, the recent policy initiatives to improve services through a partnership between HM Prison Service and the NHS in England and Wales, and two matters of particular – current – concern in prisons: the management of suicide and self-harm, and the transfer of those who are seriously ill into health and care services outside prisons.

A history of mental health provision in prisons

> The transformation of prisoners into patients has never done more than relieve jails of the obviously disordered. They have always had to cope with the residual problem of the prisoner whose degree of disorder, though marked enough to interfere with discipline and communication, is not sufficient to satisfy the psychiatric criteria of the day. (Walker and McCabe 1973: 38)

The role of prisons as part of the overall system of care and custody for mentally disordered offenders is far from new. In 1777, social reformer John Howard highlighted neglect, moral decay and idleness pervading prison institutions in *The State of the Prisons in England and Wales*. He noted that children, petty thieves and the mentally disordered were housed with the most experienced offenders, the mentally disordered often unintentionally providing a source of amusement for other prisoners.

During the nineteenth century efforts were made to remove some of the most obviously mentally disordered from prison, notably through the opening in 1861 of a separate wing for criminal lunatics at the Bethlem Hospital, London, followed in 1863 by the opening of Broadmoor criminal lunatic asylum. However, this initiative did not herald an end to the detention of the mentally disordered in prison as, contemporaneously, special provision was being created within the prison system for those who were not to be transferred to hospital. Accordingly, in 1864, the population of mentally disordered prisoners housed at Dartmoor prison was transferred to Millbank penitentiary in London and, in 1897, Parkhurst prison was used to house prisoners assessed as 'unfit for ordinary penal discipline because of some mental instability other than insanity' (cited in Gunn 1985: 127). In 1895, the Report of the Gladstone Committee recommended that all prison medical officers be experienced in the subject of lunacy, thus acknowledging the likelihood of the mentally disordered remaining a significant presence in prisons. The role of hospital officer was instigated in 1899, fulfilled by men drawn from the ranks of the discipline officers and provided with a brief general health care training (Bluglass 1990).

For the mentally disordered who remained in prison in the eighteenth and nineteenth centuries, 'treatment', such as it existed, was rudimentary. With moralistic overtones, links were made between disease and prior 'riotous living, sexual indulgence and intemperance' whereby prisoners 'were susceptible to disease because they were susceptible to vice' (Ignatieff 1978). Prison surgeons were called upon to expose those prisoners suspected of feigning madness, thus clearly linking medical expertise with the disciplinary structures of the prison. Sim (1990) cites examples of the use of medically sanctioned cold baths, straitjackets, electric shocks, prisoners being strapped to their beds or being housed in dark, underground cells, in order to test for true insanity or to curb the behaviour of refractory prisoners. A particular prison surgeon was defended by *The Lancet* in 1855 as a 'gentleman of integrity, of Christian feelings [and] of high professional attainments' in a report of an incident whereby the surgeon had sanctioned the use of a straitjacket for a violent prisoner, accompanied by putting salt into the prisoner's mouth in order to tranquillise him. In an echo of modern-day public and media criticism of apparently liberal regimes in prisons, medical officers at Millbank penitentiary approved further reductions in prisoners' already meagre diets in the 1820s in response to external criticism that the prison regime was not punitive enough; the result was an outbreak of scurvy and the death of 31 prisoners (Sim 1990).

In 1865 the Prisons Act was passed, legislating that each jail should have an infirmary wherein prisoners were to be examined by a medical officer at least once a week. The Act also required all new prisoners to be examined upon admission. Around this time magistrates increasingly used the practice of remanding people into custody to allow for an examination of their mental state in relation to offences with which they were charged.

As the industrialisation of the country continued throughout the nineteenth century, prison medicine expanded in this rapidly changing world to incorporate scientific explanations for criminality. Darwinian theories were employed to label criminals as atavistic throwbacks to an early stage of evolution. Criminologists, notably Cesare Lombroso, popularised this notion by describing a type of 'born criminal' in terms of their physical features, including large jaws, low sloping foreheads, high cheekbones, flattened noses and long arms (Lombroso 1876). Reflecting this, the prison medical officer adopted a position as expert in terms of criminality and immoral behaviour. An editorial in the *British Medical Journal* in 1888 declared:

> Our highest privilege is to extend our ministrations to the mind as well as the body, to offer to erring brothers the hand of help, to bring back to honesty and wisdom those who through misfortune and weakness have fallen far away from both (cited in Sim 1990: 54)

In the early part of the twentieth century, prison doctors were publishing widely on the subject of criminality and its links with mental illness, as well as giving court evidence in individual cases. Despite this there is no evidence that treatment for mental illness in prisons was becoming more sophisticated over time; in 1904 the Medical Inspector of Prisons described interventions as falling broadly into three categories: plenty of attendants, mechanical restraint or chemical restraint (Sim 1990). Even in prisoner accounts of their experiences, the position of the medical officer was made clear. In an account published in 1936, a former prisoner noted that:

> The medical officer is the most important, powerful and the best paid official in the gaol. His word overrules everybody (cited in Sim *op cit:* 68)

The Prison Medical Service instigated the role of Director of Prison Medical Services in 1946 and, when the NHS was launched in 1948, the Prison Medical Service remained a separate entity, with prison medical and hospital officers remaining employees of the Prison Service. Hospital officers were frequently, at this time, men with nursing experience from the armed forces; in women's prisons fully trained state registered nurses were employed. Specialised psychiatric units were established in some prisons, for example in Holloway, Wakefield and Wormwood Scrubs. In the latter establishment electric shock treatment was used in the 1940s in conjunction with psychotherapy, thus expanding the 'treatment' available for mentally disturbed prisoners. The 1948 Criminal Justice Act abolished corporal punishment and hard labour in prisons, replacing them with prison regimes intended toward the constructive training and rehabilitation of prisoners. Medical opinion on offenders was frequently required both pre and post sentence, increasing both the workload and influence of prison medical officers (Sim 1990). The introduction of chlorpromazine in the 1950s, although not the first drug ever to be prescribed to prisoners, was accompanied by accusations that, rather than the drugs being used to reduce symptoms of mental illness, they were instead being used widely to control behaviours likely to disrupt the prison regime (e.g. Owen and Sim 1984).

In the latter part of the twentieth century, the Prison Medical Service was the subject of much public criticism concerning not only the alleged inappropriate use of psychotropic medication on refractory prisoners, but also with regard to the numbers of suicides in prisons and overall poor standards of care (e.g. Ralli 1994). Due to its separation from the wider NHS, the service was criticised for being 'invisible' and lacking any external accountability (Smith 1984). These criticisms led to a number of high-profile publications recommending that the Prison Service hand over responsibility for healthcare in prison establishments to the wider NHS.

In 1996, prison healthcare was criticised by the then Chief Inspector of Prisons in a report entitled *Patient or Prisoner?* as an inadequate yet expensive service, provided by insufficiently trained staff who were isolated from new clinical developments (Her Majesty's Chief Inspector of Prisons 1996). The report highlighted a lack of continuity of care between prison and community, along with inadequate provision to meet the needs of specific groups of prisoners, e.g. women and young people. The Chief Inspector recommended that the NHS should assume overall national responsibility for the delivery of healthcare in prisons, with local NHS trusts charged with ensuring that adequate provision for prison healthcare was made when allocating resources to ensure equivalence, acknowledging that:

> ... prisoners are entitled to the same level of health care as that provided in society at large. Those who are sick, addicted, mentally ill or disabled should be treated ... to the same standards demanded within the National Health Service. (Her Majesty's Chief Inspector of Prisons 1996: 5)

In the year following the publication of *Patient or Prisoner?* the Health Advisory Committee (HAC) for the Prison Service published a report on the specific topic of the provision of mental healthcare in prisons, discussing equivalence in terms of the specific implications for mentally disordered prisoners (Health Advisory Committee 1997).

Acknowledging that the prison population was in fact a subset of the population as a whole, the document argued that health policies and priorities set for the wider community should apply equally in prisons. Specific to mental health, this meant that there was an expectation that in prisons, as in the community, the majority of mental health problems could be dealt with at the primary care level and that, when required, specialist mental healthcare should be delivered by multidisciplinary community mental health teams in contrast to the traditional over-reliance on input from visiting forensic psychiatrists. The Committee found that mental health services in prisons were generally delivered in an uncoordinated way and lacked the breadth of services in the community, notably in terms of multidisciplinary team input, throughcare and flexibility of response. Transfer to specialist NHS care for those prisoners most seriously ill was noted as problematic, as was ensuring aftercare upon discharge from either prison or hospital.

In two studies detailing audit findings from statutory inspections of the quality of healthcare in prisons, further evidence of an apparent inability on the part of prisons to provide adequate standards of healthcare was detailed (Reed and Lyne 1997, 2000). Both studies appraised the quality and scope of care provided, measured against a set of standards drawn up by HM Inspectorate of Prisons.

The 1997 study focused on overall standards of care provided in 19 prisons. Inspection involved visits to all healthcare areas, discussions with staff, review of local policies and consultation with prisoner-patients. The authors reported a wide variety in the quality of care provided across sites, but some problems were common to numerous prisons. None of the prisons inspected had conducted the required health needs assessment exercise, in nine of the 19 establishments, primary care services were being provided by inadequately trained doctors and none of the prisons provided a full multidisciplinary mental health team.

The authors concluded that prison healthcare was variable in scope and quality; services of the highest quality were likely to be those which had been contracted out to a local NHS general practice, with the lead GP acting as managing medical officer. Again, it was recommended that the provision of healthcare be disaggregated from the custodial mechanisms of the prison and passed over to the Department of Health.

The study published in 2000 focused specifically on the quality of inpatient care in prisons for the mentally ill. The data for the study were gathered across 13 prisons of different types, including local prisons, high-security establishments and a young offenders' institution. Using the same methodology as the earlier study, again a set of common problems was outlined.

Most inpatient units were criticised in relation to their unsatisfactory physical environment, for example poor design hampering observation and unacceptable levels of cleanliness. With regard to staffing, no unit was overseen by a doctor who had completed specialist psychiatric training and just under a quarter (24 per cent) of nursing staff or healthcare officers were mental health trained nurses. Medical and nursing staff constituted the whole of the mental health team in the majority of prisons, with little input from other disciplines.

With regard to the patients' experiences of receiving care in these inpatient units, if it is accepted that:

> ... if a prisoner with schizophrenia is to be treated according to the standards which might apply in the health service, this will involve not just medication but attention to the person's entire environment of social relationships, occupational activities and day care, with the aim of helping the individual maintain the best possible level of functioning and independence, (Grounds 1990: 39)

then the inpatient units in the study under discussion failed to address the majority of these concerns. HM Prison Service's own healthcare standards at the time stated that prisoners should, when well enough, spend 12 hours out of cell and take part in at least six hours of structured activity daily. None of the prisons inspected reached this standard. On average, prisoners were found to be out of cell for around 3.5 hours a day with long, unbroken periods of confinement at night. Limited therapeutic or diversional activities were provided, usually consisting of the opportunity to read, play pool, clean or watch television. Further concerns were expressed about the use of seclusion in prison inpatient areas, high incidences of which appeared to correlate closely to periods of restricted staff availability. For those patients awaiting transfer to NHS facilities, waits for suitable placements were protracted.

Policy change – partnership with the NHS

A formal shift in policy direction was announced in 1999 when the Prison Service and NHS Executive published *The Future Organisation of Prison Health Care*. The document was the report of the organisations' joint Working Group's deliberations upon the issues raised by *Patient or Prisoner?* (Her Majesty's Chief Inspector of Prisons 1996). The specific purpose of the document was to address the need to develop practical proposals for change to realise the much heralded aim of achieving equivalence of standards across the NHS and the Prison Service in England and Wales.

The document revisited the problems associated with providing healthcare in prison settings that had been identified repeatedly in earlier studies, accepting that, historically, healthcare in prisons was

> ... often reactive rather than proactive, over-medicalised and only excep-
> tionally based on systematic health needs assessment ... [with an]
> over-reliance on healthcare beds within prisons and a medicalised model
> of care. (Her Majesty's Prison Service/NHS Executive 1999: 8–9)

The document embraced a public health agenda, acknowledging that:

> ... prisons should not ... make it more likely that people become ill ... good
> healthcare and health promotion in prisons should help enable individuals
> to function to their maximum potential on release, which may assist in
> reducing offending. It should also reduce morbidity in a high risk sector of
> the general public with medium and long-term reductions in demands on
> the NHS. (Her Majesty's Prison Service/NHS Executive 1999: 5)

The delivery of mental healthcare was noted as an area of particular need with regard to future development. The report acknowledged that current models of mental healthcare delivery in prisons were underdeveloped, health screening was not adequately identifying those likely to be mentally disordered and care planning was unsatisfactory. In agreement with the earlier HAC report, it was reiterated that, in the wider community, most mental health problems were treated within primary care services supported, where necessary, by community mental health teams, a development largely missing from prison settings. The proposed agenda for change on these points included the need to develop services in prisons in line with NHS policy and national service frameworks, to develop ways to better identify mental disorder at reception, to develop the use of the Care Programme Approach and to adopt a community care service model, encouraging mental health outreach work on the residential wings.

The document suggested the need for HM Prison Service and the NHS to adopt 'a more collaborative and coordinated approach ... supported by a recog-nised and formal duty of partnership', acknowledging that, in reality, neither the NHS nor the Prison Service could satisfactorily provide healthcare for pris-oners without the cooperation and involvement of the other organisation. By adopting a partnership approach, the Working Group fell short of the recom-mendations of the earlier reports which overwhelmingly supported the move of prison healthcare services to be wholly within the NHS. However, the Working Group argued that, at least in the short to medium term, a partnership arrangement was in fact a more pragmatic approach to effecting change, acting as a protective factor for the healthcare interests of prisoners. In spite of the criticism heaped upon prison healthcare services historically, the separation from the NHS in terms of priority setting and budgetary control had meant that this politically unattractive population had not had to compete for limited healthcare resources with other populations which may be judged to be more publicly acceptable. The NHS has perhaps historically underfinanced other unattractive healthcare specialities, for example general and forensic mental health services, and it may be reasonable to assume that healthcare services for prisoners would have suffered a similar fate if left to fend for themselves among the competing priorities of the NHS without the support of their 'parent organisation', the Prison Service.

These developmental needs for mental health care were later encompassed in a document outlining a cross-organisational approach to mental health policy in prisons, *Changing the Outlook* (Department of Health/HM Prison Service 2001). In line with the requirement to develop a joint NHS and Prison Service policy, this document set out the proposed improvements in prison mental health care within the context of broader NHS mental health policy, the National Service Framework (NSF) for Mental Health (Department of Health 1999a).

Changing the Outlook emphasised a number of initiatives required for prison-based mental health services. It was noted that there was a need to improve health promotion in prisons through improved staff training, peer support schemes and an emphasis on developing 'healthy prisons'. Primary care mental health services were noted as limited in scope, with work needed so that it was an effective resource which could diagnose subclinical mental health issues such as stress-related problems that could then be addressed by wider agencies within the prison, treat common mental health problems, facilitate referral to specialist mental health services when clinically indicated and be engaged in chronic disease management, for example for those prisoners with psychosis or depression.

With regard to specialist mental health services, *Changing the Outlook* outlined the need to develop wing-based services, utilising a community mental health team model, supporting prisoners with more serious mental health problems on normal residential wings. This adoption of community-based healthcare would be augmented by developments in daycare services as an alternative to inpatient care, coupled with a refocusing of inpatient care so that it was used only for those with the most serious mental health problems. The adoption of the Care Programme Approach (CPA) (Department of Health 1999b) should be used to support improved throughcare and discharge planning to ensure that prisoners were discharged with appropriate aftercare plans. A target was set that, within three years, every prisoner discharged with a serious mental illness would have a community care coordinator and care plan in place. For those prisoners whose mental health problems were severe enough to necessitate transfer to hospital, the need for effective liaison with NHS services to minimise delays, ensure efficient communication to aid risk management and ensure adequate levels of aftercare if the person is readmitted to prison are also noted.

How many mentally disordered people are in prison?

Historically, the main research focus into mental health problems in prisons has taken the form of prevalence studies, all confirming overall high levels of mental disorder. The largest and most scientifically robust study conducted to date into the prevalence of mental disorder was undertaken by Singleton and colleagues (1998) on behalf of the Department of Health. The study used the same methods as had been used in a large-scale study of psychiatric morbidity in the general population (Meltzer *et al.* 1995), was conducted in all 131 prisons in England and Wales open at the time of the survey and included 3,142 prisoners. Standardised instruments for neurotic disorder, alcohol dependence and personality disorder were administered along with a set of questions used in previous private household studies to detect drug dependence and self-harm ideation. A sub-sample of participants was seen by clinicians to undergo a full clinical interview to detect psychosis and personality disorder. Data from the interviews were used to identify factors predictive of psychosis in all participants to allow a calculation of 'probable psychosis' across the whole sample.

From the clinical interviews, prevalence rates for any functional psychosis in the past year ranged from 7 per cent in the male, sentenced population, to 14 per cent in the female population. Using the algorithm devised to calculate 'probable psychosis' in the whole population, it was suggested that 21 per cent of the female remand population would probably have a psychotic disorder, as would 10 per cent of the sentenced female population, 9 per cent of male remands and 4 per cent of male sentenced prisoners. Similarly, using the clinical interview data, 78 per cent of the male remand population and 50 per cent of the female population were diagnosed as having a personality disorder. The most prevalent was antisocial personality disorder, identified in 63 per cent of male remand prisoners and 31 per cent of female prisoners. This high rate of antisocial personality disorder is perhaps not overly surprising in light of the fact that one of the diagnostic criteria to be fulfilled is criminality (American Psychiatric Association 1994).

With regard to neuroses, all types of prisoners returned high rates of symptoms such as sleep problems and worry. In common with findings from general household studies, women prisoners were significantly more likely to be positive for neurotic disorder. Additionally, for both men and women, rates of neuroses in remand prisoners were higher than the sentenced population. Seventeen per cent of male remand prisoners and 21 per cent of female remand prisoners were diagnosed as experiencing a current depressive episode, while 12 per cent of male remand and 23 per cent of female remand prisoners reported having experienced suicidal thoughts in the past week.

Assessing the treatment needs of mentally disordered prisoners

A period in prison should present an opportunity to detect, diagnose, and treat mental illness in a population often hard to engage with NHS services ... ensuring continuity of care and reducing the risk of reoffending on release. (Reed and Lyne 2000: 1033)

The prevalence study outlined above adopted very broad criteria to define mental disorder, including considerations of alcohol and drug abuse and personality disorder. Due to the breadth of the inclusion criteria employed, closer examination of overall prevalence rates is required to usefully inform policy decisions regarding the provision of treatment services. Only 5 per cent of male and 4 per cent of female remand prisoners were not diagnosed with any form of mental disorder at all, but many prisoners were diagnosed only with disorders where motivation for change and a desire for treatment are vital, for example personality disorder and substance misuse, so not all such prisoners would make demands for treatment. Similarly, disorders such as depressive episodes were not detailed in terms of severity, thus no judgment could be made as to how many prisoners would require intervention from services provided within prison settings at either primary or secondary care level, or how many would require transfer to NHS facilities.

Previous studies which tackled the question of what proportion of mentally disordered prisoners could safely and appropriately receive treatment within prisons and how many were likely to require transfer to hospital settings have produced broadly similar findings. Gunn et al. (1991) concluded that around 10 per cent of their study sample of young offenders and adult men would require care within prison and a further 3 per cent required transfer to an NHS hospital, the majority of those having being diagnosed with psychosis. Only 12 per cent of those who were psychotic were judged as suitable for care within the prison system. Similarly, in a study of male remand prisoners, Brooke et al. (1996) found that 17 per cent of their sample could be treated by prison health services, but that 9 per cent required transfer to the NHS, again dominated by those with psychosis, with nearly half of those prisoner-patients (47 per cent) being clinically suited to treatment in local, rather than secure, hospital units.

Birmingham et al. (1996) surveyed men remanded into custody at HMP Durham, and concluded that 3 per cent required immediate transfer to psychiatric hospital, including 70 per cent of those with psychosis. A further 20 per cent of the overall sample was judged to require outpatient referral to psychiatric services while remaining in prison and 6 per cent required assessment and management as an inpatient in the prison healthcare centre. Interestingly, the study team compared the results of their findings of the presence of mental disorder with the results of routine prison screening. This exercise found that only 23 per cent of prisoners identified by the research team as mentally disordered were also identified by routine prison screening. Routine screening identified a further 18 men as mentally disordered where no evidence for this was found by the researchers. Of especial concern was the fact that routine screening identified only 25 per cent of those who were acutely psychotic as having a mental disorder. These findings are important as health screening on reception provides the best, and frequently the only, timely opportunity to successfully channel mentally disordered prisoners into appropriate treatment services. If this system is ineffective, prisoners' health may quickly deteriorate further, increasing risks of vulnerability and, potentially, suicide.

A recent study assessed mental health treatment needs for adult male prisoners using referral and service provision criteria operating in mental health services in the wider community (Senior 2005). Primary care and secondary care mental health staff working in a variety of community, inpatient and specialist settings outwith prisons were asked to delineate the appropriate client groups for their services, in terms of diagnosis, symptom severity, risk factors and social and lifestyle debility caused by mental health problems. There were high levels of consensus across staff groups about the type of client each different service could effectively engage with. This consensus was distilled into a clinical protocol to assign prisoner-patients with mental health problems to an appropriate level of service.

The clinical protocol was employed as part of a large-scale mental health prevalence study conducted in a large adult male prison. This study concluded that, at any one time, 27 per cent of the population of the prison would require intervention from some form of health service for mental health problems. Fifty-five per cent of these people would need intervention from the equivalent of primary care services, 35 per cent from services equivalent to a community mental health team and 10 per cent more intense intervention, for example inpatient admission or consideration for transfer to external hospital care.

The finding from this study, that the majority of mental health needs in prison could be safely and appropriately treated at primary care level, correlates with results from the general community where it is estimated that 80 per cent of mental health issues are treated without recourse to secondary services (Department of Health/HM Prison Service 2001). In the prison-based study, the percentage of problems that could be dealt with at primary care level was 55 per cent, a lower percentage than in the general community probably due to the increased overall prevalence rates of mental illness. The fact that most services can be delivered at primary care level is acknowledged by governmental policy initiatives around mental health in prisons (Department of Health/HM Prison Service 2001); however, a policy imperative urging the development of high-quality, effective primary care is perhaps not explicitly supported in terms of the work programme agenda which states that the main vehicle for the delivery of improvements in prison mental health care will be the development of secondary care level in-reach services.

To be considered alongside these studies which quantify the likely requirements for mental health services in prisons based on assessments of actual clinical need is additional research which indicates that, *in vivo*, custom and practice unique to prison populations results in differing patterns of service usage. Marshall *et al.* (2001) audited the use of healthcare services in prisons, illustrating that both male and female prisoners consulted doctors at a rate three times more frequently than a demographically equivalent community population, and that prisoners' consultations with other healthcare workers, defined as nursing staff or healthcare officers, were at a rate 70 times greater than that at which the general community consults nurses, described as the nearest equivalent comparison. Similarly, admissions to prison inpatient settings were ten times higher for male prisoners than the general population's admission rate to inpatient care in a community sample, rising to 17 times higher for female prisoners.

Recent service provision initiatives in prison mental health services

As noted above, a number of studies have shown that only a minority of mentally ill prisoners are likely to require transfer from prison to hospital. Reflecting this, the service developments outlined in *Changing the Outlook* concentrate on improvements in prison-based service for two main groups of prisoners, those with severe and enduring mental illnesses who will not be transferred to hospital under prevailing mental health legislation and those with common mental health problems who require robust primary care services. The service improvement outlined in *Changing the Outlook* which has been most widely adopted is that of mental health in-reach.

At their inception, prison-based mental health in-reach teams were charged with developing as multidisciplinary teams, offering prisoners with severe and enduring mental illness specialised mental healthcare, similar to that provided to the wider population by community mental health teams. It was envisaged that this level of service would be required for 5,000 prisoners at any one time. Although prisoners with the most severe forms of mental illness were to be the early focus of the in-reach teams, it was expected that their introduction would eventually benefit prisoners with all types and severity of mental health problems, through a more caring and health oriented ethos being developed within prison establishments via a process of osmosis. In-reach teams' core tasks are to offer assessments of mental health needs and risk, facilitate treatment using the Care Programme Approach and, where indicated, effect referral to other services, for example primary care or substance misuse agencies. Additionally, they are to ensure that robust throughcare and discharge planning arrangements ensure that prisoner-patients are in contact with appropriate support services upon release.

During the early stages of development, the in-reach programme adopted a collaborative approach, whereby regional networks were established to share good practice examples and to support areas of change and modernisation aimed at improving clinical standards and identifying training needs. Key aims for the collaborative included improvements to care planning and throughcare arrangements for mentally disordered prisoners, improvements in transfers between prisons and NHS units for mentally disordered prisoners, and the identification and fulfilment of training needs (Department of Health/HM Prison Service 2002).

The first three years of the in-reach programme were supported by targeted funding from the Department of Health, judged sufficient to fund 300 extra mental health professionals to work in prisons. This number has been achieved (Duggan *et al.* 2005). However, emerging research evidence paints a slightly more complex picture. Early data from the evaluation of the prison in-reach project show that, at least initially, many of the supposedly 300 'additional' staff employed as part of the in-reach initiative have in fact been redeployed from the existing prison healthcare team (Shaw, in preparation). The effect of this is twofold. Firstly, redeployment of staff from one area of service to another within the same establishment does not increase the number of staff providing care. In this case it involves, at least temporarily, reducing the number of staff in already hard pressed prison primary care services. Secondly, staff who have worked within the existing prison healthcare team prior to working as part of in-reach bring with them service models and practices informed by prison-based practices rather than community-based experience, thus potentially hampering or delaying the development of services that replicate those in the wider community.

An evaluation of the in-reach collaborative approach has been published, concluding that it had not been wholly successful, with a majority of regional networks failing to make the intended contribution to the work programme (Brooker *et al.* 2005). The evaluation did, however, conclude that, overall, in-reach itself was to be judged a success, notwithstanding some problems surrounding the implementation and operation of individual services. Through questionnaires, individual interviews and focus group meetings with key informants, data were collected from which common themes emerged about the implementation and early days of the in-reach programme.

At interview, in-reach staff spoke of sometimes struggling to imbue a caring, health-oriented approach into a prison where the underlying ethos is one of discipline and punishment. Team members spoke of problems matching the prison's expectation of their service with their own operational criteria, reporting conflict around which group of patients were core clients for in-reach and which should be treated by other services. Some in-reach teams had adopted a wider operational remit than that of concentrating solely on severe and enduring mental illness, for example having routine involvement conducting assessments following incidents of self-harm. Strikingly, these were the teams most likely to report feeling overloaded by demands placed upon them, experiencing the negative effects of working with limited resources in what seemed a bottomless pit of need for mental health intervention. If in-reach services become just an assessment service, they will not be in a position to provide in-depth interventions to their supposed target group, those with serious mental illness, and will become just an additional ineffective tier of an already dysfunctional system. This example of 'mission creep' has been recently highlighted by researchers and clinicians alike as a clear danger threatening the overall effectiveness of the in-reach initiative, whereby in-reach, to thrive, should properly be regarded as one part of a comprehensive prison-based mental health service rather than the sole source of available care (Steel *et al.* 2007). This same team is due to publish the results of their three-year evaluation of the clinical efficacy of in-reach at the end of 2007 (Shaw *et al.* in preparation).

The second area of development highlighted by *Changing the Outlook* is that of primary care mental health services for prisoners. As noted above, the document acknowledges that, as in the community, the majority of prisoners' mental health problems should be safely and appropriately treatable within primary care services. However, since the publication of the document, less emphasis has been placed upon the development of primary care mental health provision than in-reach services. The Sainsbury Centre for Mental Health published a review of mental health services in London's prisons, noting that primary care mental health services were less developed than in-reach services and varied across establishments, with primary care practitioners who lacked the skills and confidence to work with prisoners, resulting in significant unmet needs in the care for common mental health problems, including depression, anxiety, emotional distress and adjustment problems (Sainsbury Centre for Mental Health 2006).

The provision of adequate mental health triage at primary care level is essential if prison in-reach services are not to find themselves on a treadmill of conducting initial assessments on all prisoners with any type or severity of mental health problem, as referral to in-reach becomes the new default option, replacing the historical practices of referring to forensic psychiatrists or admitting to the healthcare in-patient unit. Investment of time and resources into the development of clinically effective ways of delivering primary mental health care in prisons remains a pressing priority.

Suicide and self-harm – matters of particular concern

While not unique to custodial settings, the issue of self-harm and suicidal behaviour has developed a specific resonance in prison populations. This is due to both the prevalence of such behaviour and the unique management problems created in prisons as a result.

A random, large-scale, national sample of prisoners found that 7 per cent of male and 16 per cent of women sentenced prisoners reported having attempted to commit suicide in the year before interview. These figures rose to 15 per cent and 27 per cent respectively in the remand population. Similarly, 7 per cent of male and 10 per cent of female sentenced prisoners reported having committed at least one act of self-harm in their current prison term (Singleton *et al.* 1998). In a related setting, acts of self-harm cause one-third of all deaths in police custody (Blaauw *et al.* 1997; Leigh *et al.* 1998).

Despite active efforts within HM Prison Service the number of self-inflicted deaths in prison doubled between 1982 and 1998. This rise is larger than would be expected from the increase in the prisoner population in the corresponding period alone (Her Majesty's Chief Inspector of Prisons 1999). A further study found that, in the years 1999–2000, 172 serving prisoners committed suicide, nearly a third of these deaths occurring within one week of initial reception into custody, indicating the need for prison health and social services to be able to immediately mobilise effective assessment, support and preventative strategies as soon as an at-risk individual enters prison (Shaw *et al.* 2003).

In addition to studies of prison suicide by health researchers, the issue has also been discussed in criminology literature (e.g. Liebling 1993; Liebling and Ward 1993; Medlicott 2001), by statutory bodies such as HM Chief Inspector of Prisons (e.g. Tumim 1990) and by charitable organisations concerned with offender welfare (e.g. Howard League for Penal Reform 2001). Much of this work focused on offering an explanation for, and strategies to reduce, the apparently disproportionately high rate of self-inflicted deaths in prisons when compared with the general population. A recent Home Office study calculated death rates for male prisoners, offenders under community supervision and a demographically matched general population sample. Whereas the general population sample had a death rate from suicide/self-inflicted injury of 13.6 per 100,000 in 1996, the rate for prisoners was calculated as 101.9 per 100,000, with a similar level for the community offender group (Sattar 2001).

One explanation offered for this exacerbated risk is that prisons house large numbers of those who possess factors commonly associated with suicide in the general population, for example being male (McClure 1987); divorced, widowed or single (Walmsley *et al.* 1992); being unemployed (Dooley 1990; Platt and Kreitman 1984; Lewis and Sloggett 1998); having a history of deliberate self-harm (Lloyd 1990; Liebling 1992; Barraclough and Hughes 1987); having a psychiatric disorder, especially depression, schizophrenia and substance misuse (Barraclough *et al.* 1974; Singleton *et al.* 1998; Williams and Morgan 1994). Taking the factor of the high concentration of those who are opiate-dependent alone it is speculated that UK prisons, compared to their general community equivalent, have a duty of care to effectively three times as many individuals as they actually hold (Gore 1999).

Analysis of data collected during the Office for National Statistics (ONS) study of psychiatric morbidity in prisoners found eight factors which set apart those who had attempted suicide in the year before the study from those who had not. The factors were:

- age, with suicide attempters being younger;
- ethnicity, attempters being predominantly white;
- psychotic disorder, with a prevalence of between a quarter and a half of those who attempted contrasted with about 5 per cent of all prisoners;
- severe neurotic disorder, which, although common in the general prison population was more so in those who attempted suicide;
- psychotropic medication, suicide attempters being two to three times more likely to be currently receiving medication;
- time spent as a psychiatric in-patient, with male attempters up to three times, and female attempters up to six times, more likely to have previously received inpatient care;
- poor social support, with attempters having very small circles of support; and
- adverse life events such as violence or sexual abuse, attempters more likely to have experienced a variety of stressful life events, both recent and over their lifetime (Singleton *et al.* 1998).

All this evidence of exacerbated risk of suicide and self-harm in prison populations led one writer to conclude that:

> ... arguably, the prison population is carefully selected to be at risk of suicide. (Liebling 1995: 181)

Criminological theories of suicide in prisons highlight the environment itself as a likely contributory factor to increased suicide risks. Dooley (1990) reviewed all prison suicides between 1972 and 1987, finding that factors related to the prison environment were regarded as significant motivators for suicide in 40 per cent of cases. Other studies found that differences between suicide attempters and non-attempters in prison related to perceptions of their custody experiences rather than factors such as any personal or demographic differences. Suicide attempters were more likely to perceive themselves as 'worse off' than their peers in custody in terms of their experiences of opportunities for work, education and recreation. They generally tended to spend longer in their cell and found it harder to cope with imprisonment or to relieve boredom (Liebling 1993, 1995, 1998).

In 2002 the Department of Health published the *National Suicide Prevention Strategy for England*, outlining ways the government proposed to achieve a reduction of at least 20 per cent in the death rate from suicide by 2010 (Department of Health 2002). The strategy outlines six goals to achieve this aim, and these goals are inclusive of prison populations.

Goal one specifically addressed the need to reduce suicides in key high-risk groups. Prisoners are detailed as a high-risk group and the document provided key details of HM Prison Service's then current suicide prevention strategy, colloquially known as the F2052SH system. The main elements of this strategy were improved assessment, care planning and risk management, improved health screening on reception into prison to detect mental disorder, substance abuse and vulnerability to suicide/self harm and the development of peer support schemes. However, the adequacy and effectiveness of the F2052SH policy was questioned as the UK prison suicide rate continued to rise following its inception. Specifically, the system was described as a 'paper exercise' focusing on the recording of bland, ineffective care plans (Royal College of Psychiatrists 2002; Her Majesty's Chief Inspector of Prisons 1999). A new system of care and management has since been established for prisoners at risk of suicide and self-harm. ACCT (Assessment, Care in Custody and Teamwork) builds on the multidisciplinary approach to suicide prevention engendered in the F2052SH, and includes more robust initial assessments of risks and needs. New roles of assessor and case manager have been introduced, promoting accountability in ensuring the delivery of care plan elements. Furthermore, there is an emphasis on personalised care, fully engaging with prisoners in their own care, consistent involvement of appropriate staff, and quality interactions between staff and prisoners. The majority of prisons have now begun using ACCT and time will tell what effect the changes will have on the level of suicide and self-harm in prison.

As well as detailing prisoners as a priority group with regard to suicide reduction, other high-risk groups relevant to prison populations are detailed: those with current/recent contact with mental health services, those in the year following self-harm and young men. Each of these groups are represented in prison populations, increasing the relevance and applicability of the National Suicide Strategy to prisons in a way that much health-related policy before the introduction of formal NHS/HM Prison Service partnership arrangements perhaps did not. This in turn supports the view that, while the problem of suicide and self-harm may have particular resonance in prison populations, the provision of care within prisons should retain the aim of achieving equivalence with the wider community.

Transfers from prison under mental health legislation

A further pressing issue in relation to mentally disordered prisoners is the need to affect timely and appropriate transfer from prison to hospital for those whose degree of disorder is of such severity as to require specialist treatment in a non-custodial environment. Legislation exists under the current Mental Health Act

1983 allowing for prisoners to be transferred to hospital for a period of assessment or treatment, following which they may either be returned to prison to complete their sentence or be discharged directly into the community with a statutory requirement that they receive aftercare. Restrictions upon discharge from hospital can be put in place to ensure that prisoners are returned to prison if they recover so that they are not set at liberty substantially earlier than if they stayed in prison. Restriction orders can also ensure that the Home Secretary, through the Home Office Mental Health Unit, remains involved in the management of discharged prisoner-patients, allowing their recall to hospital if they become unwell or if they fail to abide by conditions placed upon their discharge, for example compliance with follow-up care.

The number of transfers from prison has risen over recent decades. In 2003, there were a total of 721 restricted patients admitted to hospital from prison (Ly and Howard 2004), although studies of prisoners' mental health treatment needs suggest that a large number of prisoners remain in prison when transfer to hospital is clinically indicated (e.g. Gunn et al. 1991; Brooke et al. 1996). In real terms, Birmingham (2003) estimated that around 2,000 of the male prison population required transfer to a psychiatric hospital. With regard to women prisoners, Rutherford and Taylor (2004) showed that, overall, fewer than 2 per cent of newly received prisoners in a large women's prison were transferred over a 12-month period; however, the number actually requiring transfer may have been between 4 per cent of the sentenced population and 13 per cent of those on remand.

Clinical research has documented difficulties in facilitating transfer to hospital. The main issue surrounding transfers concerns delays in the process, which have been found in a series of studies (e.g. Blaauw et al. 2000). Mackay and Machin (2000) showed that a decision on transfer took 50 or more days in a fifth of cases. Robertson et al. (1994) found an average delay between being accepted for an NHS bed and admission of five to six weeks – a length of time that the authors note would never occur if a patient were admitted from the community; this view is supported by the *Changing the Outlook* document (Department of Health/HM Prison Service 2001), which stated that, in some cases, prisoners had less priority than those in the community regarding admission to mental health units.

A number of factors for transfer delays have been suggested, most frequently a shortage of suitable psychiatric beds, a common and long-standing difficulty (Home Office and the Department of Health and Social Security 1975; Birmingham 1999). Among the non-completed transfers reported by Mackay and Machin (2000), over 44 per cent were due to lack of suitable bed availability. Other factors include disagreements over the required level of security (Mackay and Machin 2000), disputes over the catchment area of local hospitals (Robertson et al. 1994), reluctance of hospitals to admit prisoner-patients (Blaauw et al. 2000) and disagreements over the severity of illness (Dell et al. 1993). Studies of individual differences revealed longer waiting times for prisoners requiring high-security placements (Isherwood and Parrott 2002) and those diagnosed with personality disorder (Rutherford and Taylor 2004). Adverse effects of delays in transfer have been documented, including suicide and self-harm among waiting prisoners (Rutherford and Taylor 2004) and location in 'strip cell conditions' (Coid et al. 2003).

The final version of the Mental Health Act 2007 passed by Parliament for Royal Assent in July 2007, has not altered the procedures for transferring prisoners to psychiatric hospitals, nor does it allow for compulsory treatment in prison due to the limits the prison environment places upon holistic care and as an acknowledgement that an ability to treat prisoners against their will while they remain in custody would further reduce the impetus to transfer them to a more appropriate hospital setting. With specific reference to the difficulties noted above in securing timely and appropriate hospital placements for prisoners with personality disorders, an evaluation of the impact of wider NHS policy regarding the inclusion of those with personality disorder into mainstream services will be required to determine any positive change in practice (Department of Health 2003).

The Department of Health undertook a two-year programme of work, ending April 2007, aimed at reducing the delays encountered in transferring prisoners to hospital. The programme was supported by procedural guidelines published by the Department of Health and a Prison Service Instruction published by the Prison Service (Department of Health 2005; HM Prison Service 2006). Best practice guidelines were issued which gave help on a number of potential problems throughout the transfer process. Emphasis was placed on the need for the early identification of prisoners who may require treatment in hospital, with the premise that no delays in accessing suitable treatment should be caused by virtue of being in prison. Clear guidelines were given to allow prison staff to determine the appropriate responsible primary care trust which needed to provide local facilities or fund an out-of-area placement. Possible problems at each stage of the process were identified, and advice regarding the resolution of these problems highlighted. Consideration was given to actions required where a prisoner's condition was of especial concern, for example in cases of the refusal of food and drink. Joint work on the development of risk and urgency guidelines was undertaken between the Department of Health and the Royal College of Psychiatrists to be piloted and evaluated in a small number of prisons with the highest numbers of transfers (Fowler, personal communication). An independent evaluation of the work programme will report at the end of 2007.

Conclusion

From ignominious beginnings, prison health services are currently subject to investment in terms of a number of active work programmes focused on clinical improvement across all types of healthcare services. In terms of mental healthcare, work is underway to improve specialist mental health services through the development of secondary care in-reach teams, improved multidisciplinary management of self-harm and suicide risk, and improved rates of transfer to hospital for those most severely ill.

Further development in terms of the range and scope of mental health services is still required, notably progress on the provision of robust, accessible primary care services to provide help to the majority of prisoner-patients who experience common mental health problems which do not require specialist input. The success of developments such as in-reach is dependent on them being part of a whole, functional system of care, rather than as a 'bolt-on' to a system essentially unchanged from earlier, dysfunctional times.

The partnership between the National Health Service and HM Prison Service in England and Wales is vital to ensure the success of current and future development work, with a need for the differing cultures of both institutions to find middle ground so that the work of each is complementary, not antagonistic, to the aims of the other. Additionally, this current renaissance of interest in prison healthcare needs professional and service-user 'champions' to help it survive the slings and arrows of ever-changing political agendas and 'righteous' media indignation, so common in public debates about how our society deals with those at its fringes.

Selected further reading

Arguably the most comprehensive history of prison healthcare services, and their influence upon the development of the wider prison system, is Sim, J. (1990) *Medical Power in Prisons*. Buckingham: Open University Press.

Discipline and Punish: The Birth of the Prison by M. Foucault (Penguin, 1991) charts the development of the prison in western societies over 500 years of social and economic change.

Prison Readings edited by Jewkes, Y. and Johnston, H. (2007, Willan) provides a comprehensive, critical introduction to the main debates and dilemmas associated with prisons and imprisonment, bringing together a selection of the key readings on the subject, along with a comprehensive introduction and commentary written by the editors.

The *Handbook on Prisons* (Jewkes, Y. (ed.) Willan, 2007) is a comprehensive book exploring a wide range of historical and contemporary issues relating to prisons, imprisonment and prison management.

Among the reports worth consulting is HM Prison Service/NHS Executive (1999) *The Future Organisation of Prison Health Care* (Department of Health). This is the policy document outlining the details of the current HMPS/NHS clinical improvement partnership in England and Wales.

References

American Psychiatric Association (1994) *DSM-IV-TR: Diagnostic and Statistical Manual of Mental Disorders*. Arlington: American Psychiatric Press.

Barraclough, B. and Hughes, J. (1987) *Suicide: Clinical and Epidemiological studies*. London: Croom Helm.

Barraclough, B., Bunch, J., Nelson, B. and Sainsbury, P. (1974) 'A hundred cases of suicide: clinical aspects'. *British Journal of Psychiatry*, 125: 355–373.

Birmingham, L. (1999) 'Between prison and the community: the "revolving door psychiatric patient" of the nineties'. *British Journal of Psychiatry*, 174: 378–9.

Birmingham, L. (2003) 'The mental health of prisoners'. *Advances in Psychiatric Treatment*, 9: 191–99.

Birmingham, L., Mason, D. and Grubin, D (1996) 'Prevalence of mental disorder in remand prisoners: consecutive case study'. *British Medical Journal* 313: 1521–1524.

Blaauw, E., Kerkhof, R. and Vermunt, R. (1997) 'Suicide and other deaths in police custody', *Suicide and Life-Threatening Behaviour*, 27 (2): 153–163.

Blaauw, E., Roesch, R. and Kerkhof, A. (2000) 'Mental disorders in European prison systems: arrangements for mentally disordered prisoners in the prison systems of 13 European countries'. *International Journal of Law and Psychiatry* 23: 649–63.

Bluglass, R. (1990) 'Prisons and the Prison Medical Service', In Bluglass, R. and Bowden, P. (eds.) (1990) *Principles and Practice of Forensic Psychiatry.* London: Churchill Livingstone.

Brooke, D., Taylor, C., Gunn, J. and Maden, A. (1996) 'Point prevalence of mental disorder in unconvicted male prisoners in England and Wales'. *British Medical Journal* 313: 1524–1527.

Brooker, C., Ricketts, T., Lemme, F., Dent-Brown, K. and Hibbert, C. (2005) *An Evaluation of the Prison In-Reach Collaborative.* Report for the NHS National Programme on Forensic Mental Health Research and Development. School of Health and Related Research, University of Sheffield.

Coid, J., Petruckvitch, A., Bebbington, P., Jenkins, R., Brugha, T., Lewis, G., Farrell, M. and Singleton, N. (2003) 'Psychiatric morbidity in prisoners and solitary cellular confinement. II. Special ("strip") cells'. *Journal of Forensic Psychiatry and Psychology*, 14: 320–40.

Dell, S., Robertson, G., James, K. and Grounds, A. (1993) 'Remands and psychiatric assessments in Holloway Prison. I. The psychotic population'. *British Journal of Psychiatry*, 163: 634–40.

Department of Health (1999a) *National Service Framework for Mental Health: Modern Standards and Service Models.* London: Department of Health.

Department of Health (1999b) *Effective Care Coordination in Mental Health Services: Modernising the Care Programme Approach.* London: Department of Health.

Department of Health (1999c) *Report of the Expert Committee: Review of the Mental Health Act 1983.* London: Department of Health.

Department of Health (2002) *National Suicide Prevention Strategy for England.* London: Department of Health.

Department of Health (2003) *Personality Disorder: No Longer a Diagnosis of Exclusion.* London: Department of Health

Department of Health (2005) *Procedure for the Transfer of Prisoners to and from Hospital Under Sections 47 and 48 of the 'Mental Health Act (1983).* London: Department of Health.

Department of Health/HM Prison Service (2001) *Changing the Outlook. A Strategy for Developing and Modernising Mental Health Services in Prisons.* London: Department of Health.

Department of Health/HM Prison Service (2002) *Mental Health In-reach Collaborative Launch Document.* London: Department of Health.

Dooley, E (1990) 'Prison suicide in England and Wales 1972–1987'. *British Journal of Psychiatry* 156: 40–45.

Duggan, S., Bradshaw, R., Mitchell, D., Coffey, M. and Rogers P. (2005). 'Modernising prison mental health'. *Professional Nurse*, 20 (8), 20–22.

Foucault, M. (1991) *Discipline and Punish: the Birth of the Prison.* Harmondsworth: Penguin.

Gore, S.M. (1999) 'Suicide in prisons: reflection of the communities served, or exacerbated risk?' *British Journal of Psychiatry*, 175 (7): 50–5.

Grounds, A. (1990) 'The mentally disordered in prison'. *Prison Service Journal* Winter 1990/91: 29–40.

Gunn, J. (1985) 'Psychiatry and the Prison Medical Service'. In Gostin, L. (ed) *Secure Provision.* London: Tavistock.

Gunn, J., Maden, A. and Swinton, M. (1991) 'Treatment needs of prisoners with psychiatric disorders'. *British Medical Journal* 303: 338–341.

Health Advisory Committee for the Prison Service (1997) The *Provision of Mental Health Care in Prisons.* London: HM Prison Service.

Her Majesty's Chief Inspector of Prisons for England and Wales (1996) *Patient or Prisoner? A New Strategy for Health Care in Prisons.* London: Home Office.

Her Majesty's Chief Inspector of Prisons for England and Wales (1999) *Suicide is Everyone's Concern: a Thematic Review.* London: Home Office.

HM Prison Service (2006) *Prison Service Instruction 03/2006 Transfer of Prisoners to and from Hospital under Sections 47 and 48 of the Mental Health Act 1983*. London: HMPS.

Her Majesty's Prison Service/NHS Executive (1999) *The Future Organisation of Prison Health Care*. London: Department of Health.

Home Office and the Department of Health and Social Security (1975) *Report of the Committee on Mentally Disordered Offenders (The Butler Report)* (Cmnd 6244). London: HMSO.

House of Lords and House of Commons (2005) *Joint Committee on the Draft Mental Health Bill – First Report*. London: UK Parliament.

Howard League for Penal Reform (2001) Suicide *and Self-harm Prevention: Repetitive Self-harm Among Women and Girls in Prison*. London: The Howard League.

Ignatieff, M. (1978) *A Just Measure of Pain*. London: Macmillan.

Isherwood, S. and Parrott, J. (2002) 'Audit of transfers under the Mental Health Act from prison – the impact of organisational change'. *Psychiatric Bulletin*, 26: 368–70.

Jewkes, Y. (ed.) (2007) *The Handbook on Prisons*. Cullompton: Willan Publishing.

Jewkes, Y. and Johnston, H. (eds.) (2007) *Prison Readings*. Cullompton: Willan Publishing.

Leigh, A., Johnson, G. and Ingram, A. (1998) 'Deaths in police custody: learning the lessons'. *Police Research Series Paper 26*. London: Home Office.

Lewis, G. and Sloggett, A. (1998) 'Suicide, deprivation, and unemployment: record linkage study'. *British Medical Journal* 317: 1283–1286.

Liebling, A. (1992*) Suicides in Prison*. London: Routledge.

Liebling, A. (1993) *Suicide Attempts and Self-injury in Male Prisons: A Report Commissioned by the Home Office Research and Planning Unit for the Prison Service*. London: Home Office.

Liebling, A. (1995) 'Vulnerability and prison suicide'. *British Journal of Criminology* 35 (2): 173–187.

Liebling, A. (ed.) (1998) *Deaths of Offenders: The Hidden Side of Justice*. Winchester: Waterside Press.

Liebling, A. and Ward, T. (1993) *Deaths in Custody: International Perspectives*. London: Whiting & Birch.

Lloyd, C. (1990) 'Suicide and self-injury in prison: A literature review'. *Home Office Research Study No. 115*. London: Home Office.

Lombroso, C. (1876) *L'Uomo Delinquente*. Milan: Hoepli.

Ly, L. and Howard, D. (2004) 'Statistics of mentally disordered offenders 2003: England and Wales'. *Home Office Statistical Bulletin* 16/04. London: Home Office, Research Development and Statistics Directorate.

Mackay, R.D. and Machin, D. (2000) 'The operation of Section 48 of the Mental Health Act 1983'. *British Journal of Criminology*, 40: 727–45.

Marshall, T., Simpson, S. and Stevens, A. (2001) 'Use of health care services by prison inmates: comparisons with the community'. *Journal of Epidemiology and Community Health* 55: 364–365.

McClure, G.M. (1987) 'Suicide in England and Wales, 1975–1984'. *British Journal of Psychiatry* 150: 309–314.

Medlicott, D. (2001) *Surviving the Prison Place: Narratives of Suicidal Prisoners*. Aldershot: Ashgate Publishing.

Meltzer, H., Gill, B. and Petticrew, M. (1995) *The Prevalence of Psychiatric Morbidity among Adults aged 16–64, Living in Private Households in Great Britain*. London: Office of National Statistics.

Owen, T. and Sim, J. (1984) 'Drugs, discipline and prison medicine: the case of George Wilkinson'. In Scraton, P. and Gordon, P. *Causes for Concern: British Criminal Justice on Trial?* Harmondsworth: Penguin.

Platt, S. and Kreitman, N. (1984) 'Unemployment and parasuicide in Edinburgh 1968–1982'. *British Medical Journal* 289: 1029–1032.

Ralli, R. (1994) 'Health care in prisons'. In Player, E. and Jenkins, M. (eds) (1994) *Prisons after Woolf: Reform through Riot.* London: Routledge.

Reed, J. and Lyne, M. (1997) 'The quality of health care in prison: results of a year's programme of semi structured inspections'. *British Medical Journal* 315: 1420–1424.

Reed, J. and Lyne, M. (2000) 'Inpatient care of mentally ill people in prison: results of a year's programme of semi structured inspections'. *British Medical Journal* 320: 1031–1034.

Robertson, G., Dell, S., James, K. and Grounds, A. (1994) 'Psychotic men remanded in custody to Brixton Prison'. *British Journal of Psychiatry*, 164: 55–61.

Royal College of Psychiatrists (2002) *Suicide in Prisons* (CR99). London: Royal College of Psychiatrists.

Rutherford, H. and Taylor, P.J. (2004) 'The transfer of women offenders with mental disorder from prison to hospital'. *Journal of Forensic Psychiatry and Psychology*, 15: 108–23.

Sainsbury Centre for Mental Health (2006) *Policy Paper 5: London's Prison Mental Health Services: A Review.* London: Sainsbury Centre for Mental Health.

Sattar, G (2001) *Home Office Research Study 231: Rates and Causes of Death among Prisoners and Offenders under Community Supervision.* London: Home Office.

Senior, J. (2005) *The Development of Prison Mental Health Services based on a Community Mental Health Model.* PhD Thesis: The University of Manchester.

Shaw, J., Appleby, L. and Baker, D. (2003) *Safer Prisons A National Study of Prison Suicides 1999–2000 by the National Confidential Inquiry into Suicides and Homicides by People with Mental Illness.* London: Department of Health.

Shaw, J., Thornicroft, G., Birmingham, L., Brooker, C., Senior, J., Lathlean, J., Kendall, K. and Saul, C. (in preparation) 'Report of the national evaluation of prison mental health in-reach services'.

Sim, J (1990) *Medical Power in Prisons.* Milton Keynes: Open University Press.

Singleton, N., Meltzer, H., Gatward, R., Coid, J. and Deasy, D. (1998) *Survey of Psychiatric Morbidity among Prisoners in England and Wales.* London: Department of Health.

Smith, R. (1984) *Prison Health Care.* London: British Medical Association.

Steel, J., Thornicroft, G., Birmingham, L., Brooker, C., Mills, A., Harty, M. and Shaw, J, (2007) 'Prison mental health inreach services'. *British Journal of Psychiatry* 190: 373–374.

Tumim, S. (1990) *Report of a Review by Her Majesty's Chief Inspector of Prisons for England and Wales of Suicide and Self-Harm in Prison Service Establishments in England and Wales.* London : Stationery Office Books.

Walker, N. and McCabe, S. (1973) *Crime and Insanity in England.* (Volume 2). Edinburgh: Edinburgh University Press.

Walmsley, R., Howard, L., and White, S (1992) *The National Prison Survey 1991: Main Findings.* London: HMSO.

Williams, R. and Morgan, H.G. (eds.) (1994) *Suicide Prevention: The Challenge Confronted – A Manual of Guidance for the Purchasers and Providers of Mental Health Care (NHS Health Advisory Service Thematic Reviews.* London: Stationery Office Books.

Chapter 8

Release procedures and forensic mental health

Pete Snowden and Bettadapura Ashim

Introduction

'Discharge' from a forensic hospital or 'release' from a penal setting is an important step in the care pathway of mentally disordered offenders; in this paper we will describe the procedures and issues that are relevant in the discharge or release of such offenders.

The legislation on sentencing and release procedures from a custodial setting has been significantly overhauled with the introduction of the Criminal Justice Act (CJA) 2003 (Home Office 2003). We will describe the old legislation relevant to sentencing and release procedures prior to the CJA 2003 and the changes since the CJA 2003 that are relevant to sentencing and release.

We will set out the:

- procedures in place for the 'discharge' or 'transfer' of patients from a hospital setting;
- procedures in place for the transfer of patients from prison to hospital and from hospital to prison;
- role of various agencies involved in the release or transfer of mentally disordered offenders including the Mental Health Review Tribunals, the Parole Board, the multi-agency public protection arrangements (MAPPA) and the Probation Service;
- difficulties in the relationship between the Home Office and the responsible medical officer in the release of restricted mentally disordered offenders.
- risk assessment tools which influence release procedures.

We will describe in some detail the functions of the MAPPA and highlight the ethical issues relevant to the disclosure of information to the MAPPA. Finally, we will attempt to illustrate some of the ethical and practical issues relevant to discharge from forensic settings in two case examples.

Current policy

It is useful to consider the sentencing provisions that were in place prior to the Criminal Justice Act 2003 as a majority of *current* prisoners are subject to the provisions of the 'old' legislation as laid down in the General Statutory Sentencing framework and in the Criminal Justice Act 1991 (Home Office 1991) and amended by the Powers of Criminal Courts (Sentencing) Act 2000 (PCC – the Act 2000).

The description of the 'recent' changes to sentencing introduced by the Criminal Justice Act 2003 (Home Office 2003) will give the reader a flavour of the current release procedures that will begin to take effect as prisoners who are sentenced under the new legislation approach release.

The old legislation on sentencing and release

The government's White Paper *Crime, Justice and Protecting the Public* (Home Office 1990) set out for the first time that the role of the courts was to impose proportionate and consistent sentences while providing a general framework for sentence decision-making. The basic principle was that the severity of the sentence imposed should reflect the seriousness of the offence committed. The Criminal Justice Act 1991 set out the release provisions for offenders based on the length of the sentence (see Table 8.1).

Table 8.1 Release provisions under the 'old legislation': the Criminal Justice Act 1991 (HMSO 1991)

Sentences under 12 months	Automatic unconditional release (AUR) at the halfway point in the sentence; no licence* requirements; however, 'at risk'** for the second half of the sentence.
Sentences from 12 months to 4 years	Automatic conditional release (ACR) at the halfway point; 'on licence* to the three-quarters point; 'at risk'** for the final quarter of the sentence.
Sentences of more years than 4	Discretionary conditional release (DCR) at any point between the halfway and two-thirds point of the sentence if the Parole Board considers the risk of release acceptable. On licence* from the point of release to the three-quarters point; 'at risk'** for the rest of the sentence.

* *On licence* means that the offender is under the supervision of the Probation Service and will have to comply with various requirements, which may include living or working only where approved, attending offending behaviour programmes or being tagged. If the licence is breached the offender is liable to be recalled back into custody until the expiry of the licence.

** *At risk* means there are no positive obligations on the offender but if he commits a further offence the unexpired part of the sentence can be added to any new one for the final quarter.

The current legislation on sentencing and release: the Criminal Justice Act 2003

Changes to the legislation on sentencing

John Halliday's sentencing review (Home Office 2001) and a government White Paper *Justice for All* (2002) set out proposals for a wide ranging programme of reform of the criminal justice system. These recommendations along with several reports by the Law Commission formed the basis of the new sentencing framework introduced through the Criminal Justice Act 2003 (CJA – the Act 2003).

This piece of legislation introduced wide changes to sentencing principles and the sentencing powers of the courts. It also introduced significant changes to the law relating to police powers, bail, disclosure, allocation of criminal offences, prosecution appeals, double jeopardy, hearsay, evidence of bad character and release on licence. For example, the new law permits offences to be tried by a judge sitting alone without a jury in cases of serious or complex fraud, or where there is a danger of jury-tampering. It also expands the circumstances in which defendants can be tried twice for the same offence (double jeopardy) when 'new and compelling evidence' is introduced. Some of the other significant changes relevant to release procedures introduced by the new legislation are summarised in Table 8.2.

Changes to the legislation on release

Most prisoners (with the exception of those offenders who are deemed to pose a significant risk of serious harm to others) are 'automatically' released under licence half way through their sentence. They will be subject to licence conditions and supervision by Probation Services. They may be subject to 'recall' into prison if they breach their licence conditions.

Dangerous offenders and the introduction of public protection sentences

The new provisions for 'imprisonment for public protection' (IPP) and 'extended sentence for public protection' (EPP) for dangerous offenders have a significant impact on sentencing and release procedures.

Life sentence or imprisonment for public protection
Section 225 of the CJA 2003 introduces new legislation for 'dangerous offenders' allowing for indeterminate sentences after a single offence.

If a person aged 18 or over is convicted of a serious offence (see Box 8.1) which can receive a life sentence, the court considers that the seriousness of the particular offence justifies a life sentence and the court is of the opinion that there is a significant risk to members of the public of serious harm (see Box 8.1) by the commission of further specified offences then the court must impose a life sentence.

If a person aged 18 or over is convicted of a serious offence but it is not one which can receive a life sentence, or if the court considers the seriousness of the offence does not justify the imposition of a life sentence but nevertheless the court is of the opinion that there is a significant risk to members of the public of serious harm by the commission of further specified offences, then the court must impose a sentence of imprisonment for public protection.

Box 8.1 Serious offences and serious harm

- A 'serious offence' is committed when an offender commits an offence from a list of 'specified' offences and the offender can receive a sentence of life imprisonment or a sentence of more than ten years in respect of that offence. Part 1 of Schedule 16 of the Criminal Justice Act 2003 contains a list of 65 violent offences and 153 sexual offences which are the 'specified' offences.
- 'Serious harm' includes death or serious personal injury, whether physical or psychological.

Table 8.2 Important changes to the current legislation on sentencing and release: the Criminal Justice Act 2003

Changes	Comment
Defining the purposes of sentencing	For the first time the purposes and principles of sentencing were introduced into statute. These are: • to protect the public; • to punish the offender; • to reduce and deter crime; • to reform and rehabilitate the offender.
Defining 'statutory' aggravating factors	The seriousness of an offence (and thus the severity of the sentence) should be increased if the offender demonstrates 'hostility based upon the victim's race, religion, sexual orientation or disability'.
Increased sentence related to the use of firearms	A minimum sentence of five years and a maximum sentence of ten years for possession or distribution of prohibited weapons or ammunition.
Establishment of a Sentencing Guidelines Council	To produce comprehensive guidelines for the full range of criminal offences to 'help remove uncertainty and disparity in sentencing and give representatives of the police, prisons, probation and victims a voice in sentencing for the first time'.
Changes to the provisions for community sentences	Replaces the various community sentences with a single community order with a range of requirements. The courts can now choose from 12 different requirements such as unpaid work, alcohol treatment, drug treatment, curfew requirements and supervision requirements etc. to make up a community order.
Changes to suspended sentence orders	The new suspended sentence orders require an offender to fulfil several requirements in the community (as with a community sentence). If an offender breaches the requirements it is presumed that the suspended prison sentence is activated.
Changes to sentences over 12 months	Apart from 'dangerous' offenders, for those serving more than 12 months release is automatic at the halfway point but offenders remain on licence until the end of their sentence.
Introduction of 'custody plus' (for sentences less than 12 months)	Custodial sentences of less than 12 months will consist of a short custodial period of between two weeks and three months followed by a licence period of at least six months. The court can set requirements similar to those available under a community order for the licence period.

The imprisonment for public protection (IPP) sentence provides for release to be at a date determined by the Parole Board after the minimum term set by the court. After release, the offender remains on licence for life. It is possible at the ten-year point to request release from the licence. Under the new legislation, the court must specify a custodial period and an extension period during which the offender will remain on licence. From the halfway point of the custodial period the offender may be released if the Parole Board determines it is safe to do so, but release will not be automatic until the end of the custodial period. After release, the offender remains on licence for the unexpired term of the original sentence (if any) and for the extension period which was set by the court when imposing sentence. It is important to remember that the imprisonment for public protection sentences can be imposed in circumstances such as a less serious robbery – even by a child – and is encouraged by the statutory criteria in the case of repeat offending by an adult.

Extended sentence for public protection
Section 227 of the Criminal Justice Act introduces the extended sentence for public protection (EPP), which offers a long period of supervision on release from custody. It applies when someone is convicted of a specified offence (Part 1 of Schedule 16 of the Criminal Justice Act 2003 contains a list of 65 violent offences and 153 sexual offences which are the 'specified' offences) other than a serious offence (i.e. cannot receive a sentence of ten years) and the court considers that there is a significant risk to members of the public of serious harm. The court must impose an extended sentence of imprisonment which is equal to the aggregate of the appropriate custodial term and a further period, 'the extension period', for which the offender is to be subject to a licence. The extension period must not exceed five years in the case of a specified violent offence and eight years in the case of a specified sexual offence. The term of an extended sentence of imprisonment must not exceed the maximum term permitted for the offence. This section applies to people convicted of relatively minor offences where it is considered that there is a risk of something more serious occurring in future.

Changes to mental health treatment requirements linked to community orders and suspended sentences
The definition of 'mental disorder' in the CJA 2003 is much wider than that in the Mental Health Act 1983. It is also wider than the common law concepts of unfitness to plead, insanity and diminished responsibility, all of which remain unaltered by the CJA 2003.

Section 328 of the CJA 2003 defines 'mental disorder' as any mental illness, personality disorder or learning disability, however caused or manifested. The legislation specifies that a person is not mentally disordered by reason only of his/her:

- sexual orientation;
- sexual deviancy;
- trans-sexualism or transvestism;
- dependence on or use of alcohol or drugs;

- displaying behaviour that causes or is likely to cause harassment, alarm or distress to any other person;
- by acting as no prudent person would act.

Probation orders

Under the CJA 2003, the courts may make a probation order with an additional requirement that the offender accepts treatment by or under the direction of a medical practitioner or chartered psychologist with a view to the improvement of his mental condition (s. 230(1)). Prior to the 2003 Act such a probation order could last for a maximum of 12 months; this restriction has been removed, so the treatment requirement can now last for up to three years, the new maximum term of a probation order. To make such an order, the court must be satisfied, on the evidence of a medical practitioner approved under s. 12 of the Mental Health Act 1983 that the offender's mental condition is such that it requires and may be susceptible to treatment, but is not such as to warrant his detention under a compulsion order or (civil) compulsory treatment order. It must also be satisfied on the evidence of the practitioner who will be providing treatment that the treatment is appropriate and that arrangements have been made for that treatment (s. 230(3)(a) and (b)).

Section 207 of the CJA 2003 permits a court to include a 'mental health treatment requirement' in relation to a community order or suspended sentence order. This requires the mentally disordered offender to 'submit' to treatment by either a registered medical practitioner or a chartered psychologist (or both, for different periods) for 'the improvement of the offender's mental condition'. The Act allows for inpatient and outpatient care. The court needs to be satisfied, on the evidence of a registered medical practitioner approved for the purposes of s. 12 of the Mental Health Act 1983, that the mental condition of the offender is such that it requires and may be susceptible to treatment, but is not such as to warrant the making of a hospital order or guardianship order within the meaning of the Mental Health Act 1983. The Act also requires that the offender has indicated a 'willingness' to participate in treatment.

Procedures for discharge or release from forensic psychiatric inpatient services

A majority of patients in forensic services are detained under sections contained in Part III of the Mental Health Act 1983 which applies to people concerned in criminal proceedings or under sentence; some are detained under sections contained in Part II of the Mental Health Act which deals with patients detained under civil sections or related criminal justice legislation, such as the criminal Procedure (Insanity and Unfitness to Plead) Acts 1964 and 1991. Detained patients are legally the charge of a responsible medical officer (RMO) – a consultant psychiatrist with responsibility for their care.

The main provisions of Part III of the Mental Health Act 1983 are summarised in Table 8.3.

Table 8.3 Summary of provisions of Part III of the Mental Health Act 1983

Arrest (awaiting trial)	Court (awaiting sentence)	Sentence	Prison
Section 35 Remand to hospital for report for up to 12 weeks *OR* **Section 36** Remand to hospital for treatment for up to 12 weeks	**Section 38** Interim hospital order to evaluate response to hospital treatment for up to 6 months *OR* **Section 48/49** To transfer an unsentenced prisoner to hospital	**Section 37** Hospital order *OR* **Section 37/41** Hospital order with restriction	**Section 47/49** To transfer a sentenced prisoner from hospital with restrictions on his discharge

The Mental Health Review Tribunal in England and Wales

The Mental Health Review Tribunal is one of the largest tribunals operating in England and Wales, dealing with approximately 24,000 applications and 13,000 hearings every year. It is an independent judicial body that operates under the provisions of the Mental Health Act 1983 and the Mental Health Review Tribunal Rules 1983. The tribunal's main purpose is to review the legality of a patients' detention under the Mental Health Act and to direct the discharge of any patient for whom the statutory criteria for discharge have been satisfied. Each tribunal is constituted by a Legal President, a medical member and a lay member. The Lord Chancellor in consultation with the Secretary of State for health makes appointments to the panel. Each individual tribunal consists of a legal member, medical member and a lay member. The legal members are usually senior legal practitioners, but for patients restricted under s. 41 or s. 49 of the Mental Health Act, they are Circuit Judges or one of a small number of Recorders who are also Queen's Counsel. The medical member is required to be a Member or a Fellow of the Royal College of Psychiatrists and have held an appointment as a consultant psychiatrist for at least three years. The lay member is considered to represent society and bring a balance to the tribunal. All the members participate in the making of decisions and, although the legal member drafts and signs the written record, this is done after taking into account the contributions of the other members. If the members do not all agree then a decision of the majority of members of the Tribunal is taken as the decision of the Tribunal. Twenty-eight per cent of all patients detained under the Mental Health Act 1983 are of a minority ethnic group (Department of Health 2006). The fact that the rates of compulsory detention in the UK are higher in those of African-Caribbean background and, to varying degrees, higher also in some other ethnic minority groups has been recognised for several years (Churchill *et al.*1999; Audini and Lelliott 2002; Harrison 2002). These very groups are seriously under-represented in the membership of the MHRT (Morris 2000). Further, it was recently reported in Parliament that:

... the MHRT does not keep information on the ethnicity of patients who come before it, so it is not possible to assess any differential impact of MHRT decisions ... we have little information on the impact of the [Mental Health] Act on any patient group, especially those with heightened vulnerability, such as children, old people and people from black and minority ethnic groups. (Hansard 2007)

Discharge from s. 37 of the Mental Health Act 1983

Patients detained under s. 37 of the Mental Health Act may be discharged by their RMO or they may apply to the Mental Health Review Tribunal or to a hearing of the hospital managers for discharge.

Discharge from s. 38 of the Mental Health Act 1983

Section 38 of the Mental Health Act allows doctors to admit patients to hospital for up to a year for a trial of treatment. If it becomes clear that treatment is inappropriate, then the patient may return to court for re-sentencing. If treatment is appropriate, then the court may later impose a hospital order under s. 37. There is no appeal to a Mental Health Review Tribunal.

Discharge from s. 41 of the Mental Health Act 1983

The purpose of s. 41 of the Mental Health Act – a restriction order – is to protect the public from serious harm. Under the provisions of s. 41, a patient detained on a hospital order (under s. 37 of the Mental Health Act) will not be allowed to leave the hospital without the Home Secretary's permission. The order can be made without limit of time or for a defined period and is imposed in a Crown Court or a higher court. The person must have been convicted of an offence for which imprisonment is a possible penalty. A patient cannot be discharged from the restriction order by the RMO without the consent of the Home Office. The MHRT has the power of absolute discharge of such a patient because the President of the Tribunal for such a restricted patient will be a legal professional (usually a judge of at least equal standing to the legal member of the Crown Court or higher court which made the original detention order).

Absolute discharges are uncommon; most restricted patients leave hospital under a conditional discharge either from the MHRT or with the agreement of the Home Office. These conditions can stipulate compliance with treatment and the patient can be recalled to hospital under a Home Office warrant if their mental state or behaviour deteriorates.

Discharge after transfer from prison to hospital

Prisoners serving a sentence or on remand can be transferred from prison to hospital under ss. 47 and 48 of the Mental Health Act 1983. A transfer direction made under s. 47 has the same effect as a s. 37 hospital order made by a court.

In practice, patients transferred under s. 47 of the Mental Health Act 1983 are usually subject to a restriction order under s. 49 of the Mental Health Act 1983. Patients are discharged from s. 47 of the Mental Health Act in the same way as from a s. 37 hospital order (if no restrictions are imposed under s. 49). This in practice means that the person may be detained in hospital for longer than their prison sentence, usually under a 'notional' s. 37 (s. 37(N)). If a patient is restricted under s. 49 of the Mental Health Act, they can be returned to prison at any time up to the end of their sentence.

Section 48 of the Mental Health Act applies to the transfer to hospital of prisoners on remand. The criteria for such transfers are the same as for s. 47, and in addition 'The prisoner is deemed in urgent need of such treatment'. Section 48 is terminated when the court makes its final decision about the outcome of the case. A restriction order under s. 49 of the Mental Health Act 1983 works in conjunction with a s. 47 or 48 transfer direction in the same way as a s. 41 restriction order. The Home Secretary may terminate the restriction at any time. The patient may also be discharged from hospital with consent of the Home Secretary.

Discharge after detention under the Criminal Procedure (Insanity) Act 1964 and Criminal Procedure (Insanity and Unfitness to Plead) Act 1991

The Criminal Procedure (Insanity) Act 1964 and Criminal Procedure (Insanity and Unfitness to Plead) Act 1991 provide for hospital treatment for those found 'unfit to plead' and 'not guilty by reason of insanity'. If the accused is found, following a trial of the facts, to have carried out the offence in question, then the court has a range of options including a notional hospital order with restrictions. The procedure for discharge from hospital is similar to discharge from a hospital order.

Aftercare under s. 117 of the Mental Health Act 1983

Section 117 of the Mental Health Act 1983 imposes a statutory duty on both local social services authorities and the District Health Authority to provide aftercare for certain groups of patients who are detained in hospital under the provisions of Part II and Part III of the Mental Health Act 1983. Section 117 applies to persons who are detained under s. 3 or s. 37 of the Mental Health Act 1983, or transferred to hospital from prison under s. 47 or 48 of the 1983 Mental Health Act and then cease to be detained and leave hospital.

Section 117 requires that prior to discharging a detained patient, a multidisciplinary meeting initiated by the responsible medical officer (RMO) must take place. The meeting should include the patient's RMO, social worker, the GP or their representative, the community psychiatric nurse, the patient and their relative, friend or advocate, and other relevant professionals involved in the patient's care. The list of other professionals may include occupational therapist, housing officer, the police or probation staff. At the meeting a care coordinator must be identified and the appropriate agency must agree to accept the responsibilities required by this role. The care coordinator may be any professional involved in the patient's care, depending on the balance of needs, and their relationship with the patient. At the meeting, a care plan (within the remit of the Care Planning Approach) should be designed and agreed, taking into account the wishes/views of the patient, their carer and/or their representative.

Mental health professionals may become involved in the new multi-agency public protection arrangements (MAPPA) because of the statutory duties of their employers. These duties will include certain groups of patients, including those who are due to be released after receiving a hospital order or who have received a custodial sentence for particular offences. MAPPA arrangements are discussed in detail in the following section with a particular focus on the issues of confidentiality.

Probation Service

The National Offender Management Service (NOMS) is the umbrella term for the Prison Service and the National Probation Service (NPS). NOMS was set up to lead and coordinate all the services that work with offenders with a stated objective of achieving 'the maximum possible reduction of reoffending'.

The NPS supervises around 200,000 adult offenders in the community at any given time (of whom 90 per cent are men and about 9 per cent from ethnic minorities). Some patients who are discharged from forensic services will be under the supervision of the Probation Service.

Function of the Parole Board

Parole is a form of discretionary release which includes a period of supervision in the community under licence conditions. Prisoners who are thought to present an 'acceptable risk' to the public are granted parole. The decision to grant parole is taken by the Parole Board and, in some cases, the Home Secretary. (The Home Secretary is usually involved in any decision involving a prisoner who has served more than 15 years; it is possible for the Parole Board to override the Home Secretary's view if they choose to do so.)

The Parole Board was established in 1968 under the Criminal Justice Act 1967. It became an independent executive non-departmental public body on 1 July 1996 under the Criminal Justice and Public Order Act 1994. As explained above, the Criminal Justice Act 2003 has radically altered the parole process. Under the CJA 2003 release at the halfway point of a sentence will be automatic for all but the most dangerous offenders.

Tagging

The Home Detention Curfew (HDC) scheme was introduced as part of the Crime and Disorder Act 1998 and came into force in January 1999. The scheme was intended to ease the transition of prisoners from custody to the community by allowing suitable prisoners to be released up to two months before their normal release date, provided that they comply with an electronically monitored curfew for that period. It is one of the largest electronic monitoring schemes in the world and in the first year of operation itself some 16,000 prisoners were placed on HDC.

Satellite tagging is perhaps the next generation of electronic tagging; this has recently been trialled with offenders in four centres across England and Wales and a trial is currently underway in the Netherlands for mentally disordered offenders discharged from a hospital setting. While there are no firm plans, it is possible that satellite tagging will be used in the future to monitor restricted patients when they are released into the community.

With a few exceptions, most prisoners serving a sentence of three months or more and less than four years are eligible for HDC. Prisoners are assessed by the

Probation Service in terms of risk and to confirm that they have suitable accommodation before being released on a tag. An analysis of the use of HDC has revealed that women and older prisoners are more likely to be released on a tag (40 per cent of eligible female prisoners compared with 29 per cent for male prisoners). Black prisoners were marginally more likely than white to be granted HDC (31 per cent compared to 29 per cent), but South Asian (51 per cent) and Chinese and other (39 per cent) inmates are much more likely to be released on a tag. The average period spent on HDC was 45 days, and this according to the Home Office represents a significant saving (Dodgson *et al.* 2001).

The main limitations of tracking (electronically or by satellite) are that they provide information only about the location of the subject but give no information about his/her activities. Additionally, recent media coverage has demonstrated that there is evidence which shows that those being tagged can circumvent the tagging arrangement by a range of techniques. At the same time the company responsible for the tagging has no authority of enforcement when the terms of tagging have been broken, requiring close relationships between the tagging company and the police.

Risk assessment tools relevant to release or discharge

OASys
The Offender Assessment System (shortened to OASys and pronounced 'oasis'), is described as a standardised process for the assessment of offenders and has been developed jointly by the National Probation Service (NPS) and the Prison Service (National Probation Service 2003). It is hoped that OASys will improve the quality of risk assessments by introducing a structured, research-based approach to assessing an offender's likelihood of reconviction, the criminogenic factors associated with offending and the risk of harm he or she presents.

OASys was commissioned in 1998, after a Home Office review concluded that 'no single existing risk/needs assessment system had all the properties necessary to support the key aims of reducing reoffending and protecting the public'. OASys focuses on six principles:

1 Targeting high and medium risk offenders
2 Targeting criminogenic needs
3 Addressing responsivity
4 Using appropriate treatment methods
5 Maintaining program integrity
6 Being community based.

OASys is designed to be administered repeatedly and assessments are usually reviewed every four, six or 12 months.

Tools used in hospitals
Though risk assessment and management are integral parts of forensic work, the theoretical analysis of both risk assessment and management is relatively underdeveloped (Dixon and Oyebode 2007). There are several actuarial tools used to assess risk in routine clinical practice (see Chapter 10 for greater detail). These assessments play a central part in the decisions to discharge patients from hospital-based settings.

The HCR-20 is the best known and best researched, empirically based guide to risk assessment:

- Ten **H**istorical items
- Five **C**linical items and
- Five **R**isk management items (see Table 8.4).

This tool was developed by examining the research literature to determine which variables are important in the prediction of violence and also by consultation with clinicians. However, it is important to note that while it is good at predicting future risk, its effectiveness at managing the risk once known, has yet to be fully evidenced.

Table 8.4   Items in the HCR-20 risk assessment scheme

Sub-scale	Items
Historical Scale	
H1	Previous violence
H2	Young age at first violent incident
H3	Relationship instability
H4	Employment problems
H5	Substance use problems
H6	Major mental illness
H7	Psychopathy
H8	Early maladjustment
H9	Personality disorder
H10	Prior supervision failure
Clinical Scale	
C1	Lack of insight
C2	Negative attitudes
C3	Active symptoms of major mental illness
C4	Impulsivity
C5	Unresponsive to treatment
Risk Management Scale	
R1	Plans lack feasibility
R2	Exposure to destabilisers
R3	Lack of personal support
R4	Non-compliance with remediation attempts
R5	Stress

Another widely used actuarial tool for the prediction of violence is the Violence Risk Appraised Guide (VRAG) (Webster *et al.* 1994; Quinsey *et al.* 1998). This tool was developed using data from patients detained in a Canadian secure hospital along with follow-up data pertaining to violent behaviour collected from Royal Canadian Mounted Police files. Twelve variables including Hare's Psychopathy Checklist Score (Hare 1991), age at index offence, degree of victim injury and history of alcohol abuse are included (see Table 8.5).

Table 8.5 Items used in the VRAG

Psychopathy checklist (PCL-R) score
Elementary school maladjustment
DSM-III diagnosis of personality disorder
Age at index offence
Lived with both parents to 16 (except for death of parent)
Failure on prior conditional release
Non-violent offence score
Marital status
DSM-III diagnosis of schizophrenia
Victim injury
History of alcohol abuse
Female victim

One of the newest tools for the assessment of the risk of sexual violence is the 'RSVP' (Risk for Sexual Violence Protocol) (Hart *et al.* 2003). The RSVP, an update on the older 'Sexual Violence Risk-20' (SVR-20 – Boer *et al.* 1997, includes static and dynamic factors for the assessment of the risk of sexual violence.

Controversies in release procedures

Multi-agency public protection arrangements and information sharing

One of the relatively recent but significant controversies concerning professionals involved in the release/discharge of mentally disordered offenders is the requirement to 'share information' under the multi-agency public protection arrangements (MAPPA). The MAPPA were introduced with the aim of reducing the risk to the general public from reoffending by convicted sexual and violent offenders after their release into the community. The MAPPA are aimed primarily at those being released from prison but are also applicable to mentally disordered offenders subject to hospital orders, guardianship or have been being found to be under a disability (unfit to plead) or not guilty by reason of insanity.

Health authorities, primary care trusts and NHS trusts, have a *statutory* requirement to 'cooperate' with MAPPA. Such cooperation includes participation in aspects of the MAPPA process and may include the provision of information. The main function of the MAPPA is case-related work involving different agencies in the assessment and management of risks posed by relevant offenders. This is focused upon those who pose the highest risks or whose management is problematic or complex, so that this will allow attention and resources to be provided according to the level of risk.

Legal framework for MAPPA
Sections 67 and 68 of the Criminal Justice and Court Services Act 2000 placed a statutory duty on the police and the Probation Service (the 'responsible

authority') in England and Wales to 'establish arrangements for the purpose of assessing and managing the risks posed in that area' by people previously convicted of sexual and violent offences and to monitor the effectiveness of such arrangements. They also have a duty to produce an annual report to the Home Secretary detailing the arrangements.

Section 325 of the Criminal Justice Act 2003 expanded the remit of the MAPPA arrangements by including the Prison Service as 'a responsible authority'. The CJA 2003 also introduced a mutual 'duty to cooperate' between the responsible authority and the following agencies: social services departments, health authorities and strategic health authorities, primary care trusts, NHS trusts, local education authorities, youth offending teams, local housing authorities, registered social landlords and providers of electronic monitoring services.

In April 2003, under powers contained in s. 67(6) of the Criminal Justice and Court Services Act 2000, the Home Secretary issued a guidance document on multi-agency public protection arrangements (Home Office 2003) which gives guidance to the responsible authorities on how their MAPPA duties should be discharged and in establishing cooperative arrangements with other agencies.

Section 325(3) of the Criminal Justice Act 2003 specifies that health agencies have a duty to 'cooperate in the establishment by the responsible authority' of MAPPA. Doubts have been raised as to whether the duty to cooperate extends beyond the setting-up of MAPPA and whether the word 'establish' could be understood as involving longer-term participation (Hewitt 2004). Although this issue remains to be clarified, it is assumed that the legislation may encompass a longer-term duty to participate in MAPPA.

Table 8.6 Number of MAPPA offenders in the community by category (% change)

	2005/06	2004/05	2003/04	2002/03
Registered sex offenders (RSOs)	29,973 (3.38%)	28,994 (18%)	24,572 (14.22%)	21,513
Violent offenders and other sex offenders	14,317 (13.07%)	12,662 (−0.72%)	12,754* (−56.9%)	29,594
'Other' offenders	3,363 (14.54%)	2,936 (35.55%)	2,166 (20.2%)	1,802
Totals	47,653 (6.86%)	44,592 (12.91%)	39,492 (−25.36%)	52,909

Current MAPPA statistics

The recent annual report of the MAPPA (National Probation Service 2006: Table 2) indicates that 47,653 offenders in England and Wales fell within the MAPPA of which 29,993 were registered sex offenders and 14,317 were 'violent and other sexual offenders' (see Table 8.6). This represents an increase of about 7 per cent from the previous year. Of the total, less than 5 per cent were assessed as posing the highest risk or greatest risk-management difficulty and were as a consequence managed by referral to a multi-agency public protection panel (MAPPP).

It is intended that a database will be maintained of all MAPPA cases in England and Wales, and that this should be through the use of the Violent and Sex Offender Register (ViSOR), a database currently being developed for police and probation authorities in England and Wales. Research has shown that 32 per cent of first-time murderers and 36 per cent of serious sexual offenders had no previous convictions (Soothill *et al.* 2002), and this has cast some doubts on the ability of MAPPA in reducing crime.

The MAPPA framework incorporates four overlapping and complementary functions as outlined below:

Function 1: Identification of MAPPA offenders

Multi-agency public protection arrangements cover people who have been convicted of certain criminal offences. People whose behaviour suggests a serious risk to the public but who have never been convicted of a sexual or violent offence cannot under the current legislation be dealt with by the MAPPA process. MAPPA offenders fall within three categories, specified in s. 327 of the Criminal Justice Act 2003:

- *Registered sex offenders.* This includes those offenders who are required under Part 2 of the Sexual Offences Act 2003 to register as sex offenders.
- *Violent and other sex offenders.* These offenders are those who have both been sentenced for sexual offences or certain violent offences since 1 April 2001 or were serving a sentence for such an offence on 1 April 2001 and received a sentence of 12 months or longer. It also includes patients subject to a hospital order or guardianship, either under the Mental Health Act or after being found under a disability (unfit to plead) or not guilty by reason of insanity.
- *Other offenders.* This includes those 'who, by reason of offences committed by them ... are considered by the responsible authority to be persons who may cause serious harm to the public'. The final category appears to be broad, and the guidance document (Home Office 2003) states that 'any reference ... to protecting the public from serious harm shall be construed as a reference to protecting the public from death or serious personal injury, whether physical or psychological, occasioned by further such offences committed by him'. Those who fall within this category are likely to have committed serious sexual or violent offences *prior* to the introduction of the CJA 2003.

By definition, all MAPPA cases will fall into one of the three categories described above. The great majority of offenders considered by MAPPA come from within the prison system, but some will have received hospital disposals. The duty of other agencies to cooperate with the responsible authority is likely to include the notification of the names of all MAPPA offenders. This means that mental health trusts have to keep a list of all those given hospital disposals who fulfil the criteria for MAPPA inclusion.

The issue of MAPPA classification will need to be incorporated into the New Care Programme Approach (CPA) procedures (which are under review in England), both for those who meet the conviction criteria for sexual and violent offences and for patients who may fall into the category of 'other offences'.

Function 2: Information sharing

The effectiveness of risk assessment depends upon the availability of comprehensive information, and this in turn depends on the effectiveness of information-sharing arrangements. The guidance issued by the Home Secretary in April 2003 outlines principles for the sharing of information with the responsible authority by other MAPPA agencies. The guidance states that the principles 'not only ensure compliance with the law, but are also aimed at promoting trust between agencies. That trust must be nurtured and sustained by professional integrity and by procedures which ensure that the process of sharing information is safe and secure'.

The principles that govern information sharing is that information sharing must have lawful authority, be necessary, be proportionate and done in ways which ensure the safety and security of the information shared, and be accountable.

It is assumed in the guidance document (Home Office 2003) that the duty to cooperate (initially incorporated in the Criminal Justice Act 2003) will provide the legal authority for a trust to provide information to the MAPPA, and that necessity and proportionality criteria will be met. The Criminal Justice Act 2003 specifies that cooperation 'may include the exchange of information'. Health authorities and trusts are only obliged to cooperate 'to the extent that such cooperation is compatible with the exercise by those persons of their functions under any other enactment'. The new Act *does not* override the common law duty upon doctors to protect patient confidentiality, or the duties to preserve confidentiality imposed by the Data Protection Act and the Human Rights Act. The new Act does not create any new powers for doctors or health agencies with respect to the release of information, nor does it change the threshold for the release of information without a patient's consent.

The guidance, however, states that the 'responsible authority' is statutorily obliged to make any information in its possession available to the Parole Board. There will be certain circumstances where the 'responsible authority' will deem it necessary to pass on information to third parties beyond the MAPPA process, for example to, individual members of the public. The guidance sets out stringent conditions which must be met before such disclosure can be permitted. This raises significant issues in relation to medical confidentiality.

Function 3: The assessment of risk

There are two standard assessment tools for the assessment of offenders used by the Probation and Prison Services. These are the OASys (Offender Assessment System) and the Risk Matrix. OASys provides a standardised categorisation of risk; further, it may flag up the need for a mental health assessment. The OASys categorisation of risk indicates the likely subject of that harm (the public, prisoners, a known adult, children, staff or self).

The categories of risk assessment in the MAPPA are:

- **Low.** No significant current indicators of risk of harm.
- **Medium.** There are identifiable indicators of risk of harm. Potential to cause harm is present if there is a change in circumstances (for example, failure to take medication, loss of accommodation, relationship breakdown and drug or alcohol misuse).

- **High.** There are identifiable indicators of risk of *serious* harm. The potential event could happen at any time and the impact would be serious.
- **Very high.** There is an *imminent* risk of serious harm. The potential event is more likely than not to happen immediately and the impact would be serious.

The guidance recognises that other agencies, such as health, will have different forms of risk assessment and these may combine the actuarial and the clinical risk. It is stated that each agency should have agreed risk assessment tools and procedures and that the results of these should be provided to form part of the MAPPA risk assessment.

Function 4: Risk management
It is recognised by the MAPPA guidance that risk management is a complex and difficult task, and that risk is a dynamic variable influenced by a variety of factors and circumstances, which will need regular monitoring. Risk management is commenced by agreeing one of three 'levels' of involvement (described below):

- *Level 1: Ordinary risk management.* This is the level used for day-to-day cases where the risks posed by the offender can be managed by a single agency. Offenders in this category would have been assessed as presenting a low level of risk. Most MAPPA cases are likely to be in this level. In a health setting, case management needs for individuals at level 1 would be met by the 'standard' Care Programme Approach.
- *Level 2: Local inter-agency risk management.* This level is intended to be used where the active involvement of more than one agency is required for the management of risk and the risk of harm is not deemed to warrant level 3 arrangements as the risk is not imminent and does not require the engagement of a range of agencies at senior level. The arrangements at level 2 are intended to be more than *ad hoc* and to involve permanent representation from the core agencies, supplemented by representatives from others, when required. The risk management needs of psychiatric outpatients subject to level 2 MAPPA will also be met by 'standard' follow-up within the Care Programme Approach.
- *Level 3: Multi-agency public protection panels (known as MAPPP or MAPP).* Multi-agency protection panels are constituted for the most serious cases. These are usually offenders who are assessed as posing a 'high or very high risk of causing serious harm' or 'present risks that can only be managed by a plan which requires close co-operation at senior level due to the complexity of the case and/or because of the unusual resource commitment that it requires'. Further cases where the risk is not assessed as high or very high but the likelihood of media scrutiny is high usually fall into this group. Most cases under the MAPPP (level 3) will concern offenders released from prison. Psychiatric outpatients are only likely to reach this level where supervision arrangements are breaking down and there is thought to be a high risk of serious harm to the public.

At level 3 (MAPPPs), senior representation is stressed and the guidelines recommend that representatives have the authority to make decisions about committing resources and that they 'understand the strategies for minimising or reducing the risk of serious harm'.

It is pointed out in the guidance document that level 2 and level 3 MAPPA meetings do not engage in case management (which remains the responsibility of individual organisations). The MAPPA cannot subvert the authority or fetter the discretion of healthcare professionals. MAPPA meetings are administrative arrangements, whose role is to coordinate a multi-agency response and to ensure that arrangements exist for risk management and for its implementation and review. The aim is to 'make the coordinated outcome greater than the sum of its parts'.

Deregistering a case from MAPPA

Those fulfilling the MAPPA inclusion criteria for sexual and violent offences can only be subject to MAPPA until the end of their period of registration or the end of statutory supervision. Where individuals are still considered to constitute a risk of serious harm to the public at the point when they would normally leave the MAPPA, they can be considered for inclusion within the MAPPA under the category of 'other offenders'.

The ethical dilemma for clinicians of the MAPPA culture

The roles of mental health professionals include identification of relevant MAPPA cases, participation in level 2 and level 3 MAPPA meetings and in the provision of information. In addition, the guidance document states that personnel from MAPPA agencies will have an important role to play in bringing their expertise to bear upon individual MAPPA cases, and an advisory role in aiding understanding by MAPPA agencies of specialist issues involved in risk assessment and management. MAPPA meetings may also serve as a source of information about patients previously known to mental health services who otherwise may not have come to the attention of mental health professionals.

MAPPA is ultimately an instrument for public protection, not for providing healthcare – in fact the guidance document emphasises 'victim focus'. It may be good practice to involve the offender in the MAPPA process, but this is not mandatory and it does not extend to an individuals presence at MAPPA meetings or to legal representation at the MAPPA. The MAPPA may take decisions which interfere with an individual's freedom. There is no right to appeal against the decisions of a MAPPA meeting, although police and probation services operate formal complaints procedures which are open to those wishing to register a complaint. There is, however, the option to seek a judicial review of a MAPPA decision.

There is no additional funding provided by the Home Office for the implementation of MAPPA by the responsible authority or for the agencies with an obligation to cooperate. Health authorities and primary care trusts are required to develop appropriate arrangements within existing funding; this obviously means that other aspects of patient care may be compromised.

Guidance issued by the Department of Health, *Confidentiality: NHS Code of Practice* (2003), requires all health professionals to owe a duty of confidentiality to their patients. A duty is also owed to patients under Article 8 of the European Convention on Human Rights (ECHR 2003), which confers a right to respect for private and family life. The Data Protection Act 1998 also imposes a duty to only disclose patient-identifying information with the prior consent of the patient, unless certain conditions are satisfied.

Breaching of confidentiality is only permissible under certain conditions. The Royal College of Psychiatrists (2006) in its guidelines issued to the profession states that: 'It may sometimes be justifiable for a doctor to pass on patient information without consent or statutory authority'. The Royal College lists such situations as follows:

- where serious harm may occur to a third party, whether or not a criminal offence, e.g. threat of serious harm to a named person;
- where a doctor believes a patient to be the victim of abuse and the patient is unable to give or withhold consent to disclose;
- where, without disclosure, a doctor would not be acting in the overall best interests of a child or young person who is his/her patient and incapable of consenting to disclosure;
- when, without disclosure the task of preventing or detecting a serious crime by the police would be prejudiced or delayed;
- when, without disclosure, the task of prosecuting a serious crime would be prejudiced or delayed (e.g. a patient tells you that he killed someone several years ago);
- where a doctor has a patient who is a health professional and has concerns over that person's fitness to practise and poses a serious danger to patients in his or her care;
- where a doctor has concerns over a patient's fitness to drive.

The College further states:

> Each case must be considered on its merits – the test being whether the release of information to protect the public interest (which includes protecting members of the public) prevails over the duty of confidence to the patient. This is a matter of judgement that may be finely balanced. Such a balancing judgement would need to take into account the various legal responsibilities at stake, including the duty of confidence to the individual and the public interest in the health service maintaining confidence. Consideration will need to be given as to whether the harm that could result from disclosure (e.g. the possible damage to the relationship of trust or the likelihood of non-compliance with a programme of health care intervention in the future) is likely to be outweighed by the positive benefit.
>
> (Royal College of Psychiatrist 2006)

Health services have an interest in the prevention of harm to the general public by patients. The importance of information sharing and multi-agency working has been emphasised in a long series of public inquiries into serious incidents involving those under the care of statutory agencies.

In constructing new inter-agency arrangements each agency should be aware of the professional boundaries of the others. These issues are discussed in the additional Home Office guidance issued in 2004 (NPS 2004). Each NHS trust with responsibilities for psychiatric services will need to agree a protocol for information exchange with the strategic management board of the MAPPA in the local area. In drawing up and negotiating such a protocol, the following issues should be taken into account:

- Whether information release is justified should be assessed – merely because a request for information comes from the MAPPA does not in itself justify the release of information.
- For patients who are no longer under psychiatric care but have served a period of imprisonment for a sexual or violent crime in the past, health professionals continue to have a duty of confidentiality.
- The health professional (not the MAPPA) has to decide whether or not a given situation justifies the release of confidential information. The health professional will have to consider all the information available to him and to the MAPPA meeting before taking a decision.
- The revised MAPPA guidance issued in April 2004 (NPS 2004) clarifies that the MAPPA process cannot require health professionals to disclose information unless the criteria described have been met.
- Where a professional is of the view that the release of information is justified, he must seek the consent of the patient to its release unless there is an increased risk of harm by doing so.
- The judgment as to enhancement of risk or inhibition of an investigation must be made by the clinician: it is not permissible simply to accept the view of an outside agency. Consent should be sought in writing. The uses to which the information may be put must be set out clearly. Adoption of a standard consent form agreed by the trust will constitute good practice. Merely because a patient consents to information being released may not be sufficient grounds to do so. Informed consent gives the authority to release information but does not make it obligatory, for the professional's care towards the patient should include forming a view as to whether disclosure is in the patient's best interests. The patient's consent to the release of information still requires the professional to make a judgment, based upon his own expertise and judgment, as to the facts of the case.
- Confidential information can only be released in spite of a patient's wishes where that information is necessary to prevent or detect a 'serious crime'. The risk must be serious and the probability of its occurring must be high.
- A propensity to cause harm is unlikely to be sufficient grounds for disclosure if the risk is not immediate. Each case must be considered individually and membership of a particular group (e.g. sex offenders) cannot in itself be sufficient. Similarly, the fact that someone is conditionally discharged from a restriction order will not in itself indicate any reason for disclosure. Conditionally discharged patients will have been deemed safe for release into the community by the Home Secretary or a Mental Health Review Tribunal.
- Professionals should consider whether the risk can be contained by the therapeutic relationship rather than by disclosure, and whether disclosure would cause the treating team to lose the opportunity to monitor the activities and risk that the patient pose. The professional must be mindful that there are circumstances in which disclosure may increase the risk of harm.
- If a patient does not have the capacity to consent to the release of information, a judgment must be made as to whether that incapacity is likely to be permanent. If so then the professional should make a judgment in the patient's best interests, including the public interest of disclosure. Incapacity is most likely to be permanent in brain injury, learning difficulties, and very

rarely in treatment-resistant mental illness. If the incapacity is likely to be time-limited, then the psychiatrist should make a judgment whether to await recovery of capacity and if such a delay is not appropriate, the case should be treated as though consent was refused.

- The informal provision of information, such as verbally in conversation or on the telephone, is subject to the same restrictions as the provision of written information.

Agreement should be sought in advance that the professionals who prepare any documents to assist the MAPPA will be consulted before the information is released to third parties.

Modern psychiatric practice consists of multidisciplinary teamworking, with treating teams including doctors, nurses, psychologists, occupational therapists and social workers. Each professional is subject to different line-management structures and to different professional codes with respect to patient confidentiality. Social service departments are under a statutory duty to cooperate with MAPPA, and this will affect hospital social workers who are employed by social service departments. Requests from the MAPPA for information might be addressed to any member of the multidisciplinary team. Protocols should apply to all disciplines.

The evolution of MAPPA

MAPPA arrangements are in a relatively early phase of their development. It is important that the basic framework of the relationship with health services is clearly defined so that mutually beneficial arrangements can be established.

Early experiences of MAPPA indicate some intrusive demands for information and a tendency to be over-inclusive in cases considered appropriate for levels 2 and 3. There have also been reports of real benefits of involvement with the MAPPA. Indications are that the process will focus more clearly in the future on cases of serious risk. Despite the framework for including relevant offenders given hospital disposals in the MAPPA process, it is unlikely that the MAPPA will wish to incorporate patients receiving hospital disposal, unless a clinical decision has been reached that they cannot be managed within the CPA process. It is also likely that a clearer understanding will develop of the uses and limitations of information exchange with health agencies. MAPPA arrangements will need to be introduced as part of a gradual process, particularly given that no extra resources have been provided for the process.

Relationship with the Home Office

A second area of controversy and ethical dilemma is the so called 'partnership' between the Home Office and the professionals caring for mentally disordered offenders. It has been suggested that there is no real 'partnership' on the grounds that the overriding interest of the Home Office in a patient's mental health is solely in terms of its impact on the risk of harm to others (Eastman 2006).

The Home Secretary for England and Wales oversees the treatment of mentally disordered offenders subject to restriction orders. The Home Secretary has numerous powers in relation to these patients, for example without the Home Secretary's permission the responsible medical officer cannot grant a restricted patient leave from hospital, nor can the RMO discharge a patient or transfer the patient to another hospital. The Home Secretary's permission is also required to recall a restricted patient from the community and return a restricted patient to prison.

There are currently about 4,600 patients subject to a restriction order and this has almost doubled from 2,337 in 1993 (Srinivas *et al.* 2006). Of these 4,600 patients, about 720 are in high secure hospitals and 1,270 are in the community. A little over 10 per cent (550) are female. A majority (69 per cent) of restricted patients have a sole diagnosis of mental illness and about 13 per cent have a conviction for a sexual offence. The Mental Health Unit at the Home Office (on behalf of the Home Secretary) handles all applications and requests involving restricted patients. In 2004–05, the Unit took over 15,000 decisions in relation to restricted patients including reviewing 6,380 reports, preparing 4,005 statements for mental health review tribunals and assessing 2,548 requests for leave. The Mental Health Unit was also involved in the transfer of 872 patients from prison to hospital and in the recall of 160 patients from the community into a secure hospital (Srinivas *et al.* 2006).

Implications for practice

Box 8.2   Scenario 1

A 22-year-old man is convicted of the rape of his work colleague at an office party. The judge adjourns the case for psychiatric reports to advise on 'dangerousness'. The psychiatrist uncovers from the medical records that the offender had committed sexual offences on a previous partner but did not receive a conviction as charges were not pressed. At interview the offender informs the psychiatrist that he occasionally has intrusive thoughts of sexual violence. The psychiatrist does not think that the offender is 'treatable'; he does not recommend a hospital order. He, however, believes the offender fulfils the criteria for a diagnosis of dissocial personality disorder.

What would be the impact on the sentence given by the court if the psychiatrist includes in his report to the court, information about Mr Smith's past offences?

Section 225 of the Criminal Justice Act 2003 introduces new legislation for 'dangerous offenders' allowing for indeterminate sentencing based on risk after a single offence. Offences must be one of the 'specified offences' which includes a list of violent offences, including arson and sexual offences. The indeterminate sentences include 'imprisonment for public protection' (IPP), which is 'a sentence of imprisonment for an indeterminate period, subject to the provisions of the Crime (Sentences) Act 1997'. If a person aged 18 or over is convicted of a serious offence but it is not one which can receive a life sentence, or if the court considers that the seriousness of the offence does not justify the imposition of a life sentence but nevertheless the court is of the opinion that there is a significant risk to members of the public of serious harm occasioned by the commission of further specified offences, then the court must impose a sentence of imprisonment for public protection (IPP).

Section 229 of the Criminal Justice Act 2003 describes what information the courts can consider before making an IPP or an extended sentence for public protection (EPP). In essence, any information put before the courts can be considered in making the order.

Professionals should be mindful that the consequences for defendants held to be 'dangerous' are severe especially when preparing reports for the court when the outcome will not be a hospital order. Many psychiatric reports describe past unconvicted violent or sexual behaviour along with other behaviours that could increase risk of reoffending (such as substance misuse or non-compliance with treatment or intrusive thoughts). All this information could be taken into account in sentencing; professionals will need to be able to show that the information and opinions are accurate and robust. Professionals also need to consider how robust instruments like the HCR-20 are in predicting 'reoffending' as the standardised instruments predict the risk of 'reconviction'. Reports will probably be subject to much greater challenge and scrutiny; the argument will be that the background history included as 'routine' in the report is inaccurate or that the professional is giving a view on risk beyond their competence.

Box 8.3 Scenario 2

A 46-year-old man received a hospital order with restrictions for the manslaughter of his mother. His solicitors have applied to the Mental Health Review Tribunal (MHRT) for an absolute discharge. The patient's probation officer wishes to refer the matter to the MAPPP in the event that he is discharged and has requested the clinical team to provide a summary document outlining the risk issues.

What is the position of the professionals in relation to their duty to share information with the MAPPP? Should they seek consent from the patient before sharing information?

MAPPA is an instrument for public protection, not for providing healthcare – in fact the guidance document emphasises 'victim focus'. All health professionals owe an 'ethical' duty of confidentiality to their patients. A duty is also owed to patients under Article 8 of the European Convention on Human Rights (ECHR 2004), which confers a right to respect for private and family life. The health professional has to decide whether or not a given situation justifies the release of confidential information.

The revised MAPPA guidance issued in April 2004 clarifies that the MAPPA process cannot require health professionals to disclose information. Where a professional is of the view that the release of information is justified, he must seek the consent of the patient in writing to its release unless there is an increased risk of harm by doing so. Even if a patient gives his consent for the release of data, it still requires the professional to make a judgment, based upon his own expertise and judgment as to the facts of the case whether the release of information is appropriate.

Clinicians should 'reveal only the minimum of information necessary to achieve the objective' (BMA 1999). Making available detailed reports or whole files is not good practice; only relevant pieces of information should be disclosed. Such information may be contained in a brief document as a separate communication and documents prepared for other purposes such as an admission/discharge summaries or a report for a Mental Health Review Tribunal should not be routinely copied to the MAPPA.

Conclusion

Release from custody or discharge from a hospital setting into the community are important steps in the care pathway of mentally disordered offenders. Recent high-profile cases where mentally disordered offenders go on to commit offences after release into the community have fuelled public fears and prompted changes to legislation. The Criminal Justice Act 2003 provides for indeterminate sentences for public protection (IPP). These are life sentences in all but name and can be used in situations where life sentences were previously not available. Professionals should be cautious in advising the courts about dangerousness especially when they are not recommending treatment in hospital, as the consequences for defendants held to be 'dangerous' are so severe. Decisions about release should ideally be made nearer the time of release rather than when sentence is passed to reflect the fact that risk is 'dynamic' and should be assessed periodically. However, clinicians must be wary of making predictions of reoffending based on standardised risk assessment tools.

The new multi-agency public protection arrangements are increasingly relevant when considering the discharge or release of mentally disordered offenders. The arrangements place health professionals alongside police and probation officers in discussing their patients and in managing the risks they pose. The health professionals should be aware of the ethical problems and the legal rules that apply. For example, the legal rule in W. v. Egdell [1990][1] that, without breach, there would be a significant risk of serious harm to the public must guide any decisions to breach medical confidentiality. Multi-agency working can rapidly result in blurring of the distinction of purpose, with all participants pursuing what seems the joint venture of public protection.

There is an inequality in the balance of power between health professionals and the Home Office in respect of restricted patients, both parties have differing agendas. The core of the professional's role is treatment of patients, while the focus of the Home Office is public protection.

Selected further reading

Ward, R. and Davies, O. (2003) *Criminal Justice Act 2003: A Practitioner's Guide*, New Law Series. Bristol: Jordans, is a comprehensive analysis of the Criminal Justice Act, including the text of the Act.

Hodgins, S. and Müller-Isberner, R. (eds) (2000) *Violence, Crime and Mentally Disordered Offenders: Concepts and Methods for Effective Treatment and Prevention*, Wiley Series in Forensic Clinical Psychology. Chichester: Wiley, summarises the treatment options available for mentally disordered offenders.

Eastman, N. and Peay, J. (1999) *Law without Enforcement: Integrating Mental Health and Justice*. Oxford: Hart, highlights the different ethical, moral and legal dilemmas associated with current mental health legislation in the UK, and advances the 'effectiveness' debate.

Note

1 *W. v. Egdell* (1989) All England Law Reports; 1989 Nov 9; [1990] 1: 835–53.

References

Audini, B. and Lelliott, P. (2002) 'Age, gender and ethnicity of those detained under Part II of the Mental Health Act 1983', *British Journal of Psychiatry*, 180: 222–6.

BMA (1999) *Confidentiality and Disclosure of Health Information*. London: British Medical Association.

Boer, D.P., Hart, S., Kropp, P.R. and Webster, C.D. (1997) *Manual for Sexual Violence Risk – 20 Professional Guidelines for Assessing Risk of Sexual Violence*. Burnaby, Canada: Simon Fraser University, Mental Health, Law, and Policy Institute.

Churchill, R., Wall, S., Hotopf, M., Wessely, S. and Buchanan, A. (1999) *A Systematic Review of Research Relating to the Mental Health Act (1983)*. London: Department of Health.

Department of Health (2003) *Confidentiality: NHS Code of Practice*. London: DoH. See: http://www.dh.gov.uk/en/Publicationsandstatistics/Publications/PublicationsPolicy AndGuidance/DH_4069253

Department of Health (2006) *Plans to Amend the Mental Health Act 1983 – Race Equality Impact Assessment*. London: DoH. See: http://www.dh.gov.uk/en/Consultations/ Closedconsultations/DH_4135812

Dixon, M. and Oyebode, F. (2007) 'Uncertainty and risk assessment', *Advances in Psychiatric Treatment*, 13: 70–8.

Dodgson, K., Goodwin, P., Howard, P., Llewellyn-Thomas, S., Mortimer, E., Russell, N. and Weiner, M. (2001) *Electronic Monitoring of Released Prisoners: An Evaluation of the Home Detention Curfew Scheme*, Home Office Research Study No. 222. London: Home Office.

Eastman, N. (2006) 'Can there be true partnership between clinicians and the Home Office? Invited commentary on ... The Home Office Mental Health Unit', *Advances in Psychiatric Treatment*, 12: 459–61.

ECHR (2003) *Convention for the Protection of Human Rights and Fundamental Freedoms as amended by Protocol No. 11*. Council of Europe. See: http://conventions.coe.int/ Treaty/en/Treaties/Html/005.htm

Hansard (2007) Lord Patel of Bradford, 17 January, col. 734. See: http://www.publications. parliament.uk/pa/ld200607/ldhansrd/text/70117-0014.htm

Hare, R. D. (1991) *The Hare Psychopathy Checklist – Revised*. Toronto: Multi-Health Systems.

Harrison, G. (2002) 'Ethnic minorities and the Mental Health Act', *British Journal of Psychiatry*, 180: 198–9.

Hart, S. D., Kropp, R., Laws, D. R., Klaver, J., Logan, C. and Watt, K. A. (2003) *The Risk for Sexual Violence Protocol (RSVP) – Structured Professional Guidelines for Assessing Risk of Sexual Violence*. Burnaby, Canada: Simon Fraser University, Mental Health, Law, and Policy Institute.

Hewitt, D. (2004) 'MAPPA reading: the NHS must now help the police to assess risk', *NHSLA PCT Bulletin*, Issue 5, March.

Home Office (1990) *Crime, Justice and Protecting the Public*. See: http://www.bopcris. ac.uk/bopall/ref21788.html

Home Office (2001) *The Halliday Report: Making Punishments Work: Review of the Sentencing Framework for England and Wales*. London: HMSO. See: http://www.home-office.gov.uk/documents/312280/

Home Office (2003) *MAPPA Guidance*. See: http://www.probation.homeoffice. gov.uk/files/pdf/MAPPA%20Guidance.pdf

Morris, F. (2000) 'Review of Tribunals: Consultation Paper'. See: http://www.barcouncil.org.uk/assets/documents/Part2MentalHealthReviewTribunal.doc

National Probation Service (2003) *OASys: The New Offender Assessment System.* See: http://www.probation.homeoffice.gov.uk/files/pdf/Info%20for%20sentencers%203.pdf

National Probation Service (2004) *Extension of MAPPA Guidance.* See: http://www.probation.homeoffice.gov.uk/files/pdf/MAPPA%20Guidance%20Update%202004.pdf

National Probation Service (2006) *A National Overview of the Multi-Agency Public Protection Arrangements 2001–2006.* See: http://www.probation.homeoffice.gov.uk/files/pdf/MAPPA%20-%20The%20First%20Five%20Years.pdf

Quinsey, V. L. E., Harris, G. T., Rice, M. E. and Cormier, C. A. (1998) *Violent Offenders: Appraising and Managing Risk*, 1st edn. Arlington, VA: American Psychiatric Association.

Royal College of Psychiatrists (2006) *Psychiatrists and Multi-Agency Public Protection Arrangements: Guidelines on Representation, Participation, Confidentiality and Information Exchange.* See: http://www.rcpsych.ac.uk/members/currentissues/publicprotection.aspx#conf

Soothill, K., Francis, B., Ackerley, E. and Fligelstone, R. (2002) *Murder and Serious Sexual Assault: What Criminal Histories Can Reveal about Future Serious Offending*, Police Research Series No. 144. London: Home Office. See: http://www.homeoffice.gov.uk/rds/prgpdfs/prs144.pdf

Srinivas, J., Denvir, S. and Humphreys, M. (2006) 'The Home Office Mental Health Unit', *Advances in Psychiatric Treatment*, 12: 450–8.

Webster, C. D., Harris, G. T., Rice, M. E., Cormier, C. and Quinsey, V. L. (1994) *The Violence Prediction Scheme: Assessing Dangerousness in High Risk Men*, 1st edn. Toronto: University of Toronto Press.

Part 3

Developing a Knowledge Base – Key Issues in Forensic Mental Health

Keith Soothill

Developing a knowledge base in a subject is a pivotal exercise. That is why around one half of the chapters in this volume reside in this Part. Developing a knowledge base means grappling with the known but also recognising that there is much that is unknown. Some regard the evidence base in the forensic mental health field as sparse. However, it sometimes becomes less so when the available material is systematically drawn together and assessed; that is the task that the contributors attempt to do. Nevertheless, having said all that about evidence, there are also conceptual issues to confront.

The title of Chapter 9 has words – 'diagnosis', 'medical model' and 'formulation' – that all indicate conceptual approaches to labelling problems of mental or physical health. Pamela J. Taylor and John Gunn remind us that 'they are subject to change with time and fashion'. But we need them, for such words provide a shorthand way of communicating about the health problems we are facing. However, their chapter also provides a cautionary tale. They note how current approaches to diagnosis tend to be categorical, and served by standard sets of criteria laid out in manuals. Taylor and Gunn maintain that these have value for research, but less value in clinical practice and should be used with the utmost caution in conjunction with any aspect of the law. In their terms, they have utility rather than validity. Even more pertinently, they argue that misuse of diagnosis, whether through ignorance or design, can be dangerous as well as potentially unethical. In effect, they are pointing to the ongoing tension between medical terminology and legal terminology.

All this is good preparation for Chapter 10 where Mike Doyle and Mairead Dolan focus on 'Understanding and managing risk'. They argue that assessing and managing risk to others from forensic patients is fundamental to the practice of mental health professionals in forensic services. In recent years clarifying the risk of violence that an individual poses has become a paramount consideration for forensic mental health professionals and services, but the authors remind us that many other risks confront forensic mental health services, including risk of self-harm, suicide, absconding, fire-setting and exploitation. Assessing risk is a delicate area as the task is becoming subject to increasing scrutiny and possible litigation. In an important section on therapeutic risk-taking, they note that forensic mental health services and clinicians who work within them must take risks and striking the right balance between the rights of the person and the safety of others is crucial. In essence, risk decisions need to be made in a manner which can be reasonably justified given the salient information that the clinician or the service had available to them at that time.

Philip Fennell's two carefully documented chapters take us to the heart of the legal framework. Together they explain how detention and compulsory community powers under mental health and criminal justice legislation are used in the management of risk to self and to others. Again it is a changing framework and in Chapter 11 Fennell discusses the impact of the European Convention on Human Rights on psychiatric detention and compulsory treatment in the community. The chapter goes on to consider how non-offender patients may be detained and treated in hospital or may be subject to compulsory powers in the community. In other words, the focus is on the civil provisions for compulsory admission and treatment. While Chapter 11 focuses on the possibilities of diverting people from the criminal justice system, Chapter 12 focuses on the legal framework when the person is 'captured' by that system. The chapter considers the special procedures applicable when a prosecution is brought against a mentally disordered or mentally vulnerable suspect. It goes on to explore the use of criminal justice legislation to sentence mentally disordered offenders. Much of the recent legislation in this area is contentious. The steady development of 'public protection sentencing', culminating in the protective sentencing provisions of the Criminal Justice Act 2003, has enormous ethical and practical implications.

The assessment and treatment of offenders with intellectual and developmental disabilities has a long history. Indeed, in Chapter 13 William R. Lindsay and John L. Taylor point to the historical unease about assessing and managing people with intellectual disabilities and their potential for crime. In fact, the shift of emphasis has been enormous following the policies of deinstitutionalisation whereby long-stay institutions for this population were closed. Nowadays, far more individuals with intellectual disability gain access to a comprehensive range of exposures in community settings. Lindsay and Taylor focus on some significant developments in the treatment of offenders with intellectual disabilities. Despite some concerns about methodological shortcomings in this area of research, this seems to be an area where some advances, albeit perhaps not widely recognised, have been made.

The next three chapters seem to cover somewhat similar territory but with very different aims. As Kevin Howells, Michael Daffern and Andrew Day quite rightly claim in Chapter 14, aggression and violence pose major problems for forensic mental health services, for the criminal justice system and for society in general. What these authors manage to do is to focus on the psychology of aggression, the study of which has played an important part in the rapidly growing discipline of academic psychology. However, they also consider other topics such as aggression in psychiatric disorders, in mental health institutions, in those with personality disorders and in those requiring psychological or psychiatric treatment. They note that these two literatures are still largely separate. The need for the convergence of mental health and psychological/behavioural models is usefully raised in this chapter. Understanding the conceptual distinctions between the approaches certainly helps.

Mary McMurran in Chapter 15 focuses more explicitly on the management and treatment of people with personality disorders. As McMurran highlights, this is an area where much work still needs to be done in terms of theoretical understanding, classification, aetiology, assessment, treatment and prevention. But she identifies that the most pressing need is what is termed translational research, that is the translation of science as applied in practical applications. There is little doubt that those with personality disorders cause more psychological harm to themselves and others than perhaps any other category discussed in this book. The prerequisite in effecting a translation from science to applications is in developing an understanding of what one is talking about. McMurran manages to elucidate what is meant by personality disorder, examine how personality disorders are assessed and identify effective treatments.

In Chapter 16 Sheilagh Hodgins focuses specifically on the criminality among persons with severe mental illness, and most particularly those with schizophrenia and schizo-affective disorder. The line now seems to be drawn in that those with schizophrenia and schizo-affective disorder are at an albeit small but increased risk of committing future violence compared to the general population. Certainly the evidence is forthcoming in this chapter and Hodgins argues that 'Currently, mental health policy and practice in the UK does not take account of this evidence.' In other words, she is raging against a complacency that assumes too readily that there is not a knowledge base in this area. Her coherent claim is that that there is such knowledge and that one needs to do something about it.

Substance abuse no longer has the ring of novelty that it may have had, say, 40 years ago. In Chapter 17 Mary McMurran clarifies these issues. While there are substance-specific offences, such as trafficking drugs, manufacturing certain chemical substances and selling alcohol to people under a specified age, these activities are not within the purview of forensic mental health professionals. In contrast, in mental health services, it is usually crimes that are in some way related to the individual's intake of drugs that are the focus. McMurran warns against attempts to decide whether alcohol or drugs *cause* crime. In fact substance abuse in mentally disordered offenders is usually part of a cluster of problems experienced by a generally disadvantaged group. McMurran's currency is one of probabilities, recognising that substance use may increase the likelihood of criminal behaviour in a number of ways. She argues that substance misuse needs to be targeted within forensic mental health populations and not seen as simply a problem to be dealt with by specialist teams. Indeed, when we consider that the majority of mental health patients in inner-city London have either a comorbid alcohol or drug abuse (or both), then the term dual diagnosis loses all meaning. If the norm is comorbidity then why bother setting up separate psychiatric and drug and alcohol services? Common sense would tell us that they should be integrated.

Sexual offending has elicited much interest and concern in recent years provoking responsive legislation. However, the knowledge base needs to be constantly reviewed. Madelaine Lockmuller, Anthony Beech and Dawn Fisher focus more specifically on sexual offenders with mental health problems. They consider the causal role of mental illness in sexual offending, broadly taking the view that the motivation to offend is related to factors other than mental illness and that the risk of individual offending is roughly the same whether they are well or unwell. The implication is that the approach to assessing and treating sexual offenders with comorbid mental health problems should be determined by what works with offenders without mental health problems. While these authors do not attempt to generalise to other kinds of offences, they do highlight the importance of embracing important conceptual issues in relation to forensic work.

Chapter 9

Diagnosis, medical models and formulations

Pamela J. Taylor and John Gunn

Introduction

The most important idea for the reader is that the terms 'diagnosis', 'medical model' and 'formulation' all indicate conceptual approaches to labelling problems of mental or physical health. As abstract concepts, they have no physical reality, although physical or bodily changes may be part of the presentation. They are subject to change with time and fashion. Jaspers (1946) captured the risk from a tendency to reify concepts: '... error begins where *instead of the idea there is an apparent accomplishment of the idea.*' Nevertheless, diagnostic approaches have a number of functions – in particular they provide a shorthand way of communicating about the health problems presented between doctors, and they should facilitate communication about needs for services of various kinds and about treatment and its likely outcome.

Diagnosis, medical modelling and formulation can certainly have powerful effects on communication, but can obscure as well as enlighten, and may be just as likely to be used to exclude needy people from services as to make useful service links for them. They should be used to provide simple reassurance that a cluster of health problems constitutes a state that has been previously recognised, so that at the least the sufferer would be entitled to understanding and support, and at best to treatment which will bring relief, even cure. However, they can be misused to stigmatise. Among their properties is their potential for compartmentalising a person's problems in a useful medical way, but there is a risk that their power can be used to overwhelm the individual; the tendency to refer to people as 'epileptics' or 'schizophrenics' or 'psychopaths' creates a different environment around the person compared with such phraseology as 'a teacher with epilepsy', 'a mother with schizophrenia' or 'a paediatrician with a personality disorder'.

For people who present to forensic mental health services, the situation may become more complex still. In court, lawyers and clinicians may find themselves divided by an apparently common language. There may be open argument not only about diagnosis, but also a range of legal terminology which sounds like clinical terminology, and even overlaps with it, but is not clinical. This can cause further obfuscation or barriers to care and treatment. In the criminal court, concepts of insanity are still used, albeit rarely. Both in the criminal courts and in clinical settings, the terminology of 'psychopathic disorder' is still valid when applied to legal grounds for detention but has long since been removed as a legitimate clinical term even if clinicians still use it from time to time in clinical practice when they have feelings of irritation, dislike or fear of a particular patient or group of patients. To add to the confusion, a not dissimilar term has been reintroduced into clinical, especially forensic clinical, practice. 'Psychopathy' is used as a label for one extreme category on a particular rating scale. It has some reliability and validity as a clinical descriptor but, perhaps in part coloured by the form of the word and of the words used for its constituent elements, it commonly becomes a term of despair, usually leading to clinical rejection. Given the potential power of diagnosis, medical modelling and formulation, it is important to explore what these terms mean and to consider both their value and their limitations.

An abstraction

The Oxford English Dictionary tells us that diagnosis is 'the identification of a disease by means of a patient's symptoms'. This implies that we know what a 'disease' is, and that it is a thing of substance. Scadding (1967: 877–82), a physician, defined disease as:

> ... the sum of the abnormal phenomena displayed by a group of living organisms in association with a specified common characteristic, or set of characteristics, by which they differ from the norm for their species in such a way as to place them at a biological disadvantage.

Both the most widely used diagnostic manuals for mental disorder – the World Health Organisation (WHO) (1992) [*International*] *Classification of Mental and Behavioural Disorders* (ICD) and the American Psychiatric Association (APA) (1994) *Diagnostic and Statistical Manual of Mental Disorders* (DSM) retain the spirit of Scadding's definition. '"Disorder" is not an exact term, but is used here to imply the existence of a clinically recognisable set of symptoms or behaviour associated in most cases with distress and interference of personal functions' (WHO 1992). The DSM definition is almost identical but adds 'or with a significantly increased risk of suffering death, pain, disability, or an important loss of freedom'. Both are clear about exclusion criteria too – that social deviance or conflict alone or a culturally sanctioned response to an event should not be classified as disease or disorder.

So far so good, but giving a name to a cluster of symptoms and signs which have a certain consistency in occurring together, even when those symptoms and signs can be described reliably, is not necessarily of practical value, nor does it necessarily stand the test of time. For about 400 years up to the beginning of the twentieth century, there was a prominent and horrible disease in young women called 'chlorosis' (lit. green sickness), also known as 'the virgin's sickness'. Loudon, the medical historian, noted:

Until the middle of the 19th century there was ... No general agreement on the cause of the disease; then, after the development of haematology it was believed to be a form of hypochromic anaemia confined to young women. When the mystery of its aetiology seemed to have been solved, however, it was succeeded by another mystery: chlorosis, which had reached 'epidemic proportions' throughout the 18th and 19th centuries, suddenly began to decline at the beginning of this century. Within two decades it had to all intents and purposes disappeared. (Loudon 1980: 1669–75)

He went on to list the reported symptoms of chlorosis, and suggested that the term referred to problems which we would now classify as two different conditions: anaemia and anorexia nervosa. He is fascinated by the use of 'green' in the terminology of the period, noting that although the sufferer's skin was typically recorded as taking on a greenish colour, it is possible that originally the term green meant of tender age, youthful or immature.

Any idea that such imaginative, even descriptive labelling was confined to the nineteenth century or before would be quashed by a glance at the current diagnostic manuals for mental disorder and their immediate predecessors. Blashfield and Fuller (1996), in their article on predicting DSM-V, had a lot of fun at the expense of the 'clinical empiricism' of the DSM system, but with a serious point. They entered data from DSM-IV and its four predecessors (DSM-I, DSM-II, DSM-III, DSM-III-R) into linear regression models to predict the characteristics of DSM-V, including date of publication, number of pages, total number of categories, total number of diagnostic criteria, the colour of the cover (it will be brown), who would be in charge of the task force to create DSM-V and the revenues it would generate. The serious point is that the first manual, in 1952, listed 128 disorders, 94 of them with diagnostic criteria, and thereafter there was linear growth in both to 357 listed disorders, 201 with diagnostic criteria, in DSM-IV by 1994. This contrasts with the landmark paper of Feighner and colleagues (1972) in which the authors insisted that there were only 16 valid categories of mental disorder.

This hints at the long-standing tensions about the nature and purpose of diagnosis. Jaspers (1946) captured much of this with respect to psychosis. From ancient times, one school of thought held to the idea of 'unitary psychosis', denying disease entities in favour of the concept of variations in a single state, influenced variously by person, passage of time and context. The opposing school construed the psychoses as natural disease entities which are clearly distinct on presentation, course and cause, and with no transition between them. Kraepelin (1919) is credited with the most enduring distinction – between manic-depressive/bipolar disorder and 'dementia praecox'/schizophrenia. Robins and Guze (1970) and Kendler (1980) are among the most rigorous subsequent categorisers. The ICD and DSM initiatives seemed to confirm that the 'disease entity' model was on the ascendant. Notwithstanding practical advantages in the categorical approach for research and substantial epidemiological work appearing to underpin it (e.g. Regier *et al.* 1998), much of the twentieth century dissent has come from academic psychiatrists. Kendell (1987) continued to maintain awareness of the limitations of the categorical model, while Crow (1990) advanced a dimensional and continuous formulation. Craddock and

Owen (2005) put their marker down for the new millennium, arguing that the evidence from genetic research is against Kraepelinian/categorical modelling. Their evidence is impressive: schizophrenia and the more affective psychotic illnesses co-occur in families generally and among twins, some chromosomal region anomalies have been found to be shared between the two broad psychosis groups and genes have been identified which appear to convey risk for both categories of disorder. Jaspers, though, was ahead of the field:

> The original question: are there only *stages and variants* of one unitary psychosis or is there a series of *disease-entities* which we can delineate, now finds its answer: *there are neither.* The latter view is right in so far that the idea of disease-entities has become a fruitful orientation for the investigation of special psychiatry. The former view is right in so far that no actual disease-entities exist in scientific psychiatry. (Jaspers 1946: 570)

Reliability, validity and utility of diagnosis

In spite of all the difficulties, efforts persist to make definition and measurement in medicine as scientific as possible. The purpose of a diagnosis is to allow people with knowledge of the diagnostic language to use just a word or two to convey to each other several messages about the person said to have the diagnosis. From the diagnosis it should be possible to know something of what to expect in the appearance or presentation of the person, something of what will happen to the person untreated, something about effective treatments or even cure, and possibly something about the cause of the condition. It follows that the reliability with which a diagnosis is made is very important. This is partly what has fuelled the manual approach to diagnosis, with its attendant selection of structured interviews, and a requirement, at least for research purposes, that anyone using these interviews is trained to do them to a specified standard and then regularly updates those skills.

Kendell *et al.* (1971) demonstrated the extent to which diagnoses even of the psychoses varied within and between countries prior to the introduction of structured interviews and explicit diagnostic criteria. The Present State Examination (PSE) (Wing *et al.* 1974) followed, and was successful in improving reliability as it evolved over the years into the Schedule for Clinical Assessment in Neuropsychiatry (SCAN) (Wing *et al.* 1998; WHO 1999). In the USA, a family of similar Structured Clinical Interviews for DSM has been developed – SCID-I for 'Axis I' disorders (illnesses and adjustment disorders, substance misuse disorders, sexual and gender identity disorders, 'other conditions that may be a focus of clinical attention' and developmental disorders other than personality disorder and mental retardation) and SCID-II for 'Axis II' disorders (personality disorders and mental retardation) (see American Psychiatric Publishing Inc. 2007 for the range of interviews and manuals). For some conditions, while good reliability is achievable between two or more observers at any one point in time (inter-rater reliability), reliability over time (test-retest reliability) has been harder to attain, and with the personality disorders is only really achievable with the overarching concept, tending to be poor with individual subcategories (Bronisch 1992; Bronisch and Mombour 1994; Westen and Arkowitz-Westen 1998).

If attaining reliability in psychiatric diagnosis has been a struggle, validity has proved a challenge too far for all but a tiny group of disorders. Traditional concepts of validity include 'predictive validity', 'concurrent validity' and 'content validity'. Predictive validity more or less equates with prognosis and is one of the more valued aspects of diagnosis, although carrying all the limitations of any risk prediction. Concurrent validity is, in effect, reliability against a gold standard. Diagnosis in physical medicine has proved easier to validate in this respect, because in so many cases, real physical entities underlying the symptoms and signs are detectable and their significance understood. Psychiatry is not really in this position. Many problems presenting as mental and behavioural problems are not known to have an underlying physical reality in the same sense that the tubercle bacillus underlies tuberculosis or blood cell deformities and shortages underlie the anaemias. Where such knowledge is available, it illustrates further how divorced the abstraction of disease may be from its physical cause. A plethora of clinical presentations, for example, is caused by just one creature – the tubercle bacillus; outcomes are variable too. Labour to isolate only those people with precisely similar diagnostic criteria and deciding that only these had tuberculosis would now seem ridiculous. Equally, similar presentations are no evidence of the same underlying condition; precisely similar shades of pallor, precisely the same rates of breathlessness and precisely the same level of exhaustion on exercise do not mean that the people concerned have the same disease.

Some are ever hopeful that 'one day' physical evidence – perhaps a blood or urine test, perhaps a lumbar puncture - will be found for all mental and behavioural problems and that diagnosis in psychiatry will be as dependent on such tests and other technology as diagnosis is in internal medicine. It is arguable that this will not happen in the foreseeable future, because of a range of barriers. First, we already know from observation of conditions with known causes – for example, mental states after intoxication with a variety of substances or in the course of high fever or under grave hormonal imbalance – that mental states can appear similar, regardless of cause. Secondly, if we acknowledge that the brain is a complex organ, even when abnormalities of structure or function are found through ever more sophisticated technologies, it is generally far from clear whether changes are causative, compensatory, compounding or coincidental. Van Os (2001), for example, has argued that measurable cognitive dysfunction among people with schizophrenia constitutes the factor that leads them to fail to cope with their psychosis and present to psychiatric services rather than necessarily being characteristic of the psychosis. Thirdly, the interplay between physical and social factors in determining the onset and form of psychiatric disorders is considerable. Although, for example, substantial research energies – with results – are poured into discovering the genetic predisposition to schizophrenia, the social and traumatic antecedents of schizophrenia are also receiving more attention (Read et al. 2005).

The concept of content validity covers the capacity of the concept to represent all of the content of a particular construct – and none of another. This is why operational definitions generally incorporate exclusion criteria as well as inclusion criteria, but still, as Kendell and Jablensky (2003) point out, such validity remains elusive for almost all psychiatric disorders. They go on to stress, however, that this is no reason to discard diagnoses so long as they have 'utility', and set out a range of ways in which our current diagnostic concepts may be useful. We covered some at the beginning of the section, in the statement of purpose of diagnosis. While they consider that current categories are useful for some aspects of research and practice, however, they regard them as of little use for legal practice. The introduction to DSM-IV (American Psychiatric Association 1994) also includes an explicit paragraph about the risks of using its categories, criteria and textual descriptions for legal purposes.

The politics of diagnosis

Psychiatry is particularly prone to its diagnostic systems changing with fashion and being used for political purposes within and outside the health care environment. In the absence of underlying pathological realities that can be confirmed in the laboratory or scanning department, psychiatric diagnoses tend to be made by consensus of psychiatric opinion, rather in the way that chlorosis was a diagnosis made by consensus in earlier centuries. In other words, traditions develop about the ways in which particular symptoms group together in a significant number of patients so that they can be called a 'syndrome'. This may not be as perverse as it sounds, providing any such labelling is explicitly to assist in an individual clinical situation or to create a testable hypothesis. It is when such tentative creations are transferred from the probabilistic climate of clinical or research practice to the binary certainties of the courts or tabloid journalism that problems arise.

A US public debate on whether 'extreme bias' can be an illness (Vedantam 2005) leads into just such a dilemma. 'Extreme bias' is a euphemism in itself; it means prejudice – racial prejudice, gay prejudice, religious prejudice – pretty much any form of ignorant, ugly attitude. On one side a group of clinicians have begun to argue that people with apparently profound beliefs of this kind are very impaired and could benefit from treatment, so they also need a special category within DSM-V; the other concerns range from 'are you pathologising all of life?' to 'you would allow hate-crime perpetrators to evade responsibility … they could use it as a defence', with yet others countering that paedophilia is classed as a disorder but not admissible as a defence to child molestation. This could be an indication of how the linear growth of categories in DSM occurred, and underscores the need for caution so often disregarded in court not to get trapped there into arguments about whether an individual fits a particular diagnostic category or not.

At the simplest level, one might argue that insofar as 'extreme bias ideas/beliefs' are 'truly pathological' in an individual, there is already a category of disorder which should capture this: delusional disorder. The argument, already raised, that in these circumstances having fewer categories for diagnosis rather than one for every variant of a symptomatic presentation, is powerful. Here, for example, there is already a wealth of literature on whether there are sufficient grounds to regard delusional disorder as a diagnostic entity in itself (e.g. Hoff 2006) and of serious debate about what constitutes its core feature – the nature of delusion (e.g. Kräupl Taylor 1979) – and about possibly distinctive psychological processes that may underpin this symptom (e.g. Bentall and Taylor 2006). Here, then, a clinical diagnosis is thought to be useful on the basis of the sufferer having a single, persistent symptom that is interfering with his or her life. Would it be helpful to have more of this kind of thing? Probably not. The question is particularly pertinent, however, for forensic mental health practitioners, and indeed for anyone working in clinical practice with people who have isolated ideas or perceptual experiences that are outside the mainstream and troubling them. Link and Stueve (1994), on comparing over 500 psychiatric patients and over 500 never treated community controls, showed that the relationship between 'threat/control-override symptoms' (as rated on the Psychiatric Epidemiology Research Interview (PERI), Dohrenwend *et al.* 1986) were associated with violence regardless of patient status. Mojtabai (2006) analysed self-report data from 38,132 people in the US national household survey on drug abuse and found not only that over 5 per cent of this sample reported psychotic symptoms, but also that people reporting any such experience were more than five times as likely to report having been violent to an intimate partner and more than five times as likely to report having had an arrest for violence. Mojtabai is cautious about inferring psychotic illness from reports of psychotic symptoms rated by non-clinicians, but Poulton *et al.* (2000) had already noted their predictive power with respect to onset of psychotic illness.

Stigmatic and dangerous use of diagnosis

Just as diagnosis incorporates inclusion and exclusion criteria, so diagnosis can be used to stigmatise and exclude from services as well as to provide the basis for drawing into services. The fact that mental disorders may not only be associated with impaired capacity for doing things but, with violent behaviour makes this potentially dangerous for the community. Part of the problem is that words which may have some legitimate clinical meaning have entered everyday language, and clinicians as well as lay people may use them pejoratively.

Perhaps the most notorious of psychiatric terms in this respect is 'psychopath'. The word has a long and chequered history originally meaning somebody with mental pathology, then being reserved for people with a certain kind of personality pathology, then becoming a legal term, but for many years now it has also been used in a derogatory manner to refer to someone who is not liked and certainly to be rejected. Sometimes it is used as an equivalent for 'evil doer' or monster rather than a fellow human being. Although it had a fairly innocuous beginning the word 'psychopathy' is not now used in the official classifications of psychiatric disease but has been revived by the Psychopathy Checklist (Hare *et al.* 1990), a psychology test based on the characteristics outlined by Cleckley (1976) in a published volume of case histories. The psychometrics of this scale are subject to periodic revision and debate, but there is undoubtedly something useful in the concept (Cooke *et al.* 2004, 2005). Nevertheless, the terminology must raise questions about just why it seems commonly associated with poor prognosis.

Imagine meeting a person with the following characteristics: glibness/superficial charm, grandiose sense of self-worth, need for stimulation/proneness to boredom, pathological lying, cunning/manipulative, lack of remorse or guilt, shallow affect, callous/lack of empathy, parasitic lifestyle, poor behavioural controls, promiscuous sexual behaviour, early behavioural problems, lack of realistic, long-term plans, impulsivity, irresponsibility, failure to accept responsibility for own actions, many short term marital relationships, juvenile delinquency, revocation of conditional release, and criminal versatility. These are the twenty items of the revised Psychopathy Checklist. Do you think you would like a person with, say ten of these characteristics? Would you be open and honest with him, even adopt an objective scientific attitude, or would you become clinically defensive, and if you intended to see him as a patient, prepare for a complex game of out-psyching the psychopath. (Maier 1990: 766–9)

Years later, Bowers (2002) extracted accounts from English high-security hospital nursing staff about the qualities in patients which would lead them to consider their patients as 'bad', 'evil' or 'monstrous' and provide barriers to treating them. Such patients had 'not been abused as children', 'their index offence had been serious violence against vulnerable victims', 'had been planned in advance', 'they refused treatment in hospital', 'they showed no remorse' *and* 'they appeared to be nice people'. Many of the patients about whom they were speaking had participated in an unrelated study about what they wanted in services and staff characteristics. Most had extensive experience of both hospital and prison; most wanted treatment although preferred the idea of prison to hospital because they assumed it would mean a fixed period of detention. The staff characteristic wanted by over 80 per cent of the patients was a caring and understanding attitude. One other quality (experience) was mentioned by 48 per cent and no other by more than 20 per cent (Ryan *et al.* 2002). The patients were not asked how they would respond to being described in the terms of psychopathy, but we have experienced individual patients express alarm at the prospect, fear about personality tests, despondency at the label and the commonly observed fact that those who acquire it are frequently rejected from psychiatric services, and terror at the thought of being caught up in the 'dangerous and severe personality disorder' net.

Such problems are not confined to people who have personality disorders. If a psychiatric patient is unpopular or deviant or badly behaved then he or she is likely to acquire this diagnosis and, as a result, be rejected from services on the grounds that 'we have no facilities for treating personality disordered patients'. This mechanism may work even against patients who have clear symptoms of psychosis, including delusions and hallucinations. Two cases which are in the public domain illustrate this point.

The first case is that of Sharon Campbell, who killed her former social worker, Isabel Schwartz (Spokes 1988). As is so often the case during the onset of schizophrenia, there was some initial doubt about Ms Campbell's diagnosis (Table 9.1): 'It is difficult to know whether we are dealing with a paranoid reaction in a somewhat abnormal personality, or whether we are dealing with a case of schizophrenia'. Two years of attempts to work with a young woman who was repetitively violent and who refused antipsychotic medication because it made her put on weight led to diagnostic certainty by 1982: 'not schizophrenia'. This is rather striking for a group of professionals who are generally not good at recording significant negatives. Presumably this was to emphasise that Ms Campbell should not be regarded as suitable for admission; this was extended a month later to 'personality disorder', and in the same month there was a further explicit statement that she was having no psychiatric symptoms and, particularly, that she had no indication of psychotic illness. By October 1983 she was having 'personality and social difficulties'. After the killing in 1984, clinicians regarded her diagnosis as unequivocally one of schizophrenia and she was subsequently hospitalised indefinitely.

Table 9.1 Consecutive diagnoses for Sharon Campbell

June 1980	Depression with paranoid features
December 1980	?abnormal personality /schizophrenia
August 1982	?paranoid psychosis (borderline)
	?paranoid personality
	?schizophrenia
25 August 1982	Not schizophrenia
September 1982	Personality disorder
July 1983	Paranoid personality disorder
	Severely disturbed adolescent
19 July 1983	No psychiatric symptoms
August 1993	No indication of psychotic illness
October 1983	Personality difficulty and social difficulties
6 July 1984	KILLED ISABEL SCHWARTZ
Later July 1984	*Schizophrenia*

It can be seen from this that while a diagnosis is normally expected to benefit a patient in leading to understanding and effective treatment it can also be used negatively to stigmatise and reject. It must always be borne in mind that diagnoses are to some extent socially constructed, they vary with time and place and they can be used politically to gain or withhold treatment. Perhaps this was an isolated case? Far from it. Christopher Clunis stabbed a complete stranger in public and without warning (Ritchie *et al.* 1994).

A glance at Table 9.2 will show that a man who had been diagnosed as suffering from paranoid schizophrenia in 1986 had his diagnosis changed several times over the next seven years, but most consistently until late 1992 he had been regarded as having a psychotic illness, whatever its cause. His risk to others in the context of his illness was clear, but an abrupt change of attitude to his problems and being given a diagnostic label which could facilitate his rejection from services closely preceded the tragic killing. After the killing of Jonathan Zito and his admission to a secure psychiatric hospital, once again there was no doubt on the part of clinicians that he had paranoid schizophrenia, as previously recognised in 1986. Jayne Zito, Jonathan Zito's widow, founded a charitable trust in her husband's name to facilitate learning from such cases, and they continue to present from time to time. Much is made about the importance of improved risk assessment, but the latest report of the National Confidential Inquiry into homicides and suicides (2006) makes it plain how few cases would be avoided by this means. Has diagnostic acumen improved in such cases? A survey of an annual resident cohort of 2006 in one medium-secure unit of people admitted with schizophrenia or similar psychosis after serious violence, showed that about one-third had had previously changing diagnoses, often seriously disadvantaging their access to other health services (Shetty *et al.* 2007).

The terms 'psychopath' and 'personality disorder' can, then, have serious disadvantages both for a patient so labelled and for his or her relatives, friends and the wider community too. The reason for this is that the diagnosis is prominently concerned with perceived actions, and it is often difficult to elicit the thoughts or feelings of the presenting patient, even if the clinician has a mind to do so. Many diagnoses that are primarily 'behavioural' in this way create practical, ethical and legal problems. People suffering from primary paraphilias suffer even more disadvantage in terms of access to services. The diagnosis of paedophilia in particular brings no advantages at all, but rather stigmatises the man and implies that he is either a lawbreaker already or likely to become so. In any case, services are not available until the person has actually offended, and even then there is rarely the advantage of the treatment plan being offered outside of the prison environment. In Britain there are very few facilities that offer any prospect of treatment, even though the condition is recognised as a psychiatric disease and treatments are available in a few specialised centres.

Table 9.2 Consecutive diagnoses for Christopher Clunis

1986	Paranoid schizophrenia
	Attempted to hit sister
29.06.87	Schizophrenia with negative features
02.07.87	Schizophrenia or drug induced psychosis
24.07.87	Depression
01.01.88	Hit fellow patient
	Drug induced psychosis, or 'manipulation for a bed'
May 88	Found with knife – threatened violence
29.03.88	Psychotic or schizoaffective illness
03.05.88	Schizophrenia, drug induced psychosis or organic illness
25.05.89	?attempted strangulation
07.06.89	Lunged at police with knife
	Paranoid schizophrenia
02.07.89	Threatened to stab another patient
06.07.89	Threatened to stab another patient
29.09.89	Punched patient, grabbed a knife
February 1990	Tried to gouge patient's eye out
July 1990	Physical abuse to fellow employees
14.08.90	Struck resident with walking stick
23.03.91	Chased residents with carving knife
23.07.91	Schizophrenia
24.07.91	Fight with another patient
05.05.92	Paranoid psychosis
14.08.92	Paranoid schizophrenia
26.08.92	(Diabetes)
10.09.92	*Normal mental state, abnormal personality*
17.12.92	KILLED JONATHAN ZITO
1993	*Paranoid schizophrenia*

Legal issues

So far we have considered diagnoses as though they existed almost exclusively in a medical or health environment. That is never true and it's especially not true in forensic psychiatry. The mentally disordered offender not only is subject to medical controls and attitudes but also to legal ones as well.

The uncertainties and changeabilities of medical diagnosis do not fit well into the legal arena. The law tends to work on an all-or-none basis. Defendants are usually either guilty or not guilty. It may be critical in a criminal case to show whether a defendant was present at the scene of a crime or not. This is done by putting the evidence and arguments for him/her being there and the opposite arguments for him/her not being there. After the arguments have been heard, judgment is made between them by a magistrate, or judge or jury. Once the judgment has been made, this will be treated as a legal fact. This process does involve testing of evidence, but it is a long way from the scientific method and a long way from the generally tentative and probabilistic methods of medicine. Nevertheless, the law tries to constrain medical diagnoses within its own framework or else invent pseudodiagnostic concepts such as 'insanity' in the criminal courts, or 'nervous shock' in the civil courts, or 'mental illness', 'psychopathic disorder', 'mental impairment' and 'severe mental impairment' in mental health legislation. 'Abnormality of mind' is another, a concept required in order to reduce a criminal charge from murder to manslaughter and thus open the possibility to sentences other than life imprisonment. 'Abnormality of mind' is defined as 'the state of mind so different from the ordinary human being's that the reasonable man would term it abnormal'. This is a definition produced by the Court of Appeal to ensure that the concept of abnormality of mind could be a wide one, to be determined by a jury. The advantage of 'diagnostic terms' peculiar to the law, from the lawyer's point of view, is that they can be defined in statute, and then, as necessary, modified formally through legal process of a new judgment, usually tested in a higher court. The modifications may employ expert witnesses, but they are ultimately legal modifications to a legal decision. It is worth emphasising that, ultimately, such 'legal diagnoses' are never made by doctors. Doctors, psychologists and others may provide clinical evidence, but the final decision is by lawyers or lay people.

It is useful to take 'nervous shock' as an example. This has been defined as requiring three elements. The plaintiff must be suffering from 'a positive psychiatric illness', a chain of causation between the negligent act and the psychiatric illness must be clearly established, and a chain of causation must have been 'reasonably foreseeable' by the reasonable man. Much of this has nothing to do with medical diagnosis, but the court will certainly want medical evidence about 'a positive psychiatric illness'. One of the commonest illnesses used as a qualification for the diagnosis of nervous shock is posttraumatic stress disorder. In reality this is a somewhat nebulous, fluctuating disability with a wide variety of features. Inevitably, however, lawyers try to pin down diagnosis; they are delighted to find a menu of criteria in the diagnostic manuals, e.g. the latest version of the Diagnostic and Statistical Manual (DSM), even though, we stress again, the manual itself warns that the diagnostic definitions within it should not be used for legal purposes as they were defined for research purposes.

Legal acknowledgment of the limitations of the classification systems in the UK was put clearly during a *civil* process: the arbitration for compensation which took place after the sinking of the *Herald of Free Enterprise* in 1987. It was ruled that the arbitration panel should decide what constituted a psychiatric illness *without reference to the standard manuals*.

> 'We [the arbitration panel] were asked by the claimants to make a finding that DSM-III-R contains a suitable guide to the diagnosis of PTSD ... While we are anxious to be as helpful as possible to the parties, we do not feel able to be as dogmatic about this point as the claimants would wish to be ... PTSD is a very recent concept and, just as DSM-III was revised in 1987, further research and experience may necessitate revision in the future. When considering the cases involved in this arbitration, there did not appear to be much dispute that, in very general terms, DSM-III-R contains a useful guide to diagnosis, provided that it is not construed as a statute, but more a document which gives a guide to diagnosis. In particular, it seemed to us the passages concerning the time of commencement or duration of symptoms were unduly arbitrary. (Ogden *et al.* 1989: 37–9)

In the UK, in the criminal courts, most mental health evidence is entered at the sentencing phase. Here, the ethical problems for psychiatrists are mounting. Use of terms such as 'personality disorder', or 'paedophilia', particularly when there is some indication of dangerousness but little treatability, has long been recognised as a factor in the judge imposing a life sentence when that possibility is available (Thomas 1979). For England and Wales, the indeterminate public protection order (a life sentence in effect), under the Criminal Justice Act 2003, opens up more dilemmas. The psychiatrist may well be expected to add an opinion on 'dangerousness' to that of diagnostic status. Psychiatrists have been asked questions about dangerousness for many years but now they have been joined in the courts by psychologists and judges are aware that an increasing number of risk assessment tools are available. The diagnostic process in these circumstances thus goes way beyond the giving of a label, it embraces the fairly traditional medical skill of prognostication, but with the serious problem that, particularly by giving spurious numerical weight to such risk, 'expert opinion' may lead to a higher level of punitive response rather than to treatment. Further, there is little understanding in a courtroom that the prognosis is a dynamic and changing process, principally for the patient's benefit.

Formulation

Diagnosis and strict operational criteria are useful for communicating about assessment and for research, but neither is ideal for treatment. This is where 'formulation' comes into its own. Westen (1997), having surveyed over 1,800 psychiatrists and psychologists, was able to show the difference between clinical practice and other assessment needs. He was focusing on personality disorder, but it is arguable that the same principles apply to people presenting for help with almost any condition. Treating clinicians do not find it helpful to ask only direct questions based on diagnostic criteria, they prefer listening to narratives and observing the presenting person's behaviour towards them in the consulting room. They want then to generate a formulation which is more specific to the individual case, and which takes account of the disorder, interpersonal relationships and wider social circumstances and disabilities. They want, in effect, to be able to tell an individual's story. A potential problem with this is that it can be simply idiosyncratic when the ideal is that it should be systematic and reproducible too.

Westen's solution was the development of an assessment tool for personality disorder which allowed clinicians to formalise their assessment through matching descriptors of their patient derived from the clinical interaction to a set of 200 standard descriptors (Westen and Shedler 1999).

A group led by Manfred Cierpka and Gerd Rudolf in Heidelberg have adapted a psychoanalytic approach, resulting in a system of 'Operational Psychodynamic Diagnostics' (OPD) (OPD Taskforce 2001, 2006). Originally designed for use principally with patients who presented with somatising disorders, the approach could be applied to people with any disorder, and the latest version incorporates some elements specific for offender patients. OPD offers a system for organising assessment across five axes, with the principal goal of informing and focusing psychotherapy, but it has potential coincidental value in helping clinicians to understand and deal with the complexities of their relationships with challenging patients. A minimum of one hour of semi-structured interview is required, but generally ratings are based on more than this. It is founded in psychodynamic principles, but without relying on technical language or being allied to a particular school. It is necessary to be trained in its use in order to be able to apply it effectively, but it is not necessary to have had a psychodynamic training. Axis V allows for mapping onto DSM/ICD systems. Axis III and axis IV have the most resonance with psychodynamic principles, and are perhaps most difficult for those without psychodynamic training to rate; they cover inner conflict and personality structure. A problem in rating offender patients is that while they have conflicts, they are often unable to internalise them. Aspects of personal structures to be rated include capacity for self-perception, self-regulation, communication and attachment. Axis I is an essential precursor to establishing treatment, dealing as it does with the patient's presenting problems, his or her perceptions of those problems, personal resources or strengths and the strengths or tensions in his or her social networks. It clarifies both the specifics of the problems for treatment and the patient's readiness to deal with them. Axis II is the interpersonal axis. It assists in the definition of four aspects of the patient – the patient's habitual experience of self, the patient's habitual experience of others, the therapist/investigator's habitual experience of the patient and the therapist/investigator's habitual experience of him- or herself while relating to the patient. Ratings are made according to given criteria and can be recorded simply as a series of four lists, or diagrammatically as a circumplex model, or as a classic, narrative formulation.

Conclusions

Diagnoses and formulations are primarily methods for transmission of information about the nature, causes and likely outcomes of presentations of problems with health to the person presenting with those problems and between others about that person and his or her problems. Within the medical model, they should principally serve the patient. However, the terminologies often do not convey the same or even any meaning to other members of the clinical team who are not trained in making diagnoses (e.g. nurses). Current approaches to diagnosis tend to be categorical and served by standard sets of criteria laid out in manuals. These have value for research but less value in clinical practice and should be used with the utmost caution in conjunction with any aspect of the law. They have utility rather than validity. Unfortunately, as a result, they may be used against presenting persons as well as strictly on their behalf. Some conditions are particularly associated with violence and there is some evidence to suggest that misuse of diagnosis through diagnostic gymnastics, whether through ignorance or design, can be dangerous as well as potentially unethical. Further care must be taken in translation between medical terminology and legal terminology. For those committed to offering treatment, it is arguable that the more individualised process of formulation is more useful than diagnosis. Methods of improving the rigour of formulation are emerging but have yet to be evaluated for their specific relevance for offender patients.

Selected further reading

Up-to-date texts for further reading are included in the references and will not be repeated here. Here we draw attention to three important older texts which give a historical perspective in which to set the modern debate.

Kraepelin, E. (1919) *Dementia Præcox*, trans. R. M. Barclay, ed. G. M. Robertson. Edinburgh: E. & S. Livingstone is a classic text which describes the first attempt at approaching phenomenology by the observation of groups of patients using a scientific approach.

Jaspers, K. (1946) *Allgemeine Pathologie*, English trans. of the 7th (1946) edn J. Hoenig and M. W. Hamilton (1963) *General Psychopathology*. Manchester: Manchester University Press remains the phenomenological bible of psychiatry and should be in every clinician's library.

Kräupl Taylor, F. (1979) *Psychopathology: Its Causes and Symptoms*. Romney Marsh: Quartermaine provides the last practical detailed description of psychopathology in phenomenological terms before DSM swept these traditional ideas away.

References

American Psychiatric Association (APA) (1994) *Diagnostic and Statistical Manual of Mental Disorders*, 4th edn. Washington, DC: APA.

American Psychiatric Publishing Inc. (2007) For all DSM manuals, SCID interviews and manuals, see: http://www.appi.org/dsm.cfx (last accessed 28 march 2007).

Bentall, R.P. and Taylor, J.L. (2006) 'Psychological processes and paranoia: implications for forensic behavioural science', *Behavioral Sciences and the Law*, 24: 277–94.

Blashfield, R.K. and Fuller, A.K. (1996) 'Predicting the DSM-V', *Journal of Nervous and Mental Disease*, 184: 4–7.

Bowers, L. (2002) *Dangerous and Severe Personality Disorder: Response and Role of the Clinical Team*. London and New York: Routledge.

Bronisch, T. (1992) 'Diagnostic procedures of personality disorders according to the criteria of present classification systems', *Verhaltungstherapie*, 2: 140–50.

Bronisch, T., and Mombour, W. (1994) 'Comparison of the diagnostic checklist with a structure interview for DSM-III-R and ICD-10 personality disorders', *Psychopathology*, 27: 312–20.

Cleckley, H.R. (1976) *The Mask of Sanity*. Saint Louis, MO: Mosby.

Cooke, D.J., Michie, C., Hart, S. D. and Clark, D. (2004) 'Reconstructing psychopathy: clarifying the significance of antisocial and socially deviant behaviour in the diagnosis of psychopathic personality disorder', *Journal of Personality Disorders*, 18: 337–57.

Cooke, D.J., Michie, C., Hart, S.D. and Clark, D. (2005) 'Searching for the pan-cultural core of psychopathic personality disorder', *Personality and Individual Differences*, 39: 283–95.

Craddock, N. and Owen, M. (2005) 'The beginning of the end for the Kraepelinian dichotomy', *British Journal of Psychiatry*, 186: 364–6.

Crow, T. J. (1990) 'The continuum of psychosis and its genetic origins. The sixty-fifth Maudsley lecture', *British Journal of Psychiatry*, 156: 788–97.

Dohrenwend, B.P., Levav, I. and Shrout, P.E. (1986) 'Screening scales from the Psychiatric Epidemiology Research Interview (PERI)', in M.M. Weissman, J.K. Myers and C.E. Ross (eds), *Community Surveys of Psychiatric Disorders*. New Brunswick, NJ: Rutgers University Press.

Feighner, J.P., Robins, E., Guze, S.B., Woddruff, R.A., Winokur, G. and Munoz, R. (1972) 'Diagnostic criteria for use in psychiatric research', *Archives of General Psychiatry*, 26: 57–63.

Hare, R.D., Harpur, T.J., Hakstian, A.R., Forth, A.E., Hart, S.D. and Newman, J.P. (1990) 'The revised psychopathy checklist: descriptive statistics, reliability, and factor structure', *Psychological Assessment: A Journal of Consulting and Clinical Psychology*, 2: 338–41.

Hoff, P. (2006) 'Delusion in general and in forensic psychiatry – historical and contemporary aspects', *Behavioral Sciences and the Law*, 24: 241–55.

Jaspers, K. (1946) *Allgemeine Pathologie*, English trans. of the 7th edn (1946) J. Hoenig and M. W. Hamilton (1963) *General Psychopathology*. Manchester: Manchester University Press.

Kendell, R.E. (1987) 'Diagnosis and classification of functional psychosis', *British Medical Bulletin*, 43: 499–513.

Kendell, R.E. and Jablensky, A. (2003) 'Distinguishing between the validity and utility of psychiatric diagnosis', *American Journal of Psychiatry*, 169: 4–12.

Kendell, R.E., Cooper, J.E., Gourlay, A.J., Copeland, J.R., Sharpe, L. and Gurland, B.J. (1971) 'Diagnostic criteria of American and British Psychiatrists', *Archives of General Psychiatry*, 25: 123–30.

Kendler, K.S. (1980) 'The nosologic validity of paranoia (simple delusional disorder): a review', *Archives of General Psychiatry*, 37: 699–706.

Kraepelin, E. (1919) *Dementia Præcox*, trans. R.M. Barclay, ed. G.M. Robertson. Edinburgh: E. & S. Livingstone.

Kräupl Taylor, F. (1979) *Psychopathology: Its Causes and Symptoms*. Romney Marsh: Quartermaine.

Link, B. and Stueve, A. (1994) 'Psychotic symptoms and the violent/illegal behaviour of mental patients compared to community controls', in J. Monahan and H.J. Steadman (eds), *Violence and Mental Disorder: Developments in Risk Assessment*. Chicago: Chicago University Press, pp. 137–59.

Loudon, I.S.L. (1980) 'Chlorosis, anaemia, and anorexia nervosa', *British Medical Journal*, 281: 1669–75.

Maier, G. J. (1990) 'Psychopathic disorders: beyond the counter-transference', *Current Opinion in Psychiatry*, 3: 766–9.

Mojtabai, R. (2006) 'Psychotic-like experiences and interpersonal violence in the general population', *Social Psychiatry and Psychiatric Epidemiology*, 41: 183–90.

National Confidential Inquiry (2006) *Five Year Report of the National Confidential Inquiry into Suicide and Homicide by People with Mental Illness*. See: http://www.medicine.manchester.ac.uk/suicideprevention/nci/Useful/avoidable_deaths_full_report.pdf (last accessed 8 January 2007).

Ogden, M., Wright, M. and Crowther, W. (1989) 'Report of an arbitration concerning the claims of 10 passengers survived the capsize of the "Herald of Free Enterprise"', *Personal and Medical Injuries Law Letter*, 5: 37–9 (104).

OPD Task Force (2001) *Operational Psychodynamic Diagnostics*. Seattle, Toronto, Bern and Göttingen: Hogrefe & Huber.

OPD Taskforce (2006) OPD-2. *Das Manual für Diagnostik und Therapieplanung*. Bern: Verlag Hans Huber.

Poulton, R., Caspi, A., Moffitt, T. E., Cannon, M., Murray, R. and Harrington, R. (2000) 'Children's self-reported psychotic symptoms and adult schizophreniform disorder: a 15-year longitudinal study', *Archives of General Psychiatry*, 57: 1053–8.

Read, J., van Os, J., Morison, A.P. and Ross, C.A. (2005) 'Childhood trauma, psychosis and schizophrenia: a literature review with theoretical and clinical implications', *Acta Psychiatrica Scandinavica*, 112: 330–50.

Regier, D.A., Kaelber, C.T., Rae, D.S., Farmer, M.E., Knauper, B., Kessler, R.C. and Norquist, G. S. (1998) 'Limitations to diagnostic criteria and assessment instruments for mental disorder', *Archives of General Psychiatry*, 55: 109–5.

Ritchie, J.H., Dick, D. and Lingham, R. (1994) *The Report of the Inquiry into the Care and Treatment of Christopher Clunis*. London: HMSO.

Robins, E. and Guze, S.B. (1970) 'Establishment of diagnostic validity in psychiatric illness: its application to schizophrenia', *American Journal of Psychiatry*, 126: 983–7.

Ryan, S., Moore, E., Taylor, P. J., Wilkinson, E., Lingiah, T. and Christmas, M. (2002) 'The voice of detainees in a high security setting on services for people with personality disorder', *Criminal Behaviour and Mental Health*, 12: 254–68.

Scadding, J.G. (1967) 'Diagnosis: the clinician and the computer', *Lancet*, 2: 877–82.

Shetty, A., Jaywickrama, D., Jones, G., Dunn, E. and Taylor, P. J. (2007) *Unusual challenging behaviour and equivocal diagnosis: a threat to receipt of appropriate healthcare for offenders?* Poster presentation, Royal College of Psychiatrists Annual Forensic Faculty Meeting, Prague, February.

Spokes, J. (1988) *Care and Aftercare of Miss Sharon Campbell*, Cm 440. London: HMSO.

Thomas, D. A. (1979) *Principles of Sentencing*, 2nd edn. London: Heinemann.

van Os, J., Hanssen, M., Bijl, R. V. and Volleburgh, W. (2001) 'Prevalence of psychotic disorder and community level of psychotic symptoms: an urban rural comparison', *Archives of General Psychiatry*, 58: 663–8.

Vedantam S. (2005) 'Psychiatry ponders whether extreme bias can be an illness', *Washington Post*, 10 December.

Westen, D. (1997) 'Divergences between clinical and research methods for assessing personality disorders: implications for research and the evolution of axis II', *American Journal of Psychiatry*, 154: 895–903.

Westen, D. and Arkowitz-Westen, L. (1998) 'Limitations of axis II in diagnosing personality pathology in clinical practice', *American Journal of Psychiatry*, 155: 1767–71.

Westen, D. and Shedler, J. (1999) 'Revising and assessing axis II, Part I: developing a clinically and empirically valid assessment method; Part II: toward an empirically based and clinically useful classification of personality disorders', *American Journal of Psychiatry*, 156: 258–72, 273–85.

Wing, J.K., Cooper, J.E. and Sartorius, N. (1974) *The Description and Classification of Psychiatric Symptoms: An Instruction Manual for the PSE and CATEGO System*. London: Cambridge University Press.

Wing, J.K., Sartorius, N. and Üstün, T.B. (1998) *Diagnosis and Clinical Measurement in Psychiatry: The SCAN System*. Cambridge: Cambridge University Press.

World Health Organisation (1992) *The ICD-10 Classification of Mental and Behavioural Disorders*. Geneva: WHO.

World Health Organisation (1999) *Schedules for Clinical Assessment in Neuropsychiatry*. Geneva: WHO.

Chapter 10

Understanding and managing risk

Mike Doyle and Mairead Dolan

Introduction

Assessing and managing risk to others from forensic patients is fundamental to the practice of mental health professionals in forensic services. Although the link between mental disorder and risk to others is nothing new (Monahan 1992), in recent times there has been increasing concern in the United Kingdom in relation to violent behaviour. Over the past two decades a relatively small yet significant number of incidents involving people with mental illness have received considerable media attention (e.g. Ritchie *et al.* 1994; NHS London 2006), and this has left a strong impression of the potential dangerousness to the public from individuals with various forms of mental disorder. A recent report (National Confidential Inquiry 2006), highlighted the fact that patients recently in contact with mental health services commit around 9 per cent of all homicides in England and Wales, which translates to 52 homicides per year and 30 by people diagnosed with schizophrenia. Findings like this fuel concern about perceived failures in provision of effective treatment and management and the overall competence of mental health services to prevent violent behaviour (Reed 1997). These perceived failures could be linked in the minds of the public with the perception of inadequate service provision, and with the growing concern that the public are not adequately protected from dangerous individuals by current legislation.

Violence risk assessment and management are the principle justifications for the existence of specialised forensic services, and must be conducted proficiently and documented accurately if they are to reflect a high standard of clinical practice. However, risk assessment is an inexact science. Ultimately the decision on the level of risk is based on clinical judgment. As clinical decisions on risk are made at all stages of the clinical care process (Department of Health (DoH) 2000), it is important that forensic clinicians have a clear rationale and structure underpinning their approach to risk assessment and management. When considering the task of risk assessment, it is important to remind ourselves that it involves an assessment of the *behaviour* of concern, the *potential damage or harm* likely from that behaviour and the *probability* that it will happen (Scott 1977).

This chapter will focus on the background to violence risk assessment, the evidence-base for risk factors and practical implications related to assessing the risk of violence to others posed by users of forensic mental health services.

A structured process of risk assessment and management will be described and clarified by the use of a case example. To conclude, areas for future developments in research and practice will be considered. The focus of this chapter is violence. The operational definition throughout this chapter will be consistent with the definition of violence provided by Webster *et al.* (1997: 24) as actual, attempted or threatened physical harm that is deliberate and non-consenting. This includes violence against victims who cannot give full, informed consent, fear-inducing behaviour where threats may be implicit or directed at third parties, and all forms of sexual assault.

Background

In the past there has been substantial debate and controversy about the ability of the mental health professionals when predicting violence. In the 1970s and 1980s, it was argued that the mental health professional's predictions of dangerous behaviour were 'wrong about 95 per cent of the time' (Ennis and Emery 1978), and Faust and Ziskin (1988) argued that the accuracy of the judgments of psychologists and psychiatrists did not necessarily surpass that of laypersons. The possible reasons as to why predictions of violence have been so poor will now be considered by reviewing approaches to violence risk assessment in mental health services.

Clinical approach 'first generation'

Historically the most common approach used is unstructured clinical or professional judgment. This approach involves professional 'opinion' or judgments where there is complete discretion over which information should be considered, and there are no constraints on the information the assessor can use to reach a decision (Grove and Meehl 1996). This has the advantage of being flexible allowing a focus on case-specific influences and violence prevention (Hart 1998). Nonetheless, the clinical approach has been criticised for being unstructured, informal, subjective and impressionistic (Grove and Meehl 1996) and is plagued by various sources of bias and error as information is highly dependent upon interviewing, observation and self-report (Kemshall 1996: 13). Hart (1998) also highlighted several weaknesses of unstructured clinical judgement. First, there tends to be a lack of consistency or agreement across assessors with low inter-rater reliability. Second, assessors may fail to specify why or how they reach a decision, making it difficult for others to question that decision. Third, there is little evidence that decisions made using this approach are accurate and many observers have attributed the inaccuracy of clinicians' judgments on risk to the unstructured nature of the clinical approach (e.g. Monahan 1981).

Research studies have examined the accuracy of predictions made by clinicians using a predominately clinical approach. Some well-known examples are 1970s studies such as Steadman and Cocozza (1974) and Thornberry and Jacoby (1979). Later studies include Holland *et al.* (1983), Sepejak *et al.* (1983), Lidz *et al.* (1993), Menzies *et al.* (1994) and Belfrage (1998). The body of knowledge generated by these studies suggests that while clinicians' assessments of risk are not as exceedingly poor as the most pessimistic debaters argued, there seems to be general agreement that clinical risk predictions are only slightly above chance and the competence varies greatly between clinicians (Lidz *et al.* 1993). Monahan (1981) published an influential review of 'first-generation research' involving clinical, unstructured approaches to violence prediction in which he strongly criticised the accuracy of this approach and later concluded that the upper bound level of accuracy that the best risk assessment technology could achieve was of the order of 0.33 indicating that clinicians were accurate in no more than one out of three predictions of violence (Monahan 1984). Monahan (1981) cited a number of errors clinicians make when assessing violence risk which lead to inaccurate predictions. These included lack of specificity about the criterion being assessed (i.e. unclear definition of what is to be assessed), relying on illusory correlations, failure to incorporate situational or environmental information and, probably the most common error, ignoring statistical base rate information (Monahan 1981: 58). The inference was that prediction could be improved by incorporating research evidence into the assessment process by integrating statistical information on valid predictive relationships into clinical practice (Monahan 1981: 125). Monahan (1984) drew the lines of a 'second-generation' of theory and policy aimed at identifying a valid array of actuarial risk markers for violence risk assessment. Integrating statistical evidence into violence prediction has been termed the actuarial approach and is now briefly described.

Actuarial approach 'second generation'

The actuarial approach to violence risk assessment is typified by assessors reaching judgments based on statistical information according to fixed and explicit rules. 'Second-generation' research on actuarial violence risk assessment among the mentally disordered evolved in an attempt to overcome methodological and conceptual problems. In recent times the notion of 'dangerousness' has been replaced by the continuum of 'risk', thereby recognising that the subject matter is continuous and dynamic in nature rather than discrete and static. The focus of research, and to some degree practice, has moved from assessing the inherent 'quality' of dangerousness to a focus on individual 'actions'; namely violent behaviour (Monahan 1981; Steadman *et al.* 1993; Gunn 1996). The focus on the concept of risk has led to a third line of inquiry referred to as 'experimental predictions studies' (Otto 1992). These studies do not describe or represent current clinical practice, but rather identify potential predictor variables and possible predictive methods, formulas or techniques. The most common approach is to compile a checklist of a number of predictors or factors, each of which is allotted a score. The sum of the risk factors is an 'actuarial' graduated probability measure, representing the amount of risk attributed to the individual.

Actuarial judgments are based on specific assessment data selected because they have been demonstrated empirically to be associated with violence and coded in a predetermined manner (Hart 1998; Kraemar *et al.* 1997). There seems to be little doubt from research that the actuarial approach is statistically superior to unstructured clinical judgment, as it improves the predictive accuracy (Monahan 1981; Dawes *et al.* 1989). In a meta-analysis of 136 studies that compared clinical versus actuarial prediction, eight resulted in greater predictive accuracy for the clinical method, 64 showed more accurate prediction for the actuarial method, and 64 showed no difference (Grove and Meehl 1996). However, there are limitations to the approach which have been summarised by Hart (1998). Firstly, actuarial approaches tend to focus the assessment on a limited number of factors thus ignoring potentially crucial case-specific, idiosyncratic factors. Secondly, there is a tendency to focus on relatively static factors which are immutable, therefore leading to passive predictions. Thirdly, actuarial approaches may exclude crucial risk factors on the basis they have not been proven empirically even though they may be entirely logical (e.g. homicidal threats) (Hart 1998). Fourthly, actuarial approaches tend to be optimised to predict a specific outcome over a specific time period in a specific population, leading to non-optimal, even bizarre decisions when applied in different settings (Gottfredson and Gottfredson 1986). There is also the conflict between the concept of 'prediction' and that of risk management. The function of actuarial prediction methods is simply that – prediction. Risk assessment in mental health services is broader and has to link closely with management and prevention. This is reported by Moore (1996: 28) who highlights the paradox between the poor performance of clinicians in predicting violent behaviour which may be largely accounted for by under-reporting of violence and the paradox that successful prediction leads to prevention and thus the prediction proves itself wrong. Put another way, if a clinician predicts that someone is going to be violent then they usually have a duty to intervene in some way to prevent the violence. In this sense referring to violence prediction is misleading as clinicians are ethically and legally bound to prove themselves wrong when they predict violence (Hart 1998). In a recent review, Heilbrun (2002) considered the aim of violence risk assessment in mental health services. He emphasised that the purpose of risk assessment is to manage and 'prevent' rather than 'predict' violence. This illustrates an important distinction between the research and clinical perspectives. In research the aim is to identify variables that are predictive of violence, whereas in clinical practice similar variables are used to estimate the risk to others in order to develop plans to prevent the violent act. If clinicians reach a judgment that an individual is a high risk of violence and subsequently the individual does not become violent, from a research perspective the clinician has made a false positive error. However, in reality they may have been instrumental in ensuring effective preventative measures to minimise the risk of violence, paradoxically rendering their original judgment ('prediction') inaccurate. Finally, actuarial risk assessment tends to disengage clinicians from the clinical process therefore minimising the role of professional judgment (Hart 1998).

Structured professional judgment 'third generation'

Clinicians are mainly concerned with the clinical reality of assessing and managing risk rather than the research task of prediction. Both clinical and actuarial approaches have definite advantages and disadvantages. The debate as to which approach is most relevant to clinical practice is complex. However, it would appear that a combination of the clinical and actuarial approach is warranted. Such an alternative 'third-generation' approach, referred to as empirically validated, structured decision-making (Douglas et al. 1999a) or structured clinical/professional judgment (Douglas et al. 2003) attempts to bridge the gap between the scientific (actuarial) approach and the clinical practice of risk assessment. With structured professional judgment, the emphasis is on developing evidence-based guidelines or frameworks, which promote systemisation and consistency, yet are flexible enough to account for case-specific influences and the contexts in which assessments are conducted. Such guidelines can promote transparency and accountability yet encourage use of professional discretion and are based on sound scientific knowledge, yet are practically relevant (Hart 1998; Douglas et al. 1999a). This approach also moves the emphasis from one of prediction to risk management where prevention and treatment issues are considered, and the conditions under which the risk will increase and decrease are highlighted. This approach also recognises the reality that the process of clinical risk assessment is a dynamic and continuous process which is mediated by changing conditions (see Doyle 2000: 144).

In support of the structured professional judgment approach, Webster et al. (1997) argue that clinical risk management can be improved significantly if: assessments are conducted using well-defined published schema (structure); agreement between assessors is good, through their training, knowledge and expertise; prediction is for a defined type of violent behaviour over a set period; violent acts are detectable and recorded; all relevant information is available and substantiated; and finally, actuarial estimates are adjusted only if there is sufficient justification.

In summary, structured professional judgment involves a broad assessment approach which is rooted in evidence that for the most part has been validated by research (Douglas et al. 1999a). To facilitate this approach instruments need to be developed that are grounded in well substantiated research that may improve the clinical practice of risk assessment (Borum 1996).

Structured professional judgment approach to clinical risk management

The stages of clinical risk assessment and management may be conceptualised as an ongoing process. This process has been described as a risk management cycle (Doyle 2000), and is usually implicit in the provision of good quality healthcare and integrated into the Care Programme Approach (DoH 2000). The basis of any assessment relies on the accumulation of reliable information and consideration of valid risk factors. The reality of clinical practice is that tests and scales can help to inform clinical judgment, not replace it as ultimately it is people, not tests, who make decisions. The structured professional judgment approach attempts to bridge the gap between the scientific (actuarial) approach and the clinical practice of risk assessment. This approach emphasises the need to take account of past history, objective measures, current presentation, context/environment and protective factors, and recognises the reality that the process of clinical risk assessment is a dynamic and continuous process which is mediated by changing conditions (see Doyle 2000; Dolan and Doyle 2000). This type of approach has been referred to as the 'guidance not gospel approach' (Swets et al. 2000) and there is evidence to suggest that this approach is warranted to structure clinicians' risk judgments and that this may be superior to unaided clinical judgement (Doyle and Dolan 2006; Douglas et al. 1999a; Borum 1996).

Recently, Doyle and Duffy (2006) proposed a sequential five-step approach to risk management in mental health services which adopts an explanatory rather than a predictive model (Table 10.1) designed to:

- structure professional risk judgments;
- utilise evidence-based guidance and to foster an evidence-based approach;
- enhance understanding of origins, development and maintenance of risk behaviour;
- involve the person being assessed;
- identify targets for intervention; and
- facilitate defensible decision-making and positive risk-taking.

Table 10.1 Five-step structured professional judgment approach to risk management

Step 1:	**Case information**	
	History, mental state, substance use	
Step 2:	**Presence of risk factors**	
	Historical, current, contextual	
Step 3:	**Presence of protective factors**	
	Historical, current, contextual	
Step 4:	**Risk formulation**	
	Nature, severity, imminence, likelihood, risk reducing/enhancing	
Step 5:	**Management plan**	
	Treatment, management, monitoring, supervision, victim safety planning	

The focus here is on violence, although this five-step framework can equally be applied to other risks such as suicide or sexual violence. The *first step* (see Table 10.1) is concerned with accumulating information about the individual, being mindful of the need for multiple assessment methods and the use of different sources of information. *Step 2* involves identifying historical and current risk factors relating to the outcome of concern, e.g. self-harm, violence. *Step 3* supplements *Step 2* by identifying past and present protective factors associated with a decreased risk. It is important for assessors to not only consider risk factors present but also the protective factors that might mitigate against or restrain the person from becoming violence. These tend to be neglected in risk prediction studies and therefore have limited supporting evidence, yet these are crucial in clinical practice when reaching judgments regarding future risk. Recent structured professional guidelines have made explicit reference to protective factors in adolescent risk (e.g. Borum *et al.* 2000) and risk of sexual violence (Hart *et al.* 2003). Protective factors could include compliance with treatment, good support from friends, family and services or restrictions on movements (see Table 10.3 below). *Step 4* is the stage where the risk information already collected in Steps 1–3 is analysed in an attempt to gain a better understanding and formulation of the person's current risk. When considering the task of risk assessment, it is important to remind ourselves that it involves an assessment of the *behaviour* of concern, the *potential damage or harm* likely from that behaviour and the *probability* that it will happen (Scott 1977). The risk formulation stage resembles attempts to conceptualise risk behaviours for treatment purposes (e.g. Novaco 1994; Linehan 1993). Recently, Huessman (1998) developed a unified social information processing model which similarly linked events, schemas and emotional states to provide an information processing framework which explained the role of cognitions in aggression. An idiosyncratic, personalised risk formulation of this type has been found to be crucial for understanding problems and risks and for providing a framework for interventions (Persons and Tompkins 1997). The risk formulation should inform *Step 5* where management interventions are developed into a risk management plan.

The five-step approach is meant to be broad in its applicability to different service settings. The approach is practice-based in that it attempts to both reflect existing clinical practice while enhancing the utility of a structured evidence-based approach to risk management. These five steps are outlined in the case example in Box 10.1.

Box 10.1 Case example – John*

Background
John is a 38-year-old man who has been resident in a forensic medium secure unit for 18 months. He was admitted to the unit following an index offence of grievous bodily harm of a community psychiatric nurse who was visiting him at home. At this time he was described as withdrawn, suspicious and preoccupied, experiencing auditory hallucinations commanding him to assault the CPN. John believed at the time that the CPN was planning to inject him with poison.

John has a history of schizophrenia from age 20. The onset of his illness appeared to be precipitated by the death of his parents in a car crash. John was completing his degree at university at the time. He has been admitted to psychiatric hospital on four occasions since which included a short spell in a medium secure unit on transfer from a district hospital psychiatric unit, due to an assault on nursing staff.

He married when he was 26. His wife was also a user of mental health services and their relationship was described as volatile. They divorced six years ago. The relationship produced two children who are now cared for by long-term foster parents. John has weekly contact with his children and receives regular visits from his brother and sister who live locally.

John's mental state has improved significantly since he commenced clozapine 12 months ago, although he regularly complains about weight gain, fatigue and excess salivation, which he attributes to side-effects of the clozapine. His mental state generally is stable, although he can become very anxious when ruminating about lack of progress and his prolonged stay within the medium secure unit.

The clinical team are considering transferring John to a lower dependency open ward within the medium secure service. There are mixed views within the clinical team about this plan and regarding the risks that John poses to others. Therefore a multidisciplinary team meeting has been arranged to assess his current risk using the HCR-20 Violence Risk Assessment Guide. The team completed the HCR-20 collaboratively. In order to develop a shared understanding and risk formulation, each item is rated by consensus using a rating of whether the item is present/relevant yes/no or partially present/relevant.

HCR-20 historical items
Items definitely present included previous violence, early age of first violent incident, major mental illness and prior supervision failure. Items partially present included substance use problems, relationship instability and employment problems.

HCR-20 clinical items
These were rated based on the time period of three months prior to the risk assessment meeting. All of the clinical items – lack of insight, negative attitude, active symptoms of major mental illness, impulsivity and unresponsiveness to treatment – were partially present in this time.

Risk management items
The risk management items were rated in two ways in the context of John (1) remaining on the current medium secure locked ward and (2) being transferred to the open ward. It was felt that John would be more of a risk in the open ward area due to less feasibility of plans and exposure to stabilisers in open ward.

Additional *risk factors* included concern about his children, hostility towards some female members of staff in the past and irritating side effects of medication. *Protective factors* identified include good control over aggressive and violent impulses with no violent incidents for 12 months, motivated for discharge, utilises effective anxiety management techniques and appears to respond well to structured environment.

Formulation of risk
Almost all violence committed has been against staff involved in his care and management with several incidents of violence towards staff in the past. Main triggers of violence appear to be as a result of deteriorating mental state, poor insight and the onset of paranoid thoughts and voices commanding him to harm others. At these times his behaviour appears to be motivated by fear and feeling vulnerable. It is unlikely he is in imminent risk as he has not been violent for 12 months and therefore his current risk to others in the unit would be low. Warning signs that might signal violence include increased agitation, pacing and constant demands upon staff. It is likely that perceived failure or bad news would increase his risk as would decrease of his privileges as he has responded angrily to request refusals in the past. Some difficulty engaging with staff in the past and failure to engage in any form of trusting relationship is likely to increase his risk. Risk reducing factors might be continuing contact with his children and development of a rehabilitation plan that sets out both short- and long-term achievable goals.

Risk management plan
Develop a rehabilitation plan that sets out small achievable goals that would include gradual transfer to open ward and eventual discharge to community placement. This plan includes psychosocial interventions aimed at increasing insight into his illness, enhancing coping strategies, medication management, identifying relapse signature and signature risk signs and developing relapse prevention action plan.

* Please note that 'John' referred to in this case example is fictitious.

Table 10.2 Risk and protective factors for violence

Category of risk factor	Risk factor
Individual: what the person is	• Age • Gender • Ethnicity • Anger • Impulsiveness • Personality
Clinical: what the person has	• Mental illness • Persecutory delusions • Misidentification delusions • Threat/control-override symptoms • Command hallucination • Personality disorder • Psychopathy • Substance abuse
Historical: What the person has done	• Prior crime and violent behaviour • Recency • Frequency • Severity • Pattern
Experiential: What has been done to the person	• Pathological family environment • Victim of childhood abuse • Childhood victimiser/delinquent
Protective factors	• Responding to treatment • Compliance with treatment • Good insight • Good rapport and therapeutic alliance • Regular contact with services • Good social networks • No interest in or knowledge of weapons • Fear of own potential for violence

Risk factors for violence

Research on how clinicians assess risk and how accurate they are in predicting violent behaviour is certainly valuable, yet unless research can independently verify the predictive value of risk factors, their actual, as opposed to perceived, usefulness in violence risk assessment will remain unknown. Until clinicians are better informed of the factors that are actuarially associated with violent behaviour there is little chance of improving the accuracy of risk assessments (Monahan and Steadman 1994: 7).

Risk factors that are linked with an increase in violence are included in many different instruments and guidelines (see Douglas *et al.* 1999a). Monahan (2006) provides us with a useful framework to categorise four different types of risk factor for violence, related to (1) individual risk factors: what the person *is;* (2) clinical risk factors: what the person *has;* (3) historical risk factors: what the person *has done;* (4) experiential risk factors: what *has been done* to the person. These factors are illustrated in Table 10.2 and are considered in more detail in Chapter 16 (this volume).

Mental disorder may well be a small, albeit significant risk factor for violence. It is argued here that the link between mental disorder and violence is most likely to depend upon the presence, type and severity of psychotic symptoms such as delusions and auditory hallucinations (Eronen *et al.* 1998). In terms of psychotic symptoms, the dimensions of delusions and auditory hallucinations that are recommended areas for risk assessment are provided in Table 10.3.

Table 10.3 Dimensions of delusions and auditory hallucinations recommended for consideration in risk assessment

Positive symptom	Dimensions
Delusions	• Do they feel under threat? • Conviction in belief • Focused on a particular identified person • Misidentification delusions • Preoccupation and search for evidence • Distress caused belief • Planned pre-emptive action on belief • Response to hypothetical contradiction
Auditory hallucinations	• Commanding • Beliefs about the voices: – malevolent/benevolent/omnipotent • Can they recognise who it is? • Do they know why they are doing it? • Response – dismiss – distract – focus – obey • Distress caused by voice • Negative content • Disruption to life

Risk assessment guidelines and tools

A number of tools and evidence-based guidelines have been developed to inform judgments about future risk (see Table 10.4) and to facilitate a structured professional judgement approach to risk management in clinical mental health services (e.g. Webster *et al.* 1997; Borum *et al.* 2000; Hart *et al.* 2003). The choice of framework used to guide assessments will depend on many factors including type of risk, service configuration, availability of trained raters and the context in which the risk assessment is being conducted. Although by no means exhaustive, a selection of the established evidence-based tools and frameworks frequently referred to in the risk literature are listed in Table 10.4 and will be briefly described.

Table 10.4 Items in violence risk assessment tools and guidelines

PCL-R (Hare 1991)	PCL: SV (Hart et al. 1995)	HCR-20 (V2) (Webster et al. 1997)	VRAG (Webster et al. 1994)	Violence risk scale (Wong and Gordon 2000) Static	Violence risk scale (Wong and Gordon 2000) Dynamic
1 Glibness/superficial charm (1)	1 Superficial (1)	H1 Previous violence	1 PCL-R score	1 Current age	1 Violent lifestyle
2 Grandiose sense of self-worth (1)	2 Grandiose (1)	H2 Young age at first violent incident	2 Elementary school maladjustment	2 Age at first violent conviction	2 Criminal personality
3 Need for stimulation/ proneness to boredom (2)	3 Manipulative (1)	H3 Relationship instability disorder	3 DSM-III diagnosis personality	3 No. of young of offender convictions	3 Criminal attitudes
4 Pathological lying (1)	4 Lacks remorse (1)	H4 Employment problems	4 Age at index offence	4 Violence throughout lifespan	4 Work ethic
5 Conning/ manipulative (1)	5 Lacks empathy (1)	H5 Substance misuse problems	5 Lived with both parents to age 16	5 Prior release failures or escapes	5 Criminal peers
6 Lack of remorse or guilt (1)	6 Does not accept responsibility (1)	H6 Major mental illness	6 Failure on prior conditional release	6 Stability of family upbringing	6 Interpersonal aggression
7 Shallow affect (1)	7 Impulsive (2)	H7 Psychopathy (PCL-R/PCL: SV)	7 Non-violent offence score		7 Emotional control
8 Callous/lack of sympathy (1)	8 Poor behaviour controls (2)	H8 Early maladjustment	8 Marital status		8 Violence in institution

PCL-R (Hare 1991)	PCL: SV (Hart et al. 1995)	HCR-20 (V2) (Webster et al. 1997)	VRAG (Webster et al. 1994)	Violence risk scale (Wong and Gordon 2000)	
				Static	**Dynamic**
9 Parasitic lifestyle (2)	9 Lacks (goals) (2)	H9 Personality disorder	9 DSM-III diagnosis of schizophrenia		9 Weapon use
10 Poor behavioural controls (2)	10 Irresponsible (2)	H10 Prior supervision failure	10 Victim injury (index offence)		10 Insight into cause of violence
11 Promiscuous sexual behaviour	11 Adolescent antisocial behaviour (2)	C1 Lack of insight	11 History of misuse		11 Mental disorder
12 Early behavioural problems (2)	12 Adult antisocial behaviour (2)	C2 Negative attitudes	12 Female victim (index offence)		12 Substance use
13 Lack of realistic long-term goals (2)		C3 Active symptoms of major mental illness			13 Stability of relationships
14 Impulsivity (2)		C4 Impulsivity			14 Community support
15 Irresponsibility (2)		C5 Unresponsive to treatment			15 Release to high-risk situations
16 Failure to accept responsibility		R1 Plans lack feasibility			16 Violence cycle

Table 10.5 (continued)

PCL-R (Hare 1991)	PCL: SV (Hart et al. 1995)	HCR-20 (V2) (Webster et al. 1997)	VRAG (Webster et al. 1994)	Violence risk scale (Wong and Gordon 2000)	
				Static	**Dynamic**
17 Many short-term marital relationships		R2 Exposure to destabilisers			17 Impulsivity
18 Juvenile delinquency (2)		R3 Lack of personal support			18 Cognitive distortion
19 Revocation of conditional release (2)		R4 Non-compliance with remediation attempts			19 Compliance with community supervision
20 Criminal versatility		R5 Stress			20 Security level of institution

Key
PCL-R = Psychopathy Checklist (Revised)
PCL: SV = Psychopathy Checklist (Screening Version)
HCR-20 (V2) = Historical/Clinical/Risk Management 20-item Scale, Version 2 (H1–10 relate to history, C1–5 to clinical and R1–5 to risk)
VRAG, Violence Risk Appraisal Guide.

(1) = factor 1 loading
(2) = factor 2 loading

Psychopathy Checklist Revised and Screening Versions

The Hare Psychopathy Checklist (PCL), Hare Psychopathy Checklist: Revised (PCL-R) (Hare 1991) and more recently the Psychopathy Checklist: Screening Version (PCL:SV) (Hart *et al.* 1995) are measures that assess the construct of psychopathy. The PCL was based on global ratings from Cleckley's *Mask of Sanity* checklist and was developed to provide a more reliable measure of psychopathy. Later, the original 22-item PCL symptom construct rating scale was revised to the 20-item PCL-R (Hare 1991). The 20 PCL-R items are listed in Table 10.4. Each item is scored on a three-point scale: 0 = 'item does not apply'; 1= 'item applies somewhat'; 2 = 'item definitely applies'. Total scores can range from 0–40 and scores of 30 or more are considered diagnostic of psychopathy. Cross-cultural comparisons in North American and European samples have found the underlying core of the disorder essentially the same and there appears to be good cross-cultural generalisability of the construct. However, due to possible suppression/facilitation of psychopathic features and cultural differences, it has been recommended that a cut-off score of greater than 25 on the PCL-R, rather than 30, is more appropriate for European and UK samples (Cooke and Michie 1999).

The screening version of the PCL-R was designed with several key requirements in mind. It needed to be conceptually and empirically related to the PCL-R, psychometrically sound, based on a symptom construct scale, sensitive to non-forensic samples and shorter than the PCL-R. The 12 items (see Table 10.4) are divided into Part 1 interpersonal and affective symptoms and Part 2 social deviance symptoms, in accordance with Factors 1 and 2 of the 20-item PCL-R. The scale is scored in the same way as the PCL-R. Overall the PCL:SV is conceptually and empirically related to the PCL-R, psychometrically sound, based on a symptom construct scale and sensitive to non-forensic samples.

Numerous studies have found psychopathy, as measured by the PCL, PCL-R and PCL:SV, to be highly predictive of future violent behaviour and treatment outcome in criminal, forensic psychiatric and civil psychiatric settings (Salekin *et al.* 1996; Hemphill *et al.* 1998). Dolan and Doyle (2000) reviewed the evidence for the PCL scales as predictors of violence and found that psychopathy significantly predicted criminal and violent recidivism in forensic and psychiatric samples. The impressive predictive validity of psychopathy is reinforced by findings from the largest violence prediction prospective study of its type. The MacArthur Violence Risk Assessment Study (MacVRAS) considered the predictive validity of 134 risk factors for community violence in a civil psychiatric sample in the USA. They found that a score >12 on the PCL: SV was the best predictor of community violence by non-forensic patients in the first 20 weeks and one year after discharge (Monahan *et al.* 2000). In the UK psychopathy has been found to be significantly predictive of inpatient violence post-admission (Doyle *et al.* 2002; (Dolan and Davies 2006)) and community violence post-discharge (Doyle and Dolan 2006b).

Staff using the PCL-R and PCL:SV obviously need extensive training and qualifications, and the completion of the scales can take several hours. As a result, it is not uncommon for the PCL scales to be omitted from other risk scales and tools due to these practical difficulties (e.g. Monahan *et al.* 2001). However, wherever possible it is strongly recommended that the psychopathy item of violence risk scales is always completed to enhance the accuracy of risk judgments (Webster *et al.* 2002).

Historical Clinical and Risk – 20 Items (HCR-20 Version 2) Violence Risk Assessment Scheme

The Historical Clinical and Risk – 20 Items (HCR-20: Webster *et al.* 1997) is a scheme based on sound scientific knowledge and intended to be practically relevant. The HCR-20 is a broadband violence risk assessment instrument with potential applicability to a variety of settings. The conceptual scheme of the HCR-20 aligns risk factors into past, present and future. The HCR-20 takes its name from these three scales – historical, clinical, risk management – and from the number of items which equal 20 (see Table 10.4). In research the items are scored 0 = item not present, 1 = possible presence of item, 2 = item definitely present, although the authors have advised against using numerical prediction in clinical practice (Douglas *et al.* 2003). The historical variables represent the more or less static ground factors included in earlier actuarial tools. The clinical variables are meant to reflect risk in light of current presentation, state of symptoms, insight and attitudes. The Risk management variables represent a systematised appraisal of future risk including plan feasibility, social network support and contextual factors. In research, once all 20 items have been scored, the risk score is calculated with a range of 0–40. For research purposes this score can then be interpreted as an indication of future risk for violence. Many studies have used the HCR-20 in violence risk research in forensic and non-forensic mental health and prison settings. In a review by Dolan and Doyle (2000) the HCR-20 demonstrated significant predictive accuracy in civil and forensic settings and evidence suggests that the HCR-20 demonstrates good predictive validity in North American and European samples (Douglas *et al.* 2006). In the UK it has been found to significantly predict community violence post-discharge (Doyle and Dolan 2006b). It has also been found to have superior predictive validity relative to the screening version of Hare's psychopathy checklist (Douglas *et al.* 1999b; Doyle and Dolan 2006b) and is valid in males and females and inpatients diagnosed with schizophrenia and personality disorder. Recent research compared numerical prediction with professional risk judgments using high, medium and low risk categories. The HCR-20 was more predictive when structuring professional judgments compared to when it was used to calculate a numerical probability figure (Douglas *et al.* 2003). Also a recent prospective post-discharge follow-up study in England found the HCR-20 scores changed over time reflecting the changing level of violence risk (Doyle 2006b). Therefore, in clinical practice it is recommended that the HCR-20 is best used periodically as a professional guideline to structure clinical assessments while promoting transparency, accountability and encouraging use of professional discretion.

Finally, as with other structured risk assessments, it should be noted that the level of supervision provided on release can attenuate the predictive accuracy of the HCR-20 for post discharge violence. This was demonstrated by Dolan and Khawaja (2004), who noted that the HCR-20 predicted self-report violence and readmission, but not officially recorded violence, as supervising staff were using readmission as as effective management strategy. Previous writers in this field have noted this phenomenon (Hart 1998; Douglas *et al.* 2003).

Violence Risk Appraisal Guide

Due to the well documented predictive validity of the PCL-R/PCL:SV it is understandable that they have been integrated into actuarial violence risk assessment schemes and instruments. One such actuarial instrument is the Violence Risk Appraisal Guide (VRAG) (Webster *et al.* 1994). The VRAG was developed following research into 618 men who had committed a serious or violent offence and who had an opportunity to recidivate following discharge. Fifty variables were considered for inclusion as predictors because they had previously been found to be related to violent or general recidivism in previous studies. These variables reflected demographic information, criminal history, psychiatric history and childhood history. The outcome variable was violent recidivism, either incurring a new charge for a criminal offence against persons or if the person was returned to an institution for violent behaviour within a seven-year period. Multiple regression procedures were used to identify 12 variables for the final instrument and the 12 items were attributed integer weights ranging from –5 to +12 (Table 10.4). Scores range from –26 to +38. The VRAG has been found to be predictive of recidivism in different samples (Harris *et al.* 2002). Due to reliance on the presence of previous convictions for rating three of the items, it may be better suited to forensic and prison samples.

Violence Risk Scale

A scale specifically designed to assess the risk of violent recidivism in forensic patients was developed by Wong and Gordon (2006). The Violence Risk Scale (VRS) was developed based on the conception that to provide a comprehensive evaluation of an individual's risk for violent recidivism, it is necessary to assess both the static and dynamic factors that are empirically or theoretically related to violent recidivism. The VRS Version 2 consists of six static or historical factors and 20 dynamic or changeable factors (see Table 10.4). Each item is rated on a four-point scale 0–3 against descriptive criteria. It has been used effectively to evaluate the effect of treatment on risk in a violence prevention programme in Canada and the authors report that research to date indicates that the VRS has demonstrated strong predictive validity for violent recidivism over a two-year follow-up period. The VRS moves the field to a 'fourth generation' in risk assessment where risk assessment not only involves reaching risk judgments but also identifies treatment targets linked to violence (Wong and Gordon 2006). As yet the published data to support the VRS as a valid instrument for violence risk assessment remains limited. 'Recent work by our group (Dolan and Fullam 2007) in a sample of male secure psychiatric inpatients indicated that the VRS-2 and HCR-20 total scale scores correlated very highly, supporting the notion that the VRS-2 is a measure of violence risk. Both the HCR-20 and the VRS-2 could distinguish between violent and non-violent subgroups with reasonable effect size. There were highly significant correlations between the scales on the rating of items measuring comparable variables. In addition, both measures were predictive of violence at 12-month follow-up, but the HCR-20 clinical sub score was the most robust contributor in the summary regression analysis. Our results offer preliminary evidence that the VRS-2 is a reasonably valid measure of violence risk and that it could be useful for research in this area. Its promise would seem to lie in its comprehensive evidence-based background, its practical format, its direct link to risk management and its ability to evaluate the impact of treatment strategies.'

Therapeutic risk-taking

Most definitions of risk nearly always include reference to the likelihood ('possibility') of a harmful outcome ('danger or harm'). However, some definitions make reference to the likelihood of outcomes that may be beneficial. For example, '[risk is] the possibility of beneficial and harmful outcomes and the likelihood of their occurrence in a stated timescale' (University of Manchester 1996). This definition is particularly pertinent for clinicians making decisions that involve taking risks. Risk-taking is a particular form of decision-making and is commonplace in forensic mental health services. Clinicians in forensic services are expected to make decisions aimed at protecting the public while at the same time ensuring the patient's rights are safeguarded and their recovery and rehabilitation are promoted. The dilemma for forensic clinicians is that the focus not only needs to be on risk but also on the strengths of the patient (Morgan 2000).

Reaching a decision about what interventions are required to minimise risk has fittingly been described as a high-order skill as decision-makers not only need to remember the different outcomes possible, but also how beneficial or harmful they might be, how likely they are to occur and the reliability of the data producing the information (Carson 1996). Risk-taking arises in clinical practice when decisions need to be made about what measures should be implemented to reduce risks, especially when attempting to promote the independence of patients (Ryan 1993).

Forensic mental health services and clinicians who work within them must take risks. There are many examples of risk decisions that cannot be avoided, including decision to admit, granting leave, placement within unit, level of observation, visitor restrictions and discharge planning. The complexities of the risk decision-making process can be illustrated using the example of the decision about whether to implement special observations. There are obvious benefits of special observations such as closer supervision, better opportunities for assessment, proactive interventions and a more rapid response in times of crisis. However, there will also be potential harms in terms of intrusion on patient's personal space, lack of independence and an infringement on freedom. The harms and benefits of the intervention need to be considered before a defensible decision is made. Likewise very often clinicians are faced with dilemmas regarding sharing of information and child protection issues where striking the right balance between the rights of the person and the safety of others is crucial. Clearly, therapeutic risk-taking must follow careful assessment and planning, where the outcome of such decisions indicate that risks to the patient and others can be managed safely and that the outcome will be an improvement in the patient's quality of life and mental health. Prior to implementing risk management measures, clinicians need to carefully weigh up the harms and benefits associated with implementing risk management against the harms and benefits of inaction (Carson 1990). This is very important for the patient, but careful consideration and documentation of the harms and benefits of a decision will also improve the defensibility of the clinician if something goes wrong. Risk decisions need to be made in a manner which can readily be justified (Carson 1996). A review date should be agreed to review the measures implemented, usually as part of the care planning review process. In addition, a number of good practice points have been recommended to facilitate defensible risk decision-making (Doyle 2000; Morgan 2000; Carson 1997) to improve the likelihood of benefits for the patient while protecting individual clinicians and the organisations where they work. These include:

- using a systematic approach to risk management;
- multidisciplinary decision-making;
- peer reviews of difficult cases and management problems;
- clinical supervision;
- maintaining professional boundaries;
- professional development;
- evidence-based practice;
- guidelines on confidentiality and sharing information;
- risk policy acknowledging need for therapeutic risk-taking;
- no-blame culture;
- good communication and clear documentation;
- involving patients as much as possible in planning treatment and care;
- reporting and recording incidents.

Future considerations

In this chapter we have reviewed effective risk assessment and management while attempting to strike a balance with the reality of clinical practice. In the future, the link between the science and the art of violence risk assessment and management will need to be strengthened further by research. Evidence-based practice is obviously important to prove the efficacy of different approaches and interventions, but of at least equal importance is the need for clinicians to be able to demonstrate the effectiveness of approaches to risk management through practice-based evidence. To this end, more implementation evaluation will need to take place to investigate if the advances made in the development of more structured approaches to risk assessment and management result in improved outcomes in practice.

The quality and systematic nature of risk assessments is becoming an increasingly important aspect in inquiries into clinical practice following untoward events. Guidelines such as the HCR-20 and the VRS have value in enhancing the rationale for clinical risk judgments. By reviewing change in clinical and risk management items it may also be possible to assess the impact of current interventions and monitor progress while systematically tracking change in all key domains that have been identified as treatment targets. The latter approach should make intuitive sense to clinicians and reflect good clinical practice in risk assessment.

There is clearly a need to use a combination of strategies to characterise individual violence risk in the long, medium and short term, and this can only be done if clinical teams have a good knowledge and understanding of idiosyncratic historical, clinical and risk management factors that apply to individual cases. The move towards a 'fourth generation' of research and practice is promising and there is a need to examine and refine our understanding of the factors that confer protection against risk of subsequent violent behaviour over and above pharmacological and specialist psychological treatments. In future research consideration needs to be given to the influence of idiosyncratic factors such as peer group, social factors and level of monitoring and supervision.

In risk prediction the research question is aimed at determining the predictive accuracy of whether a person will be violent. However, in clinical practice there is a need to get an understanding of why the person might be a risk before prescribing treatment and management interventions to minimise the risk. Therefore future research in this area should aim to be theory-based. Evidence-based risk formulations should better explain reasons for risk, identify idiosyncratic 'causative' rather than risk factors, aid risk communication and result in formulation-based interventions (Doyle and Dolan 2006a).

This chapter has focused on the assessment and management of violence in adults. It should be noted there is a growing evidence base for the utility of new adolescent violence risk assessment tools such as the Structured Assessment of Violence Risk in Youth (SAVRY) (Borum, Bartel and Forth 2006). The SAVRY is composed of 24 items in three risk domains (Historical Risk Factors, Social/Contextual Risk Factors, and Individual/Clinical Factors), drawn from existing research and the professional literature on adolescent development as well as on violence and aggression in youth. Similar to adult measures the SAVRY helps assist in structuring an assessment so that a final professional judgment can be formulated about a youth's level of risk. To date there is limited UK psychometric data on the SAVRY but we have recently demonstrated its total risk score and risk rating showed moderate predictive accuracy for both violent and general recidivism in male adolescent offenders released from custody and moderate predictive accuracy for institutional infractions (Dolan and Rennie 2007 a, b in press).

Many other risks confront forensic and general mental health services, including risk of self-harm, suicide, sexual violence, absconding, fire-setting and exploitation. These areas warrant ongoing empirical investigation equivalent to research on violence risk. See the Department of Health (2007) guidance on best practice in managing risk.

Finally, it would appear that the provision of forensic services and the assessment and management of risk is likely to be subjected to increasing scrutiny and possible litigation. Therefore forensic services need to focus more on clarifying their systems for risk management, with a strong emphasis on structuring approaches to therapeutic risk-taking and risk decision-making generally.

Selected further reading

Douglas, K., Cox, D. and Webster, C. (1999a) 'Violence risk assessment: science and practice', *Legal and Criminological Psychology*, 4: 194–4 provide a thorough overview of emerging professional guidelines designed to support structured professional judgment in several risk areas.

Hart, S.D. (1998) 'The role of psychopathy in assessing risk for violence: conceptual and methodological issues', *Legal and Criminological Psychology*, 3: 121–37 highlights the strengths and weaknesses of psychopathy and critiques the value of violence risk prediction in clinical practice.

Heilbrun, K. (2002) 'Violence risk: from prediction to risk management', in D. Carson and R. Bull (eds), *Handbook of Psychology in Legal Contexts*, 2nd edn. John Wiley & Sons, pp. 127–43 describes recent conceptual, empirical and practical advances in risk management, and discusses the strategies that might yield important further advances.

Monahan, J., Steadman, H., Silver, E., Appelbaum, P., Robbins, P., Mulvey, E., Roth, L., Grisso, T. and Banks, S. (2001) *Rethinking Risk Assessment: The MacArthur Study of Mental Disorder and Violence*. Oxford: Oxford University Press describes the largest and most rigorous violence risk assessment study conducted to date and explain the method of developing a practical evidence based tool.

Swets, J., Dawes, R. and Monahan, J. (2000) 'Psychological science can improve diagnostic decisions'. *Psychological Science in the Public Interest*, 1 (1): 1–26 provide a detailed overview of reasons why statistical prediction rules are not utilised fully in clinical practice, including in violence risk assessment.

Best Practice in Managing Risk. Principles and evidence for best practice in the assessment and management of risk to self and others in mental health services. Department of Health, June 2007.

References

Belfrage, H. (1998) 'Making risk predictions without an instrument. Three years experience of the new Swedish law on mentally disordered offenders', *International Journal of Law and Psychiatry*, 21, 59–64.

Blom-Cooper, L., Hally, H., Murphy, E. (1995) *The Falling Shadow: One Patient's Mental Health Care 1978–1993*. London: Duckworth.

Borum, R. (1996) 'Improving the clinical practice of violence risk assessment', *American Psychologist*, 51 (9): 945–56.

Borum, R., Bartel, P. and Forth, A. (2000) *The Structured Assessment of Violence Risk in Youth (SAVRY)*. Florida: Psychological Assessment Resources (PAR), Inc.

Borum, R., Bartel, P., and Forth, A., (2006) *Structured Assessment of Violence Risk in Youth (SAVRY)*. Assessment division of PEARSON.

Carson, D. (ed.) (1990) *Risk Taking in Mental Disorder: Analyses, Policies and Practical Strategies*. Chichester: SLE Publications.

Carson, D. (1996) 'Developing models of risk to aid co-operation between law and psychiatry', *Criminal Behaviour and Mental Health*, 6: 6–10.

Carson, D. (1997) 'Good enough risk taking', *International Review of Psychiatry*, 9: 303–8.

Cooke, D.J. and Michie, C. (1999) 'Psychopathy across cultures: North America and Scotland compared', *Journal of Abnormal Psychology*, 108: 58-68.

Dawes, R.M., Faust, D. and Meehl, P.E. (1989) 'Clinical versus actuarial judgement', *Science*, 243: 1668–74.

Department of Health (2000) *Effective Care Co-ordination in Mental Health Services: Modernising the Care Programme Approach. A Policy Booklet*. London: DoH.

Dolan, M. and Doyle, M. (2000) 'Violence risk prediction: clinical and actuarial measures and the role of the psychopathy checklist', *British Journal of Psychiatry*, 177: 303–11.

Dolan, M. and Khawaja, A. (2004) 'The HCR-20 and post-discharge outcome in male patients and discharged from medium security in the UK', *Aggressive Behavior*, 30: 469–83.

Dolan, M. and Davis, G. (2006) 'Psychopathy as a predictor of outcome in schizophrenia', *Schizophrenia Research*, 81(2–3): 277–81.

Dolan, M. and Fullham, R. (2007) 'The validity of the Violence Risk Scale', 2nd Edition (VRS-2) in a British Forensic Inpatient Sample, *Journal of Psychiatry & Psychology*, 18(3): 381–93.

Dolan, M. and Rennie, C. (2007a in press) 'The Structured Assessment of Violence Risk in Youth as a Predictor of Recidivism in a United Kingdom Cohort of Adolescent Offenders With Conduct Disorder'. *Psychological Assessment*.

Dolan, M. and Rennie, C. (2007 b in press) 'The accuracy of the SAVRY in predicting institutional infractions in a UK cohort of adolescent offenders with conduct disorder'. *Journal of Forensic Psychiatry and Psychology*.

Douglas, K., Cox, D. and Webster, C. (1999a) 'Violence risk assessment: science and practice', *Legal and Criminological Psychology*, 4: 194–84.

Douglas, K., Ogloff, J., Nicholls, T. and Grant, I. (1999b) 'Assessing risk for violence among psychiatric patients: the HCR-20 Violence Risk Assessment Scheme and the Psychopathy Checklist: Screening Version', *Journal of Consulting and Clinical Psychology*, 6: 917–30.

Douglas, K. S., Ogloff, J. R. and Hart, S. D. (2003) 'Evaluation of a model of violence risk assessment among forensic psychiatric patients', *Psychiatric Services*, 54 (10): 1372–9.

Douglas, K., Guy, L., Weir, J. (2006) *HCR-20 Violence Risk Assessment Scheme: Overview and Annotated Bibliography*, 12 January. University of South Florida.

Doyle, M. (2000) 'Risk assessment and management', in C. Chaloner and M. Coffey (eds), *Forensic Mental Health Nursing: Current Approaches*. London: Blackwell Science, pp. 140–70.

Doyle, M. and Dolan, M. (2006a) 'Evaluating the validity of anger regulation problems, interpersonal style, and disturbed mental state for predicting inpatient violence', *Behavioral, Sciences and the Law*, 24 (6): 783–98.

Doyle, M. and Dolan, M. (2006b) 'Predicting community violence from patients discharged from mental health services', *British Journal of Psychiatry*, 189: 520–6.

Doyle, M. and Duffy, D. (2006) 'Assessing and managing risk to self and others', in the National Forensic Nurses' Research and Development Group (eds), *Aspects of Forensic Mental Health Nursing: Interventions for People with Personality Disorder*. London: Quay Books, ch. 10.

Doyle, M. Dolan, M.C. and McGovern, J. (2002) 'The validity of North American risk assessment tools in predicting inpatient violent behaviour in England', *Legal and Criminological Psychology*, 7 (2): 141–54.

Ennis, B. J. and Emery, R. D. (1978) *The Rights of Mental Patients*, revised edn. New York: Avon Books.

Eronen, M., Angermeyer, M. and Schulze, B. (1998) 'The psychiatric epidemiology of violent behaviour', *Social Psychiatry and Psychiatric Epidemiology*, 33: 13–23.

Faust, D. and Ziskin, J. (1988) 'The expert witness in psychology and psychiatry', *Science*, 241: 31–5.

Gottfredson, S. and Gottfredson, D. (1986) 'Accuracy of prediction models', in A. Blumstein *et al.* (eds), *Criminal Careers and 'Career Criminals'*, Washington, DC: National Academy Press, pp. 212–90.

Grove, W. and Meehl, P. (1996) 'Comparative efficiency of informal (subjective, impressionistic) and formal (mechanical, algorithmic) prediction procedures: the clinical-statistical controversy', *Psychology, Public Policy and Law*, 2: 293–323.

Grubin, D. (1997) 'Predictors of risk in serious sex offenders', *British Journal of Psychiatry*, 170: 17–21.

Gunn, J. (1996) 'Let's get serious about dangerousness', *Criminal Behaviour in Mental Health*, Supplement: 51–64.

Hare, R.D. (1991). *The Hare Psychopathy Checklist–Revised*. Toronto: Multi-Health Systems.

Harris, G., Rice, M. and Cormier, C. (2002) 'Prospective replication of the Violence Risk Appraisal Guide in predicting violent recidivism among forensic patients', *Law and Human Behavior*. 26 (4): 377–92.

Hart S.D. (1998) 'The role of psychopathy in assessing risk for violence: conceptual and methodological issues', *Legal and Criminological Psychology*, 3: 121–37.

Hart, S., Cox, D. and Hare, R. (1995) *The Hare PCL:SV: Psychopathy Checklist: Screening Version*. New York: Multi-Health Systems.

Hart, S., Kropp, P.R., and Laws, D.R., with Klaver, J., Logan, C. and Watt, K.A. (2003) *The Risk for Sexual Violence Protocol (RSVP): Structured Professional Guidelines for Assessing Risk of Sexual Violence*. Vancouver, BC: Institute Against Family Violence.

Heilbrun, K. (2002) 'Violence risk: from prediction to risk management', in D. Carson and R. Bull (eds), *Handbook of Psychology in Legal Contexts*, 2nd edn. John Wiley & Sons, pp. 127–43.

Hemphill, J.F., Hare, R.D. and Wong, S. (1998) 'Psychopathy and recidivism: a review', *Legal and Criminological Psychology*, 3: 139–70.

Holland, T.R., Holt, N., Levi, M. and Beckett, G.E. (1983) 'Comparison and combination of clinical and statistical predictions of recidivism among adult offenders'. *Journal of Applied Psychology*, 68: 203–11.

Huessmann, L.R. (1998) 'The role of social information processing and cognitive schema in the acquisition and maintenance of habitual aggressive behavior', in R. Geen and E. Donnerstein (eds), *Human Aggression: Theories, Research and Implications for Social Policy*. New York: Academic Press, pp. 73–109.

Kemshall H. (1996) *Reviewing Risk: A Review of Research on the Assessment and Management of Risk and Dangerousness: Implications for Policy and Practice in the Probation Service*. London: Home Office.

Kraemer, H., Kazdin, A., Offord, D., Kesler R., Jensen, P. and Kupfer, D. (1997) 'Coming to terms with the terms of risk', *Archives of General Psychiatry*, 54: 337–43.

Lidz, C., Mulvey, E. and Gardner, W. (1993) 'The accuracy of predictions of violence to others', *Journal of the American Medical Association*, 269: 1007–11.

Linehan, M.M. (1993) *Cognitive-Behavioral Treatment of Borderline Personality Disorder*. New York: Academic Press.

Menzies, R., Webster, C.D., McMain, S., Staley, S. and Scaglione, R. (1994) 'The dimensions of dangerousness revisited. Assessing forensic predictions about violence', *Law and Human Behaviour*, 18: 1–28.

Monahan, J. (1981) *Predicting Violent Behaviour*. Sage Library of Social Research. Beverley Hills, CA: Sage.

Monahan, J. (1984) 'The prediction of violent behaviour: toward a second generation of theory and policy', *American Journal of Psychiatry*, 141: 10–15.

Monahan, J. (1992) 'Mental disorder and violent behaviour: perceptions and evidence', *American Psychologist*, April: 511–21.

Monahan, J. (2006) 'A jurisprudence of risk assessment: forecasting harm among prisoners, predators and patients', *Virginia Law Review*, 92 (3).

Monahan, J. and Steadman, H. (eds) (1994) *Violence and Mental Disorder: Developments in Risk Assessment*. Chicago: University of Chicago Press.

Monahan, J., Steadman, H., Silver, E., Appelbaum, P., Robbins, P., Mulvey, E., Roth, L., Grisso, T. and Banks, S. (2001) *Rethinking Risk Assessment: The MacArthur Study of Mental Disorder and Violence*. Oxford: Oxford University Press.

Moore, B. (1996) *Risk Assessment: A Practitioner's Guide to Predicting Harmful Behaviour*. London: Whiting & Birch.

Morgan, S. (2000) *Clinical Risk Management: A Clinical Tool and Practitioner Manual*. London: Sainsbury Centre for Mental Health.

National Confidential Inquiry (2006) *Avoidable Deaths: Five-year Report of the National Confidential Inquiry into Suicide and Homicide by People with Mental Illness*. University of Manchester.

NHS London (2006*) The Independent Inquiry into the Care and Treatment of John Barrett. October*. London: South West London Strategic Health Authority.

Novaco, R. (1994) 'Anger as a risk factor for violence among the mentally disordered', in J. Monahan and H. Steadman (eds), *Violence and Mental Disorder: Development in Risk*

Assessment. Chicago: University of Chicago Press, pp. 21–59.

Otto, R.K. (1992) 'Prediction of dangerous behavior: a review and analysis of "second generation" research', *Forensic Reports*, 5: 103–33.

Persons, J. and Tompkins, M. (1997) 'Cognitive behavioural formulation', in T.D. Eells (ed.), *Handbook of Psychotherapy Case Formulation*. New York: Guilford Press. pp. 314–39.

Reed, J. (1997) 'Risk assessment and clinical risk management: the lessons from recent inquiries', *British Journal of Psychiatry*, 170 (suppl. 32): pp. 4–7.

Ritchie, J.H., Dick, D. and Lingham, R. (1994) *The Report of the Enquiry into the Care and Treatment of Christopher Clunis*. London: HMSO.

Ryan, T. (1993) 'Therapeutic risks in mental health nursing', *Nursing Standard*, 24: 29–31.

Salekin, R.T., Roger, R. and Sewell, K.W. (1996) 'A review and meta-analysis of the Psychopathy Checklist and Psychopathy Checklist–Revised: predictive validity of dangerousness', *Clinical Psychology: Science and Practice*, 3: 203–15.

Scott, P. (1977) 'Assessing dangerousness in criminals', *British Journal of Psychiatry*, 131: 127–42.

Sepejak, D., Menzies, R.J., Webster, C.D. and Jensen, F.A. (1983) 'Clinical predictions of dangerousness: two-year follow-up 408 pre-trial forensic cases', *Bulletin of the American Academy of Psychiatry and Law*, 11: 171–81.

Steadman, H. J. and Cocozza, J. J. (1974) *Carers of the Criminally Insane: Excessive Social Control of Deviance*. Lexington, MA: Lexington Books.

Steadman, H. J. and Halfon, A. (1971) 'The Baxstrom patients: backgrounds and out-comes', *Seminars in Psychiatry*, 3: 376–86.

Steadman, H., Monahan, J., Applebaum, D., Grisso, T., Mulvey, E., Roth, L., Clark Robbins, P. and Klassen, D. (1993) 'From dangerousness to risk assessment: implications for appropriate research strategies', in S. Hodgins (ed.), *Crime and Mental Disorder*. Newbury Park, CA: Sage, pp. 39–62.

Swets, J., Dawes, R. and Monahan, J. (2000) 'Psychological science can improve diagnostic decisions', *Psychological Science in the Public Interest*, 1 (1): 1–26.

Thornberry, T.P. and Jacoby, J.E. (1979) *The Criminally Insane. A Follow-up of Mentally Ill Offenders*. Chicago: University of Chicago Press.

University of Manchester (1996) *Learning Materials on Mental Health Risk Assessment*. School of Psychiatry and Behavioural Sciences.

Wang, E. and Diamond, P. (1999) 'Empirically identifying factors related to violence risk in corrections', *Behavioral Sciences and the Law*, 17: 377–89.

Webster, C.D., Douglas, K., Eaves, D. and Hart, S. (1997) *HCR-20: Assessing Risk for Violence – Version 2*. Vancouver, BC: Simon Fraser University.

Webster, C., Harris, G., Rice, M., Cormier, C. and Quinsey, V. (1994) *The Violence Prediction Scheme: Assessing Dangerousness in High Risk Men*. Toronto: University of Toronto, Centre of Criminology.

Webster, C.D., Muller-Isberner, R. and Fransson, G. (2002) 'Violence risk assessment: using structured clinical guidelines professionally', *International Journal of Mental Health*, 1 (2): 185–93.

Wong, S. and Gordon, A. (2006) 'The validity and reliability of the Violence Risk Scale: a treatment friendly violence risk assessment tool', *Psychology, Public Policy and Law*, 12 (3): 279–309.

Chapter 11

Mental health law and risk management

Philip Fennell

Aims

This chapter and Chapter 12 explain how detention and compulsory community powers under mental health and criminal justice legislation are used in the management of risk to self and to others. This chapter begins with an analysis of the principal drivers of mental health policy in relation to mentally disordered people in general and mentally disordered offenders in particular. There is then a brief outline of the impact of the European Convention on Human Rights on psychiatric detention and compulsory treatment in the community. This is followed by an examination of the stages of the criminal justice process from arrest through to imprisonment where a mentally disordered person may be diverted from the criminal justice system to psychiatric care whether in hospital or in the community. The Mental Health Act 1983 (the 1983 Act) provides separate procedures for detaining non-offender and offender patients. Under Part 2 of the 1983 Act, non-offender patients may be detained and treated in hospital or may be subject to compulsory powers in the community. This chapter deals with Part 2 and the civil provisions for the compulsory admission and treatment. Under Part 3, mentally disordered offenders may be sentenced to a hospital order by a criminal court or transferred from prison to hospital by the Home Secretary's warrant. Restrictions may be placed on their discharge from hospital, and offender patients may be subject to compulsory powers in the community. The provisions of Part 3 and the sentencing powers under which mentally disordered offenders may be sent to prison are dealt with in Chapter 12.

Introduction: the policy context

Before embarking on any discussion of the law it is important to be aware of the policy context. Managing risk to others has always been a primary driver of mental health legislation. The 1983 Act authorises compulsory admission to hospital of anyone who suffers from mental disorder of a nature or degree warranting detention, where detention is necessary in the interests of the person's own health or safety or for the protection of others. Hence dangerousness to self or others is not a legal prerequisite of detention which may be justified on the broad paternalist grounds of the person's own health.

Criminal justice policy towards mentally disordered people accused of crime rests on three basic principles (Fennell 1991; Laing 1999). The first, exemplified in the Police and Criminal Evidence Act 1984, was that mentally disordered suspects should be subject to special safeguards surrounding their treatment in custody, since they may be particularly prone to make false confessions. The second, elaborated in Home Office Circular 66/90, is that mentally disordered suspects and offenders should be diverted away from the penal system and into the health and social care system. Two ideas underpin the second principle: (1) that mental disorder may reduce the person's culpability for their criminal acts; and (2) that they will be vulnerable to suicide and self-harm. The third principle, which has come to dominate the discourse of mental health law reform since the early 1990s, is that the public requires protection against the risk posed by mentally disordered people.

The psychiatric system has a very limited capacity to rescue vulnerable mentally disordered prisoners from the vicissitudes of the prison system. It is estimated that a significant proportion of the prison population suffer from mental health problems, with over half of female and three-quarters of male prisoners suffering from personality disorders, neurotic disorders being found in 40 per cent of male prisoners and 76 per cent in females, 6 per cent of male sentenced prisoners and 13 per cent of all female prisoners were estimated to have a schizophrenic illness, and between 1 and 2 per cent of prisoners have affective psychosis (Brooker et al. 2002: 8). Given these high levels of psychiatric morbidity in the prison population, and the high risk of suicide and self-harm, it is important to recognise the limits of any policy of diversion of mentally disordered offenders from prison to hospital.

The prison population in England and Wales is over 80,000. Between 1954 and 2004 the total number of inpatient beds in psychiatric hospitals fell from a peak of 154,000 to 32,400 in 2004 (Warner 2005: 37). On 31 March 2006 there were 14,600 patients detained in hospital, of whom 12,100 were in National Health Service hospitals (including the three high-security special hospitals Ashworth, Broadmoor and Rampton), and 2,500 in private hospitals. In 2005–06 there were 27,353 admissions under powers of detention in the Mental Health Act 1983, 1,664 of which were under the offender provisions of the Act. Although these official figures need to be treated with caution, both the prison system and the psychiatric hospital system are clearly running at full stretch, and the capacity of the psychiatric system to cope with treating greater numbers of mentally disordered offenders is strictly limited.

The Joint Pre-Parliamentary Scrutiny Committee on the Mental Health Bill 2004 (2005: paras 18–22) identified three principal drivers of mental health policy: reducing stigma and promoting social inclusion; management of risk to the public and to sufferers themselves; and protection of human rights. The policies of combating stigma, and promoting service user involvement in the planning and delivery of mental health services are reflected in the National Service Frameworks (Department of Health 1999a; Welsh Assembly Government 2001), and the Report from the Office of the Deputy Prime Minister's Social Exclusion Unit (2004), where the Prime Ministerial foreword notes the need for 'determined action to end the stigma of mental health – a challenge not just for government, but for all of us'. At the European level combating the stigma and social exclusion suffered by mentally disordered people is reflected most recently in Recommendation (2004)10 of the Committee of Ministers of the Council of Europe to member states concerning the protection of the human rights and dignity of persons with mental disorder. The United Kingdom government has reserved the right not to comply with this recommendation (Winterton 2004).

The risk management/public protection agenda has come to prominence as a result of a number of well-publicised inquiries into homicides by people who have been receiving psychiatric services. Most notable among these were the killing of Jonathan Zito by a stranger, Christopher Clunis, who suffered from schizophrenia, and the conviction in 1996 of Michael Stone, who had a personality disorder and was addicted to drugs and alcohol, for the murders of Lyn and Megan Russell. The inquiry into the care of Christopher Clunis (Ritchie *et al.* 2004: 106) identified a woeful catalogue of failure to provide adequate supervision for Clunis, that there had been no s. 117 aftercare plan, and that the authorities had failed to manage or oversee provision of health and social services for him.

The Report of the Independent Inquiry into the Care and Treatment of Michael Stone carried out on behalf of the South East Coast Strategic Health Authority was completed in 2002 but not published until September 2006 (South East Coast Strategic Health Authority 2006). The Stone case has been used in support of the argument for removal of the so-called 'treatability test', the precondition of detention of people with personality disorder, that medical treatment in hospital must be likely to alleviate or prevent deterioration in the patient's condition. These and other homicide inquiries have led to a desire on the part of government to strengthen the powers of mental health professionals to require patients with mental illness to accept medication in the community, and to reduce the obstacles to detention of people with personality disorder who pose a risk to other people.

Although the legal and policy framework of diversion remains in place, Bartlett and Sandland (2007: 199) refer to a 'sea change' in the attitude of the government. Its proposals for detention of dangerous people with severe personality disorder (DPSPD) represent in their view a cardinal example of 'a shift towards a greater use of a criminalised rather than a medicalised model of mental disorder, or a markedly increased emphasis on risk management and control over care and treatment'.

The Mental Health Act 2007 received Royal Assent on 19 July 2007. This was the government's third attempt to introduce major reform of the 1983 Act. The current process of reform began in 1999 with the Richardson Committee Report (Department of Health 1999b), which recommended a completely new Mental Health Act including a set of statutory principles to which professionals would have to have regard in implementing the Act. The government responded with a two-volume White Paper (Department of Health 2000) *Reforming the Mental Health Act 1983* and *High Risk Patients*, which rejected many of the Richardson Committee proposals, among them that the legislation should include a requirement to have regard to such principles such as non-discrimination and proportionality. A draft Bill based on the White Paper was published in 2002 and was strongly opposed by mental health professionals and voluntary organisations, principally on the grounds that it reflected a risk management, criminal justice dominated model of mental health care (Fennell 2002). A further draft Bill in 2004, very similar to the 2002 version, was subject to strong criticism by the Joint Pre-Parliamentary Scrutiny Committee (2005) (Fennell 2005). The Mental Health Act 2007 is an amending Act grafted onto the basic framework of the 1983 Act rather than a comprehensive new code. It will introduce a broader definition of mental disorder, recast the criteria for compulsion, and establish new powers of supervised community treatment (SCT), and new statutory roles of approved mental health professional (AMHP) (to replace the approved social worker (ASW)) and responsible clinician (RC) (to replace the responsible medical officer (RMO)). The proposed amendments in the 2007 Act are discussed at relevant points throughout this chapter.

The Human Rights Act 1998

The Human Rights Act 1998 requires all public authorities to act compatibly with rights under the European Convention on Human Rights. Article 5(1) of the Convention specifies the grounds on which a person may be deprived of liberty, which include 5(1)(a) 'lawful detention of a person after conviction by a competent court' and 5(1)(e) 'lawful detention of persons of unsound mind, alcoholics or drug addicts or vagrants'. No one may be deprived of liberty on grounds of 'unsoundness of mind' unless this is done in compliance with 'a procedure prescribed by law'.

In *Winterwerp* v. *The Netherlands* (1979: para. 37) the European Court of Human Rights laid down three important substantive and procedural requirements for lawful detention of persons of unsound mind:

(1) Except in emergencies, the individual must reliably be shown to be suffering from a true mental disorder on the basis of objective expertise.
(2) The mental disorder must be of a kind or degree justifying confinement.
(3) Those carrying out the detention must satisfy themselves at intervals that the criteria for detention continue to be met.

Winterwerp established that detention must be a proportionate response to the patient's circumstances, and this has been further emphasised in subsequent case law (*Litwa* v. *Poland* (2001)).

The *Winterwerp* requirements are met in the detention procedures under the 1983 Act. Admission of non-offender patients is by administrative process, based on professional expertise and checks and balances. Only an approved social worker (ASW) with specialised mental health training or the patient's nearest relative may apply for detention, supported by two medical recommendations, one from a person recognised under s. 12 of the 1983 Act as having appropriate psychiatric expertise. When the Mental Health Act 2007 Act comes into force the power to make an application will be taken over by an approved mental health professional (AMHP). Appropriately trained nurses, psychologists, occupational therapists and social workers will be eligible to be AMHPs. The ASW presents those medical recommendations, 'the objective medical evidence of a true mental disorder of a kind or degree warranting detention' to the 'competent authority', who in England and Wales are the hospital managers. The hospital managers have the duty to review the detention at reasonable intervals and to discharge if the criteria are not met. An application may only be made if the treatment cannot be provided without detention, reflecting the principle of proportionality. Nothing in Article 5 or the case law requires admission to be authorised by a court or tribunal, so the current admission procedures are Convention compliant (*HL* v. *United Kingdom* (2004)). Offenders who are sentenced by a competent court following conviction of a criminal offence are lawfully detained for Convention purposes.

Article 5(4) entitles detainees to take proceedings by which the lawfulness of detention must be decided speedily by a court and release ordered if it is not lawful. In *X* v. *United Kingdom* (1981: 189) the Strasbourg Court held that the court or tribunal reviewing the lawfulness of psychiatric detention must be able to review the applicability of the *Winterwerp* criteria. If they are not met, the court must have the power to direct the patient's discharge. Review of the 'lawfulness' of detention must be carried out in light of domestic legal requirements, the Convention and the principle of proportionality. Article 5(4) review is shared between the High Court which reviews the formal legality of decisions to detain and renew detention and by Mental Health Review Tribunals (MHRTs) which review the continued applicability of the *Winterwerp* criteria and have the power to direct discharge. Prisoners who are subject to life sentences have the right under Article 5(4) to a review of their continued dangerousness, and these cases are reviewed by the Parole Board, which operates in a similar way to the MHRTs. The right to challenge detention is considered in Chapter 12.

Article 5(1)(e) imposes a 'negative' obligation on the state and its agents not to detain someone arbitrarily. It also imposes 'positive' obligations relating to the conditions in which a person is detained. The positive obligation under Article 5(1)(e) is that where a person is detained on grounds of unsoundness of mind, that detention must take place in a hospital, clinic or similar suitable institution (*Aerts* v. *Belgium* 2000). Recent Strasbourg case law suggests that prisoners with severe mental disorder are entitled either to appropriate treatment in prison or to be transferred out to a psychiatric hospital. In *Riviére* v. *France* (2006) the Court held that the prohibition of inhuman or degrading treatment in Article 3 had been infringed and that:

> [P]risoners with serious mental disorders and suicidal tendencies, even if these had not to date been acted upon, required special measures to ensure that they received humane treatment for their condition, regardless of the seriousness of the offence of which they had been convicted. In the instant case, the applicant's continued detention without medical supervision appropriate to his current condition had entailed particularly acute hardship and caused him distress or adversity of an intensity exceeding the unavoidable level of suffering inherent in detention.

Articles 5 and 3 provide a basic floor of rights for prisoners and detained psychiatric patients. Article 5 only applies to deprivations of liberty, where those having care of the patient have complete and effective control over the patient's residence, movement, treatment, assessment and contacts with other people (*HL* v. *United Kingdom* 2004).

By contrast, treatment under compulsory powers, whether in hospital or the community, falls within the right to respect for physical integrity which is part of private life under Article 8. This means requirements to accept treatment may be justified under Article 8(2) if they are in accordance with the law and are necessary in a democratic society to protect health, or the rights and freedoms of others, or to prevent crime. In *L v. Sweden* (1988), the European Commission on Human Rights held that granting the patient leave from detention subject to a requirement that she take her medication was justified as necessary in a democratic society to protect her health. The evidence was that L had ceased medication in the past and her mental health had seriously deteriorated as a result. Article 8 has a less developed case law than Article 5 and provides less scope for challenge to a provision authorising compulsory treatment in the community.

Detained patients have rights to second opinions under Part 4 of the Mental Health Act 1983 if they are treated without consent with certain treatments. Non-offender patients detained in hospital for 28 days, assessment or for up to six months renewable for treatment have the right to a statutory second opinion if they are to be given medicines or electro-convulsive therapy (ECT) as treatment for mental disorder. The same applies to offender patients sentenced to hospital orders with or without restrictions, and to patients who have been transferred from prison. Only in an emergency may a patient be given ECT without consent or a second opinion. The Mental Health Act 2007, s. 58A introduces a right for capable patients to refuse ECT, which means that, other than in an emergency, ECT may not be given if the patient is assessed as retaining capacity to make the treatment decision and is refusing. A patient only becomes eligible for a second opinion for medicine after taking the medicine for three months, and medicine may be given without consent under the 1983 Act even if the patient is capable and refuses.

Patients in the community will have their treatment authorised by a second opinion appointed doctor (SOAD) under Part 4A of the 1983 Act, introduced by the Mental Health Act 2007. The requirement of a SOAD certificate authorising medicines or ECT applies unless the treatment is required in an emergency or, in the case of medicines, less than one month has elapsed since the CTO was made. Part 4A applies aspects of the decision-making framework of the Mental Capacity Act 2005 to treatment under the Mental Health Act and permits treatment in the community of a community patient if:

- the treatment is immediately necessary and the patient is capable and consents to the treatment;
- the treatment is immediately necessary and there is consent from someone authorised under the Mental Capacity Act 2005 to make decisions on the patient's behalf;
- the patient lacks capacity and force is not necessary to secure compliance; or
- emergency treatment needs to be given, using force if necessary, to a patient who lacks capacity.

The second opinion system applies to treatment for mental disorder only. Patients subject to detention, guardianship or a CTO are entitled to seek review of the continued need for such compulsory powers before a Mental Health Review Tribunal (MHRT).

Diversion from the criminal justice system under mental health legislation

Mental disorder

In order to be dealt with under the 1983 Act a person must be suffering or appear to be suffering from 'mental disorder'. Section 1(2) of the 1983 Act defines mental disorder as 'mental illness, arrested or incomplete development of mind, psychopathic disorder, and any other disorder or disability of mind'. This general definition applies to short-term powers of admission for assessment or remand by a criminal court for reports (MHA 1983: ss. 2, 4, 35), the doctors and nurses holding power under s. 5, and the powers to remove to a place of safety under ss. 135 and 136. A person may not be treated as mentally disordered by reason only of promiscuity, immoral conduct, sexual deviancy, drug or alcohol dependence. There must be some accompanying mental disorder, such as depression or personality disorder, before a person exhibiting one of these behaviours may be treated as mentally disordered (MHA 1983: s. 1(3)).

Detention under long-term powers authorising detention for six months or more, such as civil admission for treatment (MHA 1983: s. 3) or under a hospital order made by a criminal court (MHA 1983: s. 37), requires that the patient be suffering from mental disorder in one of four forms; mental illness, psychopathic disorder, mental impairment or severe mental impairment. These concepts are narrower in scope than the general definition, which is, of 'mental illness, psychopathic disorder, arrested or incomplete development of mind and any other disorder or disability of mind', which applies to the shorter-term powers discussed above. The three principal differences are: first the absence of the catch-all 'any other disorder or disability of mind'; second the fact that, with the exception of mental illness, detainable mental disorder requires abnormally aggressive or seriously irresponsible conduct; and third the fact that detention on grounds of psychopathic disorder or mental impairment requires that medical treatment be certified to be likely to alleviate or prevent deterioration in the patient's condition. These issues are dealt with in the discussion of detention for treatment under s. 3 below.

When the Mental Health Act 2007 (MHA 2007) comes into force in October 2008 a new definition of mental disorder will be introduced. In future it will mean 'any disorder or disability of the mind' (MHA 2007: s. 1(2)). A person will not be able to be treated as mentally disordered (except for the purposes of detention under 72 hour powers (MHA 1983: ss. 4, 5, 135, 136), detention for assessment (s2), or remand for reports (s35)) by reason of learning disability unless they exhibit abnormally aggressive or seriously irresponsible behaviour. Learning disability means 'a state of arrested or incomplete development of the mind which includes significant impairment of intelligence and social functioning' (MHA 2007: s. 2(3))

The exclusions stating that a person may not be treated as mentally disordered by reason only of promiscuity, immoral conduct or sexual deviancy have been removed by the 2007 Act. They have been replaced by a provision stating that dependence on alcohol or drugs shall not be considered to be a mental disorder for the purposes of the Act (MHA 2007: s. 3). The government's intention is to remove perceived obstacles to the detention of sex offenders under mental health legislation and allow detention on grounds of paedophilia without the need to find another accompanying mental disorder.

Powers to remove a mentally disordered person to a place of safety: Mental Health Act 1983, ss. 135–136

Under s. 136 of the 1983 Act a constable who finds a person in 'a place to which the public have access' who appears to be mentally disordered and to require immediate care and control may, if he thinks it is necessary in that person's interests or for the protection of others, take the person to a place of safety. The person need not be mentally disordered; the constable need only have a reasonable belief that this is the case. The definition of mental disorder applicable to this section is broad 'mental illness, arrested or incomplete development of mind, psychopathic disorder, and any other disorder or disability of the mind'. This power applies to people with learning disability who are not abnormally aggressive or seriously irresponsible in their conduct. The MHA 2007 amends it to 'any disorder or disability of the mind'. This power applies to people with learning difficulties who are not abnormally aggressive or seriously irresponsible in their conduct. The evidence suggests that the police are reasonably good at assessing the presence of mental disorder. Rogers (1990: 229) found a 95 per cent correlation between police assessments of mental disorder and later assessments done by psychiatrists.

The s. 136 power may be exercised in a public place. In *Carter v. Commissioner of Police for the Metropolis* (1975) the Court of Appeal held that the communal balcony of a block of flats was a place to which the public have access. The powers of the police to enter private premises to prevent a breach of the peace are preserved by s. 17(6) of the Police and Criminal Evidence Act 1984, provided any police action is a proportionate response in all the circumstances (*McLeod v. United Kingdom* (1999).

Section 135(1) of the 1983 Act confers a power on a magistrate to issue a warrant authorising a police office to enter private premises, using force if necessary, to remove the person to a place of safety. A warrant may only be granted where information has been laid on oath by an ASW stating reasonable cause to suspect that a person believed to be suffering from mental disorder has been or is being ill-treated, neglected or kept otherwise than under proper control, or is living alone and unable to care for himself. Section 135(2) confers a power on magistrates to grant a warrant authorising entry onto premises to remove a patient who is already liable to be detained under the Mental Health Act and take them back to hospital or to the place where they are required to reside under the terms of mental health guardianship or supervised discharge.

The purpose of removal to a place of safety under s. 136 or s. 135(1) is to enable a doctor and an approved social worker to assess the patient, to decide whether he should be admitted to hospital, either informally or under compulsion, and to make any other necessary arrangements for his care and treatment. The authority for detention under these sections expires when these arrangements have been made or after 72 hours, whichever is the earlier.

In *R (Anderson) v. HM Coroner for Inner North Greater London* (2004), Collins J. held that:

The powers contained in s. 136 of the 1983 Act to remove to a place of safety inevitably require that the person concerned can be kept safe in the sense that harm to himself or others is prevented until he can be seen by a doctor and, if necessary, given some form of sedation … A police officer in exercising his powers under s. 136 is entitled to use reasonable force. If someone is violent, he can be restrained.

A place of safety is defined in s. 135(6) as residential accommodation provided by a local social services authority, a hospital, a police station, a mental nursing home or residential home for mentally disordered persons, or any other suitable place the occupier of which is willing temporarily to receive the patient. The Mental Health Act Code of Practice states that the identification of preferred places of safety is a matter for local agreement between the local social services authority, district health authority and the Chief Officer of Police, whose task it is jointly to establish a clear local policy (Department of Health and Welsh Office 1999: 10.1, 10.5). However, as a general rule the Code expresses a preference for detention of a person thought to be suffering from mental disorder in a hospital rather than a police station. In formulating local policy, regard is to be had to the impact different types of place of safety may have on the person and on the outcome of the assessment.

During 2005–06 there were 5,495 admissions under s. 136 where the place of safety was a hospital, 3,092 men and 2,403 women. During the same period there were 382 admissions to hospitals under s. 135, 224 men and 158 women. This compares with 27,353 total compulsory admissions under all other provisions of the MHA 1983 (National Statistics Information Centre 2007: Tables 1 and 5). The Mental Health Act Code of Practice states that a record of the person's time of arrival must be made immediately he reaches the place of safety, and that as soon as he is no longer detained under the Act he must be advised of the fact. It also advises that it is good practice, where a hospital is the place of safety, for the managers to devise and use a form for recording the end of a person's detention under this provision (para. 10.7).

There are no figures relating to the use of police stations as places of safety. Where an individual has been arrested by the police under s. 136 he is entitled to have another person informed of his arrest and whereabouts, and where he is detained in a police station as the place of safety he has a right of access to legal advice (Police and Criminal Evidence Act 1984: ss. 56, 58; Mental Health Act Code, para. 10.9). Code of Practice C issued under the Police and Criminal Evidence Act 1984 (PACE Code C) governs the detention, treatment and questioning of persons by police officers, and applies to people removed to a police station under s. 136.

Paragraph 3.16 of PACE Code C deals specifically with s. 136 and states that:

It is imperative that a mentally disordered or otherwise mentally vulnerable person, detained under … s. 136 be assessed as soon as possible. If that assessment is to take place at the police station, an approved social worker and a registered medical practitioner shall be called to the station as soon as possible in order to interview and examine the detainee. Once the detainee has been interviewed, examined and suitable arrangements made for their treatment or care, they can no longer be detained under s. 136. A detainee must be immediately discharged from detention under s. 136 if a registered medical practitioner, having examined them, concludes they are not mentally disordered within the meaning of the Act.

Whether or not the detainee has been detained under s. 136, if the person appears to be suffering from a mental disorder the custody officer must make sure the person receives appropriate clinical attention as soon as reasonably practicable (PACE Code C, para. 9.5). Where an assessment under s. 136 is taking place at a police station the custody officer must consider whether an appropriate healthcare professional should be called to conduct an initial clinical check on the detainee. This applies particularly when there is likely to be any significant delay in the arrival of a suitably qualified medical practitioner (PACE Code C, para. 9.6). If a detainee requests a clinical examination, an appropriate healthcare professional must be called as soon as practicable to assess the detainee's clinical needs (PACE Code C, para. 9.8).

Box 11.1 Case example

Daniel is found in the street unclothed, uttering seemingly delusional incantations at passers by and running in the traffic, putting himself at risk. He appears to be mentally disordered and to require immediate care and control, so a constable can remove Daniel if he considers it necessary in his best interests to a place of safety where he can be assessed with a view to admission to hospital either as a voluntary or a detained patient. This assessment could take place in a police station or a hospital. The priority here would be to secure the prompt attendance of an ASW and a doctor to carry out an assessment. If the place of safety is a police station, an appropriate adult should be requested to attend also. If Daniel had been waving a knife in a threatening manner and frightening passers-by, he could still be removed both in his own best interests and for the protection of others. He could be diverted from prosecution by informal or compulsory admission under the Mental Health Act, or he could be charged with the offence of threatening behaviour or possibly assault. If the latter course is chosen an appropriate adult will need to be summoned before questioning begins.

Informal admission

The 1983 Act is based on the principle that, wherever possible, patients should be admitted to hospital on an informal basis and powers of compulsion should be used as a last resort. Section 131 states:

> Nothing in this Act shall be construed as preventing a patient who requires treatment for mental disorder from being admitted to any hospital or mental nursing home ... without any application, order or direction rendering him liable to be detained under this Act ...

Approximately 250,000 admissions to psychiatric hospitals take place every year. Over 90 per cent of all admissions to mental illness and mental handicap hospitals and units are informal (Bartlett and Sandland 2007: 111). The Mental Health Act Code of Practice states that where a patient is willing to be admitted informally, this should in general be arranged, and compulsory admission powers should only be exercised in the last resort (Department of Health and Welsh Office 1999: 2.7):

> Informal admission is usually appropriate when a mentally capable patient consents to admission, but not if detention is necessary because of the danger a patient presents to himself or others. Compulsory admission should be considered where the patient's current mental state, together with reliable evidence of past experience, indicates a strong likelihood that he will change his mind about informal admission prior to his actual admission to hospital with a resulting risk to his health or safety or that of other persons.

Informal patients are free to leave hospital at any time (they need not seek permission from their doctor or anyone else although it is desirable to inform the hospital staff), unless a holding power under s. 5 is invoked. During 2005–06 (National Statistics Information Centre 2007: Table 3) 72 per cent of the 5,385 patients taken to hospital as a place of safety under s. 136 for whom outcome figures were available became informal patients after assessment, and the remaining 28 per cent were detained under the civil powers of detention, either s. 2 for up to 28 days assessment or s. 3 for up to six months for treatment.

In the case study Daniel appears to present a danger to himself and to other people, and his apparent psychotic symptoms seem likely to render him incapable of consenting to admission. He would probably be unable by reason of mental disorder or disability to understand and retain information relevant to the decision or to weigh it in the balance to arrive at a decision (Mental Capacity Act 2005: s. 3). It is therefore more likely that he would be admitted compulsorily under s. 2 or s. 3 of the 1983 Act. If the degree of control to be exercised over Daniel's residence, movement, treatment and assessment reaches a degree and intensity so as to amount to a 'deprivation of liberty', and Daniel lacks capacity, and he does not pose a risk to others, and deprivation of liberty is in his best interests, he may fall within the Bournewood provisions for deprivation of liberty in Schedules 1A and A1 in the Mental Capacity Act 2005 to be introduced by the MHA 2007, s. 50 in March 2009.

Application for compulsory admission of someone who is already an inpatient

A patient who initially consents to admission but later seeks to leave hospital may be restrained from doing so using the doctor's or the nurse's holding power under s. 5 of the 1983 Act.

The doctor's (and approved clinician's) holding power

Section 5(2) confers a holding power on the registered medical practitioner in charge of the treatment of an inpatient in any hospital, not necessarily a psychiatric one. Inpatient for the purposes of this section does not include anyone who is already liable to be detained or who is a community patient under the 1983 Act. Section 9 of the MHA 2007 will extend that power to 'approved clinicians'

(ACs) who may be a mental health nurse, psychologist, social worker or occupational therapist. If the doctor (or approved clinician) considers that an application for compulsory admission needs to be made, s/he should furnish a report to the hospital managers to that effect. Where this happens, the patient may be detained in hospital for a period of 72 hours from the time when the report was furnished.

The power may be used in the case of a person receiving treatment for a physical condition in a general hospital, provided s/he is an inpatient. Section 5(3) permits the doctor (or approved clinician) in charge of the patient's treatment to nominate 'one (but not more than one) other registered medical practitioner (or approved clinician) on the staff of the hospital to act for him ... in his absence'. The purpose of detention is to enable the assessment necessary for admission under either s. 2 or s. 3 to take place. Section 5(2) should not therefore be seen as an independent power of short-term detention but as a *holding power* to enable a full assessment to be made. This being so, arrangements for such an assessment should be set in train immediately the holding power is implemented.

The nurse's holding power

The second power is the so-called *nurse's holding power* under s. 5(4). This enables a nurse of the prescribed class to hold an inpatient in a psychiatric ward or hospital for not more than six hours, during which time the doctor in charge of the patient's treatment or his or her deputy should attend to determine whether the managers should be furnished with a report under s. 5(2). The nurses' holding power can only be used *where the patient is receiving treatment for mental disorder as an inpatient*. The grounds for its use are:

- that the patient is suffering from mental disorder to such a degree that it is necessary for his or her health or safety or for the protection of others that s/he be immediately restrained from leaving hospital; and
- that it is not practicable to secure the immediate attendance of a practitioner (or clinician) for the purpose of furnishing a report under s. 5(2).

For purposes of this power, 'mental disorder' includes learning disability without abnormally aggresive or seriously irresponsible conduct. The nurse's holding power may only be used to restrain the patient from leaving hospital. Where a patient requires restraint but is not showing any inclination to leave the hospital, staff must rely on common law powers to prevent a breach of the peace, or statutory powers under the Criminal Law Act 1967 or the Medical Capacity Act 2005.

Section 3(1) of the Criminal Law Act 1967 allows a person to use 'such force as is reasonable in the circumstances in the prevention of crime'. The common law allows for reasonable force to be used in self-defence, for the defence of others or to prevent a breach of the peace. Reasonable steps to prevent the breach of the peace can include detaining the person against his will (*Albert* v. *Lavin* 1982). A breach of the peace can take place in either a public or a private place where a person is in fear of being harmed through an assault, an affray, an unlawful assembly or other disturbance (*R* v. *Howell* 1982). These powers can only be used to justify detention or restraint insofar as it is reasonably necessary, and only for so long as the risk of breach of the peace or crime subsists. Hence they would not authorise seclusion to continue after the risk had passed.

Sections 5 and 6 of the Mental Capacity Act 2005 provide a legal defence for anyone who takes action that is in the best interests of a person who lacks capacity in relation to the decision to remain in hospital. This includes reasonable restraint where the restraint is imposed to prevent harm to the patient and is a proportionate response both to the likelihood of harm and the severity of the harm. In order for the action to be lawful the person taking it must have taken reasonable steps to determine whether the person has capacity in relation to the relevant decision, must reasonably believe that the person indeed lacks capacity, and must reasonably believe that what they are doing is in the person's best interests.

Admission for assessment

Section 2 of the Act provides for compulsory admission for assessment for up to 28 days. An application may be made by an approved social worker or the patient's nearest relative, supported by two medical recommendations, one of which must come from a doctor approved under s. 12 of the 1983 Act as having expertise in the diagnosis or treatment of mental disorder. The patient must be suffering from mental disorder of a nature or degree which warrants his detention in hospital for assessment or for assessment followed by medical treatment for at least a limited period. For admission for assessment it is not necessary to specify that the patient is suffering from any of the statutory categories of mental disorder. Hence the patient may be admitted as suffering simply from 'mental disorder' in the broad sense, which includes arrested or incomplete development of mind (learning disability) and any other disorder or disability of mind. This means that, in contrast to the position under s. 3 admissions, a person with a learning disability who does not exhibit abnormally aggressive or seriously irresponsible conduct may be detained under s. 2 for up to 28 days. This possibility will remain following the entry in force of the MHA 2007, s. 2(2).

It must also be certified that the patient ought to be detained in the interests of his health *or* safety *or* for the protection of other persons. Where the patient meets the 'mental disorder of a nature or degree' criterion, detention may be implemented if necessary in the interests of the patient's own health (including mental health) and it is not necessary to wait until s/he is overtly dangerous to self or others. It is a common misconception that patients need to present some threat to their own safety or that of others before compulsory admission is possible. The Mental Health Act allows detention on 'strong paternalist' grounds. A person may be detained in the interests of their own health.

A patient who is detained under s. 2 may be given treatment for mental disorder without consent, including medicines or electro-convulsive therapy (ECT), under the provisions of Part 4 of the MHA 1983. Of the 27,353 total formal admissions from the community during 2005–06, 15,265 were for assessment with or without treatment under s. 2 (National Statistics Information Centre 2007: Table 1). In addition 3,425 informal inpatients in NHS hospitals and 45 in private hospitals were detained for assessment under s. 2. A further 2,723 informal NHS patients and 104 private patients were held under s. 5 of the Act and subsequently admitted for assessment. This makes a grand total of 21,552 uses of s. 2 during 2006 (National Statistics Information Centre 2007: Table 4).

In the case example there are reasonable grounds to believe that Daniel has a mental illness. If he is expressing delusional ideas and running in the traffic he would certainly appear to be suffering from mental illness of a kind or degree which warrants detention in the interests of his own health and his safety. It could also be said that detention is necessary for the protection of others to prevent him from causing an accident. If he is also waving a knife at passers-by detention would certainly also be necessary for the protection of others.

Admission for treatment

Section 3 of the 1983 Act provides for compulsory admission for treatment for up to six months renewable for a further six months and thereafter for periods of 12 months at a time. An application may be currently made by either the nearest relative or an ASW. When the 2007 Act comes into force an application will be able to be made by the nearest relative or an approved mental health professional (AMHP) and must be supported by medical recommendations given by two medical practitioners, one of which must come from a s. 12 approved doctor. In 2006 there were 8,435 admissions direct to NHS hospitals in England under s. 3, and 712 direct to private hospitals. In addition 5,467 informal inpatients in NHS hospitals and 87 in private hospitals were transferred from informal status to detention under s. 3. A further 3,034 NHS and 66 private hospital informal patients were made subject to s. 5 holding powers and then detained under s. 3. This makes a grand total of 16,936 s. 3 detentions in NHS hospitals and 865 in the private sector (National Statistics Information Centre 2007: Table 4).

The criteria which must be met currently are as follows:

- the patient must be suffering from one of four forms of mental disorder: mental illness, severe mental impairment, psychopathic disorder or mental impairment;
- the mental disorder must be of a nature or degree which makes it appropriate for the patient to receive medical treatment in a hospital; and
- in the case of psychopathic disorder or mental impairment, such treatment must be likely to alleviate or prevent deterioration of his condition; and
- it must be necessary in the interests of his health or safety or for the protection of other persons that he should receive such treatment and that it must be the case that the treatment cannot be provided unless he is detained under this section.

Mental disorder

Detention for treatment under s. 3 requires that the patient be suffering from mental disorder in one of four forms: mental illness, psychopathic disorder, mental impairment or severe mental impairment. These concepts are narrower in scope than the general definition – 'mental illness, psychopathic disorder, arrested or incomplete development of mind and any other disorder or disability of mind' – which applies to the shorter-term powers discussed above. The two principal differences are, first, the absence of the catch-all 'any other disorder or disability of mind', and, second, the fact that psychopathic disorder, mental impairment and severe mental impairment require abnormally aggressive or seriously irresponsible conduct. The consequence is that a learning disabled person without abnormally aggressive or seriously irresponsible conduct cannot be detained under this power. This will continue to be the case under the MHA 2007, even though it will dispense with these subcategories of mental disorder for the purposes of s. 3 and will replace them with the definition 'any disorder or disability of mind', applicable to all uses of compulsory powers under the Act.

Nature or degree

The mental disorder must be of a nature or degree warranting detention. In *R* v. *Mental Health Review Tribunal for the South Thames Region ex parte Smith* (1999) Popplewell J held that 'the word nature refers to the particular mental disorder from which the patient suffers, its chronicity, its prognosis, and the patient's previous response to … treatment. The word degree refers to the current manifestation of the patient's disorder.' In *Smirek* v. *Williams* (2002: para. 19) Hale LJ said that

> [W]here there is a chronic condition, where there is evidence that the patient will deteriorate if medicine is not taken, I find it impossible to accept that it is not a mental illness of a nature or degree which makes it appropriate for the patient to be liable to be detained in hospital for medical treatment if the evidence is that, without being detained in hospital, the patient will not take the treatment.

The test may therefore be satisfied if there is a patient with an illness of a serious nature, where the patient is not showing any severe symptoms, but where the patient has ceased taking medication and there is a history of serious relapse when medication is stopped. The illness, although not currently of a degree making detention appropriate, may nevertheless be of a sufficiently serious nature to satisfy the test.

The mental disorder must be of a nature or degree making it appropriate for the patient to receive treatment *in a hospital*. This means that the intention must be for the patient to receive treatment as an inpatient. In *R* v. *Hallstrom ex parte W* (1986) McCullough J said that 'Admission for treatment under s. 3 is intended for those whose condition is believed to require treatment as an inpatient.' Section 3 cannot therefore be used when the intention is that the patient will be detained for a purely nominal period before being sent home on leave under s. 17, and where the true purpose of the admission is to provide authority to impose treatment in the community.

Treatability: the likelihood that treatment will alleviate or prevent deterioration in the patient's condition

If a person with a classification of psychopathic disorder or mental impairment is to be detained for treatment or under a hospital order, it must be certified that medical treatment in hospital is likely to alleviate or prevent deterioration in the patient's condition. This is the so-called 'treatability' test which will be significantly changed by the MHA 2007. Medical treatment is broadly defined in the

1983 Act. Section 145 states that it 'includes nursing, care, habilitation and reha-bilitation under medical supervision'. As the definition is inclusive, this is not an exhaustive list, and treatment also clearly includes treatments expressly mentioned in Part 4 of the 1983 Act such as medicines and ECT. Section 7 of the 2007 Act changes the definition of medical treatment by adding after 'nursing and care' 'psychological intervention and specialist mental health habilitation, rehabilitation and care'. The addition of psychological interventions makes clear that treatments for personality disorder such as cognitive behaviour therapy are included within medical treatment. Medical treatment for mental disorder must have the purpose of alleviating, or preventing a worsening of the disorder or one or more of its symptoms or manifestations.

As the leading authority on the practical application of the 1983 Act has remarked, given the wide interpretation in the case law of the treatability test (Jones 2006: 42), 'it is difficult to imagine the circumstances that would cause a patient to fail it.' In *Reid* v. *Secretary of State for Scotland* (1999: 493) Lord Hope held that the provision gives effect to the policy that people with psychopathic disorder or mental impairment 'should only be detained under compulsory powers if there is a good prospect that the treatment they will receive there will be of benefit.' His Lordship went on to hold that the term treatment was (1999: 497) 'wide enough to include treatment which alleviates or prevents deteriora-tion in the symptoms of the disorder, not the disorder itself.' Lord Hutton (1999: 515) held that the test could be satisfied where 'anger management in the struc-tured setting of the State Hospital in a supervised environment resulted in the patient being less physically aggressive.'

Despite the breadth of the treatability test, the government sees it as a fault line in the legislation which enables psychiatrists to decide that a person with psychopathic disorder who might be dangerous to others should not be detained because they are not treatable. The effect of the case law is that a person who is being contained as a detained patient in the structured environ-ment of a hospital may be held to be treatable. Nevertheless, in the 2007 Act, in addition to adopting a general definition of mental disorder – 'any disorder or disability of mind' – for all durations of detention, the government has decided to replace the current treatability test with a new requirement that treatment is available for the patient which is 'appropriate in his case, taking into account the nature and degree of the mental disorder and all other circumstances of his case' (MHA 2007: s. 4)

The government sees this as having the advantage that the treatability crite-rion will be met even if a patient with a personality disorder refuses to cooperate with psychological treatments such as cognitive behavioural therapy which require active participation by the patient.

Necessary in the interests of the patient's health or safety or for the protection of others and the treatment cannot be provided unless he is detained under this section

A patient need not be dangerous to him or herself or others in order to be detained. If detention in hospital is necessary in the interests of only one of the goals listed: health (including mental health) *or* safety *or* the protection of others, this criterion will be met. The requirement to certify that the treatment cannot be provided without detention reflects the European Convention principle of proportionality or the US principle of the least restrictive alternative, namely that treatment should be provided if possible in the setting which imposes the least restrictions on the patient's freedom.

Treatment in the community following detention under s. 3

The 1990s saw increasing legal recognition of the problem of the unfortunately named 'revolving door' patient who gets well on medication but once discharged ceases to take it and relapses. Instead of using mental health guardianship to provide a framework for compulsion in the community, the psychiatric profession's preferred solution is extended leave from compulsory detention as a means of requiring acceptance of medication outside hospital (MHA 1983: s. 17). A patient can be required to accept medication as a condition of leave and recalled to hospital in the event of non-compliance. Detention must be renewed at intervals and a problem arose if the patient was in the community when the time came to renew detention. To overcome this, patients would be recalled from the community to hospital for one night to have their detention renewed and would then be sent on leave for a further six or 12 months until the detention next required renewal. By this ingenious device, a long-term community treatment order was fashioned out of the power to grant leave from detention. However, the obligation to accept treatment while resident in the community could only be imposed on someone who has already been detained, since only a detained patient can be granted leave.

In *R v. Hallstrom* (1986), Justice McCullough declared unlawful two widely used practices in psychiatry. The first was that of compulsorily admitting patients for treatment under s. 3 of the MHA 1983 when there was no intention that they should receive inpatient treatment for mental disorder. Such patients would be sent on leave under s. 17 of the Act shortly after admission, subject to the condition that they took their medication. This was declared unlawful on the grounds that one of the conditions of admission is that the patient must need treatment in hospital for their mental disorder and that the treatment cannot be provided unless they are detained. It remains unlawful to detain a patient in the first place when there is no intention to provide any inpatient treatment. The second practice at issue in *Hallstrom* was that of returning patients on leave under s. 17 to hospital for one night, renewing their detention and discharging them the next day subject to the condition that they continue to take their medication. The judge held that a patient's detention could not be renewed unless it was intended that they should receive treatment in hospital as an inpatient. The implication of this was a limit on the duration of a patient's subjection to compulsory powers in the community. Legislation providing for supervised discharge, introduced to overcome the effect of *Hallstrom*, has been little used.

Subsequent case law has almost completely reversed the effect of *Hallstrom*. It provides that a patient's detention can be renewed as long as a patient needs some treatment at a hospital, not necessarily as an inpatient. First, in *B v. Barker Havering and Brentwood NHS Trust* (1999) the Court of Appeal held that it was lawful to renew the detention of a patient even though she spent only two nights a week in hospital, Lord Woolf holding that (at para. 113) 'As long as treatment viewed as a whole involves treatment as an inpatient the requirements of the section can be met.' Then, in *R (DR)* v. *Merseycare NHS Trust* (2002), the patient was receiving no inpatient treatment while on leave, but was receiving treatment in hospital as an outpatient. Justice Wilson held that the only relevant question to renewal was whether a significant component of the treatment of the plan for the claimant was for treatment in hospital. That treatment did not have to be as an inpatient.

By the time these later cases were decided, supervised discharge had already been introduced in 1995 by the Mental Health (Patients in the Community) Act 1995, following the exposure of failures of community care in cases such as that of Christopher Clunis. Supervised discharge provides a power to subject a patient over 16 to supervision in the community if this person is not a restricted patient (see this volume Chapter 12) and is currently subject to detention under one of the provisions of the 1983 Act justifying detention for six months or longer. The patient must be suffering from mental illness, mental impairment, severe mental impairment or psychopathic disorder. There must be substantial risk of serious harm to the health or safety of the patient or the safety of other persons or of the patient being seriously exploited, if he or she were not to receive the aftercare services to be provided for him or her after they leave hospital. The patient's subjection to aftercare under supervision must be likely to help to secure that they receive the aftercare services. Supervised discharge may require the patient to live at a specified place, to grant access to mental health professionals and to attend at a specified place for treatment, education or training. If the patient does not attend as required he or she may be forcibly taken and conveyed to the relevant place (MHA 1983: ss. 25A–H). These provisions will be repeated by the MHA 2007.

In *R (DR)* v. *Merseycare NHS Trust* (2002), which so markedly increased the scope of extended leave, the argument was put that supervised discharge should have been at least considered, if not used in preference to extended leave. The judge rejected this argument, stating that it was a (2002: para. 33)

[C]entral feature, regarded by many as a central deficiency, of the provisions for aftercare under supervision that, although under s. 25D(3)(b) and (4) a patient can be required to attend the place where he is due to receive the treatment and to allow himself to be conveyed there, he cannot be required to actually take the medication. If he refuses to take it, the power to administer it compulsorily arises only when he has again been made liable to be detained by the properly cumbersome procedures set by s. 3 of the Act.

The Mental Health Act 2007 repeals ss. 25A–J of the 1983 Act and replaces them with a new regime of powers (ss. 17A–G) to impose supervised community treatment. The necessary pre-conditions of making a community treatment order will be:

• the patient is suffering from mental disorder (any disorder or disability of mind) of a nature or degree which makes it appropriate for him to receive medical treatment;
• it is necessary for his health or safety or for the protection of other persons that he should receive such treatment;

- subject to his being liable to be recalled, such treatment can be provided without his continuing to be detained in a hospital;
- it is necessary that the responsible clinician should be able to exercise the power to recall the patient to hospital (the Bill said necessary for the patient's health or safety or for the protection of others – the Act simply says necessary);
- appropriate medical treatment is available for him.

The order will be made by the patient's RC with the agreement of an AMHP. Before making an order the responsible clinician must give priority to the risk of deterioration, and the risk of non-compliance with medication if the patient were not to remain in detention. She or he must *'in particular* [emphasis added] consider, having regard to the patient's history of mental disorder and any other relevant factors, what risk there would be of a deterioration of the patient's condition if he were not detained in a hospital (as a result, for example, of his refusing or neglecting to receive the medical treatment he requires for his mental disorder) (MHA 2007: s. 17).

The Mental Health Bill 2006 would have specified the obligations on patients as follows:

- that the patient reside at a particular place;
- that the patient make himself available at particular times and places for the purposes of medical treatment;
- that the patient receive medical treatment in accordance with the responsible clinician's directions;
- that the patient makes himself available for examination;
- that the patient abstain from particular conduct.

Most noteworthy on the list of conditions was the obligation to receive medical treatment, rather than as before to attend a specified place for the purpose of medical treatment, and the obligation to desist from specified conduct, a condition which has led to the contention that this amounts to the psychiatric equivalent of the antisocial behaviour orders (ASBOs) introduced by s. 1 of the Crime and Disorder Act 1998. Section 32 of the MHA 2007 does not list the types of condition which may be applied. Instead it provides, without listing the types of condition, that a community treatment order must 'specify conditions to which the patient is to be subject.' Any conditions must be agreed between the RC and the AMHP. The only limitation on the scope of the obligations is that the RC and AMHP must agree that the conditions are 'necessary or appropriate' for:

- ensuring that the patient receives medical treatment;
- preventing risk of harm to the patient's health or safety;
- protecting other persons.

There are several disturbing factors of this power from a human rights point of view. First is that the scope of the conditions and limitations on personal freedom is left to the discretion of healthcare professionals, subject only to loose requirements as to purpose which would allow conditions that the patient desist from specified conduct. This was supposedly one of the government's concessions during the debates on the 2006 Bill. The 2007 Act, if anything, allows more scope for expansion of the powers, as long as they can be necessary or appropriate for treatment or to prevent risk to self or others. The 'necessary or appropriate' test is lax indeed. 'Necessary and appropriate' would have required the professionals to address their minds to whether the conditions were necessary and whether they were appropriate. As it is one may question what sort of condition might not be necessary but would be appropriate and vice versa. There is no power to seek review before the MHRT of the need for specified conditions. However, the patient may apply to the MHRT on the grounds that one or more of the conditions for making an order are not met. The MHRT must direct discharge if it is not satisfied that (MHA 2007: Sched., para. 21):

- the patient is then suffering from mental disorder or mental disorder of a nature or degree which makes it appropriate for him to receive medical treatment; or
- that it is necessary for his health or safety or for the protection of other persons that he should receive such treatment; or
- that it is necessary that the responsible clinician should be able to exercise the power to recall the patient to hospital; or
- that appropriate medical treatment is available for him.

In deciding whether it is satisfied that the power of recall is necessary the MHRT must '*in particular* consider, having regard to the patient's history of mental disorder and any other relevant factors, what risk there would be of a deterioration of the patient's condition if he were to continue not to be detained in a hospital (as a result, for example, of his refusing or neglecting to receive the medical treatment he requires for his mental disorder)'.

The tribunal is also under a duty to discharge on an application by the nearest relative if not satisfied that the patient if discharged would be likely to act in a manner dangerous to self or to others.

Although failure to comply with conditions will not lead to automatic recall, a patient who fails to comply with any of the conditions may be recalled to hospital and held there for up to 72 hours. If they do not agree to comply within that period, the community treatment order will be revoked and they will resume status as a detained patient. Like its predecessor, supervised discharge under ss. 25A–H, supervised community treatment under ss. 17A–G will be available for patients who have been detained under s. 3, and also for offender patients subject to hospital orders or transfer directions without restrictions (MHA 1983: ss. 37 and 47).

We might ask why a responsible clinician would choose a community treatment order in preference to using the equally broad power to send the patient on extended leave under s. 17. This allows the RC, without the need for an AMHP's agreement, to grant leave 'subject to such conditions as the RC considers necessary in the interests of the patient or for the protection of other persons'. Section 33(2) of the 2007 Act states that extended leave under s. 17 of more than seven days may not be granted, unless the responsible clinician first considers whether the patient should be dealt with under s. 17A instead. The obligation is to consider using s. 17A, not to actually use it. It may be that the Code of Practice will contain strong exhortation to use s. 17A in preference to s. 17 There is nothing in the Act to stop the RC considering s. 17A but deciding to use s. 17 instead.

Guardianship

Guardianship applications in respect of non-offender patients are made under s. 7 of the 1983 Act by either the nearest relative or an ASW. Two medical recommendations are necessary. The nearest relative may block a guardianship application but unreasonable objection will be grounds for displacement by the county court under s. 29. The patient must be suffering from mental illness, severe mental impairment, mental impairment or psychopathic disorder of a nature or degree warranting reception into guardianship. In addition, guardianship must be necessary in the interests of the patient's welfare or for the protection of others. Section 8 of the Act sets out the three powers conferred on the guardian. These are:

- to require the patient to reside at a specified place;
- to require the patient to attend specified places for medical treatment, occupation, education or training;
- to require access to be given to the patient by a doctor, approved social worker or other specified person.

Although the great hope of both the Mental Health Act 1959 and the 1983 Act in terms of providing the underpinning of compulsion necessary to enforce community care, guardianship has never been much used. In England there are about 900 patients subject to guardianship at any time, and around 450 new cases are initiated each year (National Statistics Information Centre 2006: Tables 1–2). In 2006 in England there were 934 people under s. 7 guardianship, and 45 under guardianship orders made by a criminal court under s. 37. For Wales the equivalent figures for 2005 were 85 people under s. 7 guardianship and 21 under guardianship orders made by a criminal court under s. 37 (Local Government Data Unit Wales 2005).

The small numbers under guardianship may change with the MHA 2007 which extends guardianship to anyone who suffers from 'any disorder or disability of mind', although the exclusion remains in relation to learning disabled people who do not exhibit abnormally aggressive or seriously irresponsible conduct. (Schedule 3, para 3(5)) broadens the powers of the guardian by introducing a new power to take and convey a person to their required place of residence under guardianship alongside the power which already exists to return a guardianship patient who has absconded to their place of residence.

Concluding remarks on civil powers under the Mental Health Act

In 1990 the Home Office issued Circular 66/90 Provision for Mentally Disordered Offenders to encourage a policy of diversion of mentally disordered offenders from custody (Fennell 1991). We have seen how the civil powers in Part 2 of the 1983 Act to detain patients and to subject them to compulsory community powers provide ample scope to divert a person who has committed a minor criminal offence, or even one who has not yet committed an offence, away from the criminal justice system and to manage any risk they may pose without recourse to prosecution. In the case example outlined above, Daniel could have been detained for assessment under s. 2. At the end of the 28-day assessment period, he could have been detained, again on application by a social worker supported by two medical recommendations, for up to six months (renewable) for treatment (MHA 1983: s. 3). It seems highly likely that he suffers from a mental illness. Under the 2007 Act he will be detainable if he suffers from a mental disorder. Under the 1983 Act and the 2007 Act amendments the treatment must be necessary in the interests of his health or safety or for the protection of others, and it must be also certified that the treatment he needs cannot be provided without detention. This would be the case if he is without insight, unlikely to accept voluntary admission and prone to assault others. Finally, appropriate treatment must be available.

Daniel's psychiatrist would have had the power to discharge him from hospital. As a way of ensuring that he continued to accept treatment, his psychiatrist could instead send him on extended leave, subject to a condition that he accept medication (MHA 1983: s. 17). If he did not comply, he could be recalled to hospital. Alternatively, he could have been made subject to supervised discharge on the grounds that there was a substantial risk that he might cause serious harm to others. This would mean that he could be required to attend any place for treatment, and if he did not, could be taken and conveyed there in custody, and assessed for possible readmission to hospital in the event of continued non-compliance (MHA 1983: s. 25A). From October 2008 a CTO under the supervised community treatment powers in ss. 17A–17H will be possible is he suffers from a mental disorder which warrants treatment in the interests of his health and safety or for the protection of others, appropriate treatment is available, and it is necessary for him to be subject to the RC's power of recall. Guardianship under s. 7 could have been considered if Daniel had been assessed as not needing inpatient treatment but instead as being likely to survive in the community with health and social services support within a framework of compulsory powers. This would enable the team to work with him to achieve as independent a life as possible without it being necessary for him to have spent time as a detained patient, as is the case with extended leave, supervised discharge or supervised community treatment.

This chapter has considered the use of the non-offender provisions in Part 2 of the 1983 Act to divert patients from the criminal justice system. Chapter 12 will consider the factors determining whether a mentally disordered offender will be prosecuted, examines the special procedures which apply to mentally disordered and mentally vulnerable suspects and defendants, and explores the sentencing and other disposals available in such cases.

Selected further reading

An excellent contextual discussion of mental health law in general is to be found in P. Bartlett and R. Sandland (2007) *Mental Health Law Policy and Practice*, 3rd edn. Oxford: Oxford University Press.

A complete annotated text of the Mental Health Act 1983, its supporting regulations, Code of Practice and Mental Health Act Commission Guidance Notes is provided by R. Jones in *The Mental Health Act Manual*. London: Sweet & Maxwell, now in its 10th edition. The manual is a superb reference work for practitioners.

P. Fennell (2007) *Mental Health: The New Law*. Bristol: Jordans is an up-to-date summary of the changes introduced by the Mental Health Act 2007 into the Mental Health Act 1983, the Mental Capacity Act 2005 and the Domestic Violence Crime and Victims Act 2004.

Statutes

Crime and Disorder Act 1998
Criminal Law Act 1967
Human Rights Act 1998
Mental Capacity Act 2005
Mental Health Act 1959
Mental Health Act 1983
Mental Health Act 2007
Mental Health (Patients in the Community) Act 1995
Police and Criminal Evidence Act 1984

Cases cited

Aerts v. *Belgium* [2000] 29 EHRR 50
Albert v. *Lavin* [1982] AC 346
B v. *Barker, Havering and Brentwood NHS Trust* [1999] 1 FLR 106
Carter v. *Commissioner of Police for the Metropolis* [1975] 1 WLR 507
HL v. *United Kingdom* (2004) Judgment of the European Court of Human Rights 5 October 2004; [2005] 40 EHRR 32
L v. *Sweden* (1988) European Commission on Human Rights Decisions and Reports Vol. 61, pp. 62–91
Litwa v. *Poland* (2001) EHRR 53; (2000) 63 BMLR 199
McLeod v. *United Kingdom* [1999] 27 EHRR 493
R v. *Hallstrom ex parte W (No. 2)* [1986] 2 All ER 306
R v. *Howell* [1982] 2 QB 416
R v. *Law Thompson* [1997] CrimLR 674
R v. *Mental Health Review Tribunal for the South Thames Region ex parte Smith* [1999] COD 148
R (Anderson) v. *HM Coroner for Inner North Greater London* [2004] EWHC 2729
R (DR) v. *Merseycare NHS Trust* (2002) Queen's Bench Division Administrative Court, Wilson J; (2002) All ER (D) 28 (Aug) 7 August 2002
Reid v. *Secretary of State for Scotland* [1999] 1 All ER 481
Rivière v. *France*, Judgment of 11 July 2006
Smirek v. *Williams* [2002] MHLR 38
Winterwerp v. *The Netherlands* (1979–80) 2 EHRR 387
X v. *United Kingdom* (1981) 4 EHRR 188

References

Bartlett, P. and Sandland, R. (2007) *Mental Health Law Policy and Practice*, 3rd edn. Oxford: Oxford University Press.

Brooker, C., Repper, J., Beverley, C., Ferriter, M. and Brewer, N. (2002) *Mental Health Services and Prisoners: A Review*. Available at: http://www.dh.gov.uk/en/Publications andstatistics/Publications/PublicationsPolicyAndGuidance/DH_4084149

Department of Health (1999a) *National Service Framework for Mental Health: Modern Standards and Service Models*. London: DoH. Accessible at: http://www.doh.gov.uk/pub/docs/doh/mhmain.pdf

Department of Health (1999b) *Report of the Expert Committee Review of the Mental Health Act 1983* (Richardson Committee Report). London: DoH.

Department of Health (2000) *Reforming the Mental Health Act 1983 and High Risk Patients*, Cm 5016-1 and 2. London: DoH.

Department of Health and Welsh Office (1999) *Mental Health Act 1983 Code of Practice*. London: TSO.

Fennell, P. (1991) 'Diversion of mentally disordered offenders from custody', *Criminal Law Review*, 333–48.

Fennell, P. (2001) 'Reforming the Mental Health Act 1983: "joined up compulsion"', *Journal of Mental Health Law*, June, 5–20.

Fennell, P. (2005) 'Protection! Protection! Protection! The government's response to the Joint Parliamentary Scrutiny Committee on the Mental Health Bill 2004', *Journal of Mental Health Law*, November, 19–34.

Joint Pre-Parliamentary Scrutiny Committee (House of Lords and House of Commons) (2005) *Report on the Draft Mental Health Bill, Session 2004–2005*, HL Paper 79-1, HC 95-1, Session 2004–05.

Jones, R. M. (2006) *Mental Health Act Manual*, 10th edn. London: Sweet & Maxwell.

Laing, J. M. (1999) *Care or Custody*. Oxford: Oxford University Press.

Local Government Data Unit Wales (2005) 'People who are subject to guardianship under Section 7 or Section 37 of the Mental Health Act 1983', *Personal Social Services Statistics Wales 2005*. Available at: http://www.unedddatacymru.gov.uk/Documents/

National Statistics Information Centre (NSIC) (2007) 'In-patients formally detained in hospitals under the Mental Health Act 1983 and other legislation, NHS Trusts, Care Trusts, Primary Care Trusts and Independent Hospitals, England; 1995–96 to 2005–06'. Available at: http://www.ic.nhs.uk/statistics-and-data-collections/health-and-lifestyles/mental-health/in-patients-formally-detained-in-hospitals-under-the-mental-health-act-1983-and-other-legislation-nhs-trusts-care-trusts-primary-care-trusts-and-independent-hospitals;-2005-06

Office of the Deputy Prime Minister (2004) *Report of the Social Exclusion Unit on Mental Health and Social Exclusion*. London: ODPM.

Ritchie, J. H., Dick, D. and Lingham, R. (1994) *The Report of the Inquiry into the Care and Treatment of Christopher Clunis*. London: HMSO.

Rogers, A. (1990) 'Policing mental disorder: controversies, myths and realities', *Social Policy and Administration*, 24: 226.

South East Coast Strategic Health Authority (2006) *The Report of the Independent Inquiry into the Care and Treatment of Michael Stone*. Available at: http://www.southeastcoast.nhs.uk/news/MS-Report-21.09.06.pdf

Warner, L. (2005) 'Acute care in crisis', in the Sainsbury Centre for Mental Health, *Beyond the Water Towers: The Unfinished Revolution in Mental Health Services* 1985–2005, London: Sainsbury Centre for Mental Health, pp. 37–47.

Welsh Assembly Government (2001) *Strategy Document for Adult Mental Health Services in Wales: Equity, Empowerment, Effectiveness, Efficiency*. Cardiff: Welsh Assembly Government.

Winterton, R. (2004) *Hansard*, HC Debates, 20 October 2004.

Chapter 12

The law relating to mentally disordered persons in the criminal justice system

Philip Fennell

Aims

Chapter 11 discussed the possibilities for using the civil powers in the Mental Health Act 1983 (the 1983 Act) to divert people from the criminal justice system. This chapter considers the special procedures applicable where a prosecution is brought against a mentally disordered or mentally vulnerable suspect, and goes on to discuss the provisions of Part 3 of the 1983 Act whereby mentally disordered offenders may be diverted from custody and the sentencing powers under criminal justice legislation whereby they may be sent to prison. Under Part 3, mentally disordered offenders may be remanded to hospital, sentenced to a hospital order or hospital direction by a criminal court or transferred from prison to hospital by the Home Secretary's warrant. Restrictions may be placed on discharge from hospital, and offender patients may be subject to compulsory powers in the community. The number of restricted patients detained in hospital at any one time has gone up from 1,864 in 1980 to 3,395 in 2005–06, of whom 779 had been transferred from prison, 212 had been found unfit to plead and 42 found not guilty by reason of insanity.

This chapter also explores the use of criminal justice legislation to sentence mentally disordered offenders. The advantage from the point of view of risk management of detention in hospital over detention in prison used to be that the former offered greater possibilities for indeterminate detention. However, in recent years there has been a steady development of 'public protection sentencing', culminating in the protective sentencing provisions of the Criminal Justice Act 2003. Ashworth (2005: 218) summarises, these developments:

> The 2003 Act has introduced a regime of three 'dangerousness' measures of ascending severity – extended sentences, imprisonment for public protection, and life imprisonment – supported by a legislative framework that obliges courts to impose such sentences in given circumstances.

The chapter concludes with a discussion of what has been described as a 'convergence' between the legal frameworks of hospital and prison detention. This has been driven, on the one hand, by the imperative of risk management and, on the other, by the need to comply with the European Convention on Human Rights (Fennell and Yeates 2002).

The decision to proceed with a criminal investigation in respect of a mentally disordered suspect will be taken by the police in the first instance in the light of the public interest as defined in the Code for Crown Prosecutors. The decision to prosecute a mentally disordered suspect triggers the use of special interview procedures, may lead to the use of special procedures at trial, may involve decisions about criminal responsibility and may culminate in the use of a hospital rather than a penal disposal.

The decision to prosecute

In most cases, the Crown Prosecution Service (CPS) is responsible for deciding whether a person should be charged with a criminal offence and, if so, what that offence should be, and the decision is made in accordance with the Code for Crown Prosecutors (Crown Prosecution Service: 2004) and the Director of Public Prosecutions Guidance on Charging. The CPS applies a two-stage test (Crown Prosecution Service 2004 para: 5.1). The first question is evidentiary and asks whether there is a 'realistic prospect of conviction', or in other words whether a jury or bench of magistrates or judge hearing a case alone, properly directed in accordance with the law, is more likely than not to convict the defendant of the charge alleged. The second question is whether a prosecution is needed in the public interest. The general principle here is that (Crown Prosecution Service 2004: para. 5.1) 'A prosecution will usually take place unless there are public interest factors tending against prosecution which clearly outweigh those tending in favour, or it appears more appropriate in all the circumstances of the case to divert the person from prosecution'.

The Code for Crown Prosecutors (Crown Prosecution Service 2004: para. 5.10 f–g) states that factors weighing against proceeding to trial could include where:

(f) prosecution is likely to have a bad effect on the victim's physical or mental health, always bearing in mind the seriousness of the offence; or
(g) the defendant is elderly or is, or was at the time of the offence, suffering from significant mental or physical ill health, unless the offence is serious or there is real possibility that it may be repeated ... Crown Prosecutors must balance the desirability of diverting a defendant who is suffering from significant mental or physical ill health with the need to safeguard the general public.

So if the offence is not serious and is unlikely to be repeated the public could be adequately safeguarded by a decision to admit as a voluntary patient or under civil powers rather than proceed to prosecution. The decision to investigate a criminal offence will be made by the police in the light of this guidance. The weightiest factor in the decision to prosecute a mentally disordered suspect rather than divert them from the criminal justice system will be the seriousness of the alleged offence. If the police decide to proceed to interview a mentally disordered or mentally vulnerable suspect in relation to a criminal offence, an 'appropriate adult' must be present.

The appropriate adult

PACE Code C (para. 3.15) states that if a detainee in a police station is mentally disordered or otherwise mentally vulnerable, the custody officer must, as soon as practicable, inform an appropriate adult of the grounds for their detention and their whereabouts, and ask the adult to come to the police station to see the detainee. The primary role of the appropriate adult is to ensure that no undue pressure is put on the suspect. The appropriate adult is not to act simply as an observer and this is to be explained to him or her. The Code states that the role has three aspects: (1) to advise the person being questioned; (2) to observe whether or not the interview is being conducted properly and fairly; and (3) to facilitate communication with the person being interviewed (PACE Code C: para. 11.17).

An appropriate adult in the case of someone who is mentally disordered or mentally vulnerable can be (1) a relative, guardian or other person responsible for their care or custody; (2) someone experienced in dealing with mentally disordered or mentally vulnerable people but who is not a police officer or employed by the police; or (3) failing these, some other responsible adult aged 18 or over who is not a police officer or employed by the police (PACE Code C: para. 1.7(b)). Explanatory Note 1D of PACE Code C states that it may be appropriate if the appropriate adult is someone with qualifications in looking after mentally disordered people, but that if the suspect prefers a relative to a better qualified stranger, that wish should 'if practicable' be respected. A person should not be the appropriate adult if they are suspected of involvement in the offence, a victim, a witness or otherwise involved in the investigation. Nor should someone be an appropriate adult if they have received admissions in relation to the offence from the suspect, as appropriate adults are not covered by legal professional privilege. A solicitor or independent custody visitor may not be an appropriate adult if they are present in the police station in either of those capacities (PACE Code C: Explanatory Notes 1B–1E).

Unless an urgent interview can be authorised by a superintendent or higher rank, a mentally disordered person must not be interviewed or asked to sign a statement without an appropriate adult attending (PACE Code C: para. 11.15). The only exception is where an officer of at least the rank of superintendent certifies that delay will involve a serious risk of interference with evidence, harm to persons or serious loss or serious damage to property. Even then questioning may not continue in the absence of the appropriate adult once sufficient information to avert the risk has been received. A record must be made of the grounds for any decision to begin an interview in such circumstances (PACE Code C: para. 11.1(a), 11.18–11.20).

The PACE Code refers to appropriate adults being necessary for mentally vulnerable detainees who, because of mental state or capacity, may not understand the significance of what is said and of questions and their replies, as well as for those suffering from mental disorder meaning 'mental illness, arrested or incomplete development of mind, psychopathic disorder and any other disorder or disability of mind'. The Code states that when the custody officer has any doubt about the mental state or capacity of a detainee, that detainee should be treated as mentally vulnerable and an appropriate adult called.

The Notes for Guidance to PACE Code C (para. 11C) recognise the vulnerability of mentally disordered suspects, observing that while they:

> ... are often capable of providing reliable evidence, they may, without knowing or wishing to do so, be particularly prone to provide information which is unreliable, misleading or self-incriminating. Special care should therefore be exercised in questioning such a person and the appropriate adult should always be involved if there is any doubt about a person's mental state or capacity.

Consequences of failure to have an appropriate adult present at interview

Three sections of the Police and Criminal Evidence Act 1984 relate to the admissibility of confession evidence. Only s. 77 refers directly to any form of mental disorder. Although the PACE Code refers to mental vulnerability and mental disorder, s. 77 of the Police and Criminal Evidence Act 1984 refers to the narrower concept of mental handicap ('arrested or incomplete development of mind which includes significant impairment of intelligence and social functioning'), stating that where the case against a defendant depends wholly or substantially on a confession by him and the judge is satisfied: (1) that he is mentally handicapped; and (2) that the confession was not made in the presence of an independent person, the judge must warn the jury that there is a special need for caution before convicting the accused in reliance on the confession. The decision as to whether a suspect is mentally handicapped is to be based on medical evidence (*R* v. *Ham* (1995)). Although a solicitor cannot be an appropriate adult, a solicitor was held to be an independent person for the purposes of this section (*R* v. *Lewis (Martin)* (1996)).

Section 77 of PACE merely requires the judge to warn the jury of the need for caution before relying on a confession and the warning is only required where the suspect was mentally handicapped and an appropriate adult was not present. Sections 76 and 78 allow for confessions to be excluded entirely, and one of the grounds on which they may be excluded is failure to provide an appropriate adult. Section 76(2) provides that where it is represented to the court that a confession may have been (1) obtained by oppression of the person who made it, or (2) in consequence of anything said or done which was likely, in the circumstances existing at the time, to render the confession unreliable, the burden is on the prosecution to show beyond reasonable doubt that the confession was not improperly obtained (notwithstanding that it may be true). Failure to secure the presence of an appropriate adult is unlikely to amount to oppression, unless there is a strong degree of hectoring of a mentally vulnerable suspect. However, it may amount to something said or done which was likely to render the confession unreliable under s. 76(2)(b) (*R* v. *Everett* (1988); *R* v. *Moss* (1990)). Under s. 78(1) in any proceedings the court may refuse to allow evidence on which the prosecution proposes to rely to be given if it appears to the court that, having regard to all the circumstances, including the circumstances in which the evidence was obtained, the admission of the evidence would have such an adverse effect on the fairness of the proceedings that the court ought not to admit it. The attitude of the courts to the effect of failure to provide an appropriate adult on fairness has varied. In some cases it has led to exclusion (for example, *R* v. *Aspinall* (1999)), in others not (for example, *R* v. *Law Thompson* (1997)).

Sentencing of mentally disordered offenders

The Mental Health Act 1983 Code of Practice asserts that (Department of Health and Welsh Office 1999: para. 3.1):

> Those subject to criminal proceedings have the same right to psychiatric assessment and treatment as other citizens. The aim should be to ensure that everyone in prison or police custody who is in need of medical treatment which can only satisfactorily be given in a hospital ... is admitted to such a hospital.

Moreover, the Code (para. 3.2) makes it clear that a prison healthcare centre is not a hospital within the meaning of the 1983 Act. As it is not a hospital and as prisoners are not detained under the 1983 Act they may not be given treatment for mental disorder without consent using the powers and second opinion safeguards in Part 4 of the 1983 Act. But there is convergence in the regimes in terms of legal powers to treat without consent. Treatment for mental disorder may be given to prisoners using restraint and force under ss. 5 and 6 of the Mental Capacity Act 2005 if the person lacks capacity and restraint and treatment are necessary and proportionate responses to prevent harm to the patient. Although ss. 5 and 6 are said to codify the common law doctrine of necessity, the statute and supporting Code of Practice show clearly that treatment may be given without consent outside hospital settings, using force or the threat of force if necessary, where the patient lacks capacity. Under common law, treatment which is immediately necessary and a proportionate response to prevent the patient from harming others may be given using restraint, whether or not the person retains capacity (*R (Munjaz)* v. *Ashworth Hospital* Court of Appeal (Hale LJ)).

Even after a decision has been made to proceed to trial for a criminal offence there are still ample opportunities for mentally disordered offenders to be diverted away from the prison system to psychiatric hospital (be that high, medium or low security) or to psychiatric supervision in the community

Mental condition at time of remand: remand to hospital

The Mental Health Act 1983 introduced three powers with regard to mentally disordered offenders: the power to remand an accused person for reports on his mental condition under s. 35, which was used 135 times in 2005–06; the power to remand for psychiatric treatment under s. 36, used 17 times in 2005–06; and the power to impose an interim hospital order under s. 38, used an unknown number of times in 2005–06 (National Statistics Information Centre 2007). As Bartlett and Sandland (2007: 220) note: 'When the numbers remanded under both ss. [35 and 36] are compared to the thousands of mentally disordered people remanded to prison for medical assessments, the underuse of the power to remand to hospital is truly shocking.'

There are certain common features to the remand powers. No court can make a remand order unless it is satisfied, on the evidence of the doctor (or, under the MHA 2007, the 'approved clinician' (AC)) who would be responsible for making the report (s. 35(4)) or who would be in charge of his case (s. 36(7)), or some other person representing the hospital managers, that arrangements have been made for the patient's admission to hospital within seven days of the remand order being made.

Remand is for 28 days in the first instance, but the accused may be further remanded for periods of 28 days up to a maximum of 12 weeks in all. The court can extend the remand of someone remanded under s. 35 in his absence (as long as he is represented in court) if it is satisfied on the evidence of the doctor (or, under the MHA 2007, the AC) preparing the report, that a further remand is necessary in order to complete the psychiatric assessment (MHA 1983: s. 35(5), (6)).

In the case of someone remanded for treatment under s. 36, remand may be extended if the court is satisfied on the report of the responsible medical officer (or, under the MHA 2007, the AC) that further remand is warranted. A person remanded for reports is entitled to commission at his own expense an independent report from a doctor, or under the MHA 2007 any other AC and to apply to the court for his remand to be terminated. Remand patients have no right to apply for discharge to a Mental Health Review Tribunal (MHRT).

Remand for a psychiatric report under s. 35

In recognition of the fact that remand to prison may lead to a high risk of suicide in mentally vulnerable people, s. 35 of the Act provides for remand to hospital for reports where the court is satisfied that (1) there is reason to suspect that the accused is suffering from mental illness, psychopathic disorder, severe mental impairment or mental impairment; and (2) it would be impracticable for a report to be made on his mental condition if he were remanded on bail.

A Crown Court may remand an accused person awaiting trial or who has been arraigned for an offence punishable by imprisonment and has not yet been sentenced. In relation to the magistrates, 'accused person' has two meanings. First, it includes anyone who has been convicted by the court of an offence punishable with imprisonment. Second, it includes any person charged with such an offence if the court is satisfied that either (1) he did the act or made the omission charged, or (2) he has consented to the making of the remand. Evidence is required from one doctor, who must be approved by the Secretary of State as having special experience in the diagnosis or treatment of mental disorder (MHA 1983: s. 54(1)). The diagnostic threshold for remand is not high. There need only be reason to suspect that the accused is suffering from one of the four forms of mental disorder. The Mental Health Act 2007 will allow remand if there is reason to suspect that the accused is suffering from mental disorder, the new definition being 'any disorder or disability of mind.'

The Code of Practice on the Mental Health Act 1983 states that a report prepared in pursuance of s. 35 (as currently applicable) should contain a statement of whether a patient is suffering from one or more of the four specified forms of mental disorder identifying its relevance to the alleged offence. This will change when the broad definition of mental disorder (any disorder or disability of mind) in s. 1 of the Mental Health Act 2007 is introduced. The report should not comment on guilt or innocence. The report should include relevant social factors and any recommendations on care and treatment including where and when it should take place and who should be responsible (Department of Health and Welsh Office 1999: para. 17.4). The Mental Health Act 2007 (s. 10(2)) will allow reports to be prepared not just by doctors but also by approved clinicians who might be nurses, psychologists, social workers or occupational therapists.

A person remanded under s. 35 is not subject to the consent to treatment provisions in Part 4 of the Act (MHA 1983: s. 56(1)(b)) and therefore retains the common law right to refuse treatment. The Code of Practice advises that where a patient remanded under s. 35 is thought to be in need of medical treatment for mental disorder under Part 4 of the Act, consideration ought to be given to referring the patient back to court with an appropriate recommendation, and with an assessment of whether the patient is in a fit state to attend court. It goes on to suggest that if there is delay in securing a court date, and depending on the patient's mental condition, consideration should be given to whether the patient meets the criteria of s. 3 (Department of Health and Welsh Office 1999: para. 17.3). There are various legal issues in relation to detaining a remanded person under civil powers in order to acquire a right to treat compulsorily, most notably that Parliament clearly provided a separate power to remand for treatment which is subject to stricter criteria, and a patient could appeal successfully against detention under the civil powers, but still remain detained under the remand power (Fennell 1991; Bartlett and Sandland 2007: 221–2).

The Mental Capacity Act 2005 introduces the possibility that a person remanded for reports could be given treatment without consent for mental disorder. Under s. 5 a defence is available in relation to any action based on treatment without consent to anyone who has taken reasonable steps to carry out an assessment of a patient's capacity reasonably believes that the person lacks capacity and reasonably believes that the treatment is in the person's best interests. Restraint (use or threat of force) can also be justified if necessary and proportionate to prevent harm to the incapacitated person under s. 6 of the 2006 Act. Under s. 3 of the 2005 Act a person's capacity is to be assessed by asking whether there is any mental disability ('disturbance or disability of mind or brain') which renders him unable to communicate a decision, unable to understand and retain relevant treatment information, or unable to use and weigh that information in the balance as part of the process of arriving at a decision. This definition may mean that a person who retains cognitive function and can communicate and understand and retain treatment information long enough to make a decision may still lack capacity if some emotional disturbance of mental functioning, such as depression, renders them unable to weigh the information in the balance to make a decision.

Remand for treatment under s. 36

Remand for treatment may be used to provide treatment before trial and hence potentially avoid an accused person being found unfit to plead. The definition of accused person for this power is any person who is in custody awaiting trial for an offence punishable with imprisonment (other than murder), or who at any time before sentence is in custody in the course of a Crown Court trial. A remand order for treatment may only be made by the Crown Court on the evidence of two doctors, one of whom must be approved by the Secretary of State as having special experience in the diagnosis or treatment of mental disorder. The court must be satisfied that the accused is suffering from mental illness or mental impairment of a nature or degree which makes it appropriate for him to be detained in hospital for medical treatment (MHA 1983: ss. 36(1) and 54(1)). The Mental Health Act 2007 will allow remand for treatment if there is reason to suspect that that accused is suffering from mental disorder, the new definition being 'any disorder or disability of mind'. The test will be that (1) the patient is suffering from mental disorder ('any disorder or disability of mind') of a nature or degree which makes it appropriate for him to be detained in a hospital for medical treatment; and (2) appropriate medical treatment is available to him. A person remanded for treatment is subject to Part 4 of the 1983 Act and so may be given medicine for mental disorder or electro-convulsive therapy without consent, subject to the statutory second opinion procedure in s. 58. An accused person remanded for treatment has no right to apply for discharge to a Mental Health Review Tribunal (MHRT).

Because the sentence is fixed by law, a person accused of murder cannot be remanded for treatment under s. 36 (s. 36(2)). However, s. 3(6A) of the Bail Act 1976 allows the court to impose the following conditions of bail:

- that the accused must undergo examination by two doctors for psychiatric reports to be prepared; and
- that he must attend an institution or place as the court directs for that purpose and comply with any other directions from the doctors.

Section 36 was only used 17 times in 2005–06. It remains to be seen whether the broader definition of mental disorder will lead to an increase in its use.

Interim hospital order under s. 38

Either the Crown Court or a magistrates' court may make an interim hospital order on the evidence of two doctors (one of whom must be approved under s. 12) that the relevant criteria are met. Currently the court must be satisfied that the diagnostic criterion is met, that the offender is suffering from mental illness, psychopathic disorder, severe mental impairment or mental impairment. The court must also be satisfied that there is reason to suppose that the mental disorder is such that it may be appropriate for a hospital order to be made. The Mental Health Act 2007 will open the possibility for patients suffering from any disorder or disability of mind to be subject to interim hospital orders.

The main uses for s. 38 were intended to be following trial where doubt remained about precise diagnosis or to assess whether medical treatment in hospital was likely to alleviate or prevent deterioration in the condition of a person with a classification of psychopathic disorder or mental impairment. It is unclear how much s. 38 has been used because the statistical bulletins place it in a category of 'other sections' including provisions which allow committal to hospital by a Crown Court pending final disposal of the case, and allowing courts martial to commit members of the armed services to hospital. Patients admitted under these other sections during 2005–06 totalled 166.

The court must be satisfied on the evidence of the responsible medical officer who would be in charge of treatment (under the Mental Health Act 2007 this will be the 'responsible clinician who would have overall responsibility for his case') or hospital managers that arrangements have been made for the patient's admission to hospital within 28 days (s. 38(4)). An interim hospital order is for an initial period of 12 weeks which may be renewed at 28-day intervals thereafter up to a maximum of 12 months on the written or oral evidence of the responsible medical officer (under the Mental Health Act 2007 this will be the 'responsible clinician'). The court may terminate the order if, having considered the evidence of the responsible medical officer (under the Mental Health Act 2007 this will be the responsible clinician), it decides to deal with the offender in some other way. The court can renew the interim order or make a full hospital order in the absence of the patient, provided he is represented in court (s. 38(2), (6)). A patient on an interim hospital order is subject to the consent to treatment provisions in Part 4 of the Act, and so may be given medicine for mental disorder or electro-convulsive therapy without consent, subject to the statutory second opinion procedure in s. 58. Patients on interim hospital orders are not entitled to apply to an MHRT for discharge.

Mental condition at the time of the offence

The offender's mental condition at the time of the offence can have a bearing on disposal of a mentally disordered offender. Mentally disordered offenders have traditionally been exempt from ordinary penal measures on the grounds that they are not criminally responsible for their behaviour (not guilty by reason of insanity), that their responsibility for doing or being a party to a homicide is diminished by abnormality of mind (diminished responsibility), or that they are unable to understand the course of the proceedings at their trial and contribute to their defence (unfit to plead). Each of these may lead to a psychiatric rather than a penal disposal.

The insanity defence

Section 2 of the Trial of Lunatics Act 1883 provides for a special verdict of not guilty by reason of insanity to be returned where a person was insane at the time the offence was committed. The definition of insanity remains the McNaghten rules laid down by Tindal C J in the decision of the House of Lords in McNaghten's Case. For the defence to be made out (1843: 201):

It must be clearly proved that, at the time of committing the act, the accused was labouring under such a defect of reason from disease of the mind that he did not know the nature and quality of the act, or so as not to know that what he was doing was wrong.

There are two key issues here. The first is the fit between the nineteenth century concept of disease of the mind and modern psychiatric knowledge. The second is the fact that a person must be labouring under a very severe defect of reason to be entitled to the defence that they did not know the nature and quality of their act (the example often given is chopping someone with an axe believing them to be a block of wood). Similarly, there must be a severe defect of reason if someone knows the nature and quality of their act (for example, killing someone), but does not know that it is wrong. An important question here is whether a person will be entitled to the special verdict if they know something is legally wrong (homicide) but believe that it is morally justified because they have a delusional belief that the victim is the embodiment of the devil. Is it enough if their defect of reason from disease of the mind stops them from knowing that their actions are morally wrong? Mackay *et al.* (2006: 405–7) have noted that in 68 of 100 special verdict cases in their research the psychiatrists interpreted wrong to mean 'morally wrong' and the courts were prepared to accept this wider approach. Professor Mackay succeeded in persuading the Royal Court of Jersey in *Attorney-General* v. *Prior* (2001) to adopt a definition of insanity which is more in keeping with modern medical thinking. A person would be entitled to the insanity defence if, 'at the time of the offence, his unsoundness of mind affected his criminal responsibility to such a degree that the jury consider that he ought not to be found criminally responsible'. Bartlett and Sandland (2007: 241) comment that given the Mental Health Act Commission view that the McNaghten rules are (2005: para. 5.21) 'offensive, and no longer meaningful in either a clinical or a common language context it is difficult ... to dispute the preferability of [the Jersey] test over the McNaghten approach.' The insanity defence is used between ten and 15 times per year, and is most often used with serious offences against the person. If the offence is homicide, the defence may seek to plead guilty to manslaughter on grounds of diminished responsibility rather than rely on the insanity defence.

The insanity defence may be raised by the defence, the prosecution or the court. If the defendant raises the issue, the burden is on him to satisfy the jury on the balance of probabilities. If the issue is raised by the prosecution, the prosecution must satisfy the jury beyond reasonable doubt that the defendant was insane at the time of the offence. Until the Criminal Procedure (Insanity and Unfitness to Plead) Act 1991 (the 1991 Act) the automatic consequence of a special verdict was that the defendant was subject to a hospital order with restrictions on discharge without limit of time. For that reason if for no other, the defence was little used by defendants. However, it could be raised by the prosecution.

This happened in *R* v. *Sullivan* (1983). Sullivan assaulted someone while he was in the throes of an epileptic seizure. He sought to rely on the defence of non-insane automatism, which if successful would have led to an acquittal. The prosecution stated that, if he relied on this defence, they would contend that the facts relied on showed the insanity defence to be applicable. If the prosecution were to succeed in satisfying the jury that the insanity defence applied Sullivan would face indeterminate detention under a restriction order. He pleaded guilty. The House of Lords held that the prosecution had been within its rights to seek to raise insanity as the true defence applicable since epilepsy could be a disease of the mind.

Following concerns that the insanity defence might be imposed in cases where the defendant did not have what psychiatrists would accept as a true mental disorder in accordance with modern principles of medicine, but suffered instead from epilepsy (*R v. Sullivan*) or hypoglycaemia (as in *R v. Hennessy* (1989)), s. 1 of the 1991 Act provides that that a jury shall not return a special verdict except on the written or oral evidence of two medical practitioners, one of whom must be approved under s. 12. This effectively means that unless a psychiatrist certifies that the person is suffering from a true mental disorder there will not be a special verdict.

Since the Criminal Procedure (Insanity and Unfitness to Plead) Act 1991 a Crown Court which finds a defendant not guilty by reason of insanity is no longer bound to impose a restriction order without limit of time. The Domestic Violence Crime and Victims Act 2004 (s. 24) inserts a new s. 5 into the Criminal Procedure (Insanity) Act 1964 Act setting out the three disposal options available to the court:

- to make a hospital order under s. 37 of the 1983 Act, which can also be accompanied by a restriction order under s. 41 of that Act;
- to make a supervision order; or
- to order the absolute discharge of the accused.

Where the sentence for the offence is fixed by law the 1991 Act provides that there must be a restriction order without limit of time if the Mental Health Act criteria for making a restriction order are met (Criminal Procedure (Insanity and Unfitness to Plead) Act 1991: Sched. 1, para. 2(2)). If those criteria are not met, the court may only make a supervision order or discharge the defendant absolutely. This is most likely to apply in a case where the defendant is found unfit to plead because of a physical disorder rather than a case where the defendant is found on psychiatric evidence to be not guilty by reason of insanity. A supervision order requires the supervised person to be under the supervision of a supervising officer (social worker or probation officer) for a specified period of not more than two years. A supervision order may require the supervised person to submit to treatment by or under the direction of a registered medical practitioner. The court may only make a supervision order if satisfied that, having regard to all the circumstances of the case, the making of such an order is the most suitable means of dealing with the accused, that the supervising office is willing to supervise, and that arrangements have been made for the treatment which will be specified in the order. A supervision order may include a condition that the supervised person shall submit to medical treatment aimed at improving his mental condition. This may be either treatment as a non-resident patient at a specified institution or treatment under the direction of a specified doctor. The court must be satisfied on the evidence of two doctors, one of them s. 12 approved, that the mental condition of the supervised person requires and may be susceptible to treatment but is not such as to warrant the making of a hospital order under s. 37 of the 1983 Act.

A supervision order may also include a condition that the supervised person submit to medical treatment designed to improve his medical condition other than his mental condition. This may be either treatment as a non-resident patient at a specified institution or treatment under the direction of a specified doctor. This option is only available where the court is satisfied on the written or oral evidence of two or more doctors that because of his medical condition, other than his mental condition, the supervised person is likely to pose a risk to himself or others and the condition may be susceptible to treatment.

If the doctor in charge of mental or other medical treatment considers that the treatment may be more conveniently given in or at an institution or place which is not specified in the original order where the person will receive treatment under the direction of a doctor, he may, with the consent of the supervised person, make arrangements for that treatment to take place. This may include treatment as a resident patient. Notice must be given to the supervising officer. The supervised person's consent is required for the change of arrangement, but once the change is made, the treatment provided for by the arrangements shall be deemed to be treatment to which he is required to submit in pursuance of the supervision order. A supervision order may also include requirements as to residence but before imposing a residence requirement, the court must consider the home surroundings of the supervised person.

The insanity defence is available in respect of any offence. The legislation on the special verdict applies to Crown Court trials. White (1991) has argued that the insanity defence is also available in the magistrates' court and that a defendant who establishes it there is entitled to an acquittal. The argument has been accepted by some magistrates.

The plea of diminished responsibility

Section 2 of the Homicide Act 1957 provides for the plea of diminished responsibility to a charge of murder. The effect of successfully raising it is that a homicide conviction is reduced from murder with the mandatory life sentence to manslaughter where the sentence is within the judge's discretion. However, this does not necessarily mean that a hospital order will be imposed. The jury must be satisfied on the balance of probabilities that the accused is suffering from such abnormality of mind (whether arising from a condition of arrested or retarded development of mind or any inherent cause or induced by disease or injury) as substantially impaired his mental responsibility for his acts or omissions in doing or being a party to the killing. The court will accept pleas of guilty to manslaughter except in cases where medical opinion is divided or is open to challenge (*R v. Cox* (1968); *R v. Vinagre* (1979))

The first question is whether there is an abnormality of mind. This is a question for the jury to decide on the balance of probabilities, based on medical evidence. In *R v. Vinagre* (1979) the Crown Court accepted the defendant's plea of guilty to manslaughter on the basis that his Othello syndrome or pathological jealousy was an abnormality of mind which substantially impaired his responsibility for killing his wife. The trial judge sentenced him to life imprisonment. The Court of Appeal dismissed his appeal against sentence. Lawton LJ expressed scepticism about Othello syndrome and emphasised the importance of medical evidence before the court would accept a plea of diminished responsibility (*R* v. *Vinagre* (1979): 107):

> However much the concept of Othello syndrome has entered modern psychiatric medicine, this is not one which appeals to this Court … [P]leas to manslaughter on the grounds of diminished responsibility should only be accepted when there is clear evidence of mental imbalance.

A leading case showing that personality disorder can be an abnormality of mind is *R* v. *Byrne* (1960). Byrne was diagnosed as a sexual psychopath. He had strangled and mutilated a young girl in a hostel. Three doctors agreed he was a sexual psychopath. The judge did not allow the defence of diminished responsibility to go to the jury. Lord Parker CJ contrasted 'abnormality of mind' with 'defect of reason' in the McNaghten rules, stating that abnormality of mind means (1960: 5):

> [A] state of mind so different from that of ordinary human beings that the reasonable man would term it abnormal. It appears to us to be wide enough to cover the mind's activities in all its aspects, not only the perception of physical acts and matters and the ability to form a rational judgment whether an act is right or wrong, but also the ability to exercise will-power to control physical acts in accordance with that rational judgment.

Byrne's appeal was allowed and a verdict of manslaughter on grounds of diminished responsibility substituted although this did not affect his life sentence.

The second question is whether the abnormality of mind arises from a condition of arrested or retarded development of mind or any inherent cause or induced by disease or injury. Arrested or retarded development of mind includes learning disability. Any inherent cause could include personality disorders. Induced by disease could include psychotic illnesses with strong delusions and hallucinations, depressive illness and severe reactive depression. Induced by injury would include mental disorder brought on by head injury. Bluglass and Bowden (1990: 207) report that there have been cases where premenstrual syndrome has been successfully used as grounds for a finding of diminished responsibility, but there must be a well-recorded medical history substantiating the diagnosis. There will also need to be good evidence of abnormal mental state at the time of the offence showing that the effects of the disorder were severe enough to impair substantially the defendant's criminal responsibility for homicide.

Reactive depression or mental disturbances brought on by prolonged abuse or extreme stress could amount to an abnormality of mind. Two cases in point are so-called 'battered woman syndrome' and 'mercy killings'. In *R* v. *Ahluwalia* (1992) Kiran Ahluwalia's husband had abused her for years. Finally, in 1989, after being threatened with an iron and with other physical violence, she chose to retaliate. While her husband was sleeping she doused him with petrol and set fire to him. He died of his injuries a week later. Ahluwalia was convicted of murder and given a tariff of 12 years. She won her appeal against her conviction on the grounds of diminished responsibility. A psychiatric report commissioned by her original team not produced at her trial clearly stated that she suffered from endogenous depression at the time of the offence. Although a retrial was ordered, the Crown commissioned its own psychiatric reports and accepted her plea of guilty to manslaughter on grounds of diminished responsibility. The judge substituted a shorter prison sentence which, as she had spent three years three months in jail, she was deemed to have already served and was released in 1992. Later, in *R v. Hobson* (1997) evidence of two psychiatrists that the defendant was suffering from battered woman syndrome was accepted by the Court of Appeal as being capable of forming the basis of a diminished responsibility plea. Her conviction was quashed and a new trial ordered.

There have also been several mercy killing cases where family members have killed suffering relatives. The defendant in *R v. Mawditt* (2005) suffocated his terminally ill wife of 50 years, and received a three-year conditional discharge following conviction of manslaughter on grounds of diminished responsibility. Medical reports showed him to have been suffering from extreme stress and a depressive condition. In *R v. Gardner* (2005) the defendant killed his parents after looking after them for a significant number of years. His verdict of diminished responsibility was based on a depressive illness. In *R v. Wragg* (2006) too the defendant had suffocated his son, who suffered from Hunter Syndrome, with a pillow. His responsibility was diminished and he was found guilty of manslaughter because "the pressure of looking after Jacob, his failing marriage and the horrors he witnessed in Iraq led him to a state of mind in which he believed his son had 'come to the end of the road'".

As to the relevance of alcohol or drug intoxication at the time of the offence, in *R v. Gittens* Lord Lane CJ said that the jury should be directed to disregard the effect of alcohol or drugs since these were not 'due to inherent causes'. The jury should then consider (1984: 703):

> [W]hether the combined effect of the other matters which do fall within the section amounted to such an abnormality of mind as substantially impaired the defendant's mental responsibility ...

In *R v. Dietschmann* (2003) the defendant had killed a man in a savage attack. At the time, he was suffering from an abnormality of mind in the form of an adjustment disorder brought on by depressed grief reaction to bereavement, but was also extremely drunk. At the trial the judge directed the jury that it was up to the defendant to satisfy them that he would still have killed as he had done even if he had not taken drink, and that he would have been under diminished responsibility from abnormality of mind when he did so. This involves the hypothetical subtraction from the equation of the effects of alcohol on the defendant's conduct. This will never be an exact science as the effects of alcohol on each individual may differ markedly. It would also be hard to establish the defence since most juries would be reluctant to accept that ingestion of large quantities of alcohol would not be a significant cause of violent conduct.

The House of Lords took a more generous approach, holding that the defendant did not have to establish that even if he had not had any drink he would still have killed as he did. Section 2(1) referred to substantial impairment which did not require the abnormality of mind to be the sole cause of the defendant's acts in doing the killing. Even if he would not have killed if not drunk, the causative effect of the drink did not prevent the abnormality of mind from substantially impairing his responsibility for the homicide. The abnormality of mind did not have to be the sole cause of the impaired responsibility. The case was remitted to the Court of Appeal which ordered a retrial.

The third issue is whether the defendant's 'responsibility' was 'substantially impaired'. The first question here is what is meant by 'responsibility'. In *R v. Byrne* Lord Parker C J offered this definition (1967: 5):

[T]he expression 'mental responsibility for his acts' points to a consideration of the extent to which the accused's mind is answerable for his physical acts which must include a consideration of the extent of his ability to exercise will-power to control his physical acts.

This meant that the defence was available to someone with a personality disorder. The term mental responsibility was strongly criticised in the Butler Report (1975: para. 19.5) for creating confusion as to whether it refers to 'legal responsibility' or 'moral responsibility'. Mackay (1995: 192) expressed concerns that medical witnesses were being asked to give evidence on the moral responsibility of the defendant when they have no more expertise in this area than a layperson. Mackay's concerns were echoed by Baroness Murphy (2007: cols 1700–01) in the House of Lords debate on homicide law: 'Psychiatrists do not feel qualified to pontificate on degrees of responsibility, though they may be qualified to pontificate on abnormality of mind. So often it comes down to making a judgment on a sliding scale of moral quality.'

On the question of 'substantially' in *R v. Lloyd* (1967: 178) Edmund Davies J said this:

Substantial does not mean total, that is to say, the mental responsibility need not be totally impaired, so to speak, destroyed altogether. At the other end of the scale substantial does not mean trivial or minimal. It is something in between and Parliament has left it to you and other juries to say on the evidence was the mental responsibility impaired, and, if so, was it substantially impaired?

As Murphy puts it, although in the early 1990s diminished responsibility was used about 130 times a year (2007: col. 1700):

[T]he numbers have dropped off to 20 or 30 a year, and perhaps that is no bad thing ... [P]sychiatrists agree that the defence of diminished responsibility is rather a blot on their practice. It is far better to use psychiatric evidence at the sentencing stage – if the judiciary has the freedom over sentencing – when a specialist opinion can be considered without the unseemly legal argument over the minutiae of the language used to describe types of abnormality of mind.

The Mental Health Act Commission (MHAC) (2006: 369) reports that 'the number of diminished responsibility verdicts peaked about 25 years ago and has been tailing away ever since. The MHAC also reports (2007: 375–6) that of the 515 diminished responsibility verdicts between 1992 and 2002–03, 182 (35 per cent) resulted in prison sentences rather than hospital. Of the prison sentences 27 per cent were life sentences, one person had a sentence of more than ten years, 45 per cent were between four and ten years and 27 per cent were less than four years. One of the significant findings reported by the MHAC (2007: 370) is 'the surprising fact that diminished responsibility verdicts no longer account for the majority of Mental Health Act hospital orders subsequent to a manslaughter verdict. After 1999–2000 "other" manslaughter verdicts (most likely provocation) account for over 80 per cent of hospital orders'.

The plea of infanticide

Infanticide is defined in s. 1 (1) of the Infanticide Act 1938 as:

> Where a woman by any wilful act or omission causes the death of her child being a child under the age of twelve months, but at the time of the act or omission the balance of her mind was disturbed by her not having fully recovered from the effect of giving birth to the child or by reason of the effect of lactation consequent upon the birth of the child, then … she shall be guilty … of infanticide, and may for such offence be dealt with and punished as if she had been guilty of the offence of manslaughter of the child.

This replaced the definition in the Infanticide Act 1922 which only applied to a 'newly born' child. It enables women charged with child killing when in the throes of post natal depression or any other severe mental illness to escape conviction for murder.

Unfitness to plead

A defendant in a Crown Court will be under disability in relation to his or her trial ('unfit to plead') 'if unable to plead to the indictment, to understand the proceedings so as to be able to challenge jurors, to understand and give evidence, and to make a proper defence' (R v. Pritchard (1836)). If the defendant raises the issue, the burden is on him or her to satisfy the judge on the balance of probabilities. If the issue is raised by the prosecution, the prosecution must satisfy the judge beyond reasonable doubt that the defendant is under disability (Criminal Procedure (Insanity) Act 1964: s. 4, as amended by Domestic Violence Crime and Victims Act 2004: s. 22).

The Criminal Procedure (Insanity and Unfitness to Plead) Act 1991 (the 1991 Act: s. 4A(2)(b)) provides for 'a trial of the facts' to take place where a defendant is found to be unfit to plead. A full trial will not take place, but a jury will be required to determine whether they are satisfied beyond reasonable doubt that the defendant did the act or made the omission charged against him as an offence regardless of the existence of any necessary *mens rea*. If they are satisfied that the defendant did the act or made the omission charged, they must make a finding to that effect; if they are not so satisfied, they are obliged to return a verdict of acquittal. Where the defendant is found guilty 'on the facts', the powers of sentence are the same as for a special verdict of not guilty by reason of insanity.

Paragraph 13 of Home Office Circular 93/91 states: 'Where an accused person is found unfit to be tried he should always be legally represented during the trial of the facts. There may be cases where the accused, because of his mental disorder, repudiates his legal representative prior to, or during the trial of the facts'. The court should appoint a lawyer to put the case for the accused who may properly be entrusted to pursue his or her interests. This could include someone who has previously represented the accused or any other person whom the court considers appropriate, for example a solicitor known to the court to have experience in such matters. The Official Solicitor has let it be known that he is prepared to act as the legal representative of an accused person during a trial of the facts.

The Domestic Violence Crime and Victims Act 2004 has made a number of changes. First, as we have seen, it reduces to three the disposal options available to the court. These are:

- to make a hospital order under s. 37 of the 1983 Act , which can also be accompanied by a restriction order under s. 41 of that Act;
- to make a supervision order; or
- to order the absolute discharge of the accused.

Second, it clarifies that for a hospital order to be made the criteria in s. 37 need to be satisfied. If a restriction order is to be imposed it must be necessary for the protection of the public from serious harm. Third, the court can direct admission, and does not have to rely on the Secretary of State to do so. Fourth, in appropriate cases remand powers under ss. 35 and 36 and interim orders under s. 38 are available to the court. Finally, the Home Secretary is empowered to remit for trial a patient detained under s. 37/41 following a finding of unfitness to plead, if satisfied that they can now properly be tried.

Mental condition at time of sentencing

The effect of mental disorder on criminal responsibility or fitness for trial is confined to small numbers of cases. Its effect on sentencing disposal is manifest in many thousands of cases. In some of these the result will be that an offender is not imprisoned but is instead admitted to hospital under Part 3 of the Mental Health Act 1983. In others, especially where there is a personality disorder, the result may be an enhanced prison sentence under the Criminal Justice Act 2003. Once a defendant is convicted or has been found to have committed the act constituting the offence, they may be given a community disposal, a prison sentence or a hospital order. A patient may be diverted to the psychiatric system at the sentencing stage. This may be done under the 1983 Act by a hospital or a guardianship order or by using a community order under the 2003 Act.

Since the Mental Health Act 1959, hospital orders have been a key method of disposal of mentally disordered offenders. Department of Health figures (NSIC

2007: 17) show a long-term decline in unrestricted hospital orders over the life-time of the 1983 Act. In 1995–06, 536 such orders were made; since then the annual figure has been between 300 and 350, the number for 2005–06 being 322, with a further 322 hospital order with restrictions on discharge being imposed. The key question in the decision to impose a hospital order is whether the offender is suffering from mental disorder *at the time of sentencing*, not whether his mental disorder had any bearing on the offending behaviour. In making a hospital order the court is not concerned with criminal responsibility or the defendant's fitness to participate in the trial; the person has usually already been tried and convicted. The only relevant considerations are his mental condition and the need for psychiatric treatment in hospital at the time of sentencing. The 1983 Act also provides for the transfer of mentally disordered prisoners (whether on remand or serving a sentence) from prison to hospital on the authority of a Home Secretary's warrant. In 2005–06, 704 prisoners were trans-ferred from prison to hospital.

The Criminal Justice Act 2003 now provides a general framework for sentenc-ing offenders, with disposals ranging from community sentences to provisions for sentencing dangerous offenders. Hospital orders and transfers to psychiatric hospital from prison continue to be governed by the Mental Health Act 1983. Section 142(1) of the 2003 Act requires any court dealing with an offender to have regard to five purposes of sentencing. These are:

- the punishment of offenders;
- the reduction of crime (including its reduction by deterrence);
- the reform and rehabilitation of offenders;
- the protection of the public; and
- the making of reparation by offenders to persons affected by their offences.

This section does not apply to offenders under 18, to offenders convicted of murder, of certain firearms offences or offences requiring a custodial sentence, who are subject to the dangerous offender provisions in ss. 225–8 of the Act, or where the court makes a hospital order, an interim hospital order or a hospital direction under Part 3 of the Mental Health Act 1983.

Sections 167–73 of the 2003 Act provide for the establishment of the Sentencing Guidelines Council (SGC) and require criminal courts to have regard to any relevant SGC guideline when sentencing an offender. The Act does not provide that any one purpose of sentencing listed should be more important than any other. It is for the sentencing court to determine the manner in which they apply in accordance with SGC guidance.

The sentencing court must begin by considering the seriousness of the offence. The assessment of seriousness is intended to determine whether any of the sentencing thresholds in the Act has been crossed, indicating that a commu-nity, custodial or other sentence is appropriate, and is intended to be the key factor in deciding the severity of the requirements of any community sentence the duration of any prison sentence or the level of any fine.

Seriousness has two components, each of which must be considered by the court. They are (Criminal Justice Act 2003: s. 143(1)): 'the offender's culpability in committing the offence and any harm which the offence caused, was intended to cause, or might foreseeably have caused'. Culpability relates to intention to cause harm. Factors indicating significantly lower culpability include mental illness or disability and youth or age where it affects the responsibility of the defendant (Sentencing Guidelines Council 2004a: para 1.25). Harm is widely defined to include situations where harm is not suffered by individuals or the community but there is a risk of harm from the offending behaviour.

Community sentences

There are two thresholds for imposing a community sentence. The first is s. 148(1), designed to ensure that cases which should generally be dealt with by way of discharge or fine are not dealt with by community sentence. It provides as follows:

> A court must not pass a community sentence on an offender unless it is of the opinion that the offence, or the combination of the offence and one or more offences associated with it, was serious enough to warrant such a sentence.

The second threshold is s. 151 which states that a court may pass a community sentence where it is satisfied that such an order would be in the interests of justice and the offender has since the age of 16 been fined on three or more occasions, even though their offence is not serious enough to justify a community sentence and their previous convictions would not justify such a sentence. The Sentencing Guidelines Council (2004b: para. 1.1.10) advises 'great care ... in assessing whether a community sentence is appropriate, since failure to comply with conditions could result in a custodial sentence'.

Section 147 of the 2003 Act defines a community sentence as a sentence which consists of or includes: (1) a community order; or (2) one or more youth community orders. Section 177 sets out 12 forms of community order which a court may attach to a community sentence for an offender over the age of 18. These include:

- an unpaid work requirement (s. 199);
- an activity requirement (s. 201);
- a programme requirement (s. 202);
- a prohibited activity requirement (s. 203);
- a curfew requirement (s. 204);
- an exclusion requirement (s. 205);
- a residence requirement (s. 206);
- a mental health treatment requirement (s. 207);
- a drug rehabilitation requirement (s. 209);
- an alcohol treatment requirement (s. 212);
- a supervision requirement (s. 213); and
- in a case where the offender is aged under 25, an attendance centre requirement (s. 214).

The most pertinent for present purposes is the 'mental health treatment require-ment' (Criminal Justice Act 2003: s. 207). A court may not impose a mental health treatment requirement unless satisfied on the evidence of a s. 12 doctor that the offender's mental condition requires and may be susceptible to medical treatment but not so as to warrant a hospital or guardianship order. The court must be satisfied that arrangements have or can be made for the treatment intended to be specified in the order, and the offender must have expressed willingness to comply with the requirement.

A mental health treatment requirement requires the offender to submit, during a period specified in the order, to treatment by or under the supervision of a doctor or a chartered psychologist (or both) 'with a view to the improve-ment of the offender's mental condition'. A community order can require treatment as an outpatient where the offender must accept treatment as a non-resident patient at any institution specified in the order, or treatment by or under the direction of such registered medical practitioner or chartered psychol-ogist as may be specified. Treatment may be required as a resident patient in an independent nursing home or care home within the meaning of the Care Standards Act 2000 or a hospital, but not in a high-security hospital. Beyond the above listed specifications, the court may not specify in the order the nature of the treatment to be given.

Section 208 empowers the doctor or psychologist in charge of treating an offender's mental condition under a mental health treatment requirement to arrange transfer where the offender consents and where the clinician is of the opinion that part of the treatment given by or under the direction of a doctor or a psychologist can be better or more conveniently given in or at an institution or place which is not specified in the relevant order. The requirement to accept treatment at the new location applies as if it had been part of the original order. Interestingly, the arrangements to transfer may provide for the offender to receive part of his treatment as a resident patient in an institution or place 'notwithstanding that the institution or place is not one which could have been specified for that purpose in the relevant order'. It is not clear whether this is intended to authorise admission to a high-security hospital, which is not a power available to the court on making the initial order.

Section 179 and Schedule 8 deal with breach. Schedule 8 provides that where the responsible officer considers that an offender has failed to comply with a community order without reasonable excuse, he must issue a warning specify-ing the breach, stating that it is unacceptable and that if there is a further breach within 12 months the offender will be liable to be brought before a court. If within that period the responsible officer considers there has been a further breach without reasonable excuse, he must lay an information before the magis-trates or bring the matter before a Crown Court. The court may then deal with the offender as if for the original offence by attaching more onerous require-ments to the community sentence, or by imprisoning the offender if the original offence was punishable by imprisonment. If an offender over 18 has wilfully and persistently failed to comply with the requirements of the order, the magis-trates or the Crown Court may impose a sentence for the original offence of up to 51 weeks even though that offence was not punishable by imprisonment. In deciding what to do in the event of persistent and wilful non-compliance, the court must take into account the extent to which the offender has complied with the requirements of the community order.

Imprisonment

The threshold requirement for a sentence of imprisonment is set out in the Criminal Justice Act 2003, s. 152(2):

> The court must not pass a custodial sentence unless it is of the opinion that the offence, or the combination of the offence and one or more offences associated with it, was so serious that neither a fine alone nor a community sentence can be justified for the offence.

Section 157 requires any court to obtain and consider a medical report before passing a custodial sentence on an offender who is or who appears to be mentally disordered within the meaning of the Mental Health Act 1983. The medical report may be made or submitted orally or in writing by a doctor approved under s. 12 of the 1983 Act by the Secretary of State as having special experience in the diagnosis or treatment of mental disorder. However, the obligation is not absolute and does not apply if, in the circumstances of the case, the court is of the opinion that it is unnecessary to obtain a medical report, or in any case where the sentence is fixed by law.

Where the offender appears to be mentally disordered, unless the sentence is fixed by law, the court must consider any information (whether or not it is in a report) relating to the offender's mental condition and the likely effect of a custodial sentence on the person's mental condition and on any treatment which may be available for it. Failure to obtain and consider a report does not invalidate any custodial sentence, but any court considering an appeal against sentence must obtain a medical report if none was obtained by the court below, and must consider any report obtained by it or by the court below.

Sentencing under the dangerous offender provisions

Chapter 5 of Part 12 of the 2003 Act (ss. 224–36) contains provisions relating to the sentencing of dangerous offenders. These provisions allow for dangerous offenders guilty of specified serious offences to be sentenced to life imprisonment, imprisonment for public protection or an extended sentence. Schedule 15 specifies the sexual and violent offences which render an offender eligible for dangerous offender sentencing. Section 37(1A) of the Mental Health Act 1983 provides that nothing in ss. 225–8 of the Criminal Justice Act 2003 shall prevent a court from making a hospital order under s. 37(1) of the 1983 Act. So if the court is satisfied that the criteria for making a hospital order are met, an offender need not be dealt with under the dangerousness sentencing provisions of the 2003 Act.

If an offender has committed a specified offence and meets the criterion of dangerousness, the court must impose a life sentence, imprisonment for public protection or an extended sentence. An offender is dangerous where the court is 'of the opinion that there is a significant risk to the public of serious harm occasioned by the commission by him of serious offences'. 'Serious harm' means death or serious personal injury, whether physical or psychological. Section 229 governs the way in which the courts are to assess dangerousness. In all cases the court must take into account any available information before it about the offences, about any pattern of behaviour of which it may form part and about the offender. Section 229(3) creates a presumption of dangerousness where an offender over 18 has previously been convicted of a relevant offence. The court must assume risk of serious harm to the public unless the court considers, after considering the information outlined above, that it would be unreasonable to conclude that there is such a risk.

As Ashworth observes (2005: 210), the requirement that the court find a significant risk of serious harm is an attempt to comply with Article 5 of the European Convention on Human Rights. However, he goes on to describe (2005: 214–15) the s. 229(3) presumption as a 'draconian provision' since there is no requirement that the previous offence be recent or be similar to or related to the offence for which the offender is now being sentenced. He questions whether the presumption is compatible with European Convention Articles 5 (protection against arbitrary detention) and 6 (right to a fair trial) since 'in principle the court ought to be able to assess freely the degree of risk to the public rather than being constrained by a presumption'.

Section 225(1) specifies the circumstances where a court is required to impose either a life sentence or imprisonment for public protection. First the offender must have been convicted of a serious offence and the court must be of the opinion that there is a significant risk to the public of serious harm occasioned by the commission by him of serious offences.

Life sentences

Section 225(2) requires the court to impose a life sentence if the offence is one which potentially carries a sentence of life imprisonment and the court considers that the seriousness of the offence or of the offence and other offences associated with it is such as to justify a life sentence. In sentencing the offender the court should specify the minimum term which the offender will serve, usually half the term which would be proportionate to the offence minus any time spent on remand (*Attorney-General's Reference No. 3 of 2004 (Akuffo)* [2005]: 240). Once the minimum term has expired the offender's eligibility for release will be determined by the Parole Board using the criteria of risk in Part 2 of the Crime (Sentences) Act 1997. This means that the offender will be released when the Parole Board is satisfied that detention is no longer necessary for the protection of the public.

Imprisonment for public protection: indeterminate sentences

If the case falls within s. 225(1) but not s. 225(2), the court must impose a sentence of imprisonment for public protection for an indeterminate period. Section 225(2) will not apply if the offence is one for which a life sentence is unavailable or where the court does not think the offence has reached the threshold of seriousness sufficient to justify a life sentence. However, the consequences may be little different from a sentence of life imprisonment in that the court sets a minimum term commensurate with the seriousness of the offence. After this period has expired, the prisoner will remain in prison until the Parole Board is satisfied that detention is not longer necessary for the protection of the public. If released, the offender will be on life licence, which will only be lifted if the Parole Board decides that it is no longer necessary for the protection of the public.

Extended sentences

Where a person over 18 is convicted of a specified offence, and s. 225 does not apply, s. 227 requires the court to impose an extended sentence where it considers that there is a significant risk to members of the public of serious harm occasioned by the commission by the offender of further specified offences. An extended sentence is the sum of the appropriate custodial term (which should be proportionate to the seriousness of the current offence) and an 'extension period' for which the offender is to be subject to a licence and which is of such length as the court considers necessary for the purpose of protecting members of the public from serious harm occasioned by the commission by him of further specified offences.

There would therefore be nothing to stop the appropriate custodial term for the offence being two years and the extension period being up to five years in the case of a specified violent offence or up to eight years in the case of a specified sexual offence. As Ashworth (2005: 212) notes:

> Whereas life imprisonment and imprisonment for public protection may only be imposed where the offence is both a specified offence and a serious offence – meaning that the relevant statutory maximum is ten years or more – the extended sentence applies to all specified offences which are not serious offences – meaning that the relevant statutory maximum is between two and ten years

The term of an extended sentence must not exceed the maximum term permitted for the offence (Criminal Justice Act 2003: s. 227(5)). The offender is eligible for release after serving half the custodial term, but this depends on the Parole Board expressing itself satisfied that confinement in prison is no longer necessary for the protection of the public. An offender who cannot satisfy the Parole Board that detention is no longer necessary to protect the public will remain in prison for the whole of the extension period. If released by the Parole Board the prisoner will be on licence and subject to recall for the remainder of the extension period.

As noted above, nothing in ss. 225–8 of the Criminal Justice Act 2003 shall prevent a court from making a hospital order under s. 37(1) of the 1983 Act. So if the court is satisfied that the criteria for making a hospital order are met, an offender need not be dealt with under the dangerousness sentencing provisions of the 2003 Act and may be given a hospital order instead.

The hospital order (Mental Health Act 1983: s. 37)

A hospital order sentences a mentally disordered person to detention in hospital for treatment rather than in gaol. A hospital order may be imposed without restrictions in which case the patient's responsible clinician may discharge the patient without recourse to higher authority. If a restriction order is imposed by a Crown Court (see below) the patient may not be discharged by the responsible clinician but the Home Secretary or the MHRT may direct discharge. In 1995–96, 536 hospital orders without restrictions on discharge were made. This figure has declined to 322 in 2005–06. At the same time the number of restriction orders was 321 in 1995–96, declined to 235 in 2003–04 and has since risen to 322 in 2005–06. This is the first time that there have been equal numbers of non-restricted and restricted hospital orders made during the year.

If sent to prison a mentally disordered person can only be treated under the terms of the Mental Capacity Act 2005 ss. 5 and 6 which authorise treatment without consent of a person who lacks capacity and who needs treatment in his own best interests, and authorises restraint of a mentally incapacitated person where necessary and a proportionate response to prevent harm to the person. A person, whether or not they lack capacity, may also be treated without consent under common law, where restraint and treatment may be authorised where they represent the minimum force necessary to prevent that person from harming others.

In *Munjaz* v. *Mersey Care NHS Trust* (2003: para. 46) Hale LJ said as follows:

> There is a general power to take such steps as are reasonably necessary and proportionate to protect others from the immediate risk of significant harm. This applies whether or not the patient lacks the capacity to make decisions for himself. But where the patient does lack capacity, there is also the power to provide him with whatever treatment or care is necessary in his own best interests.

People detained under long-term powers in the MHA 1983 may be given treatment without consent subject to the second opinion safeguards in Part 4 of the Act.

A hospital order may be made by magistrates or by the Crown Court. The Crown Court can make an order if the person is convicted of an offence punishable with imprisonment, except in the case of murder (for which the sentence is fixed by law) (MHA 1983: s. 37(1)). A magistrates' court can make a hospital order without recording a conviction if the person is suffering from mental illness or severe mental impairment, and the court is satisfied that he committed the act with which he is charged (MHA 1983: s. 37(3)). One of the two doctors giving evidence must be approved under s. 12 of the 1983 Act. An order authorises detention for up to six months in the first instance, renewable for a further six months and then for periods of one year at a time. Under the Mental Health Act 2007 the old categories of mental disorder will cease to be relevant and the court will be required to be satisfied that:

- the offender is suffering from mental disorder ('any disorder or disability of the mind') of a nature or degree making it appropriate for him to be detained in hospital for medical treatment; and
- that appropriate treatment is available for him.

The court must also be of the opinion, having regard to all the circumstances, including the nature of the offence and the character and antecedents of the offender, and to other methods of dealing with him, that the most suitable method of disposing of the case is by means of a hospital order. Even if the criteria for making a hospital order are met, the court still has considerable discretion to consider other alternatives such as a dangerous offender sentence. Guidance was given by the Court of Appeal in *R v. Birch* (1989: 215) on the circumstances where prison might be chosen as an alternative for a patient found to be suffering from mental disorder. The first is where the offender is dangerous and there is no suitable secure hospital bed. The second is where there was an element of culpability for the offence which merited punishment. This might happen where there is no connection between the mental disorder and the offence, or where the offender's responsibility for the offence is diminished but not extinguished. In *R v. Drew* (2003) the House of Lords held that under both national law and the European Convention case law a sentence of imprisonment could be imposed on a mentally disordered defendant who was criminally responsible and fit to be tried.

Appropriate treatment can include psychological treatment, care, habilitation and rehabilitation and is defined as treatment which is intended to alleviate or prevent deterioration in the patient's condition. The new definition of mental disorder means that people with learning disability (subject to the presence of abnormally aggressive or seriously irresponsible conduct), people with mental illness and people with personality disorders (who are thought to benefit most from psychological interventions such as cognitive behaviour therapy) may be detained if their disorder is of a nature or degree making it appropriate for them to be detained for treatment.

A hospital order cannot be made unless the court is satisfied, on the evidence of the approved clinician who would have overall responsibility for his case or the hospital managers, that arrangements have been made for the patient's admission to hospital within 28 days Thus the hospital has the discretion to decide whether to admit an offender; in some cases under the 1959 Act, mentally disordered people were sentenced to imprisonment because hospitals have refused to accept them. Section 39 of the 1983 Act therefore empowers a court considering making a hospital order, an interim hospital order or a hospital direction with a restriction direction to request the primary care trust or health authority where the person resides or last resided or any other health authority or primary care trust which appears to be appropriate to furnish the court with such information as they can reasonably obtain with respect to the hospital or hospitals in their area or elsewhere where arrangements could be made for the admission of the offender. The trust or authority approached by the court must comply with any such request.

The effect of a hospital order is similar to that of an admission for treatment as a non-offender under s. 3 with some exceptions; the most important is that a hospital order patient cannot be discharged by his nearest relative. A hospital order can be made with or without a s. 41 order imposing restrictions on discharge.

Restriction order (Mental Health Act 1983: s. 41)

Where a hospital order has been made, a Crown Court may make a restriction order. A magistrates' court has no power to make a restriction order, but if the criteria are met, it may commit an offender over 14 years of age to the Crown Court where a restriction order can be made. The evidence of one of the two doctors supporting the hospital order must have been given orally. In 2005-6 Department of Health figures indicate that 322 hospital orders with restriction orders were made by courts (NSIC 2007: 17). Home Office data show that in 1995 there were 1,548 patients subject to restriction orders resident in hospitals under detention, 264 of whom were women. By 2005 that figure had risen to 2,344, where 411 of whom were women (Home Office 2007: 4)

The grounds for making a restriction order are that it appears to the court, having regard to the nature of the offence, the antecedents of the offender and the risk of his committing further offences if set at large, that a restriction order is necessary for the protection of the public from serious harm. The Court of Appeal in *R* v. *Birch* (1989) held that the sentencing court is required to assess the seriousness of the risk not that he will reoffend, but the risk that, if he does, the public will suffer serious harm. The harm in question need not be limited to personal injury, nor need it relate to the public in general, but the potential harm must be serious, and a high possibility of the recurrence of minor offences will not be sufficient.

Where the medical opinion is unanimous that a restriction order should be imposed and there is a secure bed, a decision not to impose a hospital order should not be made because of concerns about risk to the public should the offender be released (*R* v. *Howell* (1985)). However, if the doctors giving medical evidence are not unanimous about a hospital disposal, the sentencing decision is for the judge to resolve in the light of all the evidence and the circumstances of the case (*R* v. *Reid* (2005)).

The 1983 Act provided for restriction orders to be made for either a specified period or without limit of time. The courts had adopted the practice that restriction orders should usually be made without limit of time unless doctors can confidently assert that recovery will take place within a certain period (*R* v. *Gardiner* (1967)). The possibility of a time limited restriction order has been removed by the Mental Health Act 2007, and all future restriction orders will be without limit of time.

The effect of a restriction order is that a patient's detention does not need to be renewed by the hospital managers. Detention carries on, subject to a requirement on the responsible clinician to submit a report at least once a year 'on that person'. The patient cannot be granted leave of absence, transferred or discharged by the responsible clinician or hospital managers without the consent of the Home Secretary. This is dealt with by the Mental Health Unit in the Ministry of Justice. If the patient is discharged with Ministry of Justice permission this may be absolutely or subject to conditions. Except in rare cases (such as extreme age) where the offender is assessed as posing no risk, conditional discharge will be the route chosen.

Restriction order patients used to have only limited rights to challenge detention. A patient detained for treatment under the civil power (s. 3) or by a criminal court under a hospital order (s. 37) has the right to apply for discharge to an MHRT. The MHRT must order discharge if not satisfied (1) that the patient is suffering from mental disorder of a nature or degree warranting detention , or (2) that detention is necessary in the interests of the patient's health or safety or for the protection of others, or (3) that appropriate treatment is available. Under the 1959 Act restriction order patients did not have this right. They could only ask the Home Secretary to refer their case to an MHRT, and the tribunal did not have the power to order release, only to advise the Home Secretary to exercise his power of discharge.

The MHRT's lack of power to order discharge was held in X v. *United Kingdom* (1981) to breach the requirement in Article 5(4) that a person detained because of unsoundness of mind must be able, at intervals, to seek review of the lawfulness of their detention before a court or tribunal *with the power to order release*. The 1983 Act authorises an MHRT to order the absolute or conditional discharge of a restriction order patient if not satisfied that the conditions of detention are met (mental disorder of a nature or degree warranting confinement). This introduced the possibility that an offender patient might persuade a tribunal to discharge him when the Ministry of Justice Mental Health Unit still considered discharge to pose too great a risk, removing absolute ministerial control over the duration of detention of offenders sentenced to restriction orders without limit of time.

In R v. A (2005) the Court of Appeal held that the risk that an offender might be released prematurely by an MHRT is not a ground for a court to pass a life sentence rather than making a restriction order, since the composition and powers of the MHRT and the Parole Board panels are 'closely analogous'. Each consists of a legally qualified president who has experience in the criminal courts, a psychiatrist and a lay member. The figures show that since 1990 the MHRT gives many more conditional discharges than the Home Secretary. In 2002, of the 357 conditional discharges of restricted patients 280 were by the MHRT and 77 were by the Home Office Mental Health Unit. This has been the pattern for the past decade.

The restriction order with its conditional discharge option is seen as an effective means of risk management. Reoffending rates in terms of serious sexual offences or violent offences of the 717 patients conditionally discharged between 1999 and 2003 are assessed by the Home Office as averaging 2 per cent (Home Office 2007: 14).

A restriction order patient can be discharged by the Home Secretary or an MHRT either absolutely or subject to conditions. If the patient is given an absolute discharge, both the hospital and restriction orders cease to have effect and s/he cannot be recalled to hospital. If a patient's discharge is conditional, s/he may, for example, be directed to live in a specified place, to attend for treatment and to accept treatment by or under the direction of the responsible clinician. Because it may be a condition of discharge that the patient must accept treatment for mental disorder, a conditionally discharged restricted patient is not eligible to seek review of treatment by a second opinion doctor under Part 4 of the 1983 Act.

The Home Office says it should be notified by the responsible clinician in the case of a conditionally discharged patient where:

- there appears to be a risk to the public;
- contact with the patient is lost;
- the patient is unwilling to cooperate with supervision;
- the patient needs further inpatient treatment; or
- the patient is charged with an offence.

A conditionally discharged restricted patient may be recalled to hospital by the Home Secretary or by the responsible clinician at any time while the restriction order is in force but, unless it is an emergency recall, there must be medical evidence of mental disorder warranting confinement (*James Kay* v. *United Kingdom* (1998)). The patient must be informed that s/he is being recalled to hospital at the time, and a further explanation of reasons for recall must be given as soon as is reasonably practicable (Jones 2006: 266). The case of a conditionally discharged restricted patient who is recalled to hospital must be referred by the Home Secretary to an MHRT within a month of his return to hospital.

Guardianship order (Mental Health Act 1983: s. 37)

As Jones (2006: 230) points out, 'Little use has been made of guardianship orders by the courts', with figures running at under 30 cases per year. In 2006 in England there were 66 patients under guardianship orders (NSIC 2006: Tables 1–2; Local Government Data Unit Wales 2005). The diagnostic criterion for making an order are that the offender must be 16 or over and suffering from one of the four forms of mental disorder of a nature or degree which warrants his reception into guardianship. This will change with the 2007 Act, the new test being whether the patient suffers from any disorder or disability of mind warranting reception into guardianship. A learning disabled person may only be given a guardianship order if their disorder is associated with abnormally aggressive or seriously irresponsible conduct on his or her part. The court enjoys wide discretion to decide whether guardianship is 'suitable', since it must be of the opinion, having regard to all the circumstances, including the nature of the offence and the character and antecedents of the offender and to other methods of dealing with him, that the most suitable method of disposing of the case is by means of a guardianship order.

The medical evidentiary requirements for making a guardianship order are virtually the same as for a hospital order. The court enjoys similar powers to request information to those available for hospital order cases. Under s. 39A, a court considering making a guardianship order will be empowered to request the local social services authority (or any other social services authority considered by the court to be appropriate): (1) to inform the court whether it or any person authorised by it is prepared to receive the patient into guardianship; and (2) if so, to give such information as it reasonably can about how it or the other person could be expected to exercise guardianship powers.

Transfer to hospital of sentenced prisoners (ss. 47 and 49)

Section 47 allows for the transfer of a sentenced prisoner to hospital by the Home Secretary's direction. Section 49 empowers the Home Secretary to attach a restriction direction, imposing restrictions on discharge. By far the majority of transfers are subject to restrictions. In 1995–06, 222 patients were transferred under s. 47 with restrictions under s. 49. In 2005–06 the figure was 273. The equivalent figures for s. 47 transfers without restrictions were for 1995–06: 31, and for 2005–06: 56 (NSIC 2007: 17). In 1995, 402 prisoners were resident in hospital having been transferred under s. 47 with s. 49 restrictions. Since 2003 the numbers of inpatients have begun to rise significantly, the total for 2005 being 561 (Home Office 2007: 4).

If no restriction direction is made, detention lasts for up to six months, renewable for six months and then for periods of one year at a time. If a restriction direction is made, the restrictions expire on the earliest date on which the offender would have been released from prison (the earliest release date); thereafter, the patient is detained as if he were a patient under a s. 37 hospital order without restrictions. This means that they may be discharged by the clinical supervisor or the MHRT.

Under the Mental Health Act 2007, before issuing a direction the Home Secretary must be satisfied that the prisoner is:

- suffering from mental disorder (any disorder or disability of mind); and
- the mental disorder is of a nature or degree which makes it appropriate for him to be detained in hospital for medical treatment; and
- that appropriate medical treatment is available for him; and
- having regard to the public interest and to all the other circumstances, a transfer is expedient.

The direction must be based on two medical reports, one from a doctor approved under s. 12 (s. 54(1)). The initial version of the Mental Health Act Code of Practice (1993) stated that the need for inpatient treatment of a prisoner must be identified and acted on swiftly, and contact made urgently between the prison doctor and the hospital doctor. It also emphasises that the transfer of a prisoner to hospital should not be delayed until close to his release date, since a transfer in such circumstances may well be seen by the prisoner as being primarily intended to extend his detention (paras. 3.12–3.13). These paragraphs no longer appear in the Code, but the Mental Health Act Commission (2006: 382–3) have expressed their continuing concern that transfers late in the sentence are distorting mental health law by using it for primarily public protection purposes, and that transfer should take place as soon as is therapeutically indicated rather than being delayed until risk is the primary factor.

Where the Secretary of State thinks fit, he may attach to a transfer direction a restriction direction. If a restriction direction is not given, or once it expires because the prisoner's earliest release date has passed, the offender is detained as if under a hospital order. Patients transferred from prison to hospital are entitled to make applications to have their case referred to an MHRT. If the Minister of Justice is notified by the clinical supervisor, another clinician or the MHRT that the offender no longer requires treatment in hospital, he has two options: he can either discharge an offender who would have been eligible for release on parole had he remained in prison, or he can direct that he be returned to prison to serve the remainder of his sentence. This means that the Secretary of State for Justice retains greater control over the duration of detention of a transferred prisoner with a restriction direction than he does over a restriction order patient. To comply with Article 5 of the European Convention a tribunal must have the power to discharge a restriction order patient, but because a transferred person is a prisoner, the Home Secretary may remit them to prison to serve out their term. This fact was undoubtedly one of the inspirations behind the introduction of the hospital direction and limitation direction ('hybrid order') under s. 45A (discussed below).

Transfer of unsentenced prisoners to hospital (Mental Health Act 1983: s. 48)

Section 48 provides the same power of transfer from prison to psychiatric hospital of civil prisoners, remand prisoners and prisoners detained under immigration legislation. Under the 2007 Act the Home Secretary will have to be satisfied:

- that the person is suffering from mental disorder (again the new broad definition of any disorder or disability of mind) of a nature or degree which makes it appropriate for him to be detained in hospital for medical treatment; and
- he is in urgent need of such treatment; and
- appropriate medical treatment is available for him;

The same requirements for medical reports apply to s. 48 as apply to a transfer direction under s. 47. The main difference between ss. 47 and 48 is that for the latter the need for treatment must be urgent. In 1995–06 there were 359 transfers of unsentenced prisoners with restriction directions and 51 without. In 2005–06 there were 361 with restrictions and 14 without (NSIC 2007: 17). In 1995, 183 prisoners were resident in hospital having been transferred under s. 48 with s. 49 restrictions. The figures since have been between 140 and 190 per year. The total population for 2005 was slightly up at 218 (Home Office 2007: 4). Under the 1983 Act the power is confined to people with mental illness or severe mental impairment. The 2007 Act extends it to patients with any form of disorder or disability of mind. This may prove important and may lead to increased use, since transfer of remand prisoners is an important power to rescue people who may be at risk of suicide or self-harm due to mental illness such as depression but who equally might need urgent treatment to prevent risk to self or others brought on by personality problems. Patients transferred under s. 48 may be given treatment without consent under the regime of powers and second opinions in Part 4 of the 1983 Act.

Hospital directions and restriction directions (Mental Health Act: s. 45A)

Section 45A, introduced by the Crime (Sentences) Act 1997, provides for a hospital direction and limitation direction ('hybrid order') whereby a mentally disordered offender may be given a sentence of imprisonment coupled with an immediate direction to hospital. Initially confined to people with a psychopathic disorder diagnosis, the 2007 Act will extend this to people with any disorder or disability of mind. The conditions which must be met before a court may impose a hospital and restriction direction are that there must be written or oral evidence from two doctors:

- that the offender is suffering from mental disorder;
- that the mental disorder from which the offender is suffering is of a nature or degree which makes it appropriate for him to be detained in a hospital for medical treatment; and
- that appropriate medical treatment is available for him.

The result of this is that, although directed initially to hospital, the offender has the legal status of prisoner rather than patient. This means that in the event of the mental disorder being successfully treated before the expiry of the prison sentence the offender can be returned to prison to serve the remainder of the tariff sentence. The offender is given a prison sentence which is calculated in accordance with normal sentencing principles, but is directed to hospital in the first instance. If he recovers prior to the expiry of the sentence, he will be remitted to prison to serve the remaining sentence. This avoids the problem of the MHRTs discharging patients 'early', because if the offender is no longer mentally disordered, the Secretary of State for Justice has the ultimate say in whether he returns to prison. The hybrid order was initially confined to patients with psychopathic disorder, but the Mental Health Bill 2006 extends it to anyone suffering from mental disorder in the broad sense of 'any disorder or disability of mind'.

The Mental Health Act Commission (2006: 389–94) criticised the Home Office for its suggestion that hybrid orders 'could provide a punitive element in the disposal ... to reflect the offender's whole or partial responsibility' (Home Office 1996: para. 1.6). They adopt Bartlett and Sandland's argument (2003: 307) that it is purportedly the aim of mental health disposals to divert the mentally disordered from punitive sanctions and the hybrid orders require clinicians to become involved in determining levels of criminal responsibility and to engage in the process of deciding what is a suitable punishment.

Home Office guidance has dropped reference to criminal responsibility, preferring instead to stress that the power should be used in two situations. First is where the alternative would be a mandatory life sentence under the 'two strikes and you're out' provision in the Powers of the Criminal Courts (Sentencing) Act 2000 (s. 109) which provides for, excluding exceptional circumstances, a mandatory life sentence on conviction of a second serious offence. Mental disorder is not an exceptional circumstance. The second situation is where it would be the most effective way to protect the public from further harm (Home Office 1997: para. 3). If the Home Office entertained hopes that this provision would be widely used, they have been disappointed. The courts have not used the power extensively. Since 2000 the total number of patients in hospital in any year under a hospital direction and restriction direction has never risen above 11 (Home Office 2007: 4).

The Mental Health Act Commission (2006: 392–3) remain concerned that hybrid orders, if they are to be used at all, should not become the normal disposal for any mentally disordered offender whom the court views as criminally responsible to some degree. They are also worried that imposition of punishment alongside medical treatment may undermine treatment compliance and foster a sense of 'doing time'. Moreover, since mental illness may be relapsing and episodic a return to prison might trigger relapse and result in a form of ping-pong between prison and hospital throughout the tariff period.

Victims

In keeping with the general move to increase the legal rights of victims of crime to make representations in relation to disposal and release, the Domestic Violence (Crime and Victims) Act 2004 (ss. 36–8) provide that where a person convicted of a violent or sexual offence defined in s. 45 of the 2004 Act is given a hospital order with or without restrictions or a hospital and limitation direction, the local probation board must take all reasonable steps to ascertain whether the person who appears to be the victim of the offence or who appears to act for the victim wishes to make representations about whether the offender should be subject to any conditions if discharged or wishes to receive information about any conditions which may be imposed. If the person makes representations, the local probation board must forward them to the body making the decision on discharge. The MHA 2007 extends the rights of victims to make representations about discharge to cases where the offender is given a hospital order or transfer direction without restrictions.

Concluding comments

The Department of Health (2005) Offender Mental Health Care Pathway provides a best-practice template and aims to meet two targets: first, no one with acute severe mental illness should be in prison; and, second, prisons should be safe places for other people with mental health problems, with a particular focus on the creation of in-reach services and suicide prevention. With a prison population now over 80,000, limited capacity in the psychiatric services and overcrowding rife in British jails, these goals are far from realisation. The small numbers transferred from prison of around 800 per year represents less than 1 per cent of the prison population. The 3,500 restricted patients equal just over 4 per cent of the prison population. It cannot seriously be doubted that there are many prisoners who are in need of hospital treatment for mental disorder.

There is a legal framework for diversion from the penal system, but the courts enjoy wide discretion when deciding whether there will be a hospital disposal based on therapeutic ideals or a prison disposal based on punitive ones. One of the main limiting factors is the number of beds. Court diversion teams report that the courts are much more willing to contemplate hospital treatment as a diversionary sentence than they are to accept treatment in the community. The last decade has seen the transformation of the penal system and the psychiatric system in such a way as to bring about a convergence between them. There have been two principal drivers: first, the management of risk to the public of offences committed by mentally disordered people; and second to ensure compliance with the right to freedom from arbitrary detention under Article 5 and the right to respect for physical integrity, home, privacy and family life under the European Convention on Human Rights. The risk management agenda seeks to remove obstacles in the way of ensuring that people with mental disorder who are assessed as high risk may be detained under the civil powers of admission under Part 2 of the 1983 Act. Moreover, risk management also demands that equally effective risk management is available regardless of whether a mentally disordered offender is sentenced under mental health or criminal justice legislation. These goals manifest themselves legally in a number of ways.

First, the powers under the 1983 Act as amended will include the power to detain in hospital and to require acceptance of treatment in the community by people who have committed no offence. The broader definition of mental disorder allows personality disorder to be more clearly brought within the Act. The removal of the exclusion that no one shall be treated as mentally disordered by reason only of sexual deviance brings paedophiles firmly within the purview of the Act. The extension of the definition of medical treatment to include psychological interventions clearly has personality disorder in mind. The government has refused to accept the Scottish condition of detention that the patient's judgment must be significantly impaired in relation to the decision to enter hospital. This is because of concerns that a psychiatrist might refuse to admit a patient who was assessed as high risk on the basis of an assessment that the patient's judgment was not significantly impaired. Here the government has in mind intelligent risky people with personality disorders.

Second, each system has a range of options for indeterminate detention with closely supervised discharge either via Mental Health Act restriction orders or dangerousness sentences under the Criminal Justice Act followed by release on licence subject to close supervision. The advantage of indeterminate detention has been transplanted from the psychiatric system to the penal system. Before a prisoner assessed as high risk for causing serious harm emerges from prison following a determinate sentence, he may be transferred to hospital under s. 47. If he or she falls through the net and is released, he or she will be subject to the multi-agency public protection panel system established by the Criminal Justice and Court Services Act 2000. These are joint committees including police, probation, health, social services and housing to assess and manage risks posed by violent or sexual offenders, intended to identify people who may require admission to hospital under civil powers on grounds of risk before they commit an offence.

Third, each system has a network of community powers with the capacity to impose significant limits on freedom of movement, to choose residence and to refuse treatment for mental disorder alcoholism or drug addiction. In addition any condition may be attached to a patient's community treatment order which is either necessary or appropriate to secure that the patient receives medical treatment or to prevent risk to self or others. This could include the power to impose a curfew or restrictions of movement on an individual. Here we see strong cross fertilisation between conditional discharged restricted patient status, antisocial behaviour orders (ASBOs) under the Crime and Disorder Act 1998, community orders under the Criminal Justice Act 2003 and community treatment orders under the Mental Health Act 1983 as amended. Obligations under a community treatment order may only include such limits on behaviour as are necessary to manage risk, not exactly an onerous restriction of the range of conditions which may be applied. The range of controls available under all of these measures has effectively meant that anyone subject to them is broadly in a similar position to a conditionally discharged restricted patient. Given the limits of institutional capacity to manage risk in prisons and hospitals, the reach of risk management for mentally disordered people can only be extended by moving into the community, with a wider number of professionals exercising power to renew detention and treat without consent ('responsible clinicians' rather than just doctors). This is a system where movement may be monitored from a central point using electronic tags, where there is effective technology to monitor movement and behaviour in the community, as well as to detect drug or alcohol infringements. It is not fanciful therefore to speak of the effective institutionalisation of the community through the establishment of an effective interconnected network of disciplinary and therapeutic power relationships mediated by law.

Selected further reading

A. Ashworth's book (2005) *Sentencing and Criminal Justice*. Cambridge: Cambridge University Press is the best general guide to sentencing, and offers a critical discussion of the powers of the criminal courts in the context of currents in penal policy and the European Convention on Human Rights. J. Laing's (1990) *Care or Custody: Mentally Disordered Offenders in the Criminal Justice System*. Oxford: Oxford University Press offers a thoughtful analysis of the policy of diversion of mentally disordered offenders from custody. An excellent analysis of mental condition defences to criminal offences is found in R. Mackay's book (1995) *Mental Condition Defences in the Criminal Law*. Oxford: Clarendon Press, and the Law Commission Report (2004) *Partial Defences to Murder*, Cm 6301. London: TSO.

P. Bartlett and R. Sandland's (2007) *Mental Health Law Policy and Practice*, 3rd edn. Oxford: Oxford University Press provides an excellent contextual discussion of mental health law as it relates to mentally disordered offenders. A full up-to-date analysis of the effect of the Mental Health Act 2007 on mentally disordered offenders is to be found in P. Fennell's (2007) *Mental Health: The New Law*. Bristol: Jordans.

Statutes

Bail Act 1976
Care Standards Act 2000
Crime (Sentences) Act 1997
Crime and Disorder Act 1998
Criminal Justice Act 2003
Criminal Justice and Court Services Act 2000
Criminal Procedure (Insanity) Act 1964
Criminal Procedure (Insanity and Unfitness to Plead) Act 1991
Domestic Violence Crime and Victims Act 2004
Homicide Act 1957

Infanticide Act 1922
Mental Capacity Act 2005
Mental Health Act 1959
Mental Health Act 1983
Mental Health Act 2007
Mental Health (Patients in the Community) Act 1995
Police and Criminal Evidence Act 1984
Powers of the Criminal Courts (Sentencing) Act 2000
Trial of Lunatics Act 1883

Cases cited

Attorney-General v. *Prior* (2001) Royal Court of Jersey
Attorney-General's Reference No. 3 of 2004 (Akuffo) [2005] Cr. App. R (S) 230
James Kay v. *United Kingdom* (1998) 40 BMLR 20
McNaghten's Case [1843] X Clark and Finnelly 200
Munjaz v. *Mersey Care NHS Trust* (2003)
R v. *A* [2005] EWCA Crim 2077
R v. *Ahluwalia* [1992] 4 All ER 889, 96 Cr App Rep 133; [1993] Crim LR 63
R v. *Aspinall* (1999) 2 Cr App R 115
R v. *Birch* (1989) 11 Cr. App. Rep. (S) 202
R v. *Byrne* [1960] 3 All ER 1
R v. *Cox* (1968) Cr. App. R. 130
R v. *Dietschmann* [2003] UKHL 10; [2003] 1 All ER 897
R v. *Drew* [2003] UKHL 25
R v. *Everett* [1988] Crim LR 826
R v. *Gardner* (2003) *The Independent*, 17 May; http://web.lexis-nexis.com/professional/
    form?_index=pro_en.html&_lang=en&ut=3333627529
R v. *Gittens* [1984] QB 698
R v. *Ham* (1995) 36 BMLR 169
R v. *Hennessy* [1989] 2 All ER 9
R v. *Hobson* (1997) 43 BMLR 181
R v. *Howell* (1985) 2 Cr App R 360
R v. *Law Thompson* [1997] Crim LR 674
R v. *Lewis* (Martin) [1996] Crim LR 260
R v. *Lloyd* [1967] 1 QB 175
R v. *Mawditt* (2005) *The Times*, 3 September 2005
R v. *Moss* (1990) 91 Cr App R 37
R v. *Pritchard* (1836) 7 C & P 303
R (Munjaz) v. *Ashworth Hospital* [2003] EWCA 1036 Court of Appeal
R v. *Reid* [2005] EWCA Crim 392
R v. *Sullivan* [1983] 2 All ER 673 (HL)
R v. *Vinagre* (1979) 69 Cr App R 104
X v. *United Kingdom* (1981) 4 EHRR 188
R v. *Wragg* (2005) *The Guardian*, 13 December; http://web.lexis-nexis.com/
    professional/form?_index=pro_en.html&_lang=en&ut=3333627529

References

Ashworth, A. (2005) *Sentencing and Criminal Justice*. Cambridge: Cambridge University Press.

Bartlett, P. and Sandland, R. (2003) *Mental Health Law Policy and Practice*, 2nd edn. Oxford: Oxford University Press.

Bartlett, P. and Sandland, R. (2007) *Mental Health Law Policy and Practice*, 3rd edn. Oxford: Oxford University Press.

Bluglass, R. and Bowden, P. (1990) *Principles and Practice of Forensic Psychiatry*. London: Churchill Livingstone.

Butler (1975) *Report of the Committee on Mentally Abnormal Offenders*, Cmnd 6244. London: HMSO.

Crown Prosecution Service (2004) *Code for Crown Prosecutors*. Available at: http://www.cps.gov.uk/publications/prosecution/index.html

Department of Health (2000) *Reforming the Mental Health Act 1983* and *High Risk Patients*, Cm 5016-1 and 2. London: TSO.

Department of Health (2005) *Offender Mental Health Care Pathway*. Available at: http://www.dh.gov.uk/prod_consum_dh/groups/dh_digitalassets/@dh/@en/documents/digitalasset/dh_4102232.pdf

Department of Health and Welsh Office (1999) *Mental Health Act 1983 Code of Practice*. London: TSO.

Fennell, P. (1991) 'Double detention under the Mental Health Act 1983: a case of extra Parliamentary legislation', *Journal of Social Welfare and Family Law*, 194–208.

Fennell, P. and Yeates, V. (1996) '"To serve which master?" – criminal justice policy, community care and the mentally disordered offender', in A. Buchanan (ed.), *Care of the Mentally Disordered Offender in the Community*. Oxford: Oxford University Press, pp. 288–324.

Home Office (1996) *Mentally Disordered Offenders: Sentencing and Discharge Arrangements*. London: Home Office.

Home Office (1997) *Guidance on the Crime (Sentences) Act*, Circular 52/1997. London: Home Office.

Home Office (2007) *Statistics of Mentally Disordered Offenders 2005*, Statistical Bulletin 05/07. See: http://www.homeoffice.gov.uk/rds/pdfs07/hosb0507.pdf

Jones, R. M. (2006) *Mental Health Act Manual*, 10th edn. London: Sweet & Maxwell.

Local Government Data Unit Wales (2005) 'People who are subject to guardianship under Section 7 or Section 37 of the Mental Health Act 1983', Personal Social Services Statistics Wales 2005. Available at: http://www.unedddatacymru.gov.uk/Documents/

Mackay, R. D. (1995) *Mental Condition Defences in the Criminal Law*. Oxford: Clarendon Press.

Mackay, R. D., Mitchell, B. J. and Howe, L. (2006) 'Yet more facts about the insanity defence', *Criminal Law Review*, 399–411.

Mental Health Act Commission (2006) *In Place of Fear*, Eleventh Biennial Report 2003–2005. London: TSO.

Murphy, Baroness (2007) Hansard HL Debs 1 March 2007, cols 1700–1. Available at: http://www.publications.parliament.uk/pa/ld200607/ldhansrd/text/70301-0009.htm

National Statistics Information Centre (2006) 'Guardianship under the Mental Health Act 1983'. Available at: http://www.ic.nhs.uk/statistics-and-data-collections/health-and-lifestyles/mental-health/guardianship-under-the-mental-health-act-1983-england-2006

National Statistics Information Centre (2007) 'In-patients formally detained in hospitals under the Mental Health Act 1983 and other legislation, NHS Trusts, Care Trusts, Primary Care Trusts and Independent Hospitals, England; 1995–96 to 2005–06'. Available at: http://www.ic.nhs.uk/statistics-and-data-collections/health-and-lifestyles/mental-health/in-patients-formally-detained-in-hospitals-under-the-mental-health-act-1983-and-other-legislation-nhs-trusts-care-trusts-primary-care-trusts-and-independent-hospitals;-2005-06

Sentencing Guidelines Council (2004a) *Seriousness Guideline*. Available at: http://www.sentencing-guidelines.gov.uk/docs

Sentencing Guidelines Council (2004b) *New Sentences: Criminal Justice Act 2003 Guideline*. Available at: http://www.sentencing-guidelines.gov.uk/docs/New_sentences_guideline1.pdf

White, S. (1991) 'Insanity defences and magistrates' courts', *Criminal Law Review*, 333.

Chapter 13

Assessment and treatment of offenders with intellectual and developmental disabilities

William R. Lindsay and John L. Taylor

Introduction

In the late nineteenth and early twentieth centuries, several writers seemed convinced of a strong link between intellectual and developmental disabilities and crime (Scheerenberger 1983). In 1921, Goddard suggested that up to 50 per cent of people in prisons were 'mentally defective' while Terman (1911) wrote that 'There is no investigator who denies the fearful role of mental deficiency in the production of vice, crime and delinquency ... not all criminals are feeble minded but all feeble minded are at least potential criminals' (p. 11). Clearly there has been historical unease about people with intellectual disabilities and their potential for crime. This chapter will review the trends and developments of research in the field over the last 60 years or so.

There is no doubt that the quantity and sophistication of research investigations have increased in the last 20 years. Partly, this is due to the fact that, following policies of deinstitutionalisation, far more individuals with intellectual disability have gained access to a comprehensive range of experiences in community settings as a result of significant relocations from institutions to local settings. Previously, large institutions provided courts with a diversion option which was frequently employed. The social policy aimed at reducing the numbers in institutions has resulted in three significant changes. Firstly, more individuals with intellectual disability (ID) with potential to offend against society's laws remain living in the community; secondly, if they commit offending or abusive acts, they are more likely to be dealt with by the criminal justice system; and thirdly, the result of court considerations may be the use of a normal range of sentencing options including probation, fines, community service orders and prison. Those involved in service planning, research and clinical services have responded to these changes with a growth in services for this group of individuals, a realisation that central policy initiatives must be implemented and an upsurge in research and academic interest (Lindsay *et al.* 2004).

Prevalence of offending and recidivism

Despite the long association between crime and ID, it is not clear whether people with ID commit more or less crime than those without (Holland 2004). The main difficulty when considering prevalence of offending in people with ID is the disparity of methodology used across various studies. Studies have investigated prevalence in high-secure hospitals (Walker and McCabe 1973), prisons (MacEachron 1979), probation services (Mason and Murphy 2002), appearance at court (Messinger and Apfelberg 1961) and appearance at police stations (Lyall *et al.* 1995). Some studies have reported that particular types of offence are over-represented among offenders with ID. For example, Walker and McCabe (1973), in a study of 331 men with ID who had committed offences and been detained under hospital orders to secure provision in England and Wales, found high rates of fire-raising (15 per cent) and sexual offences (28 per cent) when compared with other groups in their secure hospital sample. On the other hand, in a more recent study Hogue *et al.* (2007) reviewed a number of characteristics of offenders with ID across community, medium/low-secure and high-secure settings. They found that the rates of arson in the index offence depended on the setting with low rates in the community setting (2.9 per cent) and higher rates in the medium/low secure setting (21.4 per cent). This indicates that the setting in which data is collected is very likely to influence the results and subsequent conclusions about the population.

In a study of individuals assessed for the New York Criminal Justice System, Messinger and Apfelberg (1961) found that about 2.5 per cent had ID. This is roughly similar to the theoretical percentage of individuals with ID in the population. MacEachron (1974) reviewed the literature on prevalence rates for offenders with ID in prisons and found a range from 2.6 to 39.6 per cent. In her own more carefully controlled study, employing recognised intelligence tests, she studies 436 adult male offenders in Maine and Massachusetts state penal institutions and found prevalence rates of ID of about 0.6 to 2.3 per cent. Variations in inclusion criteria used, particularly if those considered to be functioning in the 'borderline intelligence' range are included, can affect prevalence rates as can the method used to identify the presence of ID (e.g. IQ tests, educational history, psychiatric opinion). Therefore these filtering effects, sampling biases, location differences and variations in identification will all influence the reported offending rates across studies (Holland *et al.* 2002).

As we have indicated, these methodological issues occur in the context of significant changes in criminal justice, health and social care policies. Where there had been policies of institutionalisation, individuals are likely to be diverted prior the stage of court proceedings. Where these individuals within institutions presented significant management difficulties, they may have moved on to more secure services within the health and social system resulting in a higher percentage of people with ID in more secure settings. Studies of recidivism rates for offenders with ID suffer from the same methodological and social policy influences (Linhorst *et al.* 2003). Lund (1990), in a follow-up study of 91 offenders with ID on statutory care orders in Denmark, found a doubling of the incidents of sex offending when comparing sentencing in 1973 to 1983. He suggested that this rise may have been a result of policies of deinstitutionalisation whereby people with ID are no longer detained in hospital for indeterminate lengths of time. He concluded that those with propensities towards offending would be more likely to be living in the community and as a result were likely to be subject to the normal legal processes should they engage in offending behaviour.

Historically, studies reviewing the outcome and recidivism of offenders with ID who have received services, have a long-standing and respectable record. Wildenskov (1962) followed up 47 men with borderline IQ (IQ 70–79) who had been convicted of a variety of offences. These individuals had been treated for a period in hospital and were then followed up for 20 years. He found that the re-offending rates were 51 per cent and although one can criticise this early study for a number of methodological limitations, when one considers that his 20-year review goes back to the 1940s, it does show that interest in evaluating such services goes back over at least 60 years. In a review of 423 male patients with ID discharged from high-secure hospital, Tong and MacKay (1969) found 40 per cent reconviction rates with follow-up periods of 1–12 years and Walker and McCabe (1973) found that 39 per cent of their sample had reoffended one year after discharge. Gibbens and Robertson (1983) reviewed 250 male offenders with ID who had been on hospital orders. After a follow-up period of 15 years they found that 68 per cent of them had been reconvicted and 41 per cent had three or more reconvictions. This higher rate of reoffending was also noted by Lund (1990) where he found that 72 per cent had reoffended during a ten-year follow-up. These studies review individuals who have been in contact with services through admission to hospital or provision of a statutory care order and it is reasonable to assume that they will have received some form of treatment or management. Given the extra input implied by such service contact, it is disappointing that reoffending rates are consistent with contemporary studies of mainstream offenders who have received prison or probation sentences with no such additional support.

Some more recent studies have reported recidivism rates of offenders with ID who have presumably been subject to the policies of deinstitutionalisation. Klimecki *et al.* (1994) reported reoffending rates in previous prison inmates with ID, two years after their release. They found that overall reoffending rates were 41.3 per cent with higher rates for less serious offences. However, the lower reoffending rates (around 31 per cent) for sex offences, murder and violent offences were artificially reduced because a number of those individuals were still in prison and therefore unable to reoffend. Linhorst *et al.* (2003) followed up 252 convicted offenders with ID who had completed a case management community programme and found that 25 per cent who had completed the programme were rearrested within six months and 43 per cent of those who dropped out were rearrested during the same period. Due to lack of controlled studies involving ID and non-ID offenders, it is difficult to make direct comparisons of recidivism rates. However, Langan and Levin (2002) found that for a population of 300,000 general offenders, 30 per cent were rearrested within six months while the rearrest rate for 79,000 general offenders on probation was reported to be 43 per cent by Langan and Cunniff (1992). Therefore it would appear that, based on the limited data available for comparison purposes, recidivism rates for offenders with ID are consistent with those for populations of mainstream offenders. Given these prevalence rates and recidivism rates, we can conclude that there is a significant problem to be addressed and issues of assessment, treatment and management are of paramount importance.

Assessment issues

One of the difficulties in reviewing this field is that research currently being conducted is extensive and wide-ranging covering important social policy issues such as competence to engage with the criminal justice system, assessment of risk for future violence, assessment of mental health issues associated with offending and assessment of offence-specific behaviour. This review is therefore selective in its focus.

Competence to engage in the criminal justice process

One of the basic requirements for the practitioner, researcher or policy-maker is whether or not the individual has an intellectual disability and, if so, the extent of that disability. Often in the criminal justice process and occasionally for research purposes, there are severe time constraints on the psychological assessment. Furthermore, it is becoming increasingly the case that services may wish to screen all of their offenders to determine the prevalence of ID. At the outset, it should be remembered that all relevant bodies, including the American Psychological Association, the British Psychological Society, the American Association for Intellectual and Development Disabilities and the World Health Organisation, demand that three criteria must be met for the classification of ID. An IQ or standard score two standard deviations below the mean is only one of these, the two others being significant deficits in adaptive behaviour and onset of a disability during childhood. It is undoubtedly the case that the second of these, assessment of adaptive behaviour, is time-consuming and may require input from a third party who knows the client well. Owing to these difficulties, adaptive behaviour tends to be seldom reported in the research literature. However, it is a professional requirement to assess adaptive behaviour and it should certainly be reported in court and forensic assessments using an instrument such as the Vineland Adaptive Behaviour Scale (Sparrow *et al.* 1984).

Hayes (2002) argued that intellectual disability should be identified as early as possible in the criminal justice process. She notes that in several jurisdictions, the police have an obligation to provide special assistance to vulnerable suspects during interview and initial detention. There is also a cost of the criminal justice system in aborted cases when, at a later date, it is realised that the individual has ID and previous supportive procedures have not been implemented. She also notes the importance of the human rights of the accused with ID and that these supportive procedures should be in place as early as possible. In a more general discussion of legal issues in relation to jurisdictions in the United States, England and Wales and Australia, Baroff *et al.* (2004) conclude 'the rights of people with intellectual disabilities are given lip service, while the reality of their treatment within the criminal justice system is often unfair, unjust and harsh' (p. 63).

The Hayes Ability Screening Index (HASI: Hayes 2000) has been developed in an attempt to address the issue of early identification of the presence of ID. It takes around five minutes to administer and consists of self-report questions, a spelling subtest, a 'join the dots' puzzle and a clock drawing test. On a sample of 567 individuals with and without ID, Hayes (2002) predicted IQ and adaptive behaviour results using the HASI scores. That HASI was 82.4 per cent accurate in detecting true positives and 71.6 per cent accurate in excluding true negatives when compared to another brief intelligence test. However, a careful analysis of Hayes' (2002) data reveals that all of the errors were in the same direction and included within the population people who did not have ID. Therefore there was about a 20 per cent over-inclusion rate.

The assessment of competence to stand trial lies at the heart of the judicial process for this client group. Competence includes the ability to take a meaningful or active part in a trial, the capacity to understand the laws of society prohibiting certain actions, the capacity to understand personal responsibility and the ability to express a plea and instruct legal counsel. There are a number of assessments for understanding the procedures of court, mainly based on the criminal justice system in the USA. The Competence Assessment to Stand Trial – Mental Retardation (CAST-MR: Everington and Luckasson 1992) assesses competence in three areas related to the court system – basic legal concepts, skills to assist defence and understanding of case events. The CAST-MR was used by 45 per cent of psychologists surveyed about practices used when evaluating juvenile competence to stand trial (Ryba et al. 2003). Some of the limitations of competency assessment are summarised by Otto et al. (1998) and include the lack of underlying conceptual structure, lack of standardised administration, lack of criterion-based scoring and limited norms.

Related to competence is the issue of suggestibility of accused persons with ID during police interview. Gudjonnson (1992) argued that certain categories of people with disabilities were more susceptible to yielding to leading questions and shifting their answers under interrogation by police and, as such, were more suggestible and liable to give a false confession. Clare and Gudjonnson (1993) in a study of 20 ID participants compared with 20 participants of average intellectual ability found that participants with ID confabulated more and were acquiescent. Everington and Fulero (1999) found that participants with ID were more likely to alter their answers in response to negative feedback. Both studies concluded that people with mild ID were more suggestible under conditions of interrogative interview. However, Beail (2002) reviewed a number of studies which led him to question the link between the test situation and the real-life situation. He concluded that the Gudjonnson Suggestibility Scales (Gudjonnson 1997) which assess suggestibility through memory of a narrative story, may be limited in their applicability to criminal justice proceedings 'because the results are based on an examination of semantic memory, whereas police interviews are more concerned with episodic or autobiographical event memory. Also experienced events usually involve multi-modal sensory input, resulting in a more elaborate trace in associative memory' (p. 135). In a test of this hypothesis, White and Willner (2005) assessed 20 individuals with intellectual disability in terms of their ability to recall information from a standard passage when compared to a further 20 who were asked to recall an actual experienced event.

They found that participants recalled greater amounts of information and were significantly less suggestible in relation to the experienced situation when compared to the standard verbally presented passage.

Prediction of risk for future offences

A number of studies have emerged in the last few years which suggest that risk prediction in this population, with suitably tailored risk assessments, may be as valid as prediction for mainstream offenders. Lindsay *et al.* (2004a) conducted a study to review the predictive value of a range of previously identified variables in relation to recidivism for 52 male sex offenders with ID. The significant variables to emerge from regression models were generally similar to those variables which had been identified in mainstream studies. However, employment history, criminal lifestyle, criminal companions, diverse sexual crimes and deviant victim choice, which have been highly associated with recidivism in studies on mainstream offenders, did not emerge as predictor variables. These authors considered that this may be an indication of the way in which professionals making assessments in this field should adjust their perceptions. For example, while few individuals with ID have an employment history, they are likely to have alternative regimes of special educational placement, occupational placement and the like which make up a weekly routine of engagement with society. Non-compliance with this regime did emerge as a significant variable suggesting that individuals with ID should be judged in relation to their peers. It may be that probation officers, used to mainstream offenders and their employment histories, may consider the occupational placement of an ID offender as tedious or boring or they may make allowances for the individual on the basis of their disability. Lindsay (2005) has written of the theoretical and practical importance of engaging offenders with ID with society in the form of interpersonal contacts, occupational/educational placements and so on. Therefore to excuse an offender on the basis of their intellectual disability may be precisely the wrong thing to do. In another report on sexual offenders, Tough (2001) found that the Rapid Risk Assessment for Sex Offender Recidivism (RRASOR: Hanson 1997) had a medium effect size in predicting recidivism for a cohort of 81 participants. In addition, Harris and Tough (2004) report that they employed the RRASOR as a means of allocating sex offender referrals to their service and, by accepting referrals of only low or medium risk, they targeted limited resources on appropriate individuals.

Quinsey *et al.* (2004) conducted a rigorous assessment of the Violence Risk Appraisal Guide (VRAG: Quinsey *et al.* 1998) in a 16-month follow-up of 58 participants with ID. They found a significant predictive value with a medium effect size and that staff ratings of client behaviour significantly predicted antisocial incidents. Lindsay *et al.* (2008) have recently made the first comparison of actuarial risk assessments with a mixed group of 212 violent and sexual offenders with ID. They followed up participants for one year and found that the VRAG was a reasonable predictor for future violent incidents (auc = 0.72), the Static-99 was a reasonable predictor for future sexual incidents (auc = 0.71) and the RM2000 predicted somewhat less well for violent (auc = 0.61) and sexual (auc = 0.62) incidents. Since the RM2000 is relatively simple to use, these authors wrote that research should not be discouraged on this instrument because it has considerable potential utility if it can be found to have similar predictive ability to other assessments. However, the study did give validation to both the VRAG and Static-99 for use with this client group. Employing the same samples, Taylor et al. (2007) have reviewed the psychometric properties and predictive validity of the HCR-20 (Webster et al. 1995). They found that inter-rater reliability was acceptable at over 80 per cent agreement for all scales and Cronbach's Alpha was acceptable for the H Scale (0.75) but low for the C and R Scales (0.59 and 0.39 respectively). Exploratory factor analysis found that the H Scale constituted three factors (delinquency, interpersonal functioning and personality disorder) while the C and R Scales made up distinct separate factors. They also found that the R Scale had the highest predictive value in relation to recorded incidents over a period of a year. They concluded that the HCR was a robust instrument for guiding clinical judgment which would help clinicians to reach clinically consistent and defendable decisions.

Quinsey et al. (2004) also assessed the value of dynamic/proximal risk indicators. They found that in the month prior to a violent or sexual incident, the dynamic indicator of antisociality was significantly higher than values recorded six months prior to the incident. This, they concluded, provided the persuasive evidence of the value of dynamic assessment since the increase in dynamic risk factors one month prior to the offence could not be attributed to any bias in the light of an offence occurring. Employing a similar design, Lindsay et al. (2004b) tested the Dynamic Risk Assessment and Management System (DRAMS) on which staff made daily ratings of clients' mood, antisocial behaviour, aberrant thoughts, psychotic symptoms, self-regulation, therapeutic alliance, compliance with routine and renewal of emotional relationships. Ratings were compared between those taken on the day of incident, the day prior to the incident and a further control day at least seven days distant from an incident. Although there were only five clients with full data sets on appropriate days, there were significant increases in ratings for the day prior to the incident for mood, antisocial behaviour, aberrant thoughts and DRAMS total score. Steptoe et al. (2007) conducted a larger study on the predictive utility of the DRAMS with 23 forensic patients in a high-secure setting. Predictions were made against independently collected incident data and concurrent validity was assessed against the Ward Anger Rating Scale (WARS: Novaco and Taylor 2004). The sections of mood, antisocial behaviour and intolerance/agreeableness had significant predictive values with incidents (auc > 0.70) and there were highly significant differences, with large effect sizes, between assessments taken one or two days prior to an incident and control assessments conducted at least seven days from an incident. Therefore dynamic risk assessment appears to perform well in both concurrent and predictive validity in relation to offenders with ID.

Further developments have been conducted using a range of assessments. Hogue et al. (2007) evaluated the utility of the Emotional Problem Scale (EPS: Prout and Strohmer 1991) with 172 offenders with ID from a range of security settings. The EPS is generally considered to be a dynamic assessment of emotion and self-concept and these authors, using the assessment on only a single occasion, found that the derived scores successfully predicted recorded incidents over a period of a year. Morrissey et al. (2007a, 2007b) have investigated the utility, discriminative validity and predictive validity of the Psychopathy

Checklist – Revised (PCL-R: Hare 1991) and found that it predicted both good response to treatment and positive moves from high to medium secure conditions, both within two years of assessment. Therefore there are a number of studies, using a range of assessments, some of which are developed for this client group, which attest to the utility and validity of risk prediction for offenders with ID.

Assessment of offence specific behaviour and attitudes

A number of studies have been conducted on the assessment of offence specific variables, the majority of which have been on interpersonal problem-solving and offence-related thinking, anger and aggression, and sexual offending. Lindsay (2005) has stressed the importance of promoting social contact, interpersonal relationships and community identification in sex offenders with ID both from a practical and theoretical standpoint. Such increased social inclusion allows others to monitor the individual offender and also ensures that their views and attitudes are constantly being adjusted and even challenged by ordinary social contact. In a recent study, Steptoe *et al.* (2006) reported that although the sex offender participants had the same opportunities as other participants, they seemed to choose to take advantage of these opportunities less often than the control participants. In addition, they appeared to have more impoverished relationships than control participants but reported being quite happy with a more restricted range of relationships. This led to the conclusion that the promotion of appropriate relationships, contact with the community and pro-social influences are important areas for assessment and treatment.

Some of the most interesting work investigating issues related to interpersonal problem-solving and ID combines this with perception and attribution of aggressive intent. Basquill *et al.* (2004), in a study of 45 participants, found that when compared to non-aggressive participants, aggressive individuals made significantly more errors in their cognitive appraisal of interpersonal situations and were significantly less accurate in identifying interpersonal intent. They felt that the findings pointed to the presence of an attributional bias related to perception of aggression and hostility. Aggressive participants were also poorer in relation to social problem-solving, regardless of the type of problem presented. While this research suggests that some difficulties in interpersonal problem-solving may be related to aggression in this client group, the work of Jahoda *et al.* (2006) contradicts these findings. In a comparison of aggressive and non-aggressive individuals, they found that the former did not have deficits in the attribution of emotion. Indeed, the aggressive participants were superior in recognising hostile intent in angry protagonists and they concluded that 'this may be indicative of a greater emotional sensitivity to provocation and could support the crucial mediating role that anger plays in aggressiveness' (p. 86). This research suggests that an emphasis on self-regulation and interpersonal problem-solving in provocation situations is likely to be productive and relevant to the particular difficulties experienced by these clients.

Hamilton *et al.* (2006) have piloted the use of the Social Problem Solving Inventory – Revised (SPSI: D'Zurilla *et al.* 2000) with offenders with ID and found that if it is suitably modified it can be used reliably. In addition, they conducted a preliminary factor analysis on the 25 items and found a fairly logical and reasonably simple factor structure which conformed to the original development of the test. The SPSI has been widely used in the evaluation of mainstream offender programmes (McMurran *et al.* 2001) and in their pilot study, Hamilton *et al.* (2006) found three factors emerged accounting for 63 per cent of the variance: negative/avoidant style, positive/rational style and impulsive problem-solving style. Therefore there is emerging evidence to suggest that interpersonal relationships and interpersonal attributions may be crucial in the perpetration of offending incidents in this client group and that problem-solving style may be assessed using a suitably adapted inventory.

The work on social problem-solving and attribution has been related to aggression and violent offences and this field has been researched with greater frequency than others. Taylor (2002) has pointed out the significant impact which client aggression has on work-related factors for staff. It is therefore fitting that hostility and anger in individuals with ID is an area which has attracted a reasonable amount of research when compared to other offence-related factors. Novaco and Taylor (2004) evaluated the reliability and validity of the Novaco Anger Scale (NAS: Novaco 2003) with 129 male forensic inpatients with ID. In this study, self-report measures of anger disposition, anger reactivity and informant-related anger attributes were investigated with regard to their internal consistency, stability and concurrent and predictive validity. The NAS showed substantial intercorrelations with other measures of anger providing evidence for the concurrent validity of the instruments. WARS staff ratings for patient anger, based on ward observations, were found to have high internal consistency and to correlate significantly with the patient's anger self-reports. In addition, they recorded assaultive behaviour in hospital and found that participant's self-reports on anger were significantly related to incidents. The NAS total score was found to be significantly predictive of whether the patient had physically assaulted others in the hospital and the total number of physical assaults. This relationship held true even when age, length of stay, IQ, violent offence history and personality were held constant.

Taylor *et al.* (2004) developed the Imaginal Provocation Test (IPT) as an individual anger assessment procedure that taps key elements of the experience and expression of anger and is easily modifiable for idiographic use. With 48 participants, they found that the IPT had good internal reliability and reasonable concurrent validity with the NAS and showed responsiveness to anger management treatment. Alder and Lindsay (2007) also produced a provocation inventory which is easily accessible and usable. In a study of 114 participants with ID, a five-factor solution emerged including threat to self-esteem, locus of control, resentment, frustration and disappointment. The most important factor was threat to self-esteem which has also been found as a fundamental schema in people with ID who have difficulties with aggression by Jahoda *et al.* (2006).

Although hostile attitude and anger emerged consistently from studies assessing risk for future violent and sexual incidents (Quinsey *et al.* 2004) it is interesting that sex offenders with ID tend to show lower levels of anger than other offenders with ID. Lindsay *et al.* (2006a), in a study of 247 offenders with ID, found that sex offenders showed significantly lower levels of anger and aggression than other male offenders or female offenders. However, where anger is present, it may be a particularly potent dynamic risk factor.

In mainstream sex offender work, inappropriate sexual preference and sexual drive are considered primary motivation for the perpetration of sexual offences (Harris *et al.* 2003). For offenders with ID, some of the main inferences can be drawn from studies which have noted previous sexual offending and patterns of offending in cohorts of referred clients. Day (1994) reported in a study of 31 sexual offenders referred to his clinic that all of them had previously recorded incidents of inappropriate sexual behaviour or sexual offences. Lindsay *et al.* (2004c) found that for 62 per cent of referrals there was either a previous conviction for a sexual offence or clear documented evidence of sexual abuse having been perpetrated by that individual. When one considers that incidents of sexual abuse are met with a great deal of criticism towards the perpetrator on the part of care givers and perhaps the victim's family, this would be a considerable disincentive to further commission of additional sex offences and one might conclude that sexual drive and sexual preference are significant factors in overriding the suppression effects of previous criticism.

Although not directly relevant, Blanchard *et al.* (1999) investigated patterns of sexual offending in 950 participants. They found that those sex offenders with lower intellectual functioning were more likely to commit offences against younger children and male children. The proportion of variance was not high but this information constitutes evidence that inappropriate sexual preference may play at least some role in this client group. Cantor *et al.* (2005) presented a detailed meta-analytic study of previous reports which have included reliable data on IQ and sex offending. In a reanalysis of data on 25,146 sex offenders and controls, they found a robust relationship between lower IQ and sexual offending but, specifically, lower IQ and paedophilia. Again, the proportion of variance was not high but they hypothesised that 'a third variable – a perturbation of prenatal or childhood brain development – produces both paedophilia and low IQ' (p. 565). This information on the relationship between low IQ and sexual preference presents more persuasive evidence than the essentially anecdotal accounts of previous authors (e.g. Day 1994). Therefore sexual drive and sexual preference are likely to be important issues in assessment and treatment.

Although there appears to be more recent recognition of the importance of sexual preference, the first hypothesis advanced to account for inappropriate sexual behaviour in men with ID was that lack of sexual knowledge might lead to inappropriate sexual contact precisely because the individual is unaware of the means to establish appropriate interpersonal and sexual relationships. This hypothesis of 'counterfeit deviance' was first posited by Hingsburger *et al.* (1991). A number of studies have emerged recently testing this hypothesis. Michie *et al.* (2006) argued that a consequence of this hypothesis is that men who have committed inappropriate sexual behaviour or sexual offences should have poorer sexual knowledge than those who have not. They conducted two studies in separate centres and in both studies found that when there were significant differences between groups, the sex offenders showed higher levels of sexual knowledge than the non-sexual offenders. They then pooled the data for all 33 sex offenders and 35 control participants and found the significant positive correlation between IQ and sexual knowledge for the control group (r = 0.71) but no significant relationship between IQ and sexual knowledge for the sex offender cohort (r = 0.17). They presented two possible reasons for this finding. Firstly, by definition, all of the sex offender cohort have some experience of sexual interaction and it is unlikely that these experiences of sexual interaction are random. One might therefore conclude that these sex offenders have given some thought and attention to sexuality at least in the period prior to the perpetration of the incident. Secondly, it is possible that these individuals have a developmental history of increased sexual arousal. This in turn may have led to selective attention and interest in sexual information gained from informal sources such as newspapers and television. These behavioural and informal educational experiences would lead to a higher level of sexual knowledge suggesting an interactive effect between sexual preference and knowledge acquisition.

Talbot and Langdon (2006) also compared sexual knowledge in groups of sex offenders with ID and groups of non-offenders with ID. They found that sex offenders who had not received treatment showed no deficits in sexual knowledge when compared to non-offenders and concluded that limited sexual knowledge may not be a factor which increases the risk of committing a future sexual offence. Lunsky et al. (2007) conducted a more sensitive analysis of this issue by splitting the sexual offenders into a group of 27 participants who had committed repeated or forced offences and 16 participants who had committed inappropriate sexual behaviour such as public masturbation or inappropriate touching. They also found that the sex offender participants had higher levels of sexual knowledge than a matched group of non-offenders but the persistent, forceful offenders had a greater level of knowledge and more liberal attitudes than the inappropriate offenders who had similar conservative attitudes to the control group. They concluded that the counterfeit deviance hypothesis better accounted for the inappropriate offenders.

It is generally recognised that cognitive distortions which justify, minimise or mitigate sexual offences are crucial in the offending cycle of perpetrators. A number of assessments have been developed to assess these cognitive distortions and these developments have spread to the field of ID. Kolton et al. (2001) employed the Abel and Becker Cognition Scale (ABCS) with 89 sex offenders with ID. They found that the response options of the test needed to be changed to a dichotomous assessment to reduce extremity bias and the revised assessment preserved the psychometric integrity of the original test. Keeling et al. (2007a) revised the Victim Empathy Distortion Scale (VES: Beckett and Fisher 1994) for use with special needs sexual offenders (mean IQ 71). They found that the adapted scale correlated significantly with the original (0.78), had good internal consistency (alpha = 0.77) and good test/retest reliability (r = 0.88). It also had good convergent validity with a further test of empathy. The VES was also used in an evaluation of sex offender pathways by Langdon et al. (2007) where they found that it did not differentiate between different types of sexual offenders with ID.

In a development specific to sex offenders with ID, Lindsay et al. (2007) reported on the Questionnaire on Attitudes Consistent with Sexual Offences (QACSO). The QACSO contains a series of scales which evaluate attitudes across a range of different types of offences including rape, voyeurism, exhibitionism, dating abuse, homosexual assault, offences against children and stalking. In a study comparing sex offenders, non-sex offenders, non-offenders (all with ID) and non-ID controls, they reported that each scale had good reliability, discriminant validity and internal consistency. Lindsay *et al.* (2006b) also found that the rape and offences against children scales in particular discriminated between offenders against adults and offenders against children in the hypothesised directions with offenders against adults having significantly higher scores on the rape scale and significantly lower scores on the offences against children scale than child molesters. Langdon and Talbot (2006) also used the QACSO to assess levels of cognitive distortions in sex offenders and found that this cohort had significantly higher levels of cognitive distortions than non-offenders.

Conclusions on assessment

A number of assessment instruments have been developed to help professionals consider an individual's competence to engage with the criminal justice process. Our knowledge on static risk factors has begun to develop considerably and there have now been a few studies on the validity of risk assessments for this client group. These studies have found predictive results that are broadly consistent with the literature on mainstream offending. Studies on dynamic risk factors have confirmed their relevance in the prediction of incidents and a number of reports have demonstrated the reliability and validity of assessments of offence-related issues, notably hostility and cognitive distortions. There have also been recent important developments in research on the relevance of interpersonal factors in the development of offending incidents.

Treatment of offenders

Violence and aggression

By far the most common treatment approach for violent and aggressive behaviour has been behavioural intervention and several reviews have supported the effectiveness of these approaches (e.g. Carr *et al.* 2000). However, one difficulty in employing these approaches with offenders is that they generally require contingencies to be organised in a consistent and reliable fashion, in a controlled institutional environment with reasonable staff ratios. Such conditions contrast with those in services for offenders with ID who may be relatively high functioning, display low frequency yet very serious aggression and violence and live in relatively uncontrolled environments (e.g. community settings). In response to the need for more 'self-actualising' treatments that promote generalised self-regulation of anger and aggression, several authors have employed cognitive behavioural treatments based on the approach developed by Novaco (1975, 1994). This approach employs cognitive restructuring, arousal reduction and behavioural skills training as well as the stress inoculation paradigm (Meichenbaum 1985).

Taylor (2002) and Taylor and Novaco (2005) have reviewed numerous case and case series studies and uncontrolled group anger treatment studies involving individual and group therapy formats incorporating combinations of cognitive behavioural techniques including relaxation and arousal reduction, skills training and self-monitoring that have produced good outcomes in reducing anger and aggression which have been maintained at follow-up. Several case studies have reported successful outcomes in people with histories of aggressive behaviour in hospital and community settings (Murphy and Clare 1991; Black and Novaco 1993; Rose and West 1999). These case series have extended to demonstrations of the effectiveness of cognitive behavioural anger treatments with violent offenders with ID living in the community and involved with the criminal justice system (Allan *et al.* 2001; Lindsay *et al.* 2003). In these studies improvements have been maintained in follow-ups for up to ten years. Lindsay *et al.* (2004d) reported a controlled study of cognitive behavioural anger treatment for individuals living in the community and referred by the courts or criminal justice services. Several outcome measures were used including a provocation inventory, provocation role-plays and self-report diaries over a follow-up period of 15 months. Aggressive incidents and reoffences were also recorded for both the treatment group and the waiting list control group. There were significant improvements in anger control on all measures with significant differences between the treatment and control groups. In addition, the treatment group recorded significantly fewer incidents of assault and violence at the post-treatment assessment point (14 per cent vs. 45 per cent). There was evidence that anger management treatment had a significant impact on the number of aggressive incidents recorded in these participants in addition to improvements in the assessed psychological variables.

It should be noted that in all studies on the treatment of anger and violence (e.g. Taylor and Novaco 2005) it is always maintained that feelings of anger are appropriate in certain situations. In a series of waiting list controlled studies, Taylor *et al.* (2002a, 2004, 2005) have evaluated individual cognitive behavioural anger treatment with detained male patients who have mild-borderline ID and significant violent histories. Taylor *et al.* (2002a) reported a pilot study involving 20 detained male patients using an 18-session cognitive behavioural treatment comprising six sessions of a psycho-educational and motivational preparatory phase, followed by a 12-session treatment phase based on individual formulation of each participant's anger problems and needs that followed the cognitive behavioural stages of cognitive preparation, skills acquisition, skills rehearsal and practice *in vivo*. Participants' self-report of anger intensity to provocation was significantly lower following the intervention in a treatment condition when compared with a waiting list control. There was also limited evidence for the effectiveness of treatment provided by staff ratings of patient anger disposition and coping behaviour post-treatment. Taylor *et al.* (2005) reported on a larger-scale study with 20 participants allocated to the treatment condition while 20 served as waiting list controls. Scores on self-reported anger disposition and reactivity indices significantly improved following the intervention in the treatment group compared with scores for the control group and these differences were maintained at a four-month follow-up.

Fire-setting

As has been noted earlier, while some authors have suggested that arson is over-represented in offenders with ID, more recent evidence suggests that prevalence rates may depend on the study setting. However, it does remain an important problem and there have been a number of case studies reported on the treatment of fire-setters. Rice and Chaplain (1979) employed a social skills intervention with two groups of fire-setters, one of which was functioning in the mild-borderline ID range. Following treatment, both groups were reported to have been improved and none of the participants had reoffended at 12 months follow-up. Clare *et al.* (1992) reported a case study involving a man with mild ID who had prior convictions for arson. Following a multi-modal behavioural control and skills training intervention, significant improvements were recorded and the client was discharged to the community with no reoffending at 30 months follow-up.

Taylor *et al.* (2002b) investigated the outcome following treatment for 14 men and women with ID and arson convictions. Significant improvements were found in fire-specific, anger and self-esteem measures. Taylor *et al.* (2004) reported a further case series of four detained men with ID and convictions for arson offences. They employed a 40-session cognitive behavioural, group-based intervention that involved work on offence cycles, education about the costs associated with setting fires, training of skills to enhance future coping with emotional problems and relapse prevention plans. All participants showed a high level of motivation and improvements in attitudes with regard to personal responsibility, victim issues and awareness of risk factors associated with fire-setting. Taylor *et al.* (2006) presented a further series of case studies on six women with mild-borderline ID and histories of fire-setting who received a cognitive behavioural group intervention similar to that described by Taylor *et al.* (2004). There were improvements on all measures related to fire-specific treatment targets and all but one of the group participants had been discharged to community placements at a two-year follow-up. There were no reports of participants setting any fires or engaging in fire risk-related behaviour throughout the follow-up period. In all of these Taylor *et al.* studies, significant improvements were seen on measures of anger (the NAS) suggesting that anger or resentment may be a significant motivation for fire-setting and, as such, an important target for treatment. The other significant motivating factor identified by Taylor *et al.* (2006) was peer approval indicating that this also is an important target for intervention through social skills training in alternative ways to generate peer approval.

Sexual offending and inappropriate sexual behaviour

As with work on anger treatment, until relatively recently behavioural management approaches have been the most common psychological treatments for the management of sexual offending (Plaud *et al.* 2000). These approaches advance behavioural competency in daily living skills, general interpersonal and educational skills and specialised behavioural skills related to sexuality and offending. For example, Griffiths *et al.* (1989) developed a comprehensive behavioural management regime for sex offenders with ID. Their programme included addressing deviant sexual behaviour through education, training social competence and improving relationship skills, reviewing relapse prevention through alerting support staff and training on issues of responsibility. In a review of 30 cases, they reported no re-offending and described a number of successful case studies to illustrate their methods. Others have also described similar positive outcomes with behavioural management approaches (Grubb-Blubaugh *et al.* 1994; Plaud *et al.* 2000).

Recent developments have employed cognitive and problem-solving techniques which, in mainstream offenders, Hanson *et al.* (2002) found to produce greater reductions in recidivism rates than treatments which employed other techniques including behavioural approaches. A central assumption in cognitive therapy is that sex offenders may hold a number of cognitive distortions regarding sexuality which support the perpetration of sexual offences. Cognitive distortions fall into a number of categories including mitigation of responsibility, denial of harm to the victim, denial of intent to offend, thoughts of entitlement, mitigation through the claim of an altered state and complete denial that an offence occurred. There have been several reports which considered these cognitive processes during treatment of sexual offenders with ID. O'Conner (1996) developed a problem-solving intervention for 13 adult male sex offenders involving consideration of a range of risky situations in which offenders had to develop safe solutions for both themselves and the potential victim. She reported positive results from the intervention with most participants achieving increased community access.

Support for the centrality of cognitive distortions in the offence process came from a qualitative study of nine male sex offenders with ID by Courtney *et al.* (2006) using grounded theory techniques. In the analysis of interviews with participants, they concluded that all aspects of the offence process were linked to offender attitudes and beliefs such as denial of the offence, blaming others and seeing themselves as the victim. Therefore a crucial aspect of treatment is to explore these aspects of denial and other cognitive distortions. Lindsay *et al.* (1998a, 1998b, 1998c) reported a series of case studies on offenders with ID using a cognitive behavioural intervention in which various forms of denial and mitigation of the offence were challenged over treatment periods of up to three years. Across these studies, participants consistently reported changes in cognitions during treatment and there was evidence of low reoffending rates 4–7 years following initial conviction. Each of these papers gave examples of the way in which cognitive distortions are elicited and challenged during treatment and measures of cognitive distortions found reductions which maintained for at least one year follow-up.

Rose *et al.* (2002) reported on a 16-week cognitive behavioural treatment for five participants who had perpetrated sexual abuse. They assessed locus of control, cognitive distortions, victim empathy and knowledge of the law and the only significant change was a greater focus on external locus of control after the intervention. These authors reported no reoffending at one-year follow-up. The difficulties associated with treatment evaluations in this client group is illustrated by a treatment study of six sex offenders with ID by Craig *et al.* (2006). Following a seven-month treatment programme incorporating cognitive behavioural aspects and sex education, they found no significant improvements on any measure including assessments of sexual knowledge. They also found no further incidents of sexual offending during a twelve-month follow-up but reported that all participants received 24-hour supervision and had little opportunity to offend. Therefore, where individuals are continually supervised, the value of follow-up data will be compromised.

A further difficulty in the field is that those treatment comparisons which have been conducted have fallen well short of the standards required for experimental rigour. Lindsay and Smith (1998) compared seven individuals who had been in treatment for two or more years with another group of seven who had been in treatment for less than one year. The comparisons were serendipitous in that time and treatment reflected the probation sentences delivered by the court. Those individuals who had been in treatment for less than one year showed significantly poorer progress and were more likely to reoffend than those treated for at least two years, and they concluded that shorter treatment periods may be of limited value for this client group. Keeling *et al.* (2007b) conducted another comparison of convenience between 11 'special needs' offenders and 11 mainstream offenders matched on level of risk, victim, sex, offence type and age. The authors noted a number of limitations, including the fact that 'special needs' was not synonymous with ID and as a result they were unable to verify the intellectual differences between the mainstream and special needs populations, the fact that the treatments were not directly comparable and the fact that assessments for the special needs population were modified. There were few differences between groups post-treatment but follow-up data identified that none of the offenders (neither completers nor non-completers) in either group committed further sexual offences, although completers had a longer average post-release period. Murphy and Sinclair (2006) reported on the cognitive behavioural treatment of 52 men who had sexually abusive behaviour and mild ID. Treatment groups ran over a period of one year and there were significant improvements in sexual knowledge, victim empathy and cognitive distortions at post-treatment assessment. There were also reductions in sexually abusive behaviour at six-month follow-up. However, although the study was designed to include control participants, it was not possible to recruit participants for a range of unforeseen circumstances. Therefore, in these studies, the control comparisons have not been randomised, have been controls of convenience or researchers have not been able to gather sufficient participants.

A further series of comparisons have been made by Lindsay and colleagues between individuals who have committed sexual offences and other types of offenders with ID. Lindsay *et al.* (2004) compared 106 men who had committed sexual offences or sexually abusive incidents with 78 men who had committed other types of offences or serious incidents. There was a significantly higher rate of reoffending in the non-sex offender cohort (51 per cent) when compared to the sex offender cohort (19 per cent). In a subsequent, more comprehensive evaluation, Lindsay *et al.* (2006a) compared 121 sex offenders with 105 other types of male offenders and 21 female offenders. Reoffending rates were reported for up to 12 years after the index offence. There were no significant differences between the groups on IQ and the sex offender cohort tended to be older than the other two cohorts. Female offenders had higher rates of mental illness although rates for male cohorts were generally high at around 32 per cent. These high rates of mental illness and sex offender cohorts have been found by other researchers (Day 1994). The differences in reoffending rates between the three groups was highly significant with rates of 23.9 per cent for male sex offenders, 19 per cent for female offenders and 59 per cent for other types of male offenders. The significant differences were evident for every year of follow-up except year 1. These authors also investigated harm reduction by following up the number of offences committed by recidivists and found that for those who reoffended, the number of offences following treatment, up to 12 years, was a quarter to a third of those recorded before treatment indicating a considerable amount of harm reduction as a result of intervention. Therefore, although these treatment comparisons have been less than satisfactory in terms of their experimental design, there are some indications that treatment interventions may significantly reduce recidivism rates in sex offenders with ID. Where recidivism does occur, for all types of offenders with ID, treatment may result in fewer abusive incidents with significant amounts of harm reduction. These outcomes are considerably more positive than those reported earlier by studies reviewing recidivism and offenders with ID.

Conclusions

As with the work on assessment, there have been a number of significant developments in the treatment of offenders with ID. The most persuasive evidence has been in the field of anger treatment where structured programmes have been published and evaluated by a number of controlled comparisons. The positive outcomes have included psychological factors as well as records of aggressive incidents at up to 12 years follow-up. Similarly, with sexual offenders there have been significant advances in assessment which have allowed comparisons to be made pre- and post-intervention which has generally employed cognitive behavioural techniques to address cycles of offending and cognitive distortions. As a result, the positive evaluation outcomes for violence can be regarded with some confidence and suggest that such treatment programmes should be incorporated into the general management of violent and aggressive offenders with ID. For sex offenders, group comparison studies have been comparisons of convenience but have generally produced optimistic outcomes with lower recidivism rates over lengthy follow-up periods. However because of the considerable methodological shortcomings, these results should be treated with critical caution. There have also been some advances in the consideration of offence related issues and social problem-solving with some initial developments in assessment. Case study reports for fire-setters with ID have all provided promising outcomes and this field, particularly, requires some controlled evaluation of these treatment programmes.

Selected further reading

Griffiths, D.M., Quinsey, V.L. and Hingsburger, D. (1989) *Changing Inappropriate Sexual Behaviour: A Community-Based Approach for Persons with Developmental Disabilities.* Baltimore, MD: Paul Brooks is ideal for readers who wish to review an early text outlining some of the first principles on which treatment is based.

Lindsay, W.R., Taylor, J.L. and Sturmey, P. (2004) *Offenders with Developmental Disabilities.* Chichester: John Wiley is the most recent volume in the field with chapters on a range of assessments and treatments for offence types.

Linhorst, D.M., McCutchen, T.A. and Bennett, L. (2003) 'Recidivism among offenders with developmental disabilities participating in a case management programme', *Research in Developmental Disabilities*, 24: 210–30 is a more recent example of a study assessing the effects of treatment on recidivism.

MacEachron, A. E. (1979) 'Mentally retarded offenders prevalence and characteristics', *American Journal of Mental Deficiency*, 84: 165–76 is an early study which remains one of the best investigations into the prevalence of offenders with ID in prisons.

Taylor, J. L. and Novaco, R. W. (2005) *Anger Treatment for People with Developmental Disabilities: A Theory, Evidence and Manual Based Approach*. Chichester: Wiley is one of the strongest experimental studies into an assessment for offenders with ID.

References

Alder, L. and Lindsay, W. R. (2007) 'Exploratory factor analysis and convergent validity of the Dundee Provocation Inventory', *Journal of Intellectual and Developmental Disabilities*, 32: 190–9.

Allan, R., Lindsay, W.R., Macleod, F. and Smith, A.H.W. (2001) 'Treatment of women with intellectual disabilities who have been involved with the criminal justice system for reasons of aggression', *Journal of Applied Research in Intellectual Disabilities*, 14: 340–7.

Baroff, G.S., Gunn, M. and Hayes, S. (2004) 'Legal issues', in W.R. Lindsay, J.L. Taylor and P. Sturmey (eds), *Offenders with Developmental Disabilities*. Chichester: John Wiley, pp. 37–66.

Basquill, M.F., Nezu, C.M., Nezu, A.M. and Klein, T.L. (2004) 'Aggression related hostility bias and social problem solving deficits in adult males with mental retardation', *American Journal of Mental Retardation*, 109: 255–63.

Beail, N. (2002) 'Interrogative suggestibility, memory and intellectual disability', *Journal of Applied Research in Intellectual Disabilities*, 15: 129–37.

Beckett R. and Fisher, D. (1994) 'Victim empathy measure', in R. Beckett, A. Beech, D. Fisher and A.S. Fordham (eds), *Community-based Treatment for Sex Offenders: An Evaluation of Seven Treatment Programmes*. London: Home Office.

Black, L. and Novaco, R. W. (1993) 'Treatment of anger with a developmentally disabled man', in R.A. Wells and V.J. Giannetti (eds), *Casebook of the Brief Psychotherapies*. New York: Plenum Press.

Blanchard, R., Watson, M., Choy, A., Dickey, R., Klassen, P., Kuban, N. and Feren, D.J. (1999) 'Paedophiles: mental retardation, mental age and sexual orientation', *Archives of Sexual Behaviour*, 28: 111–27.

Cantor, J. M., Blanchard, R., Robichaud, L.K. and Christensen, B.K. (2005) 'Quantitative reanalysis of aggregate data on IQ in sexual offenders', *Psychological Bulletin*, 131: 555–68.

Carr, J.E., Coriaty, S., Wilder, D.A., Gaunt, B.T., Dozier, C.L. Britton, L.N., Avina, C., and Reed, C.L. (2000) 'A review of "noncontingent" reinforcement as treatment for the aberrant behaviour of individuals with developmental disabilities', *Research in Developmental Disabilities*, 21: 377–91.

Clare, I.C.H. and Gudjonsson, G.H. (1993) 'Interrogative suggestibility, confabulation and acquiescence in people with mild learning disabilities (mental handicap): implications for reliability during police interrogations', *British Journal of Clinical Psychology*, 37: 295–301.

Clare, I.C.H., Murphy, G.H., Cox, D. and Chaplain, E.H. (1992) 'Assessment and treatment of fire setting: a single case investigation using a cognitive behavioural model', *Criminal Behaviour and Mental Health*, 2: 253–68.

Courtney, J., Rose, J. and Mason, O. (2006) 'The offence process of sex offenders with intellectual disabilities: a qualitative study', *Sexual Abuse: A Journal of Research and Treatment*, 18: 169–91.

Craig, L.A., Stringer, I. and Moss, T. (2006) 'Treating sexual offenders with learning disabilities in the community', *International Journal of Offender Therapy and Comparative Criminology*, 50: 127–35.

D'Zurilla, T.J., Nezu, A.M. and Maydeu-Olivares, A. (2000) *Manual for the Social Problem Solving Inventory – Revised*. North Tonawanda, NY: Multi-Health Systems.

Day, K. (1994) 'Male mentally handicapped sex offenders', *British Journal of Psychiatry*, 165: 630–9.

Everington, C. and Fulero, S.M. (1999) 'Competence to confess: measuring understanding and suggestibility of defendants with mental retardation', *Mental Retardation*, 37: 212–20.

Everington, C. and Luckasson, R. (1992) *Competence Assessment for Standing Trial for Defendants with Mental Retardation*. Worthington, OH: International Diagnostic Systems.

Gibbens, T.C. and Robertson, G. (1983) 'A survey of the criminal careers of restriction order patients', *British Journal of Psychiatry*, 143: 370–5.

Goddard, H. H. (1921) *Juvenile Delinquency*. New York: Dodd, Mead.

Griffiths, D. M., Quinsey, V.L. and Hingsburger, D. (1989) *Changing Inappropriate Sexual Behaviour: A Community Based Approach for Persons with Developmental Disabilities*. Baltimore, MD: Paul Brooks Publishing.

Grubb-Blubaugh, V., Shire, B.J. and Baulser, M.L. (1994) 'Behaviour management and offenders with mental retardation: the jury system', *Mental Retardation*, 32: 213–17.

Gudjonsson, G.H. (1992) *The Psychology of Interrogations, Confessions and Testimony*. Chichester: John Wiley.

Gudjonsson, G.H. (1997) *Gudjonsson Suggestibility Scales*. Hove, Sussex: Psychology Press.

Hamilton, C., Doyle, M.C., Lindsay, W.R. and Goodall, J. (2006) 'Adaptation and psychometric evaluation of the Social Problem Solving Inventory – Revised (SPSI-R)', *Journal of Applied Research in Intellectual Disabilities*, 19: 258.

Hanson, R.K., Gordon, A., Harris, A.J.R., Marques, J.K., Murphy, W., Quinsey, V.L. and Seto, M.C. (2002) 'First report of the collaborative outcome data project on the effectiveness of psychological treatment for sex offenders', *Sexual Abuse: A Journal of Research and Treatment*, 14: 169–94.

Hare, R. D. (1991) *The Hare Psychopathy Checklist – Revised*. Toronto: Multi-Health Systems.

Harris, A.J.R. and Tough, S. (2004) 'Should actuarial risk assessments be used with sex offenders who are intellectually disabled', *Journal of Applied Research in Intellectual Disabilities*, 17: 235–42.

Harris, G.T., Rice, M.E., Quinsey, V.L., Lalumière, M.L., Boer, D. and Lang, C. (2003) 'A multi-site comparison of actuarial risk instruments for sex offenders', *Psychological Assessment*, 15: 413–25.

Hayes, S.C. (2000) *Hayes Ability Screening Index (HASI) Manual*. Sydney: University of Sydney, Behavioural Sciences in Medicine.

Hayes, S.C. (2002) 'Early intervention or early incarceration? Using a screening test for intellectual disability in the criminal justice system', *Journal of Applied Research in Intellectual Disability*, 15: 120–8.

Hingsburger, D., Griffiths, D. and Quinsey, V. (1991) 'Detecting counterfeit deviance: differentiating sexual deviance from sexual inappropriateness', *Habilitation Mental Health Care Newsletter*, 10: 51–4.

Hogue, T.E., Steptoe, L., Taylor, J.L., Lindsay, W.R., Mooney, P., Pinkney, L., Johnston, S., Smith, A.H.W. and O'Brien, G. (2006) 'A comparison of offenders with intellectual disability across three levels of security', *Criminal Behaviour and Mental Health*, 16: 13–28.

Hogue, T.E., Mooney, P., Morrissey, C., Steptoe, L., Johnston, S., Lindsay, W.R. and Taylor, J. (2007) 'Emotional and behavioural problems in offenders with intellectual disability: comparative data from three forensic services', *Journal of Intellectual Disability Research*, 51: 778–85.

Holland, A.J. (2004) 'Criminal behaviour and developmental disability: an epidemiological perspective', in W.R. Lindsay, J.L. Taylor and P. Sturmey (eds), *Offenders with Developmental Disabilities*. Chichester: John Wiley, pp. 23–34.

Holland, T., Clare, I.C.H. and Mukhopadhya, T. (2002) 'Prevalence of "criminal offending" by men and women with intellectual disability and characteristics of "offenders": implications for research and service development', *Journal of Intellectual Disability Research*, 46 (suppl. 1): 6–20.

Jahoda, A., Pert, C. and Trower, P. (2006) 'Socio-emotional understanding and frequent aggression in people with mild to moderate intellectual disabilities', *American Journal on Mental Retardation*, 111: 77–89.

Keeling, J.A., Rose, J.L. and Beech, A.R. (2007a) 'A preliminary evaluation of the adaptation of four assessments for offenders with special needs', *Journal of Intellectual and Developmental Disability*, 32: 62–73.

Keeling, J.A., Rose, J.L. and Beech, A.R. (2007b) 'Comparing sexual offender treatment efficacy: mainstream sexual offenders and sexual offenders with special needs', *Journal of Intellectual and Developmental Disability*, 32: 117–24.

Klimecki, M. R., Jenkinson, J. and Wilson, L. (1994) 'A study of recidivism among offenders with intellectual disability', *Australia and New Zealand Journal of Developmental Disabilities (Journal of Intellectual and Developmental Disabilities)*, 19: 209–19.

Kolton, D.J.C., Boer, A. and Boer, D.P. (2001) 'A revision of the Abel and Becker Cognition Scale for intellectually disabled sex offenders', *Sexual Abuse: A Journal of Research and Treatment*, 13, 217–19.

Langan, P.A. and Cunniff, M.A. (1992) *Recidivism for Felons on Probation*, Bureau of Statistics, Special Report (NCJ-134177). Washington, DC: United States Department of Justice, Bureau of Justice Statistics.

Langan, P.A. and Levin, D.J. (2002) *Recidivism of Prisoners Released in 1994*, Bureau of Statistics, Special Report (NCJ-193427). Washington, DC: United States Department of Justice, Bureau of Justice Statistics.

Langdon, P.E., Maxted, H. and Murphy, G.H. (2007) 'An evaluation of the Ward and Hudson Offending Pathways Model with sex offenders who have intellectual disabilities', *Journal of Intellectual and Developmental Disabilities*, 32: 94–105.

Lindsay, W.R. (2005) 'Model underpinning treatment for sex offenders with mild intellectual disability: current theories of sex offending', *Mental Retardation*, 43: 428–41.

Lindsay, W.R. and Smith, A.H.W. (1998) 'Responses to treatment for sex offenders with intellectual disability: a comparison of men with 1 and 2 year probation sentences', *Journal of Intellectual Disability Research*, 42: 346–53.

Lindsay, W.R., Marshall, I., Neilson, C.Q., Quinn, K. and Smith, A.H.W. (1998a) 'The treatment of men with a learning disability convicted of exhibitionism', *Research on Developmental Disabilities*, 19: 295–316.

Lindsay, W.R., Neilson, C.Q., Morrison, F. and Smith, A.H.W. (1998b) 'The treatment of six men with a learning disability convicted of sex offences with children', *British Journal of Clinical Psychology*, 37: 83–98.

Lindsay, W.R., Olley, S., Jack, C., Morrison, F. and Smith, A.H.W. (1998c) 'The treatment of two stalkers with intellectual disabilities using a cognitive approach', *Journal of Applied Research in Intellectual Disabilities*, 11: 333–44.

Lindsay, W.R., Allan, R., Macleod, F. and Smith, A. H. W. (2003) 'The treatment of six men with intellectual disabilities convicted of assault', *Mental Retardation*, 41: 47–56.

Lindsay, W.R., Elliot, S.F. and Astell, A. (2004a) 'Predictors of sexual offence recidivism in offenders with intellectual disabilities', *Journal of Applied Research in Intellectual Disabilities*, 17: 299–305.

Lindsay, W.R., Taylor, J. L. and Sturmey, P. (2004b) *Offenders with Developmental Disabilities*. Chichester: John Wiley.

Lindsay, W.R., Allan, R., Parry, Macleod, F., Cottrell, J., Overend, H. and Smith, A.H.W. (2004c) 'Anger and aggression in people with intellectual disabilities: treatment and follow-up of consecutive referrals and a waiting list comparison', *Clinical Psychology and Psychotherapy*, 11: 255–64.

Lindsay, W.R., Smith, A.H.W., Law, J., Quinn, K., Anderson, A., Smith, A. and Allan, R. (2004d) 'Sexual and non-sexual offenders with intellectual and learning disabilities: a comparison of characteristics, referral patterns and outcome', *Journal of Interpersonal Violence*, 19: 875–90.

Lindsay, W.R., Hogue, T., Taylor, J.L., Steptoe, L., Mooney, P., O'Brien, G., Johnston, S. and Smith, A.H.W. (2008) 'Risk assessment in offenders with intellectual disability: a comparison across three levels of security', *International Journal of Offender Therapy and Comparative Criminology*. 52: 90–111.

Lindsay, W.R., Steele, L., Smith, A.H.W., Quinn, K. and Allan, R. (2006c) 'A community forensic intellectual disability service: twelve year follow-up of referrals, analysis of referral patterns and assessment of harm reduction', *Legal and Criminological Psychology*, 11: 113–30.

Lindsay, W.R., Michie, A.M., Whitefield, E., Martin, V., Grieve, A. and Carson, D. (2006d) 'Response patterns on the Questionnaire on Attitudes Consistent with Sexual Offending in groups of sex offenders with intellectual disability', *Journal of Applied Research in Intellectual Disabilities*, 19: 47–54.

Lindsay, W.R., Whitefield, E. and Carson, D. (2007) 'The development of a questionnaire to measure cognitive distortions in sex offenders with intellectual disability', *Legal and Criminological Psychology*, 12: 55–68.

Linhorst, D.M., McCutchen, T. A. and Bennett, L. (2003) 'Recidivism among offenders with developmental disabilities participating in a case management programme', *Research in Developmental Disabilities*, 24: 210–30.

Lund, J. (1990) 'Mentally retarded criminal offenders in Denmark', *British Journal of Psychiatry*, 156: 726–31.

Lunsky, Y., Frijters, J., Griffiths, D.M., Watson, S.L. and Williston, S. (2007) 'Sexual knowledge and attitudes of men with intellectual disabilities who sexually offend', *Journal of Intellectual and Developmental Disability*, 32: 74–81.

Lyall, I., Holland, A.J., Collins, S. and Styles, P. (1995) 'Incidence of persons with a learning disability detained in police custody', *Medicine, Science and the Law*, 35: 61–71.

MacEachron, A.E. (1979) 'Mentally retarded offenders prevalence and characteristics', *American Journal of Mental Deficiency*, 84: 165–76.

McMurran, M., Fyffe, S., McCarthy, L., Duggan, C. and Latham, A. (2001) 'Stop and think! Social problem solving therapy with personality disordered offenders', *Criminal Behaviour and Mental Health*, 11: 273–85.

Mason, J. and Murphy, G. (2002) 'Intellectual disability amongst people on probation: prevalence and outcome', *Journal of Intellectual Disability Research*, 46: 230–8.

Meichenbaum, D. (1985) *Stress Inoculation Training*. Oxford: Pergamon Press.

Messinger, E. and Apfelberg, B. (1961) 'A quarter century of court psychiatry', *Crime and Delinquency*, 7: 343–62.

Michie, A.M., Lindsay, W.R., Martin, V. and Grieve, A. (2006) 'A test of counterfeit deviance: a comparison of sexual knowledge in groups of sex offenders with intellectual disability and controls', *Sexual Abuse: A Journal of Research and Treatment*, 18: 271–9.

Morrissey, C., Hogue, T., Mooney, P., Allen, C., Johnston, S., Hollin, C., Lindsay, W.R. and Taylor, J. (2007a) 'Predictive validity of the PCL-R in offenders with intellectual disabilities in a high secure setting: institutional aggression', *Journal of Forensic Psychology and Psychiatry*, 18: 1–15.

Morrissey, C., Mooney, P., Hogue, T., Lindsay, W.R. and Taylor, J.L. (2007b) 'Predictive validity of psychopathy for offenders with intellectual disabilities in a high security hospital: treatment progress', *Journal of Intellectual and Developmental Disabilities*, 32: 125–33.

Murphy, G. and Clare, I. (1991) 'MIETS: a service option for people with mild mental handicaps and challenging behaviour or psychiatric problems', *Mental Handicap Research*, 4: 180–206.

Murphy, G. and Sinclair, N. (2006) *Group Cognitive Behaviour Treatment for Men with Sexually Abusive Behaviour*. Paper presented to 6th Seattle Club Conference on Research and People with Intellectual Disabilities.

Novaco, R.W. (1975) *Anger Control: The Development and Evaluation of an Experimental Treatment*. Lexington, MA: Heath.

Novaco, R.W. (1994) 'Anger as a risk factor for violence among the mentally disordered', in J. Monahan and H.J. Steadman (eds), *Violence in Mental Disorder: Developments in Risk Assessment*. Chicago: University of Chicago Press.

Novaco, R.W. (2003) *The Novaco Anger Scale and Provocation Inventory Manual (NAS-PI)*. Los Angeles: Western Psychological Services.

Novaco, R.W. and Taylor, J.L. (2004) 'Assessment of anger and aggression in offenders with developmental disabilities', *Psychological Assessment*, 16: 42–50.

O'Connor, W. (1996) 'A problem-solving intervention for sex offenders with intellectual disability', *Journal of Intellectual and Developmental Disabilities*, 21: 219–35.

Otto, R.K., Poythress, N.G., Nicholson, R:A., Edens, J.F., Monahan, J., Bonnie, R.J., Hoge, S.K. and Eisenberg, M. (1998) 'Psychometric properties of the MacArthur Competence Assessment Tool – Criminal Adjudication', *Psychological Assessment*, 10: 435–43.

Plaud, J.J., Plaud, D.M., Colstoe, P.D. and Orvedal, L. (2000) 'Behavioural treatment of sexually offending behaviour', *Mental Health Aspects of Developmental Disabilities*, 3: 54–61.

Prout, H.T. and Strohmer, D.C. (1991) *Emotional Problems Scales: Professional Manual for the Behaviour Rating Scales and the Self-Report Inventory*. Lutz, FL: Psychological Assessment Resources Inc.

Quinsey, V.L., Book, A. and Skilling, T.A. (2004) 'A follow-up of deinstitutionalised men with intellectual disabilities and histories of antisocial behaviour', *Journal of Applied Research in Intellectual Disabilities*, 17: 243–54.

Quinsey, V.L., Harris, G.T., Rice, M.E. and Cormier, C.A. (1998) *Violent Offenders: Appraising and Managing Risk*. Washington, DC: American Psychological Association.

Rice, M.E. and Chaplain, T.C. (1979) 'Social skills training for hospitalised male arsonists', *Journal of Behaviour Therapy and Experimental Psychiatry*, 10: 105–8.

Rose, J. and West, C. (1999) 'Assessment of anger in people with intellectual disabilities', *Journal of Applied Research in Intellectual Disabilities*, 12: 211–44.

Rose, J., West, C. and Clifford, D. (2000) 'Group interventions for anger and people with intellectual disabilities', *Research in Developmental Disabilities*, 21: 171–81.

Rose, J., Jenkins, R., O'Conner, C., Jones, C. and Felce, D. (2002) 'A group treatment for men with intellectual disabilities who sexually offend or abuse', *Journal of Applied Research in Intellectual Disabilities*, 15: 138–50.

Ryba, N.L., Cooper, V.G. and Zapf, P.A. (2003) 'Juvenile competence to stand trial evaluations: a survey of current practices and test usage among psychologists', *Professional Psychology: Research in Practice*, 34: 499–507.

Scheerenberger, R.C. (1983) *A History of Mental Retardation*. London: Brooks.

Sparrow, S., Balla, D. and Cicchetti, D. (1984) *Vineland Adaptive Behaviour Scales Survey Form Manual*. Circle Pines, MN: American Guidance Service.

Steptoe, L., Lindsay, W.R., Forrest, D. and Power, M. (2006) 'Quality of life and relationships in sex offenders with intellectual disability', *Journal of Intellectual and Developmental Disabilities*, 31: 13–19.

Steptoe, L., Lindsay, W. R., Murphy, L. and Young, S.J. (2007) 'Construct validity, reliability and predictive validity of the Dynamic Risk Assessment and Management System (DRAMS) in offenders with intellectual disability', *Legal and Criminological Psychology* (in press).

Talbot, T.J. and Langdon, P.E. (2006) 'Locus of control and sex offenders with an intellectual disability', *International Journal of Offender Therapy and Comparative Criminology*, 50: 391–401.

Taylor, J.L. (2002) 'A review of the assessment and treatment of anger and aggression in offenders with intellectual disability', *Journal of Intellectual Disability Research*, 46 (suppl. 1): 57–73.

Taylor, J.L. and Novaco, R.W. (2005) *Anger Treatment for People with Developmental Disabilities: A Theory, Evidence and Manual Based Approach*. Chichester: Wiley.

Taylor, J.L., Novaco, R.W., Gillmer, B. and Thorne, I. (2002a) 'Cognitive behavioural treatment of anger intensity among offenders with intellectual disabilities', *Journal of Applied Research in Intellectual Disabilities*, 15: 151–65.

Taylor, J.L., Thorne, I., Robertson, A. and Avery, G. (2002b) 'Evaluation of a group intervention for convicted arsonists with mild and borderline intellectual disabilities', *Criminal Behaviour* and *Mental Health*, 12: 282–93.

Taylor, J.L., Novaco, R.W., Guinan, C. and Street, N. (2004) 'Development of an imaginal provocation test to evaluate treatment for anger problems in people with intellectual disabilities', *Clinical Psychology and Psychotherapy*, 11: 233–46.

Taylor, J.L., Novaco, R.W., Gillmer, B.T., Robertson, A. and Thorne, I. (2005) 'Individual cognitive behavioural anger treatment for people with mild-borderline disabilities and histories of aggression: a controlled trial', *British Journal of Clinical Psychology*, 44: 367–82.

Taylor, J.L., Robertson, A., Thorne, I., Belshaw, T. and Watson, A. (2006) 'Responses of female fire-setters with mild and borderline intellectual disabilities to a group based intervention', *Journal of Applied Research in Intellectual Disabilities*, 19: 179–90.

Taylor, J.L., Lindsay, W.R., Hogue, T.E., Mooney, P., Steptoe, L., Johnston, S. and O'Brien, G. (2007) 'Use of the HCR-20 in offenders with intellectual disability', submitted for publication.

Terma, L. (1911) *The Measurement of Intelligence*. Boston: Houghton Mifflin.

Tong, J.E. and MacKay, G.W. (1969) 'A statistical follow-up of mental defectives with dangerous or violent propensities', *British Journal of Delinquency*, 9: 276–84.

Tough, S.E. (2001) 'Validation of two Standard Risk Assessments (RRASOR, 1997; Static-99, 1999) on a sample of adult males who are developmentally disabled with significant cognitive deficits'. Unpublished Masters thesis, University of Toronto, Canada.

Walker, N. and McCabe, S. (1973) *Crime and Insanity in England*. Edinburgh: Edinburgh University Press.

Webster, C.D., Eaves, D., Douglas, K.S. and Wintrup, A. (1995) *The HCR-20: The Assessment of Dangerousness and Risk*. Vancouver: Simon Fraser University and British Columbia Forensic Psychiatric Services Commission.

White, R. and Willner, P. (2005) 'Suggestibility and salience in people with intellectual disabilities: an experimental critique of the Gudjonsson Suggestibility Scale', *Journal of Forensic Psychiatry and Psychology*, 1: 638–50.

Wildenskov, H.O.T. (1962) 'A long-term follow-up of subnormals originally exhibiting severe behaviour disorders or criminality', *Proceedings of the London Conference on the Scientific Study of Mental Deficiency*. London: May & Baker, pp. 217–22.

Chapter 14

Aggression and violence

Kevin Howells, Michael Daffern and Andrew Day

Aggression and violence pose major problems for forensic mental health services, for the criminal justice system and for society in general. The social and
economic costs of violence are immense. Within institutions such as hospitals
and prisons, apart from causing injury, psychological harm and stress in
patients and staff, violence can contribute to poor morale, staff turnover, job dis-
satisfaction and the elimination of a therapeutic climate in which patients or
prisoners can be assisted to change and to improve their well-being. It has been
estimated that violence in healthcare settings has direct costs of at least £69 million per annum in the United Kingdom (National Audit Office 2003; Gadon *et
al.* 2006). Within Wales, which has a population of less than 3,000,000, the Wales
Audit Office (2005) estimated the cost of violence to the NHS as £6.3 million
between 2003 and 2004. Health care workers and prison officers, in particular,
are at high risk of being assaulted in their workplace, compared to other groups
of workers (Duhart 2001).

Aggressive and violent acts and the likelihood of future violence are of particular concern for mental health professionals, particularly those working
within secure settings and also for those responsible for decision-making about
offenders in prisons and community services. Both forensic mental health services and the criminal justice system, despite differences in their core purposes
and underlying philosophies, share a responsibility for public protection
(Howells *et al.* 2004a). Developing an understanding of the causal antecedents
for aggression and violence, valid methods for their assessment and sound
strategies for their modification are necessary conditions for the public protection role and for effective services for patients and offenders themselves within
both mental health and criminal justice services. One of the themes to be developed in this chapter is that this task of dealing with violence has been
insufficiently grounded in the substantial and long-standing scientific literature
relating to aggression and has been excessively focused on psychiatric disorders
as causal factors in explaining (and hence dealing with) violent behaviour. (The
literature relating to mental disorders and criminality, including violence, is
covered in depth by Hodgins in this volume, Chapter 16.)

Locating violence within the broad knowledge-base related to aggression has
a major advantage in that aggression theory and research has been a substantial
area of activity and provides concepts and empirical findings which can be used
in the clinical setting. This state of affairs contrasts with that existing for dealing, for example, with sex offending, where clinical services for offenders

developed largely in the absence of any substantial body of knowledge and concepts about how sexual preferences and patterns of sexual behaviour might develop (see Lockmuller *et al.*, this volume, Chapter 18).

Conceptual and definitional problems

An initial task, which is particularly important in this field, is to define core terms. It is proposed here that it is useful to locate violence within the broader phenomenon of aggression, hence it is necessary to define the latter term as a starting point. It has been estimated that there are more than 200 definitions of aggression in the literature, ranging from Buss's (1961) 'a response that delivers noxious stimuli to another organism' to Baron and Richardson's (1994) 'any form of behaviour directed toward the goal of harming or injuring another living being who is motivated to avoid such treatment' (Parrott and Giancola 2006). The latter definition will be used in this chapter and has the advantage of excluding unintended acts and harmful acts the victim does not want to avoid (for example, in sadomasochism).

The confusion of aggression with related constructs of anger, hostility and violence is still common (Parrott and Giancola 2006). *Anger* refers to an *internal emotional response*, with typical psychophysiological and facial components. Anger, in turn, needs to be distinguished from *hostility* which refers to the *negative cognitive evaluation of people or events*. Both anger and hostility can give rise to the *behavioural expression* of aggression, but need not do so. Some have further distinguished emotional, affective and feelings aspects of anger (see Berkowitz 1999), but these distinctions will not be observed in the present chapter. Aggression, anger and hostility may refer to particular acts or events but may also have a *dispositional* aspect. An individual may engage in an aggressive act but may not have a general disposition (trait) to act in this way. Equally, hostility may take the form of a particular appraisal or evaluation ('he just insulted me') or it may be an ongoing, trait-like evaluation ('my boss is a pig'). These distinctions are more than academic in that they point to the need for precision in devising clinical measures for assessment of aggression or measures for use in treatment evaluation (Parrott and Giancola 2006).

The distinction between aggression (see above) and *violence* is largely based on the extent of physical harm inflicted. For Anderson and Bushman (2002), for example, violence is defined as aggression that has extreme harm as its goal and for Blackburn (1993) as the forceful infliction of physical injury. Clearly all acts of violence are aggressive but not all acts of aggression are violent. Verbal insults would generally be viewed as aggressive rather than violent. Prolonged verbal abuse of a child by a parent, similarly, is probably best labelled as aggressive rather than violent in that the harm inflicted is predominantly psychological rather than physical in nature. As such, it is no surprise that the reporting of violence or aggression upon NHS staff has been historically linked with significant problems of definition. Different trusts used different criteria. As so many definitions of violence occurred, making public health initiatives redundant as they relied upon accurate counting of violent incidents, then research also became fraught with difficulties. Consequently, in October 2005, the National Health Service Security Management Service (NHS SMS) published the first figures based on consistent definitions and this indicated that staff working in mental health and learning disability services faced a higher risk. The DoH directions (Department of Health 2003) introduced a new national reporting system based on legal definitions of physical and non-physical assault. These clarified reporting procedures to ensure a consistent approach. The definition for physical assault, which *replaces all previous definitions* used in the NHS in England, was:

> The intentional application of force to the person of another, without lawful justification, resulting in physical injury or personal discomfort (*Eisener v. Maxwell 1951, Kaye v. Robinson 1991*). (DoH 2003)

Violent offending forms a subcategory of violence, referring to acts of violence that contravene the legal code. Although it might initially appear straightforward to define a group of violent offenders (for purposes of service provision or for research) in terms of whether individuals have committed a particular offence, for example an assault, in practice, the process is highly problematic (Kenny and Press 2006). The latter authors point out the considerable behavioural differences that may exist between acts that meet a legal definition such as assault and have stressed the need for a reliable coding system for classifying violent acts and offences. There are wide variations in clinical and research practice, with violent offence/offender status sometimes ascribed on the basis of the index offence alone, at other times on the basis of the whole criminal history, at others on the basis of the predominant (most frequent) offence. Classifications such as 'violent offence' often do not discriminate the different levels of severity of violence (Kenny and Press 2006). Furthermore, there are indications that how violent offending is defined and classified affects the reported frequency and the pattern of relationship of violence to other variables (Kenny and Press 2006). There are also potential problems in relying on criminal history alone in determining a person's level of violence or whether or not they are best described as a violent offender. As Kenny and Press point out, ideally, a formal criminal history would be supplemented by self-report data (itself subject to methodological uncertainties), other records (hospital records, prison files) and other observations.

For the rest of this chapter the term *aggression* will be used to cover this broad field, with violence being included under this term. Where a particular author or study being discussed has explicitly used the term violence or violent offending, then the original term used is retained. Parrott and Giancola's (2004) point is well made that the majority of assessments of aggression in clinical settings fail to make the necessary discriminations between different types of aggression and may aggregate behaviours that substantially differ from each other and have no adequate conceptual underpinnings.

The heterogeneity of aggressive acts and aggressive actors

If our aim is to understand the factors that give rise to aggressive acts or aggressive actors then it needs to be acknowledged that both aggressive acts and aggressive actors are unlikely to be homogeneous categories. Of the many possible distinctions to be made, only a few that are particularly important are discussed here.

Aggression by males and females

There is a substantial literature indicating that males are more aggressive than females (Bennett *et al.* 2005), with recent evidence that the sex difference increases with the increasing seriousness of the aggression. Sex differences are much larger for serious violence in the 'real world', where men are the great majority of perpetrators, than in laboratory studies of less serious aggression, though differences in prevalence of aggression for males and females may be less clear-cut for violence between intimate partners (Archer 2000, 2004; Campbell 2006). There are clear indications in the literature that different antecedents may exist for male and female violence and aggression. Although recorded aggression is far more prevalent in males than in females, the prevalence of aggression among females has significantly increased in industrialised countries in recent decades, with a consequent narrowing of the gender gap (Graves 2006). The reasons for this latter phenomenon remain speculative. The important clinical issue is whether aggression and violence serve *different functions* in males than in females, that is whether the antecedent conditions (variously labelled as risk factors, needs, criminogenic needs, etc.) giving rise to aggression are different and whether the purposes or goals of aggressive acts differ for the two sexes. In an analysis of risk factors, Graves (2006) concluded that the following differences had some empirical support:

- a stronger association of aggresssion with internalising conditions such as depression in females;
- greater inhibition about aggressive behaviour in females as a result of differential socialisation;
- a stronger association of aggression with physical and sexual victimisation in females, as manifested in high levels of posttraumatic stress disorder (PTSD).

The question of whether sex differences reflect an instigatory difference (a stronger impulse towards aggression in men) or a self-regulatory difference (poorer self-control and higher impulsivity in men) has been addressed by Campbell (2006). Anger is a major instigatory factor (see below) but there is little evidence to suggest a sex difference in levels of trait anger, at least when the measure is of anger *experience* as opposed to anger *expression* (Milovchevich *et al.* 2001). There is some evidence (see Campbell 2006) that males and females may express anger in different ways, suggesting that self-regulatory mechanisms are important and that fear-based inhibition being stronger in females accounts better for sex differences in aggression than do instigatory factors.

Hostile versus instrumental aggression

Hostile (or angry) and instrumental aggression have long been distinguished in the literature. Hostile aggression typically involves a triggering frustrating event, an internal state of emotional arousal and an impulse to hurt or harm the perpetrator of the frustration. In instrumental aggression, on the other hand, the intention is to obtain some reward, usually environmental, and the perpetrator does not show emotional arousal (or cognitions) of an angry sort. A homicide in the course of an angry row provides an example of hostile aggression and the predatory use of aggression to extort money from a cashier at a service station an example of instrumental aggression. Distinctions of this sort are very common in the literature (McEllistrem 2004) though a variety of terms have been used (angry, affective, reactive, impulsive, hot-blooded versus non-angry, predatory, proactive, planned, cold-blooded and so on). The distinction has clearly influenced clinical practice, insofar as patients and offenders who are prone to hostile/reactive aggression are likely to be seen as suited to clinical interventions such as cognitive therapies for anger and emotion regulation (see discussion of treatment approaches below). It is important to acknowledge that the hostile/instrumental distinction refers to the nature of aggressive acts rather than aggressive actors. Thus a particular individual may engage in both hostile and instrumental aggressive acts or engage in only one type.

Despite the pervasiveness of this distinction and its theoretical and empirical support in the literature, it has recently been subject to sceptical critiques, particularly by Bushman and Anderson (2001). These authors question the validity of a rigid hostile/instrumental distinction because such a differentiation is confounded by the fact that controlled (planned) and automatic functioning can occur in both. The notion that anger-mediated (hostile) aggression is impulsive and unplanned is almost certainly wrong, given the importance of angry rumination – the individual may ruminate about the perceived provocation over some time before aggression occurs.

Barratt and Slaughter (1998) have shown that many aggressive acts are difficult to categorise as either hostile or instrumental. Even when *acts* can be reliably described, it may be a mistake to assume angry or instrumental aggression are reliable traits of *perpetrators*. Perpetrators may behave in both angry and instrumental ways on different occasions or may have multiple goals and functions for any one aggressive act. This latter possibility is addressed in the functional analytic methodology adopted by Daffern and colleagues (Daffern *et al.* 2007) discussed in more detail below.

Despite the problems of the hostile/instrumental dichotomy, the presence or absence of anger and other negative emotional states as an antecedent for aggressive and violent acts remains an important clinical issue. Some aggressive and violent acts can clearly occur in a 'cool' state of mind and a perpetrator whose acts were always of this sort – for example a 'Hare psychopath' (Hare 2006) – would not require forms of clinical intervention predicated on the assumption that heightened anger had lead to impulsive aggression and that angry impulses need to be controlled. Patrick (2006) has recently shown, however, that a complex picture is emerging as to the links between different facets of psychopathy and angry aggression.

Despite the Bushman and Anderson critique, the hostile/instrumental distinction is alive and kicking in many areas of aggression theory and research (see, for example, from a neuropsychological perspective, Blair 2004). Dodge's influential work on aggression in children and juveniles (Dodge and Coie 1987; Crick and Dodge 1996) similarly is based on a distinction between reactive and proactive aggression, though a mixed group is also identified. The former involves aggression in response to negative emotion elicited by perceived threat and provocation. Proactive aggression, on the other hand, involves no provocation and is motivated by the desire to obtain resources or control over others, to dominate and coerce. Berkowitz and other social learning theorists have also distinguished *reactive from instrumental* aggression (Berkowitz 1993, 1999), the former being a response to aversive or frustrating stimulation, followed by particular types of cognition.

The existence of two types of aggressive behaviour (that associated with provoking situations and that not so associated) is also emerging in current theory and empirical research on personality and aggression – see below (Bettencourt *et al.* 2006; Meloy 2006). Observational studies of animals have lead to seven categories of aggression being identified (Moyer 1968) but a distinction similar to hostile versus instrumental appears to have emerged (affective versus predatory violence) in recent animal and neuroanatomical studies (McEllistrem 2004).

The hostile/instrumental distinction in personality disorders

The hostile/instrumental distinction has relevance to personality disorder. It would appear likely that psychopathy (Hare 2006) would be associated more strongly with instrumental than with angry aggressive acts, given the 'cold', affectless nature of psychopathic individuals (Hare 2006). Cornell *et al.* (1996) compared violent offenders who had committed at least one instrumental offence with those with a history of reactive violent offences. In both the samples studied the two violent groups could be distinguished on the basis of their Hare Psychopathy score. Such studies have clear implications for treatment interventions, suggesting that the instrumentally violent psychopath has no need for anger interventions, requiring, perhaps, to learn to overcome their inhibitory deficits and related impairments in moral development (Blair 2006).

We know little, however, about types and patterns of aggression in other personality disorders such as antisocial personality disorders (APD). On the basis of their clinical descriptions, borderline personality disorder (PD) would be expected to be associated with angry, impulsive aggression, as would paranoid PD, though the author is not aware of any studies testing such hypotheses. The clinical features of paranoid PD mirror those cognitive characteristics shown to be associated with hostile aggression in other populations, for example the tendency to over-attribute hostile and malevolent causes (to others) for negative social events. Similarly the association between the trait of narcissism and angry aggression (cf. 'narcissistic rage') in general populations (Bettencourt *et al.* 2006) would suggest that hostile aggression would prevail in narcissistic PD, albeit with distinctive triggers, namely threats to self-esteem. For a review of links between personality disorders and anger, see Howells (in press).

Factors contributing to aggression

Social learning has been extensively studied and widely accepted as important in the causation of aggression. Imitation (observing acts of aggression) and vicarious reinforcement (perceiving aggression to be rewarded) are important mechanisms (Bandura 1977) as are broader mechanisms involved in the learning of aggressive scripts during childhood and adolescence (Huesmann and Miller 1994). Social learning theorists have devoted much effort to evaluating the effects of exposure to violence on television as a determinant of subsequent aggression. In broad terms, the evidence for such an effect is consistent and convincing, based on aggregate-level and individual-level studies, using cross-sectional, longitudinal, experimental and quasi-experimental methodologies. Questions of temporal order and causality in effects are difficult to address. The main reservation about this literature, from the clinical perspective of this chapter, is that expressed by Savage (2004) in an exhaustive and critical review of published work. Savage argues not only that methodological inadequacies exist that make definitive conclusions impossible but also that the dependent variables in many studies are forms of relatively minor aggression, rather than the serious acts of criminal violence which are more relevant to the present volume.

Triggering events and situations

Even for highly aggressive individuals, aggressive acts are not random but are typically responses to particular events and situations in the life of the perpetrator. It has been demonstrated that events eliciting aggression have particular features. Hostile or angry aggression, for example, is typically elicited by events that are *aversive* for the individual, often constituting situations of *frustration* in which the person is blocked in achieving important goals or where expected rewards fail to eventuate (Berkowitz 1999).

The availability of weapons is a potentially important situational trigger for violence, with evidence that weapons differ in their lethality, guns being more lethal than weapons such as knives (Hepburn and Hemenway 2004). There are considerable methodological difficulties with studies in this area creating a host of confounding factors and making it difficult to say with total confidence that the established and consistently reported association between gun ownership and acts of serious violence such as homicide is causal, though a causal interpretation is consistent with contemporary psychological models of violence (Anderson and Bushman 2002).

In an extensive analysis of links between gun ownership and gun-related homicide, Hepburn and Hemenway (2004: 438) concluded: 'most studies, cross-sectional or time series, international or domestic, are consistent with the hypothesis that higher levels of gun prevalence substantially increase the homicide rate'. Far fewer studies exist in relation to the availability of knives, which are the most commonly used weapons in the United Kingdom context. A literature does exist on situational factors in intimate partner violence, though it is acknowledged that detailed analysis of violent situations has been a neglected area (Wilkinson and Hamerschlag 2005). One way of understanding situational influences on aggression is that these factors may contribute to the breakdown of normal self-regulation skills (Baumeister *et al.* 1994).

In any event, assessment of aggression-eliciting situations, including actual or likely access to a weapon (for example, carrying a knife) and beliefs about weapon use, are likely to be as important a task for the forensic clinician as are more commonly accomplished assessments of angry emotions, mental state and aggressive personality traits.

Cognitive factors

Since the advent of the 'cognitive revolution' in psychology, particularly in clinical psychology, disordered emotions and behaviour have been increasingly viewed as, in part, the product of biases in the appraisal and construction by the person of the events to which they are exposed. Such a model has also proved relevant to understanding aggressive behaviour. For example, Crick and Dodge's (1996) model of the development of aggressive and antisocial behaviour in young people draws attention to the social information processing and other cognitive biases that are associated with aggression and violence, including biases in social attribution for negative events and attentional, goal-setting, problem-solving and representational deficits. Crick and Dodge (1996) have identified attributions of intent to harm as aggression-eliciting in reactively aggressive children. Cognitive biases also appear to associated with high anger in the general population (Hazebroek *et al*. 2001). The cognitive elicitation of hostile aggression involves a number of necessary components, including the initial obstruction of the person in achieving a personally significant goal (motivational relevance of the triggering event), the appraisal that an external agent is responsible and blameworthy and the judgment that the offensive act violates some personal, moral imperative, constituting an 'is-ought discrepancy' (Berkowitz and Harmon-Jones 2004; Hazebroek *et al*. 2001; Ortony *et al*. 1988). Appraisal that the provoking 'offence' by the other person can be effectively coped with and eliminated may also be important if anger rather than fear or sadness is to occur (Berkowitz and Harmon-Jones 2004). Subtle and indirect methods for assessing such cognitive processing biases in aggressive populations are beginning to emerge (Smith and Waterman 2003, 2004) and it is likely that this area of assessment will develop substantially in the near future.

Empathy

Empathy deficits have also been implicated as possible causal influences for offending in general and for aggressive offending in particular. Most typically, the implied mechanism for this association is a failure of emotional inhibition of aggressive acts. The non-empathic person is assumed to fail to learn to inhibit criminal or aggressive acts, because the punishing consequences of the acts (distress elicited by observing the negative effects of the acts for others) fail to occur. Empathy is a complex, multi-faceted phenomenon and, thus, empathy deficits may involve a number of different psychological processes, ranging from a perceptual failure to observe the distress at others, to a cognitive failure to take the perspective of others (Mohr *et al*. 2007), to an affective failure to experience distress at the suffering of others or a behavioural failure to act on the empathic responses that have been elicited. Jolliffe and Farrington (2004) have reported a meta-analytic investigation of the links between the cognitive and affective aspects of empathy and offending. These authors found a stronger negative relationship between cognitive empathy and offending than between affective empathy and offending and provided some support for the notion that empathy deficits are stronger in violent than in sexual offenders.

Affective and emotional states

As indicated above, the effects of cognitive processes, particularly appraisal, have dominated our understanding of hostile aggression in the past two decades and such domination has inevitably influenced thinking about the appropriate focus and content for therapeutic interventions. Cognitive behavioural therapy, the most common therapeutic approach, sits comfortably with theories which emphasise the role of cognition. Arguments have been put forward, however, that cognitive factors have been overemphasised in theoretical analyses (Berkowitz and Harmon-Jones 2004). Berkowitz (1993, 1999), one of the most influential psychological theorists in the field of anger and aggression, has argued, and produced evidence to demonstrate, that it is the *aversiveness* of the provoking event that elicits hostile aggression rather than the cognitive appraisals discussed above. Cognitions are important, from this sceptical point of view, to the extent that they make the event more aversive. Aversive events (pain, frustration, social stressors) are seen as inducing an initial state of negative affective arousal which subsequently becomes differentiated into specific emotions, such as anger or fear, depending on higher order cognitive and other processes, including other features present in the environment and body states of the person. The emphasis on negative affect as an elicitor of aggression is congruent with studies of personality and aggression (see below).

Such models have therapeutic implications, suggesting that the therapeutic strategy for reducing such acts of aggression should be broader than attempting to modify distorted cognitive appraisals. Interventions would seek to reduce the aggressive person's exposure to aversive events, to reduce the aversiveness of these events where feasible (for example through modifying the person's psychophysiological state) and to improve the person's capacity to regulate and control their negative affective arousal. Given the reciprocal relationship between environments and the person (environments shape our behaviour but we also create our environments through our own behaviours) then an obvious therapeutic strategy would be to enable aggressive individuals to change aspects of their social behaviour so as to reduce their tendency to produce aversive environments and to augment their capacity to produce positive environments.

Many traditional rehabilitative activities (enhancing work skills, improving education) can be construed as methods for enhancing the valence or affective tone of the experienced environment. Such an approach is also consistent with the 'Good Lives Model' (Ward *et al.* 2006) which provides a theoretical basis for many contemporary rehabilitation and treatment approaches in forensic settings (see Lockmuller *et al.*, present volume, Chapter 18).

Anger

The specific emotional state most frequently identified as an important antecedent for aggression has been anger (Howells 1998, in press; Novaco 1997;

Novaco *et al.* 2001). Anger is neither a necessary condition for aggression (aggression can occur without anger) nor a sufficient condition (anger can occur without aggression following) but is viewed as a contributing factor when other environmental and intrapersonal conditions are present. Anger theory (Howells 2004; Novaco and Welsh 1989) has been useful in specifying important components of anger, particularly cognitive components that may be causally significant for aggressive behaviour. The distinction (above) between trait and state aspects of anger is important. The aggressive person may or may not have high trait anger, as assessed by a psychometric test. Even where trait anger is only average it may nevertheless be the case that that the state of anger may have been critical in the pathway that led to an aggressive act (Howells *et al.* 2004b).

Behavioural inhibition, coping and self-regulatory skills

Whereas most of the factors discussed so far are of an *instigatory* nature (frustrating events, biased appraisals, negative emotions, etc.) it is possible that the difference between aggressive and non-aggressive individuals, and between occasions on which an individual behaves aggressively as opposed to ones in which he does not, lie in subsequent *self-regulatory* rather than instigatory processes. The concept of self-regulation has some overlap with the concept of *inhibition* and also with (low) *impulsivity*. Both inhibition and impulsivity are emerging as highly relevant to aggression but also as complex, multi-faceted constructs (Campbell 2006; Polaschek 2006; Wang and Diamond 1999).

Self-regulation and inhibition of aggressive impulses has become a significant area for neuropsychological investigation (Blair 2004; Davidson *et al.* 2000) with a particular focus on the orbitofrontal and ventromedial cortices (Raine 2002; Raine *et al.* 1997). Self-regulatory skills are discussed further below in the section on overcontrol.

Personality variables

As briefly decribed above, aggressive behaviour will be influenced by both situational and intrapersonal variables, both proximal and distal (historical). Some intrapersonal factors will be dispositional in character, that is they are enduring dispositions of the person or traits. The territory of long-term dispositions of this sort is usually labelled as *personality*. The important question is which personality variables, if any, influence aggression? Given the different types and patterns of aggression, as outlined above, the question might be more appropriately stated as which personality variables influence which types of aggression? A number of methodologies have been used to attempt to answer this question. These range from experimental laboratory studies in which, for example, aggression is defined in terms of delivery of electric shocks to another person to field surveys and to clinical observational studies. Each methodology has its strengths and limitations. Fortunately, a broadly similar pattern of findings has emerged across methodologies (Bettencourt *et al.* 2006).

In an important theoretical review and meta-analytic investigation Bettencourt *et al.* (2006) have tested the hypothesis that some personality variables influence aggression under both neutral and provocative conditions while others influence aggression only under provocation. Among the personality traits shown in their review of empirical work to be influential for aggression in the presence of a provocation were trait anger (defined by intensity, frequency and duration of anger reactions), type-A personality, rumination, narcissism and impulsivity. On the other hand, trait aggressiveness (a composite propensity to engage in hostile cognition, physical and verbal aggression and anger expression) and irritability influenced aggression under both neutral (no provocation) and provocation conditions.

The work of Bettencourt and colleagues has important potential clinical implications, indicating as it does that being anger-prone, a ruminator about bad events, narcissistically vulnerable to threats to self-esteem and a poor regulator of impulses require an *interaction* with provoking and frustrating circumstances if these traits are to influence the probability of aggressive behaviour occurring. In clinical treatment programmes for perpetrators of aggression and violence (such as the DSPD programme in England and Wales, Howells *et al.* 2007), risk and clinical assessments would need to include the personality traits identified by Bettencourt and colleagues (the clinical relevance of such traits would be recognised by clinicians in the field) but would also need to accommodate the fact that that provocation exposure is required. The probability and nature of provocations in the person's current and future social environment would also need to be assessed (see above).

This emphasis on the experienced environment is critical in the functional analytic approach to assessment discussed below, with its focus on determining the eliciting event for an aggressive act and also its purpose or function (Daffern *et al.* 2007). Functional analysis is also based on the premise that what constitutes a provocation will vary and that 'signature' eliciting events and goals need to be identified for the individual (Mischel 2004a).

Bettencourt *et al.* (2006) summarise their findings in terms of *provocation sensitive* and *aggression-prone* personality traits. Individuals with high scores on the latter, they suggest, have the capacity to be aggressive in the absence of provocation and demonstrate a 'cold-blooded style of aggressive behaviour' whereas the former exhibit a more hot-blooded style.

Five-factor model

Contemporary personality theory has been dominated for some years by the Five Factor Model of personality (McCrae and Costa 1987), so it is relevant to ask where the provocation-sensitive and aggression-prone traits lie within the five-dimensional space. Bettencourt *et al.* (2006) suggest provocation-sensitivity is associated with the Neuroticism dimension and aggression-prone traits with antagonism (low Agreeableness).

Psychopathy

Among the personality variables best correlated with violence in mentally disordered and non-disordered groups is Psychopathy, as typically measured by the PCL-R (Hare 2006). Hare has argued that Psychopathy is a robust risk factor in a range of forensic populations, including adult male offenders, adult female offenders, adolescent offenders, forensic psychiatric patients, including those with Axis 1 disorders, and civil psychiatric patients (for a listing of detailed studies see Hare 2006).

Skeem *et al.* (2005) addressed the issue of whether psychopathy *per se* best predicts violence or whether it is the higher order personality variables tapped by psychopathy scale items. Using a sample derived from the larger MacArthur Risk Assessment Study (Monahan *et al.* 2001), Skeem *et al.* (2005) found that the Five Factors model measures (NEO-Five-Factor Inventory) were post-dictive of violence in the mentally disordered, with Antagonism and Neuroticism being the strongest correlates of violence (cf. the conclusions of Bettencourt *et al.* (2006) above). Antagonism was shown to have moderate positive correlations with psychopathy variables, particularly Factor II. Such studies confirm the relevance of general personality variables, such as antagonism, in violence prediction. As Skeem *et al.* suggest, 'one can easily imagine how antagonism might predispose someone to violent transactions with others' given that 'antagonism is a highly interpersonal construct that includes such traits as suspiciousness, combativeness, deceptiveness, lack of empathy and arrogance' (2005: 461). It might be added that Antagonism, as defined here, is a complex and multi-faceted construct, including as it does behavioural, cognitive and affective processes. Skeem *et al.* (2005) draw attention, in particular, to cognitive biases (cf. Crick and Dodge 1996) which engender hostile aggression as possibly particularly important factors. Thus personality-based theories of this sort are congruent with broader models of anger and anger control which have become so influential in the treatment of aggressive offenders (see below). It should be noted that empirical findings relating to correlates of violence are likely to be dependent on the characteristics of the specific population being studied. The MacArthur sample referred to above, for example, included only a minority of severely mentally ill persons, with a large proportion of drug addicts and depressed addicts.

Overcontrol

It will be apparent from the above discussion that negative emotion, particularly angry emotion, is a critical variable in contemporary psychological explanations of aggression and violence, at least for the provocation-based form of aggression. It is for this reason that cognitive behavioural therapy for anger ('anger management') has become one of the most prevalent forms of intervention for perpetrators of aggression. This treatment approach is discussed in detail below. The picture painted of the aggressive individual by the research of Bettencourt and many others and by accounts of therapeutic programmes is of someone who is easily moved to anger and aggressive impulses (anger is of high frequency, intensity and duration) and who is impulsive and deficient in the control and regulation of such emotions and 'action tendencies'. Such an individual needs, clearly, to acquire self-regulatory and inhibitory skills, the latter forming a major component of many treatment programmes. While this characterisation would be accurate for many perpetrators of violence, there are several groups for whom it is inaccurate, among whom would be the 'overcontrolled' aggressor (Davey *et al.* 2005).

It is commonly observed clinically that some aggressive offenders have personality characteristics opposite to those of the high anger, high impulsivity individual. Tsytsarev and Grodnitsky (1995), for example, have described what they refer to as 'prolonged' anger arousal and an 'accumulation of affective tension which turns into an explosion of anger and rage, and is usually accompanied, or preceded, by intense feelings of humiliation and despair' (p. 104). Such individuals, it has been proposed, may normally have high inhibitions about anger experience and expression, hence the 'overcontrolled' (versus 'undercontrolled') description. This group has received some, though not extensive, attention in empirical studies (Megargee 1966; Blackburn 1971, 1993; Lang *et al.* 1987). Davey *et al.* (2005) have proposed that the overcontrolled aggressive offender type falls into two sub-types, distinguishing the *phenomenologically overcontrolled* offender, who does not report either anger-eliciting cognitions or angry emotional arousal following exposure to a frustration, from the *behaviourally overcontrolled* individual, who may experience intense anger, ruminate on and rehearse grievances but strongly inhibits behavioural expression (a distinction resembling Blackburn's (1986, 1993) *conforming* and *inhibited* types).

The work on overcontrol is important in that it, again, illustrates the heterogeneity of aggressive offenders and also identifies self-regulatory strategies as vital in understanding aggression, particularly for hostile aggression (above).

The overcontrol phenomenon has clear implications for forensic clinical practice and for treatment strategies, including issues of readiness for treatment (Howells and Day 2003; Ward *et al.* 2004), treatment targets and the assessment of risk (Davey *et al.* 2005). A major lesson to be derived from theoretical models such as those of Gross (2002) is that treatment needs to increase the flexibility and variety of self-regulatory strategies used by the aggression perpetrator.

Before leaving the topic of personality traits that may be related to aggression, the limitations of the personality approach need some comment. The work on personality and aggression is, by definition, focused on enduring traits and dispositions of the person. There exist in personality theory long-standing and influential critiques of the very notion of a trait that exists across time and across situations (Mischel, 1968; 2004a, 2004b) which draw attention to the importance of *state* (that is non-enduring) factors within the person, such as day-to day variations in emotions or cognitive appraisals, and to temporary *situational* factors that have an influence. Central to such work is the notion of the person-situation interaction (Mischel 2004a, 2004b) As suggested above, a balanced approach may be required in the clinical setting, with a fuller recognition of state, situational and interaction effects (discussed below).

Other influences

Space does not allow for a full discussion in this chapter of all the many variables shown to be important to aggressive and other antisocial behaviours. Substance misuse may be highly relevant as a causal influence (discussed by McMurran in this volume, Chaper 17) as are neurophysiological processes identified as relevant to psychopathy, personality disorder (discussed by McMurran in this volume, Chapter 15) and mental disorders (discussed by Hodgins in this volume, Chapter 16).

What is clear from the above discussion is that a wide range of person and situational variables influence human aggression and violence. Each of the domains discussed has been the subject of domain-specific theories. In addition there have been attempts to provide broad models which try to integrate findings and provide a broader framework, one which might form the basis for a comprehensive approach to the prevention and treatment of aggression. An influential example of broader model building is that provided by Anderson and Bushman (2002) in their General Aggression Model (GAM).

General Aggression Model

The GAM tries to integrate cognitive, affective, psychophysiological, behavioural, situational and personological variables. Person factors include personality traits, attitudes, beliefs, genetic and neurophysiological dispositions, schemata, behavioural scripts and what the authors label 'knowledge structures'. Some of these factors will be dispositional in nature while others are state rather than trait variables. Situational factors identified by Anderson and Bushman include aggressive cues (for example, presence of weapons), provoking and frustrating events in the environment, ingestion of alcohol and other drugs and environmental incentives to aggress.

The relevant internal states (cognition, affect and arousal) are interconnected and influence subsequent decision-making and behavioural expression. Bushman and Anderson make the point that most contemporary attempts to treat or prevent aggression 'do not address the wide range of factors that contribute to the development and maintenance of violent behaviour' (2001: 45) but suggest that approaches such as multisystemic therapy are consistent with broad analyses of causation (Henggeler *et al.* 1998).

Functional analytic approaches to assessment

The notion that aggression and violence may have multiple goals for the individual has already emerged in personality theory (Bushman and Anderson 2001; Bettencourt *et al.* 2006) but until recently has had little influence on clinical practice. In their work with aggressive psychiatric patients in high-security settings, Daffern and others (Daffern and Howells 2002; Daffern *et al.* 2007) have proposed an assessment framework for analysing the functions (goals) of a particular act of aggression, acknowledging that multiple goals may be present for any particular act and that perpetrators may have different goals for different acts. Aggressive acts are common in some forensic mental health units, particularly high-security institutions (Daffern 2007), as well as constituting one of the most frequent reasons for admission. What factors influence the occurrence of such acts is still poorly understood, but they are likely to include mental disorder variables, as well as social and psychological factors, the latter including those of a dispositional (long-term personality traits of the perpetrator) and of a situational nature (variations in the external environment and in the cognitive, affective and behavioural state of the individual).

Functional assessment approaches (Daffern and Howells 2002; Haynes and O'Brien 1998; Sturmey 1996) seek to clarify the factors responsible for the development, expression and maintenance of the patient's problem, in this case acts of aggression. There is a particular emphasis on identifying the antecedent conditions giving rise to the behaviour and to the consequences, that is the *functions* the behaviour serves for the perpetrator. Daffern *et al.* (2007) have devised the 'Assessment and Classification of Function' assessment (ACF), derived from the literature on the various functions of aggression, but applied, in this case, to the mentally disordered aggressive offender in a secure hospital. The functions included in the ACF are:

1 *Demand avoidance.* In response to demands by staff or other patients to cease or engage in an activity.
2 *To force compliance.* Following denial of a request.
3 *To express anger.* Following perceived provocation.
4 *To reduce tension (catharsis).* Arousal reduction.
5 *To obtain tangibles.* Obtain social or psychological reinforcers.
6 *Social distance reduction (attention-seeking).* From staff or other patients.
7 *To enhance status or social approval.* In response to humiliation or threats to reputation.
8 *Compliance with instruction.* Command auditory hallucination or overt instruction from another.
9 *To observe suffering.* Enjoying suffering, in absence of provocation.

In a study of 502 aggressive incidents in a high-security forensic hospital, Daffern *et al.* (2007) found that anger expression was the most frequent function but that functions differed for aggressive behaviours towards staff and those towards patients. Demand avoidance was a common function for aggression towards staff but rare for aggression towards patients. To obtain tangibles (an instrumental function) was rare for both types of incident. In an extension of the ACF to violent personality disordered patients in a high-secure setting (Daffern and Howells in press), two further categories of function have been added to the original nine functions, namely 'sensation seeking' and 'sexual gratification' to capture apparent sexual/sadistic functions occasionally occurring in this very high-risk population.

A major reason for identifying functions for aggression in this way is to suggest intervention strategies. These are likely to take the form of encouraging alternative strategies for obtaining the functional goal or to change conditions in such a way that the need to pursue the problematic goal is reduced (for examples of strategies for each goal, see Daffern *et al.* 2007).There is a need to extend such analyses to other (non-psychotic) forensic populations, including those with personality disorders and non-mentally disordered violent offenders in the criminal justice system, which would allow for comparing the functions of aggression in these different groups and settings.

Assessment and treatment issues

In many developed criminal justice systems across the world, the treatment and rehabilitation of offenders have undergone a revolution in the last 20 years. The so called 'Nothing Works' era has progressively given way to an era of moderate confidence that well planned interventions following established theoretical and empirically supported principles are capable of producing significant, if modest, change in offenders, particularly in relation to recidivism rates (Hollin 2001; Hollin and Palmer 2006; Howells, Day, Williamson *et al.* 2005; McGuire 2002, 2004). This 'movement' and literature have acquired various labels, including 'What Works' and the RNR (Risk/Needs/Responsivity) approach

(Andrews and Bonta 2003). The RNR model suggests that determination of *risk* (particularly of future violence and sexual offending), identification of the individual's *criminogenic needs* and ensuring programme *responsivity* (matching of treatment programme content and style with characteristics of the treatment participant) are core tasks in the treatment and rehabilitation of offenders and essential in recidivism reduction (Andrews and Bonta 2003).

The RNR model is highly relevant to offenders with histories of aggression and serious violence. As aggressive offenders, like sex offenders, are likely to be perceived as presenting a greater risk of harm to the community should they reoffend than, for example, property offenders, it would be expected that aggressive offenders would feature strongly in offenders identified as needing treatment under the risk principle. The criminogenic needs principle would require that the criminogenic needs of aggressive offenders be the major targets for treatment interventions, that is treatment should focus on factors demonstrated empirically to be causally or functionally related to their aggressive and violent behaviour.

There are two categories of criminogenic needs in such offenders. Aggressive offenders will share many criminogenic needs with other offender types (for example, impulsivity or having peers involved in criminal behaviour) in that many offenders are generalists rather than engaging in only one type of offending. However, they will also have criminogenic needs specific to their aggressive acts. The diverse variables discussed in previous sections of this chapter constitute some of the potentially relevant areas of criminogenic need in aggressive offenders, including environmental, cognitive, affective and behavioural factors. The Responsivity principle is not discussed in depth at this point but will be alluded to below when readiness for treatment is addressed.

The purpose of risk assessment in the RNR model is to ensure that those of highest risk are offered the most intensive treatment, with the corollary that those of low risk may require little or even no treatment resource to be dedicated to them. The development and implementation of risk assessment has become a major activity and high risk status is central to admission to some forensic services in the forensic mental health system and to some therapeutic programmes within the criminal justice system. In the recently developed DSPD services in England, for example, to be admitted the offender must be shown to pose a high risk, in combination with meeting other criteria (Howells *et al.* 2007). Risk assessment is discussed elsewhere in this volume (see Chapter 10 by Doyle and Dolan) so comment will be restricted here to only two issues that are relevant to how we conceptualise and treat aggression and violence.

The first relates to the need not to rely exclusively on dispositional, intrapersonal variables in the explanation of aggression. As briefly described above, the bias to over-attribute causality for observed behaviour to internal dispositional factors is well known within psychological theory and research, particularly that related to attributional processes. Although the extreme situationist position has generally been rejected in contemporary psychology, the importance of situational variation and of the interaction between the person and the situation is well recognised (Mischel 2004a, 2004b).

The need for dynamic risk measures (*risk state* as opposed to *risk status*) has been well described and analysed by Douglas and Skeem (2005). Exclusive reliance on static and trait variables in determining risk and criminogenic needs in forensic patients and offenders diminishes the clinical formulation of the case and the comprehensiveness and relevance of the therapeutic strategies adopted. This is not to deny that some causal factors for aggression are stable and enduring aspects of the person that are present from an early age (see, for example, the discussion by Hodgins of Type 1 aggressors in Chapter 16 of this volume).

As discussed by Douglas and Skeem (2005), risk state variables for aggression and violence are dynamic (capable of change) and comprise factors that can be demonstrated to affect the probability of an aggressive act occurring, with an emphasis on variation *over time* in violent behaviour. Thus an individual patient's aggression might be demonstrated to be more likely to occur, for example, when their internal state is one of emotional agitation, angry resentment, disinhibition through ingestion of alcohol and preoccupation with cognitions that they are being 'humiliated' by the provoking agent. Relevant state factors also lie within the violent situation (the behaviour of others, the setting, etc.).

As will be apparent, the focus on state risk is congruent with the functional analytic approach described above (Daffern and Howells 2002; Daffern *et al.* 2007). Douglas and Skeem (2005) have described assessment methodologies for state assessments. Ogloff and Daffern (in press), for example, have devised the DAST for 24-hour prediction of the probability of an aggressive incident, based on an ongoing assessment by nurses of the risk state of the individual patient. Douglas and Skeem's analysis of state risk variables plausibly related to violence includes those listed in Table 14.1.

Table 14.1 Proposed dynamic risk factors for violence

Impulsiveness
Negative affectivity
Anger
Negative mood
Psychosis
Antisocial attitudes
Substance use and related problems
Interpersonal relationships
Treatment alliance and adherence
Treatment and medication compliance
Treatment-provider alliance

Source: Douglas and Skeem (2005).

Treatment programmes for aggression and violence

Given that aggression is an important contributor to risk, it is unsurprising that treatment programmes for aggressive offenders have been developed around the world. It is surprising, however, that the treatment of aggression appears to lag behind the treatment of sex offenders (see Lockmuller *et al.* this volume, Chapter 18) in terms of the scale and extent of programme delivery, the degree of sophistication shown in the construction of programmes and in the extent of empirical evaluation of the effectiveness of the programmes. Given the high societal impact of violence it is puzzling that the treatment of violence has received so little attention, particularly in forensic mental health settings (Howells *et al.* 2004a).

Polaschek and colleagues in New Zealand have described, reviewed and critically evaluated violence programmes across the world (Polaschek 2006; Polaschek and Collie 2004; Polaschek and Reynolds 2001) as have Serin and Preston (2001) in the Canadian correctional setting. Polaschek's (2006) review describes the wide range of therapies that have been implemented, including intimate partner violence programmes, pro-feminist group programmes, cognitive-behavioural interventions, counselling approaches, anger management, aggression-replacement training, multisystemic therapy, psychopathy programmes and others. Such authors have generally concluded that, as yet, there is insufficient evidence available to determine the effectiveness of these programmes.

Treatment programmes with aggressive and violent individuals may face particular challenges which will need to be overcome if treatment is to be effective. Low *readiness for treatment* and consequent low treatment engagement, for example, have been identified as problematic in treatment interventions for these populations and such factors are likely to diminish treatment effects unless addressed (Howells and Day 2003, 2006; Howells, Day, Williamson *et al.* 2005; Ward *et al.* 2004).

Cognitive behavioural treatment for anger appears to be one of the most widely delivered interventions for violent offenders. While anger treatment is well grounded in theories of aggression and has convincing supportive evidence from meta-analytic reviews (Del Veccio and O'Leary 2004; DiGiuseppe and Tafrate 2003), it remains to be shown that it is an effective treatment for aggressive and violent offenders, as opposed to being effective for other populations with anger problems (Howells, Day, Williamson *et al.* 2005). The critical evaluation of the effectiveness of aggression and violence programmes, using adequate control groups and using randomised controlled trials or similar experimental designs (Davies *et al.* 2007) is a vital task for the future.

It could be argued that few, if any, of the treatments currently available address aggression and violence in the wide-ranging and comprehensive way that the considerable literature on aggression (some of which is reviewed in this chapter) suggests is necessary. The demonstrated heterogeneity of aggressive acts and actors, as indicated in this chapter, is also rarely addressed in devising therapeutic interventions. It is to be hoped that greater integration of aggression theory with treatment and rehabilitation practice and research, in both criminal justice and forensic mental health settings, will enhance our capacity to intervene effectively to reduce aggression and violence in the next decade.

Conclusions: the future

A recent comprehensive review of different types of violence within different populations by the WHO entitled *World Report on Violence and Health* concluded that:

Violence is often predictable and preventable ... certain factors appear to be strongly predictive of violence within given populations, even if direct causality is sometimes difficult to establish. These range from individual and family factors such as impulsivity, depression, poor monitoring and supervision of children, rigid gender roles and marital conflict to macro level factors, such as rapid changes in social structures and sharp economic downturns, bringing high unemployment and deteriorating public services. There are also local factors, specific to a given place and time, such as an increased presence of weapons or changing patterns of drug dealing in a particular neighbourhood. (WHO 2002)

In essence, we do not have a single model of violence causation; therefore, all models of violence reduction need to be considered in each individual case.

One important issue for the future is whether current psychiatric models and taxonomic systems adequately address problems of aggression and associated, cognitive, affective, self-regulatory and environmental factors. Without any doubt, acts of aggression and violence are major causes of distress for other people in the environment of perpetrators, and for society as a whole. Aggression and violence are also likely sources of distress for at least some perpetrators themselves, particularly those whose aggressive acts follow the breakdown of normal self-regulatory processes, particularly in relation to anger. In this sense (distress caused to others and to the self) aggression problems sometimes meet the underlying, fundamental criteria of psychiatric disorder in systems such as the DSM. At present, anger and aggression problems receive scant attention within the DSM and similar systems, though intermittent explosive disorder and some of the personality disorders, particularly borderline personality disorder, do include some reference to problems of aggression.

A second issue is the need for convergence of mental health and psychological/behavioural models (Howells *et al.* 2004a). It will be apparent to the reader that large sections of this chapter are devoted to the psychology of aggression, a field of academic and applied inquiry which is substantial, has a long history and has involved some of the most distinguished researchers and theoreticians in the history of psychology. Other sections of the chapter have been concerned with aggression in psychiatric disorders, in mental health institutions, personality disorders and in those requiring psychological or psychiatric treatment. These two literatures are still largely separate.

The reference point for mental health professionals and researchers in understanding aggression and violence appears often, arguably too often, to be what is known about disorders and mental illness rather than what is known about the causes, modification and prevention of aggression. The blame for this lack of mutual understanding and influence lies, arguably, in part with those working in the mainstream psychology of aggression, who have, perhaps, been slow to go beyond the laboratory walls and to observe aggression and violence at the clinical coalface. Conversely, mental health practitioners, despite disavowal of subscribing to the 'medical model', may be inclined to focus excessively on the accompanying disorder. Psychiatric and other clinical observations about aggression and violence in patients in mental health settings need to be plotted onto existing psychological models of aggression.

Selected further reading

The journal *Aggression and Violent Behavior* provides useful and scholarly reviews of what is known about aggression and violence. General principles of assessment and treatment are comprehensively discussed in C. R. Hollin, *Handbook of Offender Assessment and Treatment*. Chichester: Wiley, and in D. A. Andrews and J. Bonta, *Psychology of Criminal Conduct*, 3rd edn. Cincinnatti, OH: Anderson. Theories of aggression and of the role of emotion in aggression are discussed in detail in L. Berkowitz and E. Harmon-Jones, 'Towards an understanding of the determinants of anger', *Emotion*, 4: 107–30.

References

Anderson, C.A. and Bushman, B.J. (2002) 'Human aggression', *Annual Review of Psychology*, 53: 27–51.

Andrews, D.A. and Bonta, J. (2003) *Psychology of Criminal Conduct*, 3rd edn. Cincinnati, OH: Anderson.

Archer, J. (2000) 'Sex differences in aggression between heterosexual partners: a meta-analytic review', *Psychological Bulletin*, 126: 651–80.

Archer, J. (2004) 'Sex differences in aggression in real-world settings: a meta-analytic review', *Review of General Psychology*, 8: 291–322.

Bandura, A. (1977) *Social Learning Theory*. Englewood Cliffs, NJ: Prentice-Hall.

Baron, R.A. and Richardson, D.R. (1994) *Human Aggression*. New York: Plenum.

Barratt, E.S. and Slaughter, L. (1998) 'Defining, measuring and predicting impulsive aggression: a heuristic model', *Behavioral Sciences and the Law*, 16: 285–302.

Baumeister, R.F., Heatherton, T. F. and Tice, D.M. (1994) *Losing Control: How and Why People Fail at Self-Regulation*. San Diego, CA: Academic Press.

Bennett, S., Farrington, D.P. and Huesmann, L.R. (2005) 'Explaining gender differences in crime and violence: the importance of social cognitive skills', *Aggression and Violent Behavior*, 10: 263–88.

Berkowitz, L. (1993) *Aggression: Its Causes, Consequences and Control*. New York: McGraw-Hill.

Berkowitz, L. (1999) 'Anger', in T. Dalgleish and M. Power (eds), *Handbook of Cognition and Emotion*. Chichester: Wiley, pp. 411–28.

Berkowitz, L. and Harmon-Jones, E. (2004) 'Towards an understanding of the determinants of anger', *Emotion*, 4: 107–30.

Bettencourt, B.A., Talley, A., Benjamin, A.J. and Valentine, J. (2006) 'Personality and aggressive behaviour under provoking and neutral conditions: a meta-analytic review', *Psychological Bulletin*, 132: 751–77.

Blackburn, R. (1971) 'Personality types among abnormal homicides', *British Journal of Criminology*, 37: 166–78.

Blackburn, R. (1986) 'Patterns of personality deviation among violent offenders: replication and extension of an empirical taxonomy', *British Journal of Criminology*, 26: 254–69.

Blackburn, R. (1993) *The Psychology of Criminal Conduct*. Chichester: Wiley.

Blair, R.J.R. (2004) 'The roles of orbital frontal cortex in the modulation of antisocial behaviour', *Brain and Cognition*, 55: 198–208.

Blair, R.J.R. (2006) 'The emergence of psychopathy: implications for the neuropsychological approach to developmental disorders', *Cognition*, 101: 414–42.

Bushman, B.J. and Anderson, C.A. (2001) 'Is it time to pull the plug on the hostile versus instrumental aggression dichotomy?', *Psychological Review*, 108: 273–9.

Buss, A. (1961) *The Psychology of Aggression*. New York: Wiley.

Campbell, A. (2006) 'Sex differences in direct aggression: what are the psychological mediators?', *Aggression and Violent Behavior*, 11: 237–64.

Cornell, D. G., Warren, J., Hawk, G., Stafford, E., Oram, G. and Pine, D. (1996) 'Psychopathy in instrumental and reactive violent offenders', *Journal of Consulting and Clinical Psychology*, 64: 783–90.

Crick, N. R. and Dodge, K. A. (1996) 'Social information-processing mechanisms in reactive and proactive aggression', *Child Development*, 67: 993–1002.

Daffern, M. (2007) 'The predictive validity and practical utility of structured schemes used to assess risk for aggression in psychiatric inpatient settings', *Aggression and Violent Behavior*, 12: 116–30.

Daffern, M. and Howells, K. (2002) 'Psychiatric inpatient aggression: a review of structural and functional assessment approaches', *Aggression and Violent Behavior*, 7: 477–97.

Daffern, M. and Howells, K. (in press) 'The function of aggression in personality disordered patients', *Journal of Interpersonal Violence*.

Daffern, M., Howells, K. and Ogloff, J.R.P. (2007) 'What's the point? Towards a methodology for assessing the function of psychiatric inpatient aggression', *Behavior Research and Therapy*, 45: 101–11.

Davey, L., Day, A. and Howells, K. (2005) 'Anger, overcontrol and violent offending', *Aggression and Violent Behavior*, 10: 624–35.

Davidson, R.J., Putnam, K.M. and Larson, C. L. (2000) 'Dysfunction in the neural circuitry of emotion regulation: a possible prelude to violence', *Science*, 289: 591–4.

Davies, J., Howells, K. and Jones, L. (2007) 'Evaluating innovative treatments in forensic mental health: a case for single case methodology?', *Journal of Forensic Psychiatry and Psychology*, 18: 53–67.

Del Veccio, T. and O'Leary, D. (2004) 'Effectiveness of anger treatments for specific anger problems: a meta-analytic review', *Clinical Psychology Review*, 24: 15–34.

Department of Health (2003) 'Secretary of State Directions on work to tackle violence against staff or professionals who work in or provide services to the NHS'. London. Available from: http://www.cfsms.nhs.uk (last accessed 12 December 2006).

DiGiuseppi, R. and Tafrate, R.C. (2003) 'Anger treatment for adults: a meta-analytic review', *Clinical Psychology: Science and Practice*, 10: 70–84.

Dodge, K.A. and Coie, J. D. (1987) 'Social-information-processing factors in reactive and proactive aggression in children's peer groups', *Journal of Personality and Social Psychology*, 53: 1146–58.

Douglas, K.S. and Skeem, J.L. (2005) 'Violence risk assessment: getting specific about being dynamic', *Psychology, Public Policy and Law*, 11: 347–83.

Duhart, D.T. (2001) Violence in the Workplace, 1993–99, *Bureau of Justice Statistics: Special Report*. NCJ 190076. Washington, DC: US Department of Justice.

Gadon, L., Johnstone, L. and Cooke, D. (2006) 'Situational variables and institutional violence: a systematic review of the literature', *Clinical Psychology Review*, 26: 515–34.

Graves, K.N. (2006) 'Not always sugar and spice: expanding theoretical and functional explanations of why females aggress', *Aggression and Violent Behavior*, 11: 131–40.

Gross, J. (2002) 'Emotion regulation: affective, cognitive and social consequences', *Psychophysiology*, 39: 281–91.

Hare, R.D. (2006) 'Psychopathy: a clinical and forensic overview', *Psychiatric Clinics of North America*, 29: 709–24.

Haynes, S.N. and O'Brien, W.H. (1998) 'Functional analysis in behavioral therapy', *Clinical Psychology Review*, 10: 649–68.

Hazebroek, J., Howells, K. and Day, A. (2001) 'Cognitive appraisals associated with high trait anger', *Personality and Individual Differences*, 30: 31–45.

Henggeler, S.W., Schoenwald, S.K., Borduin, C.M., Rowland, M.D. and Cunningham, P. B. (1998) *Multisystemic Treatment of Antisocial Behaviour in Children and Adolescents*. New York: Guilford.

Hepburn, L.M. and Hemenway, D. (2004) 'Firearm availability and homicide: a review of the literature', *Aggression and Violent Behavior*, 9: 417–40.

Hollin, C.R. (ed.) (2001) *Handbook of Offender Assessment and Treatment*. Chichester: Wiley.

Hollin, C.R. and Palmer, E.J. (eds) (2006) *Offending Behaviour Programmes: Development, Application and Controversies*. Chichester: Wiley.

Howells, K. (1998) 'Cognitive-behavioural interventions for anger, aggression and violence', in N. Tarrier, A. Wells and G. Haddock (eds), *Treating Complex Cases: The Cognitive Behavioural Therapy Approach*. Chichester: Wiley, pp. 295–318.

Howells, K. (in press) 'Angry affect, aggression and personality disorder', in M. McMurran and R. Howard (eds), *Personality, Personality Disorder and Risk of Violence*. Chichester: Wiley.

Howells, K. and Day, A. (2003) 'Readiness for anger management: clinical and theoretical issues', *Clinical Psychology Review*, 23: 319–37.

Howells, K. and Day, A. (2006) 'Affective determinants of treatment engagement in violent offenders', *International Journal of Offender Therapy and Comparative Criminology*, 50: 174–86.

Howells, K., Day, A. and Davey, L. (2005) 'The future of offender rehabilitation', in D. Chappell and P. Wilson (eds), *Issues in Australian Crime and Criminal Justice*. Chatswood: LexisNexis Butterworths, pp. 419–34.

Howells, K., Day, A. and Thomas-Peter, B. (2004a) 'Treating violence: forensic mental health and criminological models compared', *Journal of Forensic Psychiatry and Psychology*, 15 (3): 391–406.

Howells, K., Day, A. and Wright, S. (2004b) 'Affect, emotions and sex offending', *Psychology, Crime and Law*, 10: 179–95.

Howells, K., Krishnan, G. and Daffern, M. (2007) 'Challenges in the treatment of DSPD', *Advances in Psychiatric Treatment*, 13: 325–32.

Howells, K., Day, A., Williamson, P., Bubner, S., Jauncey, S., Parker, A. and Heseltine, K. (2005) 'Brief anger management programs with offenders: outcomes and predictors of change', *Journal of Forensic Psychiatry and Psychology*, 16: 296–311.

Huesmann, L.R. and Miller, L.S. (1994) 'Long-term effects of repeated exposure to media violence in childhood', in L.R. Huesmann (ed.), *Aggressive Behavior: Current Perspectives*. New York: Plenum, pp. 153–86.

Joliffe, D. and Farrington, D. P. (2004) 'Empathy and offending: a systematic review and meta-analysis', *Aggression and Violent Behavior*, 9: 441–76.

Kenny, D.T and Press, A.L. (2006) 'Violence classifications and their impact on observed relationships with key factors in young offenders', *Psychology, Public Policy and Law*, 12: 86–105.

Lang, R., Holden, R., Langevin, R., Pugh, G. and Wu, R. (1987) 'Personality and criminality in violent offenders', *Journal of Interpersonal Violence*, 2: 179–95.

McCrae, R.R. and Costa, P.T. (1987) 'Validation of the five factor model of personality across instruments and observers', *Journal of Personality and Social Psychology*, 52: 81–90.

McEllistrem, J.E. (2004) 'Affective and predatory violence: a bimodal classification system of human aggression and violence', *Aggression and Violent Behavior*, 10: 1–30.

McGuire, J. (ed.) (2002) *Offender Rehabilitation and Treatment: Effective Programmes and Policies to Reduce Re-offending*. Chichester: Wiley.

McGuire, J. (2004) 'Commentary: promising answers and the next generation of questions', *Psychology, Crime and Law*, 10: 335–45.

Megargee, E. (1966) 'Undercontrolled and overcontrolled personality types in extreme antisocial aggression', *Psychological Monographs*, 80: 1–116.

Meloy, J.R. (2006) 'Empirical basis and forensic application of affective and predatory violence', *Australian and New Zealand Journal of Psychiatry*, 40: 539–47.

Milovchevich, D., Howells, K., Drew, N. and Day, A. (2001) 'Sex and gender role differences in anger: an Australian community study', *Personality and Individual Differences*, 31: 117–27.

Mischel, W. (1968) *Personality and Assessment*. New York: Wiley.

Mischel, W. (2004a) Towards an integrative science of the person', *Annual Review of Psychology*, 55: 1–22.

Mischel, W. (2004b) 'Towards an integrative model for CBT: encompassing behaviour, cognition, affect and process', *Behavior Therapy*, 35: 185–203.

Mohr, P., Howells, K., Gerace, A., Day, A. and Wharton, M. (2007) 'The role of perspective taking in anger arousal', *Personality and Individual Differences*, 43: 507–18.

Monahan, J., Steadman, H. J. and Silver, E. (2001) *Rethinking Risk Assessment: The MacArthur Study of Mental Disorder and Violence*. New York: Oxford University Press.

Moyer, K.E. (1968) 'Kinds of aggression and their physiological basis', *Communications in Behavioral Biology*, 2: 65–87.

National Audit Office (2003) *A Safer Place to Work: Protecting NHS Hospital and Ambulance Staff from Violence and Aggression*. Report by the Controller and Auditor General HC 527, Session 2002–2003: 27 March.

Novaco, R.W. (1997) 'Remediating anger and aggression with violent offenders', *Legal and Criminological Psychology*, 2: 77–88.

Novaco, R.W. and Welsh, W.N. (1989) 'Anger disturbances: cognitive mediation and clinical prescription', in K. Howells and C.R. Hollin (eds), *Clinical Approaches to Violence*. Chichester: Wiley.

Novaco, R. W., Ramm, M. and Black, L. (2001) 'Anger treatment with offenders', in C. R. Hollin (ed.), *Handbook of Offender Assessment and Treatment*. Chichester: Wiley.

Ogloff, J.R.P. and Daffern, M. (in press) 'The assessment of risk for inpatient aggression in psychiatric inpatients: introducing the Dynamic Appraisal of Situational Aggression: Inpatient Version', *Behavioral Sciences and the Law*.

Ortony, A., Clore, G.L. and Collins, A. (1988) *The Cognitive Structure of Emotions*. New York: Cambridge University Press.

Parrott, D.J. and Giancola, P.R. (2006) 'Addressing "the criterion problem" in the assessment of aggressive behaviour: development of a new taxonomic system', *Aggression and Violent Behavior*, 11: 280–99.

Patrick, C. J. (2006) 'Back to the future: Cleckley as a guide to the next generation of psychopathy research', in C. J. Patrick (ed.), *Handbook of Psychopathy*. New York: Guilford Press, pp. 605–17.

Polaschek, D.L.L. (2006) 'Violent offender programmes: concept, theory and practice', in C.R. Hollin and E.J. Palmer (eds), *Offending Behaviour Programmes: Development, Application and Controversies*. Chichester: Wiley, pp. 113–54.

Polaschek, D.L.L. and Collie, R.M. (2004) 'Rehabilitating serious violent adult offenders: an empirical and theoretical stocktake', *Psychology, Crime and Law*, 10: 321–34.

Polaschek, D.L.L. and Reynolds, N. (2001) 'Violent offenders: assessment and treatment', in C.R. Hollin (ed.), *Handbook of Offender Assessment and Treatment*. Chichester: Wiley, pp. 415–31.

Raine, A. (2002) 'Biosocial studies of antisocial and violent behaviour in children and adults: a review', *Journal of Abnormal Child Psychology*, 30: 311–26.

Raine, A., Buchsbaum, M. and Lacasse, L. (1997) 'Brain abnormalities in murderers indicated by positron emission tomography', *Biological Psychiatry*, 42: 495–508.

Raine, A., Meloy, J.R., Bihrie, S., Stoddard, J. and Buchbaum, M.S. (1998) 'Reduced prefrontal and increased subcortical brain functioning assessed using positron emission tomography in predatory and affective murderers', *Behavioural Sciences and the Law*, 16: 319–32.

Savage, J. (2004) 'Does viewing violent media really cause criminal violence? A methodological review', *Aggression and Violent Behavior*, 10: 99–128.

Serin, R.C. and Preston, D.L. (2001) 'Designing, implementing and managing treatment programs for violent offenders', in G.A. Bernfeld, D.P. Farrington and A.W. Leschied (eds), *Offender Rehabilitation in Practice*. Chichester: John Wiley & Sons.

Skeem, J.L., Miller, J.D., Mulvey, E., Tiemann, J. and Monahan, J. (2005) 'Using a Five-Factor lens to explore the relation between personality traits and violence in psychiatric patients', *Journal of Consulting and Clinical Psychology*, 73 (3): 454–65.

Smith, P. and Waterman, M. (2003) 'Processing bias for aggression words in forensic and non-forensic samples', *Cognition and Emotion*, 17: 681–701.

Smith, P. and Waterman, M. (2004) 'Role of experience in processing bias for aggressive words in forensic and non-forensic populations', *Aggressive Behavior*, 30: 105–22.

Sturmey, P. (1996) *Functional Analysis in Clinical Psychology*. Chichester: Wiley.

Tsytsarev, S. and Grodnitsky, G. (1995) 'Anger and criminality', in H. Kassinove (ed.), *Anger Disorders*. Philadelphia: Taylor & Francis, pp. 91–108.

Wales Audit Office (2005) *Protecting NHS Trust Staff from Violence and Aggression*. Wales Audit Office.

Wang, E.W. and Diamond, P.M. (1999) 'Empirically identifying factors related to violence risk in corrections', *Behavioral Sciences and the Law*, 17: 377–99.

Ward, T., Day, A., Howells, K. and Birgden, A. (2004) 'The multifactor offender readiness model', *Aggression and Violent Behavior*, 9: 645–73.

Ward, T., Mann, R. E. and Gannon, T. A. (2006) 'The good lives model of offender rehabilitation: clinical implications', *Aggression and Violent Behavior*, 11: 87–107.

WHO (2002) *World Report on Violence and Health*. Available from: http://www.who.int/violence_injury_prevention/violence/world_report/en/full_en.pdf (last accessed 12 December 2006).

Wilkinson, D.L. and Hamerschlag, S.J. (2005) 'Situational determinants in intimate partner violence', *Aggression and Violent Behavior*, 10: 333–61.

Chapter 15

Personality disorders

Mary McMurran

Introduction

Over recent years, the management and treatment of people with personality disorders has become a major issue in both non-forensic and forensic mental health services. In 1998, Michael Stone was convicted of murdering Dr Lin Russell and her 6-year-old daughter, Megan, and attempting to murder Megan's 9-year-old sister, Josie.[1] During his trial it was revealed that he had sought help from a forensic mental health service, but help was not forthcoming because Stone was diagnosed as suffering from an untreatable personality disorder. Although Stone could have been treated as an outpatient, under mental health legislation a person suffering from a personality disorder needs to be considered treatable to permit admission to hospital.

Recognising the possibility that had Stone received treatment he may not have committed these attacks, a number of changes were initiated in service provision for people with personality disorders. First, non-forensic mental health services were seen as points of early intervention for people with personality disorders, potentially preventing risk of harm by otherwise untreated patients. In a document entitled *Personality Disorder: No Longer a Diagnosis of Exclusion* (National Institute of Mental Health for England 2003), general mental health services were instructed not to exclude people with personality disorders from treatment, but rather to develop services for this particular group.

Second, forensic mental health services, jointly with the Home Office, developed new services for dangerous offenders with severe personality disorders (Department of Health and Home Office 1999, 2000b). Special units have been built in secure psychiatric hospitals and prisons in which this group of personality disordered offenders are now assessed and treated. These offenders do not have to volunteer for this treatment; they may be sent to these services to have their motivation worked upon.

Finally, there were changes made to mental health legislation in England and Wales (Department of Health and Home Office, 2000a). Among those changes, two are of specific relevance here. The first was the removal of the need for treatability to be proven before people with mental disorder may be detained, thus permitting the detention of people with untreatable personality disorders. Second, the treatment plan required under the new legislation may be formulated to address risk, even if the underlying disorder is not directly treated, which can be interpreted as permitting the detention of people with personality disorders for risk management (Fennell 2001). Widespread resistance, particularly on the grounds that patients' rights to protection against arbitrary detention were sacrificed to the public safety agenda (Fennell 2005), led to delays but there was very little revision of the contentious aspects of the Bill which received Royal Assent in summer 2007.

The costs involved in attempts to change mental health legislation and in developing services for 'dangerous and severely personality disordered offenders' (DSPD) have been exorbitant. Start-up costs for DSPD services were £126 million over a three-year period, with an estimated annual cost of between £130,000 and £180,000 per patient thereafter (Barrett *et al.* 2005; Batty 2002). It would be reasonable to assume that this investment was directed at a mental health problem that clinicians could reliably diagnose and treat. This is, however, far from being the case. Diagnoses of personality disorders are of dubious validity, show poor reliability and are of limited utility in that they rarely indicate what treatments might be effective. Not surprisingly, there are critics of the entire concept of personality disorders. The aims of this chapter are to elucidate what is meant by personality disorder, examine how personality disorders are assessed and identify effective treatments. The emphasis here is on offenders who are diagnosed as suffering from personality disorder, and so the relevance of personality disorder to offenders and their offending will be examined.

Personality disorder, offenders and offending

What is personality disorder?

Personality disorders are psychiatric conditions described in the two major diagnostic classification systems, the current versions of which are the Diagnostic and Statistical Manual of Mental Disorders IV (DSM-IV: American Psychiatric Association 1994, 2000), in which personality disorders are contained within Axis II,[2] and the International Classification of Diseases 10 (ICD-10: World Health Organisation 1992). DSM-IV defines personality disorder as:

> An enduring pattern of inner experience and behaviour that deviates markedly from the expectations of the individual's culture, is pervasive and inflexible, has an onset in adolescence or early adulthood, is stable over time, and leads to distress or impairment. (American Psychiatric Association 1994: 629)

ICD-10 defines personality disorder as:

> ... deeply ingrained and enduring behaviour patterns, manifesting themselves as inflexible responses to a broad range of personal and social situations. They represent either extreme or significant deviations from the way the average individual in a given culture perceives, thinks, feels, and particularly relates to others. Such behaviour patterns tend to be stable and to encompass multiple domains of behaviour and psychological functioning. They are frequently, but not always, associated with various degrees of subjective distress and problems in social functioning and performance. (World Health Organisation 1992: 200)

Table 15.1 DSM-IV and ICD-10 personality disorders

DSM-IV	ICD-10
Cluster A	
Paranoid	Paranoid
Distrust; suspiciousness	Sensitivity; suspiciousness
Schizoid	Schizoid
Socially and emotionally detached	Emotionally cold and detached
Schizotypal	No equivalent
Social and interpersonal deficits; cognitive or perceptual distortions	
Cluster B	
Antisocial	Dissocial
Violation of the rights of others	Callous disregard of others; irresponsibility; irritability
Borderline	Emotionally unstable
Instability of relationships, self-image, and mood	(a) Borderline – Unclear self-image; intense, unstable relationships
	(b) Impulsive – Inability to control anger; quarrelsome; unpredictable
Histrionic	Histrionic
Excessive emotionality and attention-seeking	Dramatic; egocentric; manipulative
Narcissistic	No equivalent
Grandiose; lack of empathy; need for admiration	
Cluster C	
Avoidant	Anxious
Socially inhibited; feelings of inadequacy; hypersensitivity	Tense; self-conscious; hypersensitive
Dependent	Dependent
Clinging; submissive	Subordinates personal needs; needs constant reassurance
Obsessive-compulsive	Anankastic
Perfectionist; inflexible	Indecisive; pedantic; rigid
Personality disorder not otherwise specified (NOS)	Personality disorder, unspecified
	This is undefined in ICD-10, although it is said to include character neurosis NOS and pathological personality NOS
PDNOS 1	Mixed personality disorders
Traits of several different personality disorders are present but the criteria are not met for any single disorder	Features of several disorders with no predominant set of symptoms
PDNOS 2	Other specific personality disorders
The general criteria for personality disorder are met but the person has a disorder that is not included in the list (e.g., passive-aggressive)	Includes eccentric, *haltlose* (i.e., drifting, aimless and irresponsible lifestyle), immature, narcissistic, passive-aggressive, and psycho-neurotic

The personality disorders are listed in Table 15.1, with a brief description of the key features of each. In DSM, disorders that commonly co-occur are grouped in three clusters: Cluster A – odd or eccentric (paranoid, schizoid and schizotypal); Cluster B – dramatic or flamboyant (antisocial, borderline, histrionic and narcissistic); and Cluster C – anxious or fearful (avoidant, dependent and obsessive-compulsive).

The personality disorders of DSM and ICD are not an exhaustive list but are a narrow group compared with the personalities generally recognisable in people at large and describe maladaptive conditions that are of interest to clinicians (Stone 1993). If an individual does not fit those maladaptive conditions specifically listed in DSM and ICD, a diagnosis is still possible using the categories 'personality disorder not otherwise specified (PDNOS)', 'mixed' and 'other', a practice that Tyrer (2006: 20) calls the 'ultimate diagnostic dissociation'. Clinicians and researchers have considerable latitude in setting criteria for these unspecified disorders yet their use is by no means uncommon (Verheul and Widiger 2004).

Having defined personality disorder in general, definitions of 'personality disordered offenders' now need to be clarified.

Personality disordered offenders

Having a psychiatric diagnosis of personality disorder can have medico-legal significance in that an offender may thus be diverted from the criminal justice system to mental health services. In England and Wales, this requires that an offender is legally classified as suffering from 'psychopathic disorder' under the terms of the Mental Health Act 1983. The Act defines psychopathic disorder as 'a persistent disorder or disability of mind which results in abnormally aggressive or seriously irresponsible conduct'.

A 'persistent disorder or disability of mind' in this context may be taken to mean a personality disorder, although this is an interpretation of the phrase, not an explicit legal requirement. Somewhat confusingly, the medico-legal term 'psychopathic disorder' is not the same as 'psychopathy', which is a particular type of personality that will be described later. To avoid confusion, the former will be referred to as legal psychopathy and the latter as clinical psychopathy.

Providing the personality disorder is treatable (but see proposed changes mentioned earlier), and depending upon the perceived level of risk of harm to self or others, the person legally classified as suffering from psychopathic disorder may be detained involuntarily in hospital for treatment or treated in the community by virtue of a compulsory treatment order. However, most personality disordered offenders are not legally classified or diagnosed as personality disordered and are found in criminal justice settings, such as prison and probation services.

People legally classified as suffering from psychopathic disorder are a heterogeneous group who may be diagnosed with any one or more of the personality disorders in DSM-IV or ICD-10. The complete range of personality disorders has been shown in patients in maximum-security psychiatric hospitals and in prisoners (Coid 1992; Coid et al.1999; Dolan and Mitchell 1994; Reiss et al. 1996; Singleton et al. 1998).

Clinical psychopathy

There is no personality disorder called 'psychopathy' in the major diagnostic systems. ICD-10 lists dissocial personality disorder, with criteria that are largely those traits originally identified by Cleckley (1941) as defining psychopathy, namely lack of guilt, lack of anxiety, inability to learn from punishment, impoverished emotions, inability to form lasting emotional ties, egocentricity and superficial charm. DSM-IV lists antisocial personality disorder, based upon more behavioural criteria, namely law-breaking, recklessness and irresponsibility.

Hare (1991) incorporated both personality traits and behavioural criteria in his definition of psychopathy, and these form the basis of the Psychopathy Checklist – Revised[3] (PCL-R). The PCL-R consists of 20 items (see Table 15.2) which are scored from interview, official records and corroborative checks with significant others. Each item is scored absent (0), somewhat applicable (1) or definitely applicable (2), with the resultant total score ranging from 0 to 40, where a higher score indicates a greater degree of psychopathy. Hare (1991, 2003) recommends a cut-off point of 30 for determining psychopathy, although other cut-offs may be appropriate in different cultures (Cooke 1995). The use of cut-offs to diagnose psychopathy implies that the condition is a taxon, that is a distinct class whose members differ in some discrete way from non-members. The dichotomous approach leads to the identification of 'the psychopath', with its pejorative connotations, rather than an individual with a certain degree of psychopathic traits. There is currently insufficient evidence to conclude that psychopathy is a taxon, and there is evidence of value in scoring psychopathy on a continuum.

Table 15.2 Items of Hare's (1991) Psychopathy Checklist – Revised

1.	Glibness/superficial charm
2.	Grandiose sense of self-worth
3.	Need for stimulation/proneness to boredom
4.	Pathological lying
5.	Conning/manipulative
6.	Lack of remorse or guilt
7.	Shallow affect
8.	Callous/lack of empathy
10.	Parasitic lifestyle
11.	Poor behavioural controls
12.	Promiscuous sexual behaviour
13.	Early behaviour problems
14.	Lack of realistic long-term goals
15.	Impulsivity
16.	Irresponsibility
17.	Failure to accept responsibility for actions
18.	Many short-term marital relationships
19.	Juvenile delinquency
20.	Revocation of conditional release
21.	Criminal versatility

Within the PCL-R, two factors were originally identified: Factor 1 – affective and interpersonal characteristics such as grandiosity, selfishness and callousness; and Factor 2 – an antisocial, irresponsible and parasitic lifestyle (Hare *et al.* 1990). More recent analyses by Cooke and Michie (2001) indicated that seven items relating to criminality and disapproved behaviours could be removed to leave a purer personality model of psychopathy. They found a superordinate construct of psychopathy, with three constituent factors: (1) arrogant and deceitful interpersonal style; (2) deficient affective experience; and (3) impulsive and irresponsible behavioural style. However, excluding antisocial behaviour from the construct of psychopathy may be to exclude an important dimension, and others favour retaining this factor on both theoretical and statistical grounds (Hare 2003; Vitacco *et al.* 2005).

What is 'severe' personality disorder?

Given that dangerous offenders may be assessed and treated in specialist services for those with severe personality disorder, one would expect there to be a clear definition of what 'severe' means in this respect. There is, in fact, no agreement about what severe personality disorder is.

Tyrer and Johnson (1996) examined a graded system for classifying the severity of personality disorder based upon the number of conditions diagnosed and whether or not these were from the same cluster. This system predicted symptoms and outcomes in 163 psychiatric patients in treatment: patients with complex personality disorders had the highest level of symptoms and improved least. This system is shown in Table 15.3, with 'severe' personality disorder added as an extra to this empirically derived list (Tyrer 2006) and defined as two or more personality disorders from different clusters, one of which is Cluster B, that create 'gross societal disturbance' (Royal College of Psychiatrists 1999).

Table 15.3 Classification of severity of personality disorder (after Tyrer 2006)

Level	Classification	Criteria
0	No personality disorder	Does not meet criteria for personality disorder
1	Personality difficulty	Meets sub-threshold criteria for one or more personality disorders
2	Simple personality disorder	One or more personality disorders within one cluster
3	Complex personality disorder	Two or more personality disorders from different clusters
4	Severe personality disorder	Two or more personality disorders from different clusters (including B) plus gross societal disturbance

Source: after Tyrer (2006).

Including 'gross societal disturbance' as a defining feature of severe personality disorder highlights the fact that it is a category designed for troublesome people. A severe personality disorder label thus permits the coercion of troublesome people into treatment, with the primary objective of public protection. For many mental health professionals this is at odds with their professional obligation to work in the best interests of their patients.

Prevalence of personality disorders

In a recent study of a representative sample of the UK general population ($N = 626$), using a structured clinical interview, the prevalence of personality disorder was identified as 4.4 per cent, with men more likely to have a personality disorder (5.4 per cent) than women (3.4 per cent) (Coid *et al.* 2006). Obsessive-compulsive personality disorder was the most common disorder found in the general population.

Compared with the general population, the prevalence of any personality disorder in prisoners is considerably higher. Using a structured interview with 505 prisoners in England and Wales, Singleton *et al.* (1998) identified personality disorders in 78 per cent of remanded males, 64 per cent of sentenced males and 50 per cent of women prisoners. antisocial, paranoid and borderline personality disorders were most common. A review of 28 prison surveys that assessed personality disorder, representing a total of 13,844 prisoners, showed that 65 per cent of men were diagnosable with any personality disorder and 47 per cent with antisocial personality disorder, with the figures for women being 42 per cent and 21 per cent respectively (Fazel and Danesh 2002).

In the late 1990s, the proportion of patients in UK secure hospitals classified as having psychopathic disorder was around 41 per cent (Taylor *et al.* 1998), and the admission rate was decreasing (Jamieson *et al.* 2000). This may now be on the increase with the new special units for dangerous people with severe personality disorder in Rampton and Broadmoor Hospitals, each with 70 places (DSPD Programme 2005).

The prevalence of psychopathy has been identified in a sample of 728 adult male prisoners in England and Wales as 4.5 per cent with a PCL-R score of 30 or more, and 13 per cent with a score of 25 or more, the latter being the statistically derived European cut-off (Hare *et al.* 2000). It is worth emphasising that psychopathy is not equivalent to antisocial personality disorder. While most offenders who meet the criteria for psychopathy will likely also meet the criteria for antisocial personality disorder, the opposite is not true: nowhere near all of those who meet the criteria for antisocial personality disorder will meet the criteria for psychopathy.

Personality disorder and offending

Compared with mentally ill offenders, those classified as psychopathically disordered are more likely to reoffend after discharge from hospital (Bailey and MacCulloch 1992; Steels *et al.* 1998). Jamieson and Taylor (2004) list methodological problems with reconviction studies of mentally disordered offenders in that discharged patients may not be in the community where they are actually at risk of offending, follow-up periods are often short, and the figure reported is often the proportion of a sample that reoffends rather than the more useful calculation of time to reconviction. In their 12-year follow-up of a cohort of 204 patients discharged from UK high-security hospitals in 1984, Jamieson and Taylor (2004) found that 38 per cent were reconvicted, 26 per cent for a serious offence. The odds of committing a serious offence were seven times higher for those classified as psychopathically disordered compared with those classified as mentally ill. The time to reconviction after discharge did not differ by legal classification.

In their general population sample, Coid *et al.* (2006) noted that people with Cluster B disorders, compared to those without, were ten times more likely to have had a criminal conviction and almost eight times more likely to have spent time in prison. This elevation of criminal risk was not evident for those with Cluster A and C disorders.

Among all the DSM personality disorders, Hiscoke *et al.* (2003) identified offenders with antisocial, borderline and schizoid personality disorders as most likely to be reconvicted of a violent crime. Coid *et al.* (1999) identified those with antisocial personality disorder as versatile across the offending spectrum (violence, sex, acquisitive and damage), those with borderline personality disorder specialising in arson and criminal damage (as well as self-harm) and the others primarily committing violent offences.

Concerning clinical psychopathy, a meta-analysis of studies using the PCL-R showed that offenders defined as psychopaths were three times more likely than non-psychopaths to commit further offences and about four times more likely to commit further violent offences (Hemphill *et al.* 1998). Correlations between Factor 2 and general recidivism were stronger than for Factor 1, and both factors correlated equally with violent recidivism. Personality disorder diagnoses were not as accurate as PCL-R scores at predicting recidivism.

Hare *et al.* (2000) followed up 278 offenders for two years after release from prisons in England and Wales, and compared high and low PCL-R scorers, using a cut-off of 25. Of the high scorers, the reconviction rate was 82 per cent for general offences and 38 per cent for violent offences, with the rates for low PCL-R scorers being 40 per cent and 3 per cent respectively, these differences being highly significant.

Personality disorder diagnosis

Mention has already been made about problems with personality diagnoses and these will be elucidated here.

Categorical diagnosis

DSM-IV and ICD-10 personality disorders are diagnosed categorically; that is a person has or does not have a diagnosis. In DSM-IV, there is a statement that 'a categorical approach to classification works best when all members of a diagnostic class are homogeneous, when there are clear boundaries between classes, and when the different classes are mutually exclusive' (p. xxii). In personality diagnoses, none of these pertain.

Homogeneity is impossible because for any diagnosis a set of criteria is provided, with a diagnosis requiring a positive identification of only a subset of these criteria (i.e. diagnoses are polythetic). Arithmetically, there are 247 ways of meeting the criteria for borderline personality disorder, and 848 ways of meeting the antisocial personality disorder criteria (Arntz 1999; Widiger and Trull 1994). Hence, people with the same diagnosis may have very different problem profiles.

There is overlap in the criteria for personality disorders, hence boundaries are unclear and classes are not mutually exclusive. For example, aggression is diagnostic of both antisocial and borderline personality disorders, and hostility defines eight other disorders (Widiger and Trull 1994). Furthermore, there is overlap between criteria for personality disorders and other psychiatric conditions. For example, schizotypal personality disorder and Axis I psychotic disorders share diagnostic commonalities (odd beliefs, disorganised speech), as do borderline personality disorder and Axis I biopolar disorder (affective dysregulation). The result of this is that there is considerable comorbidity or co-occurrence of different personality disorders with each other and of personality disorders with major mental disorders. This may reflect some connection among co-occurring disorders, or there may be diagnostic overlap because of a flaw in the diagnostic system (Livesley 1998).

Comorbid or co-occurring disorders

Multiple personality disorders are frequently observed. Of those in a general population sample who were diagnosed as suffering from personality disorder, the mean number of personality disorders was 1.92, with 53.5 per cent having one disorder, 21.6 per cent two disorders, 11.4 per cent three disorders and 14 per cent between four and eight diagnoses (Coid et al. 2006). Coid (1992) identified an average of almost three personality disorders per person for men legally classified as psychopathically disordered, and almost four for women.

A high prevalence of Axis I disorders was identified in the lifetime of personality disorder patients admitted to secure psychiatric care in England and Wales (Coid et al. 1999). Comorbidity was particularly evident in relation to substance misuse disorders, with rates of comorbid depression also being high. Specific personality disorder diagnoses were differentially related to Axis I disorders, with antisocial personality disorder strongly associated with substance misuse and organic syndromes; borderline personality disorder with mania, depression, epilepsy and substance misuse; paranoid with brief psychosis and substance misuse; and dependent with depression and anxiety. Similar comorbidities were found in prisoners (Singleton et al. 1998). Interestingly, Coid et al. (2006) found that people with Cluster A and B personality disorders who sought help from mental health services did so for their Axis I disorders rather than their personality disorders, and they concluded that the development of personality disorder treatment services may not be as necessary as the government thinks.

There is also evidence that a substantial number of people with mental illness also have personality disorders. In a community sample, 28 per cent were identified as having comorbid personality disorder, with all disorders represented (Moran et al. 2003). In a survey of special hospital patients, Taylor et al. (1998) found that over one quarter of those with schizophrenia also had a personality disorder. The situation is similar for prisoners, where evidence of a functional psychosis increased the odds of having a personality disorder (Singleton et al. 1998). A small percentage of learning disabled offenders may also have a personality disorder (Taylor et al. 1998).

There are clinical implications of comorbidity, as Blackburn (2000) noted. First, because comorbidity is common, forensic mental health clinicians may be well advised always at least to screen all patients (including those with mental illness and learning disability) for all personality disorders. Second, treatments should take into account multiple diagnoses. This is important not only so that treatment for personality problems can be introduced, but also because personality disorder is widely held to influence the course of and complicate the treatment of other disorders (Bloom and Wilson 2000; Verheul *et al.* 1998). Where there are multiple diagnoses, clinicians appear to prioritise one disorder over another (Westen 1997) and research into how this works would be beneficial. Finally, there are implications in relation to interpreting research on personality disorders when 'pure' cases of any personality disorder are a rarity.

Validity of personality disorder diagnoses

The issues mentioned above call into question the validity of personality diagnoses. Livesley (2001) commented on the shortcomings of diagnostic categories in relation to a number of types of validity. Content validity is poor, in that the criteria for a diagnostic category often do not adequately describe what clinicians consider to be important in a disorder. Construct validity is poor in that diagnoses do not produce homogeneous groups (internal validity) nor do they produce groups that are distinct from other diagnostic groups (external validity). Diagnoses also have poor predictive validity in terms of aetiology and course. Because of all these validity problems, personality disorder diagnoses have very little clinical utility in terms of identifying effective treatments.

Reliability of personality disorder diagnosis

Descriptions of personality disorders in DSM and ICD consist of a mixture of both psychological traits and behaviour, leading to doubt as to whether diagnoses identify 'true' personality disorders (i.e. traits) or social deviance (i.e. behaviour). The reliability of clinical diagnoses of personality disorders has been improved by focusing on behaviours, with the diagnosis of antisocial personality disorder being particularly reliable (Stone 1993). However, reliance on observable behaviour as a means of identifying a personality disorder may sacrifice construct validity.

Psychiatrists may diagnose personality disorders by clinical interview, with reference to the relevant DSM or ICD criteria. This method shows poor inter-rater reliability for specific diagnoses, although agreement about the presence or absence of any personality disorder is somewhat higher (Zimmerman 1994). Reliability of diagnosis is improved by using structured interviews with strict scoring guidelines. These interview schedules present questions matching the diagnostic criteria contained in DSM or ICD and provide scoring systems that identify a diagnosis or otherwise. Interview schedules show improved test-retest reliability and inter-rater reliability over clinical diagnosis, yet this is still only moderately good (Zimmerman 1994). There is good agreement between interview schedules on continuous scores, yet diagnostic concordance is only moderate, and so none should be taken as superior (van Elzen and Emmelkamp 1996).

A complete review of these interview schedules is beyond the scope of this chapter. The most commonly used are listed in Table 15.4. In addition, two major self-report measures of personality are listed. These are recommended for use prior to lengthy interviews to help focus on those disorders that are likely to need comprehensive assessment (Widiger and Samuel 2005).

Table 15.4 Structured diagnostic assessments

Assessment	Authors	Publisher	DSM/ICD
Interview schedules			
International Personality Disorder Examination (IPDE)	Loranger (1997)	Psychological Assessment Resources	DSM-IV/ICD-10
Personality Assessment Schedule-I	Tyrer (2000)	Author	ICD-10
Personality Disorder Interview-IV	Widiger *et al.* (2005)	Psychological Assessment Resources	DSM-IV
Structured Clinical Interview for DSM-IV Axis II Personality Disorders (SCID-II)	First *et al.* (1997)	American Psychiatric Publishing	DSM-IV
Structured Interview for DSM-IV Personality (SIDP-IV)	Pfohl *et al.* (1997)	American Psychiatric Publishing	DSM-IV
Self report measures			
Millon Clinical Multi-Axial Inventory-III (MCMI-III)	Millon *et al.* (1994)	Multi-Health Systems, Inc.	Does not map onto DSM or ICD
Minnesota Multiphasic Personality Inventory-2 (MMPI-2)	Hathaway and McKinley (1989)	Multi-Health Systems, Inc.	Does not map onto DSM or ICD

Despite what has just been said about clinical versus structured interviews, a survey of UK forensic services relating to their admission of personality disordered offenders found that less than half conducted a formal personality assessment, and of those that did, the instruments used in the assessment varied widely, addressing personality structure, general health and specific psychological problems such as anger and self-esteem (Milton 2000). The use of structured diagnostic instruments was rare, and Milton (2000) recommends that clinicians should use them.

These shortcomings raise the question of whether there is any point at all in categorical personality disorder diagnosis, or if the whole enterprise is but a fool's errand.

Alternative models of personality disorder diagnosis

Personality disorder categories are not firmly grounded in theory, nor are they empirically based (Livesley 1998). Some critics say that personality disorder categories are so flawed that the best option is to abolish them and start afresh, but most pragmatists recognise that so much has been invested in them that they are very likely here to stay (Blackburn 2000; Livesley 1998). The approach now gathering momentum, and predicted as the basis of DSM-V and ICD-11, is a dimensional approach. But which dimensions should be used?

A prototype approach to personality disorder diagnosis

Shedler and Westen (2004) studied how clinicians conceptualise personality disorders using the Shedler-Westen Assessment Procedure-200 (SWAP-200). This consists of 200 personality descriptors that the clinician sorts into eight categories, 0 for not at all like the patient up to 7 which is highly like the patient, in a fixed distribution, where half the items must be placed in the least like category and ever fewer in each category ending with eight items in the most like category. They found that clinicians need more than the eight or nine items given in DSM-IV adequately to describe a personality disorder, with 15 to 20 items more accurately capturing the essence of any such disorder. The items that are extra to DSM usually relate to inner experience, these being the very attributes that DSM avoids in efforts to improve reliability and minimise overlap. Shedler and Westen (2004) suggest that providing a larger number of descriptors accords more with the clinical reality of a disorder. Although some disorders share core features, permitting clinicians to judge a patient's condition by looking at the whole picture rather than recording the presence or absence of a number of criteria actually reduces overlap.

In this manner, Shedler and Westen (2004) elicited hypothetical prototypes, that is the pure form of a disorder, from experienced clinicians. Descriptions of the prototype are presented narratively and the clinician rates how closely the patient in question fits the prototype on a scale of 1 to 5, where 1 is no match and 5 is a prototypical case, giving both a dimensional score and a categorical diagnosis (score 4 or 5). In comparison with categorical diagnoses, the prototype matching method showed less comorbidity and was rated easier to use by clinicians. This method was as good as categorical diagnoses at predicting a patient's functioning, treatment response and aetiological variables (Westen *et al.* 2006).

Shedler and Westen's (2004) research also indicated the need for revisions to the number of distinct diagnoses. Schizoid and schizotypal personality disorders were empirically indistinguishable and could be represented by one disorder. Avoidant and dependent personality disorders showed substantial overlap and had depression and dysphoria at their core, indicating that a single depressive or dysphoric personality disorder may be a better category. Of particular relevance here are findings relating to antisocial personality disorder, where the criteria generated accorded closely with those used to define clinical psychopathy.

Trait approaches

Trait approaches to the study of personality and personality disorder focus on those basic dispositions that give rise to overt patterns of behaviour and subjective experience, both normal and abnormal. There are a number of hierarchical trait models, postulating between two and seven higher order domains each of which is described by a lower order set of traits or facets.

The trait model most widely studied in relation to DSM diagnoses is Costa and McCrae's (1992) Five Factor Model. In this, personality is deemed to be hierarchically structured along five broad dimensions (the Big Five), these being Neuroticism (N), Extraversion (E), Openness to experience (O), Agreeableness

(A) and Conscientiousness (C), with each dimension consisting of a number of more specific traits or facets. Statistical relationships have been observed between DSM disorders and the Big Five in many studies.

Saulsman and Page (2004) conducted a meta-analysis of 12 studies that correlated DSM personality diagnoses with the Big Five personality domains, finding that virtually all personality disorders are characterised, to differing degrees, by a positive relationship with Neuroticism and a negative relationship with Agreeableness. Additionally, histrionic and narcissistic are high on Extraversion; schizoid, schizotypal and avoidant are low on Extraversion; antisocial is low on Conscientiousness; and obsessive-compulsive is high on Conscientiousness. A case has been advanced for using the framework of the Five Factor Model to understand variants of psychopathy, with key features being low Agreeableness and Conscientiousness, high Extraversion, and low anxiety along with high hostility and impulsiveness, these being facets of Neuroticism (Miller and Lynam 2003).

Despite research indicating relationships between traits and diagnoses, integration of dimensional trait models with DSM or ICD personality disorders has not yet been crystallised, although proposals for a number of dimensional classifications have been suggested (Widiger and Simonsen 2005). Correlational studies are of limited help in integrating two conceptually different models, since they do not help identify what aspects of the global diagnostic categories relate to specific traits and what the nature of any relationship might be (Livesley and Lang 2005). Furthermore, trait assessments may not capture all the information necessary to identify personality disorder (Livesley and Lang 2005).

Livesley and Lang (2005) suggest that personality disorder is more than just extreme scores on trait dimensions, and that this extra aspect is that the structure of personality (i.e. traits) prevents the achievement of life tasks. That is, traits are related to disorder by virtue of how they influence the processes that determine an individual's functioning.

Biopsychosocial developmental approaches to personality disorder

In DSM and ICD, there are no personality disorder categories for children or adolescents, yet adult personality disorders are said to have their origins early on in life. Furthermore, the study of adult dispositional traits does not explain the patterns of experience and behaviour that comprise personality. This requires an understanding of the social and psychological processes whereby personality traits come to be expressed as a pattern of thoughts, feelings and behaviours.

It is clear that our understanding of personality disorders can be advanced through a developmental approach, looking into the role of childhood and adolescent antecedents to adult personality disorder. Of course, this approach requires that personality disorders are valid and reliable categories. In addition, a theoretical underpinning to the research helps identify relevant variables for inclusion in any study.

Research into individual differences in infants and children focuses on temperament, which consists of stable characteristics that appear early on in life. There are different components of temperament, including sociability, emotionality, activity, attention and impulsivity which map to a considerable degree onto the Big Five (Mervielde et al. 2005). These domains of temperament may have biological bases, linked to neural systems governing functions such as behavioural activation, behavioural inhibition, affect regulation and attention, but neuroscience cannot fully explain the complex phenomena of temperament and personality (Paris 2005). Even at an early age there is an interaction between the individual and his or her environment, such that individual differences can never be explained by genetics or neurobiology alone. It is the interaction between traits and experiences over the life span that helps us understand personality, whether disordered or not.

One personality disorder that has been thoroughly investigated, and is of high relevance in this chapter, is antisocial personality disorder. Several longitudinal studies have identified factors associated with the emergence, escalation, persistence and desistance from antisocial behaviour. Farrington (2005) summarises the most important risk factors in his review of the childhood origins of antisocial behaviour, with temperament characteristics evident as early as 3 years of age. Risk factors are: early impulsivity, low intelligence, poor parental supervision, harsh and erratic discipline, maltreatment by parents, parental conflict, lone mother, disrupted families, antisocial parents, large families, low socio-economic status, low commitment to school, poor educational attainment and delinquent peers. Of interest are the processes by which these risk factors increase the likelihood of antisocial personality disorder in adulthood, which Farrington (2005) conceptualises in his Integrated Cognitive Antisocial Potential (ICAP) theory. The individual has antisocial potential and the likelihood of actual antisocial behaviour is a function of traits (e.g. impulsivity) interacting with social factors (e.g. family management, peer associations) and opportunities for pro-social and antisocial activities (e.g. employment, neighbourhood) via mechanisms such as attachment, self-regulation, cognitive development, skills acquisition and labelling.

In understanding psychopathy from a multi-level, developmental perspective, reviewers acknowledge a genetically based emotional dysfunction as central (Blair *et al.* 2006; Saltaris 2002). The core emotional dysfunction is not itself affected by social or environmental factors, but these do play their part in the development of aggression and antisocial behaviour. The processes implicated in the development of antisocial behaviour in psychopaths include lack of distress at another's discomfort, lack of fear, poor impulse control and information processing abnormalities.

Treatment

Targets of treatment for personality disordered offenders

An examination of the effectiveness of treatments for personality disordered offenders requires first that we decide what it is we are aiming to treat. Is it the personality disorder, the socially deviant behaviour, or both? Must the personality disorder be connected with the antisocial behaviour in such a way that to ameliorate the disorder reduces risk?

There are ethical objections to 'treating' people for violation of social norms, and therapists need to balance competing responsibilities to the individual patient, the institutional context and society. Blackburn (1993, 2002) believes that because it is the mental disorder that causes the offender to be diverted to the mental health system, the target should be the alleviation of the disorder, although reduced recidivism will be one indication of successful outcome in the case of personality disorder. He says that it should be the mediators of antisocial behaviour that are targeted in treatment. In the criminal justice system, the ultimate target may be the antisocial behaviour, but here too it would be the mediators of that behaviour that would be addressed in the process. The net result is that treatment programmes for personality disordered offenders in mental health services and in the criminal justice system would probably be indistinguishable, although the ultimate service evaluation criterion might differ between the two settings.

The difficulty is the precise identification of the mediators of antisocial behaviour in personality disordered offenders. In terms of diagnoses, within DSM-IV there is the statement that 'a diagnosis does not carry any necessary implications regarding the causes of an individual's mental disorder or its associated impairments' (American Psychiatric Association 1994: xxiii). People diagnosed with any personality disorder or group of personality disorders are heterogeneous in terms of their developmental background, thoughts, emotions and current behaviour, and there is no way of saying from the diagnosis alone what the treatment goals should be and what type of treatment will suit them best. The same problem pertains to the relationship between personality disorder and offending: a personality disorder diagnosis does not say what offences a person may commit, what the level of risk is and how that risk may be addressed in treatment. Some critics would say that a personality disorder diagnosis is of very limited value in identifying treatment goals and that an analysis of the individual's behaviour in historical and current contexts, including cognitive, behavioural and psychosocial elements, is more productive (Rice and Harris 1997).

Case conceptualisations

A case conceptualisation or problem formulation is important in making sense of the individual's problems, assessing risk and identifying appropriate treatment targets. As well as describing the nature of the client's problem or problems, information relating to personality traits, psychosocial development and current environmental variables are important. Information in all of these domains should be integrated within a theoretical framework to present working hypotheses about antecedents to and maintaining factors of aspects of the problem. Targets for intervention are identified and, as therapy progresses, the working hypotheses may change.

Westen and Shedler (1999) are particular supporters of case conceptualisations in relation to personality disorders. Individual problem formulations help the practitioner identify targets for intervention, direct the assessment of clinically relevant issues both for further investigation and for evaluation of progress in therapy (e.g. anger, self-esteem, motivation to change), and indicate what style of intervention might be most effective in light of the person's personality and cognitive capabilities (e.g. intelligence, neuropsychological status and information processing skills). Furthermore, individual formulations contribute to the identification of risk factors.

Treatment of personality disorders

There is an extensive literature on the treatment of personality disorders, although published studies are not always of impeccable methodological rigour. In a systematic review of treatments for people with personality disorder, Duggan and colleagues (2005) articulated some of the problems in making sense of the body of evidence. First, diagnostic groups cannot be taken as comparable across studies, given the variety of methods of assessment of personality disorder and their low convergent validity. Second, there are studies of groups which would likely have a high proportion of personality disordered individuals in them, but personality disorder has not been formally diagnosed (e.g. offenders, substance abusers, disturbed adolescents). Third, various outcomes of personality disorder treatment are presented and there is no agreement about whether the aim should be to change personality structure, behaviour or general functioning.

Overall, Duggan *et al.* (2005) identified just 29 methodologically acceptable randomised controlled trials of treatments for people with personality disorder: 16 psychopharmacological treatments (10 for borderline, 2 antisocial, 1 avoidant and 3 mixed personality disorders) and 13 psychological treatments (7 for borderline, 1 antisocial, 2 avoidant and 3 mixed personality disorders). Clearly, this body of treatment research is strongly biased toward borderline personality disorder.

Pharmacotherapy

Duggan *et al.* (2005) identified antidepressants and antipsychotics as most commonly used in studies of treatment for borderline personality disorder, with antidepressants appearing to have most effect in reducing anger and hostility, and antipsychotics appearing to have most effect in reducing schizotypal symptoms and improving overall functioning. In studies of antisocial personality disorder treatment, the aim is commonly to reduce substance use but there is insufficient evidence for the effectiveness of any particular medication with this population. The wealth of research that focuses directly on substance misuse treatment clearly has much to offer in informing treatment for this population. In mixed populations, as for borderline personality disorder, there is some evidence that antidepressants reduce anger and hostility.

Psychological treatments for personality disorders

Meta-analyses of treatment outcomes for personality disorders show a strong positive effect of treatment (Cohen's d^4 0.80 to 1.39), with both cognitive-behavioural and psychodynamic approaches showing good effects (Liechsenring *et al.* 2004; Perry *et al.* 1999).

Dialectical behaviour therapy (DBT) for women with borderline personality disorder is the most widely evaluated treatment. DBT is based on the premise that the borderline personality disorder is typified by a failure to regulate emotions, which has developed as a result of a biologically based emotional vulnerability in combination with an invalidating environment, that is where the child's private experiences are denied, contradicted or punished by significant others (Linehan 1993a, 1993b). A combination of group and individual therapies, over a period of around a year, focuses on motivation, self-acceptance, distress tolerance, emotion regulation and interpersonal effectiveness.

In women substance abusers with borderline personality disorder randomly allocated to DBT or treatment as usual, DBT proved superior in reducing substance use, preventing treatment drop-out and improving global adjustment (Linehan *et al.* 1999). Another randomised controlled study with women patients with borderline personality disorder showed that those in DBT were significantly more likely to remain in treatment compared with those in treatment as usual, and DBT significantly reduced self-harming behaviours, particularly in those with high baseline frequencies of self-harm, whereas those in treatment as usual showed deterioration (Verheul *et al.* 2003). Results were maintained six months after the end of treatment, although the differences between treatment and control groups narrowed (van den Bosch *et al.* 2005).

DBT has also been used with apparent success with offender populations. Mentally disordered women offenders in a secure psychiatric hospital showed reduced self-harm, suicidal ideation, depression and dissociative experiences, along with improved survival and coping beliefs, after DBT (Low *et al.* 2001). Women prisoners who completed 12 months of DBT showed global positive change in borderline symptoms, improved emotion control, reduced impulsivity and increased internal locus of control (Nee and Farman 2005).

In summary, DBT is an efficacious treatment for women with borderline personality disorder, although better designed research is needed for patients in forensic settings and in relation to criminal outcomes.

Other cognitive-behavioural treatments for borderline personality disorder have shown themselves effective in randomised controlled trials, particularly those that target core beliefs or schemas. Schema-focused therapy (Giesen-Bloo *et al.* 2006) has proven more effective than transference-focused therapy in retaining patients in treatment and reducing the severity of the disorder. Davidson *et al.* (2006) showed that adding cognitive-behavioural therapy to treatment as usual reduced suicidal acts, anxiety and distress. Bateman and Fonagy (1999) compared psychodynamic psychotherapy of 18 months' duration with general psychiatric treatment, finding that the treatment group became less depressed, decreased self-harming behaviours, reduced their days in hospital and improved their social functioning, whereas the control group either did not change or deteriorated. The treatment group maintained these gains and showed some further improvement at follow-up 18 months after treatment (Bateman and Fonagy 2001).

Some interventions have been evaluated with groups of people with a variety of personality disorders. In one sample of people with a mixture of personality disorders, Huband *et al.* (2007) showed improved social functioning and anger control in those randomised to receive psychoeducation plus social problem-solving therapy compared with those receiving treatment as usual.

Interventions with people detained under mental health legislation are usually mixed groups. Often, these abide by the 'what works' principles, that is targeting criminogenic needs through structured cognitive-behavioural treatment programmes (Andrews 1995). Hughes *et al.* (1997) evaluated a programme for male legal psychopaths detained in a maximum security hospital that consisted of group therapies targeting assertiveness, self-esteem, cognitive skills, problem-solving and emotional awareness. The nine patients who completed the programme showed global positive change, although there was a significant negative correlation between PCL-R Factor 1 scores and clinical improvement. A programme at Broadmoor Hospital for young male patients, most of whom were legal psychopaths, combined cognitive-behaviour therapy and psychodynamic psychotherapy, run both individually and in groups (Reiss *et al.* 1996). A comparison of a treated and a matched untreated group showed that, among those discharged into the community, similar numbers in each group committed a further serious offence, but a higher proportion of those treated in the unit showed a good social outcome, and this was predictive of not reoffending.

Therapies for personality disordered men in a secure unit focusing on social problem-solving and managing anger and aggression have led to improvements in these areas (McMurran *et al.* 1999, 2001a, 2001b). These improvements are indicative that treatment is progressing effectively, but only long-term follow-up will tell regarding rehabilitation and recidivism.

Therapeutic communities

Therapeutic communities (TCs) aim to address maladaptive interpersonal styles in a democracy where residents confront each other with the impact of their behaviours. In a study of hospitalised personality disordered patients, Copas *et al.* (1984) found that, at three- and five- year follow-ups, fewer TC participants had further convictions or hospitalisations compared with those assessed but not admitted, and those who stayed in the TC for nine months or longer fared best. In a study of TC participants at the same hospital, Dolan (1997) measured changes in symptomatology, showing a highly significant reduction in psychological distress. A study comparing men admitted to HMP Grendon with those referred but not admitted reported fewer reconvictions for the treated group, although statistical significance did not reach what is normally considered to be an acceptable level (Marshall 1997).

McMurran *et al.* (1998) examined the criminal recidivism of predominantly personality disordered offenders who had either participated in a hospital-based TC for an average of 17 months or had been rejected after an assessment period averaging two months. At a mean follow-up time of almost five years, there was a significant reduction in crime for the whole sample when comparing pre-admission and post-discharge offences, but there were no significant differences between the two groups in terms of reconvictions, suggesting that the TC intervention had no effect on offending and that personality disordered offenders improved regardless.

There is evidence that TCs have done more harm than good with some mentally disordered offenders. Rice *et al.* (1992) carried out a retrospective evaluation of a TC in a maximum security institution for mentally disordered offenders, matching the TC participants with a comparable assessment-only group. Follow-up at a mean of 10.5 years after discharge showed a modest overall degree of success for the TC (success being defined as no reconviction, revocation of parole or reincarceration), but those TC participants scoring 25 or more on the PCL-R showed higher rates of recidivism, particularly violent recidivism, than a comparable non-treated group. That is, treatment in a TC made 'psychopaths' worse than if they had had no treatment at all. This study has, however, been criticised in that the treatment practices within the TC were unusual and not comparable with modern practices. However, in his meta-analysis of treatments for psychopaths, Salekin (2002) found that TCs were the least effective approach.

Many practitioners believe that TCs have value in treating personality disordered offenders, but very careful attention needs to be paid to who is selected, what is addressed and how the TC operates, if harm is to be avoided (McMurran *et al.* 1998). That said, concept TCs for substance-abusing offenders in prisons show good outcomes, with 35 methodologically sound studies of TC or milieu therapy for adults, with almost 11,000 participants, giving a positive mean effect size of 0.14 (Lipton *et al.* 2002). This is important given the strong association between substance use and antisocial personality disorder.

Treatment of clinical psychopathy

Evidence regarding the effectiveness of treatment for clinical psychopathy is equivocal. In one meta-analysis of treatment outcome, high PCL-R scorers were shown to benefit least from psychological therapies (Garrido *et al.* 1996). However, benefiting less is not the same as not benefiting at all, and in a later meta-analysis of treatments for psychopathy Salekin (2002) found that treatment can be effective, with cognitive-behavioural therapies and psychodynamic approaches showing particular promise.

On the other hand, Hare *et al.* (2000), in their follow-up of British prisoners, identified that those scoring high on PCL-R Factor 1 were more likely to recidivate if they had been in cognitive-behavioural treatment, education or vocational training than if they had not been in any of these while in prison. D'Silva *et al.* (2004) addressed the question of whether treatment does indeed make high PCL-R scorers worse in a systematic review. Most of the outcome studies they identified were methodologically inadequate, and overall as many indicated improvement as indicated deterioration, hence no firm conclusions can yet be drawn about the treatability of those with high psychopathy scores. Given the high risk of recidivism of this group, there is a need for attention to how treatments may be designed with reference to their personality characteristics so that outcomes are improved (Hemphill and Hart 2002).

Conclusion

There is much work to be done in all areas of personality disorder studies: theoretical understanding, classification, aetiology, assessment, treatment and prevention. Overall, research needs to be of better quality to answer the questions posed. Perhaps the most pressing need is in what is termed translational research, that is the translation of science into practical applications. This is important because people with personality disorders are people with difficulties, living with family members or partners who may struggle to cope, being treated by mental health professionals who need the skills to maintain helping relationships and deliver effective treatments. The not inconsiderable intellectual exercise of understanding personality disorders is, in fact, an endeavour aimed at improving lives.

Acknowledgement

This chapter is adapted, with permission, from a report entitled *Personality Disorders* published in 2002 in the National Programme on Forensic Mental Health Research and Development's Expert Paper series (see: http://www.nfmhp.org.uk/expertpaper.htm).

Selected further reading

Alwin, N., Blackburn, R., Davidson, K., Hilton, M., Logan, C. and Shine, J. (2006) *Understanding Personality Disorder: A Report by the British Psychological Society*. Leicester: British Psychological Society, is a readable overview, with references to offenders with personality disorder throughout.

Livesley, W. J. (ed.) (2001) *Handbook of Personality Disorders*. New York: Guilford, is the most comprehensive text on the theory, aetiology, assessment and treatment of personality disorders and includes a chapter on forensic issues by Stephen Hart.

The National Institute of Mental Health in England (2003) *Personality Disorder: No Longer a Diagnosis of Exclusion* London: Department of Health (available from: http://www.dh.gov.uk/en/Publicationsandstatistics/Publications/PublicationsPolicyAndGuidance/DH_4009546) provides information about the government's intentions for the delivery of personality disorder services within general mental health and forensic settings.

Duggan, C., Adams, C., McCarthy, L., Fenton, M., Lee, T., Binks, C. and Stocker, O. (2005) *Finally, a Systematic Review of the Effectiveness of Pharmacological and Psychological Treatments for Those with Personality Disorder*. Liverpool: National Programme on Forensic Mental Health Research and Development (available from: http://www.nfmhp.org.uk/MRD per cent2012 per cent2033 per cent20Final per cent20Report.pdf) is the most comprehensive and up-to-date examination of all the treatment research.

Notes

1 Stone was retried and reconvicted in 2001, and lost an appeal in 2005.
2 Axis I – Clinical disorders: Axis II – Personality disorders and mental retardation (the term used in DSM-IV)' Axis III – General medical conditions; Axis IV – Psychosocial and environmental problems; Axis V – Global assessment of functioning.
3 There are now several variants on the PCL-R, including a screening version (PCL:SV: Hart *et al.* 1995), a research version the (P-SCAN: Hare and Hervé 1999) and a youth version (PCL: YV: Forth *et al.* 2003).
4 Cohen's d is an effect size statistic calculated by subtracting the post-treatment mean from the pre-treatment mean and dividing by the pooled standard deviations. An effect size of 0.20 is considered small, 0.50 medium and 0.80 large.

References

Alwin, N., Blackburn, R., Davidson, K., Hilton, M., Logan, C. and Shine, J. (2006) *Understanding Personality Disorder: A Report by the British Psychological Society*. Leicester: British Psychological Society.

American Psychiatric Association (1994) *Diagnostic and Statistical Manual of Mental Disorders*, 4th edn. Washington, DC: APA.

American Psychiatric Association (2000) *Diagnostic and Statistical Manual of Mental Disorders*, 4th edn, text revision. Washington, DC: APA.

Andrews, D. (1995) 'The psychology of criminal conduct and effective treatment', in J. McGuire (ed.), *What Works: Reducing Re-offending*. Chichester: Wiley.

Arntz, A. (1999) 'Do personality disorders exist? On the validity of the concept and its cognitive-behavioral formulation and treatment', *Behaviour Research and Therapy*, 37: S97–S134.

Bailey, J. and MacCulloch, M. (1992) 'Characteristics of 112 cases discharged directly to the community from a new special hospital and some comparisons of performance', *Journal of Forensic Psychiatry*, 3: 91–112.

Barrett, B., Byford, S., Seivewright, H., Cooper, S. and Tyrer, P. (2005) 'Service costs for severe personality disorder at a special hospital', *Criminal Behaviour and Mental Health*, 15: 184–90.

Bateman, A. and Fonagy, P. (1999) 'Effectiveness of partial hospitalization in the treatment of borderline personality disorder: a randomized controlled trial', *American Journal of Psychiatry*, 156: 1563–9.

Bateman, A. and Fonagy, P. (2001) 'Treatment of borderline personality disorder with psychoanalytically oriented partial hospitalization: an 18-month follow-up', *American Journal of Psychiatry*, 158: 36–42.

Batty, D. (2002) 'Risky view', *Guardian*, April 17. Retrieved 27 December 2006 from http://society. guardian.co.uk/mentalhealth/story/0,,685442,00.html

Blackburn, R. (1993) 'Clinical programmes with psychopaths', in K. Howells and C.R. Hollin (eds), *Clinical Approaches to the Mentally Disordered Offender*. Chichester: Wiley.

Blackburn, R. (2000) 'Classification and assessment of personality disorders in mentally disordered offenders: a psychological perspective', *Criminal Behaviour and Mental Health*, 10: S8–S32.

Blackburn, R. (2002) 'Ethical issues in motivating offenders to change', in M. McMurran (ed.), *Motivating Offenders to Change: A Guide to Enhancing Engagement in Therapy*. Chichester: Wiley.

Blair, R.J.R., Peschardt, K.S., Budhani, S., Mitchell, D.G.V. and Pine, D.S. (2006) 'The development of psychopathy', *Journal of Child Psychology and Psychiatry*, 47: 262–75.

Bloom, J.D. and Wilson, W.H. (2000) 'Offenders with schizophrenia', in S. Hodgins and R. Müller-Isberner (eds), *Violence, Crime and Mentally Disordered Offenders*. Chichester: Wiley.

Cleckley, H. (1941) *The Mask of Sanity*. St Louis, MO: Mosby.

Coid, J. (1992) 'DSM-III diagnosis in criminal psychopaths: a way forward', *Criminal Behaviour and Mental Health*, 2: 78–9.

Coid, J., Kahtan, N., Gault, S. and Jarman, B. (1999) 'Patients with personality disorder admitted to secure forensic psychiatry services', *British Journal of Psychiatry*, 175: 528–36.

Coid, J., Yang, M., Tyrer, P., Roberts, A., and Ullrich, S. (2006) 'Prevalence and correlates of personality disorder in Great Britain', *British Journal of Psychiatry*, 188: 423–31.

Cooke, D.J. (1995) 'Psychopathic disturbance in the Scottish prison population: the cross-cultural generalisability of the Hare Psychopathy Checklist', *Psychology, Crime and Law*, 2: 101–8.

Cooke, D.J. and Michie, C. (2001) 'Refining the construct of psychopathy: towards a hierarchical model', *Psychological Assessment*, 13: 171–88.

Copas, J., O'Brien, M., Roberts, J. and Whiteley, S. (1984) 'Treatment outcome in personality disorder', *Personality and Individual Differences*, 5: 565–73.

Costa, P.T. and McCrae, R. R. (1992) *Revised NEO Personality Inventory and the NEO-Five Factor Inventory (NEO-FFI) Professional Manual*. Odessa, FL: Psychological Assessment Resources.

Davidson, K.M., Norrie, J., Tyrer, P., Gumley, A., Tata, P., Murray, H. and Palmer, S. (2006) 'The effectiveness of cognitive behaviour therapy for borderline personality disorder: results from the borderline personality disorder study of cognitive therapy (BOSCOT) trial', *Journal of Personality Disorders*, 20: 450–65.

Department of Health and Home Office (1999) *Managing Dangerous People with Severe Personality Disorder: Proposals for Policy Development*. London: Department of Health.

Department of Health and Home Office (2000a) *Reforming the Mental Health Act Part I: The New Legal Framework*. Norwich: Stationery Office.

Department of Health and Home Office (2000b) *Reforming the Mental Health Act Part II: High Risk Patients*. Norwich: Stationery Office.

Dolan, B. (1997) 'A community based TC: the Henderson Hospital', in E. Cullen, L. Jones and R. Woodward (eds), *Therapeutic Communities for Offenders*. Chichester: Wiley.

Dolan, B. and Mitchell, E. (1994) 'Personality disorder and psychological disturbance of female prisoners: a comparison with women referred for NHS treatment of personality disorder', *Criminal Behaviour and Mental Health*, 4: 130–43.

D'Silva, K., Duggan, C. and McCarthy, L. (2004) 'Does treatment really make psychopaths worse? A review of the evidence', *Journal of Personality Disorders*, 18: 163–77.

DSPD Programme (2005) *Dangerous and Severe Personality Disorder (DSPD) High Secure Services for Men: Planning and Delivery Guide*. London: Department of Health, Home Office and HM Prison Service. Retrieved 27 December 2006 from: http://www.dspdprogramme.gov.uk/media/pdfs/High_Secure_Services_for_Men.pdf

Duggan, C., Adams, C., McCarthy, L., Fenton, M., Lee, T., Binks, C. and Stocker, O. (2005) *A Systematic Review of the Effectiveness of Pharmacological and Psychological Treatments for Those with Personality Disorder*. Liverpool: National Programme on Forensic Mental Health Research and Development.

Farrington, D.P. (2005) 'Childhood origins of antisocial behaviour', *Clinical Psychology and Psychotherapy*, 12: 177–90.

Fazel, S. and Danesh, J. (2002) 'Serious mental disorder in 23,000 prisoners: a systematic review of 62 surveys', *The Lancet*, 359: 545–50.

Fennell, P. (2001) 'Reforming the Mental Health Act 1983: "joined up compulsion"', *Journal of Mental Health Law*, June: 5–20.

Fennell, P. (2005) 'Protection! Protection! Protection! Déjà vu all over again. The government response to the Parliamentary Scrutiny Committee', *Journal of Mental Health Law*, November: 110–22.

First, M.B., Gibbon, M., Spitzer, R.L., Williams, J.B.W. and Benjamin, L.S. (1997) *Structured Clinical Interview for DSM-IV Axis II Personality Disorders*. Arlington, VA: American Psychiatric Publishing.

Forth, A.E. Kosson, D.S. and Hare, R.D. (2003) *The Psychology Checklist: Youth Version*. Toronto: Multi-Health Systems.

Garrido, V., Esteban, C. and Molero, C. (1996) 'The effectiveness in the treatment of psychopathy: a meta-analysis', in D.J. Cooke, A.E. Forth, J. Newman and R.D. Hare (eds), *International Perspectives on Psychopathy*, Issues in Criminological Psychology No. 24. Leicester: British Psychological Society.

Giesen-Bloo, J., van Dyck, R., Spinhoven, P., van Tilburg, W., Dirksen, C., van Asselt, T., Kremers, I., Nadort, M. and Arntz, A. (2006) 'Outpatient psychotherapy for borderline personality disorder: randomized trial of schema-focused therapy vs transference-focused therapy', *Archives of General Psychiatry*, 63: 649–59.

Hare, R.D. (1991) *The Hare Psychopathy Checklist – Revised*. North Tonawanda, NY: Multi-Health Systems.

Hare, R.D. (2003) *The Hare Psychopathy Checklist – Revised*, 2nd edn. North Tonawanda, NY: Multi-Health Systems.

Hare, R.D. and Hervé, H.F. (1999) *Hare P. SCAN Research Version*. Toronto: Multi-Health Systems.

Hare, R.D., Clark, D., Grann, M. and Thornton, D. (2000) 'Psychopathy and the predictive validity of the PCL-R: an international perspective', *Behavioral Sciences and the Law*, 18: 623–45.

Hare, R.D., Harpur, T. J., Hakstian, A.R., Forth, A.E., Hart, S.D. and Newman, J.P. (1990) 'The Revised Psychopathy Checklist: reliability and factor structure', *Psychological Assessment*, 2: 338–41.

Hart, S.D., Cox, D. N. and Hare, R. D. (1995) *The Hare Psychopathy Checklist: Screening Version*. Toronto: Multi-Health Systems.

Hathaway, S.R. and McKinley, C. (1989) *Minnesota Multiphasic Personality Inventory-2*. North Tonawanda, NY: Multi-Health Systems.

Hemphill, J.F. and Hart, S.D. (2002) 'Motivating the unmotivated: psychopathy, treatment, and change', in M. McMurran (ed.), *Motivating Offenders to Change: A Guide to Enhancing Engagement in Therapy*. Chichester: Wiley.

Hemphill, J.F., Hare, R.D. and Wong, S. (1998) 'Psychopathy and recidivism: a review', *Legal and Criminological Psychology*, 3: 139–70.

Hiscoke, U.L., Långström, N., Ottosson, H. and Grann, M. (2003) 'Self-reported personality traits and disorders (DSM-IV) and risk of criminal recidivism: a prospective study', *Journal of Personality Disorders*, 17: 293–305.

Huband, N., McMurran, M., Evans, C. and Duggan, C. (2007) 'Social problem solving plus psychoeducation for adults with personality disorder: a pragmatic randomised clinical trial', *British Journal of Psychiatry*, 190: 307–13.

Hughes, G., Hogue, T., Hollin, C. and Champion, H. (1997) 'First-stage evaluation of a treatment programme for personality-disordered offenders', *Journal of Forensic Psychiatry*, 8: 515–27.

Jamieson, E., Butwell, M., Taylor, P. and Leese, M. (2000) 'Trends in special (high-security) hospitals. I: Referrals and admissions', *British Journal of Psychiatry*, 176: 253–9.

Jamieson, L. and Taylor, P. J. (2004) 'A reconviction study of special (high security) hospital patients', *British Journal of Criminology*, 44: 783–802.

Liechsenring, F., Rabung, S. and Liebing, E. (2004) 'The efficacy of short-term psychodynamic psychotherapy in specific psychiatric disorders: a meta-analysis', *Archives of General Psychiatry*, 61: 1208–16.

Linehan, M.M. (1993a) *Cognitive-Behavioral Treatment of Borderline Personality Disorder*. New York: Guilford Press.

Linehan, M.M. (1993b) *Skills Training Manual for Treating Borderline Personality Disorder*. New York: Guilford Press.

Linehan, M.M., Schmidt, H., Dimeff, L.A., Craft, J.C., Kanter, J. and Comtois, K.A. (1999) 'Dialectical behaviour therapy for patients with borderline personality disorder and drug-dependence', *American Journal on Addictions*, 8: 279–92.

Lipton, D.S., Pearson, F.S., Cleland, C.M., and Yee, D. (2002) 'The effects of therapeutic communities and milieu therapy on recidivism', in J. McGuire (ed.), *Offender Rehabilitation and Treatment: Effective Programmes and Policies to Reduce Re-offending*. Chichester: Wiley.

Livesley, W.J. (1998) 'Suggestions for a framework for an empirically based classification of personality disorder', *Canadian Journal of Psychiatry*, 43: 137–47.

Livesley, W.J. (2001) 'Conceptual and taxonomic issues', in W. J. Livesley (ed.), *Handbook of Personality Disorders: Theory, Research, and Treatment*. New York: Guilford Press.

Livesley, W.J. and Lang, K.L. (2005) 'Differentiating normal, abnormal, and disordered personality', *European Journal of Personality*, 19: 257–68.

Loranger, A.W. (1997) *The International Personality Disorder Examination*. Odessa, FL: Psychological Assessment Resources.

Low, G., Jones, D., Duggan, C., Power, M. and MacLeod, A. (2001) 'The treatment of deliberate self-harm in borderline personality disorder using dialectical behaviour therapy: a pilot study in a high security hospital', *Criminal Behaviour and Mental Health*, 29: 85–92.

McMurran, M., Egan, V. and Ahmadi, S. (1998) 'A retrospective evaluation of a therapeutic community for mentally disordered offenders', *Journal of Forensic Psychiatry*, 9: 103–13.

McMurran, M., Egan, V., Richardson, C. and Ahmadi, S. (1999) 'Social problem-solving in mentally disordered offenders: a brief report', *Criminal Behaviour and Mental Health*, 9: 315–22.

McMurran, M., Charlesworth, P., Duggan, C. and McCarthy, L. (2001a) 'Controlling angry aggression: a pilot group intervention with personality-disordered offenders', *Behavioural and Cognitive Psychotherapy*, 29: 473–83.

McMurran, M., Fyffe, S., McCarthy, L., Duggan, C. and Latham, A. (2001b) '"Stop and Think!" – social problem solving therapy with personality-disordered offenders', *Criminal Behaviour and Mental Health*, 11: 273–85.

Marshall, P. (1997) *A Reconviction Study of HMP Grendon Therapeutic Community, Research Findings No. 53*. London: Home Office Research and Statistics Directorate.

Mervielde, I., De Clercq, B., De Fruyt, F. and van Leeuwen, K. (2005) 'Temperament, personality, and developmental psychopathology as childhood antecedents of personality disorders', *Journal of Personality Disorders*, 19: 171–201.

Miller, J.D. and Lynam, D.R. (2003) 'Psychopathy and the Five-Factor Model of personality: a replication and extension', *Journal of Personality Assessment*, 81: 68–178.

Millon, T., Millon, C. and Davis, R. (1994) *MCMI-III*. North Tonawanda, NY: Multi-Health Systems.

Milton, J. (2000) 'A postal survey of the assessment procedure for personality disorder in forensic settings', *Psychiatric Bulletin*, 24: 254–7.

Moran, P., Walsh, E., Tyrer, P., Burns, T., Creed, F. and Fahy, T. (2003) 'Impact of comorbid personality disorder on violence in psychosis: report from the UK 700 trial', *British Journal of Psychiatry*, 182: 129–34.

National Institute of Mental Health for England (2003) *Personality Disorder: No Longer a Diagnosis of Exclusion*. London: Department of Health.

Nee, C. and Farman, S. (2005) 'Female prisoners with borderline personality disorder: some promising treatment developments', *Criminal Behaviour and Mental Health*, 15: 2–16.

Paris, J. (2005) 'Neurobiological dimensional models of personality: a review of the models of Cloninger, Depue, and Siever', *Journal of Personality Disorders*, 19: 156–70.

Perry, J.C., Banon, E. and Ianni, F. (1999) 'Effectiveness of psychotherapy for personality disorders', *American Journal of Psychiatry*, 156: 1312–21.

Pfohl, B., Blum, N. and Zimmerman, M. (1997) *Structured Interview for DSM-IV Personality (SIDP-IV)*. Arlington, VA: American Psychiatric Publishing.

Reiss, D., Grubin, D. and Meux, C. (1996) 'Young "psychopaths" in special hospital: treatment and outcome', *British Journal of Psychiatry*, 168: 99–104.

Rice, M.E. and Harris, G. T. (1997) 'The treatment of mentally disordered offenders', *Psychology, Public Policy, and Law*, 3: 126–83.

Rice, M.E., Harris, G. T. and Cormier, C.A. (1992) 'An evaluation of a maximum security therapeutic community for psychopaths and other mentally disordered offenders', *Law and Human Behavior*, 16: 399–412.

Royal College of Psychiatrists (1999) *Offenders with Personality Disorder*. London: Gaskell.

Salekin, R.T. (2002) 'Psychopathy and therapeutic pessimism: clinical lore or clinical reality?', *Clinical Psychology Review*, 22: 79–112.

Saltaris, C. (2002) 'Psychopathy in juvenile offenders: can temperament and attachment be considered as robust developmental precursors?', *Clinical Psychology Review*, 22: 729–52.

Saulsman, L.M. and Page, A.C. (2004) 'The five-factor model and personality disorder empirical literature: a meta-analytic review', *Clinical Psychology Review*, 23: 1055–85.

Shedler, J. and Westen, D. (2004) 'Refining personality disorder diagnosis: integrating science and practice', *American Journal of Psychiatry*, 161: 1350–65.

Singleton, N., Meltzer, H., Gatward, R., Coid, J. and Deasy, D. (1998) *Psychiatric Morbidity among Prisoners*. London: Office of National Statistics.

Steels, M., Roney, G., Larkin, E., Jones, P., Croudace, T. and Duggan, C. (1998) 'Discharged from special hospital under restrictions: a comparison of the fates of psychopaths and the mentally ill', *Criminal Behaviour and Mental Health*, 8: 39–55.

Stone, M.H. (1993) *Abnormal Personalities: Within and Beyond the Realm of Treatment*. New York: Norton.

Taylor, P.J., Leese, M., Williams, D., Butwell, M., Daly, R. and Larkin, E. (1998) 'Mental disorder and violence', *British Journal of Psychiatry*, 172: 218–26.

Tyrer, P. (2000) 'Personality Assessment Schedule: PAS-I (ICD version)', in P. Tyrer (ed.), *Personality Disorders: Diagnosis, Management and Course*. London: Arnold.

Tyrer, P. (2006). 'Deconstructing personality disorder', *Quarterly Journal of Mental Health*, 1: 20–4.

Tyrer, P. and Johnson, T. (1996). 'Establishing the severity of personality disorder', *American Journal of Psychiatry*, 153: 1593–7.

van den Bosch, L.M.C., Koeter, M.W.J., Stijnen, T., Verheul, R. and van den Brink, W. (2005). 'Sustained efficacy of dialectical behaviour therapy for borderline personality disorder', *Behaviour Research and Therapy*, 43: 1231–41.

van Elzen, C.J.M. and Emmelkamp, P.M.G. (1996) 'The assessment of personality disorders: implications for cognitive and behavior therapy', *Behaviour Research and Therapy*, 34: 655–68.

Verheul, R. and Widiger, T. A. (2004) 'A meta-analysis of the prevalence and usage of the Personality Disorder Not Otherwise Specified (PDNOS) diagnosis', *Journal of Personality Disorders*, 18: 309–19.

Verheul, R., van den Brink, W. and Hartgers, C. (1998) 'Personality disorders predict relapse in alcoholic patients', *Addictive Behaviors*, 23: 869–82.

Verheul, R., van den Bosch, L.M.C., Koeter, M.W.J., De Ridder, M.A.J., Stijnen, T. and van den Brink, W. (2003) 'Dialectical behaviour therapy for women with borderline personality disorder: 12 month, randomised clinical trial in The Netherlands', *British Journal of Psychiatry*, 182: 135–40.

Vitacco, M.J., Neumann, C. S. and Jackson, R.L. (2005) 'Testing a four-factor model of psychopathy and its association with ethnicity, gender, intelligence, and violence', *Journal of Consulting and Clinical Psychology*, 73: 466–76.

Westen, D. (1997) 'Divergences between clinical and research methods for assessing personality disorders: implications for research and the evolution of Axis II', *American Journal of Psychiatry*, 154: 895–903.

Westen, D. and Shedler, J. (1999) 'Revising and assessing Axis II. Part I: Developing a clinically and empirically valid assessment method', *American Journal of Psychiatry*, 156: 258–72.

Westen, D., Shedler, J. and Bradley, R. (2006) 'A prototype approach to personality disorder diagnosis', *American Journal of Psychiatry*, 163: 846–56.

Widiger, T.A. and Samuel, D.B. (2005) 'Evidence-based assessment of personality disorders', *Psychological Assessment*, 17: 278–87.

Widiger, T.A. and Simonsen, E. (2005) 'Alternative dimensional models of personality disorder: finding a common ground', *Journal of Personality Disorders*, 19: 110–30.

Widiger, T.A. and Trull, T.J. (1994) 'Personality disorders and violence', in J. Monahan and H.J. Steadman (eds), *Violence and Mental Disorder: Developments in Risk Assessment*. Chicago: University of Chicago Press.

Widiger, T.A., Mangine, S., Corbitt, E.M., Ellis, C.G. and Thomas, G.V. (2005) *Personality Disorder Interview-IV*. Odessa, FL: Psychological Assessment Resources.

World Health Organisation (1992) *10th Revision of the International Classification of Diseases (ICD-10)*. Geneva: WHO.

Zimmerman, M. (1994) 'Diagnosing personality disorders: a review of issues and research methods', *Archives of General Psychiatry*, 51: 225–45.

Chapter 16

Criminality among persons with severe mental illness

Sheilagh Hodgins

The prevalence of criminality among persons with severe mental illness

Persons with severe mental illness[1] (SMI) (Hodgins *et al.* 1996), and most particularly those with schizophrenia and schizo-affective disorder, are at increased risk, as compared to the general population, to commit violent crimes. This is a robust finding. It has been reported by several independent research groups working in industrialised (Arseneault *et al.* 2000; Brennan *et al.* 2000; Tiihonen *et al.*1997; Wallace *et al.* 2004) and underdeveloped countries (Volavka *et al.* 1997) with distinct cultures and health, social service and criminal justice systems, who have examined different cohorts and samples using various experimental designs including prospective, longitudinal investigations on birth cohorts (Arseneault *et al.* 2000; Brennan *et al.* 2000; Tiihonen *et al.*1997) and population cohorts (Wallace *et al.* 2004), follow-up studies comparing patients and their neighbours (Belfrage 1998), random samples of incarcerated offenders (Fazel and Danesh 2002), and complete cohorts of homicide offenders (Erb *et al.* 2001). A recent study showed that among people living in the community, the presence of psychotic symptoms in the absence of a psychotic disorder was associated with increased risk of aggressive behaviour (Mojtabai 2006). Much less is known about the prevalence of violent criminality among persons with major affective disorders than among those with schizophrenia. The few existing studies suggest a weak relationship (Arseneault *et al.* 2000; Brennan *et al.* 2000).

The results of the studies reviewed above are remarkably consistent. They tell us four important facts about offending by persons with SMI. One, while the increase in the risks associated with SMI (that is the odds ratios comparing crime rates among persons with SMI and persons in the general population) for non-violent and violent offending and for homicide reported in various studies are similar (Hodgins 1998), the proportions of persons with SMI who offend differ across countries and time periods. For example, in a Swedish birth cohort, 14.6 per cent of the men and 6.3 per cent of the women with SMI were convicted for at least one violent crime before their 30th birthday (Hodgins 1992). In a larger Danish birth cohort followed for 13 years longer, 11.3 per cent of the men and 2.8 per cent of the women with schizophrenia had at least one conviction for a violent crime (Brennan *et al.* 2000). In a more recent study of a large cohort of patients with schizophrenia in Denmark, 68 per cent had at least one conviction for a violent crime (Kramp 2004). In a study of a series of cohorts of patients with schizophrenia studied in the state of Victoria, Australia from 1975 to 1995, between 15 and 25 per cent had at least one conviction for a violent crime. Therefore the proportions of people with SMI who commit crimes vary by place and time period. Two, while studies consistently report that the prevalence of SMI among incarcerated offenders exceeds the prevalence for gender and age-matched subjects in the general population, the proportions of inmates with SMI vary from country to country, and from one time period to another, depending on the laws and policies that are in place concerning diversion of persons with SMI from prisons (Hodgins and Côté 1995). Three, while many more men than women with SMI commit crimes, SMI – and most particularly schizophrenia – confers a greater risk for violent crime among women than among men (Brennan *et al.* 2000). Four, while people with schizophrenia are responsible for approximately ten times more homicides than people without schizophrenia (Erb *et al.* 2001), few offenders with SMI have committed homicides and most have committed repeated assaults (e.g. Hodgins *et al.* 2005).

The prevalence of aggressive behaviour among persons with SMI

In concert with the evidence showing that persons with SMI, and most particularly those with schizophrenic disorders, are more likely than those without these disorders to commit violent crimes, there is a growing body of evidence on aggressive behaviour towards others by people with schizophrenia. In these studies aggressive behaviour is reported by patients, treatment staff and/or collateral informants using detailed protocols (see, for example, Steadman *et al.* 1998). The prevalence of assaultive behaviour varies depending on sample characteristics and length of the study period. For example, in a British study of outpatients with psychosis, 20 per cent assaulted another person in a two-year period (Walsh *et al.* 2001). In a US study of men with schizophrenic disorders admitted to psychiatric wards, 40.2 per cent had assaulted in the ten weeks prior to admission (Monahan *et al.* 2001).[2] In another US study of patients with schizophrenia recruited into a recent trial of medications, 19.1 per cent had committed an assault in the previous six months (Swanson *et al.* 2006). While rates vary from one study to another, they demonstrate that a significant minority of people with psychotic disorders, and most particularly with schizophrenia, present persistent aggressive behaviour.

Society's response to crime and aggressive behaviour among persons with SMI

Despite this growing body of evidence, mental health policies fail to recognise that aggressive behaviour and violent criminality are problems for a proportion of persons with SMI, and most particularly for those with schizophrenia. For example, in the UK neither the National Service Framework for Mental Health (Department of Health 1999) nor the NICE clinical guidelines for schizophrenia (Royal College of Psychiatrists and British Psychological Society 2003) take account of the evidence concerning the increased vulnerability associated with SMI for engaging in violent crime or assaultive behaviour. While policy remains mute on the topic, health services in the UK and throughout Europe have responded to the situation by dramatically increasing the number of forensic beds (Priebe *et al.* 2005) and incarcerating large numbers of persons with SMI in prisons (Davies 2004a, 2004b, 2004c). Most patients in forensic services are men with schizophrenia who have been in and out of general adult psychiatric services for many years while they were committing criminal offences (Hodgins and Müller-Isberner 2004). Mental health care for persons with SMI that is provided by general adult services does not address antisocial and criminal behaviour, but rather focuses, almost exclusively, on providing medication to reduce psychotic symptoms.

Between July 2004 and April 2005, we conducted a study of the patients with SMI on all general psychiatric adult wards of an inner-city mental health trust. Interviews were completed with patients and their key workers. We used the MacArthur Community Violence Interview to assess aggressive behaviour and victimisation and we obtained criminal records from both the Home Office and the Police National Computer database. The mean age of the patients was 38.5 years, most had previous admissions, three-quarters had a diagnosis of schizophrenia, 60 per cent presented a substance misuse problem and 56 per cent were admitted involuntarily. The prevalence of convictions for criminal offences was high (any crime – 68.3 per cent of the men and 27.1 per cent of the women; violent crime – 46.7 per cent of the men and 16.5 per cent of the women). The offenders had committed, on average, ten offences and two violent offences (Hodgins *et al.* 2007a).

Neither mental health policy nor practice, nor criminal justice policy, is consistent with the scientific evidence that has accumulated regarding criminality and aggressive behaviour among persons with SMI. Consequently, persons with these disorders fail to receive interventions designed specifically to reduce illegal behaviours until after many years of treatment in general adult psychiatric services they are finally transferred to a forensic service. Such services, however, are limited in number because they are very costly. For example, in the mental health trust where the study described above was conducted, a bed in a medium secure unit is estimated to cost £160,000 per year and patients stay, on average, four years. In this trust, forensic services take 31 per cent of the budget for adult mental health care and treat only 5 to 10 per cent of the patients. Consequently, the failure of general mental health services to intervene at illness onset to reduce aggressive and other illegal behaviours contributes to the growing numbers of forensic beds and to stigma against all persons afflicted with SMI (Hodgins *et al.* 2006a).

Why are persons who develop schizophrenic disorders at increased risk of committing crimes and engaging in aggressive behaviour towards others?

Similar to offenders in the general population, offenders with schizophrenia constitute a population that is heterogeneous with respect to both criminal offending and the correlates of offending. Knowledge about the origins of criminal offending in the general population has exploded since investigations began to focus on subgroups defined by age of onset and persistence of antisocial behaviour. Available data suggest that a similar approach to the study of offenders with schizophrenia may prove useful for beginning to unravel the aetiology of both the violence and the schizophrenia and for the development of effective treatment programmes.

As in the general population, age at first offence identifies groups of offenders with schizophrenia that differ as to patterns of criminal activities and the factors associated with offending. In order to describe offenders with schizophrenia and to illustrate the heterogeneity of this population, data are presented from the Comparative Study of the Prevention of Crime and Violence by Mentally Ill Persons (Hodgins et al. 2006b). Two hundred and twenty-four men with schizophrenia discharged from general and forensic psychiatric hospitals in four sites in Canada, Finland, Germany, and Sweden were examined. Each site is responsible for all of the mentally ill persons who commit crimes within a large geographic catchment area. Consecutive discharges of patients with a diagnosis of SMI from the forensic psychiatric hospitals serving the catchment areas were asked to participate. Patients with same sex and diagnoses and similar age being discharged from a general psychiatric hospital in the same geographic region were also recruited into the study. In the weeks preceding discharge, interviews with the participants were undertaken by research team psychiatrists to assess diagnoses, symptoms, substance misuse history, personality traits and history of antisocial behaviour. Information on psychiatric and criminal histories was extracted from official files. Family members and treatment staff corroborated information provided by patients and records. The men with schizophrenia were divided into five groups, one group with no record of criminal activity and four groups of offenders classified by age at first crime.

As can be seen in Table 16.1, the five groups differ as to the number and the types of crimes that they have committed. While 100 per cent of those who began offending before age 18 and 84.3 per cent of those whose first offence was committed between the ages of 18 and 23 had been convicted of non-violent offences, this was true of less than 60 per cent of those who began offending at later ages. The average number of non-violent offences decreased dramatically with the age of first crime. This association between age at first crime and frequency and persistence of non-violent offending has been observed in other samples of men with schizophrenia (Tengström et al. 2001; Tengström et al. 2004). While almost all the offenders had committed at least one violent crime, the average number of violent offences decreased with the age of first offence. This was not true for homicide. The highest prevalence (37 per cent) of homicide offenders was found among those who began offending after age 30, as compared to 17 per cent of those who began offending before age 18 and 15 per cent of those who began offending between 18 and 22 years of age. Other studies have also found that a proportion of homicide offenders with schizophrenia have no history of crime prior to the onset of illness (Erb et al. 2001).[3] Some homicide offenders with schizophrenia have a long history of illness before the homicide, while others develop schizophrenia at a relatively late age, fail to receive care until after the murder and then respond well to neuroleptic treatment (see, for example, Beaudoin et al. 1993; Erb et al. 2001). As can be observed in the table, many of the characteristics of the offenders with schizophrenia varied by age at first crime, notably prevalence of co-morbid diagnoses of illicit drug use disorders and of antisocial personality disorder (APD), levels of psychosocial functioning, psychiatric history, characteristics in childhood and adolescence, and prevalence of criminality among fathers and brothers.

Table 16.1 Comparisons of five groups of men with schizophrenia based on age at first crime

	Age at first crime					
	a No crime (n = 57)	b < 18 years (n = 39)	c 18–22 years (n = 51)	d 23–30 years (n = 53)	e 31 and older (n = 41)	Test
Mean age (in years)	34.52 (SD = 9.57)	35.38 (SD = 9.34)	36.15 (SD = 11.60)	39.01 (SD = 8.71)	48.21 (SD = 10.63)	X^2 (4, N = 238) = 41.04, p = .000 e > a, b, c, d d > a
Comorbid diagnoses						
% Alcohol abuse/dependence	40.7% (22)	66.7% (26)	64.7% (33)	56.6% (30)	61.0% (25)	X^2 (4, N = 238) = 8.82, p = .066
% Drug abuse/dependence	27.8% (15)	64.1% (25)	66.7% (34)	47.2% (25)	22.0% (9)	X^2 (4, N = 238) = 30.74, p = .000 b > a, e c > a, d, e d > a, e
% Antisocial personality disorder	9.3% (5)	53.9% (21)	35.3% (18)	9.4% (5)	9.8% (4)	X^2 (4, N = 238) = 41.50, p = .000 b > a, d, e c > a, d, e
Psychosocial functioning						
Mean score global assessment of functioning	43.86 (SD = 10.76)	47.10 (SD = 11.70)	48.40 (SD = 14.77)	52.66 (SD = 11.60)	52.46 (SD = 13.67)	X^2 (4, N = 232) = 15.52, p = .004 d > a, b e > a
% Never employed (excluding sheltered workshop)	68.5% (37)	35.9% (14)	27.5% (14)	17.0% (9)	14.6% (6)	X^2 (4, N = 238) = 7.96, p = .093

Table 16.1 (continued)

| | Age at first crime | | | | | |
	a No crime (n = 57)	b < 18 years (n = 39)	c 18–22 years (n = 51)	d 23–30 years (n = 53)	e 31 and older (n = 41)	Test
% had intimate partner	37.0% (20)	28.2% (11)	25.5% (13)	49.1% (26)	61.0% (25)	$X^2(4, N = 238) = 16.27$, p = .003 d > b, c e > a, b, c
% successfully completed obligatory military service	50.0% (14)	90.0% (18)	69.0% (20)	55.2% (16)	34.4% (11)	$X^2(4, N = 138) = 17.88$, p = .001 b > a, d, e c > e
Psychiatric history						
Mean age at onset of schizophrenia (in years)	22.96 (SD = 7.15)	21.03 (SD = 6.70)	21.60 (SD = 4.81)	23.02 (SD = 6.29)	32.10 (SD = 9.65)	$X^2(4, N = 203) = 36.71$, p = .000 e > a, b, c, d
Mean age at first hospitalisation (in years)	24.02 (SD = 7.62)	21.00 (SD = 6.07)	22.47 (SD = 7.49)	24.32 (SD = 6.38)	33.20 (SD = 10.16)	$X^2(4, N = 237) = 46.87$, p = .000 e > a, b, c, d
Mean length of all hospitalisations (months)	3.15 (SD = 3.00)	15.41 (SD = 13.84)	11.26 (SD = 11.55)	15.63 (SD = 21.48)	21.49 (SD = 31.06)	$X^2(4, N = 238) = 57.40$, p = .000 b > a c > a d > a e > a
Criminal history						
% with at least one non-violent offence	0	100.0% (39)	84.3% (43)	58.5% (31)	53.7% (22)	$X^2(4, N = 238) = 116.57$, p = .000 b > a, c, d, e c > a, d, e d > a e > a

Table 16.1 (continued)

| | Age at first crime | | | | | |
	a No crime (n = 57)	b < 18 years (n = 39)	c 18–22 years (n = 51)	d 23–30 years (n = 53)	e 31 and older (n = 41)	Test
Mean number of non-violent offences	0	22.85 (SD = 29.02)	11.20 (SD = 20.15)	4.45 (SD = 9.31)	2.05 (SD = 3.01)	X^2 (4, N = 238) = 116.78, p = .000 b > a, c, d, e c > a, d, e d > a e > a
% with at least one violent offence	0	87.2% (34)	78.4% (40)	88.7% (47)	90.2% (37)	X^2 (4, N = 238) = 139.78, p= .000 b > a c > a d > a e > a
Mean number of violent offences	0	5.69 (SD = 6.18)	4.35 (SD = 7.81)	2.53 (SD = 2.64)	1.95 (SD = 1.92)	X^2 (4, N = 238) = 103.39, p = .000 b > a, d, e c > a d > a e > a
% who committed at least one homicide	0	15.4% (6)	13.7% (7)	18.9% (10)	36.6% (15)	X^2 (4, N = 238) = 23.78, p = .000 e > a, b, c d > a b > a c > a

Criminality among persons with severe mental illness

Table 16.1 (continued)

Age at first crime

	a No crime (n = 57)	b < 18 years (n = 39)	c 18–22 years (n = 51)	d 23–30 years (n = 53)	e 31 and older (n = 41)	Test
Aggressive behaviour						
% hurt victim so badly that inhospital treatment was required	17.3% (9)	63.2% (24)	40.4% (19)	50.9% (27)	52.5% (21)	X^2 (4, N = 230) = 23.19, p = .000 b > a, c c > a d > a e > a
Parents and Siblings						
% with a mentally ill father or brother(s)	28.9% (15)	21.1% (8)	39.1% (18)	17.0% (8)	25.0% (10)	X^2 (4, N = 223) = 6.71, p = .152
% with a mentally ill mother or sister(s)	40.7% (22)	21.1% (8)	47.8% (22)	40.4% (21)	32.5% (13)	X^2 (4, N = 230) = 7.34, p = .119
% with a criminal father or brother(s)	20.8% (11)	31.6% (12)	36.2% (17)	11.5% (6)	12.2% (5)	X^2 (4, N = 231) = 13.16, p = .0.11 b > d, e c > d, e
% with a criminal mother or sister(s)	5.7% (3)	13.2% (5)	6.4% (3)	3.9% (2)	2.4 (1)	X^2 (4, N = 231) = 4.78, p = .311
% with father or brother(s) with substance abuse	38.9% (21)	55.3% (21)	48.9% (23)	38.5% (20)	39.0% (16)	X^2 (4, N = 232) = 4.04, p = .400

Table 16.1 (continued)

	Age at first crime					
	a No crime (n = 57)	b < 18 years (n = 39)	c 18–22 years (n = 51)	d 23–30 years (n = 53)	e 31 and older (n = 41)	Test
% with mother or sister (s) with substance abuse	24.5% (13)	18.4% (7)	28.6% (14)	25.0% (13)	12.2% (5)	X^2 (4, N = 233) = 4.23, p = .376
Childhood and adolescence						
% below average in elementary school	26.9% (14)	28.9% (11)	42.6% (20)	21.2% (11)	12.5% (5)	X^2 (4, N = 299) = 11.09, p = .026 c > d, e
% with conduct disorder	5.6% (3)	48.7% (19)	37.3% (19)	13.2% (7)	7.3% (3)	X^2 (4, N = 238) = 39.89, p = .000 b > a, d, e c > a, d, e
Mean number of CD symptoms before age 15	0.65 (SD = 1.22)	3.13 (SD = 2.85)	2.12 (SD = 2.07)	1.08 (SD = 2.00)	.68 (SD = 1.61)	X^2 (4, N = 241) = 44.76, p = .000 b > a, d, e c > a, d, e
Substance abuse before 18	33.3% (17)	73.7% (28)	57.5% (27)	46.2% (24)	12.5% (5)	X^2 (4, N = 228) = 35.54, p=. 000 b > a, d, e c > a, e d > a, e a > e
% Treatment before age 18	25.5% (13)	34.2% (13)	31.9% (15)	21.2% (11)	7.3% (3)	X^2 (4, N = 229) = 10.33, p=. 035 a > e b > e c > e

A typology of offenders with schizophrenia

We have proposed a typology of offenders with schizophrenic disorders based on age of onset and persistence of antisocial behaviour. Type I, the early-start offenders, display conduct problems from a young age that escalate in severity and frequency as they grow up. A second type of offender with schizophrenia displays no antisocial behaviour prior to illness onset, but a stable pattern of aggressive behaviour thereafter. A third type displays no antisocial behaviour before illness onset or for many years thereafter, and then engages in very serious violence towards others. The available evidence suggests that these three types differ as to both aetiology and response to treatment.

Early-start offenders with schizophrenia: Type I

For reasons that are currently unknown, conduct disorder (CD)[4] prior to age 15 is associated with an increased risk of developing schizophrenia (Robins 1993; Robins *et al.* 1991). A recent investigation of a population cohort examined this association prospectively and found that 40 per cent of those who developed schizophrenic disorders by age 26 had displayed CD prior to age 15 (Kim-Cohen *et al.* 2003). In clinical samples of persons with schizophrenia, the prevalence of CD varies depending on where the sample is recruited. For example, among well functioning individuals with schizophrenia living in the community, 23 per cent of the men and 17 per cent of the women were found to have presented CD prior to age 15. In a sample of men with schizophrenia who had been found not guilty by reason of insanity for a criminal offence, 27 per cent displayed CD prior to age 15. Among a representative sample of men with schizophrenia who were convicted for a criminal offence and received a sentence of two years or longer, 62 per cent met criteria for CD prior to mid-adolescence (Hodgins *et al.* 1998). As can be seen in Table 16.1, the earlier the age at first crime, the greater the proportion of the offenders with schizophrenia who had presented CD in childhood.

Among persons with schizophrenia, CD prior to age 15 is associated with criminality and aggressive behaviour into middle age. Among the 248 men who participated in our international study and who are described in Table 16.1, 52 met criteria for CD before age 15. At the time official criminal records were collected the men were aged on average 38.6 years (SD = 11.1). A diagnosis of CD prior to age 15 was positively associated with the number of convictions for non-violent crimes (odds ratio = 3.70, 2.11–6.50) and for violent crimes (odds ratio = 2.64, 1.63–4.26) committed during adulthood. More surprisingly, as presented in Figure 16.1, the number of CD symptoms present prior to age 15 was positively – and linearly – related to the number of convictions. These relationships between CD prior to age 15 and subsequent lifetime offending remained significant after controlling for lifetime diagnoses of substance misuse disorders (Hodgins *et al.* 2005). (We will return to this issue.) This finding is consistent with results of a number of other studies (Crocker *et al.* 2005; Fulwiler and Ruthazer 1999; Mueser *et al.* 2006).

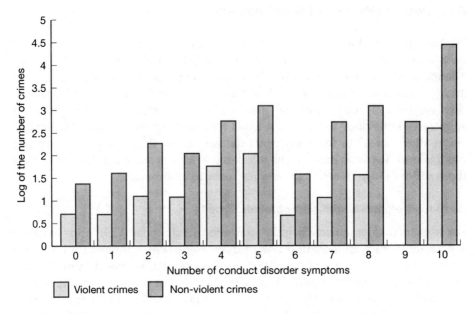

Figure 16.1 Number of non-violent and violent crimes as a function of the number of conduct disorder systems

For two years after discharge, these men were interviewed at six-monthly intervals and asked to provide samples of hair and urine for drug testing. The percentages of participants who were reported to have engaged in aggressive behavior during each six-month period was low (7.5 per cent, 8.9 per cent, 8.3 per cent, 10.3 per cent). There was no evidence that aggressive behaviour in one period was related to participation in the subsequent interview. The diagnosis of CD and the number of CD symptoms were associated with increases in the risk of aggressive behaviour during the 24-month follow-up period, after controlling for lifetime diagnoses of substance use disorders, current alcohol and drug use, and compliance with medication (Hodgins *et al.* 2005). This finding has now been replicated in a US study of patients enrolled in a medication trial (Swanson *et al.* 2006) and in a UK sample of patients with SMI (Hodgins *et al.* in press).

In industrialised western countries, almost all adolescents with CD misuse alcohol and/or illicit drugs at earlier ages than other children (Robins and McEvoy 1990) and behavioural genetic studies indicate that the genetic contribution to early-onset and stable conduct problems includes a vulnerability for substance misuse (Krueger *et al.* 2002). In other words, substance misuse is one aspect of early onset antisocial behaviour that remains stable across the life-span. The available evidence shows that men with schizophrenia and a history of conduct problems going back to childhood almost always present substance misuse disorders that had onset in adolescence (Fulwiler *et al.* 1997; Moran and Hodgins 2004; Mueser *et al.* 1999). Importantly, however, as described above, among men who develop schizophrenia after presenting CD, it is the early presentation of conduct problems rather than past or current substance misuse that is associated with criminality. Most studies that have examined the links between substance misuse and violence did not measure childhood conduct problems (Eronen *et al.*

1996; Steadman *et al.* 1998; Wallace *et al.* 2004). Those that did found that it was the childhood conduct problems, rather than the substance misuse, that was associated with offending (Hodgins *et al.* 2005; Rice and Harris 1995; Swanson *et al.* 2006; Tengström *et al.* 2004). These results suggest that among offenders with schizophrenic disorders who have a history of conduct problems since at least mid-adolescence, successful treatment of substance misuse would not eliminate offending and aggressive behaviour. Rather, in this sub-type of offenders with schizophrenia interventions that target the long-standing pattern of antisocial behaviour would be required to reduce offending (Mueser *et al.* 2006).

Early-start offenders with schizophrenic disorders are distinguished from other offenders with schizophrenia, and from other persons with the disorder, not only by their patterns of crime and aggressive behaviour but also by characteristics present before illness onset. Using the sample of 248 men with schizophrenic disorders from our international study that is described above, those who had presented CD as compared to those who had not had more fathers and brothers with criminal records and substance misuse problems, more mothers and sisters with substance misuse problems, more of them had obtained below average marks as early as elementary school, fewer completed high school and more reported experiencing physical abuse before age 12 (Hodgins *et al.* 2005). To date, there is no evidence that the presentation of schizophrenia differs among those with a prior history of CD (Hodgins *et al.* 2005; Mueser *et al.* 2006). There are some intriguing findings, however, suggesting that men with CD who subsequently develop schizophrenia are less compromised neurologically than other men with schizophrenia (Naudts and Hodgins 2005). These findings tentatively suggest that one of the reasons why those with prior CD are able to engage in various types of offending, for example buying and selling illicit drugs, is that they present a higher level of cognitive skills than others with the disorder.

No antisocial or aggressive behaviour prior to illness onset: Type II

We know little about this type of person with schizophrenia. We do know, however, from a great deal of research on general population samples that it is very rare for adults with no prior history of conduct problems to begin committing criminal offences or to begin engaging in aggressive behaviour towards others. This can be clearly seen, for example, by examining the non-disordered subjects in the birth cohort studies that examined the associations between mental disorders and offending (Hodgins 1992; Hodgins *et al.* 1996; Moffitt *et al.* 2002). When repeated aggressive behaviour does onset in adulthood, it is often associated with a brain disorder or brain damage, for example caused by excessive and prolonged use of alcohol. Among the 248 men with schizophrenia recruited into our international study, those whose criminal careers began after the onset of schizophrenia, as compared to the early starters, by middle age had committed many fewer non-violent offences and fewer violent offences, fewer of them had fathers or brothers with criminal records but similar proportions of both male and female relatives with substance misuse problems. In childhood and adolescence, they presented almost no conduct problems, and academic performance was better, consistent with findings from other studies (Mueser *et al.* 2006). While some studies have reported that these offenders present particularly serious problems with illicit drug use (Mueser *et al.* 1999, 2006), our findings did not support this conclusion.

No antisocial or aggressive behaviour prior to illness onset, or for years after, and then a violent offence: Type III

This type of offender attracts a great deal of attention from the media because they typically seriously harm, even kill, another person seemingly 'out of the blue'. Their existence and low numbers, however, are evident in most studies (Erb *et al.* 2001; Hodgins *et al.* 2005). They obtain low ratings on risk assessment instruments such as the Historical, Clinical, Risk Scale (Webster *et al.* 1997) because they have no history of childhood problems or prior antisocial or aggressive behaviour, and few, if any, clinical or risk signs assessed by this instrument. Based on anecdotal evidence from clinicians who had assessed such patients shortly after they had assaulted or killed someone, we hypothesised that for reasons that are currently unknown, these patients become extremely callous and insensitive to others prior to the assault. It is well known that among both animals and humans, callousness releases the usual constraints on aggressive behaviour. Consequently, if due to changes in the brain related to schizophrenia such individuals become callous, and then, for example, a family member or carer annoys them, they simply strike out. Using the data from the international sample described above, we found that callousness (measured by four items on the PCL-R) was associated with violent crime independently of a lifetime history of antisocial behaviour and substance misuse (Sunak *et al.* in preparation). We hypothesise that among people with schizophrenia the level of callousness fluctuates over time as do positive and negative symptoms of psychosis, reflecting ongoing changes in the brain.

Conclusions regarding the typology of offenders

The above findings suggest that this typology may be useful for guiding research into the aetiology of offending among persons with schizophrenia and for studies designed to identify effective treatments.

Symptoms and violence

Many mental health professionals believe that psychotic symptoms drive violent behaviour, at least in some patients with schizophrenia. There is some evidence to support this belief. For example, by examining 128 of the men with schizophrenia from the international study described above, we found that positive symptoms and threat-control-override (TCO) symptoms were associated with significant increases in the risk of aggressive behaviour after controlling for comorbid APD[4] and substance misuse or high Psychopathy Checklist scores (PCL-R) (Hare 1991) and substance misuse (Hodgins *et al.* 2003). A similar US study reported that in a sample of persons with SMI, the affect and thought disturbance subscales of the Brief Psychiatric Rating Scale (BPRS) were associated with violence (Crocker *et al.* 2005). In a sample comprised mainly, but not exclusively, of patients with SMI who had recently been admitted to a forensic ward, the BPRS scores predicted aggressive behaviour on the ward (Gray *et al.* 2003). Further, evidence is accumulating to show that second-generation neuroleptic medications are effective in reducing aggressive behaviour both among inpatients (Volavka *et al.* 2004) and patients living in the community (Swanson *et al.* 2004a, 2004b). Since the principal effect of these medications is to reduce positive symptoms of psychosis, these findings also suggest that high levels of psychotic symptoms are associated with aggressive behaviour.

The results of other investigations, however, do not concur (Appelbaum *et al.* 2000; Bjørkly 2002a, 2002b; Hersch and Borum 1998). In an exhaustive review of studies examining the associations between psychotic symptoms and aggressive behaviour, Bjørkly (2002a) concluded that there is evidence that persecutory delusions increase the risk of violence in some patients, that persecutory delusions associated with emotional distress increase the risk of aggressive behaviour and that there is limited evidence that TCO symptoms are associated with violence. Further, he found no evidence to support the proposition that hallucinations *per se* are associated with violence, but hallucinations ordering violence against others increase the risk. Finally, he concluded that the evidence of a combined effect of hallucinations and delusions on aggressive behaviour is inconclusive (Bjørkly 2002b).

The results of studies of the association of symptoms and aggressive behaviour may differ simply because the definitions and sources of information about violence vary widely, from self-reports of aggressive behaviour to convictions for a violent crime, to reports of aggressive incidents by ward staff (see, for example, Naudts and Hodgins 2005).

The available evidence suggests that in order to understand the role that psychotic symptoms may play with regard to aggressive behaviour, it is essential to distinguish between aggressive behaviour that occurs during an acute episode of psychosis on an inpatient psychiatric ward from aggressive behaviour that occurs in the community. All of the evidence that has been reviewed in this chapter so far concerned crime and aggressive behaviour that occurred in the community. Some studies focus exclusively on inpatients in an acute phase of illness (Krakowski and Czobor 2004; Newhill *et al.* 1995; Steinert 2002), others focus on inpatients in a stablised phase of illness (Tengström *et al.* 2006; Hodgins *et al.* 2003), while others focus on patients who are living in the community (Appelbaum *et al.* 2000; Crocker *et al.* 2005; Hodgins *et al.* 2003; Newhill *et al.* 1995). Results suggest that both the phase of illness and the living situation may influence the association between psychotic symptoms and violence. Importantly, the factors that correlate with violence on acute inpatient wards such as confusion and thought disorder but not gender (Krakowski and Czobor 2004; Newhill *et al.* 1995; Steinert 2002;) differ from those associated with aggressive behaviour in the community.

Studying the role of psychotic symptoms in aggressive behaviour among people with SMI living in the community presents a methodological challenge as it requires that psychotic symptoms are measured before the aggressive behaviour. Many of the studies that suggest that psychotic symptoms are associated with violence assessed symptoms after the violence occurred and thus confounded antecedents and consequences (Taylor 1985; Link and Stueve 1994).

Other methodological features of the studies examining psychotic symptoms and aggressive behaviour may explain the contradictory results, as noted by several authors (Appelbaum *et al.* 2000; Bjørkly 2002a, 2002b; Hodgins *et al.* 2003; Stompe *et al.* 2004). One, the samples of patients studied often include both those with schizophrenia and those with major affective disorders (Appelbaum *et al.* 2000; Crocker *et al.* 2005; Gray *et al.* 2003) and sometimes those with a primary diagnosis of personality disorder (Gray *et al.* 2003) or substance use disorders (Appelbaum *et al.* 2000). Psychotic symptoms may be differentially associated with violence in schizophrenia as opposed to mania or personality disorder. A second feature of previous studies that may explain why results differ is the way in which psychotic symptoms are assessed. This influences the number and type of symptoms that are elicited, as does the source of information (Appelbaum *et al.* 2000; Bjørkly 2002c). Three, persecutory delusions (Buchanan *et al.* 1993; Wessely *et al.* 1993; Taylor 1985) and threat/control-override (TCO) symptoms (Appelbaum *et al.* 1999) may only be associated with violence when negative affect is also present, yet many studies assess only psychotic symptoms and fail to measure other symptoms such as depression and anxiety.

A final reason why the results concerning the role of psychotic symptoms and violence may be contradictory is the failure of most studies to control for previous history of violence. One study controlled for previous violence by using Psychopathy Checklist Screening Version scores (PCL – SV) (Hart *et al.* 1995) and found that PCL scores and not symptoms were related to future violent behaviour (Appelbaum *et al.* 2000). In this study, only 17 per cent of the participants had a primary diagnosis of schizophrenia.

We examined the associations between symptoms of psychosis, anxiety and depression and aggressive behaviour among the men with schizophrenia in our international study during the two-year period when they were living in the community. During four sequential six-month periods, symptoms were assessed at the beginning of the period and used to predict aggressive behaviour that occurred in the subsequent six months. Predictions of aggressive behaviour from symptoms and changes in symptoms were calculated for each period, controlling for APD and substance misuse defined as either a self-report of use, detection of drugs in hair or urine, or a refusal to provide samples of hair and urine.

The present investigation offers several advantages with respect to the methodological issues previously discussed. The sample is relatively large (n = 248), and homogeneous with respect to principal diagnosis (schizophrenia or schizo-afffective disorder) and sex (all men). Symptoms and changes in symptoms were measured prospectively. We hypothesised that a sudden change in symptom levels, as well as the absolute levels, might trigger aggressive behaviour. We measured anxiety and depression in addition to psychotic symptoms. We focused on aggressive behaviour in the community reported by either the participant or a collateral informant and experienced – and specifically trained – psychiatrists rated symptoms on standardised and validated scales. We assessed the impact of patients' histories of antisocial behaviour as indexed by a diagnosis of APD and we measured substance misuse both objectively (hair and urine samples) and subjectively. As recommended (McNiel *et al.* 2003), predictions were made for relatively short periods (six months).

We conducted a series of regression models[5] to estimate the association between psychotic symptoms and aggressive behaviour in the subsequent six months. In the first model, we entered site, type of hospital at discharge – forensic or general – and presence or absence of a diagnosis of APD. In the second stage, we entered alcohol and drug use defined as a self-report or a refusal to provide samples of hair and urine or traces of illicit drugs in hair and/or urine. In the third model, we entered the number of clinically relevant positive and negative symptoms as assessed using the Positive and Negative Symptom Scale (PANSS) (Kay *et al.* 1987), the number of clinically relevant negative symptoms, the number of TCO symptoms (see Link and Stueve 1994), the total score on the Hamilton Rating Scale for Depression (Hamilton 1960) and the score on the anxiety item of the PANSS. In the fourth model, we entered the changes in symptoms in the six months preceding the measure of aggressive behaviour. The results are presented in Table 16.2. The most important finding is the number of variables that did not predict aggressive behaviour, including alcohol and drug use, TCO symptoms, negative symptoms and depression symptoms. Only four predictors remained in the final model. The risk of aggressive behaviour was increased six times by a diagnosis of APD,[4] and one and a half times by the number of clinically relevant positive symptoms, by the change in the level of positive symptoms and by the presence of anxiety. These results again demonstrate that a history of antisocial behaviour going back to at least mid-adolescence is a strong predictor of aggressive behaviour among middle-aged men with schizophrenic disorders who are being treated in the community. Positive symptoms of psychosis that were measured prospectively and anxiety had a much weaker, but statistically significant, association with aggressive behaviour. Future studies may provide more clinically relevant findings if they focus on the role of symptoms in triggering aggressive behaviour among different subtypes of patients with schizophrenia, and if symptoms are measured more frequently.

Victimisation

At the beginning of this chapter, we described a sample of inpatients with SMI from an urban mental health trust that we have assessed. During the six months prior to admission, 56.7 per cent of the men and 48.2 per cent of the women reported being victims of physical assaults. These findings add to a growing body of evidence showing that persons with SMI are at increased risk of being victims of aggressive behaviours and crimes after controlling for socio-demographic factors (Silver *et al.* 2005; Teplin *et al.* 2005; Walsh *et al.* 2003). While rates of victimisation vary from place to place (Honkonen *et al.* 2004), the correlates are usually found to be similar and include the victim's own aggressive behaviour towards others, illicit drug use, comorbid personality disorder, symptomatology and homelessness. A recent study showed that both current victimisation and childhood maltreatment contributed to substance misuse, demoralisation and increased levels of psychotic symptoms among persons with SMI (Shahar *et al.* 2004). It may be that certain environments foster, even teach, the use of aggressive behaviour to resolve conflicts and to solve problems. Research is urgently needed to understand the link between victimisation and aggressive behaviour among persons with SMI and to identify the factors associated with reductions in both. To date, only one study has addressed this issue and found that adherence to treatment that resulted from community treatment orders for patients with SMI was associated with a reduction in victimisation (Hiday *et al.* 2002).

Table 16.2 Statistically significant predictions, expressed as odds ratios, of aggressive behaviour in the community

| | Odds ratios (95% confidence intervals) for aggressive behaviour | | | |
	Model 1	Model 2	Model 3	Model 4
Stage 1: Stable characteristics (n = 773)				
Forensic general	2.20 (1.12, 4.35)			
APD	5.01 (2.53, 9.95)	5.37 (2.55, 11.29)	5.43 (2.38-12.39)	6.07 (2.64, 13.95)
Stage 2: Alcohol and/or drug use (n = 705)				
Alcohol self-report				
Illicit drug use				
Stage 3: Symptoms (n = 675)				
Positive symptoms				1.49 (91.20, 1.84)
Negative symptoms				
TCO symptoms				
Depression symptoms[A]				
Anxiety symptoms			1.58 (1.13, 2.21)	1.58 (1.13, 2.22)
Stage 4: Change in symptoms (n = 672)				
Change in positive symptoms				1.45 (1.23, 171)
Change in negative symptoms				
Change in TCO symptoms				
Change in depression symptoms				
Change in anxiety symptoms				

A. Square root of the total score on the Hamilton Rating Scale for Depression

The effects of treatment in reducing and preventing crime and aggressive behaviour among persons with schizophrenia

There are no randomised controlled trials (RCTs) of treatments aimed at reducing offending or aggressive behaviour among persons with schizophrenia. A small body of evidence is emerging, however, that identifies treatments worth testing in an RCT. Naturalistic follow-up studies of patients discharged from forensic hospitals document low rates of criminal recidivism (for a review, see Heilbrun and Peters 2000; Maden *et al.* 2004; Steels *et al.* 1998). Using the data described above on the international sample, we found that during the two years after discharge the forensic patients engaged in less aggressive behaviour and presented lower levels of symptoms than those discharged from general adult psychiatric wards. The findings could not be explained by community treatment orders or probation orders (Hodgins *et al.* 2007b). Since most of the men with schizophrenia in forensic hospitals had been treated, often for many years, in general adult services prior to admission to a forensic hospital, the findings do suggest that something goes on in the forensic hospitals that has long-term and positive consequences. The follow-up studies of patients discharged from forensic hospitals suggest that specialised forensic community care has a positive association with good outcome (Heilbrun and Peters 2000). There is also evidence from the US that community orders requiring patients to comply with treatment (i.e. taking medication), if left in place for at least 18 months, are associated with reductions in aggressive behaviour (Swartz and Swanson 2004). Evidence concerning a positive effect of second-generation neuroleptic medications on reducing aggressive behaviour of patients in the community is beginning to accumulate (Swanson *et al.* 2004a, 2004b). Taken together, the evidence strongly suggests, but does not prove, that when mental health professionals treat the illness and simultaneously assess and manage the risk of violence reductions in aggressive behaviour are evident. Since positive and other symptoms do seem to be associated with increasing the vulnerability for aggressive behaviour, an integrated programme of treatment provided by one clinical team is necessary to both assure optimal control of symptoms, psychosocial functioning and an absence of offending and aggressive behaviour.

Conclusions

There is now robust evidence that persons with SMI, particularly those with schizophrenia, are at increased risk of engaging in aggressive behaviour towards others and non-violent and violent crime. Currently, mental health policy and practice in the UK does not take account of this evidence. Consequently, large numbers of patients in general adult psychiatric services are committing crimes, assaulting others and experiencing victimisation. A few are transferred to very expensive forensic inpatient services and, after discharge, criminal recidivism is low. Future research into the causes of the vulnerability for crime and aggressive behaviour needs to be theoretically driven and test hypotheses. The typology of offenders presented here may prove to be a useful heuristic tool. Studies of the effectiveness of various interventions will also advance knowledge more quickly if they fully characterise the patients who benefit and those who do not from the intervention being tested.

Selected further reading

The paper by Crocker, A. G., Mueser, K. T., Drake, R. E., Clark, R. E., McHugo, G. J. and Ackerson, T.H.. (2005) 'Antisocial personality, psychopathy, and violence in persons with dual disorders', *Criminal Justice and Behavior*, 32 (4): 452–76, describes a sample of persons with schizophrenia and demonstrates how early-onset conduct problems continue to be associated with antisocial behaviour in adulthood.

The study by Hodgins, S. and Müller-Isberner, R. (2004) 'Preventing crime by people with schizophrenia: the role of psychiatric services', *British Journal of Psychiatry*, 185: 245–50, describes pathways into forensic care for persons with schizophrenia. It demonstrates that most forensic patients are treated, often for many years, in general psychiatry where their criminal activities are ignored. Finally, after a very serious offence they are transferred to forensic care.

The study by Hodgins, S., Müller-Isberner, R. and Allaire, J. (2006) 'Attempting to understand the increase in the numbers of forensic beds in Europe: a multi-site study of patients in forensic and general psychiatric services', *International Journal of Forensic Mental Health*, 5 (2): 173–84, demonstrates that inattention by general adult forensic services to antisocial and aggressive behaviour of persons with schizophrenia may be an important reason for the increase in the numbers of forensic psychiatric beds.

The paper by Hodgins, S., Tiihonen, J. and Ross, D. (2005) 'The consequences of conduct disorder for males who develop schizophrenia: associations with criminality, aggressive behavior, substance use, and psychiatric services', *Schizophrenia Research*, 78: 323–35, describes a sample of persons with schizophrenia and demonstrates that conduct disorder prior to age 15 is associated with violent and non-violent offending through middle age.

Notes

1 Severe mental illness includes schizophrenia, schizo-affective disorder, major depression, bipolar disorder and other non-drug and alcohol-related psychoses. These disorders onset in late adolescence or early adulthood and in the great majority of cases remain chronic throughout life. For a further discussion, see Hodgins and Janson (2002). Throughout this chapter, the term schizophrenia refers to both schizophrenia and schiz-affective disorder.
2 Calculated from the data that are publicly available.
3 It is important to note that two recent UK studies of homicide offenders cannot address this issue. Shaw *et al.* (2006) investigated the psychiatric histories of persons convicted of homicide and therefore could not identify homicide offenders with SMI who received no treatment prior to the killing. Maden (2006) examined persons with SMI who committed a homicide while in psychiatric care.
4 A diagnosis of conduct disorder prior to age 15 is a necessary part of the diagnosis of Antisocial Personality Disorder according to DSM criteria.
5 We investigated predictors of aggressive behaviour using a multi-stage stepwise logistic regression with within-subject correlated error. Estimations were by means of the Generalised Estimating Equations (GEE). In the first stage, site (country), type of

hospital, forensic or general, and APD were entered into the model. In the second stage alcohol and drug use in the same period were entered stepwise into the model, using an Enter criterion of p < .15 and an Exit criterion of p > .20. In the third stage, positive, negative, TCO, depression and anxiety symptoms in the previous period were entered stepwise into the model, using the same criteria. In the fourth stage, change scores (difference between current and previous period) of positive, negative, TCO, depression and anxiety symptoms were entered stepwise into the model, again using the same criteria.

References

Appelbaum, P.S., Robbins, P.C. and Roth, L.H. (1999) 'Dimensional approach to delusions: comparison across types and diagnoses', *American Journal of Psychiatry*, 156: 1938–43.

Appelbaum, P.S., Robbins, P.C. and Monahan, J. (2000) 'Violence and delusions: Data from the MacArthur Violence Risk Assessment Study', *American Journal of Psychiatry*, 157: 566–72.

Arseneault, L., Moffitt, T.E., Caspi, A., Taylor, P.J. and Silva, P.A. (2000) 'Mental disorders and violence in a total birth cohort: results from the Dunedin Study', *Archives of General Psychiatry*, 5: 979–86.

Beaudoin, M.N., Hodgins, S. and Lavoie, F. (1993) 'Homicide, schizophrenia, and substance abuse or dependency', *Canadian Journal of Psychiatry*, 38: 541–6.

Belfrage, H.A. (1998) 'Ten-year follow-up of criminality in Stockholm mental patients: new evidence for a relation between mental disorders and crime', *British Journal of Psychiatry*, 38: 145–55.

Bjørkly, S. (2002a) 'Psychotic symptoms and violence towards others – a literature review of some preliminary findings: Part 2. Hallucinations', *Aggression and Violent Behavior*, 7: 605–15.

Bjørkly, S. (2002b) 'Psychotic symptoms and violence towards others – a literature review of some preliminary findings: Part 1. Delusions', *Aggression and Violent Behavior*, 7: 617–31.

Bjørkly, S. (2002c) 'SCL-90-R profiles in a sample of severely violent psychiatric inpatients', *Aggressive Behavior*, 28: 446–57.

Brennan, A., Mednick, S.A., and Hodgins, S. (2000) 'Major mental disorders and criminal violence in a Danish birth cohort', *Archives of General Psychiatry*, 57: 494–500.

Buchanan, A., Reed, A., Wessely, S., Garety, P., Taylor P. and Grubin, D. (1993) 'Acting on delusions, II: The phenomenological correlates of acting on delusions', *British Journal of Psychiatry*, 163: 77–81.

Crocker, A.G., Mueser, K.T., Drake, R.E., Clark, R.E., McHugo, G.J. and Ackerson, T.H. (2005) 'Antisocial personality, psychopathy, and violence in persons with dual disorders', *Criminal Justice and Behavior*, 32 (4): 452–76.

Davies, N. (2004a) 'Scandal of society's misfits dumped in jail', *Guardian*, 6 December.

Davies, N. (2004b) 'Trapped in a cycle of self-harm and despair for want of a psychiatric bed', *Guardian*, 7 December.

Davies, N. (2004c) 'Wasted lives of the young let down by jail system', *Guardian*, 8 December.

Department of Health (1999) *National Service Framework for Mental Health: Modern Standards and Service Models*. London: Department of Health.

Erb, M., Hodgins, S., Freese, R., Müller-Isberner, R. and Jöckel, D. (2001) 'Homicide and schizophrenia: maybe treatment does have a preventive effect', *Criminal Behaviour and Mental Health*, 11: 6–26.

Eronen, M., Hakola, O. and Tiihonen, J. (1996) 'Factors associated with homicide recidivism in a 13-year sample of homicide offenders in Finland', *Psychiatric Services*, 47 (4): 403–6.

Fazel, S. and Danesh, J. (2002) 'Serious mental disorder in 23 000 prisoners: a systematic review of 62 surveys', *Lancet*, 259: 545–50.

Fulwiler, C. and Ruthazer, R. (1999) 'Premorbid risk factors for violence in adult mental illness', *Comprehensive Psychiatry*, 40 (2): 96–100.

Fulwiler, C., Grossman, H., Forbes, C. and Ruthazer, R. (1997) 'Early-onset substance abuse and community violence by outpatients with chronic mental illness', *Psychiatric Services*, 48: 1181–5.

Gray, N.S., McGleish, A., MacCulloch, M.J., Hill, C. and Timmons, D. (2003) 'Prediction of violence and self-harm in mentally disordered offenders: a prospective study of the efficacy of HCR-20, PCL-R, and psychiatric symptomatology', *Journal of Consulting and Clinical Psychology*, 71 (3): 443–51.

Hamilton, M. (1960) 'A rating scale for depression', *Journal of Neurology and Neurosurgery and Psychiatry*, 23: 56–62.

Hare, R. (1991) *The Hare Psychopathy Checklist – Revised*. Toronto: Multi-Health Systems.

Hart, S.D., Cox, D.N. and Hare, R.D. (1995) *The Hare Psychopathy Checklist: Screening Version (PCL:SV)*. Toronto: Multi-Health Systems.

Heilbrun, K. and Peters, L. (2000) 'Community-based treatment programmes', in S. Hodgins and R. Müller-Isberner (eds), *Violence, Crime and Mentally Disordered Offenders: Concepts and Methods for Effective Treatment and Prevention*. Chichester: John Wiley & Sons, pp. 193–215.

Hersch, K. and Borum, R. (1998) 'Command hallucinations, compliance, and risk assessment', *Journal of the American Academy of Psychiatry and the Law*, 26: 353–9.

Hiday, V.A., Swartz, M.S., Swanson, J.W., Borum, R. and Wagner, H.R. (2002) 'Impact of outpatient commitment on vicitimization of people with severe mental illness', *American Journal of Psychiatry*, 159: 8.

Hodgins, S. (1992) 'Mental disorder, intellectual deficiency and crime: evidence from a birth cohort', *Archives of General Psychiatry*, 49: 476–83.

Hodgins, S. (1998) 'Epidemiological investigations of the associations between major mental disorders and crime: methodological limitations and validity of the conclusions', *Social Psychiatry and Epidemiology*, 33 (1): 29–37.

Hodgins, S. and Côté, G. (1995) 'Major mental disorder among Canadian penitentiary inmates', in L. Stewart, L. Stermac and C. Webster (eds), *Clinical Criminology: Toward Effective Correctional Treatment*. Toronto: Solliciteur général et Service correctionnel du Canada, pp. 6–20.

Hodgins, S. and Janson, C.G. (2002) *Criminality and Violence among the Mentally Disordered: The Stockholm Metropolitan Project*. Cambridge: Cambridge University Press.

Hodgins, S. and Müller-Isberner, R. (2004) 'Preventing crime by people with schizophrenia: the role of psychiatric services', *British Journal of Psychiatry*, 185: 245–50.

Hodgins, S., Mednick, S.A., Brennan, P., Schulsinger, F. and Engberg, M. (1996) 'Mental disorder and crime: evidence from a Danish birth cohort', *Archives of General Psychiatry*, 53: 489–96.

Hodgins, S., Toupin, J. and Côté, G. (1998) 'Schizophrenia and antisocial personality disorder: a criminal combination', in L.B. Schlesinger (ed.), *Explorations in Criminal Psychopathology: Clinical Syndromes with Forensic Implications*. Springfield, IL: Charles C. Thomas, pp. 217–37.

Hodgins, S., Hiscoke, U.L. and Freese, R. (2003) 'The antecedents of aggressive behavior among men with schizophrenia: a prospective investigation of patients in community treatment', *Behavioral Sciences and the Law*, 21: 523–46.

Hodgins, S., Tiihonen, J. and Ross, D. (2005) 'The consequences of conduct disorder for males who develop schizophrenia: associations with criminality, aggressive behavior, substance use, and psychiatric services', *Schizophrenia Research*, 78: 323–35.

Hodgins, S., Müller-Isberner, R. and Allaire, J. (2006a) 'Attempting to understand the increase in the numbers of forensic beds in Europe: a multi-site study of patients in forensic and general psychiatric services', *International Journal of Forensic Mental Health*, 5 (2): 173–84.

Hodgins, S., Muller-Isberner, R., Tiihonen, J., Repo-Tiihonem, E., Eronen, M., Eaves, D., Hart, S., Webster, C., Levander, S., Tuninger, E., Ross, D. and Kronstrand, R. (2007b). 'A comparison of general and forensic patients with schizophrenia living in the community', *International Journal of Foresic Mental Health* 6(1): 63–75.

Hodgins, S., Tengström, A., Östermann, R., Eaves, D., Hart, S. and Konstrand, R. (2006b) 'An international comparison of community treatment programs for mentally ill persons who have committed criminal offences', *Criminal Justice and Behavior*, 20 (10): 1–26.

Hodgins, S., Alderton, J., Cree, A., About, A. and Mak, T. (2007a) 'Aggressive behaviour, victimisation, and crime among severely mentally ill patients requiring hospitalisation', *British Journal of Psychiatry* 191: 343–350.

Hodgins, S., Cree, A., Alderton, J., and Mak, T. (in press) 'Conduct disorder in severe mental illness: associations with aggressive behaviour, crime and victimisation', *Psychological Medicine*.

Honkonen, T., Henriksson, M., Kolvisto, A.-M., Stengard, E. and Salokangas, R.K.R. (2004) 'Violent victimization in schizophrenia', *Social Psychiatry and Psychiatric Epidemiology*, 39 (8): 606–12.

Kay, S. R., Fiszbein, A. and Opler, A. (1987) 'The positive and negative syndrome scale (PANSS) for schizophrenia', *Schizophrenia Bulletin*, 13: 261–76.

Kim-Cohen, J., Caspi, A., Moffitt, T.E., Harrington, H.L., Milne, B.J. and Poulton, R. (2003) 'Poor juvenile diagnoses in adults with mental disorder: developmental followback of a prospective longitudinal cohort', *Archives of General Psychiatry*, 60: 709–17.

Krakowski, M. and Czobor, P. (2004) 'Gender differences in violent behaviours: relationship to clinical symptoms and psychosocial factors', *American Journal of Psychiatry*, 161 (3): 459–65.

Kramp, P. (2004) 'Editorial: schizophrenia and crime in Denmark', *Criminal Behaviour and Mental Health*, 14: 231–7.

Krueger, R.F., Hicks, B.M., Patrick, C.J., Carlson, S.R., Iacono, W.G. and McGue, M. (2002) 'Etiologic connections among substance dependence, antisocial behavior, and personality: modeling the externalizing spectrum', *Journal of Abnormal Psychology*, 111 (3): 411–24.

Link, B. G. and Stueve, A. (1994) 'Psychotic symptoms and the violent/illegal behavior of mental patients compared to community controls', in J. Monahan, and H. J. Steadman (eds), *Violence and Mental Disorders: Developments in Risk Assessment*. Chicago: University of Chicago Press, pp. 137–60.

McNiel, D.E., Gregory, A.L., Lam, J.N., Binder, R.L. and Sullivan, G.R. (2003) 'Utility of decision support tools for assessing acute risk of violence', *Journal of Consulting and Clinical Psychology*, 71: 945–53.

Maden, A., Scott, F., Burnett, R., Lewis, G.H. and Skapinakis, P. (2004) 'Offending in psychiatric patients after discharge from medium secure units: prospective national cohort study', *British Medical Journal*, 328 (7455): 1534.

Maden, T. (2006) *Review of Homicides by Patients with Severe Mental Illness*. See: National Institute for Mental Health Care Services Improvement Partnership: http://www.nimhe.csip.org.uk/silo/files/review-of-homicides-by-patients-with-severe-mental-illness.pdf

Moffitt, T.E., Caspi, A., Harrington, H. and Milne, B.J. (2002) 'Males on the life-course-persistent and adolescence-limited antisocial pathways: follow-up at age 26 years', *Development and Psychopathology*, 14: 179–207.

Mojtabai, R. (2006) 'Psychotic-like experiences and interpersonal violence in the general population', *Social Psychiatry and Psychiatric Epidemiology*, 40: 1–8.

Monahan, J., Steadman, H.J., Silver, E., Appelbaum, P.S., Robbins, P.C. and Mulvey, E.P. (2001) *Rethinking Risk Assessment*. The MacArthur Study of Mental Disorder and Violence. New York: Oxford University Press.

Moran, P. and Hodgins, S. (2004) 'The correlates of co-morbid antisocial personality disorder in schizophrenia', *Schizophrenia Bulletin*, 30 (4): 791–802.

Mueser, K.T., Rosenberg, S.D., Drake, R.E., Miles, K.M., Wolford, G. and Vidaver, R. (1999) 'Conduct disorder, antisocial personality disorder and substance use disorders in schizophrenia and major affective disorders', *Journal of Studies of Alcohol*, 60: 278–84.

Mueser, K.T., Crocker, A.G., Frisman, L.B., Drake, R.E., Covell, N.H. and Essock, S.M. (2006) 'Conduct disorder and antisocial personality disorder in persons with severe psychiatric and substance use disorders', *Schizophrenia Bulletin*, 32 (4): 626–36.

Naudts, K. and Hodgins, S. (2005) 'Neurobiological correlates of violent behaviour among persons with schizophrenia', *Schizophrenia Bulletin*, 32: 562–72.

Newhill, C.E., Mulvery, E.P. and Lidz, C.W. (1995) 'Characteristics of violence in the community by female patients seen in a psychiatric emergency service', *Psychiatric Services*, 46 (8): 785–9.

Priebe, S., Badesconyi, A., Fioritti, A., Hansson, L., Kilian, R. and Torres-Gonzales, F. (2005) 'Reinstitutionalisation in mental health care: comparison of data on service provision from six European countries', *British Medical Journal*, 330: 123–6.

Rice, M.E. and Harris, G.T. (1995) 'Psychopathy, schizophrenia, alcohol abuse, and violent recidivism', *International Journal of Law and Psychiatry*, 18 (3): 333–42.

Robins, L.N. (1993) 'Childhood conduct problems, adult psychopathology, and crime', in S. Hodgins (ed.), *Mental Disorder and Crime*. Newbury Park, CA: Sage, pp. 173–93.

Robins, L.N. and McEvoy, L.T. (1990) 'Conduct problems as predictors of substance abuse', in L.N. Robins and M. Rutter (eds), *Straight and Devious Pathways from Childhood to Adulthood*. Cambridge: Cambridge University Press, pp. 182–204.

Robins, L.N., Tipp, J. and Przybeck, T. (1991) 'Antisocial personality', in L.N. Robins and D. Regier (eds), *Psychiatric Disorders in America: The Epidemiological Catchment Area Study*. New York: Macmillan/Free Press, pp. 258–90.

Royal College of Psychiatrists and British Psychological Society (2003) *Schizophrenia: Full National Clinical Guideline on Core Interventions in Primary and Secondary Care*, developed by the National Collaborating Centre for Mental Health; commissioned by the National Institute for Clinical Excellence, UK. London and Leicester: Royal College of Psychiatrists and British Psychological Society.

Shahar, G., Wisher, A., Chinnman, M., Sells, D., Kloss, B. and Tebes, J. K. (2004) 'Trauma and adaptation in severe mental illness: the role of self-reported abuse and exposure to community violence', *Journal of Trauma and Dissociation*, 5 (1): 29–47.

Shaw, J., Hunt, I.M., Flynn, S., Meehan, J., Robinson, J. and Bickley, H. (2006) 'Rates of mental disorder in people convicted of homicide: National clinical survey', *British Journal of Psychiatry*, 188: 143–7.

Silver, E., Arseneault, L., Langley, J., Caspi, A. and Moffitt, T.E. (2005) 'Mental disorder and violent victimization in a total birth cohort', *American Journal of Public Health*, 95: 2015–21.

Steadman, H.J., Mulvey, E.P., Monahan, J., Robbins, P.C., Appelbaum, P.S. and Grisso, T. (1998) 'Violence by people discharged from acute psychiatric inpatient facilities and by others in the same neighborhoods', *Archives of General Psychiatry*, 55 (5): 393–401.

Steels, M., Roney, G., Larkin, E., Jones, P., Croudace, T. and Duggan, C. (1998) 'Discharged from special hospital under restrictions: a comparison of the fates of psychopaths and the mentally ill', *Criminal Behaviour and Mental Health*, 8: 39–55.

Steinert, T. (2002) 'Prediction of inpatient violence', *Acta Psychiatrica Scandinavica*, 106: 133–41.

Stompe, T., Ortwein-Swoboda, G. and Schanda, H. (2004) 'Schizophrenia, delusional symptoms and violence: the threat/control-override concept re-examined', *Schizophrenia Bulletin*, 30 (1): 31–44.

Sunak, S., Blackwood, N. and Hodgins, S. (in preparation) 'Deficient affective experience and violence in schizophrenia'.

Swanson, J.W., Swartz, M.S. and Elbogen, E.B. (2004a) 'Effectiveness of atypical antipsychotic medications in reducing violent behavior among persons with schizophrenia in community-based treatment', *Schizophrenia Bulletin*, 30 (1): 3–20.

Swanson, J.W., Swartz, M.S., Elbogen, E.B. and Van Dorn, R.A. (2004b) 'Reducing violence risk in person with schizophrenia: olanzaine versus risperidone', *Journal of Clinical Psychiatry*, 65: 1666–73.

Swanson, J.W., Swartz, M.S., Van Dorn, R.A., Elbogen, E.B., Wagner, H.R. and Rosenheck, R.A. (2006) 'A national study of violent behavior in persons with schizophrenia', *Archives of General Psychiatry*, 63: 490–9.

Swartz, M.S. and Swanson, J.W. (2004) 'Involuntary outpatient commitment, community treatment orders, and assisted outpatient treatment', *Canadian Journal of Psychiatry*, 49: 585–91.

Taylor, P.J. (1985) 'Motives for offending among violent and psychotic men', *British Journal of Psychiatry*, 147: 491–8.

Tengström, A., Hodgins, S. and Kullgren, G. (2001) 'Men with schizophrenia who behave violently: the usefulness of an early versus late starters typology', *Schizophrenia Bulletin*, 27: 205–18.

Tengström, A., Hodgins, S., Grann, M., Långström, N. and Kullgren, G. (2004) 'Schizophrenia and criminal offending: the role of psychopathy and substance misuse', *Criminal Justice and Behavior*, 31 (4): 1–25.

Tengström, A., Hodgins, S., Müller-Isberner, R., Jöckel, D., Freese, R. and Özokyay, K. (2006) 'Predicting violent and antisocial behavior in hospital using the HCR-20: the effect of diagnoses on predictive accuracy', *International Journal of Forensic Mental Health Services*, 5: 39–54.

Teplin, L., McClelland, G.M., Abram, K.M. and Weiner, D.A. (2005) 'Crime victimization in adults with severe mental illness: comparison with the National Crime Victimization Survey', *Archives of General Psychiatry*, 62: 911–21.

Tiihonen, J., Isohanni, M., Rasanen, P., Koiranen, M. and Moring, J. (1997) 'Specific major mental disorders and criminality: a 26-year prospective study of the 1996 Northern Finland birth cohort', *American Journal of Psychiatry*, 154 (6): 840–5.

Volavka, J., Laska, E., Baker, S. and Meisner, M. (1997) 'History of violent behaviour and schizophrenia in different cultures. Analyses based on the WHO study on Determinants of Outcome of Severe Mental Disorders', *British Journal of Psychiatry*, 171: 9–14.

Volavka, J., Czobor, P., Nolan, K. A., Sheitman, B., Lindenmayer, J. P. and Citrome, L. (2004) 'Overt aggression and psychotic symptoms in patients with schizophrenia treated with clozapine, olanzaphin, risperidone, or haloperidol', *Journal of Clinical Psychopharmacology*, 24: 225–8.

Wallace, C., Mullen, P. E. and Burgess, P. (2004) 'Criminal offending in schizophrenia over a 25-year period marked by deinstitutionalization and increasing prevalence of comorbid substance use disorders', *American Journal of Psychiatry*, 161 (4): 716–27.

Walsh, E., Gilvarry, C., Samele, C., Harvey, K., Manley, C. and Tyrer, P. (2001) 'Reducing violence in severe mental illness: randomised controlled trial of intensive case management compared with standard care', *British Medical Journal*, 323 (10): 1–5.

Walsh, E., Moran, P., Scott, C., McKenzie, K., Burns, T. and Creed, F. (2003) 'UK700 Group. Prevalence of violent victimisation in severe mental illness', *British Journal of Psychiatry*, 183: 233–8.

Webster, C.D., Douglas, K.S., Eaves, D. and Hart, S.D. (1997) *HCR-20: Assessing Risk for Violence (Version 2)*. Vancouver, BC: Simon Fraser University.

Wessely, S., Buchanan, A., Reed, A., Cutting, J., Everitt, B.G.P. and Taylor, P.J. (1993) 'Acting on delusions. I: Prevalence', *British Journal of Psychiatry*, 163: 69–76.

Chapter 17

Substance abuse

Mary McMurran

Introduction

The possession, sale and use of certain substances is against the law, either completely or under certain circumstances, hence there are substance-specific offences, such as trafficking drugs, manufacturing certain chemical substances and selling alcohol to people under a specified age. Seen as rational if unwise choices, these activities are not within the purview of forensic mental health professionals. In mental health services, it is usually crimes that are in some way related to the individual's intake of drugs that are the focus. In understanding the connection between substance use and crime, we first need to acknowledge the range of behaviours to which each of these terms refer. Substance use refers to a range of psychoactive substances, both legal and illegal, taken in a variety of ways, and with different effects on the individual. Crime also refers to a range of activities, with differing targets and varying levels of harm to others.

It is important to note at the outset that attempts to decide whether alcohol or drugs *cause* crime are likely to be fruitless. The issue is better addressed in terms of probabilities, and the question that should be addressed is: 'What type of substance used in what kind of way under what conditions by a person with which characteristics might increase the likelihood of what sort of behaviour?' This allows consideration of all types of substances (legal, illegal and prescribed), taken orally, nasally or intravenously, in various locations and in certain company, by people with specific personality problems or mental health difficulties, who have a history of high-risk behaviours.

Where illegal drugs are concerned, the crimes of principal concern are acquisitive offences, these being most closely associated with the use of heroin and crack cocaine (Stewart *et al.* 2000). The economic necessity hypothesis is that drug-related crimes are committed to support a habit. In a sample of UK offenders in drug treatment, Turnbull *et al.* (2000) found the average annual expenditure on drugs to be £21,000 per person, a sum that reveals why many drug users may need to commit acquisitive crimes.

By contrast, the main concern regarding alcohol relates to crimes of violence. The psycho-pharmacological effects of alcohol adversely affect attention, threat perception, information processing, reasoning, problem-solving and impulse control so that the likelihood of violence is increased (see reviews by Chermack and Giancola 1997; Graham *et al.* 1998; McMurran 2002, 2007). Furthermore, the circumstances in which people drink typically present increased likelihood of meeting with provocations to anger and aggression. One type of violence is that which commonly occurs in and around city-centre licensed premises at weekend closing times, where both perpetrator and victim are likely to be male (Lang *et al.* 1995). Intimate partner violence, which is most likely to be perpetrated by men against women, is another major area of concern. Alcohol use has been identified as a strong risk factor for domestic violence in a meta-analysis of studies of risk (Stith *et al.* 2004). In both types of violence, not only is the assailant likely to be intoxicated, but so is the victim of violence (Lindqvist 1991).

Although the focus is generally on drugs and acquisitive offending and alcohol and violence, some drugs are associated with violence by the individual who uses, particularly crack-cocaine (Home Office 2002; Parker and Auerhahn 1998). Although generally attracting less attention, the cost of supporting a habit of heavy drinking may drive some people to commit acquisitive offences (McMurran and Cusens 2005).

In this chapter, as befits a text on forensic mental health, the focus is largely on substance use as it relates to mentally disordered offenders. Legal and diagnostic issues will be covered briefly, then substance use will be covered in relation to offenders with personality disorder, mental illness and intellectual disability in turn, concluding with a section on treatment. Issues relating to substance misuse in the broadest sense will be examined, including acute intoxication, problematic use and dependence.

Intoxication and legal defence

In law, voluntary intoxication with alcohol or drugs is not accepted as a defence for crimes of basic intent, these being crimes where proof is required only that the defendant committed the act, with no need to prove that harm was intended (Haque and Cumming 2003). For example, in a case of simple criminal damage (basic intent), the defendant's intoxication would not be seen as mitigation, regardless of any claim that the behaviour was out of character, and the law would hold him or her fully responsible for the criminal act.

In crimes of specific intent, that is where there is an intention to cause harm (*mens rea*), intoxication may be used in defence. The defendant may not have been intent on harming another but may have behaved recklessly because he or she was intoxicated. For example, in a case of criminal damage where it is suspected that the intention was to cause harm to another, such as tampering with the safety of someone's car so that the driver would be likely to crash (specific intent), then the defendant's intoxication could be used as mitigation if it meant that the intent to harm was not present. In such a case, the crime would be reduced from criminal damage with intent to one of simple criminal damage. However, intent to harm may be present along with intoxication, for example where drink is taken to give courage to commit the crime, and intoxication is clearly not a mitigating factor in such a case.

An insanity defence may be used where there is delirium tremens or a drug-induced psychosis. A defence of diminished responsibility for a charge of murder could be lodged on the grounds of brain damage as a result of substance use or drinking, or if intoxication is held to be involuntary through dependence on drugs or alcohol (Haque and Cumming 2003).

Diagnosis of substance use disorders

Although substance use disorders exist within diagnostic systems, namely the International Classification of Diseases-10 (ICD-10; World Health Organisation 1992), and the Diagnostic and Statistical Manual of Mental Disorders-IV (DSM-IV; American Psychiatric Association 1994), people whose problems stem exclusively from alcohol or drug consumption are explicitly excluded from the detainable categories of mental disorder in the Mental Health Act 1983. This exclusion will also apply in proposed amendments to the Act. The major diagnostic categories in ICD-10 and DSM-IV, along with brief descriptions of each, are listed in Table 17.1. In this chapter, the term substance misuse will be used as an umbrella term to refer to intoxication, harmful use or dependence.

Table 17.1 Substance use disorders

Disorder	Description
Intoxication	A transient condition following administration of the substance resulting in disturbances in consciousness, cognition, perception, affect or behaviour.
Harmful use/abuse	A pattern of use causing damage to health, risk of accident, legal or social problems.
Dependence	A feeling of compulsion to take the substance; impaired control over use; tolerance to the substance's effects; experience of withdrawal when intake is reduced or stopped; focus on getting and using, with progressive neglect of other activities; persistence in use regardless of evident harm.
Withdrawal	A substance-specific syndrome due to the reduction or cessation of substance use, including physical and psychological distress, cognitive impairment and sleep disturbances.
Substance-induced psychosis	Hallucinations or delusions that occur after substance use, which the user does not recognise as substance-induced.

It is worth noting here that there is some controversy over the nature of addiction and dependency. It is incontrovertible that some people find themselves overwhelmed by the need to drink or take drugs, have great difficulty reducing or stopping their substance use and eventually do themselves serious harm, even unto death. The controversy lies largely in how these phenomena are explained. Implicated in addiction or dependence are a whole range of genetic, neurological, emotional, behavioural, cognitive, familial, social and cultural factors and the relative importance of the contribution of each of these domains is often disputed. Space prohibits examining the arguments here, and interested readers are referred to other texts (Davies 1997; McMurran 1994; West 2006).

Mental disorder and substance misuse

The co-occurrence of mental disorder and substance misuse is of interest to forensic mental health professionals in that these categories of problem combined in an individual may increase the risk of crime, particularly the risk of serious violent crime, and may militate against effective treatment. These concerns require that professionals understand the epidemiology, aetiology, risk and treatability of both mental disorder and substance misuse, so that services may be fashioned to meet the clinical needs of this population. Although the term 'dual diagnosis' is frequently used to refer to mental illness and substance use, a broader perspective will be taken here to include all three mental disorder categories represented in the mental health legislation of England and Wales, namely personality (psychopathic) disorder, mental illness and intellectual disability (mental impairment/severe mental impairment). These disorders are the grounds for detention and treatment of offenders in health services, so each of the three broad categories of mental disorder is relevant to the work of forensic mental health professionals. Furthermore, these mental disorders are not mutually exclusive in that a person may suffer from two or even all three together, meaning that professionals require knowledge of all three conditions.

Personality disorder and substance misuse

Offenders with personality disorders are of considerable concern, since personality disorder is a predictor of serious recidivism (Bailey and MacCulloch 1992; Bonta et al. 1998; Steels et al. 1998). Personality disorder and substance misuse are commonly co-occurring problems, and this relationship requires closer scrutiny.

Prevalence of co-occurring personality disorders and substance misuse

General population samples

In a US general population sample (N = 43,093), 15 per cent had at least one personality disorder, and of these 16 per cent had current alcohol use problems and 7 per cent current drug use problems (Grant et al. 2006). Of those with an alcohol use disorder, 29 per cent also had a personality disorder, and among those with a drug use disorder the figure was 48 per cent, in both cases the relationship being with antisocial, histrionic and dependent personality disorders. Analysis of data from 626 members of a UK general population estimated a prevalence of personality disorder of 4 per cent (Coid et al. 2006). The odds of alcohol dependence was substantially increased for those in Cluster B (i.e. antisocial, borderline, histrionic and narcissistic) (adjusted odds ratio 4.21), as was the likelihood of a criminal conviction (adjusted odds ratio 10.6). Those in Cluster A (i.e. paranoid, schizoid and schizotypal) were also more likely to be alcohol dependent (adjusted odds ratio 1.61), but those in Cluster C (i.e. avoidant, dependent and obsessive compulsive) were less likely to be alcohol dependent (adjusted odds ratio 0.36). The likelihood of drug dependence was elevated for all personality clusters (adjusted odds ratios of 1.32, 1.87 and 1.93 for Clusters A, B and C respectively). The three major conclusions are that, in a general population sample, if you have a substance use disorder you are likely also to have a personality disorder, drug use is associated with higher levels of personality pathology compared with alcohol, and alcohol and crime are associated most strongly with the externalising personality disorders (Cluster B).

Substance abuse treatment samples

Looking at samples of substance abusers in treatment, Verheul *et al.* (1995) reviewed 50 studies of co-occurrence of substance misuse and personality disorders finding a median prevalence of co-occurrence of 61 per cent, with illicit drug users showing higher personality disorder prevalence rates than problem drinkers. Verheul *et al.* (1995) identified all personality disorders co-occurring, although the association was particularly strong between substance misuse and antisocial and borderline personality disorders. Data from 278 patients in four urban UK drug and alcohol services in 2001/2002 showed a different profile to that suggested by Verheul *et al.* (1995). Positive ratings for at least one personality disorder were recorded for 37 per cent of drug-dependent patients and 53 per cent of alcohol-dependent patients, with drug-dependent patients most commonly impulsive (16 per cent) and dissocial (10 per cent), whereas alcohol-dependent patients were most commonly anxious/avoidant (27 per cent), with dependent (16 per cent), dissocial (11 per cent), and borderline (10 per cent) also featuring (Bowden-Jones *et al.* 2004).

Among substance misusers, the co-occurrence of antisocial personality disorder is twice as likely for men as for women, and most likely in users of multiple substances, i.e. alcohol plus illicit drugs (Flynn *et al.* 1996). In substance misusers, there is also high degree of co-occurrence of antisocial with other personality disorders, particularly borderline, with multiple personality pathology associated with severity of substance misuse (Cecero *et al.* 1999).

Furthermore, co-occurring mood disorder is about three times higher in substance misusers with a personality disorder diagnosis than without (Kokkevi *et al.* 1998). antisocial personality disorder with lifetime depression is associated with severity of dependence (Cecero *et al.* 1999), and there is evidence that alcohol misuse, either alone or with illicit drugs, is associated with disorders of anxiety and depression (Flynn *et al.* 1996).

To summarise, in clinical samples, the co-occurrence of personality disorder and substance misuse is higher than in general population samples, and, as one would expect, there is evidence of higher levels of multiple problems, including mood disorders. In the UK at least, those with alcohol problems appear to show more personality pathology than those with drug problems, with both externalising and anxiety problems featuring. Those with antisocial personality disorder diagnoses are predominantly male, users of many substances and with other personality problems. Treatment samples are selected on the basis of having certain problems, hence the difference between them and general samples. Criteria for admission to services vary, which may explain differences between US and UK studies.

Forensic samples

UK prisons contain high proportions of personality disordered offenders, with an unsurprising predominance of antisocial personality disorder (Singleton *et al.* 1998). Data from UK prisons also show high prevalence of substance misuse, with around 60 per cent of male prisoners and almost 40 per cent of female prisoners being alcohol abusers, and 80 per cent of men and 60 per cent of women having used drugs (Singleton *et al.* 1998). Dependence rates in remand prisoners are 12 per cent of men and 6.5 per cent of women alcohol dependent, and 19 per cent of men and 29 per cent of women drug-dependent (Brooke *et al.* 1998). However, in one remand sample, 52 per cent were deemed to have a need for substance abuse treatment (Hardie *et al.* 1998)

Hospitalised offenders also show high rates of personality disorder (Coid *et al.* 1999; Reiss *et al.* 1996). In studies of the UK special hospital population, the incidence of co-occurring substance misuse in those diagnosed as personality disordered is identified as 14 per cent in one study (Taylor *et al.* 1998) and 18 per cent in another, with 4.5 per cent of these latter substance misusers being drug dependent and 6.4 per cent being alcohol dependent (Corbett *et al.* 1998). The authors of these studies suggest that the figures are likely to be an underestimate, due either to failure to inquire about or document substance misuse or to under-reporting by patients.

The supposition that we underestimate the extent of co-occurrence is borne out by data from Coid *et al.*'s (1999) study of patients in secure settings, where substance misuse was determined from the patients' histories rather than whether a diagnosis was recorded. By this method, 53 per cent of personality disordered patients were judged as having a lifetime alcohol misuse diagnosis, and 47 per cent were considered to have a lifetime drug misuse diagnosis. Also, Quayle *et al.* (1998) found that 42 per cent of secure hospital patients claim to have been drinking at the time of their index offence.

Examining the overlap

High rates of diagnostic co-occurrence raise the question of whether there is overlap between diagnoses, so that the observation of high levels of co-occurrence of substance misuse and personality disorders is a tautology (Rounsaville *et al.* 1998). Substance misuse is a defining criterion of some personality disorders, and some personality disorder features can be directly or indirectly related to substance misuse, for example irritability, irresponsibility and affective instability. In a study aimed at teasing out specific from common factors, when substance-related symptoms were excluded from personality disorder diagnoses percentages drop but the incidence of co-occurrence remained high (Rounsaville *et al.* 1998). This suggests that personality disorder diagnoses are not simply another way of measuring substance-related behaviours, although substance misuse may make underlying personality traits more evident.

Personality disorder, substance misuse and crime

While there is an association between personality disorder, substance misuse and crime, not all personality disorders or substance misuse problems increase the likelihood of crime (substance-specific crimes apart). Substance use may exacerbate underlying personality traits, but this will not always increase the risk of crime. People with problems in the anxious cluster, for example, may drink or use drugs with little or no consequences to anyone other than themselves.

In a longitudinal study of a community sample, the relationship between anti-social personality and substance use was explained to a substantial degree by shared traits of impulsivity and antagonism (Lynam *et al.* 2003). Looking at psychopathy, as measured by Hare's Psychopathy Checklist – Revised (PCL-R; Hare 2003), it is clear that the antisocial factor is key in the relationship between substance use and crime. In a study of people in treatment for alcohol problems, those scoring high on the PCL-R and those diagnosed as suffering from antisocial personality disorder formed two largely distinct groups, with the antisocial personality disorder sub group having greater alcohol problems, drug problems and criminal activity (Windle 1999). Patrick *et al.* (2005) have shown that a broad externalising construct, which includes alcohol and drug abuse, relates to antisocial lifestyle scores (Factor 2) of the PCL-R and not deviant personality traits (Factor 1). This corroborates the findings of an earlier study of prisoners in minimum security by Smith and Newman (1990), in which substance misuse was shown to be related to Factor 2 of the PCL-R and not Factor 1.

Antisocial personality disorder, substance misuse and crime, particularly violent crime, share highly similar risk factors across the lifespan, starting with early childhood signs of difficult temperament, aggression and hyperactivity, with progression to conduct disorder in childhood (Af Klinteberg *et al.* 1993; Loeber 1988; Maughan 1993). Poor parental supervision, harsh discipline and parental conflict contribute further to the risk of antisocial behaviour, including substance use (see reviews by Farrington 2005; McMurran 1996).

Mental illness and substance misuse

High rates of co-occurrence of severe mental illness, such as schizophrenia or bipolar disorder, and substance misuse are evident in non-forensic samples. An epidemiological survey of the general population in the US identified co-occurrence rates of 47 per cent in people with schizophrenia, 56 per cent in those with bipolar disorder and 32 per cent for those with affective disorders (Regier *et al.* 1990). These percentages represent odds of having a substance misuse disorder for people with a psychiatric diagnosis compared with those without of 4.6 times higher for people with schizophrenia, 6.6 times higher for those with bipolar disorder and 2.6 times higher for those with affective disorder. Alcohol disorders were twice as prevalent as other drug disorders.

Among a sample of referrals to a London community forensic service, 57 per cent had a diagnosis of substance misuse and of those 37 per cent had a co-occurring mental illness (Isherwood and Brooke 2001). In a UK regional secure unit, 62 per cent of schizophrenic patients were identified as problematic substance users (Wheatley 1998). Among special hospital patients suffering from schizophrenia, between 8 per cent and 15 per cent have co-occurring substance misuse disorders in English samples (Corbett *et al.* 1998; Taylor *et al.* 1998), but as high as 41 per cent in a Scottish sample (Steele *et al.* 2003). Alcohol-related problems have been identified in 18 per cent of English male special hospital patients (Thomas and McMurran 1993) and 54 per cent in a similar Scottish sample (Steele *et al.* 2003). In Thomas and McMurran's (1993) sample, alcohol abusers showed more serious criminality and were responsible for a disproportionately high number of murder and manslaughter offences. Reasons for relatively low prevalence rates in English special hospital patients remain unclear, but, as with personality disordered patients, it is strongly suspected that substance misuse is under-recorded.

Among prisoners, 19 per cent of receptions have been identified as suffering from a mental illness (Birmingham *et al.* 2000). Compared with psychiatric inpatients matched for age, sex and diagnosis, prisoners suffering from major schizophrenic and affective disorders show a higher incidence of substance abuse and, although they show better psychosocial functioning, they tend to be more violent (Côté *et al.* 1997).

Relationships between substance use and mental illness

Stress-vulnerability models of schizophrenia hold that some people are psychobiologically vulnerable to mental illness and that stressors of various types can trigger psychiatric disorder, with substance use being one stress factor. People with a mental illness use substances for the same reasons as most other people, for example mood management, alleviating boredom, lack of alternative activities and association with substance using peers. They may, however, have more risk factors for substance misuse than most, in that they are more prone to low moods, are less likely to be gainfully employed, may live in neighbourhoods where substances are more readily available, and they are more likely to befriend people who drink or use drugs. Those with better premorbid adjustment are those most likely to have a substance abuse disorder, possibly because they are more sociable and therefore more exposed to drinking and drug-using opportunities. Despite a persistent belief in the self-medication hypothesis, there is no strong evidence that mentally ill people choose specific drugs to medicate specific symptoms, but rather that, like most people, they use what is most readily available in their social context, typically alcohol and cannabis (Lehman *et al.* 1994; Mueser *et al.* 1992).

The supersensitivity hypothesis holds that people with a mental illness are exceptionally susceptible to the effects of drugs and alcohol (Mueser *et al.* 1998). Patients with schizophrenia appear to experience more adverse effects of substances at lower levels of consumption than non-mentally ill people, and are less successful in maintaining symptom-free use (Drake and Wallach 1993). Cognitive theories of schizophrenia emphasise the role of cognitive processes in explaining abnormal thoughts and perceptions and, as stated earlier, substance use in itself impairs cognitive functioning, with such impairment being potentially permanent, which may add to the risk of mental illness (Mueser *et al.* 1992). Once mental illness is being treated, substance use may interact with prescribed medication to limit, or even negate, its effectiveness.

Prospective studies of substance users to see if they develop mental illness, and long-term follow-up studies of people diagnosed as mentally ill following substance abuse, indicate that although substance use may trigger psychiatric disorder, there is little evidence that thereafter the mental illness differs from a condition that develops without the aid of substances, although the onset of substance-induced mental illness is at a younger age (Mueser *et al.* 1998). Nevertheless, substance misuse can contribute to increased symptom severity, speedier relapse to mental illness, and more numerous complicating problems, such as poor psychosocial adjustment (Bartels *et al.* 1995).

Many drugs induce transient psychotic symptoms that are similar to those found in schizophrenia, for example hallucinogens can induce a variety of psychotic symptoms, cannabis can induce panic and paranoia, and alcohol withdrawal can cause hallucinations and delusions. It is important to distinguish acute and transitory psychoses from chronic psychiatric conditions before a medico-legal disposal is made. Johns (1997) points out that diagnostic confusion should be avoided by attempting to distinguish true psychosis from the following conditions: intoxication mimicking functional psychosis, withdrawal states and chronic hallucinosis induced by substance misuse. Hodge (2000) notes that 'transitory' symptoms can last as long as substance use persists, take some time to remit and reinstate quickly if substance use starts again, all of which can lead to a mistaken diagnosis of a primary, rather than a secondary, mental illness.

Mental illness, substance use and crime

General population studies

Acts of violence are committed by people without mental illness and sometimes also by people with mental illness. Swanson (1994) examined a subset of 7,000 members of a general population sample studied longitudinally, who were given a psychiatric examination and whose violent behaviour was recorded, and found that 9 per cent of the entire group had been seriously violent at some time in their lives, rising to 18 per cent when less serious violence was included. Looking only at violence in the previous year, 1.2 per cent of the population with no disorder had been seriously violent compared with 3.8 per cent of those with a mental illness (schizophrenia or affective disorder). The overall likelihood of violence was low. The odds of having been seriously violent in the past year were three times higher for those with schizophrenia or a major affective disorder compared to those without a mental illness. Thus mental illness does increase the likelihood of violence, but, since the overall likelihood of violence is low, the incidence multiplied by three is still relatively low. People who abused alcohol and drugs were nine times more likely to have been seriously violent in the past year, and those with both mental illness and substance use problems were 13 times more likely to have been seriously violent in the previous year.

Again studying a birth cohort, alcohol-abusing male schizophrenics were 25 times more likely to commit violent crimes than mentally healthy men, whereas the risk for violence of schizophrenic men who did not abuse alcohol was only four times that for mentally healthy men (Räsänen *et al.* 1998).

Gender differences have been reported by Brennan *et al.* (2000), who studied a 1944 Danish birth cohort ($N = 335,990$), of whom about half were male and half female. Only 3 per cent of females compared with 11 per cent of males with schizophrenia were violent. The odds of violent arrest were 4.6 for men and 23.2 for women with schizophrenia. The figures for affective disorder were 5 per cent prevalence in men and 0.5 per cent in women, with the odds of violent arrest 2 and 4 respectively. Only those who were hospitalised could be examined for secondary substance abuse problems ($N = 7,962$). Controlling for marital status, socio-economic status and secondary diagnosis of substance abuse removed the relationship between affective disorder and violence, although the relationship between schizophrenia and violence remained (odds ratio 2.0 for men and 7.5 for women).

The conclusions are as follows:

1. Most people are not violent.
2. Most mentally ill people are not violent.
3. The overall incidence of violence is low, but nevertheless serious mental illness increases the risk of violence.
4. People with substance abuse disorders, particularly alcohol abuse, are much more likely to be violent than are people with a mental illness.
5. Having a major mental illness plus a substance abuse disorder presents the highest risk for violence.
6. As is true generally, women are less violent than men, nonetheless all of the foregoing statements are true for women.

Clinical samples

Since most people with a mental illness are not violent and are not hospitalised, sampling hospital patients gives a biased picture about the relationship between mental illness and violent crime (Brennan *et al.* 2000), yet it is nonetheless important to examine this important subgroup. Hodgins *et al.* (1999) followed up psychiatric patients for two years after discharge, finding that more of those patients suffering from major affective disorders than from schizophrenia committed violent offences, and that drug use but not antisocial personality disorder predicted violence in this group. Hence, from the studies by Brennan *et al.* (2000) and Hodgins *et al.* (1999), it appears that substance abuse largely explains the violence of people with affective disorder.

Among schizophrenic special hospital patients with a substance use disorder who had committed a violent or homicidal index offence, 43 per cent claim to have taken drugs or alcohol at the time of the offence, a smaller proportion than that for personality disordered patients, but nonetheless of a magnitude that causes concern (Corbett *et al.* 1998). Medication non-compliance adds to the risk of violence in mentally ill people with a substance abuse problem, although not in those without a substance misuse problem (Farabee and Shen 2004; Swartz *et al.* 1998). Furthermore, in this group violence is most strongly associated with drinking, and the predictors of violence are being male, young and of low socioeconomic status.

Mental illness and personality disorder

As we saw in the previous section, personality disorder and substance use are strongly connected, particularly where there is a pathway of early temperament problems, flourishing into childhood conduct disorder and persisting into adult antisocial personality disorder. A similar pathway has been identified in some mentally ill offenders, and those who have a criminal history that antedates the onset of mental illness have been called the 'early-starter' type (Hodgins *et al.* 1998). This contrasts with cases where offending emerges concurrently with psychiatric symptoms, this type of mentally ill offender being called 'late-starters' (Hodgins *et al.* 1998).

Patients with mental illness and antisocial personality disorder are more likely to have a substance abuse disorder than mentally ill patients without a personality disorder (Hodgins *et al.* 1998). Walsh *et al.* (2004) in a prospective study of 271 UK patients with schizophrenia over two years found the best predictors of violence to be alcohol abuse, having received special education as a child and previous violence.

Childhood conduct disorder has been found to predict later schizophrenia and bipolar disorder, and increased rates of antisocial personality disorder have been identified in both of these major mental disorders (Carlson and Weintraub 1993; Robins and Price 1991). Hodgins *et al.* (2005) examined the consequences of conduct disorder in males who developed schizophrenia. In a sample of 248 men hospitalised with schizophrenia, 21 per cent ($N = 52$) received a retrospective diagnosis of conduct disorder. Compared with the rest of the sample, members of this subgroup performed worse at school, were more likely to use substances and had a family background of crime, substance misuse and physical abuse. A diagnosis of conduct disorder increased the risk of violent crime twofold. Even after taking into account a lifetime diagnosis of substance misuse, the association between conduct disorder and adult violence remained evident. This suggests that underlying personality explains most of the violence and that substance misuse is not the main culprit. The authors concluded that conduct disorder in childhood or early adolescence is associated with criminal behaviour and substance use in adulthood, and that the course of antisocial behaviour runs parallel to schizophrenia.

Information from 961 young adult participants in a longitudinal study from birth showed that three diagnoses were related to violence: alcohol dependence marijuana dependence and a schizophrenia-spectrum disorder (Arseneault *et al.* 2000). The elevations of risk relative to participants with no diagnosis were 1.9, 3.8 and 2.5 respectively. Analyses were conducted to explain this risk using three variables: substance use before offending, excessive threat perception, and adolescent conduct disorder. All three variables explained some of the variance in each case. Where people with a diagnosis of schizophrenia were concerned, the primary variables in explaining risk of violence were adolescent conduct disorder and threat perception. Regarding threat perception, a relationship between a tendency to see the world as threatening and violence has been described by Link and Stueve (1994) as threat/control-override; that is, violence is related to those symptoms that 'cause a person to feel threatened or involve the intrusion of thoughts that can override self controls' (p. 155). While the threat/control override hypothesis was supported by Arseneault *et al.* (2000), other studies have not supported this as a predictor of violence in people with schizophrenia (Walsh *et al.* 2004).

Intellectual disability and substance misuse

In a survey of community intellectual disability teams in Northern Ireland, mental health professionals identified 67 adult substance abusers, representing just 0.8 per cent of the population served (Taggart *et al.* 2006). Of these, all were alcohol abusers and 13 (19 per cent) were also abusers of other substances, mainly cannabis ($N = 8$) and prescribed medication ($N = 4$). Compared with non-abusers, these abusers were of mild to moderate intellectual disability, younger and living in more independent accommodation. For the majority, acute intoxication was associated with verbal aggression (70 per cent), and physical aggression and offending were not uncommon (45 per cent and 34 per cent respectively).

Reviews of alcohol use acknowledge that among people with learning disabilities the levels of abstinence are high and the levels of problematic drinking are correspondingly low. However, of those that do use alcohol a high proportion are prone to misuse (McGillicuddy and Blane 1999; Simpson 1998). Those that do misuse alcohol appear similar to other populations in that they are mostly single males living alone, who are more likely to smoke tobacco, use soft drugs, experience consequent work problems and get into trouble with the law, commonly with offences such as public intoxication, disturbing the peace, assault, indecent exposure, breaking and entering, and driving while intoxicated (Krishef and DiNitto 1981; McGillicuddy and Blane 1999).

There is relatively little literature on the role of alcohol and drugs in the lives of people with intellectual disabilities; rather, research focuses largely on rates of use in comparison with that of non-disabled populations (McGillicudy 2006). Suppositions have been made regarding why people with intellectual disabilities drink, and these include a desire to join 'normal' society, meet people and fill one's leisure time, but these suppositions are not empirically supported (Simpson 1998).

Treatment

There is a wide range of effective treatments for substance misuse, including detoxification, maintenance prescription, antagonist prescription, therapeutic communities, motivational enhancement therapy, counselling and psychotherapy, cognitive-behaviour therapies, family and relationship therapies, community reinforcement and combinations thereof (National Institute on Drug Abuse 1999).

Alcohol and drug education has a dubious reputation, with some very well-designed and comprehensively researched school-based programmes proving ineffective (Rosenbaum and Hanson 1998), although commentators in the UK have taken a more optimistic approach, saying that community-based, multi-component, and interactive programmes can be effective (Allott *et al.* 1999). Obviously, what works with school pupils and adult offenders may differ entirely, but the message seems to be that education is only successful when it broadens out into what approaches a comprehensive cognitive-behavioural skill-based programme.

A meta-analysis of outcomes of treatments for substance misusing offenders in US prisons, published between 1968 and 1996, indicated that interventions that were ineffective were boot camps (a militaristic experience intended to shock young people into mending their ways) and drug counselling (Pearson and Lipton 1999). Thirty-five methodologically sound studies of therapeutic community or milieu therapy for adults, with almost 11,000 participants, gave a positive mean effect size of 0.14 (Lipton *et al.* 2002a). Lipton *et al.*'s (2002b) meta-analysis of 68 methodologically acceptable behavioural and cognitive-behavioural programmes with over 10,000 participants gave a positive mean effect size of 0.12. Separate analyses revealed that the 23 evaluations of behavioural programmes (i.e. without the cognitive element) produced a mean effect size of 0.07, and that for 44 cognitive-behavioural programmes was 0.14. Effect sizes of 0.12 and 0.14 are quite respectable in comparison with most interventions in offender treatments. Other approaches which showed promise, but with too few studies to draw strong conclusions, were methadone maintenance for offenders addicted to heroin, substance abuse education and 12-step programmes (Pearson and Lipton 1999).

What works in the US may not work in the UK, and so Perry *et al.* (2006) identified studies of UK criminal justice interventions to reduce crime, identifying only methodologically acceptable evaluations. In drug and alcohol treatments, only seven methodologically acceptable studies of drug treatments were identified, and just three for alcohol interventions (McMurran 2006). Methadone maintenance was effective in reducing acquisitive crime (Coid *et al.* 2000; Keen *et al.* 2000; Parker and Kirby 1996), although other studies showed that prescription of pharmaceutical heroin (diamorphine) was superior over methadone at keeping people in treatment and reducing crime (McCusker and Davies 1996; Metrebian *et al.* 2001). Haynes (1998) compared offending of probation service referrals before and after referral to a drug treatment service, finding a reduction in serious offences of violence and burglary, although there was an increase in less serious property offences. Of participants in a 12-step therapeutic community for drug and alcohol misusers in prison, significantly fewer graduates than non-graduates had been reconvicted at 13 months (Martin and Player 2000). Success in treatment for drug users was associated with attending treatment (Haynes 1998; Martin and Player 2000), abstaining from the illicit drug of choice (Martin and Player 2000; Metrebian *et al.* 2001), finding employment (Parker and Kirby 1996) and being female (Parker and Kirby 1996).

Regarding alcohol interventions, Baldwin and colleagues (1991) examined the effectiveness of a 12-hour alcohol education course for male young offenders on average 14 months after release, finding significant decreases in drinking and offending against the person in those treated compared with a no-treatment comparison group. Singer (1991) evaluated a six-session alcohol education course for young offenders, finding that the actual reconviction rate for high-risk offenders was lower than expected 12 months after completing the course. McMurran and Boyle (1990) investigated the effectiveness of a behavioural self-help manual with male young offenders, finding no significant difference in reconviction at 15 months after release between no intervention, those given the manual to read alone and those who had the contents of the manual presented to them. Clearly, no general conclusion may be drawn from so few studies.

Personality disordered substance misusers

Personality disordered substance misusers in general substance misuse treatment programmes are frequently singled out for study. Treatment gains are generally less with personality disordered compared to non-personality disordered substance misusers, yet treatment does lead to reduced substance misuse and symptomatology over time (Brooner *et al.* 1998; Cecero *et al.* 1999; Kokkevi *et al.* 1998; Linehan *et al.* 1999). Substance misuse treatment has also been shown to reduce crime in those with antisocial personality disorder, although not those with borderline personality disorders (Hernandez-Avila *et al.* 2000). Looking at specific traits, motivational enhancement therapy is particularly effective with clients who are high in anger (Project MATCH Research Group 1997).

People with co-occurring personality disorder, particularly antisocial personality disorder, are more likely to drop out of substance abuse treatment, but there is evidence that this may actually be related to depression rather than personality disorder (Kokkevi *et al.* 1998). Since treatment completion is important to a good outcome, it is crucial to assess for and treat depression in substance misusers, with or without personality disorders, although it is worth bearing in mind that withdrawal from substances may actually be the cause of low mood. Nevertheless, antisocial personality disordered people who complete substance abuse treatment, as they often do when the treatment is compulsory, show good outcomes (Hernandez-Avila *et al.* 2000).

Mentally ill substance abusers

Minkoff (1989: 1031) remarked that designers of programmes for the treatment of co-occurring mental illness and substance misuse face the challenge of developing 'an integrated treatment philosophy that incorporates both mental health and substance abuse treatment in a unified conceptual and programmatic framework'. This integrated approach to treatment helps avoid failing the patient whose mental health problems are not addressed by the drug services and whose drug problems are not addressed by psychiatric services (Seivewright *et al.* 2004), and helps avoid conceptual clashes, for instance where the patient is held personally responsible for one problem and not the other (Mueser *et al.* 1992). Integrated dual disorder treatment programmes require at least a close liaison between psychiatric and drug teams, but preferably the same team of clinicians treating both mental illness and substance misuse (Drake *et al.* 1993; Seivewright *et al.* 2004).

Within the overarching principle of integrated treatment, effective interventions with mentally ill substance abusers include assertive outreach, motivating people to change, intensive supervision, attention to broader issues in life such as relationships, work, leisure and accommodation, and a longitudinal approach, bearing in mind that there can be relapses to both mental illness and substance misuse (Drake *et al.* 1993; Graham 2004). Integrated treatments are proving effective in engaging clients, decreasing substance use, increasing remission and decreasing hospitalisation.

A randomised, controlled, single blind clinical trial of an integrated treatment for people with co-occurring schizophrenia and substance misuse addressed patient-carer dyads in their homes (Barrowclough *et al.* 2001; Haddock *et al.* 2003). The intervention included motivational interviewing to promote motivation to change, individual cognitive-behaviour therapy to ameliorate delusions and hallucinations, and a family intervention to promote a family response that was supportive of therapeutic gains. Seventeen patient-caregiver dyads completed the integrated treatment and 15 were given routine care over nine months. Overall, the group receiving the novel treatment showed more improvement in global functioning, positive symptoms, and relapse to substance use at 12 months post-treatment. Improvements in global functioning were maintained at 18 months post-treatment (Haddock *et al.* 2003). Comparing integrated with parallel treatment, Mangrum *et al.* (2006) examined outcomes for 216 randomly allocated clients. The integrated treatment, which included assertive engagement, close monitoring, and a range of treatments tailored to the individual's needs, was more effective in reducing hospitalisation and arrests.

Although integrated treatments show promising results, these are not common in forensic mental health settings. Chandler *et al.* (2004) highlight some of the challenges in implementing integrated treatments in criminal justice settings, namely the pre-eminence of security matters over treatment, the fact that mental illness treatment can be compulsory but substance misuse treatment cannot, and that some types of treatment (e.g. methadone maintenance) are not acceptable to some criminal justice personnel. Drake *et al.* (2006) note the need for further attention to treatment models for forensic dual diagnosis clients, in that both the dual disorder *and* criminality require attention. Looking specifically at mentally ill substance users who commit violent offences, the research indicates that the explanations for violence differ across disorders, hence interventions need to be tailored accordingly (Arsenault *et al.* 2000). Research by Hodgins *et al.* (2005) indicates that early interventions to prevent the development of conduct disorder may be useful. Conduct disorder is associated with features that may actually contribute to the development of schizophrenia. Children with conduct problems may lack the psychological and emotional resources to cope with the prodromal symptoms of schizophrenia, and in turn they are likely to use alcohol and illicit drugs which may trigger the illness. In adulthood, this subgroup of antisocial mentally ill persons requires interventions to target antisocial thinking and behaviour. Using interventions developed with non-mentally disordered offenders that target violence risk factors is indicated (Harris and Rice 1997; Bonta *et al.* 1998), and the effectiveness of such interventions is currently being evaluated (Fahy *et al.* 2004). Research by Arseneault *et al.* (2000) suggests that some people with schizophrenia may benefit from cognitive therapies directed at reducing threat perception.

Intellectually disabled substance users

Compared with that for non-disabled people, substance misuse treatment for people with intellectual disabilities is typically simpler, more behavioural, less confrontative, more directive, more educational, of longer duration and more likely to involve the client's family (Krishef and DiNitto 1981). Rather than using an altogether different approach, it seems more that styles of presentation and interaction are modified to suit the needs of people with intellectual disabilities, for example by being highly interactive and using material with visual impact (McGillicuddy and Blane 1999; McMurran and Lismore 1993). There is also evidence that a shift in emphasis may be appropriate, for instance by focusing on developing a range of leisure activities as alternatives to drinking in pubs (Lindsay *et al.* 1991). Substance misuse treatment is not, however, readily available to people with intellectual disabilities, perhaps because of the effort involved in adapting treatment programmes, the need for intensive individual work and the disconnectedness of substance misuse and learning disability services (Campbell *et al.* 1994). Like services for people with co-occurring mental illness and substance abuse, closer liaison between staff working in these two areas could prove helpful (Clarke and Wilson, 1999).

Conclusion

Substance misuse in mentally disordered offenders may be part of a cluster of problems experienced by this generally disadvantaged group. Treatment of substance misuse is indicated for the general health and well-being of forensic patients. Other commonly co-occurring problems, such as mood disorders, need to be assessed, not only because they require direct treatment but also because of the implications of these issues for the effectiveness of other treatments. Substance use may increase the likelihood of criminal behaviour in a number of ways depending on who is taking what substance in what way and in what context. Underlying personality traits may be the main explanatory factor for personality disordered and mentally ill patients alike. Substance misuse may exaggerate or exacerbate traits that are implicated in antisocial behaviour, such as impulsivity and aggression. Substance misuse needs to be targeted in forensic mental health populations and care should be taken that this issue is not sidestepped because it is seen as outwith the remit of forensic mental health services, being the lot of drug and alcohol teams, or as lacking urgency, where those in secure settings are not currently drinking or using drugs.

Acknowledgement

This chapter is adapted, with permission, from a report entitled *Dual Diagnosis of Mental Disorder and Substance Misuse* published in 2002 and 2007 in the National Programme on Forensic Mental Health Research and Development's Expert Paper series (see http://www.nfmhp.org.uk/expertpaper.htm).

Selected further reading

Gossop, M., Marsden, J. and Stewart, D. (2001) *NTORS after Five Years: Changes in Substance Use, Health and Criminal Behaviour During the Five Years after Intake*. London: National Addiction Centre (see: http://www.dh.gov.uk/en/Publicationsandstatistics/Publications/PublicationsPolicyAndGuidance/DH_4084908), is a prospective longitudinal study of people recruited to treatment services showing that drug use and crime does reduce substantially.

McMurran, M. (2006) 'Drug and alcohol programmes: concept, theory and practice', in C. R. Hollin and E. J. Palmer (eds), *Offending Behaviour Programmes: Development, Application and Controversies*. Chichester: Wiley, is a critical overview of current interventions in criminal justice systems.

McMurran, M. (2006) 'Alcohol and drug treatments', in A. E. Perry, C. McDougall and D. P. Farrington (eds), *Reducing Crime: The Effectiveness of Criminal Justice Interventions*. Chichester: Wiley, is an evaluation of the best designed research in UK criminal justice.

References

Af Klinteberg, B.A., Andersson, T., Magnusson, D. and Stattin, H. (1993) 'Hyperactive behavior in childhood as related to subsequent alcohol problems and violent offending: a longitudinal study of male subjects', *Personality and Individual Difference*, 15: 381–8.

Allott, R., Paxton, R. and Leonard, R. (1999) 'Drug education: a review of British Government policy and evidence on effectiveness', *Health Education Research: Theory and Practice*, 14: 491–505.

American Psychiatric Association (1994) *Diagnostic and Statistical Manual of Mental Disorders*, 4th edn. Washington, DC: American Psychiatric Association.

Arseneault, L., Moffitt, T.E., Caspi, A., Taylor, P.J. and Silva, P.A. (2000) 'Mental disorders and violence in a total birth cohort', *Archives of General Psychiatry*, 57: 979–86.

Bailey, J. and MacCulloch, M. (1992) 'Patterns of reconviction in patients discharged directly to the community from a special hospital: implications for aftercare', *Journal of Forensic Psychiatry*, 3: 445–61.

Baldwin, S., Heather, N., Lawson, A., Robertson, I., Mooney, J. and Braggins, F. (1991) 'Comparison of effectiveness: behavioural and talk-based courses for court-referred young offenders', *Behavioural Psychotherapy*, 19: 157–92.

Barrowclough, C., Haddock, G., Tarrier, N., Lewis, S. W., Moring, J., O'Brien, R., Schofield, N. and McGovern, J. (2001) 'Randomized controlled trial of motivational interviewing, cognitive behaviour therapy and family intervention for patients with co-morbid schizophrenia and substance use disorders', *American Journal of Psychiatry*, 158: 1706–13.

Bartels, S.J., Drake, R.E. and Wallach, M.A. (1995) 'Long-term course of substance use disorders among patients with severe mental illness', *Psychiatric Services*, 46: 248–51.

Birmingham, L., Gray, J., Mason, D. and Grubin, D. (2000) 'Mental illness at reception into prison', *Criminal Behaviour and Mental Health*, 10: 7–87.

Bonta, J., Law, M. and Hanson, K. (1998) 'The prediction of criminal and violent recidivism among mentally disordered offenders: a meta-analysis', *Psychological Bulletin*, 123: 123–42.

Bowden-Jones, O., Iqbal, M.Z., Tyrer, P., Seivewright, N., Cooper, S., Judd, A. and Weaver, T. (2004) 'Prevalence of personality disorder in alcohol and drug services and associated comorbidity', *Addiction*, 99: 1306–14.

Brennan, P.A., Mednick, S.A. and Hodgins, S. (2000) 'Major mental disorders and criminal violence in a Danish birth cohort', *Archives of General Psychiatry*, 57: 494–500.

Brooke, D., Taylor, C., Gunn, J. and Maden, A. (1998) 'Substance misusers on remand to prison – a treatment opportunity?', *Addiction*, 93: 1851–6.

Brooner, R.K., Kidorf, M., King, V. L. and Stoller, K. (1998) 'Preliminary evidence of good treatment response on antisocial drug abusers', *Drug and Alcohol Dependence*, 49: 249–60.

Campbell, J.A., Essex, E.L. and Held, G. (1994) 'Issues in chemical dependency treatment and aftercare for people with learning difficulties', *Health and Social Work*, 19: 63–70.

Carlson, G.A. and Weintraub, S. (1993) 'Childhood behaviour problems and bipolar disorder – relationship or coincidence', *Journal of Affective Disorders*, 28: 143–53.

Cecero, J.J., Ball, S.A., Tennen, H., Kranzler, H.R. and Rounsaville, B.J. (1999) 'Concurrent and predictive validity of antisocial personality disorder subtyping among substance users', *Journal of Nervous and Mental Disease*, 187: 478–86.

Chandler, R.K., Peters, R.H., Field, G. and Juliano-Bult, D. (2004) 'Challenges in implementing evidence-based treatment practices for co-occurring disorders in the criminal justice system', *Behavioral Sciences and the Law*, 22: 431–48.

Chermack, S.T. and Giancola, P.R. (1997) 'The relation between alcohol and aggression: an integrated biopsychosocial conceptualisation', *Clinical Psychology Review*, 17: 621–49.

Clarke, J.J. and Wilson, D.N. (1999) 'Alcohol problems and intellectual disability', *Journal of Intellectual Disability Research*, 43: 135–9.

Coid, J., Kahtan, N., Gault, S. and Jarman, B. (1999) 'Patients with personality disorder admitted to secure forensic psychiatry services', *British Journal of Psychiatry*, 175: 528–36.

Coid, J., Carvell, A., Kittler, Z., Healey, A. and Henderson, J. (2000) *The Impact of Methadone Treatment on Drug Misuse and Crime, Research Findings No. 120*. London: Home Office.

Coid, J., Yang, M., Tyrer, P., Roberts, A. and Ullrich, S. (2006) 'Prevalence and correlates of personality disorder in Great Britain', *British Journal of Psychiatry*, 188: 423–31.

Corbett, M., Duggan, C. and Larkin, E. (1998) 'Substance misuse and violence: a comparison of special hospital inpatients diagnosed with either schizophrenia or personality disorder', *Criminal Behaviour and Mental Health*, 8: 311–21.

Côté, G., Lesage, A., Chawsky, N. and Loyer, M. (1997) 'Clinical specificity of prison inmates with severe mental disorders', *British Journal of Psychiatry*, 170: 571–7.

Davies, J.B. (1997) *The Myth of Addiction*, 2nd edn. Amsterdam: Harwood.

Drake, R.E. and Wallach, M.A. (1993) 'Moderate drinking among people with a severe mental illness', *Hospital and Community Psychiatry*, 44: 780–2.

Drake, R.E., Bartels, S.J., Teague, G.B., Noordsy, DL. and Clark, R.E. (1993) 'Treatment of substance abuse in severely mentally ill patients', *Journal of Nervous and Mental Disease*, 181: 606–11.

Drake, R.E., Morrissey, J.P. and Mueser, K.T. (2006) 'The challenge of treating forensic dual diagnosis clients: comments on "Integrated treatment for jail recidivists with co-occurring psychiatric and substance use disorders"', *Community Mental Health Journal*, 42: 427–32.

Fahy, T., Clarke, A.Y. and Walwyn, R. (2004) 'Controlled study of a cognitive skills intervention to reduce offending behaviour in forensic patients with psychotic illness', *Schizophrenia Research*, 67 (Suppl. S Feb. 15): 9–10.

Farabee, D. and Shen, H. (2004) 'Antipsychotic medication adherence, cocaine use and recidivism among a parolee sample', *Behavioral Sciences and the Law*, 22: 467–76.

Farrington, D.P. (2005) 'Childhood origins of antisocial behavior', *Clinical Psychology and Psychotherapy*, 12: 177–90.

Flynn, P. M., Craddock, S.G., Luckey, J.W., Hubbard, R.L. and Dunteman, G.H. (1996) 'Comorbidity of antisocial personality and mood disorders among psychoactive substance-dependent treatment clients', *Journal of Personality Disorders*, 10: 56–67.

Graham, H.L. (2004) *Cognitive-Behavioural Integrated Treatment (C-BIT): A Treatment Manual for Substance Misuse in People with Severe Mental Health Problems*. Chichester: Wiley.

Graham, K., Leonard, K.E., Room, R., Wild, T.C., Pihl, R. O., Bois, C. and Single, E. (1998) 'Current directions in research on understanding and preventing intoxicated aggression', *Addiction*, 93: 659–76.

Grant, B.F., Stinson, F.S., Dawson, D.A., Chou, S.P., Ruan, W.J. and Pickering, R.P. (2006) 'Co-occurrence of 12-month alcohol and drug use disorders and personality disorders in the United States', *Archives of General Psychiatry*, 61: 361–8.

Haddock, G., Barrowclough, C., Tarrier, N., Moring, J., O'Brien, R., Schofield, N., Quinn, J., Palmer, S., Davies, L., Lowens, I., McGovern, J. and Lewis, S. (2003) 'Cognitive-behavioural therapy and motivational intervention for schizophrenia and substance misuse', *British Journal of Psychiatry*, 183: 418–26.

Haque, Q. and Cumming, I. (2003) 'Intoxication and legal defences', *Advances in Psychiatric Treatment*, 9: 144–51.

Hardie, T., Bhui, K., Brown, P. M., Watson, J. P. and Parrott, J.M. (1998) 'Unmet needs of remand prisoners', *Medicine, Science and the Law*, 38: 233–6.

Hare, R.D. (2003) *The Hare Psychopathy Checklist – Revised*, 2nd edn. North Tonawanda, NY: Multi-Health Systems.

Harris, G.T. and Rice, M.E. (1997) 'Mentally disordered offenders: what research says about effective service', in C.D. Webster and M.A. Jackson (eds), *Impulsivity: Theory, Assessment and Treatment*. New York: Guilford.

Haynes, P. (1998) 'Drug using offenders in south London: trends and outcomes', *Journal of Substance Abuse Treatment*, 15: 449–56.

Hernandez-Avila, C.A., Burleson, J.A., Poling, J., Tennen, H., Rounsaville, B.J. and Kranzler, H.R. (2000) 'Personality and substance use disorders as predictors of criminality', *Comprehensive Psychiatry*, 41: 276–83.

Hodge, J. E. (2000) Personal communication.

Hodgins, S., Côté, G. and Toupin, J. (1998) 'Major mental disorder and crime: an etiological hypothesis', in D.J. Cooke, A.E. Forth and R.D. Hare (eds), *Psychopathy: Theory, Research and Implications for Society*. Dordrecht: Kluwer.

Hodgins, S., Lapalme, M. and Toupin, J. (1999) 'Criminal activities and substance use of patients with major affective disorders and schizophrenia: a 2-year follow-up', *Journal of Affective Disorders*, 55: 187–202.

Hodgins, S., Tiihonen, J. and Ross, D. (2005) 'The consequences of Conduct Disorder for males who develop schizophrenia: associations with criminality, aggressive behaviour, substance use and psychiatric services', *Schizophrenia Research*, 78: 323–35.

Home Office (2002) *Tackling Crack: A National Plan*. London: Home Office.

Isherwood, S. and Brooke, D. (2001) 'Prevalence and severity of substance misuse among referrals to a local forensic service', *Journal of Forensic Psychiatry*, 12: 446–54.

Johns, A. (1997) 'Substance misuse: a primary risk and a major problem of comorbidity', *International Review of Psychiatry*, 9: 233–41.

Keen, J., Rowse, G., Mathers, N., Campbell, M. and Seivewright, N. (2000) 'Can methadone maintenance for heroin-dependent patients retained in general practice reduce criminal conviction rates and time spent in prison?', *British Journal of General Practice*, 50: 48–9.

Kokkevi, A., Stefanis, N., Anastasopoulou, E. and Kostogianni, C. (1998) 'Personality disorders in drug abusers: prevalence and their association with Axis I disorders as predictors of treatment retention', *Addictive Behaviours*, 23: 841–53.

Krishef, C.H. and DiNitto, D.M. (1981) 'Alcohol abuse among mentally retarded individuals', *Mental Retardation*: 19: 151–5.

Lang, E., Stockwell, T., Rydon, P. and Lockwood, A. (1995) 'Drinking settings and problems of intoxication', *Addiction Research*, 3: 141–9.

Lehman, A.F., Myers, C. P., Corty, E. and Thompson, J. (1994) 'Severity of substance use disorders among psychiatric inpatients', *Journal of Nervous and Mental Disease*, 182: 164–7.

Lindqvist, P. (1991) 'Homicides committed by abusers of alcohol and illicit drugs', *British Journal of Addiction*, 86: 321–6.

Lindsay, W.R., Allen, R., Walker, P., Lawrenson, H. and Smith, A.H.W. (1991) 'An alcohol education service for people with learning difficulties', *Mental Handicap*, 19: 96–100.

Linehan, M.M., Schmidt, H., Dimeff, L.A., Craft, J.C., Kanter, J. and Comtois, K.A. (1999) 'Dialectical behavior therapy for patients with borderline personality disorder and drug-dependence', *American Journal on Addictions*, 8: 279–92.

Link, B.G. and Stueve, A. (1994) 'Psychotic symptoms and the violent/illegal behavior of mental patients compared to community controls', in J. Monahan and H. J. Steadman (eds), *Violence and Mental Disorder*. Chicago: University of Chicago Press.

Lipton, D.S., Pearson, F.S., Cleland, C.M. and Yee, D. (2002a) 'The effects of therapeutic communities and milieu therapy on recidivism', in J. McGuire (ed.), *Offender Rehabilitation and Treatment: Effective Programmes and Policies to Reduce Re-offending*. Chichester: Wiley, pp. 39–77.

Lipton, D.S., Pearson, F.S., Cleland, C.M. and Yee, D. (2002b) 'The effectiveness of cognitive-behavioural treatment methods on offender recidivism', in J. McGuire (ed.), *Offender Rehabilitation and Treatment: Effective Programmes and Policies to Reduce Re-offending*. Chichester: Wiley, pp. 79–122.

Loeber, R. (1988) 'Natural histories of conduct problems, delinquency and associated substance use', in B.B. Lahey and A.E. Kazdin (eds), *Advances in Clinical Child Psychology*, Vol. 11. New York: Plenum.

Lynam, D.R., Leukefeld, C. and Clayton, R.R. (2003) 'The contribution of personality to the overlap between antisocial behavior and substance use/misuse', *Aggressive Behavior*, 29: 316–31.

McCusker, C. and Davies, M. (1996) 'Prescribing drug of choice to illicit heroin users: the experience of a UK community drug team', *Journal of Substance Abuse Treatment*, 13: 521–31.

McGillicuddy, N.B. (2006) 'A review of substance use research among those with mental retardation', *Mental Retardation and Developmental Disabilities Research Reviews*, 12: 41–7.

McGillicuddy, N.B. and Blane, H. T. (1999) 'Substance use in individuals with mental retardation', *Addictive Behaviors*, 24: 869–78.

McMurran, M. (1994) *The Psychology of Addiction*. London: Taylor & Francis.

McMurran, M. (1996) 'Substance use and delinquency', in C.R. Hollin and K. Howells (eds), *Clinical Approaches to Working with Young Offenders*. Chichester: Wiley, pp. 209–35.

McMurran, M. (2002) 'Alcohol, aggression and violence', in J. McGuire (ed.), *Offender Rehabilitation and Treatment*. Chichester: Wiley.

McMurran, M. (2006) 'Alcohol and drug treatments', in A. Perry, C. McDougall and D. Farrington (eds), *Reducing Crime: The Effectiveness of Criminal Justice Interventions*. Chichester: Wiley.

McMurran, M. (2007) 'Alcohol and aggressive cognition', in T.A. Gannon, T. Ward, A. R. Beech and D. Fisher (eds), *Aggressive Offenders' Cognition: Theory, Research and Practice*. Chichester: Wiley

McMurran, M. and Boyle, M. (1990) 'Evaluation of a self-help manual for young offenders who drink', *British Journal of Clinical Psychology*, 29: 117–19.

McMurran, M. and Cusens, B. (2005) 'Alcohol and acquisitive offending', *Addiction Research and Theory*, 13: 439–43.

McMurran, M. and Lismore, K. (1993) 'Using video-tapes in alcohol interventions for people with learning disabilities', *Mental Handicap*, 21: 29–31.

Mangrum, L.F., Spence, R.T. and Lopez, M. (2006) 'Integrated versus parallel treatment of co-occurring psychiatric and substance use disorders', *Journal of Substance Abuse Treatment*, 30: 79–84.

Martin, C. and Player, E. (2000) *Drug Treatment in Prison: An Evaluation of the RAPt Treatment Programme*. Winchester: Waterside Press.

Maughan, B. (1993) 'Childhood precursors of aggressive offending in personality disordered adults', in S. Hodgins (ed.), *Mental Disorder and Crime*. Newbury Park, CA: Sage.

Metrebian, N., Shanahan, W., Stimson, G.V., Small, C., Lee, M., Mtutu, V. and Wells, B. (2001) 'Prescribing drug of choice to opiate dependent drug users: a comparison of clients receiving heroin with those receiving injectable methadone at a West London drug clinic', *Drug and Alcohol Review*, 20: 267–76.

Minkoff, K. (1989) 'An integrated treatment model for dual diagnosis of psychosis and addiction', *Hospital and Community Psychiatry*, 40: 1031–6.

Mueser, K.T., Bellack, A.S. and Blanchard, J.J. (1992) 'Comorbidity of schizophrenia and substance abuse: implications for treatment', *Journal of Consulting and Clinical Psychology*, 60: 845–56.

Mueser, K.T., Drake, R.E. and Wallach, M.A. (1998) 'Dual diagnosis: a review of etiological theories', *Addictive Behaviors*, 23: 717–34.

National Institute on Drug Abuse (1999) *Principles of Drug Addiction Treatment: A Research-Based Guide*, NIH Publication No. 99-4180. Rockville, MD: National Institute on Drug Abuse. Available at: htp://www.nida.nih.gov/PDF/PODAT/PODAT.pdf

Parker, H. and Kirby, P. (1996) *Methadone Maintenance and Crime Reduction on Merseyside*, Police Research Group, Crime Detection and Prevention Series, Paper 72. London: Home Office.

Parker, R.N. and Auerhahn, K. (1998) 'Alcohol, drugs and violence', *Annual Review of Sociology*, 24: 291–311.

Patrick, C.J., Hicks, B.M., Krueger, R.F. and Lang, A.R. (2005) 'Relations between psychopathy facets and externalizing in a criminal offender sample', *Journal of Personality Disorders*, 19: 339–56.

Pearson, F.S. and Lipton, D.S. (1999) 'A meta-analytic review of the effectiveness of corrections-based treatments for drug abuse', *Prison Journal*, 79: 384–410.

Perry, A., McDougall, C. and Farrington, D.P. (eds) (2006) *Reducing Crime: The Effectiveness of Criminal Justice Interventions*. Chichester: Wiley.

Project MATCH Research Group (1997) 'Project MATCH secondary a priori hypotheses', *Addiction*, 92: 1671–98.

Quayle, M., Clark, F., Renwick, S.J., Hodge, J. and Spencer, T. (1998) 'Alcohol and secure hospital patients', *Psychology, Crime and Law*, 4: 27–41.

Räsänen, P., Tiihonen, J., Isohanni, M., Rantakallio, P. Lehtonen, J. and Moring, J. (1998) 'Schizophrenia, alcohol abuse and violent behaviour: a 26-year follow up study of an unselected birth cohort', *Schizophrenia Bulletin*, 24: 437–41.

Regier, D.A., Farmer, M.E., Rae, D.S., Locke, B.Z., Keith, S.J., Judd, L.L. and Goodwin, F.K. (1990) 'Comorbidity of mental disorders with alcohol and other drug abuse: results from the Epidemiologic Catchment Area study', *Journal of the American Medical Association*, 264: 2511–18.

Reiss, D., Grubin, D. and Meux, C. (1996) 'Young "psychopaths" in a special hospital: treatment and outcome', *British Journal of Psychiatry*, 168: 99–104.

Robins, L.N. and Price, R.K. (1991) 'Adult disorders predicted by childhood conduct problems: results from the NIMH Epidemiologic Catchment Area project', *Psychiatry*, 54: 116–32.

Rosenbaum, D.P. and Hanson, G.S. (1998) 'Assessing the effects of school-based drug education: a six year multilevel analysis of project D.A.R.E.', *Journal of Research in Crime and Delinquency*, 35: 381–412.

Rounsaville, B.J., Kranzler, H.R., Ball, S., Tennen, H., Poling, J. and Triffleman, E. (1998) 'Personality disorders in substance abusers: relation to substance abuse', *Journal of Nervous and Mental Disease*, 186: 87–95.

Seivewright, N., Iqbal, M.Z. and Bourne, H. (2004) 'Treating patients with comorbidities', in P. Bean and T. Nemetz (eds), *Drug Treatment: What Works?* London: Routledge.

Simpson, M.K. (1998) 'Just say "no"? Alcohol and people with learning difficulties', *Disability and Society*, 13: 541–55.

Singer, L.R. (1991) 'A non-punitive paradigm of probation practice: some sobering thoughts', *British Journal of Social Work*, 21: 611–26.

Singleton, N., Meltzer, H., Gatward, R., Coid, J. and Deasy, D. (1998) *Psychiatric Morbidity among Prisoners*. London: HMSO.

Smith, S.S. and Newman, J.P. (1990) 'Alcohol and drug abuse-dependence disorders in psychopathic and non-psychopathic criminal offenders', *Journal of Abnormal Psychology*, 99, 430–9.

Steele, J., Darjee, R. and Thomson, L.D.G. (2003) 'Substance dependence and schizophrenia in patients with dangerous, violent and criminal propensities: a comparison of co-morbid and non-co-morbid patients in a high secure setting', *Journal of Forensic Psychiatry and Psychology*, 14: 569–84.

Steels, M., Roney, G., Larkin, E., Jones, P., Croudace, T. and Duggan, C. (1998) 'Discharged from special hospital under restriction: a comparison of the fates of psychopaths and the mentally ill', *Criminal Behaviour and Mental Health*, 8: 39–55.

Stewart, D., Gossop, M., Marsden, J. and Rolfe, A. (2000) 'Drug misuse and acquisitive crime among clients recruited to the National Treatment Outcome Research Study (NTORS)', *Criminal Behaviour and Mental Health*, 10: 10–20.

Stith, S.M., Smith, D.B., Penn, C.E., Ward, D.B. and Tritt, D. (2004) 'Intimate partner physical abuse perpetration and victimization risk factors: a meta-analytic review', *Aggression and Violent Behavior*, 10: 65–98.

Swanson, J.W. (1994) 'Mental disorder, substance abuse and community violence: an epidemiological approach', in J. Monahan and H.J. Steadman (eds), *Violence and Mental Disorder: Developments in Risk Assessment*. Chicago: University of Chicago Press.

Swartz, M.S., Swanson, J.W., Hiday, V.A., Borum, R., Wagner, H.R. and Burns, B.J. (1998) 'Violence and severe mental illness: the effects of substance abuse and nonadherence to medication', *American Journal of Psychiatry*, 155: 226–31.

Taggart, L., McLaughlin, D., Quinn, B. and Milligan, V. (2006) 'An exploration of substance misuse in people with intellectual disabilities', *Journal of Intellectual Disability Research*, 50: 588–97.

Taylor, P. J., Leese, M., Williams, D., Butwell, M., Daly, R. and Larkin, E. (1998) 'Mental disorder and violence', *British Journal of Psychiatry*, 172: 218–26.

Thomas, G. and McMurran, M. (1993) 'Alcohol-related offending in male special hospital patients', *Medicine, Science and the Law*, 33: 29–32.

Turnbull, P.J., McSweeney, T., Webster, R., Edmunds, M. and Hough, M. (2000) *Drug Treatment and Testing Orders: Final Evaluation Report, Home Office Research Study No. 212*. London: Home Office.

Verheul, R., van den Brink, W. and Hartgers, C. (1995) 'Prevalence of personality disorders among alcoholics and drug addicts: an overview', *European Addiction Research*, 1: 166–77.

Walsh, E., Gilvarry, C., Samele, C., Harvey, K., Manley, C., Tattan, T., Tyrer, P., Creed, F., Murray, R. and Fahy, T. (2004) 'Predicting violence in schizophrenia', *Schizophrenia Research*, 67: 247–52.

West, R. (2006) *Theory of Addiction*. Oxford: Blackwell.

Wheatley, M. (1998) 'The prevalence and relevance of substance use in detained schizophrenic patients', *Journal of Forensic Psychiatry*, 9: 114–29.

Windle, M. (1999) 'Psychopathy and antisocial personality disorder among alcoholic inpatients', *Journal of Studies on Alcohol*, 60: 330–6.

World Health Organisation (1992) *The ICD-10 Classification of Mental and Behavioural Disorders*. Geneva: World Health Organisation.

Chapter 18

Sexual offenders with mental health problems: epidemiology, assessment and treatment

Madelaine Lockmuller, Anthony Beech and Dawn Fisher

Introduction

The debate regarding the causal role of mental illness in sexual offending is represented, on the one hand, by the view that individuals who have a mental illness commit sexual offences because of factors specific to acute illness. For example, Jones *et al.* (1992) describe how psychosis may play a causative role in offending through direct experiences such as command hallucinations or sexual delusions and suggest that this type of offender is not at risk of offending when not acutely unwell. Risk reduction could, therefore, be achieved by treating the symptoms of psychosis directly. The opposing view is that the motivation to offend is related to factors other than acute psychosis and that the risk of the individual offending is roughly the same whether they are well or unwell; a number of studies conclude that mental illness/psychosis alone is not sufficient to explain the mechanism by which most mentally ill sexual offenders offend (Phillips *et al.* 1999; Baker and White 2002). We would broadly ascribe to the latter view and suggest that treating the symptoms of psychosis alone may not be enough to reduce the risk of offending (Lockmuller *et al.* in preparation) as there is, in fact, limited evidence for a direct link between command hallucinations/sexual delusions and sexual offending; Taylor and Smith (1999) found that 22 per cent of a sample of 80 men who were experiencing psychotic symptoms at the time of their index sexual offence had apparently responded to directly related symptoms.

Therefore in this chapter we focus on the aetiology and current evidence base for assessment and treatment of sexual offenders with mental health problems. When referring to mental health problems, we are in fact describing individuals with severe and enduring mental health problems (generally a psychotic/mental illness) rather than short-lived or transient mental health symptoms or indeed personality disorder. It is worth noting though that the former group often have a comorbid personality disorder. In the chapter, we explain a multi-factorial model of sexual offending, discuss motivation to offend and review psychological assessment and treatment approaches for adult male sexual offenders. Due to a paucity of research specific to offenders within the forensic mental health services, it is necessary to refer to research on offenders within the UK prison system who may not present with significant mental health problems; the limitation and generalisation of the information available is discussed, controversies in the area highlighted and future directions for research are proposed.

Sexual offending by females is not addressed in this chapter; this is an emerging area that requires further research (see Davin *et al.* 1999 and Ford 2006 for an exploration of this area). In order to illustrate some of the points raised in the chapter we will be referring to a specific case example, Noel, and ask the reader to hold him in mind when reading the chapter (see Box 18.1).

Nature, prevalence and epidemiology

In 2005 across England and Wales, there were 4,808 adult males convicted of a sexual offence against an adult (2,259) or a child (2,549) with a further 1,600 cautioned. This figure has remained relatively consistent, apart from a small drop in 2000, since 1995 and accounts for around 1 per cent of all recorded crime in the UK (Home Office 2006). The figure for female offenders suggests about 100 convictions or cautions for sexual offences in 2005 (Home Office 2006). In comparison the number of sex offenders admitted to hospital, including high security and any other psychiatric hospital in England or Wales, in 2004 (the latest published figure at the time of writing) was 94, with 403 (12 per cent of the total population) detained patients in total in the psychiatric system at the end of December 2004 (Home Office 2006). While this is a much smaller number it seems disproportionately large given that a number of authors have concluded that major/florid mental illness is rare among serious sex offenders (Chiswick 1983).

So what do we mean by a sexual offender? Sexual offenders are a heterogeneous group and attempts have been made to classify offenders by victim type, offence type, motivation and approach by a number of authors (Knight and Prentky 1990; Ward and Hudson 2000). Table 18.1 gives an outline of the type of offenders we will be referring to in this chapter. Motivation to offend varies according to the individual's unique developmental, environmental and personality characteristics and is addressed later when we discuss theories of sexual offending but broadly this can include: primary sexual interest in children, dysfunctional beliefs and cognitions about sex and victim groups, anger, deviant sexual interests/arousal, poor intimacy and social competence skills, sadism and problems with early sexual development.

Box 18.1 Case study Noel

Noel's early childhood was positive with no particular difficulties during his early school years. At the age of eleven, his father died from cancer and his mother became depressed and distant from her three sons. Noel found it difficult to talk to his mother about his grief and thus did not express any of the difficult feelings he was experiencing. He tried to look after his brothers and mother but felt that he was unable to cope with this responsibility.

Noel became interested in girls in his teens and found that he was able to develop sexual relationships quite easily. At the age of 14 he developed a significant relationship with a female peer in which he found emotional and sexual comfort. Noel developed the idea that sex with women was easy to achieve. He decided to end this relationship as he believed that he was too young to settle down and at this time began to use drugs and alcohol quite extensively. Noel then developed a new relationship but was disappointed by the lack of sex. At this point Noel began to regret terminating the relationship with his former girlfriend, whom he still occasionally saw and had sex with. Noel found it difficult to talk about his feelings with his new partner as he wanted to avoid conflict. He began to find the relationship claustrophobic and irritating but did nothing to either solve the problems or end the relationship. He also began to have casual one-night stands with other women. At this time he also began to expose himself from his bedroom window to a neighbour, which he found exciting.

Noel's partner became pregnant unexpectedly creating financial difficulties for the couple. Since leaving school Noel had not been employed and tended to spend his days writing music, playing his guitar and taking drugs. This caused arguments with his partner and eventually the relationship broke down. Noel then moved into a mobile home out of town, causing him to become isolated. After a year a new female neighbour moved into the mobile home next door. Over a period of a year Noel began to believe that the neighbour had feelings for him even though these had never been expressed and he barely knew her. During this time Noel also began to develop auditory hallucinations of women being raped and people arguing. Noel also experienced the voice of his neighbour whom he believed was telling him that she wanted to be in a relationship with him. His mother precipitated a referral to a psychiatrist but Noel masked his symptoms at assessment. Noel began to stare at his neighbour's mobile home for long periods of time and on occasions exposed himself to her through the kitchen window. Following a complaint by the neighbour's husband, Noel decided to approach the neighbour regarding her feelings for him. He broke into her home and raped her.

Assessment indicated that Noel was suffering from schizophrenia and he was detained in a secure hospital. His illness remitted quickly following appropriate pharmacological treatment but he continued to deny that he had raped the victim, insisting that she had consented to sex. After seven years of detention he began to accept responsibility. Noel engaged in a variety of occupational and therapeutic activities that increased his confidence and social skills but he remained unclear about the precipitants to his offence. He then engaged in a two-year programme of individual cognitive-behavioural therapy designed to address offence-specific factors and was successfully rehabilitated back into the community after 14 years of detention.

Table 18.1 Sexual offenders – offence types

Offence type	Victim	Motivation (examples only)
Child abuse (can be non-contact through to penetrative)	Child, related or unrelated, male or female, age-specific. Some offenders 'crossover' between sex, age and relatedness	• Primary or fixated sexual interest in children (paedophilia) • Preferred partner is not available • Belief in entitlement to sex
Rape	Adult, male or female, who does not give permission to commit penetrative sexual acts	• Sexual • Anger • Sadistic (Or a combination of above)
Sexual murder	Anyone who is murdered during commission of sexual offence	• Murdering to prevent disclosure of sexual offence • Find murder arousing
Internet offences (there may be different types of Internet offenders but it is unclear at this time)	Most commonly children-content of illegal sexual material downloaded from the Internet – 'child pornography'	• Direct contact offences – motivation to sexually offend but have not done so yet • Compulsively drawn to collect indecent images of children with no intention of engaging in contact offences
Exhibitionism (non-contact offence)	Anyone who is exposed to the offender's genitals from a distance	• Need for but fear of intimacy • Stress relief • Can influence the degree of risk of more serious contact offences presented by the offender

The relationship between mental illness and sexual offending

A model of sexual offending behaviour will be outlined later but in general, theories propose multi-factorial causation to sexual offending (e.g. Ward and Siegert 2002; Ward and Beech 2006) and outline that neither deviant sexual preference nor mental illness alone are sufficient in explaining motivation to sexually offend. Given this, are mentally ill offenders similar to the non-mentally ill offenders that populate our prisons?

A review of the research literature on mentally ill sexual offenders reveals some common findings. Many studies have found that mentally ill sexual offenders, like their non-mentally ill counterparts, had experienced a disrupted/dysfunctional early life, and poor schooling, demonstrated poor

449

interpersonal and social skills (Chesterman and Sahota 1998b; Baker and White 2002), had a lack of sexual experience or poor sexual knowledge and were preoccupied with sex (Cournos *et al.* 1994; Phillips *et al.* 1999). Ward and Siegert (2002) suggest that not all sexual offenders lack self-esteem but that some actually have a sense of entitlement. This type of grandiosity may be manifested by mentally ill offenders, perhaps confused with or indistinct from delusional beliefs but still present when active features of illness have remitted. Some studies report that mentally ill sex offenders and non-mentally ill offenders have both sexual and non-sexual pre-convictions with a minority reporting no prior history of sexually inappropriate or criminal behaviour (Taylor and Smith 1999). Mentally ill sex offenders, then, appear to have some characteristics in common with their non-mentally ill counterparts.

Some mentally ill sex offenders have clearly been identified as not suffering from psychosis at the time of their offending and the majority of studies conclude that mental illness/psychosis alone is not sufficient to explain the mechanism by which most mentally ill sexual offenders offend (Phillips *et al.* 1999; Smith 2000; Baker and White 2002). Chesterman and Sahota (1998a) suggest that illness may act as a potentiator (factor increasing vulnerability/ propensity to offend) in the context of other variables. The other variables that have been highlighted in the literature include social and psychological factors such as ineffective social and interpersonal skills, antisocial behaviour, personality disorder, anger and sexually deviant interests. These characteristics have been explored in the non-mentally ill offender (Beech *et al.* 1998; Perkins and Bishopp 2003) and considerable progress has been made in understanding the aetiology of sexual offending in this group. However, there are fewer studies that have explored similar precipitants in the mentally ill and attempts to draw direct comparison between the psychological profiles of the two groups are rare. Chesterman and Sahota (1998c) initiated this process with their psychometric assessment of mentally ill and non-mentally ill sex offenders and mentally ill non-offenders in which they found similar levels of cognitive distortion regarding sexual behaviour between the groups. Two further studies (Epstein unpublished thesis; Lockmuller *et al.* in preparation) indicate similar psychometric profiles for the two groups in terms of social competence and pro-offending attitudes;[1]; the results of the latter study, however, are tempered by the finding that mentally ill non-offenders also demonstrated a similar psychometric profile but with higher levels of pro-offending attitudes.

The current lack of clarity about the relationship between mental illness and sexual offending often results in offence-specific behaviours remaining untreated and an inadequate approach to risk management being practised in mental health settings. Offenders are still discharged having completed no offence-focused therapy. The high number of offenders not in contact with psychiatric services at the time of relapse and offending (Chesterman and Sahota 1998b) and the poor treatment compliance of those who offend in the context of mental illness (Phillips *et al.* 1999) highlight that current monitoring and relapse prevention are deficient for this group and this requires attention in the future.

As we argue that the mechanisms underlying sexual offending are broadly similar for mentally ill and non-mentally ill individuals, we will now report the latest ideas regarding the aetiology of sexual offending in non-mentally ill offenders and describe how it might relate to mentally ill sexual offenders.

Sexual offender theory

Theories of sexual offending and deviant behaviour have developed from a number of perspectives. Many clinicians, however, would agree that social learning theory and behavioural theories of conditioning through reinforcement are key to our understanding of sexually assaultative behaviour. How these factors actually operate to precipitate sexually deviant behaviour, however, is not well understood. As there is no current theoretical perspective that specifically focuses on the role of mental illness/mental health problems in sexual offending, these mechanisms can only be understood in the context of current theories of offending among individuals who are not identified as having significant mental health problems. In this chapter, we focus on one theory in detail – the Pathways Model of child sexual abuse by Ward and Siegert (2002) – which takes a 'theory knitting' perspective (i.e. it amalgamates the best features of previous theories of sexual offending, such as those proposed by Hall and Hirschman 1992; Marshall and Barbaree 1990[2]). While this theory has been developed with child sexual abuse in mind, we would propose that this theory can also be applied to adult sexual assault.

The Pathways Model suggests that the clinical phenomena evident among child molesters are generated by four distinct and interacting psychological mechanisms: *intimacy and social skills deficits*, *distorted sexual scripts*, *emotional dysregulation* and *cognitive distortions* (pro-offending attitudes about forced sexual contact with others). Each mechanism generates a specific offence pathway and describes offenders with different psychological and behavioural profiles that have separate underlying deficits and for whom the origins of the behaviour may differ. The number and type of factors that precipitate the motivation to offend and the type of offence behaviour will vary depending on the pathway's particular developmental course (Beech and Ward 2004). We will now look at each of these pathways in more detail.

Each distinctive pathway has a primary dysfunctional mechanism that precipitates a specific set of problems and can be identified as the primary cause of the sexual offending behaviour. The primary mechanism, however, must also interact with the other three mechanisms in order to precipitate a sexual offence. In other words, all offending involves the components of emotional dysregulation, intimacy problems, cognitive distortions and arousal. The model, therefore, proposes that there may be causal mechanisms that when occurring in isolation could be considered to be functioning normally but when interacting with the primary causal mechanism exert a dysfunctional effect.

In each pathway the primary causal or dysfunctional mechanism is thought to be different:

- *Intimacy deficits pathway.* Individuals are thought to possess normal sexual scripts but to offend at times when, for example, their preferred partner is not available or during periods of emotional loneliness or when they have been rejected – they may then have a temporary distortion in their sexual script.
- *Deviant sexual scripts pathway.* Individuals may have subtle or gross distortions in their developmental learning and in their understanding or

experience of sex (scripts) that interact with a set of dysfunctional ideas and beliefs, known as schemas, about relationships (e.g. relationships are seen as purely sexual).

- *Emotional dysregulation pathway.* Individuals are thought to possess normal sexual scripts but are ineffective at regulating and containing emotional arousal.
- *Distorted cognitions pathway.* Individuals may not have distorted sexual scripts but behave in antisocial ways and exhibit pro-criminal or pro-offending attitudes.

A fifth pathway is proposed that consists of individuals for whom there is no primary mechanism but where all dysfunctional mechanisms exert an equally powerful effect. These individuals are thought to have distorted sexual scripts that may relate to childhood experiences of sexual abuse or exposure to sexually deviant material or experiences, which then precipitate deviant fantasy. The presence of the other dysfunctional mechanisms in addition to these distorted scripts leads to impaired judgments about children and their capacity to make informed decisions about sex. Further to this, the effects of problems in emotional regulation and intimacy deficits compound their management of antisocial and pro-offending attitudes and capacity to inhibit offending behaviour. Ward and Siegert suggest that this group contains those individuals that could be thought of as 'pure paedophiles' – those with a primary sexual interest in children. Offending occurs when the appropriate set of triggers or stimuli are present, such as the presence of a victim, and the opportunity to offend does not conflict with other goals at the time.

Ward and colleagues (Ward *et al.* 2006) suggest that this model has clinical utility as it highlights clearly defined areas of dysfunction that could be addressed using psychological intervention and offers a clear theoretical perspective for offenders to begin to understand their own behaviour. Development of a clear framework for understanding offending and, therefore, to address the psychological, contextual and biological precipitants to deviant sexual behaviour is essential in order to attempt to prevent further offending or, in clinical terms, to prevent relapse to offending behaviours.[3] In fact the four different pathways have a lot in common with the four areas of dynamic risk (see below) described by Thornton (2002).

Application to offenders with mental illness

This model explains sexual offending as multi-factorial in causation and in the manifestation of specific behaviours. Factors such as psychosis are not addressed independently but could be considered to be related to emotional dysregulation. This would suggest that there is no need for independent theories to explain offending by individuals with severe and enduring mental health problems including mental illness. The role of psychosis may be relevant at different points in the cycle of offending. It may be that it has a disinhibitory effect (Smith 2000) and so, in terms of the Pathways Model, psychosis may be responsible for a reduction in the capacity to regulate emotional states or to challenge distorted cognitions about sex or victims of sexual assault. Psychosis may have a role as one of a number of proximal precipitating factors rather than as a single or independent causative factor. In terms of the Pathways Model, psychosis alongside distorted sexual scripts may increase the likelihood of offending as mechanisms to inhibit the behaviour (e.g. the desire to act on deviant fantasy) are compromised. Psychosis may also play a causative role in offending through direct experiences such as command hallucinations or sexual delusions (Jones *et al.* 1992) but only in the minority of mentally ill offenders. It is likely that the nature of the delusions, i.e. sexual, experienced by our case example Noel, were determined by the development of distorted sexual scripts and distorted beliefs about sex during adolescence that were then proximally precipitated by loneliness and poor social functioning at the time (social competence). His use of drugs reduced his capacity to inhibit his behaviour and when faced with a situation that was dissonant with his beliefs (i.e. complaints about his behaviour from the woman whom he perceived was in love with him), high levels of anger (emotional dysregulation) became the final triggering variable for the offence.

In the next section of the chapter we will outline current notions about risk assessment in mainstream sexual offender populations as this again sets a framework for thinking about risk assessment in sexual offenders with mental health problems.

Assessment of sexual offenders

We have already discussed how the motivation of offenders to commit acts of sexual assault may vary according to a range of personality, developmental, environmental, social/cultural and psychosexual or physiological factors. In order to gain a clear understanding of the offender's motivation to offend, the precipitants to an offence and the factors that perpetuate or maintain the offending, a comprehensive assessment of all of these potential factors is required. The focus of the assessment may differ according to the question being posed. Typically we want to answer one or all of three questions:

- What is the risk of reoffending and level of dangerousness of the offender and to whom and when do they pose this risk?
- How do we understand the offender's behaviour and what are the treatment targets and types of intervention required?
- How effective have our interventions been and what is the longer-term prognosis?

All of these questions require that a clinical assessment is conducted but additional aspects related specifically to risk are also required.

A key issue to consider during assessment is that sexual offenders generally demonstrate high levels of denial (Marshall 1994). This can range from complete denial of responsibility to minimisation of aspects of the offence, such as how much the victim was harmed. There are many factors that can influence an offender's decision to deny aspects of the offending behaviour. These could include factors such as shame and fear of the consequences of admitting in terms of both criminal procedures and response of family and friends. Assessment of denial and minimisation is, therefore, essential and can be aided by the use of witness statements for comparison with the offender's account, the use of specific psychometric measures to evaluate general and offence-specific openness (often termed 'lie' or social desirability scales) and through a detailed functional analysis of the offence behaviours. Multiple sources of information rather than those that rely solely on the offender's self-disclosures are essential. It is also important to develop a non-judgmental but non-collusive approach with the offender to enable them to feel comfortable about making disclosures. Much useful information about the offender's attitudes, thoughts, beliefs and actual behaviour can be gained through careful and sensitive questioning. It is sensible to hear the information being given without making comment on its reliability or challenging its accuracy in order to obtain as clear a picture as possible of the offender's real thoughts and beliefs about what has happened. Assumptive questioning techniques and motivational interviewing strategies (Miller and Rollnick 1991) can also be very helpful.

Most qualitative information about offending is gained from clinical interview with offenders but this method of assessing offenders is susceptible to the effects of deception and also to compliance. It is wise to assume that an offender is unlikely to fully disclose all aspects of their offending behaviour until engaged in long-term treatment, if at all. In this respect, much of the goal of a treatment intervention is to conduct further more detailed assessment to clarify the picture presented. A further issue to consider with mentally ill offenders is that they may attribute their behaviour solely to their illness and have very little insight initially as to other contributory factors. Sometimes this is another method of denial and avoidance of the painful process of confronting their offending behaviour. However, it may also be genuine and it may be necessary to question them more sensitively initially. Our case example Noel continued to deny that his offence was non-consensual for seven years despite his psychosis remitting many years earlier. Once in an appropriate treatment programme, he was able to address the minimisation of his offence and the impact on his victim and also revealed further offences that he had committed as an adolescent and young adult. At this point he had already been detained in hospital for 11 years.

Clinical assessment

The time required for assessment will vary according to the offender's motivation to engage, their mental state and level of cognitive functioning but it would be unusual to be able to gather the required information in less than six hours and usually takes considerably longer. For fuller details of the key components to clinical assessment of sexual offenders the reader is referred to Morrison *et al.* (1994) and Briggs *et al.* (1998). A comprehensive clinical assessment should include the following (see Table 18.2 for full information):

- *family background and early developmental experiences* – in detail and including the offender's qualitative experience of their early life;
- *psychosexual history* – including positive and negative experiences, social relationships in general, capacity to relate to others, deviant arousal;
- *psychiatric history* – including experiences that did not require formal intervention;

- *functional analysis of offending behaviour* – precipitants, behaviour engaged in, consequences of and other reinforcers of the behaviour;
- *forensic history* – full history of offending including convictions and cautions;
- *attitude to offending* – including issues of denial, minimisation, justification, cognitive distortions, victim empathy/understanding;
- *psychometric assessment* – of personality, sexual behaviour/interests, social competence, denial/malingering, socially desirable responding, mental health, thinking patterns/schemas (and suggestibility and cognitive functioning if appropriate);
- *collateral information* – including previous reports from mental health, probation, social services, education department, criminal justice system (criminal record, witness statements).

All of these factors are important in being able to develop a psychological formulation (a structured hypothesis using psychological factors) of the offending behaviour and the offender. While developing a formulation it is useful to keep a model of sexual offending in mind – our chosen model is the Pathways Model – in order to ensure that information has been collected in all of the areas that sexual offenders are thought to present problems: emotional dysregulation, cognitive distortions, social competence and distorted sexual scripts. In developing a formulation, a clear understanding of the function of the offending behaviour is key. This can be informed by applying a functional analysis.

Functional analysis

This is a clinical tool used to investigate the antecedents, behaviours and consequences of the offence. This allows an assessment to be made of the process of the offence and the offence pathway that characterises the offending for that individual. Hence, this type of analysis is an important first step in ascertaining the type of goals and strategies a sexual offender has toward offending. This information will be gained from careful questioning about the offence(s) during clinical assessment. Currently one of the most useful frameworks is called a 'Decision Chain' (Ward *et al.* 1995) – see Figure 18.1. This model has tended to supersede earlier frameworks such as Finkelhor's (1994) preconditions or Wolf's (1984) offence cycle. A Decision Chain is a sequence of choices leading to an offence. Each choice is characterised in terms of the situation it took place in, the thoughts that made sense of and responded to the situation and the emotions and actions that arose from these thoughts. Thus in any analysis of offence behaviours it is important to take account of the diversity in offending and to accommodate individuals whose firmly entrenched beliefs about the legitimacy of sexual contact with children or forced sex with adults lead them to experience positive emotions during the offence process. Decision Chains have the advantage that they can represent with equal facility offences that spring from negative emotional states and poor coping strategies (as in the Wolf cycle) and those where these negative factors are not involved (Laws 1999; Ward and Hudson 1996).

Table 18.2 Clinical assessment of sexual offenders

Assessment area	Content of area to be assessed
Family background	• Family of origin: parents/siblings – age/health, occupation, relationship past and current, experience of them, discipline, care giving, forensic and psychiatric history • Significant others: extended family • Bereavements and loss, time in care or away from home, financial situation • Physical, sexual, emotional abuse
Education	• Include primary and secondary education • Learning problems, behaviour problems – is client literate/numerate? • Changes in school, attitude to school/learning • Relationship with peers, teachers • Bullying, fighting, expulsion, running away, truanting, • Racism, effects of disability or special needs • Exams/qualifications achieved, hopes for the future e.g. career/job
General issues/problems	• Reflection on childhood: did they feel happy, loved, treated equally, what would they have changed? • General problems: head injury, disabilities, involvement of educational psychologist, welfare officer, other specialist services, early childhood problems e.g. enuresis, effect of above on peer/sibling relationships, cultural/religious issues
Employment	• Longest job, type of work, unemployment length/reason for it, general attitude to working • Unfulfilled ambitions/disappointments/further or higher education, plans for future
Relationships (social and sexual)	• Friendships: close friends or acquaintances only, happy/satisfied with friendships, difficulties, shyness, bullying, social isolation • Sexual development and identity: from child to adult, sexual problems, adverse experiences, level of experience, satisfaction with relationships, info. about partners, deviant interests, attitude to women, violence and sex, fantasy
Forensic history	• Criminal record, number and type of offences, chronology, escalation, disposal, specific attention to motivation/triggers to violence, planning/opportunism, offences committed but not charged with • Functional analysis-most recent offence • Attitude to offending, understanding, motivation to change

Addictive behaviours (drugs, alcohol, gambling)	• Consumption level/frequency, type of drugs/alcohol used, financing of use, effect, attitude towards this behaviour now, relationship to offending, presence in offence chain, attempts to change
Psychiatric and medical history	• Previous contact with psychiatric services, assessments and admissions, diagnosis, specifically ask about depression/anxiety/OCD, family history, specific problems presented by above, undiagnosed problems • Previous contact with psychiatric services, assessments medical history current and past, neurological issues, impact on life
Formulation	• Vulnerability/early experience factors, precipitating and maintaining factors, schemas/beliefs, critical incidents • Relationship of mental health issues to offending • Risk factors

Up-to-date thinking about the offence process should be drawn from the work of Ward and Hudson (1998, 2000) who suggest that it is possible to classify offenders according to one of four different routes to offending. These routes are different to those described in the Pathways Model earlier as they are about the process of the offence rather than the motivation or developing precipitants as described in the Pathways Model. The groups/routes are defined by the individual offender's goal towards deviant sex (i.e. avoidant or approach), and the selection of strategies designed to achieve their goal (i.e. active or passive). The *avoidant* goal offender is described as having a commitment to restraint as the overall goal is one of avoidance. However, self-regulation deficiencies such as inadequate coping skills (under-regulation) or inappropriate strategies (misregulation) ultimately result in goal failure. Consequently, negative affective states and covert planning characterise the avoidant pathway. For the *approach* goal offender, positive affective states, explicit planning and the presence of distorted attitudes about victims and offending behaviour typify the process leading to offending.

Further to this, the *active approach* offender seeks opportunities to offend and actively sets up the situation in which to offend. The *passive approach* offender, however, while motivated to offend, only does so when the opportunity presents itself. With the *avoidant active* offender the active pathway is one in which the offender makes an effort to avoid offending while the *avoidant passive* offender would prefer not to offend but does nothing to prevent himself. In terms of our case example, we would classify Noel as an *avoidant passive* offender. Assessment of approach/ avoidant and active passive strategies can be partly informed by the checklist developed by Bickley and Beech (2002). This checklist is at the moment fairly brief but at least can act as a guide to offence analysis.

In addition to the information gained through clinical assessment it can be useful to administer psychometric measures.

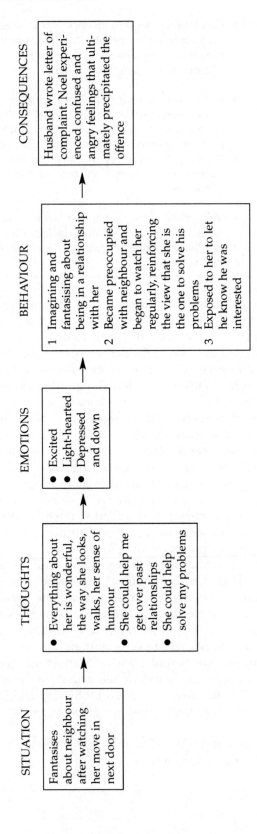

Figure 18.1 Functional analysis: a link in Noel's decision chain

Psychometric assessment

The publication of the Sex Offender Treatment Evaluation Project (STEP) reports (Barker and Morgan 1993; Beckett *et al.* 1994; Beech *et al.* 1998; Beech *et al.* 2005) have highlighted the usefulness of psychometric measures, mostly self-report questionnaires, in enhancing clinical assessment of adults who sexually assault children. The most recent report suggests that psychometric assessment is less useful with adults who have committed offences of rape and/or offences that are sadistic in nature.

Self-report measures can be a useful addition to clinical assessment. The advantage of this type of measure is that they enable a comparison to be made between different offenders and the general population thus enabling an objective but comparative profile of the individual's beliefs, attitudes, behaviours and personality to be established. The disadvantages are that the measures are open to 'faking' and to the effects of acquiescence and compliance, they may lead to inappropriate generalisations about the offender and are not suitable for individuals who may be cognitively impaired or whose verbal skills are poor. Certainly they can provide a substantial amount of information about an offender in a relatively short space of time and can often reveal information that an offender may be too embarrassed to speak directly about (for example, specific paraphilias, sexual problems or a lack of sexual knowledge). It is important that any practitioner who applies these measures has a good conceptual understanding of the utility of psychometrics and also of the reliability/validity of the measures used. They should be interpreted alongside, and as a method of enhancing, clinical assessment and not as stand-alone measures. There are also other methods of assessing sexual interest including physiological measures such as the Penile Plethysmograph (PPG), which measures changes in penile tumescence in reaction to different visual material, and Affinity, which measures the individual's viewing time of visually presented material. The former is available at specific sites in the UK (including Broadmoor Hospital) and the latter by contacting the author David Glasgow.

Beech, Fisher and Beckett constructed a package of questionnaires designed to assess adults who offend against children as part of the national Sex Offender Treatment Evaluation Project (STEP); an adolescent version is also available. The Sex Offender Assessment Pack (SOAP) is widely used within the UK but there are other measures that are useful additions to this and that are more appropriate to offenders who assault adults. For a population with a mental health/illness presentation, measures that help to differentiate between implicit beliefs (Ward 2000) or schemas and psychotic beliefs can also be useful (for example, Young's Schema Questionnaire and subscales of the Millon Clinical Multi-Axial Inventory and the Personality Assessment Inventory). Beech, Fisher and Ward (2005) point out, however, that more valuable information about implicit theories can be gained through narratives given by the offender during clinical assessment. Table 18.3 contains details of these measures.

Once significant information about the offender has been collected, the question of dangerousness and future risk can be addressed.

Table 18.3 Psychometric measures

Assessment Area	Measures
Sexual interest and attitudes	• Multiphasic Sex Inventory (Nichols and Molinder 1984)* • Hanson Sex Attitudes Questionnaire (Hanson *et al.* 1994)
Distorted attitudes	• Justifications Scale of the MSI • Abel and Becker Cognitions Scale (Abel *et al.* 1984) • Schema Questionnaire (Young 1990)
Attitudes supportive of sexual assault	• Bumby RAPE and MOLEST scales (Bumby 1996) • Children and Sex: Cognitive Distortions Scale (Beckett 1987)* • Burt Rape Scales – including adversarial sexual attitudes, acceptance of interpersonal violence against women etc. (Burt 1980) • Hostility Towards Women Scale (Check 1984)
Intimacy deficits and socio-affective problems	• Children and Sex: Emotional Congruence Scale* • UCLA Loneliness Scale (Russell, Peplau and Cutrona 1980)* • Social Response Inventory (Keltner, Marshall and Marshall 1981)* • Locus of Control Scale (Nowicki 1976)* • Multi-Dimensional Self-Esteem Inventory (MSEI) (O'Brien and Epstein 1983) • Social Problem Solving Inventory (D'Zurilla *et al.* 2002) • Stait Trait Anger Expression Inventory 2 (Spielberger 1999)
Empathy	• Victim Distortions Scales (Beckett and Fisher 1994)* • Rapist Empathy Measure (Marshall and Fernandez 2002) • Interpersonal Reactivity Index (Davis 1980)*
Denial/deception	• Sex Offence Information Questionnaire Revised (Hogue 1998) • Paulhus Deception Scale (Paulhus 1999) • Subscales of MSI, MSEI, PAI and MCMI 3 • Personal Reaction Inventory (Greenwald and Satow 1970)*
Self-management/ self-regulation problems	• Psychopathy Checklist Revised – Factor 2, which measures lifestyle impulsivity (Hare 1991) • Barratt Impulsivity Scale (Barratt 1994)
Personality	• Millon Clinical Multiaxial Inventory III (MCMI III) (Millon 1997) • Personality Assessment Inventory (PAI) (Morey 1991)
Relapse prevention	• Relapse Prevention Questionnaire (Beckett, Fisher, Mann and Thornton, 1997)*

* indicates measures from the SOAP

Risk assessment

In the risk assessment of sexual offenders clinicians typically use clinical judgment, actuarial prediction or some combination of these approaches to assess the future risk of a convicted sexual offender. However, actuarial assessment may not provide enough qualitative information to aid the clinician in determining the appropriate areas for psychological intervention with a specific offender and thus psychological formulation, including functional analysis, and dynamic risk assessment are also essential to treatment planning.

Actuarial risk assessment

The most commonly employed actuarial risk prediction instruments for sexual offenders rely almost exclusively on historical or *static* risk factors that cannot change, such as previous convictions for sexual offences, identified lack of long-term intimate relationships and general criminality. This information will be gained mostly from formal documentation such as a criminal record. These and other factors have been identified in various empirical studies reported by, for example, Hanson and Thornton (2000), who describe the development and validation of Static-99, and Thornton *et al.*(2003), who describe the development and validation of Risk Matrix 2000. Currently, actuarial risk prediction is the most accurate method of risk prediction available for use with sexual offenders (Hanson *et al.* 2003).

Actuarial assessment provides guidance as to the general band of risk that an offender falls into (e.g. low, medium, high, very high) and is based on cumulative research evidence that is used to develop a coding system for risk level.

Formalised risk measures

Probably the most well known actuarial instruments in the UK are the following:

- *Static-99* (Hanson and Thornton 2000). As its name implies, Static-99 is based solely on static factors. It consists of ten items: prior sex offences, prior sentencing occasions, convictions for non-contact sex offences, index non-sexual violence, prior non-sexual violence, unrelated victims, stranger victims, male victims, lack of a long-term intimate relationship and if the offender is aged under 25 on release (or now, if the offender is in the community).
- *Risk Matrix 2000* (RM2000: Thornton *et al.* 2003). The Risk Matrix 2000 has separate indicators for risk of sexual recidivism, non-sexual assault and overall violence. The Prison, Probation and Police Services in England and Wales have adopted the scale nationally. The first stage involves three static items: age at commencement of risk, sexual appearances and total criminal appearances. Points are awarded and the offender placed into one of four categories (low, medium, high or very high). The second stage of RM2000 requires rating on four aggravating factors: male victim, stranger victim, non-contact sexual offences and lack of a long-term intimate relationship. If two aggravating factors are present the risk category is raised one level and if all four are present the risk is raised two levels.
- *The Sex Offence Risk Appraisal Guide* (SORAG: Quinsey *et al.* 1998). SORAG is less frequently used in the UK and was developed in Canada. It is designed to predict violence committed by sexual offenders. SORAG has 14 items that

cover: living with both biological parents until age 16, school maladjustment, alcohol problems, evidence of a sustained intimate relationship, non-violent criminality, violent criminality, previous sexual contact convictions, convictions against girls under 14 only, failure on prior conditional release, age at index offence, evidence of personality disorder, schizophrenia, evidence of deviant sexual preferences and psychopathy (as defined by the Psychopathy Checklist – Revised – Hare 1991). This scale's average predictive accuracy is slightly poorer than Static-99 (Hanson *et al.* 2003). The scale may, however, have particular advantages in samples where personality disorder and strong deviant sexual preferences vary independently of prior sexual convictions (Beech *et al.* 2003).

Dynamic risk assessment

In an attempt to overcome the limitations of purely static actuarial instruments and to take into account the fact that risk may be reduced through treatment, some researchers have developed classification schemes that additionally incorporate *dynamic* factors, i.e. clinical/psychological risk factors that are amenable to change (Beech *et al.* 2003). Probably the most up-to-date thinking in this area is by Thornton (2002) who suggests four domains[4] of psychological problems that are related to the future commission of sexual offences. These are:

- *sexual interests* that are broadly deviant, such as arousal to children or to sexualised violence;
- *distorted attitudes* that are supportive of sexual assault, such as child abuse supportive beliefs or adversarial sexual attitudes;
- a level of *socio-affective functioning* that leads to lack of emotionally intimate relationships with adults and excessive emotional over-identification with children;
- *self-management* problems, leading to lifestyle impulsiveness and/or dysfunctional coping.

In the general criminological literature such long-term psychological problems are characterised as *criminogenic need* factors. This means that they have been identified as being related to recidivism and that addressing them during psychological treatment may reduce dynamic risk (Andrews and Bonta 2003).

Hanson and Harris (2000) have described another set of risk factors, which they term *acute dynamic* risk factors. These risk factors include evidence of severe emotional disturbance or crisis, hostility, substance abuse and rejection of supervision. These could be regarded as proximal/contextual characteristics that may precipitate or signal the onset of offending. These are different to the *stable dynamic/criminogenic need* factors that are also important in maintaining offending behaviour.

Assessment of the likelihood of sexual offending, therefore, should be broad and involve more than a simple documentation of the level of risk. It should also contribute information that can guide risk management. The types of risk factors to be assessed, therefore, can be helpfully collated into categories:

- *dispositional factors* (i.e. stable dynamic risk factors) such as psychopathic or antisocial personality characteristics;

- *historical factors* (i.e. static risk factors) such as adverse developmental events, prior history of crime and violence, prior hospitalisation and poor treatment compliance;
- *contextual antecedents to violence* (i.e. acute dynamic risk factors) such as deviant social networks, lack of positive social supports and victim access;
- *clinical factors* such as psychiatric diagnosis, poor cognitive functioning and substance abuse.

Comprehensive risk assessment for any type of future sexual or non-sexual violence should seek to determine the presence or absence of each category of these risk factors (McGuire 2000) and can be conducted by combining information from formal actuarial assessments with clinical assessment.

Formalised risk measures

There are a number of different measures available but those that would have greatest relevance for a forensic mental health population include the following:

- *The Risk for Sexual Violence Protocol* (RSVP: Hart *et al.* 2003). This is a 22-item measure that categorises items into five domains: sexual violence history, psychological adjustment, mental disorder, social adjustment and manageability. In coding each item, the measure requires three areas of coding including presence in the past, presence currently and relevance to future risk management; further evaluation of each area is achieved through determining whether a factor is definitely present, partially present or not present at all. This coding system can be helpful when thinking about the causal role that a risk factor may play in respect to violence, in treatment planning and in developing risk management strategies/plans. These measures also allow further consideration of an individual's likely risk through the development of risk scenarios that are hypotheses about what type of offence the individual under assessment may be likely to commit. The authors describe this as 'scenario-based risk assessment' that is intended to inform decision-making in the development of risk management plans.
- *The Sexual Violence Risk-20* (SVR-20: Boer *et al.* 1997). The SVR-20 has items which cover psychosocial adjustment, sexual offences and future plans. The 20 items are as follows: deviant sexual preference, victim of child abuse, level of psychopathy, major mental illness, substance abuse, suicidal or homicidal ideation, relationship problems, employment problems, violent non-sexual offences, general criminality, supervision failure, high frequency of sex offences, range of sex offences, physical harm to victim, use of weapons, escalation in frequency or severity of sex offences, extreme denial or minimisation of sex offences, pro-offending attitudes, lack of realistic plans and negative attitude towards intervention. It also allows for the addition of three extra items that are not historical items but can be considered as dynamic: acute mental disorder, recent loss of social support network and frequent contact with potential victims. The SVR-20 is regarded as a 'judgment after review' instrument by its authors, in that the scale is intended to provide a list of items that have been shown by research to be indicative of reconviction. This

allows the assessor to weight items in accordance with each individual situation. This of course means that the instrument's accuracy will vary depending on the judgment of the clinician applying it. While this scale is still in use, the RSVP is in fact a more up-to-date version of the SVR-20.

Of course, all dynamic risk assessment tools require formal training before a clinician is considered qualified to administer them and it is also good practice for clinicians to have had significant experience in working with issues of risk and with offenders before interpreting the information provided by this type of assessment.

Psychological intervention

Overview of current approaches

Our understanding of sexual offending and approach to treating offenders has increased considerably in the last ten years. The publication of the Woolf Report[5] in 1990 prompted progress in the appropriate disposal of sex offenders and the establishment of a standardised treatment programme within the Prison Service, the Sex Offender Treatment Programme (SOTP) that now treats approximately 1,000 offenders per year in 26 English and Welsh prisons. The Home Office commissioned a national research project to evaluate the effectiveness/outcome of the programme (the Sex Offender Treatment Evaluation Project – STEP), which has now published four volumes of research results. The STEP reports have had a significant impact on treatment delivery for sexual offenders. The STEP research has offered valuable evidence on which to base our practice of sex offender treatment of adults who molest children and the most recent volume investigated the impact of the SOTP on men who have offended against adult victims, specifically rapists and sexual murderers. This latter report established that the current prison SOTP has had an impact on men who have committed offences of rape and sexual murder but that there were treatment needs outstanding for this group following completion of the standard Core programme. The STEP research has contributed significantly to a growing body of research that suggests a strong evidence base for intensive and long-term cognitive-behavioural intervention for sexual offenders (Hanson *et al.* 2002; Friendship *et al.* 2003). Cognitive-behavioural treatment has been shown in the 'What Works' literature (McGuire 1995) to be the most effective method of treating offenders. Primarily the goal of treatment is to reduce the risk of reoffending in the future but this includes attention to factors that increase life satisfaction and encourage the development of skills that enable offenders to lead safer and more fulfilling lives without resorting to dysfunctional and deviant patterns of behaviour.

In the Prison Service and in some community probation-run treatment programmes in the UK, interventions for sexual offending are delivered as group treatment programmes that have been designed using a structure and format based on cognitive-behavioural principles (e.g. Core 2000 – the general programme for most offenders, the Extended programme – applied after Core for offenders with further treatment needs, and the Rolling programme – for offenders with fewer treatment needs than Core). While most research has focused on group treatment programmes, the same concepts and processes can be adapted for use in individual therapy and it is likely that offenders in forensic mental health settings may require some individualised therapy alongside group work. The STEP studies have suggested that the amount of treatment required will depend on the level of deviancy of the offender – deviancy is established by applying Beech's deviancy algorithm (1998) to the results of specific psychometric measures. Offenders classed as high deviancy require more hours of intervention (160+) than low deviancy offenders to effect change in key areas.

Considerations in a forensic mental health setting

We have already addressed the issue of the similarity in presentation and the applicability of theories of sexual abuse to offenders with mental illness when compared with non-mentally ill offenders and we would propose that similar treatment approaches should be used with both groups. However, there are specific factors relating to the experience of psychosis that will need to be taken into account when planning a treatment programme for an individual with mental illness/severe and enduring mental health problem. The most important feature to consider is the impact of psychosis on cognitive or *neuropsychological functioning*. Neuropsychological abnormalities have been reported consistently in individuals with a diagnosis of schizophrenia. Most consistently reported symptoms are impairments in memory, learning and in executive functioning (Heinrichs and Zakzanis 1998). These symptoms have also been observed in individuals who are unmedicated, suggesting that impairments are due to the direct effects of psychosis rather than to the psychotropic medication used to treat it. These impairments will have a direct influence on the individual's capacity to learn new ideas and strategies for managing their behaviour, to hold in mind different ideas at one time, to sustain their attention and to problem-solve. Frith (1992) has also suggested that some key features of schizophrenia are due to the inability to monitor the beliefs and intentions of others and this could have an impact on the capacity to perspective-take and to develop empathy. These latter two factors are common features of sexual offender presentation and key issues in therapeutic intervention. Interventions for this group will often need to be conducted over a longer period of time, with frequent rehearsal of key concepts and adaptation of some of the more demanding tasks.

Other factors to consider include the potential effects of some *psychotropic medications*, such as tiredness or drowsiness; the *remission/relapse* pattern of the illness for some offenders (this may interfere with consistency of treatment delivery and have an impact on capacity to retain learning); and *detention under the MHA 1983*, as this is based on presentation of active symptoms of an illness and need for treatment of those symptoms rather than of psychological disorders. This may lead to offenders being discharged part-way through psychological treatment programmes and motivation to engage may significantly reduce following discharge when there are limited incentives for the offender to attend.

Key components of intervention

Research (Beech *et al.* 1998) indicates that in delivering interventions to sexual offenders, the primary treatment targets (those most relevant to reoffending) are those areas considered under the heading of *pro-offending attitudes* – this includes: cognitive distortions, justification/minimisation of behaviour and of harm, non-acceptance of responsibility, poor victim empathy and lack of relapse prevention skills. Secondary but still key treatment targets include areas under the heading of *social competence* – social skills, problem-solving, intimacy, emotional regulation and general empathy. Our formulation and risk assessment of an offender will further direct us to those areas that require particular attention for a specific individual; in our case example, Noel's distortions regarding his victim reduced significantly following his acceptance that the sexual contact was non-consenting and this occurred prior to cognitive-behavioural treatment. Assessment and formulation during the early stages of a cognitive-behavioural programme revealed further offences and the presence of deviant arousal from a younger age than had been known previously. This directed the treatment towards intensive exploration of early beliefs about women and sexuality (distorted sexual scripts) that helped Noel to further understand that his offending was not just a product of psychosis and that he needed to develop skills to prevent relapse of both his illness and of his distorted ideas about sex.

Pro-offending attitudes

Cognitive distortions and patterns of dysfunctional thinking

It has been well documented that sex offenders typically hold beliefs about their offending that allow them to justify and rationalise their behaviour (Murphy 1990). Work on raising awareness of these thinking errors (cognitive distortions) and enabling individuals to recognise and challenge their own distorted thinking should usually be addressed early on in a programme but will require continued attention throughout treatment as offenders begin to develop a greater awareness of the precipitants to their behaviour. The work attempts to identify the underlying causes of distorted thinking, thought to be a core set of dysfunctional schema held by the offender (Ward *et al.* 1997). Ward and Keenan (1999) suggest that an example of such a schema, and a belief that arises from it, would be seeing children as sexual beings and believing that sexual contact between adults and children is not harmful. These schemas are examined and deconstructed using cognitive techniques such as debating the arguments for and against a belief where the offender is required to argue against a belief that he holds. As offenders can be more defensive when exploring their own beliefs it can be useful to focus on non-offence-related examples first in order to help the offender to learn about the concept of distorted thinking and how it affects behaviour in a less challenging way. With some offenders, the work required to achieve this is longer-term. Beech, Fisher and Ward (2005) and Beech, Ward and Fisher (2006) describe the work of several authors on the classification of and intervention with implicit beliefs (or schemas).

Lack of victim empathy

It is recognised that many sexual offenders lack empathy for others but research suggests that this may be specific to their own victims rather than a general empathy deficit (Fernandez *et al.* 1999). This suggests that empathy is a potential block to abusive behaviour and that increasing empathy could make it less likely that an offender will act on an impulse to sexually assault a potential victim. Empathy development should be addressed once distortions have been successfully worked with, otherwise an offender may feel attacked and react defensively, potentially regressing to a victim stance themselves. The Woolf Report (1990) noted that sex offenders had a tendency to leave prison with the view that they had been victims of undue punishment when distorted beliefs about their offending and victims had not been addressed. Exercises to address empathy deficits include role plays where the offender plays a member of the victim's family, or the victim themselves, describing the long-term impact of the assault on their life, constructing hypothetical apology letters to victims, watching video material of adult victims talking about the long-term impact of their childhood abusive experiences on them, etc.

Feedback from men who have assaulted children and who have been through cognitive-behavioural treatment suggests that the victim empathy component of the UK prison programme, which includes role-play, has had the most profound effect in terms of their understanding of the harm caused to their victims (Beech *et al.* 1999). With our case example, while Noel had a good understanding intellectually of the harm that was caused to victims of sexual assault, a significant shift occurred in his emotional experience of and understanding for his victim following a facilitated role-play task in which he played the role of his victim one year on from the assault. Offenders who do benefit from this aspect of treatment may find that increased empathy can also lead to increased guilt and negative feelings about themselves. It is, therefore, important not to undertake this work until the offender has sufficient personal resources to take on the responsibility for his behaviour and to follow this aspect of treatment with exercises to help manage these feelings.

Deviant sexual arousal
A key factor in working with deviant sexual arousal is addressing deviant fantasy. Fantasy is important for sexual offenders because it is thought to reinforce deviant behaviour by stimulating interest in deviant images and sensitising the offender to deviant behaviours (Wolf 1984). Not all offenders experience primary arousal to deviant fantasies. Many will have appropriate fantasies and are offending due to appropriate sexual outlets being unavailable to them. This is typically where distorted thinking is employed to justify their behaviour. In this situation, behaviour can be most successfully addressed through modification of these distortions and by enhancing skills in problem-solving to enable the offender to find more appropriate ways of meeting their sexual needs. Individuals who are only aroused by deviant activity and have no interest in appropriate sexual activity will remain strongly motivated to offend. For those individuals it may be necessary to employ fantasy modification techniques to attempt to modify the type of images or sexual contact that they are aroused to; this could include masturbatory reconditioning, covert sensitisation, satiation or ammonia aversion. However, there is limited evidence for the efficacy of these techniques (Laws and Marshall 1991) and they should only be employed when the clinician is sure that the offender genuinely wants to change their behaviour and is applying the technique correctly. Otherwise there is a risk of actually reinforcing the use of deviant images. In some instances, such as when the offender wants to change their behaviour but fantasy modification is unsuitable, anti-libidinal medication can be of help.

Social competence

This field of treatment covers a wide range of areas that relate to the efficacy of an individual's social functioning. While these areas can be addressed in direct offence-focused work it is also important that offenders engage in a range of therapeutic activities designed to enhance self-efficacy and life skills. In a forensic mental health setting, occupational therapy has a key role to play in the development of social competence. Positive therapeutic relationships with nursing staff and other members of the multidisciplinary team are also important in modelling appropriate social behaviours and for fostering the development of problem-solving skills.

Self-esteem

Low self-esteem is regarded as a problem for many sexual offenders; Fisher *et al.* (1999) found significantly lower levels of self-esteem in child abusers compared to non-offenders. It is thought that this may contribute to their offending and hinder progress in therapy. Marshall *et al.* (1997) found that enhancement of self-esteem facilitated the attainment of a number of specific treatment goals and was associated with reductions in deviant arousal. Self-esteem appears to be linked to how the individual relates to others and copes with life and it is likely that improvements in these areas will lead to a corresponding increase in self-esteem. Beech and Mann (2002) report that the general literature on self-esteem suggests that those who have low self-esteem are more likely to see themselves as not being in control of their lives (external locus of control) and, therefore, refuse to take responsibility for their own actions, making it less likely that they will exhibit self-regulatory behaviour. Ward and Siegert (2002) also argue that many offenders actually have high self-esteem marked by views of entitlement but this is perhaps more common among men who commit rape than among those who assault children. There are many different methods of working with self-esteem but the enhancement of general life skills such as managing finances, self-care, work skills and the development of interests and satisfactory social relationships are key goals. The reader is referred to Fennell (1999) for further information.

Intimacy deficits

Marshall (1989) has proposed that deficits in intimacy cause sex offenders to seek sexual satisfaction with either children or non-consenting adults. He further argues (Mulloy and Marshall 1999) that sex offenders identify all types of intimacy with sex and thus think that sexual behaviour of any kind will meet their intimacy needs. Certainly evidence suggests that men who assault children report higher levels of emotional loneliness and fear of intimacy and/or isolation than non-offenders (Fisher *et al.* 1999). Lack of intimacy, it could also be argued, can lead to increases in deviant fantasy, which for a number of child abusers is an important precursor to sexual offending (Swaffer *et al.* 2000). Work on intimacy skills can be achieved through the development of general social interaction skills throughout a programme of treatment but the most change may occur once the offender is in 'real-life' situations in which he is interacting with peers with whom he may develop a relationship. In our case example, the significant work on intimacy skills was conducted with Noel following his discharge from hospital and was at its most effective when he began to make new friends and meet women in his own environment. He was able to bring real-life scenarios to his session and problem-solve or discuss how to manage the feelings that this precipitated for him.

Assertiveness difficulties

Research evidence that child abusers are lacking in assertion skills is somewhat mixed and recent evidence (Fisher *et al.* 1999) suggests that it is only fixated child abusers (those with a primary interest in children) who are under-assertive. Where formulation indicates that assertiveness is an area for intervention then techniques that use behavioural practice, modelling and problem-solving skills are useful. The primary goal in enhancing skills in assertion, whether to reduce passive behaviour or regulate aggressive behaviour, is to help offenders to learn socially appropriate ways of meeting their needs, to be more effective in their daily life and to be able to resolve conflict appropriately.

Management of negative emotional states

Many sex offenders do not cope effectively with negative mood states (e.g. anger, boredom, humiliation, resentment, anxiety and depression) and use sexual thoughts and behaviours to cope (Cortoni *et al.* 1997). Teaching effective coping strategies for dealing with emotional states should include work on identifying early signs of heightened arousal including physiological symptoms and negative thinking, use of cognitive techniques to challenge cognitions and to identify alternative positive or calming cognitions, solution-focused approaches to resolving difficulties likely to precipitate negative emotional states, positive self-talk and relaxation. It is important to note that some offenders commit offences when in a positive emotional state. This should be clearly identified during assessment and may require different techniques for management.

Problem-solving deficits

Barbaree *et al.* (1988) examined the problem-solving abilities of sex offenders and reported that while they could identify as many potential solutions to problems as did non-offenders, they typically chose an inadequate solution. Barbaree *et al.* report that sex offenders often have poor general problem-solving skills and have developed inadequate generic coping styles, rather than simply being deficient in specific skills. In addition to poor coping strategies, disorganised irresponsible lifestyle and poor impulse control has also been found to be a characteristic of some sex offenders and one which is predictive of reoffending (Thornton 2002). Offenders who attend the prison SOTP are usually referred to the cognitive problem-solving course Enhanced Thinking Skills. This group intervention teaches a variety of techniques through experiential learning for solving everyday difficulties; offenders are given a 'reference manual' of different techniques that they can then refer to when faced with difficulties in the future. This intervention is being used increasingly in forensic mental health settings but requires adaptation in terms of the intensity and length of each session for this client group.

Relapse prevention

This area of work requires the offender to identify the precursors (thoughts, moods, situations) to his offending. Once these 'warning signs' have been identified the aim of this module of therapy is to empower the offender to develop appropriate self-management skills to prevent relapse. Thus offenders develop both an awareness of the risk factors for reoffending and appropriate strategies to cope safely with these factors.

The traditional model of relapse prevention has recently been criticised as not taking into account the fact that there are different paths to relapse. The application of Ward and Hudson's (2000) self-regulation model and classification of offenders into approach/avoidant, passive/active is thought to be more useful in guiding the clinician to the identification of appropriate treatment targets and motivation to offend, which can improve risk assessment and management.

Assessment and formulation will help the clinician to identify other factors specific to the offender that may need addressing to further manage the risk of reoffending. For some offenders, it may be necessary to address issues related to their own abuse during child or adulthood and this could include difficulties that have arisen due to poor attachment relationships with caregivers. These issues may be touched upon during a programme of cognitive-behavioural treatment but are likely to require separate therapeutic interventions following the successful completion of offence-focused work.

Current policy

The political implications of increasing public concern about sexual offenders residing in the community and the perceived risk to children in particular have had a significant impact upon the UK government's approach to managing sex offenders, particularly those deemed to have a dangerous and severe personality disorder. A number of new legislative measures for the punishment and management of sex offenders have been introduced in the past ten years. In 1997 the Sexual Offenders Act introduced the Sex Offender Register that required all new convicted or cautioned sexual offenders to notify the police of their address and any subsequent changes to this. This was subsequently updated to the Violent and Sex Offenders Register (ViSOR) in 2003 and allows police and probation services to access information notifying them of offender location and other demographic information in order to aid successful detection of crime. The 1998 Crime and Disorder Act introduced new civil orders, sex offender orders (now known as Sexual Offence Prevention Orders (SOPO)), to increase the powers of the police to manage and monitor offenders whose behaviour in the community gives them reasonable cause for concern. In 2003 a new sexual offenders act was introduced that expanded the number and type of offences that could be prosecuted including non-contact offences such as abuse of a position of trust and inciting or causing a child to engage in sexual activity. Multi-agency public protection arrangements (MAPPA) have been introduced and strengthened, allowing better cooperation between the police and other agencies involved with sexual offenders in managing high-risk individuals. In 2002 a National Crime Squad and National Crime Intelligence Service was established, dedicated to 'help the fight against sexual crime' (*Protecting the Public* – paper presented to Parliament by the Home Secretary 2002: 7). The government has also significantly increased the resources that are allocated to treating this group and consequently the Probation Service can now offer structured group-based intervention programmes designed specifically to modify sex offenders' deviant cognitions and behaviours. In parallel, the number of medium-secure and low-secure beds available in the NHS for offenders with mental illness have been significantly increased (Fender 2000) and, consequently, access to appropriate treatments for this group has improved.

Controversial issues

We introduced this chapter by discussing the controversy regarding the role of mental illness in sexual offending, whether causative or merely contributory. While, anecdotally, there is still opinion that the mental illness is the primary motivating factor for individuals with psychosis, the weight of evidence (e.g. Baker and White 2002) and theoretical basis for models of sexual offending suggest that psychosis may be just one of a number of static and dynamic factors relevant to sexual offending behaviour.

Another key controversy in this area is whether offence-focused treatment for adults who commit sexual offences is actually effective. Harkins and Beech (2007) highlight the difficulty at the centre of the controversy, which is that there are methodological shortcomings to many of the studies that examine treatment effectiveness and different opinions as to the degree to which these flaws should be tolerated. Differences in methodology create problems for meta-analytic studies and in general studies have reached varying conclusions from significant (Lösel and Schmucker 2005) to no significant treatment effect (Marques *et al.* 2005). Treatment effectiveness, using recidivism rates as the primary outcome measure, is yet to be conclusively demonstrated.

Further to this, some studies have found that self-esteem and victim empathy are unrelated to recidivism rates (e.g. Hanson and Bussière 1998) and thus some authors would argue that these are, therefore, not legitimate treatment targets (Hanson and Morton-Bourgon 2004). We would argue that the meta-analyses leading to this finding do not allow consideration to be given to individual differences in the goals and motivation of an offender. For example, we would expect a sadistic offender to have insight into the impact of their offending on their victim as this forms part of their motivation to offend but this doesn't mean that they care about victims or that caring is a mediator to offending for this particular individual. Also, if we refer back to Ward and Hudson's (1998, 2000) self-regulation model and approach-avoidant offender typology, we can see that some offenders are motivated by positive affective states and some by negative affective states, demonstrating that individual differences are important. Some research studies do not sufficiently highlight individual effects.

The subject of community notification of the whereabouts of sexual offenders has been a fervently debated topic in the media in recent years. Some sections of the public believe that they would have a greater chance of protecting their children if they were to know the location of convicted sexual offenders. However, research by the NSPCC in 2001 and 2006 (Fitch 2001; Lovell 2006) looked into the proposal for a 'Sarah's Law' based on the US community notification scheme to assess its effectiveness in improving child safety. This research found that there was, at the time, little evidence that open access to sex offender registers actually enhanced child safety. We would argue that the so-called 'driving underground' of adults who assault children presents a greater risk to the community because individuals who may otherwise have sought help from statutory agencies are left unmonitored and untreated. A further problem with community notification is the risk that less attention is then paid by the public to identifying, and therefore protecting their children from, unknown/unconvicted offenders who may be more of a risk to their families.

Future considerations

Research with forensic mental health populations has been limited, although recent studies have precipitated the process of examining this group more closely (e.g. Lockmuller *et al.* in preparation). However, these have tended to be small-scale studies and there are few if any outcome studies that include this population when researching treatment effectiveness. This is hampered by the lack of consistency in the type of treatment programmes delivered within these settings and thus limited capacity for valid and reliable comparison.

There has been criticism levelled at the model or philosophy of sex offender treatment programmes in that some authors would consider that standard cognitive-behavioural programmes based on a risk need model focus more on offender deficits than on their strengths (Ward and Brown 2004). Ward and Brown (2004) suggest that a number of important conceptual issues in sexual offender treatment are not adequately addressed by this approach, these include the importance of adopting a positive approach to treatment, the relationship between risk management and good lives, causal preconditions of therapy and the impact of therapists' attitudes toward offenders. They propose a Good Lives Model that addresses these issues and directs the focus of treatment toward a strengths-based model. We would argue that while this model is applicable to many offenders, it is still vital to focus on and address offender deficits, particularly where avoidance behaviours are central to the offending pathway. Research into the application of this model to a forensic mental health population has yet to be conducted, although one might argue that occupational therapy models of intervention have for many years been based upon a strengths-focused approach and that this is not an entirely novel approach to offender treatment.

Conclusions

In conclusion then, we would propose that the presentation of and theoretical approach to assessing and treating sexual offenders with comorbid mental health problems should be determined by what works with offenders without mental health problems. Similarities in the personality, developmental, environmental, social/cultural and psychosexual or physiological factors and thus in offence behaviours of the two groups suggest that different theoretical perspectives and thus risk management strategies are not necessary. We would further suggest that the differences that do exist are related to general individual differences in motivational, precipitating and goal-directed behaviours that would be apparent for any individual who sexually offends and are not necessarily specific to mental health status. Mental health issues may be one of a number of dynamic factors that are relevant to offending for the individual. In assessing individual differences, the techniques we would recommend include the use of clinical formulation, functional analysis, psychometric assessment and the application of the Pathways Model of sexual offending informed by the classification of the offender into Ward and Hudson's (1998, 2000) approach-avoidant typology. Risk assessment of all sexual offenders should be informed by using clinical judgment combined with more formalised assessment of static and dynamic risk factors. Intervention should utilise a cognitive-behavioural approach that focuses on addressing the dynamic risk factors that have been identified as relevant for the individual in terms of risk of recidivism. While programmatic treatment of individuals is the preferred methodology, this is not possible or appropriate for all offenders in a mental health setting and thus treatment interventions need to be flexible. All offenders require some form of relapse prevention plan that can be shared with agencies tasked with managing them when in the community, even where management alone rather than reduction of risk through treatment is possible.

Controversy regarding community notification and the philosophy underpinning the treatment of sexual offenders will likely continue for some time. Research into these areas is increasing and developing our thinking about this group of offenders, although we would suggest that more inclusion of offenders with mental health problems is required. As a developing area, we expect that our knowledge about sexual offending and how to intervene with and reduce recidivism will grow significantly in the future.

Selected further reading

We would suggest that the following books would be useful for the reader interested in this topic. For the latest on theories of sexual offending including the underpinning of assessment and treatment, Ward, T., Polaschek, D. and Beech, A. R. (2006) *Theories of Sexual Offending*. Chichester: Wiley, has some relevant chapters. Ward, T., Laws, D. R. and Hudson, S. M. (2000) *Remaking Relapse Prevention with Sex Offenders: A Sourcebook*. Thousand Oaks, CA: Sage, provides a fairly up-to-date review of the whole area of relapse prevention. Finally, Laws, D. R. and O'Donnohue, W. (2008) *Sexual Deviance: Theory, Assessment and Treatment*, 2nd edn, London: Guilford Press, provides a overview of both theoretical and assessment and treatment perspectives on different types of sexual offenders (e.g. rapists, child abusers, voyeurists, Internet offenders, female offenders, etc.).

Notes

1 Pro-offending attitudes are cognitions, beliefs and behaviours that support/condone offending and would include the failure to take responsibility for offending. Social competence refers to adequancy of social skills such as assertion, empathy, ability to cope with emotional distress and self-esteem.
2 For a fuller account and critique of these and other theories of sexual offending see Ward, Polaschek and Beech (2006).
3 More recently Ward and Beech (2006) have proposed an even more comprehensive model: the Integrated Theory of Sexual Offending. This approach builds on previous theories and attempts to present a framework for understanding the onset, development and maintenance of sexual abuse.
4 As noted above these can be seen as broadly describing the four pathways suggested by Ward and Siegert (2002).
5 The report of the inquiry into riots at Strangeways and other prisons in 1990 recommended a need for treatment for sex offenders to confront and change attitudes to their offending.

References

Abel, G.G., Becker, J.V. and Cunningham-Rathner, J. (1984) 'Complications, consent and cognition in sex between children and adults', *International Journal of Law and Psychiatry*, 7: 89–103.

American Psychiatric Association (1994) *Diagnostic and Statistical Manual of Mental Disorders*, 4th edn. Washington, DC: American Psychiatric Association.

Andrews, D.A. and Bonta, J. (2003) *The Psychology of Criminal Conduct*, 3rd edn. Cincinnati, OH: Anderson.

Baker, M. and White, T. (2002) 'Sex offenders in high security care in Scotland', *Journal of Forensic Psychiatry*, 13 (2): 285–97.

Barbaree, H.E., Marshall, W. L. and Connor, J. (1988) 'The Social Problem-solving of Child Molesters', Unpublished manuscript, Queen's University, Ontario, Canada.

Barker, M. and Morgan, R. (1993) *Sex Offenders: A Framework for the Evaluation of Community-Based Treatment*, Home Office Occasional Report. London: Home Office.

Barratt, E.S. (1994) 'Impulsiveness and aggression', in J. Monahan and H. J. Steadman (eds), *Violence and Mental Disorder: Developments in Risk Assessment*. Chicago: University of Chicago, pp. 21–79.

Beckett, R.C. (1987) *The Children and Sex Questionnaire*. Available from Richard Beckett, Room FF39, The Oxford Clinic, Littlemore Health Centre, Sandford Road, Littlemore, Oxford OX4 4XN, England.

Beckett, R.C. and Fisher, D. (1994) *Assessing Victim Empathy: A New Measure*. Paper presented at the 13th Conference of the Association for Treatment of Sexual Abusers (ATSA). San Francisco, USA.

Beckett, R.C., Beech, A.R., Fisher, D. and Fordham, A.S. (1994) *Community-Based Treatment for Sex Offenders: An Evaluation of Seven Treatment Programmes*, Home Office Occasional Report. London: Home Office.

Beckett, R.C., Fisher, D.D., Mann, R.E. and Thornton, D. (1997) 'The relapse prevention questionnaire', in H. Eldridge (ed.), *Therapists Guide for Maintaining Change: Relapse Prevention Manual for Adult Male Perpetrators of Child Sexual Abuse*. Thousand Oaks, CA: Sage.

Beech, A.R. (1998) 'A psychometric typology of child abusers', *International Journal of Offender Therapy and Comparative Criminology*, 42: 319–39.

Beech, A.R. and Fisher, D.D. (2004) 'Treatment of sexual offenders in prison and probation settings', in H. Kemshall and G. McIvor (eds), *Research Highlights in Social Work: Sex Offenders: Managing the Risk*. London: Jessica Kingsley, pp. 137–64.

Beech, A.R. and Mann, R.E. (2002) 'Recent developments in the treatment of sexual offenders', in J. McGuire (ed.), *Offender Rehabilitation: Effective Programmes and Policies to Reduce Reoffending*. Chichester: Wiley, pp. 259–88.

Beech, A.R. and Ward, T. (2004) 'The integration of etiology and risk in sexual offenders: a theoretical framework', *Aggression and Violent Behaviour*, 10: 31–63.

Beech, A.R., Fisher, D. and Beckett, R.C. (1998) *Step 3: An Evaluation of the Prison Sex Offender Treatment Programme*, Home Office Occasional Report. London: Home Office.

Beech, A.R., Fisher, D. and Beckett, R.C. (1999) *An Evaluation of the Prison Sex Offender Treatment Programme*, Home Office Occasional Report. London: Home Office.

Beech, A.R., Fisher, D.D. and Thornton, D. (2003) 'Risk assessment of sex offenders', *Professional Psychology: Research and Practice*, 34 (4): 339–52.

Beech, A.R., Fisher, D.D. and Ward, T. (2005) 'Sexual murderer's implicit theories', *Journal of Interpersonal Violence*, 20 (10): 1–24.

Beech, A.R., Oliver, C., Fisher, D.D. and Beckett, R. (2005) *Step 4: The Sex Offender Treatment Programme in Prison: Addressing the Offending Behaviour of Rapists and Sexual Murderers*, Home Office Occasional Report. London: Home Office.

Beech, A.R., Ward, T. and Fisher, D.D. (2006) 'The identification of sexual and violent motivations in men who sexually assault women: implication for treatment', *Journal of Interpersonal Violence* 21 (12): 1635–53.

Bickley, J.A. and Beech, A.R. (2002) 'An investigation of the Ward and Hudson pathways model of the sexual offence process with child abusers', *Journal of Interpersonal Violence*, 17: 371–93.

Boer, D.P., Hart, S.D., Kropp, P.R. and Webster, C.D. (1997) *Manual for the Sexual Violence Scale Risk-20*. Vancouver, BC: Simon Fraser University.

Briggs, D., Doyle, P., Gooch, T. and Kennington, R. (1998) *Assessing Men Who Sexually Abuse: A Practice Guide*. London and Philadelphia: Jessica Kingsley.

Bumby, K.M. (1996) 'Assessing the cognitive distortions of child molesters and rapists: development and validation of the MOLEST and RAPE scales', *Sexual Abuse*, 8 (1): 37–54.

Burt, M. (1980) 'Cultural myths and support for rape', *Journal of Personality and Social Psychology*, 39: 217–30.

Check, J.V.P. (1984) 'The Hostility Towards Women Scale'. Unpublished doctoral dissertation, University of Manitoba, Canada.

Chesterman, P. and Sahota, K. (1998a) 'Sexual offending in the context of mental illness', *Journal of Forensic Psychiatry*, 9 (2): 267–80.

Chesterman, P. and Sahota, K. (1998b) 'Mentally ill sex offenders in a regional secure unit. I: psychopathology and motivation', *Journal of Forensic Psychiatry*, 9 (1): 150–60.

Chesterman, P. and Sahota, K. (1998c) 'Mentally ill sex offenders in a regional secure unit. II: cognitions, perceptions and fantasies', *Journal of Forensic Psychiatry*, 9 (1): 161–72.

Chiswick, D. (1983) 'Sex crimes', *British Journal of Psychiatry*, 143: 236–42.

Cortoni, F., Heil, P. and Marshall, W.L. (1997) *Sex as a Coping Mechanism and Its Relationship to Loneliness and Intimacy Deficits in Sexual Offending*. Paper presented at 15th Annual Research and Treatment Conference of the Association for the Treatment of Sexual Offenders, Chicago.

Cournos, F., Guido, J.R., Coomaraswamy, S. Meyer-Bahlburg, H., Sugden, R. and Horwath, E. (1994) 'Sexual activity and risk of HIV infection in patients with schizophrenia', *American Journal of Psychiatry*, 151: 228–32.

D'Zurilla, T.J., Nezu, A.M. and Maydeu-Olivares, A. (2002) *Social Problem-Solving Inventory – Revised: Technical Manual*. North Tonawanda, NY: Multi-Health Systems.

Davin, P.A., Hislop, J.C.R. and Dunbar, T. (1999) *Female Sexual Abusers: Three Views*. Brandon, VT: Safer Society Press.

Davis, M.H. (1980) 'A multidimensional approach to individual differences in empathy', *JSAS Catalog of Selected Documents in Psychology*, 10: 85.

Epstein, R. (2000) 'Issues in the Assessment of Mentally Disordered Sex Offenders'. Unpublished thesis, University of Leicester.

Fender, A. (2000) *Report for National Oversight Group on High and Medium Secure Commissioning*. London: HMSO.

Fennell, M. (1999) *Overcoming Low Self-Esteem: A Self-Help Guide using Cognitive Behavioural Techniques*. London: Robinson Publishing.

Fernandez, Y.M., Marshall, W.L., Lightbody, S. and O' Sullivan, C. (1999) 'The child molester empathy measure', *Sexual Abuse: A Journal of Research and Treatment*, 11: 17–31.

Finkelhor, D. (1994) 'The international epidemiology of child sexual abuse', *Child Abuse and Neglect*, 18 (5): 409–17.

Fisher, D., Beech, A.R. and Browne, K.D. (1999) 'Comparison of sex offenders to non-sex offenders on selected psychological measures', *International Journal of Offender Therapy and Comparative Criminology*, 43: 473–91.

Fitch, K. (2006) *Megan's Law: Does it Protect Children, 2. An Updated Review of Evidence on the Impact of Community Notification as Legislated for by Megan's Law in the United States*. London: NSPCC. Available from: http://www.nspcc.org.uk/inform/publications/downloads.meganslaw2_wdf48102. pdf

Ford, H. (2006) *Women Who Sexually Abuse Children*, Wiley Child Protection & Policy Series. Chichester: Wiley.

Friendship, C., Mann, R.E. and Beech, A.R. (2003) 'Evaluation of a national prison-based treatment program for sexual offenders in England and Wales', *Journal of Interpersonal Violence*, 18: 744–59.

Frith, C.D. (1992) *The Cognitive Neuropsychology of Schizophrenia*. Hillsdale, NJ: Lawrence Erlbaum Associates.

Greenwald, H.J. and Satow, Y. (1970) 'A short desirability scale', *Psychological Reports*, 27: 131–5.

Hall, G.C.N. and Hirschman, R. (1992) 'Sexual aggression against children: a conceptual perspective of etiology', *Criminal Justice and Behavior*, 19: 8–23.

Hanson, R.K. and Bussière, M.T. (1998) 'Predicting relapse: a meta-analysis of sexual offender recidivism studies', *Journal of Consulting and Clinical Psychology*, 66: 348–62.

Hanson, R.K. and Harris, A.J.R. (2000) 'ACUTE-2000'. Unpublished manuscript, Department of the Solicitor General Canada. Available from the authors: e-mail Andrew.Harris@psepc-sppcc.gc.ca

Hanson, R.K. and Morton-Bourgon, K. (2004) *Predictors of Sexual Recidivism: An Updated Meta-analysis*, Corrections Research, Public Safety and Emergency Preparedness Canada, Ottawa, Canada. Available from: http://www.psepc-sppcc.gc.ca/publications/corrections/pdf/200402_e.pdf

Hanson, R.K. and Thornton, D. (2000) 'Improving risk assessments for sex offenders: a comparison of the three actuarial scales', *Law and Human Behaviour*, 24: 119–36.

Hanson, R.K., Gizzarrelli, R. and Scott, H. (1994) 'The attitudes of incest offenders: sexual entitlement and acceptance with children', *Criminal Justice and Behavior*, 21: 187–202.

Hanson, R.K., Morton, K.E. and Harris, A.J.R. (2003) 'Sexual offender recidivism: what we know and what we need to know', in R. Prentky, E. Janus, M. Seto, and A.W. Burgess (eds), *Sexually Coercive Behavior: Understanding and Management*. New York: Annals of the New York Academy of Sciences, Vol. 989, pp. 154–66.

Hanson, R.K., Gordon, A., Harris, A.J., Marques, J.K., Murphy, W., Quinsey, V.L. and Seto, M.C. (2002) 'First report of the collaborative outcome data project on the effectiveness of psychological treatment for sex offenders', *Sex Abuse*, 14 (2): 169–94.

Hare, R.D. (1991) *Manual for the Revised Psychopathy Checklist*. Toronto: Multi-Health Systems.

Harkins, L. and Beech, A. R. (2007) 'Measurement of the effectiveness of sex offender treatment', *Aggression and Violent Behaviour*, 12: 36–44.

Hart, S., Laws, D.R. and Kropp, P.R. (2003) 'The risk-need model of offender rehabilitation', in T. Ward, D. R. Laws, and S. M. Hudson (eds), *Theoretical Issues and Controversies in Sexual Deviance*. London: Sage, pp. 338–54.

Heinrichs, R.W. and Zakzanis, K.K. (1998) 'Neurocognitive deficit in schizophrenia: a quantitative review of the evidence', *Neuropsychology*, 12: 426–45.

Hogue, T.E. (1998) 'The Sex Offence Information Questionnaire: The Development of a Self-Report Measure of Offence Related Denial in Sexual Offenders'. Unpublished doctoral dissertation, Cardiff, University of Wales.

Home Office (2006) *Crime in England and Wales: Quarterly Update to June 2006*. London: HMSO.

Jones, G., Huckle, P. and Tanaghow, A. (1992) 'Command hallucinations, schizophrenia and sexual assaults', *Journal of Psychological Medicine*, 9: 47–9.

Keltner, A.A, Marshall, P.G. and Marshall, W.L. (1981) 'Measurement and correlation of assertiveness and social fear in a prison population', *Corrective and Social Psychiatry*, 27: 41–7.

Knight, R.A. and Prentky, R.A. (1990) 'Classifying sexual offenders: the development and corroboration of taxonomic models', in W.L. Marshall, D.R. Laws and H.E. Barbaree (eds), *Handbook of Sexual Assault*. New York: Plenum Press, pp. 23–49.

Laws, D.R. (1999) 'Relapse prevention: the state of the art', *Journal of Interpersonal Violence*, 14: 285–302.

Laws, D.R. and Marshall, W.L. (1991) 'Masturbatory reconditioning with sexual deviates: an evaluative review', *Advances in Behaviour Research and Therapy*, 13: 13–25.

Lockmuller, M.A., Beech, A.R., Fisher, D. and Fleetwood, K. (in preparation) 'A comparison of the pro-offending attitudes and social competence of mentally ill and non-mentally ill sexual offenders'.

Lösel, F. and Schmucker, M. (2005) 'The effectiveness of treatment for sexual offenders: a comprehensive meta-analysis', *Journal of Experimental Criminology*, 1: 117–46.

Lovell, E. (2001) *Megan's Law: Does it Protect Children?* London: NSPCC.

McGuire, J. (1995) *What Works: Reducing Reoffending*. Chichester: Wiley.

McGuire, J. (2000) 'Explanations of criminal behaviour', in J. McGuire, T. Mason and A. O'Kane (eds), *Behaviour, Crime and Legal Processes: A Guide for Legal Practitioners*. Chichester: Wiley, pp. 135–59.

Marques, J.K., Wiederanders, M., Day, D.M., Nelson, C. and van Ommeren, A. (2005) 'Effects of a relapse prevention program on sexual recidivism: final results from California's Sex Offender Treatment and Evaluation Program (SOTEP)', *Sexual Abuse: A Journal of Research and Treatment*, 17: 79–107.

Marshall, W.L. (1989) 'Intimacy, loneliness and sexual offenders', *Behaviour, Research and Therapy*, 27: 491–503.

Marshall, W.L. (1994) 'Treatment effects on denial and minimisation in sex offenders', *Behavior Research and Therapy*, 32: 559–64.

Marshall, W.L. and Barbaree, H.E. (1990) 'An integrated theory of the etiology of sexual offending', in W.L. Marshall, D.R. Laws and H.E. Barbaree (eds), *Handbook of Sexual Assault*. New York: Plenum Press, pp. 257–71.

Marshall, W.L. and Fernandez, Y.M. (2002) *Victim Empathy, Social Self-Esteem and Psychopathy in Rapists*. Available from the authors at the Department of Psychology, Queen's University, Kingston, Ontario, Canada, K7L 3N6.

Marshall, W.L., Champagne, F., Sturgeon, C. and Bryce, P. (1997) 'Increasing the self-esteem of child molesters', *Sexual Abuse: A Journal of Research and Treatment*, 9: 321–33.

Miller, W.R. and Rollnick, S. (1991) *Motivational Interviewing: Preparing People to Change Addictive Behaviour*. London: Guilford Press.

Millon, T. (1997) *Millon Clinical Multiaxial Inventory – III Manual*, 2nd edn. Minneapolis, MN: National Computer Systems.

Morey, L.C. (1991) *The Personality Assessment Inventory Professional Manual*. Available from Psychological Assessment Resources, Inc. 16204, North Florida Avenue, Lutz, Florida 33549. Toll-free 1.800.331.8378.

Morrison, T., Erooga, M. and Beckett, R.C. (1994) *Sexual Offending Against Children: Assessment and Treatment of Male Abusers*. London: Routledge.

Mulloy, R. and Marshall, W.L. (1999) 'Social functioning', in W.L. Marshall, D. Anderson and Y. Fernandez (eds), *Cognitive-Behavioural Treatment of Sexual Offenders*. Chichester: Wiley.

Murphy, W. (1990) 'Assessment and modification of cognitive distortions of sex offenders', in W.L. Marshall, D.R. Laws and H.E. Barbaree (eds), *Handbook of Sexual Assault: Issues, Theories, and Treatment of the Offender*. New York: Plenum Press, pp. 331–42.

Nichols, H.R. and Molinder, I. (1984) *Multiphasic Sex Inventory Manual*. Available from H.R. Nichols and I. Molinder, 437 Bowes Drive, Tacoma, WA 98466.

Nowicki, S. (1976) 'The factor structure of locus of control at three different ages', *Journal of Genetic Psychology*, 129: 13–17.

O'Brien, E. and Epstein, S. (1983) *The Multidimensional Self-Esteem Inventory*. Odessa, FL: Psychological Assessment Resources.

Paulhus, D.C. (1999) *Paulhus Deception Scales: User's Manual*. New York/Ontario: Multi-Health Systems.

Perkins, D. and Bishopp, D. (2003) 'Dangerous and severe personality disorder and its relationship to sexual offending', *Issues in Forensic Psychiatry*: 24–40.

Phillips, S.L., Heads, T.C., Taylor, P.J. and Hill, G.M. (1999) 'Sexual offending and antisocial sexual behaviour among patients with schizophrenia', *Journal of Clinical Psychiatry*, 60 (3): 170–5.

Quinsey, V.L., Harris, G.T., Rice, M.E. and Cormier, C. (1998) *Violent Offenders: Appraising and Managing Risk*. Washington, DC: American Psychological Association.

Russell, D., Peplau, L.A. and Cutrona, C.E. (1980) 'The revised UCLA loneliness scale: concurrent and discriminant validity evidence', *Journal of Personality and Social Psychology*, 39: 472–80.

Smith, A.D. (2000) 'Motivation and psychosis in schizophrenic men who sexually assault women', *Journal of Forensic Psychiatry*, 11 (1): 62–73.

Spielberger, C.D. (1999) *State-Trait Anger Expression Inventory-2 (STAXI-2) Professional Manual*. Odessa FL: Psychological Assessment Resources.

Swaffer, T., Hollin, C., Beech, A., Beckett, R.C. and Fisher, D.D. (2000) 'An exploration of child sexual abusers' sexual fantasies before and after treatment', *Sexual Abuse: A Journal of Research and Treatment*, 12: 61–8.

Taylor, P.J. and Smith, A.D. (1999) 'Serious sex offending against women by men with schizophrenia', *British Journal of Psychiatry*, 174: 233–7.

Thornton, D. (2002) 'Constructing and testing a framework for dynamic risk assessment', *Sexual Abuse: A Journal of Research and Treatment*, 14: 139–54.

Thornton, D., Mann, R., Webster, S., Blud, L., Travers, R., Friendship, C. and Erikson, M. (2003) 'Distinguishing and combining risks for sexual and violent recidivism', in R. Prentky, E. Janus, M. Seto and A.W. Burgess (eds), *Sexually Coercive Behaviour: Understanding and Management*. New York: Annals of the New York Academy of Sciences, Vol. 989, pp. 225–35.

Ward, T.W. (2000) 'Sexual offenders' cognitive distortions as implicit theories', *Aggression and Violent Behaviour*, 20 (10): 1–24.

Ward, T.W. and Beech, A.R. (2006) 'An integrated theory of sexual offending', *Aggression and Violent Behaviour*, 11: 44–63.

Ward, T.W. and Brown, M. (2004) 'The good lives model and conceptual issues in offender rehabilitation', *Psychology, Crime and Law*, 10 (3): 243–57.

Ward, T.W. and Hudson, S.M. (1996) 'Relapse prevention: a critical analysis', *Sexual Abuse: A Journal of Research and Treatment*, 8: 177–200.

Ward, T.W. and Hudson, S.M. (1998) 'A model of the relapse process in sexual offenders', *Journal of Interpersonal Violence*, 13: 400–25.

Ward, T.W and Hudson, S.M. (2000) 'A self-regulation model of relapse prevention', in D.R. Laws, S. M. Hudson and T. Ward (eds), *Remaking Relapse Prevention with Sex Offenders: A Sourcebook*. Thousand Oaks, CA: Sage, pp. 79–101.

Ward, T.W. and Keenan, T. (1999) 'Child molesters' implicit theories', *Journal of Interpersonal Violence*, 14: 821–38.

Ward, T.W. and Siegert, R. (2002) 'Rape and evolutionary psychology: a critique of Thornhill and Palmer's theory', *Aggression and Violent Behaviour*, 7 (2): 145–68.

Ward, T., Polaschek, D. and Beech, A.R. (2006) *Theories of Sexual Offending*. Chichester: Wiley.

Ward, T.W., Hudson, S.M., Johnston, L. and Marshall, W.L. (1997) 'Cognitive distortions in sex offenders: an integrative review', *Clinical Psychology Review*, 17: 479–507.

Ward, T., Louden, K., Hudson, S. and Marshall, W.L. (1995) 'A descriptive model of the offence chain in child molesters', *Journal of Interpersonal Violence*, 10: 453–73.

Wolf, S. (1984) *A Multi-Factor Model of Deviant Sexuality*. Paper presented at the Third International Conference on Victimology, Lisbon, Portugal.

Woolf, The Right Hon. Lord Justice (1990) *Report of the Inquiry into Prisoner Disturbances*, April 1990, Cm 1946. London: HMSO.

Young, J.E. and Brown, G. (1990) *Young Schema Questionnaire*. New York: Cognitive Therapy Center of New York.

Young, J. and Brown, G. (2003) *Schema Questionnaire (YSQ-L2)*. Available from the Cognitive Therapy Center of New York, 36 West 44th Street, Suite 1007, New York, NY 10036.

Part 4

Skills for Forensic Mental Health Practitioners

Keith Soothill

Skills for forensic mental health practitioners are never going to be easy to master as either we don't really know what they are or practitioners are working in arenas that can be troublesome in either physical or psychological terms (or both). The court arena is not a comfortable setting; most mental health practitioners are probably relieved that they do not have to face the potential challenges of the court that their forensic colleagues may have to accept quite routinely. Indeed, anecdotal evidence within one high-secure and one medium-secure unit suggests that nurses are being 'targeted' in mental health review tribunals owing to their lack of knowledge regarding the legal process. Nevertheless, in Chapter 19 Nicola Gray and Tegwyn Williams claim that 'engaging in witness work can be highly rewarding and professionals often feel that they "made a difference" either to the case, or to society more generally'. Understanding the process and what is required is a necessary prerequisite to engaging in such work. Yet gaining such skills outside of the professions of psychiatry and psychology is a difficult and expensive task. Gray and Williams attempt to distil years of experience of being expert witnesses into a brief, but quite comprehensive, summary of the issues. It is an ideal 'road map' for anyone who might expect to engage in the practice of being an expert witness within the highly adversarial culture of the British criminal justice system.

The question of treatment interventions produces a rather different set of issues. In Chapter 21 Conor Duggan implicitly indicates that gaining skills must be accompanied by a dose of humility. Duggan maintains there is no shortage of questions when one considers 'treatment' in a forensic context. He suggests that the discourse – both in its range and its questioning of fundamentals – is unique to mental health practice, and particularly to that of forensic mental health. Whether and why this is so needs to be confronted. Essentially Duggan provides an uncomfortable and challenging journey. So, for instance, he concludes that 'we cannot be confident that (1) the most effective treatments are chosen or (2) that they are applied in the most efficient manner'. Further, he introduces the spectre of cost-effectiveness, reminding us that 'forensic mental health will have to take its place among many other health practitioners demanding resources from an ever dwindling pot'. Being a player in the market for resources is not helped by a stance that forensic mental health practitioners must often embrace. In truth, as Duggan notes, many answers must be in the 'gray' area of 'maybe' or 'I'm not sure' or (worse of all) 'I don't know'. The Socratic position of uncertainty is a brave but unsettling one for all concerned.

Since the deinstitutionalisation movement which involved the closure of many long-stay institutions, many might regard the inpatient care, treatment and management of compulsory patients as a lost art. Certainly the number in hospitals as compulsory patients has changed quite dramatically since the Mental Health Act 1959, but in many respects the imperatives remain the same. As Kevin Gournay, Richard Benson and Paul Rogers remind us in their opening sentence, 'Since Bedlam, one of the main tasks of mental institutions has been the protection of the public from the risks, real or perceived, from mental patients'. However, the mechanisms, both psychological and physical, to effect this have changed over the years. What these authors attempt to do is to identify and discuss the unique issues relevant to inpatient assessment, care and management. The theme which runs through the chapter is a sobering one. They highlight the lack of evidence to support inpatient staff and services. This is at a time when clinicians and services are constantly being challenged to be evidence-based. The chapter seems to reveal a paradox in forensic mental health. There is a demand for evidence in areas where evidence is sparse, while in areas where there is appropriate evidence the subsequent action seems sparse.

Finally, in Chapter 22 Paul Mullen focuses on 'The crimes and pathologies of passion'. It is a deliberate choice to end the book with a chapter which provides a timely reminder of some other paradoxes that need to be recognised. Firstly, he embraces topics – love, jealousy and the pursuit of justice – which the lay public would perhaps think were the lifeblood of forensic work, but which he argues have been grossly neglected. He argues that the disorders of jealousy, love and the pursuit of justice currently occupy a marginal status not only in general mental health but in forensic mental health. He maintains that this invisibility is difficult to justify as jealousy plays such an enormous role in domestic violence and homicide as just two exemplars. In fact, he argues that it is not the numbers game that is crucial here but 'has more to do with the difficulties fitting these conditions into the worldview of most mental health professionals'. While such an analysis reminds us of our early call in Chapter 1 that the boundaries of forensic mental health are 'fuzzy' and may change over time, Mullen is implicitly making a more fundamental challenge to contemporary theory and practice. In saying that the worldview of most mental health professionals just does not work in recognising the importance of these conditions, he perhaps highlights the need for reconsidering our theoretical gaze. Whenever one hears Paul Mullen as a keynote speaker at a conference, one is invariably entertained but there is usually a sting in the tail, for he makes us think. As a final flourish, that is really the task that should be accepted by us all. We need to continue to *think* about forensic mental health, what it is, where it is done, by whom it is done and to whom, when it occurs and, the most important of all questions, why! We suggest that there is still much to do in the field – thinking is not a luxury but a necessity.

Chapter 19

The expert witness: professional practice and pitfalls

Nicola Gray and Tegwn Williams

Introduction

Being an expert witness can be a daunting task, particularly for clinicians who have little experience of such work. The court process in the UK is adversarial and health professionals are not used to having their clinical opinion challenged or their professional qualifications and competencies scrutinised. However, engaging in expert witness work can be highly rewarding and professionals often feel that they have 'made a difference' either to the case or to society more generally. The aim of this chapter is to provide a brief overview of the process of being an expert witness that can serve as guidance for those who wish to engage in such work. Being committed to evidence-based practice we would wish to ground our advice and guidance within the research literature and to review research findings. However, little such research exists. There is a body of research on issues pertinent to the judicial process, for example how juries make decisions and the validity of eyewitness testimony, etc., but these issues are not what expert witnesses want to know about when embarking on the new (or relatively new) task of being an expert within the courts. For this reason we have decided that it is not possible to provide a review of research and have instead endeavoured to try to distil our years of experience (and that of a number of other professionals) of being expert witnesses into a brief, but we hope comprehensive, summary of the issues and possible pitfalls involved in such work. It must be remembered that in legal proceedings, lawyers are in charge and may use experts for their own ends which may not be what the experts expect or intend.

Context of the guidance incorporated within the chapter

There are broadly three main branches of work within the court system that may involve mental health professionals. These are criminal work, family law and civil cases (such as personal injury). As this volume relates to forensic mental health practice, this chapter will only focus upon expert witness work within the criminal justice system. There have been a number of reforms and changes to the role and responsibilities of expert witnesses within the realms of family law (e.g. the recent advent of the Protocol) and personal injury cases (e.g. the Woolf Reforms), but a comprehensive review of these changes and how they impact upon the expert witness is beyond the scope of this chapter. We also believe that to try and cover all these aspects of how the law and the expert witness intersect would be to complicate and confuse issues. It is preferable to focus on one area of law in some detail, rather than try to cover them all at the expense of detail and depth of coverage. However, it is important to flag up here that, although much of the guidance covered in this chapter is relevant to all fields of expert witness work, there also exist important differences. Clinicians engaging in expert witness work within the fields of family law and personal injury need to ensure that they understand the roles and responsibilities set out for them within the relevant fields in which they are practising.

Definition of an expert witness

Within the court there are two types of witness: expert and ordinary. An ordinary witness (i.e. a witness to fact) is only able to give factual evidence whereas an expert witness is able to give an opinion about issues relevant to their area of expertise. An expert witness is defined as someone who is qualified in a specific area (this may be in mental health, for example psychiatry, psychology or mental health nursing) and who is therefore able to provide the court with information and opinion that is outside the experience of a judge and jury. Indeed, expert witnesses are often, within the letter of instruction, warned against expressing a view about disputes regarding the facts of a case as these are for the court to decide. If expert opinion depends on issues that are under factual dispute (e.g. whether alcohol was involved in the offence) then an expert witness should express their opinion of the basis of possible alternative findings regarding the facts of the case.

The expert witness has *a duty* to provide the court with the necessary evidence for the judge and jury to be able to properly evaluate the validity of, and the weight to be placed upon, the expert witness's opinions. For psychologists this means stating the title of any psychometric tests used and including the results obtained in the form of raw or scaled scores. These are often included in an appendix to the main report, although increasingly experts are including these scores within the main body of the report. For psychiatrists this will include professional qualifications and appointments and may include experience or research of particular relevance to the case. Within the criminal courts it is common practice for a defendant to be assessed by experts for both the defence and prosecution and it is important that each are able to know and comment upon the opinions and findings of the other. However, this may not always be possible as a result of reports not being disclosed until late in the proceedings due to legal tactics.

General issues to remember when writing court reports

The English and Welsh legal system is adversarial in nature, that is lawyers present arguments and the court decides which to accept. This leads to lawyers tending to dichotomise and categorise (e.g. guilty or not guilty, insane or sane). It is their responsibility to *present their case*, which within the criminal justice system will be either designed to help acquit the defendant or help prosecute him. Barristers will therefore attempt to restate or 'spin' the evidence to fit their case. When being trained barristers are taught never to allow expert witnesses to simply confirm what is written in their reports. Instead, barristers will *state their case* (their perspective as they wish to assert it). It is the expert's role to provide their professional opinion, the barrister's role to restate that evidence so it fits with the case they are trying to establish, and the judge and jury's role to decide which version of the case they will accept. This poses two difficulties for the expert witness. First, it is unusual for a health practitioner to be able to make categorical statements and it is important that experts resist being pushed to make them. Expert witnesses must remain a member of their profession working within their respective code of conduct and should give mental health opinions, not legal ones. Often these opinions will not be black or white but shades of grey, and the expert should be robust in their defence of this. It is up to the court to then use the expert's opinion to decide upon the legal issues. For psychiatrists this can be slightly different and they are often *encouraged* by the court (if not the barristers) to give an opinion as to whether a defendant fits a given legal category (e.g. fitness to plead and stand trial, diminished responsibility). This is described further below. Second, it is important for the expert witness not to appear to change their evidence following examination and cross-examination due to pressure exerted by the barrister (as opposed to changing an opinion in the face of changing facts). We have in the past observed an expert witness appear to completely change and then re-change their opinion in the face of assertive cross-examination and re-examination. This only serves to confuse the judge and jury and to discredit the expert. If the expert witness remembers to ensure that they always prepare reports using ordinary good practice and simple language, uninfluenced by the legal setting or the demands of the legal profession, then this will help them avoid this potential pitfall. It is easy to simply restate the fact that, for example, the defendant was hearing voices at the material time of the homicide or that the defendant is highly suggestible and compliant. The court can then attempt to use this information in the pursuit of either defence or prosecution. The questions you address within the expert report will, of course, be aimed at meeting the court's needs and the presentation of your report will be somewhat different from a normal clinical report, but the process and opinion will be similar and should be based upon solid psychological/psychiatric/nursing premises and practice.

For some issues the law requires that a 'registered medical practitioner' (doctor) gives a 'medical opinion' (e.g. McNaughton rules, diminished responsibility). Many barristers/solicitors do not always understand the distinction between psychiatrists and other mental health practitioners and will, for example, frequently ask psychologists to write a report or give oral evidence on these issues. If you are not 'a registered medical practitioner' avoid this as it is both outside your field of expertise and is not legally valid.

The expert witness report

Preliminaries

The process of accepting 'instructions'

It is often the case that the first an expert will hear about a case is via a telephone call from the instructing solicitor (or occasionally from a barrister working on the case). Telephone calls are very useful and can be used to set the scene for the resulting piece of work. At this stage it is common that the letter of instruction will not yet be finalised and this means that the expert can assert some influence upon what mental health or psychological issues they can usefully address. Often the solicitor will not understand the mental health issues that *could* be addressed by an expert witness and the expert witness does not understand the legal issues. This first contact can therefore be used to explore these issues from both sides and agree on the best-fitting instructions. For example, a solicitor may be asking for a general 'psychological' or 'psychiatric' report and only after discussion about the history of the case may it transpire that the defendant has a history of head injury and epilepsy and that a neuropsychological or neuropsychiatric assessment is indicated (or that the client is a child and you only work with adults, etc.). Sometimes this conversation will highlight that you are not from the appropriate mental health discipline, or are not the right expert from within that discipline (i.e. do not have the skills required to address the specific legal issue). In this case recommend someone who does have the requisite skills. It is far better to identify that your expertise does not match what is needed in the case at this preliminary stage rather than later in the proceedings.

The solicitor will be trying to determine two things at this early stage:

1 whether are you an expert with the required expertise to address the legal issues relevant to the case;
2 whether can you assist the court within a reasonable timescale.

In practice, it is often this latter issue that determines which expert is instructed. The expert witness should use this first contact to establish four issues:

1 to gain some understanding of the case, the legal issues that the instructing body is seeking to clarify and the psychological/psychiatric/nursing issues involved;
2 decide whether your discipline can meet the court's needs;
3 think about how to address these needs within a psychological/psychiatric framework;
4 decide whether you are competent to do this.

At this stage it is important to remember that you have not yet been instructed. In a complex case the first contact telephone call can be a fairly in-depth and lengthy process (although this is not always the case, particularly when either (1) the instructing solicitor and expert witness have worked with each other previously and know what each needs/has to offer the court; or (2) the solicitor has no idea what it is they want answered, only that their client seems 'odd'). Thus, if you are not likely to be able to accept instructions (e.g. if your diary is fully booked for the next few months) then it is best to state this immediately prior to any discussion of the case. However, we find that the more helpful an expert can be at this first stage then the more likely it is that the solicitors will return to that expert in the future and the expert will feel that their time is not wasted.

Preparing a medico-legal curriculum vitae
If, during the first contact telephone call, it is established that you are an expert with the required expertise to address the legal issues relevant to the case and that you can assist the court within a reasonable timescale, then the instructing solicitor will often ask that you submit a medico-legal *curriculum vitae* (CV). This is more commonly requested within family law and personal injury cases where there is a single jointly instructed expert and where, therefore, all parties involved in the proceedings have to agree upon who that expert witness will be. The medico-legal CV is then used to compare experts sourced by different solicitors involved in the proceedings. Comparisons are primarily made on past knowledge of that expert in previous cases and the timescale within which the expert has undertaken to submit the report. Medico-legal CVs take many forms but we prefer a structure that includes professional qualifications and relevant occupational experience; relevant publications, research, teaching and training; membership of professional bodies; relevant experience as an expert witness (e.g. number of cases instructed as an expert witness, number of reports prepared and occasions on which evidence in court has been given and details of referees (normally two professionals who have experience of your competence within medico-legal contexts – one solicitor and one barrister or judge is good practice)).

Fees (if any) should be discussed at this stage.

Competence
An expert is responsible for ensuring that he or she is competent to give expert evidence. For this reason once a letter of instruction is received it is important that the expert witness read the specific instructions detailed to ensure that nothing has been included that is outside their field of expertise. Particularly within the fields of family law or personal injury where single joint instructions are received, often on behalf of multiple parties, instructions can become complex and will cover multiple issues (before being sent to the expert the draft letter of instruction will be circulated to all parties for approval and each party can decide to add to the instructions). As the majority of lawyers are not expert in mental health they frequently do not understand the distinction between different mental health professions and will include instructions that are not appropriate. If you feel that any given aspect of the instructions is outside your area of competence it is important that you notify the instructing solicitor to inform them of this fact and ask that the instructions are either amended or that another expert witness be found. In our experience this is never a major issue and solicitors will happily amend the letter of instruction to reflect your concerns and expertise.

Competence of an expert witness is assessed in respect of a combination of the following:

- *Qualifications and professional registration.*
- *Number of years post-qualification experience.* Newly qualified staff should not normally practise as expert witnesses. However, everybody has to start somewhere and it is worth both the individual and the organisation for which they work thinking about this component of continuing professional development (particularly if the role of expert witness is pivotal to the work of the organisation – e.g. within forensic mental health services). It is good practice for more recently qualified staff to gain experience of expert witness work under the guidance and supervision of more experienced colleagues. This can include shadowing their mentor throughout a piece of expert witness work and for the mentor to supervise and observe their work. One of the most useful experiences I gained within expert witness work was when an experienced colleague of mine agreed to attend court and observe my giving evidence over a period of two days and to then provide constructive feedback on my performance under examination and cross-examination. One's own view of how well (or badly!) you have performed in the witness box can be very different to that of a qualified and experienced observer and, if possible, experts should try to benefit from such valuable feedback. Expert witness training courses can also be valuable in this regard (but make sure they are provided by an accredited training provider and that the course is relevant to your discipline).
- *Experience of clinical practice in the relevant area.* Do you have practical experience or have you just read about it? The former is given vastly more weight by the court when assessing what credance to give to an expert's testimony.
- Scientific publications in relevant areas. Experts can also assert competence by dint of research and publications in peer-reviewed scientific journals. If you have an established record of research within a given area it is useful to include this information within your medico-legal CV and expert witness report to inform the court of your specific area of expertise.

Preparation and assessment

Once you have been instructed as an expert witness in the case you will receive a letter of instruction which should include a bundle of documents relating to the case. If you do not get these ask for them.

Letter of instruction

There are a number of things to check within the letter of instruction. First, be sure that you have one before starting any work! The letter of instruction is in effect the agreement between you and the instructing solicitors. It sets out the remit of your instructions and you should ensure both that you address each point of instruction and that you do not deviate from these. If, during the course of your work, you identify issues that are relevant to the case but which you are not instructed to address, it is necessary to first contact the instructing solicitor to ask whether the scope of your instructions should be amended. It is best to ensure that you have any amendments to your instructions in writing (remembering that it is in essence a legal contract) and request oral amendments (e.g. over the telephone) are confirmed in writing. If your clinical role is as part of the patient's multidisciplinary team then it is essential that you have received consent from the patient to write the expert report in order to address issues of patient confidentiality.

Be aware of who is instructing the report. In criminal cases this is often an instruction on behalf of just one party (e.g. the solicitors representing the defendant or the Crown Prosecution Service). However, if you are appointed as a 'single joint expert' (the only expert on the issue that has been jointly appointed by all parties) within family law proceedings or a personal injury case this may be on behalf of multiple parties. Regardless of who is instructing you it is essential that you provide an expert opinion independent of all those who instruct you and that your role as an independent (and unbiased) expert witness is never open to question.

The documents provided

As soon as you receive the bundle of background documentation pertinent to the case you should check a number of things. First, does the bundle contain everything listed in the index? Often administrative staff will have neglected to include part of the bundle and it is important that you ascertain that everything you should have been sent has been received. Second, does the bundle contain everything you need to see? For example, if asked to comment on a patient's mental health you should obtain a copy of their medical records; if asked to conduct a risk assessment make sure you have an up-to-date list of previous convictions. Very often all the relevant information is not included in the bundle and it is necessary to ask the instructing solicitor to obtain what you need. This can take time so make sure you inspect the bundle early rather than realising that you do not have what you need the day before you are due to see the patient!

Prior to assessing the patient, make sure that you have read all the background documentation and have made notes of the important aspects. Frequently, much of the bundle is redundant to your expert evidence and need not be noted. By making notes of the relevant and important information buried within the bundle it negates the necessity to have to reread the bundle prior to presenting your evidence in court or, for example, if the client fails to attend for interview and you have to reschedule the appointment a number of weeks after the initial evaluation. Although reading the bundle can be a laborious and frustrating process, with much information seemingly irrelevant to your task, it is very important that you do read *all* of the bundle and do not skip or skim read parts. Very important nuggets of information can be buried within it and will often only be found if the bundle is read carefully in its entirety. It is important not to assume that all important aspects of information will be clearly identified and identifiable. We have also supervised clinicians in the past who have neglected to ask for, and have not been automatically given, the background information to the case. They have therefore assessed the client 'blind' to the context and background history of the case. Such practice is indefensible and can lead to you being made to look very naive and foolish. Your clinical assessment and resulting formulation will only be as good as the information that you are given. In the context of criminal proceedings (and other aspects of legal proceedings such as family law) the defendant will be highly motivated to present him or herself in as good a light as possible, and may therefore attempt to disguise certain aspects of negative information. You should not, therefore, rely entirely on self-report. It is for this reason that it is important within your written report to clearly state on what information you have based your opinion (i.e. by listing the documents you have read, the people you have interviewed, etc.). It is equally important to list the documents that you have *not* had access to if you feel these may contain important information. This practice protects you from adverse criticism if information is brought to light in court that is inconsistent with your conclusion. It also demonstrates that you had attempted to obtain such documents but that, for whatever reason, these were not supplied to you for your professional consideration.

Professional competence

At this point in the assessment it is important to double check that you still feel competent to take the case. Are there any issues contained in the bundle that you do not feel competent to address? If so, liaise with the instructing body to clarify any questions or uncertainties you may have. Fully document these discussions on file.

Assessing the client

This part of the process is in essence no different to assessments conducted within other contexts (e.g. your routine job). However, there are a number of issues that you need to clarify.

- Determine that an adequate assessment can be made in the location where the defendant is currently placed (e.g. in prison). For example, it would be inappropriate to try to conduct a neuropsychological assessment within a busy and noisy legal visits section of a prison. It is usually possible to negotiate use of an interview room in the prison health care centre as long as you give enough notice of your intended visit.
- Think about safety issues. Is there an alarm system in use? What is the organisation's policy on safety of independent professionals? It is usually best to find out this information before the day of assessment.
- Ensure you have enough time to complete the assessment. Prison routines are strict and inflexible and it may be necessary to arrange a number of appointments to complete your assessment. Unfortunately prisons are not flexible with regard to visits to fit in with busy professional schedules. They need significant notice of a visit and will usually only allow a maximum of two hours.
- If assessing a patient in prison arrive early and bring identification and nothing other than what is absolutely necessary for the assessment (e.g. no mobile telephones).
- Be prepared to cooperate with what may appear irritating security procedures (e.g. searches).
- At the beginning of the assessment inform the patient who you are, who has instructed you and what issues you are going to try to address. Give a clear statement that the patient is free to decide to comply with the assessment or not, and that they can decide to stop the assessment at any point. Defendants can often feel coerced into complying with an assessment that they would

otherwise refuse to cooperate with if it were not for the court proceedings. It is therefore important to give patients as much information as possible about who you are and the choices they can make in order to try to obtain meaningful informed consent to the process.

- Make it clear that none of the assessment or interview will be confidential and may be presented in open court. If you are unsure that the defendant has understood this then it is necessary to persevere on the point. Many defendants assume medical confidentiality as they are familiar with this through past contact with medical and mental health professionals. If the defendant begins to disclose sensitive information (e.g. about past childhood abuse) or incriminating evidence then it is often useful to remind the defendant about the limits of confidentiality and your duty to include all relevant information in the written report so that (s)he can make an informed choice about whether to continue with the disclosure.

- From a psychiatric point of view, take a history: you should have read a lot about what others think about an individual's past. You need to understand the individual's perspective rather than second-hand views. Taking a good history is a dying skill, but going back to basics and to what you learned when training is a good base from which to work, and a thorough mental state assessment is essential. Short cuts that we all develop in rushed clinical practice have no place in a forensic assessment.

- At the end of the assessment, give as much feedback about the results of the evaluation as you feel is suitable. Inform the defendant what will happen next (e.g. you will prepare a report that will be sent to the instructing solicitor). Give the defendant an opportunity to ask any questions. It is important to factor in enough time at the end of the assessment to allow this process to occur satisfactorily and not to be rushed or interrupted by the daily routines of the organisation.

- If the defendant is in prison or secure hospital make an entry in the inmate medical record (IMR) or their medical records briefly stating the purposes of the assessment (e.g. a psychological assessment for the forthcoming court case) and how the defendant appeared to cope with the process (e.g. was cooperative and pleasant and not unduly distressed). Be very clear about any information suggestive of any risk of suicidal ideation or self-harm, or future violence (especially to a specific individual), and ensure that this is both handed over verbally to the nurse/prison officer in charge as well as in writing in the IMR/medical notes.

The written report

Once again, there is nothing intrinsically different in a report written for court proceedings as compared to a report written for normal NHS practice. However, it is important to remember two things: (1) the report is written to be read and understood by a lay audience and so it is important not to assume any knowledge about mental health or psychological issues; and (2) the report will be subject to critical appraisal within a highly adversarial system. It is therefore important to ensure that all details are correct (e.g. date, names, test scores, spellings, etc.). Barristers may use inaccuracies in reports to attempt to undermine the professional competence of the report writer. The following points are important to remember:

- Clarity is crucial. Avoid all jargon and if you use technical terms always define them in lay terms (e.g. two black eyes rather than bilateral periorbital haematomas). Define the purpose of all psychometric tests or questionnaires and explain the meaning and relevance of results. Always give an explanation of what the numbers mean (e.g. *Mr P scored in the bottom 5th percentile, that is 95 per cent of the general population would obtain a higher score than him*).
- Give concrete examples: *Mr X suffered with memory problems throughout the assessment. He was, for example, not able to remember my name despite being told this on 12 occasions throughout the course of the evaluation.*
- When making statements always indicate the source of the information and whether it was corroborated or not. For example: *The following information was obtained from interview with Mr M and none of the information given has been corroborated* or *This information was corroborated by Mr M's mother/social worker/wife.* Inaccuracies in information provided by the defendant and restated in your report without attribution can be used to undermine your credibility or professional competence unless you clearly state the source and potential limits of this information.

Structure of the report

Title page
- Patient's name
- Date of birth
- Charges
- Court
- Your name, title and qualifications

Preamble
- Clearly state who instructed you (e.g. Mr X's defence solicitors) or that the report is a joint instruction from all parties involved (as will often be the case in family law or personal injury proceedings).
- State the instructions that you were given at the beginning of the report. If these are numerous or complex it is also good practice to repeat the instructions at the end of the report in the summary, alongside your opinion on each point of instruction. This concretely demonstrates that you have clearly addressed each point of instruction within your report.
- List all the documents you have seen and audio tapes/video tapes you have had access to.
- Disclose any discussions with other professionals that you have had about the case and why that is relevant (e.g. *I have discussed the case with Dr Smith, John Doe's Responsible Medical Officer, with respect to his current diagnosis and treatment response in hospital*).
- Describe yourself, your qualifications, the pertinent aspects of your clinical experience (e.g. that you are an expert in risk assessment) and to whom you provide a clinical service. Experts sometimes include a brief medico-legal CV

as an appendix to the report, but this can equally be included as a paragraph at the beginning of a report.

- Include a statement that the defendant was informed about the purpose and lack of confidentiality of the assessment. For example: *Mr M was informed of the purpose of the assessment, its lack of confidentiality and his right to withhold information.*
- Be clear if you are unsure of any information or were not given access to any information. For example: *Mr G's account of the offence was very disjointed and it was difficult to understand what he was trying to convey* or *The prison would not disclose Mr G's list of adjudications to me and it is possible that this contains relevant information with respect to a current risk assessment of his propensity to violence.*

Body of report
- Give the information on which you rely when coming to your conclusions, whether that be history, investigations or third-party information. It helps the court if this is arranged in a logical order leading to a logical conclusion rather than an apparently random collection of facts.
- Subheadings may be useful to highlight especially important isues (e.g. substance misuse or past medical/psychiatric history).
- Do not include negative information (e.g. John Doe has no history of fits) *unless* relevant to your conclusion.
- If a psychiatrist, include details of the patient's mental state.

Opinion
- Summarise your conclusions and reiterate your main findings. Often this is the only section that certain legal professionals will read and it needs to address all the important findings and implications of your assessment.
- If you are not sure how to interpret a given finding then state the opposing positions. For example: *The large and significant discrepancy found between Mr M's verbal and performance IQ may be due to the presence of head injury or may reflect his severely disturbed education.*
- Specifically answer any question asked in your instructions.
- In a psychiatric report address issues of:
  - fitness to plead;
  - does the patient suffer with any mental disorder and, if so, what and why;
  - does any disorder fall within the terms of mental health legislation and why or, often more importantly, why not;
  - any options for treatment and why;
  - risk if related to mental disorder;
  - recommendations (if appropriate) as to disposal (e.g hospital or community treatment).

Subsequent to writing and submitting your report you may be asked to make amendments to it by the instructing solicitor. Do not amend a report unless you have made an error in fact or unless you are asked to clarify or elaborate upon an opinion that is unclear. Any requested amendment of expert *opinion* may be viewed as collusion and will undermine your role as an unbiased and independent expert witness.

Charging for the report

This is a difficult area – one to be resolved between the instructing solicitor, your employer and your conscience. When submitting your report it is good practice to submit an associated invoice to the instructing solicitor. We also recommend a good accountant. Many clinicians believe that it is good practice to have a standard scale of charges (e.g. for preparation of a report, for attendance at court, etc.) and a standard letter that sets out terms and conditions. From May 2007 VAT is chargeable on many (but not all) types of medico-legal report.

Giving evidence in court

This aspect of being an expert witness can be the most daunting element for most professionals. However, with good preparation of the case and knowledge of the court's expectations of the expert witness it can be a fulfilling and enjoyable experience. We also believe that expert witness work can be a valuable addition to continuing professional development. Placing the professional and his/her work under the scrutiny of cross-examination and critical appraisal within a public arena acts as a strong incentive for professionals to think clearly and logically, to communicate thoughts and ideas simply and clearly, to keep abreast of new developments in their discipline, and to ensure that their work has firm foundations in logic and evidence-based practice.

Be well prepared. You will have heard the old adage 'preparation is everything' and in expert witness work this is never more pertinent. It is important that prior to giving oral evidence in court your preparation includes the following:

- Know the case well. At the very least this will involve rereading your expert report, but we also find it very useful to reread our notes made on the background information sent to us prior to assessment of the patient. It is also worthwhile contacting the instructing solicitor to ensure that you have been sent all subsequent information relevant to the case (e.g. other expert witness reports). Many solicitors will send this updated information automatically and there will be a steady stream of documentation pertinent to the case being sent to you. However, other solicitors may neglect to do so and it is your responsibility to ensure that you are kept abreast of all developments in the case. We have known many cases that have had to be adjourned for a number of hours while the court waits for an expert witness to read and become familiar with other documentation so that they can give a view as to how this information impinges upon their expert opinion. This process can place the expert witness under a lot of pressure and it can be difficult to concentrate adequately knowing that the entire court is waiting for you to finish reading what can be at times a bulky and complex set of documents. The court is also often a busy and noisy environment and it can be a frustrating and stressful task trying to concentrate and formulate opinions under pressure of time with so many distractions.
- Understand the psychological/psychiatric issues you addressed and why and how you did so. This is merely a matter of professional reflection so that you

can clearly and unambiguously address the purpose of your assessment and how you set about answering the issues set out in the letter of instruction.

- Understand the legal issues that your expert evidence is seeking to inform. If possible it can be very useful to discuss your expert findings and opinions (as well as those of opposing experts) with the barrister before the case. Sometimes these conferences with counsel can be arranged for a number of weeks (or months) before the trial and at other times it may only be possible to do this immediately before you give oral evidence. In either case they can be very useful in terms of understanding the crucial issues on which you will be examined, focusing your evidence to meet the needs of the court and in gaining an in-depth understanding of the legal issues in respect of which counsel will seek to utilise your expert evidence.
- Know the limits of your professional expertise. If at the conclusion of your report the issues that you were asked to address are still unclear then state this. Try to elucidate the possible alternative opinions and the evidence for each.
- Make sure that you have read the reports of other expert witnesses and thought through the implications of their findings for your evidence and the case in general. (For example, are their conclusions consistent with your opinion or inconsistent? If inconsistent, what are the possible reasons for this inconsistency? Did the other expert have access to the same background information as you?)

Practicalities

- Dress appropriately but comfortably. It is sad but true that appearances matter.
- Arrive early and familiarise yourself with what may be an alien environment.
- Ask a court official (usually easily identifiable) which court your case is in and go there.
- Try and find a member of the team instructing you and let them know you are there; they may want to discuss issues with you.
- Be prepared for a lot of hanging around, bring a paper or a book to help pass the time and provide useful distraction from escalating anxiety.
- Find the canteen – remember carbohydrate is a useful and readily available mild tranquilliser.

Appearance in the court itself

Be observant and follow the lead of every one else. It is important that the expert witness pays attention to court etiquette. This includes standing and bowing to the judge when (s)he enters and leaves the court and using the correct terms of address to the judge (e.g. 'Your Honour', 'My Lord'). The instructing solicitor should be willing to advise you on the correct form of address and any other salient points of court etiquette. Do not be embarrassed to ask the solicitor to advise you on such issues as it is accepted that the rules of court etiquette are complex. Expert witnesses are not, in our experience, expected to automatically understand these.

Expert witnesses are allowed to sit in court while other witnesses are giving evidence and this is invaluable in terms of preparing for the types of question you are likely to be asked, setting your evidence in context, etc. Wherever possible arrange to be present in court during evidence that may be relevant to your own (e.g. this may include witnesses of fact and watching the defendant give evidence). It is also useful experience to learn from the expertise of other expert witnesses in terms of how they present their evidence and how they manage the machinations of the competing barristers.

It is important to be (or at least appear to be) confident in the witness box. If you are unfamiliar with giving evidence in court then prepare carefully beforehand (and practise with colleagues if possible) in terms of how you will look, how you will stand, the projection of your voice, what you do with your hands, etc. We all have certain mannerisms and ways of presenting ourselves when we are anxious and it is important to recognise these in yourself and do your best to use them to your advantage. One of us will always lower their voice and speak softly and slowly when anxious (a very useful characteristic) whereas the other has a tendency to stand on one leg! This is a rather embarrassing mannerism, but one which the witness box disguises in most (but not all) legal contexts.

Make sure that you use plenty of eye contact with barristers and the judge when being asked questions, but with the jury when answering. Know your evidence and do not rely on having to read from your report. Be aware of your presentation skills and speak loudly and clearly with good emphasis placed on key words. There is nothing worse than a mumbling expert witness reading aloud from a dry and boring report with no eye contact with any of the legal professionals or the jury. It is accepted court procedure to face the barrister while he/she asks you the question, but to direct your answers to the judge and jury. It may be useful to turn your entire body to the judge or jury when answering a question as this helps to prevent the appearance of a one-to-one verbal exchange between expert witness and barrister that under aggressive cross-examination can become heated and appear unprofessional. It is a good technique to place your feet facing the judge and jury when you first enter the witness box so that you have to consciously turn to face the barristers. By doing this you will automatically turn back to face the judge and jury when the barrister finishes asking you each question. If there are certain parts of your report that you think that you may have to refer back to during evidence have this clearly marked within the file so that you do not have to rifle through a large ream of paper to find the relevant section. Such prior preparation and organisation will be noticed by the judge and jury and will go some way to establishing you as an expert witness upon whom the court can rely.

Prior to attendance at court it is very useful to write a list of key points that can be used in the witness box – each point a single word if possible – that can be used as a mnemonic to assist you in remembering all the important points that you wish to make during your evidence. During presentation of your evidence you can therefore simply glance down at this list of key points that will serve as a powerful reminder. As mentioned earlier in this chapter, it is important to take the entire case file to court and into the witness box, including original psychometric tests and handwritten notes, as you may be asked to refer to them while giving oral evidence.

Confidentiality

When an expert is placed under oath as a witness no confidentiality of information exists regardless of the context in which the information was obtained. For this reason it is important to be clear with the defendant about the limits of confidentiality, and clearly state in the written report that this has been explained and accepted by the patient. However, this also applies to restricted professional information such as specific questions and scoring criteria contained within psychometric tests. When in doubt about the ethics of disclosure discuss your concerns with the judge. However, you have to follow the judge's instructions even if you think these are wrong.

Expert not advocate

As has been stated earlier, the expert witness must remember always to be clear and unbiased and that their role is to advise the court on issues that are outside the expertise of a lay person (which includes the judge, jury and barristers). For this reason it is important that expert witnesses do not become defensive or hostile when aggressively cross-examined. It is the barrister's job to use a combination of emotion and intellect to present their case and a good barrister may attempt to use your emotions to discredit you or show that you are biased. If a barrister on either side 'scores a point' then this should not hold any emotional significance for you and, if it does, you should endeavour to disguise this. Similarly, do not defend any point too stringently if it is obvious that the argument for another interpretation is stronger. Again, this will make you appear biased and unprofessional. The best experts make reasoned and balanced consideration of each issue and are willing to concede a point if the evidence points to such. We are all human and as such we all, on occasion, make mistakes (particularly if there is a piece of information that has not been disclosed to us and which changes the interpretation of a case). It is far better to acknowledge any error in interpretation, and apologise to the court for this, than to try to assertively defend a point of view or opinion that is probably not accurate. The court will respect your honesty and professionalism in such an eventuality. Expert witnesses are best served by seeking to remember that all we can be expected to do is to give our independent professional opinion to the best of our ability and to assist the court in any way possible. It is not our role to 'always be right' in our opinions or to seek to 'win the case' in one way or another. It is very easy to be drawn into the adversarial process and to lose sight of our purpose as an expert witness (that of being 'independent' and of being 'expert' in our subject area). The adversarial dynamic is powerful and can be very contagious and that can be dangerous to our professional reputation and credibility.

If your evidence is not accepted – do not worry! It does not mean your opinion was wrong. The court is an arena where each side attempts to present the most believable case. The job of the barrister is to build and present the case. The role of the judge and jury is to decide which version of the case they believe or will accept. It is important to remember that the barrister will not simply seek to allow you to confirm your evidence as written in the expert report but will seek to use aspects of the expert evidence that best builds their case. Again, the role of the expert witness is not to get drawn into the dynamics and emotion of the case (which the barristers will seek to maximise in order to sway the jury), but to give an unbiased professional opinion to the best of our ability.

It is also important that an expert does not enter the witness box ready to give a lecture. Instead allow yourself to be examined by the barrister as to the issues he/she believes are the most salient or which are under dispute. It is perfectly acceptable to be 'led' by the barrister as to the issues s/he wishes you to present as long as this does not change the substance or meaning of your evidence in any way. Indeed, we find this process very useful as it avoids the necessity to have to remember and present every point of evidence. Instead the expert need only listen, and reply, to questions presented (a far easier task), allowing the barrister to structure the evidence and ensure that only relevant information is presented to the judge and jury.

The barrister: their approach and perspective with regard to the expert witness

Barristers will use powerful non-verbal behaviour to encourage or discourage the witness in what they are saying. This can be very distracting and offputting. For example, if you are saying something that is consistent with the case they wish to establish then the barrister will nod, smile and will often use their hands to wave the witness forward and encourage more. Alternatively, if they do not like the evidence that is being presented a barrister will often use many non-verbal strategies designed to stop the witness from speaking. This will include turning away from the witness to try to break the channel of communication, they will frown and shake their head and will 'pretend' to become angry and disparaging by their facial expressions and non-verbal behaviour. I have had the experience of a barrister literally turning their back to me when I was in mid-sentence in a vain attempt to get me to stop speaking. These non-verbal signals can be very offputting to expert and lay witnesses alike and can serve to markedly increase anxiety. Barristers will also use verbal strategies to achieve the same effect. Thus, if you are saying something that reinforces their case they will often say positive, encouraging words (such as 'yes, yes' and 'good'). The most common verbal strategy if they do not want you to proceed in your evidence is to attempt to interrupt you before you have finished speaking. It can be very difficult to continue in your answer while being spoken over by an assertive barrister and to do so can make one appear rude and aggressive. In this circumstance the best technique is to turn to the judge and to ask politely that you be allowed to continue. An awareness of these techniques utilised by barristers, and being conscious of why they are used, can dilute the effect of such. This is another reason why it is very useful to face the judge and jury when replying to questions posed by the barristers. This essentially blocks non-verbal signals given out by the barrister (although the huffs and puffs and assertive body language of a disgruntled barrister in one's peripheral vision can still be very offputting). We find it useful to remember that the greater the performance of the opposing barrister the greater negative impact they fear your evidence will have upon their case in the minds of judge and jury (and therefore probably the better job you are doing!)

Barristers are trained to be aware of their non-verbal behaviour and, unless they are purposely engaging in the behaviours described above, they will try to be as impassive as they can. They are, for example, taught not to give away too much 'true emotion' in their faces. Barristers have to look as though they are totally in control of the situation so that the jury will trust them and ultimately accept their version of events. They present the facade of control by keeping a blank face at all times. They are taught that they must not look surprised or shocked by evidence or the jury will think 'oh – we have a problem here, counsel is no longer in control'. This means that the expert witness can safely dismiss all emotional expressions on behalf of the barrister in the court arena as techniques designed to more effectively present their case and to cause maximum impact upon the minds of the jury.

The role and perspective of the barrister is to assert their case – a given perspective and opinion of events that is favourable to their client (or unfavourable, if the barrister is acting for the prosecution). For barristers it is different questioning an expert witness as opposed to a witness of fact. When questioning an expert witness the barrister (who is in effect a lay person) is not able to question or put an alternate version of events, as they may be able to do about versions of facts. For example, a barrister may be able to assert that a witness to fact was not able to have a clear view of an incident due to their view being occluded or due to the distance between them being too great. However, a barrister would not be able to assert that the defendant does not, for example, have a personality disorder due to some technicality of assessment or diagnosis, etc. In order to assert this the barrister may use a variety of techniques. Three common options are as follows:

Leading you down the slippery slope

If the expert witness asserts 'if A, then B, then C' then if the barrister can discredit point A the conclusions arising from that (B and C) no longer apply. The barrister will therefore seek to get the expert to waver on point A and when and if (s)he does the barrister will then pounce and assert strongly that B and C can no longer follow. It is not the barrister's intention to 'prove' this point but only to engender a degree of doubt in the minds of the judge and jury.

An important feature of the 'slippery slope' is for the barrister to begin his/her assertion in the context of being warm, friendly and supportive. This presentational style serves to relax the witness so that they drop their defences and feel supported and understood. Another important feature of the 'slippery slope' is that the witness agrees with all the propositions leading up to the crucial 'trap'. As an expert witness these two features can act as 'warning signals' that this 'trick' is about to be played upon you: watch for a series of seemingly innocuous questions to which the obvious answer is a simple 'yes' and beware if the opposing side (the side for which your evidence does not fit) begins to be particularly warm or charming towards you. The best defence against the slippery slope is: (1) to see it coming and; (2) not to simply agree with the propositions put to you with a simple 'yes' answer, but to give caveats to each. Usually, well placed caveats can spoil the trap before it has the chance to be sprung (even if you have no idea what specific form the trap will take, which is usually the case in our experience). However, if you wait for the trap to be sprung it is normally too late to get out of it.

Attacking the message

This is to assert with the help of another expert that the opinion of the expert is not correct. This approach aims to place a different perspective on the expert witness's findings with the help of another expert who can understand the details of evidence. It is for this reason that it is very important that you receive the reports of other expert witnesses (both of the same profession and other related professions) prior to the beginning of the court case. Make notes as to what points all expert witnesses agree and what points expert witnesses disagree and try to identify reasons for any disagreements. Think about your report (and those of other expert witnesses in the case) from the perspective of both the defence and prosecution barrister. This should allow you to predict the type of questions that each will be likely to ask at trial and will be invaluable preparation for your oral evidence.

When about to give evidence in court always prepare your report and your evidence not only in terms of what your opinion is and what you have done but also in terms of what angle/perspective the opposing counsel may seek to assert. In this way you can be prepared for the arguments that the other side will raise and prepare your answers and arguments in advance. Always think about, and try to prepare for, the different opinions and perspectives of the different parties in court.

Shooting the messenger

From the witness's point of view this is a reassuring technique – it's only if the barrister cannot attack your argument he has to resort to 'shooting the messenger'. The aim of this technique is to raise doubt in the judge and jury's mind about the competence of the expert witness or their impartiality. We have discussed ways that this can be done throughout this chapter. For example, doubts about competence can be raised by finding inaccuracies in the report, such as the date that the client was assessed, spelling errors, etc. The barrister can spend a lot of time questioning an expert about their qualifications or experience, particularly about the amount of experience the expert has had in assessing the pertinent issues in the case. Doubts about impartiality can be raised by making the expert witness appear unprofessional (e.g. by getting them to become angry in the witness stand) or by questioning their balance of work (e.g. defence vs. prosecution instructions), etc. Every effort should be made to avoid falling into these easily laid traps.

Expert witness directories and training

There are now a number of expert witness directories and institutes that can provide the budding (and experienced) expert witness with advice, information and entry onto the directories. Such directories can greatly assist in becoming established on the medico-legal circuit. Examples of these are the Law Society Expert List (http://www.lawsociety.org.uk), the Expert Witness Institute (http://www.ewi.org.uk) and, for psychologists, the British Psychological Society's Directory of Experts (http://www.bps.org.uk/e-services/find-a-psychologist/directory.cfm).

There are also increasingly becoming available training courses for expert witnesses. Such training in expert witness work is always useful for attracting continuing professional development (CPD) points and may soon become obligatory (although this has not happened yet). Examples of such training providers are Bond Solon Training, who focus on providing full CPD accredited training programmes for health and social care professionals (http://www.bondsolon.com) and, on occasion, the British Psychological Society. When choosing expert witness training remember that many disciplines undertake expert witness work (from chartered accountants to civil engineers) and some training courses may be so generic as not to be very useful for healthcare professionals.

Core questions asked of mental health practitioners in the criminal courts

As a final section to this chapter we thought it would be useful to outline some core issues that mental health practitioners are asked to address within the criminal courts.

Actus reus vs. mens rea

Actus reus – that an act or omission has occurred by the identified person. Psychologists and psychiatrists rarely become involved in issues of *actus reus*.

Box 19.1 Case example 1

A defendant was charged with grievous bodily harm (GBH) after it was alleged that she caused the victim (her partner) a serious head injury by hitting him over the head with an iron. The victim never leaves hospital and a month after the incident he dies of a brain haemorrhage. The charges are altered to that of murder. The court has to prove 'beyond reasonable doubt' that: (1) the brain haemorrhage was the cause of death; and (2) the brain haemorrhage was the direct consequence of the assault.

Mens rea – that the defendant had the state of mind (e.g. 'intent') or quality of behaviour (e.g. 'acted recklessly') necessary for a particular offence. It is the *mens rea* element of an offence that psychologists and psychiatrists are most often asked to address.

Is the defendant fit to plead and stand trial?

To have a fair trial a defendant has to realise what s/he is charged with, that s/he is being tried and be able to take part in their defence. Assessment of this is an issue for the court after hearing medical evidence.

The core criteria that have to be addressed when assessing if a client is fit to plead and to stand trial are:

Can the defendant:
- know the difference between a plea of guilty and not guilty?
- comprehend the details of evidence?
- follow the court proceedings?

- know that a juror can be challenged?
- instruct legal advisors?

The opinion for fitness to plead has to be made by a 'registered medical practitioner' and thus an opinion on fitness cannot be given by a psychologist or other mental health professional. However, psychologists are often asked to comment on the criteria that constitute this ruling as the criteria are obviously concerned with cognitive ability. A formal assessment of intellectual ability and other aspects of neuropsychological function (e.g. memory) can also be very informative for an opinion on fitness to plead and stand trial.

The above issues have to be assessed in the context of the charge. Obviously some issues are easier to comprehend than others. Level of comprehension may also differ with the amount of stress that the defendant is under at the time. For example, a patient may be able to understand the relevant issues if these are explained quietly in a non-threatening environment, but totally unable to comprehend these in the highly stressful situation of a court room. This can lead to the seemingly paradoxical situation that someone can be fit to plead guilty, but unfit to plead not guilty (as in the latter circumstance they would have to attend and comprehend a trial).

Box 19.2 Case example 2

The core legal test for a finding of insanity is that the defendant does 'not know the nature and quality of the act he was doing, or if he did know it, that he did not know that what he was doing was wrong'. In clinical practice such patients are very rare. One example of a patient who was found to be insane under the McNaughton Rules was of a man with paranoid schizophrenia who held a delusional belief that the world was a cruel and wicked place and that he was a form of saviour for the good people of the world. He believed that if he were to kill someone that they would immediately be resurrected into a 'good world', where pain or suffering did not exist. He unfortunately acted on these delusional beliefs and killed two people. At trial he was found 'not to know that what he was doing was wrong' (indeed he believed that what he was doing was good) and was found to be insane under the McNaughton Rules.

The insanity defence

Legal insanity is a valid defence to many serious charges. The defence of legal insanity leads to a finding of *not guilty by reason of insanity* and as such is an acquittal. The defendant is still subject to sentencing, however, and as the defendant has been found to be legally insane this usually consists of a placement in hospital. The legal test of insanity used is the 1843 McNaughton Rules. These state:

> Every man is presumed to be sane, until the contrary be proved, and that to establish a defence on the grounds of insanity it must be clearly proved that at the time of committing the act the accused party was labouring under such a defect of reason, from disease of mind, as not to know the nature and quality of the act he was doing, or if he did know it, that he did not know that what he was doing was wrong.

The judgment of insanity has to be made in law by a 'registered medical practitioner' and thus an opinion on the McNaughton Rules cannot be given by a psychologist or other mental health professional. However, mental health professionals other than psychiatrists can be called to assess aspects of a case that would inform this judgment. In practice the defence of insanity is rarely used today.

Diminished responsibility

This defence is available only if the charge is murder. It allows a defendant to be convicted of manslaughter rather than murder and gives discretion to the judge in terms of sentencing (those convicted of murder receiving a mandatory life sentence). The Homicide Act 1957 states:

> Where a person is party to the killing of another, he shall not be convicted of murder if he was suffering from such abnormality of mind (whether arising from a condition of arrested or retarded development of mind or any inherent causes or induced by disease or injury) as substantially impaired his mental responsibility for his acts and omissions in doing or being a party to the killing.

The concept of *abnormality of mind* allows all forms of mental disorder to be considered, including mental illness, learning disability, personality disorder and head injury. Abnormality of mind has to be linked to the action either directly or indirectly to a substantial degree (substantial being legally defined as 'more than a little and less than a lot'!). Clinical judgment about the degree of association between the abnormality of mind and the behaviour of the defendant is an issue that often causes a conflict of opinion between mental health professionals. While the court may listen to experts it does not have to agree with them and the final decision is one for the jury.

Box 19.3 Case example 3

A 45-year-old man with no history of offending killed his best friend by repeatedly stabbing him. On assessment he was found to be severely depressed with associated psychotic symptoms, including auditory hallucinations. At trial he was judged to have 'abnormality of mind ... as to substantially impair his mental responsibility' by two s. 12 approved psychiatrists. He was found to have diminished responsibility and was therefore convicted of manslaughter and sentenced to reside in a secure hospital under ss. 37/41 of the Mental Health Act 1983.

What is the defendant's future risk of offending?

This issue is becoming more common as sentencing and placement are increasingly being decided on the basis of future risk as well as upon the concept of punishment. There are ethical arguments about psychiatrists making judgments as to risk of future dangerousness in the non-mentally disordered.

It is important that experts base their evaluation of risk on an evidence-based risk instrument and not solely upon unstructured clinical assessment as a large body of research now shows that the latter is unreliable (see Chapter 10 this volume on risk assessment by Doyle and Dolan). In any risk assessment one must be clear of the limitations and the generalisability (or the lack thereof) of the assessment, the context in which it was done (e.g. are you predicting risk in the community, while on parole, while in an institution, etc.). Such limitations should include a measure of the confidence intervals of the stated risk (which are normally available within the manuals that accompany the instrument) and a clear consideration of factors that might not have been covered by the instrument. In this current risk-averse culture it is always less of a risk to the professional to describe some one as risky rather than safe and this tendency to 'play safe' needs to be borne in mind.

Therefore, the expert witness should also perform a thorough review of the background history of the defendant, including information about past charges and convictions. If the defendant suffers with a mental disorder, a detailed review of past and current diagnoses and response to treatment should also be conducted. A thorough risk formulation should be developed as to whether and, if so, in what way the mental disorder relates to future risk.

Summary

We hope that this chapter has provided a useful introduction and framework for being an expert witness to those professionals who wish to engage in this challenging, but rewarding, aspect of work. We firmly believe that the practice of being an expert witness within the highly adversarial culture of the criminal justice system helps to ensure that practitioners are continually reflecting upon their clinical practice and that they endeavour to ensure that it is both evidence-based and meets the highest standards possible. There is nothing more sobering than to realise that the expert witness for the other side entirely disagrees with one's findings and opinions on a case and the resulting nagging doubt that 'they may be right'. However, the process of reflecting upon the process of how each expert arrived at their opinions, and what aspects of the assessment has led to such diverging opinions, can be highly instructive about how we practice and the reliability and validity of our work.

Chapter 20

Focusing on treatment: the main interventions and their implications

Conor Duggan

Introduction

In Ray Bradbury's *Fahrenheit 451*, the main character, the 'fireman', is employed to burn books so as to discourage people to think for themselves. As one character exclaims, 'If you don't want a man unhappy politically, don't give him two sides of the question to worry him; give him one. Or better yet, none' (Bradbury 1997: 61).

In contrast to the above, there is no shortage of questions, many with two (or more) sides to consider, when one examines 'treatment' in a forensic context. For instance, what are the relative rights of a mentally disordered offender versus those of society? Is it appropriate to coerce such an individual into treatment and to what extent does this coercion affect the outcome? Is the focus of the intervention merely to reduce the likelihood of reoffending (largely, though not exclusively, a societal good) or should it also address the psychological ill health of the individual being treated? Hence, while it is tempting, as Bradbury's character suggests, to disregard the many-sided nature of these questions, were we to do so, this would surely not only short-change ourselves as a discipline but also those that we attempt to serve.

Although there is no shortage of questions and differing answers (the latter depending particularly on the constituency being canvassed), I suggest that this kind of discourse – both in its range and its questioning of fundamentals – is unique to mental health practice, and particularly to that of forensic mental health. A question that needs to be asked then is why this area provokes so much discussion and controversy that is largely absent – certainly in other areas of medical practice? It would be difficult to imagine, for instance, cardiologists or orthopaedic surgeons having a discussion as to whether or not there is such an entity as a diseased heart or a broken limb.

Yet this questioning of the very existence of the disorder is commonplace within forensic mental health. This is not to say that there is no discussion as to whether treatment A is better than treatment B in other areas of healthcare; rather I am arguing that these discussions take place largely among professionals (sometimes within quite closely knit professional groups) where (1) there are fundamentals that are assumed by the professional groups concerned, and (2) where the laity is largely excluded. In contrast, the mental health arena appears to have a different form of discourse.

This difference between mental health and other medical practice can be variously interpreted. One interpretation is that forensic mental health practice is at the interface of a number of disciplines – so that it has to take account not only of issues that arise from mental health itself but also those that arise from several other disciplines (e.g. criminology, law, ethics) – all of which have a legitimate interest in this area. Hence it is no surprise that this area of practice is likely to generate debate on its very principles. A further benign interpretation is that mental health practice is inclusive, respectful of the various views of others – both within and outside the professions – so that it provides real attention, not only to the contributions of a wide range of professionals but also to those of patients (or 'users'). Accepting this interpretation would place mental health at the forefront of medical practice, with other areas in its slipstream. Here, the issue of 'values', 'meaning', 'inclusivity', etc. are core issues for mental health professionals in a way that they are not for other medical disciplines in the sense that the latter are happy to concentrate on improving the health of their patients rather than dwelling unduly on what improving health means. By implication, there is a common language in mental health that has not become as rarefied as it has in other areas of medical practice that it can no longer be shared with non-professionals.

An alterative interpretation is that psychiatry (and allied areas) is a primitive discipline – indeed, some might say, hardly meriting the title of a medical science at all – and that it is this failure to advance its area of discourse and become a 'science' that explains not only its inclusivity, but also its relative failure to have much of an impact on the natural history of mental disorder. I shall return to this question again later but let us content ourselves for the moment with this tension between inclusivity on one side, at the price perhaps of relative ineffectiveness on the other.

There are judgments to be made when instituting any treatment (i.e. the costs versus the benefits to the individual receiving the treatment, and the costs versus the benefits to the society that provides it). While these considerations apply to treatment delivery in general, there are additional questions to be asked when treatments are being delivered in forensic mental health. This is for two reasons. First, there is controversy as to the *purpose* of the intervention for mentally disordered offenders: specifically, is it being applied to relieve symptomatic distress (an individual benefit) or to reduce future reoffending (resulting in an individual and societal benefit)? Second, there is the *context* in which the treatment is being delivered, especially as many individuals in forensic mental health are effectively being coerced into engaging in interventions that they might otherwise choose to avoid.

Treatment appears to be the spine around which these controversial issues can be most usefully considered. The types of interventions and their effectiveness have already been considered within Part 3 of this Handbook; here I shall focus on some of their more widespread implications. Hence, I am going to consider 'treatment' in the round and examine three questions: (1) the purpose of the 'treatment', as it relates to a reduction in criminality – especially violent criminality;

(2) whether it is legitimate to coerce individuals into 'treatment' and under what circumstances this might be permitted; and (3) how effective the legal system is in protecting patients from treatment that they do not wish to have. It will be no surprise to those familiar with this field that 'value' judgments play just as much a part as the 'scientific evidence' in addressing these issues.

The purpose of 'treatment' in the forensic mental health context

As regards the purpose of the intervention for mentally disordered offenders, I believe that this debate has shifted substantially with the past decade. Many mental health professionals now recognise, for instance, that, as further reoffending by the individual will benefit neither the individual who commits the offence nor the society that suffers as a consequence, a reduction in reoffending ought to be one of the major foci of therapeutic activity. This change has arisen for two reasons: (1) the evidence linking serious mental illness with offending (and especially violent offending) has become stronger; and (2) a belated appreciation by mental health professionals of both the appropriateness and efficacy of criminological programmes for those that they treat. Let us therefore, examine the evidence for these two propositions.

Is mental disorder associated with offending, especially with violent offending?

The change of thinking linking mental disorder with crime is so remarkable that one needs to keep in mind that our currently accepted view of this positive association has replaced an equally firmly held but directly contradictory view that prevailed no less than 30 years ago (i.e. that criminality and mental disorder were not linked). It is worth quoting Beck and Wencel (1998: 1) on this point to appreciate how radical this shift in thinking has been:

> In a brief time, no more than 5 to 7 years, two major changes in thinking have been observed (in the intellectual history of psychiatry). First the revealed wisdom of a generation that held that crime and mental disorder were unrelated has been rejected. Second, and even more unusual, this belief has been replaced by its opposite. There is now substantial evidence that violent crime and Axis 1 psychopathology are meaningfully related to each other has been accepted.

Although this association between mental disorder and the likelihood of crime is now the received wisdom, one ought not to exaggerate the significance of this link. Indeed, in the same year that Beck and Wencel published their article, Bonta *et al.* (1998) reported on an important meta-analysis that tried to identify predictors of reoffending among those with mental disorder. Their conclusion was clear-cut, namely that when mentally disordered offenders reoffend, it was their criminological characteristics, rather than their mental disorder, that predicted the recurrence of reoffending. Indeed, in their review, the features of mental disorder predicted only 15 per cent of the variance in reoffending.

On the surface at least, here are two contradictory positions: mental disorder is linked to offending and mental disorder is not linked to offending. What is the explanation? One obvious candidate is that the recent studies showing a positive association have used better methodology. For instance, although the Bonta *et al.* study was a sophisticated meta-analysis, it could be criticised in that many of the studies used in their review were old and of poor quality. Hence more recent data with better methodology that have shown a convincing association between, for instance, schizophrenia with increased rates of antisocial behaviour in general and violence in particular need to take precedence (see Chapter 16 this volume by Hodgins).

The second reason is that, while a positive association has been shown in more recent studies, this association is not overwhelming (i.e. being of the order of 10 per cent in the case of schizophrenia and violence: Mullen 2006). Hence, as Beck and Wencel's statement implies, one ought to be cautious in reading too much into these positive associations for, if one could be so misled by the evidence in the 1970s into believing that mental disorder and criminality were not linked, could this not also apply 30 years later that showed the alternative?

Despite this attractive counter-culture suggestion, most commentators are now in agreement that the current evidence in the link between mental disorder and criminality is sufficiently strong that it demands to be taken seriously by mental health professionals. Moreover, they would argue that if one accepts this association, it entails an obligation on mental health professionals to reduce the risk of further reoffending in this group.

Yet, despite the strong evidence of a link between mental disorder and criminality with the implications that one ought to intervene, many mental health practitioners choose to ignore the first and not respond to the second. Indeed, forensic mental health services have been criticised for not taking criminological issues sufficiently seriously so that patients frequently continue to reoffend as their criminological needs have not been sufficiently addressed (Maden *et al.* 2004).

Why therefore, does this evidence base have so little influence on the practice of mental health professionals (see also Chapter 16 this volume by Hodgins)? One suggestion is that psychiatrists are reluctant to stigmatise their patients further by emphasising the link between mental disorder and criminality, so that they deliberately downplay its significance (Mullen 2006). Another is that mental health practitioners do not see a reduction in criminality as their immediate concern, believing that dealing with the criminological propensities of their patients is a matter for others (e.g. criminologists) to deal with. Unfortunately, this attitude may leave the mentally disordered offender in a no-man's-land – being rejected by the mental health practitioner because of their criminality and by the criminologist on the grounds of the mental disorder – so that he/she is not properly served by either discipline. A number of commentators (e.g. Howells *et al.* 2004) bemoan this 'two cultures' mentality of mental health and criminological programmes with little connection between them. Clearly this has to change and hence it is worth examining briefly the principles and efficacy of this criminological literature that exist largely independent of mental health.

The criminological or 'what works' literature

As its name implies, this literature focuses on 'what works' in reducing criminality. At the outset, it is worth noting that the question on whether rehabilitative programmes actually do reduce criminality has run a similar course to the controversy on whether or not mental disorder is positively associated with increased criminality. For instance, the present 'what works' literature was preceded by its opposite (i.e. 'nothing works' literature) in the 1970s that concluded that rehabilitation programmes in prison had '... no appreciable effect on recidivism' (Martinson 1974). However, just as improved sampling and methodological rigour established a link between mental disorder and criminality, a similar improvement in the methodology of criminal studies, associated particularly with systematic reviews and meta-analysis, led to a more positive appraisal of therapeutic programmes in criminology. This updated methodology suggests that offender programmes across the board have a positive effect in reducing recidivism.

The 'what works' approach has focused on the need principle so that changing these criminogenic needs '... should be the touchstone in working with offenders' (Andrews and Bonta 2003). While the interventions are multi-modal, reflecting that a reduction in offending is dependent on addressing many issues, cognitive behavioural approaches underpin the psychological interventions. These are based primarily on a 'deficit model' (i.e. that individuals resort to criminal activity because they lack the thinking capacity to behave otherwise – especially when emotionally aroused). This link between distorted types of cognition and crime has been found in a variety of offences including those of violence, armed robbery, substance misuse (McGuire 2004), sexual abuse (Ward *et al.* 2001) and domestic violence (Russell 2002).

The criminological literature, in contrast to that in mental health, has been exemplary in using research findings in the development of their interventions. Hence, the evidence from the various meta-analyses into what causes crime has informed the development of effective programmes. Briefly, the following features describe the essential principles of such programmes.

- The programmes focus on tackling the offender's dynamic needs, so that the elements that emerges from an offender's needs analysis that cause him/her to offend become the focus of the programme.
- Programmes are largely based on cognitive-behavioural principles so that they are carefully structured with clear aims and objectives.
- They target high-risk offenders.
- Programmes should show 'responsivity' (i.e. so that the services offered are adapted to offenders' styles, abilities and motivations).
- Programmes should show a high level of treatment integrity (i.e. that the programme actually delivers what it set out to do).
- Organisations delivering the services need to support the implementation of the programme through having well-trained staff and structures in place to deliver it.
- Ideally, programmes ought to be delivered in the community, or if they are delivered in a secure setting, then these ought to be linked with a community service.

Thus the focus here is on the *risk* that the individual poses so that the greatest resources are directed towards those at highest risk, that they address his/her criminogenic *needs* and having a *responsive* programme to meet those needs

(RNR: Andrews 1995). In passing, it is worth highlighting the contrast between the prescriptive features of this 'what works' literature with the predominant mode of psychological intervention for mentally disordered offenders hitherto used within the NHS that is largely psychoanalytically based (Cordess and Cox 1998). There are a number of features that distinguish these two approaches. For instance, the psychoanalytic model is based on a conflictual rather than the criminogenic deficit model. Similarly, the former does not focus directly on criminogenic factors; rather it is exploratory and open-ended. Much, though not all, of the former interventions take place in secure rather than open settings. Finally, the organisation has little direct interest in the therapeutic activity in the psychoanalytic approach – other then employing the therapist.

While drawing attention to these differences, my intention is not to promote one model of intervening over the other. (I have previously argued that these two approaches can be reconciled with the CBT (cognitive-behavioural therapy) approach being directed towards the needs of the patient and psychodynamic interventions being directed towards helping the staff cope with their anxieties, rather than being offered directly to the patient (Duggan 2006)). Rather, it is to highlight, yet again, the very rapid changes that have occurred within the past 30 years – this time in the orientation of service provision.

An additional implication from the principles of the 'what works' literature is that while it stresses that the most effective treatment takes place in the community rather than in secure institutions, nonetheless forensic mental health services have been focused on the provision of services in expensive residential facilities rather than in the community. While such services appear to have been developed – as much to contain individuals as to offer them interventions to treat their disorder and reduce their risk – their expansion is increasingly being questioned. As resources are limited, is this another example of services ignoring what the research evidence is telling us? In conclusion, the forensic mental health practitioner faces a challenge from the criminological literature – both as regards (1) the efficacy of their interventions and (2) the configuration of their service delivery.

Are criminogenic type programmes effective?

Recent reviews demonstrate that, while they are effective, their effect is modest. Lösel (1996), for instance, estimates their impact across the board to be of the order of 10–12 per cent. That is to say, those who engage in the active intervention are likely to reoffend about 10 per cent less than if they had no intervention. As Hollin and Palmer (2006) point out this modest effect is superior to the impact of many accepted drug interventions in medicine. For instance, the effect size in the use of aspirin to reduce heart attacks is of the order of 6.8 per cent.

While from the perspective of the individual a 10 per cent reduction in the likelihood of re-offending is a very modest effect, when spread across the population, this effect may be very significant and well worth being supported by government policy – especially if the cost of the intervention is low – as indeed it is in the case of aspirin – and the cost to the community is high – as indeed it is in the case particularly of serious offending (Aos et al. 2001).

The implications of the 'what works' literature for forensic mental health

If one accepts for the forensic practitioner targeting his/her interventions that a reduction in reoffending is a reasonable (albeit not the sole) outcome, an important question is what additional contribution does the mental disorder make to this work? More specifically, how should one define the task of the forensic practitioner in this respect?

Mullen (2002: 289) has considered this issue and usefully sets out the reasonable purview of the role of the mental health practitioner in the following passage:

> If significant associations exist between a serious mental disorder and the frequency of criminal activity; if those associations are mediated by modifiable variables; and if modifying those variables falls within the domain of mental health practice; then, and only then, may mental health practitioners properly be considered to have a role in the prevention, or at least the minimization, of offending behaviours in the seriously mentally disordered.

As helpful as this description is, it begs a number of questions. For instance, How strong does an association between mental disorder and criminal activity have to be for it to be regarded as significant? And, again, while it is easy to specify the modifiable variable in serious mental illness so that a reduction in psychosis has to be a reasonable task for a mental health practitioner, specifying the modifiable variables in other areas of practice (e.g. personality disorder) becomes less clear. The essential questions are the extent to which mentally disordered offenders differ from non-mentally disordered offenders and if it is assumed that they are different, what implications does this have for programme delivery?

To answer the first of these, if, as it appears from the literature, that the association between schizophrenia and violence that is regarded as 'significant' is of the order of 10 per cent, would we accept this as a sufficiently strong association that we might be willing to intervene? Unfortunately, this does not take us very far for, if we were to accept that everyone with schizophrenia is likely to be violent, then one would be focusing on the wrong individual nine times out of ten. What we need therefore is a more accurate description of the 10 per cent that are likely to be violent.

Hodgins (see Chapter 16 this volume) develops a typology of schizophrenia and violence that is potentially helpful. She divides the group into the following triad. In Type 1, she identifies conduct disorder in childhood that antedated the development of the severe mental illness (SMI) as the important driver toward further antisocial behaviour. It is not entirely clear (to me) whether this antecedent criminality is independent of or interacts with the subsequent development of schizophrenia and resultant violence. Perhaps, her Type 1 shows some of the futility of separating serious mental illness from and personality disorder as this most pernicious form appears to combine both; nonetheless, this is one group where one might be able to intervene preventatively.

For her Type 2 (i.e. those with SMI and a continuous pattern of aggressive behaviour, but only after the onset of the mental disorder) she is at a loss to explain the association between SMI and violence, but suggests that this may be related to prolonged substance misuse – either associated with or subsequent to the offence. Her Type 3 – often presenting with a singleton killing 'out of the blue', often a carer or acquaintance, and with no antecedent criminal activity – is explained by a change in mental state with increased callousness that is, however, short-lived. While others (e.g. Steinert *et al*. 1998) have produced a simpler dual typology that is equivalent to Hodgins' Types 1 and 3, these differences are less important here than its implications for if either of these approaches are accepted then they lead to testable conjectures that can be appropriately investigated. If sustained, they will clearly have important implications for the practice of forensic mental health. For instance, if the antecedent history has important implications for the subsequent disposal of the defendant rather than the gravity of the crime committed, then, as Hodgins suggests (see Chapter 16 this volume), her Type 1 – an individual with schizophrenia that is especially vulnerable to further serious reoffending because of his/her antecedent criminality – ought to be the focus of greater mental health intervention as compared with an individual committing a grave offence in the context of mental illness but without antecedent criminality (her Type 3) – the latter needing a more rapid discharge from the mental health system. The current problem is that these distinctions do not govern duration of stay in expensive facilities but, were they to do so, then they might free up scarce resources so that these could be targeted more efficiently.

When one turns to the second question (i.e. the implications of the cooccurrence of mental disorder in offenders for programme delivery), the relevant data are unfortunately not available because of the disconnection of the mental health and the criminological literatures. However, there is very good evidence from general psychiatry that the co-occurrence of personality disorders with other Axis 1 disorders has an adverse effect on the prognosis for the latter (Duggan and Tyrer 2002). Hence, forensic mental health practitioners have assumed (perhaps reasonably) that mentally disordered offenders have additional therapeutic needs (compared to non-mentally disordered offenders) and have adapted their therapeutic programmes accordingly. These adaptations include such increased initial motivational work that the individual is enticed into treatment, a slower pace of delivery, the sequencing of treatment so that criminogenic needs are tackled at the end of the programme, rather than early on, when the individual is best able to make use of them, etc. All of these result in a substantial increase in the duration (and cost) for programme delivery. Unfortunately, as is the case in many other areas of forensic mental practice, there is little evidence supporting whether these modifications are either desirable or necessary.

Should treatment always be offered to mentally disordered offenders?

While, on the surface, intervening to reduce further reoffending among mentally disordered offenders appears uncontroversial, it raises at least two ethical concerns. First, the implication of Hodgins' Type 1 is that early identification of the individual likely to be a persistent offender is crucial if this cycle is to be broken. While, in an ideal world, appropriate (and effective) interventions would be offered to such an individual, how confident can one be in the present climate of reduction in mental health services that this indeed will occur? Conversely, if it does not occur, is this early identification not likely to lead to further stigmatisation and exclusion from services in a group that is already highly alienated?

Second, one has to be concerned with the finding that those who drop out of treatment – having been offered it – appear to be worse off (i.e. reoffend more readily) than if they had not been offered treatment in the first place (McMurran and Theodosi 2007). There are a number of explanations for this paradoxical outcome including: (1) their failure to engage positively with treatment means that they are further stigmatised and viewed as failures when being assessed for later interventions; (2) those who fail have a further blow to their fragile self-esteem so that this had a negative impact in their self-worth. Whatever the mechanism, this is a well attested finding that needs to be taken into account in the planning of an individual's intervention. This is especially the case as there is evidence that young, hostile, uneducated men are likely to disengage from treatment (Skodol *et al.* 1983; Smith *et al.* 1995) – the very type of offender that is likely to come the way of forensic mental health services. The research evidence suggests that such individuals, if they prematurely drop out, might be harmed more by being offered services than being denied them. Hence this evidence that intervening might not be beneficial but might actually be harmful needs to be factored into the practitioner's calculus when deciding whether or not to intervene in a particular case.

Coercion into treatment

I will now consider the second question, i.e. whether and under what circumstances an individual ought to be coerced into treatment and whether this affects their response.

The conventional view of most health professionals is that treatment ought to be voluntary in order to be effective (i.e. that the individual should be offered an informed choice as to whether or not to engage in the intervention, and then only offered it if he/she agrees to participate). Despite this, it is agreed that much treatment offered in mental health settings has a degree of coercion (sometimes concealed) attached to it.

Consider, for instance, this time in a non-forensic context, whether the impact of a relationship breakdown 'coerces' or 'encourages' an individual into treatment. That is to say, is the threat of the break-up in a relationship coercive in 'forcing' one of the parties into treatment as a condition of the relationship continuing or whether he/she 'chooses' treatment in order for the relationship to continue.

Any fair reading of treatment in many mental health contexts demonstrates that there are degrees of coercion present in many of what appear to be 'voluntary' treatments (including the use of therapeutic power). The difference between such contexts and those of forensic mental health is that this is not often explicitly acknowledged in the former. To the extent therefore that forensic mental health professionals might be more likely to acknowledge overtly this asymmetric imbalance of power between themselves and those that they wish to serve, this may make them more sensitised to the use of coercion and aware of its dangers as compared with those who work in general mental health settings where the coercion is more covert. If one concludes that it would be a mistake to have a blanket ban on coercing individuals to have treatment, and recognise that in some instances this might be beneficial, what guidance can be given to promote sensible practice?

In 1994, a Group for the Advancement of Psychiatry (GAP Report 137) published the following guidelines that identified a positive outcome even when treatment was forced upon an individual. The following is a distillation of their recommendations.

- For the therapist, the following were recognised as being important:
  - The treatment itself is appropriate and effective such that there is an alliance between the coercer (i.e. the courts, family, employer, etc.) and the therapist so that both agree as to what are the patient's best interests.
  - The consequence of non-compliance (e.g. being admitted to hospital, sent to prison, etc.) must be seen as both enforceable and fair (by the patient).
  - A structure exists that ensures that the treatment indicated can be delivered (e.g. adequate funding, properly trained staff, etc.).
- For the patient, the following were recognised as being important:
  - He/she is able to understand the immediate consequences of refusing to comply with treatment.
  - He/she values what is lost in the event of not-complying.
  - He/she trusts that compliance with treatment will avert the negative consequence of not complying
  - He/she must be able to cooperate – at least minimally.
  - His/her problem is psychiatrically treatable.

Here, although though much is made of the malevolent effect of being coerced into treatment, the empirical evidence suggests that, provided certain safeguards are observed (especially with regard to the transparency of the process), this may be less of a problem than appears on the surface.

A theoretical development from psychotherapy that might advance this area is Safran and Muran's (2000) focus on therapeutic ruptures. Their position is that when working with individuals who have relationship difficulties, 'ruptures' in the therapeutic alliance are almost inevitable. Hence the question is not whether these will occur as this is guaranteed; rather it becomes how these 'ruptures' are managed. They suggest a four-fold process involving (1) an explicit recognition of the rupture – paying particular attention to changes in the therapeutic encounter that include changes in affect, increased irritation and decreased involvement. This is followed by (2) exploring the reasons for the rupture, especially the patient expressing negative feelings about the rupture. This in turn is followed by (3) the patient describing their experience of the rupture – that is validated by the therapist. This may include the therapist acknowledging that he/she may have been at fault. Finally, (4) if, for whatever reason, the above process cannot be resolved, then attention is at least given to ways in which the patient can recognise and avoid ruptures in the future.

It seems to me that within a coercive therapeutic environment (where ruptures are likely to be part of the staple diet) the process as described by Safran and Muran might be very liberating for both therapist and patient alike. For by explicitly recognising that the patient is a co-equal partner in the process and by making it transparent, this might defuse some of the animosity that is an inevitable component of such encounters.

Is the law effective in protecting a patient's rights?

The final question that I wish to consider is whether resorting to legal processes is an effective way of protecting the patient from the intrusive (and unwelcome) impact of mental health practice. In contrast to other areas of medical intervention that depend on an assessment of the individual's 'capacity' as to whether or not a form of intervention ought to be compulsorily imposed, those with mental disorder are treated differently. For instance, as Part IV, s. 63 of the 1983 Mental Health Act makes clear, the patient's consent (in treating his/her mental disorder) shall not be required '... if the treatment is given by or under the direction of the responsible medical officer'. How therefore is 'treatment' interpreted by the courts and does this interpretation provide the patient any guarantee that his/her rights to refuse a mental health intervention will be respected? The greater the latitude in this interpretation of 'treatment' by the courts, the fewer safeguards the patient has in being able to resist its imposition. I will argue that current legal processes offer little in protecting a patient's rights. Although this may seem discordant to professionals who operate within the mental health system, I believe that any fair reading of the judgments in this area suggests that these almost invariably side with the mental health professionals rather than with the patient.

There is also another phenomenon to observe and that is that in a contest between the patient's right to refuse 'treatment' and professionals' responsibility to impose it, the pendulum often swings first in the patient's direction, only for this initial judgment to be reversed in a higher court so that the *status quo* favouring the professional is re-established. I shall provide a few examples that are representative of this theme.

The *R v. Cannons Park Mental Health Tribunal* case examined whether the 'treatability test' (the test allowing for the involuntary detention of a patient with 'psychopathic disorder') was properly met (see Baker and Crighton (1995) for a full discussion). Briefly, a woman (A), who was legally detained as having 'psychopathic disorder' and who was deemed to be treatable with psychotherapy offered in a group setting, refused to engage with the treatment offered. On the basis of her unwillingness to engage with the treatment, it was argued that she was 'untreatable' and therefore that she ought to be released.

Although the Cannons Park Mental Health Tribunal accepted that this medical treatment was unlikely 'to either alleviate or prevent a deterioration in her condition' as A refused to comply, it nevertheless refused A's application to be discharged. A then applied for a judicial review to the High Court that reversed the tribunal's decision with Justice Sedley stating that '... it was never appropriate under the provisions of the 1983 Act ... for a patient to be detained in a hospital for medical treatment for psychopathic disorder if he or she is not at that point treatable'. (*R v. Cannons Park* 1994a at 491).

The case was then referred to the Court of Appeal that reversed the Sedley decision arguing that there was '... evidence before the tribunal ... that over a prolonged period of treatment, consisting at first of not more than nursing care and persuasion to accept group therapy, followed by group therapy itself was likely to prevent deterioration of her condition, even if at first some deterioration could not be avoided ... that this might eventually lead to an improvement in the patient's condition' (Justice Kennedy) (*R* v. *Cannons Park* 1994b at 682).

This definition of treatment, a definition that is reiterated later in the justices' judgment, gives those who provide the treatment an extraordinary degree of latitude. It implies, for instance, that initially treatment in hospital (defined as no more than '... nursing and includes care, habitation and rehabilitation under medical supervision') is sufficient to fulfil the criterion of treatability. Hence, for the judges at the Court of Appeal, simply being detained in hospital is sufficient in itself as a form of treatment although this enforced hospitalisation was exactly the point that was before the court for a decision. This very wide interpretation of treatment was reaffirmed in a later case of *Reid* v. *Secretary of State for Scotland* (1999), in which Lord Hope in his judgment stated that 'The definition (in s. 145(1) [i.e. of treatment] is a wide one, which is sufficient to include all manner of treatment the purpose of which may extend from *cure to containment ...*' (my italics), although in this case, 'treatability was not considered necessary for the continued detention of the individual provided other conditions were met' (*Reid* v. *Secretary of State for Scotland* 1999).

It was also clear that justices in the Cannons Park case were anxious to avoid a situation where patients could obtain their release simply by not complying with whatever treatment was prescribed for them. The Appeal judges clearly saw the unacceptable implications of this, concluding that 'Were this to be accepted, patients would deem themselves untreatable simply by withholding their co-operation. That would place the key to the patient being detained in hospital in the patient's own hands which would not have been Parliament's intention' (*R* v. *Cannons Park* 1994b).

For completeness, one must state the alternative position, namely that many have been critical, of psychiatrists in particular, who have used the same 'treatability test' as a means of avoiding treating those with personality disorder leading to their exclusion from services. Here, the mentally disordered offender with personality disorder appears to be neither protected by the law in resisting treatment that he does not want nor provided with the treatment that he needs. As Hoggett (1990) acidly remarked on psychiatrists' use of the 'treatability test' for those legally defined as having psychopathic disorder that it '... is designed to protect the hospitals from responsibility towards patients whom they do not want, but provides no protection at all for the patient who does not want the hospital.' It is clear that we need to make better provision for such individuals.

This landscape might have changed markedly in 1998 when the European Convention on Human Rights was enacted in the UK since this was a liberal reforming legislation that contained several Articles to safeguard the rights of individuals (including those with mental disorder). Specifically, Articles 3, 5 and 8 (with their *caveats*) are especially relevant for those detained involuntarily because of their mental disorder.[1]

For instance, Article 3 affirmed that 'No one shall be subjected to torture or to inhuman or degrading treatment or punishment' – a prescription that might have special applicability to those detained within a mental health facility. Similarly, Article 5 reaffirmed this right 'to liberty' but included the *caveat* for '... the lawful detention of persons for the prevention of the spreading of infectious diseases, *of persons of unsound mind, alcoholics or drug addicts*, or vagrants, (my italics). Article 8, again, proclaimed the rights of individuals to privacy with no interference by a public authority except '... in the interests of national security, public safety or the economic well-being of the country, *for the prevention of disorder or crime, for the protection of health or morals, or for the protection of the rights and freedoms of others'* (my italics).

Has the introduction of these extra rights made a difference to protecting the patient from unacceptable practice? Initially, it would seem that the answer was in the affirmative in that it asserted the court's right '...to reach its own view both as to whether this appellant is indeed capable of consenting (or refusing to consent) to the treatment programme planned for him by the Responsible Medical Officer (RMO) and depending on the court's conclusion forcible administration of such treatment [breaches any of the patient's substantive human rights]' (*R v. RMO, Broadmoor Hospital and Others ex parte Wilkinson* [2002] 1 WLR 419). As, prior to the introduction of the Convention, the court's role was to satisfy itself merely that the terms of 1983 Mental Health Act were met, now its role was extended to make up its mind on the merits of the case; hence this revision constituted a significant advance. How has this been played out in practice?

This was put to the test in the case of Wilkinson – a patient in Broadmoor – who refused to consent to receiving anti-psychotic medication, but this was nonetheless administered to him against his will. (*R v. RMO, Broadmoor Hospital and Others ex parte Wilkinson* (2001) EWCA Civ 1545). Baroness Hale appeared to acknowledge the importance of the European Convention on Human Rights when she declared:

> Whatever the position before the Human Rights Act, the decision to impose treatment without consent is a potential invasion of [the patient's] rights under Article 3 or Article 8. (*R v. RMO, Broadmoor Hospital and Others ex parte Wilkinson* [2002] 1 WLR 419 at 444)

She continued that the appellant was entitled to a proper hearing on whether treatment could be imposed upon him against his will '... having regard to the likelihood of its alleviating or preventing a deterioration of his condition ...' What evidence was the court to use in arriving at its decision?

Unfortunately for the appellant, the court turned for guidance to the European Court of Human Rights in the case of *Herczegfalfy v. Austria* (1992) 15 EHRR 437 para. 82. Here, acknowledging that the '... inferiority and powerlessness which is typical of patients confined in psychiatric hospitals calls for increased vigilance ...' so as to protect patients' rights, it was clear that the court intended to take its responsibilities seriously.

But what was to guide its decision-making? Answer 'medical necessity'. Hence, provided that it could be shown that medical necessity existed, the treatment could go ahead irrespective of the patient's wishes. How did the court satisfy itself that the '... medical necessity has been convincingly shown to exist'? This was determined by (1) the degree of certainty that the individual suffers from a treatable mental disorder, (2) the seriousness of that disorder and of the risk posed by that disorder to others, and (3) the likelihood that treatment will alleviate the patient's disorder (*R* v. *Dr M ex parte N* (2003)). Unfortunately, all of these are matters about which there is considerable debate and little certainty.

To an outsider, there appears to be an unacceptable degree of circularity in this process in that if the interventions proposed by psychiatrists are resisted by the patient and the latter appeals to the court for protection, then the evidence that is brought to bear is largely produced by psychiatrists. It certainly offered poor protection to Herczegfalfy, a psychiatric patient in an Austrian hospital who was forcibly fed and medicated and who ended up in handcuffs and broken ribs as it deemed 'medically necessary' to treat him. Looking at the process from the outside it appears that any attempts at a more liberal interpretation of the law to the benefit of the patient is almost invariably followed by whatever decision previously arrived at being reversed in favour of the professional.

England and Wales (that are subject to the same mental health legislation) are clearly not the only countries faced with difficult individuals presenting the legislature with major dilemmas. I will therefore discuss two other important cases, one in the United States and the other in Australia, where similar dilemmas were faced. In each of these cases (1) the societal need for protection trumped the inmate's need to be released and (2) further detention was justified by the presence of 'treatment'.

Kansas v. Hendricks (1997)

While this case centred on the preventative detention of those who are likely to reoffend sexually in the United States, it shares many features (and concerns) associated the provision for dangerous and severe personality disorder (DSPD) in this country. Briefly, in 1994, the State of Kansas enacted a Sexually Violent Predator Act that allowed the civil commitment (i.e. the preventative detention) of persons who, due to their 'mental abnormality' or 'personality disorder', are likely to engage in 'predatory acts of sexual violence'. The introduction of this new Act was important as it replaced the previously amended mental health code that specifically excluded antisocial personality disorder as a condition satisfying the 'severe mental disorder' criterion of civil commitment. Thus the implication of this revision was that the state had a responsibility to preventatively detain dangerous sexual offenders, independent of whether the individual's dangerousness was due to a treatable condition (Greig 2002).

Shortly after the legislation was enacted, a convicted paedophile (Leroy Hendricks), a sexual offender soon to be released from prison having served a fixed-term sentence, was deemed to be of such high risk of reoffending that he was committed to a further period of indefinite detention in order to prevent him reoffending. Hendricks challenged his continued committal and, while successful initially in a lower court, predictably had this decision reversed by the Kansas Supreme Court. The case was then referred to the US Supreme Court.

After considering the evidence, the US Supreme Court found in favour of the Kansas Supreme Court (i.e. that civil commitment was lawful) on a split 5/4 verdict. Importantly, for our purposes here, was how seriously the Chief Justices took the necessity of treatment in such cases. First, there was a statutory obligation on the state to provide treatment designed to effect recovery in such cases, with treatment itself being described as '... a kind of touchstone helping to distinguish civil from punitive purposes' (*Allen* v. *Illinois* (1986). Justice Kennedy, in his judgment, took the issue of 'treatment' even more seriously when he wrote: 'If the object or purpose of the Kansas law had been to provide treatment but the treatment provisions were adopted as a sham, or mere pretext, there would have been an indication of the forbidden purpose to punish' (US Supreme Court's Reports 1997). Although this seemed counter to the Kansas State's intent to preventatively detain a dangerous sex offender on the grounds of their dangerousness alone and irrespective of their treatability, anecdotal evidence suggests that very few sex offenders who are detained in the US satisfy the conditions that they ought to be released, suggesting the treatment has not been effective.

The Garry David case

Garry David was a prisoner coming to the end of a fixed-term prison sentence in Australia when his dramatic threats of violence on release so perturbed the Victoria state government to enact special legislation to detain him. The reason that he is relevant for our purpose is that he also suffered from 'severe personality disorder', this being illustrated by extreme acts of self-mutilation. His self-mutilation was also so extreme that it provoked an intense debate between different professional groups as to whether or not he had a mental disorder that was treatable but also as to the conclusion that if someone were to act impulsively in this way, irrespective of the consequences, it implied that he was likely to behave in a reckless and dangerous manner.

The politicians found themselves caught in a cross-fire, not only between professional groups such as psychiatrists and lawyers but by other groups in society. The broader sociological implications of this dispute are well documented by Greig (2002) but one aspect is especially worthy of comment. This involved the Victorian Prison Staff Association that threatened industrial action unless 'something was done'. To this request, the Minister for Health (Tom Roper) wryly replied: 'This phrase has been heard many times in this case, the *something* often remaining unspecified, but the *done* always referring to somebody else, and in some other place, preferably far away!'

The pressure that 'something needed to be done' is common in this field and the State Government of Victoria duly introduced 'singular' legislation, the Community Protection Act, that allowed the incarceration of Garry David in either a hospital or a prison. Thus he became explicitly what many others are in practice, namely a 'psychiatric prisoner'. Although one might accept the dictum that 'hard cases do not make good law' it appears inevitable that, under pressure from the media and the public, governments will behave in precisely that manner.

In summary, an overview of recent legislation and its interpretation by the courts suggests that, despite well-meaning attempts at a humane interpretation, once the issue of potential dangerousness to the public is raised, then liberal intentions are shelved and the *status quo* is resumed.

Conclusions

In this chapter, I have considered three questions: (1) Is the reduction of antisocial behaviour the proper business of mental health professionals and what implications does a positive answer to this question have for their practice? (2) Is coercion into treatment permissible and what are its implications? (3) Is the law effective in protecting the interests of psychiatric patients from professionals that wish to impose treatment upon them?

In summary, the answer to (1) is that while the answer is in the affirmative, it is not clear as to how (or indeed if at all) current criminological programmes need to be modified for mentally disordered offenders. Similarly, I have argued (question 2) that coercion is endemic in most mental health (and indeed to some extent in all health) practice because of the imbalance of power between the recipient and the provider of the service, so that the best protection afforded to the patient is by making the process as transparent as possible. Finally, my assessment of the evidence in (3) that, while the legal constraints of the mental health process may be irritating to mental health professionals, they offer the patient very limited protection as, when it comes to the crunch, 'medical necessity' usually trumps whatever other arguments are produced in the patient's favour.

Where does that leave us, particularly in our response to the thorny issue of preventative detention? I suggest that the best safeguard for patients who have to be involuntarily incarcerated for treatment is by delivering effective treatments for the groups for which they were designed. Paul Applebaum (1988) provided similar guidance in suggesting that 'psychiatric preventative detention' ought to be limited to (1) those patients who are treatable in the setting to which they are sent, (2) the provision of the indicated treatment, and (3) detaining individuals only as long as to accomplish the needed intervention(s). While Applebaum, as a psychiatrist, focused on his own profession, these recommendations could be generalised to other disciplines.

Two issues stand out for consideration. First, are the treatments currently employed in forensic mental health effective? This is central to Applebaum's legitimisation of preventative detention (i.e. the patient gives up his/her liberty so as to obtain treatment in return – the so called principle of reciprocity). Implicit in this exchange is that the treatments applied are effective, otherwise the patient may feel understandably short-changed. His second point, namely that the resources are in place so that the indicated treatments are actually provided, is equally important but often neglected. Thus, within forensic services at the moment, can we honestly say that we have a suitably trained staff to deliver the treatments (particularly psychological treatments) that we prescribe for detained patients? If we do not, then clearly the individual's detention is illegal.

Unfortunately, we cannot be confident that (1) the most effective treatments are chosen or (2) that they are applied in the most efficient manner. This is for two reasons: (1) the basic science underpinning most mental health interventions is weak so that, in the absence of a mechanism linking the mental disorder to offending, interventions are inevitably somewhat speculative. In the absence of significant funding for basic research into mental mechanisms (and this is likely to continue), the various professions can hardly be blamed for a lack of evidence at this level; (2) what they do have to take responsibility for, however, is critically evaluating the interventions that they do apply in properly designed trials. The evidence produced in this handbook shows significant shortfalls in evidence, certainly as regards the treatment of personality disorder, sexual offending and learning disability.

However, having effective treatments is not in itself sufficient. Such treatments must not only be effective but also must be cost-effective. Costs are often neglected in this type of discourse, yet they are crucially important. Is it fair, for instance, that a relatively small number of patients in secure hospitals are able to avail of expensive interventions, while a far larger group, perhaps with the same degree of mental disorder, languish in prison usually without any intervention? Is it also not a paradox that where the cost of care is at its highest (i.e. in secure hospitals), the risk to society is at its lowest while conversely, community mental health teams that may have to deal with equally worrying patients but in a much more exposed situation, are substantially less resourced?

As there is increasing attention to the costs and benefits of interventions within the health service so that these become more transparent, forensic mental health will have to take its place among many other health practices demanding resources from an ever dwindling pot. Government officials and policy-makers will have some difficult choices to make. One does not need a crystal ball to realise that those who can demonstrate efficacy at low cost will be at a considerable advantage.

One hopeful sign for forensic services comes from an unexpected source, namely the cost impact of the ever increasing prison population. And we are not alone in this as recently the prison budget exceeded that which the State of California spent on higher education (Didion 2003). Similarly, the cost in the UK is also likely to rise substantially due to the increased numbers of automatic life sentences now being imposed on young men who behave in a violent manner. As the only way in which such men will be able to leave custody is by being granted release by the Parole Board that will have to satisfy itself that the individual's risk has been substantially diminished, this may be an opportunity for mental health services to play a crucial role. If they are to do so, however, they will need to demonstrate that (1) a proportion of these individuals have mental health needs, (2) that such needs are linked to their offending, and (3) that the interventions offered by mental health services result in a reduction of further reoffending. Unfortunately, we are far from being able to meet these objectives at the moment.

Although forensic mental health provision is more complicated than other areas of health service delivery for the reasons given above, the same methods of determining efficacy apply. Hence health practitioners have at least the same ethical obligations as others in providing services for mentally disordered offenders that are effective and efficiently delivered. Indeed, I believe there are additional ethical imperatives as (1) in general they are dealing with a marginalised, stigmatised and poorly represented group for whom mental health professionals may be the only advocates, and (2) specifically they may be intervening without the patient's consent.

Reviewing forensic mental health practice over the past 30 years leaves me with two impressions: first that this is an area of huge uncertainty with one view being replaced with another that is diametrically opposite within a short period of time. Examples are provided by the debates on 'nothing works/what works' in criminology, the association between mental disorder and offending, and the most effective treatments for offenders. As Beck and Wencel (1998) point out such extreme changes are unusual in intellectual history. The second is that whatever view is adopted it is then held very tenaciously by those who espouse it at the time – sometimes perhaps well beyond the evidence that supports it.

One positive conclusion from the review is that when one of these positions replaces the other, it is usually because improved scientific methodology has placed the debate on a firmer footing. Conversely, prescriptions based on poor scientific methodology are likely to delay the advancement of knowledge. Hence the more recent positions ought to have greater credibility compared to those that they replace. Nonetheless, as many of our current beliefs are still based on fairly fragile evidence, they might still suffer the same consequence as those that preceded them.

I believe that one of the reasons why forensic mental health professionals hold so tenaciously to their beliefs – even when they are incorrect – is that are often forced (reluctantly) to giving a 'black or white' answer in an adversarial contest. Yet many answers are likely to be in the 'gray' area of 'maybe' or 'I'm not sure' or (worse of all) 'I don't know'; these are likely to be regarded as especially unhelpful by those in authority who have to make categorical decisions. The case of Garry David – was he bad *or* mad? – typified this problem.

However, the broad sweep of history shows that much of what we currently believe to be the case is wrong. Montaigne, for instance, in his *Apology for Raymond Sebone* warned against us becoming complacent as follows:

> Since a wise man can be mistaken, and a hundred men, and many nations, yes, and human nature is mistaken for many centuries about this and that, what assurance have we that sometimes it stops at being mistaken, and in this century it is not making a mistake? (Montaigne, cited in Frame 1958: 433)

One of the challenges for the forensic mental practitioner is being able to adopt this Socratic position of uncertainty on the one hand, while on the other being able to service a process that will constantly demand definite answers.

Selected further reading

This chapter has focused on the interface between treatment and other competing concerns. Hence it is appropriate to recommend anything written by either Paul Applebaum or by William Reid. The latter has a column on Law and Psychiatry in the *Journal of Psychiatric Practice* and has a website (http://www.reidpsychiatry.com) that addresses practical concerns. The Baker and Crighton article (1995) referenced in this chapter is a very incisive review of the 'treatability' issue on psychopathy illustrating the divide between the competing discourses of medicine and the law. Finally, the special issue of *Psychology, Crime and Law* (ed. Howells) devoted to personality disorder and offending is a useful update on therapeutic approaches in this area.

Note

1 Here, I am indebted to Ralph Stanaland (Lecturer in Mental Health Law, University of Nottingham) whose views on the effects of the European Convention on Human Rights I have drawn on widely.

Cases cited

Allen v. *Illinois* (1986) 478 US 364; 106 SCt 2988; 92 LEd 2nd 296
Herczegfalfy v. *Austria* (1992) 15 EHRR 437
Kansas v. *Hendricks* (1997) US Supreme Court No. 95-1649 (see: http://findlaw.com/us/521/346.html)
R v. *Cannons Park Mental Health Review Tribunal, ex parte A* (1994) 1 All ER 481 DC (cited as 1994a)
R v. *Cannons Park Mental Health Review Tribunal, ex parte A* (1994) 2 All ER 659 CA (cited as 1994b)
R v. *Dr M ex parte M* (2003) 1 WLR 562
R v. *RMO, Broadmoor Hospital and Others ex parte Wilkinson* (2001) EWCA Civ 1545; [2002] 1 WLR 419
Reid v. *Secretary of State for Scotland* (1999) 2 AC 512

References

Andrews, D. A. (1995) 'The psychology of criminal conduct and effective treatment', in J. McGuire (ed.), *What Works: Reducing Reoffending – Guidelines for Research and Practice.* Chichester: John Wiley & Sons, pp. 35–62.
Andrews, D. A. and Bonta, J. (2003) *The Psychology of Criminal Conduct*, 3rd edn. Cincinnati, OH: Anderson.
Aos, S., Phillips, P., Bamoski, R. and Lieb, R. (2001) *The Comparative Costs and Benefits of Programmes to Reduce Crime.* Washington State Institute for Public Policy (see: http://www.wr.gov.wsipp).
Applebaum, P. S. (1988) 'The new preventative detention: psychiatry's problematic responsibility for the control of violence', *American Journal of Psychiatry*, 145: 779–85.
Baker, E. and Crighton, J. (1995) 'Ex parte A: psychopathy, treatability and the law', *Journal of Forensic Psychiatry*, 6: 101–19.
Beck, J. and Wencel, H. (1998) 'Violent crime and Axis 1 psychopathology', in A. E. Skodol (ed.), *Psychopathology and Violent Crime.* Washington, DC: American Psychiatric Association, Chapter 1.
Bonta, J., Law, M. and Hanson, K. (1998) 'The prediction of criminal and violent recidivism among mentally disordered offenders: a meta-analysis', *Psychological Bulletin*, 123: 123–42.
Bradbury, R. (1997) *Fahrenheit 451.* New York: Del Ray.
Cordess, C. and Cox, M. (eds) (1996) *Forensic Psychotherapy: Crime Psychodynamics and the Offender Patient.* London & Philadelphia: Jessica Kingsley.
Didion, J. (2003) *Where I Was From.* New York: Knopf.
Duggan, C. (2006) 'Dynamic therapy for severe personality disorder', in C. Newrith, C. Meux and P. Taylor (eds), *Personality Disorders and Serious Offending: Hospital Treatment Models.* London: Hodder Arnold, pp. 46–160.
Duggan, C. and Tyrer, P. (2002) 'Implications of comorbid personality disorder in the treatment and outcome of common mental disorders', *Psychiatry*, 1 (1): 26–9.

Frame, D. M. (1958) *The Complete Works of Montaigne*, trans. D. M. Frame. London: Hamish Hamilton.

GAP Report 137 (1994) *Forced into Treatment: The Role of Coercion in Clinical Practice*. Washington, DC: American Psychiatric Press.

Greig, D. N. (2002) 'Neither bad nor mad. The competing discourses of psychiatry, law and politics', *Forensic Focus 20*. London: Jessica Kingsley.

Hoggett, B. (1990) *Mental Health Law*, 3rd edn. London: Sweet & Maxwell.

Hollin, C. R. and Palmer, J. (2006) 'Offending behaviour programmes: history and development', in C. Hollin and E. J. Palmer (eds), *Offending Behaviour Programmes: Development, Application, and Controversies*. Chichester: John Wiley & Sons, pp. 1–32.

Howells, K., Day, A. and Thomas Peter, B. (2004) 'Treating violence: mental health and criminological models compared', *Journal of Forensic Psychiatry and Psychology*, 15: 391–406.

Lösel, F. (1996) 'Working with young offenders: the impact of the meta-analysis', in C. R. Hollin and K. Howells (eds), *Clinical Approaches to Working with Young Offenders*. Chichester: John Wiley & Sons, pp. 57–82.

McGuire, J. (2004) *Understanding Psychology and Crime: Perspectives on Theory and Action*. Maidenhead: Open University Press/McGraw-Hill Education.

McMurran, M. and Theodosi, E. (2007) 'Is treatment non-completion associated with increased reconviction over no treatment?', *Psychology, Crime and Law*, 13: 333–43.

Maden, A., Williams, J., Stephen, C. P. Wong, S. and Leis, T. A. (2004) 'Treating dangerous and severe personality disorder in high security: lessons from the Regional Psychiatric Centre, Saskatoon, Canada', *Journal of Forensic Psychiatry and Psychology*, 15: 375–90.

Martinson, R. (1974) 'What works? Questions and answers about prison reform', *The Public Interest*, 35: 22–54.

Mullen, P. E. (2002) 'Serious mental disorder and offending behaviours', in J. McGuire (ed.), *Offender Rehabilitation and Treatment: Effective Programmes and Policies to Reduce Re-offending*. Chichester: John Wiley & Sons, pp. 289–305.

Mullen, P. E. (2006) 'Schizophrenia and violence: from correlations to preventive strategies', *Advances in Psychiatric Treatment*, 12: 239–48.

Russell, M. N. (2002) 'Changing beliefs of spouse abusers', in J. McGuire (ed.), *Offender Rehabilitation and Treatment: Effective Programmes and Policies to Reduce Re-offending*. Chichester: John Wiley & Sons, pp. 243–58.

Safran, J. D. and Muran, J. C. (2000) *Negotiating the Therapeutic Alliance: A Relational Treatment Guide*. New York: Guilford Press.

Skodol, A. E., Buckley, P. and Charles, E. (1983) 'Is there a characteristic pattern to the treatment history of clinic outpatients with borderline personality?', *Journal of Nervous and Mental Disease*, 171 (7): 405–10.

Smith, T. E., Koenigsberg, H. W. and Yeomans, Fe. (1995) 'Predictors of dropout in psychodynamic psychotherapy of borderline personality disorder', *Journal of Psychotherapy Practice and Research*, 4: 205–13.

Steinert, T., Voellner, A. and Faust, V. (1998) 'Violence and schizophrenia: two types of criminal offenders', *European Journal of Psychiatry*, 12: 153–65.

Ward, T., Hudson, S. M. and Keenan, T. R. (2001) 'The assessment and treatment of sexual offenders against children', in C. R. Hollin (ed.), *Handbook of Offender Assessment and Treatment*. Chichester: John Wiley & Sons, pp. 346–61.

Chapter 21

Inpatient care and management

Kevin Gournay, Richard Benson and Paul Rogers

Introduction

Since Bedlam, one of the main tasks of mental institutions has been the protection of the public from the risks, real or perceived, from mental patients. Security through environmental measures of containment and some form of restraint have been forever present.

Up until the mid-1800s, security was through a range of mechanical restraints, commonly used across all mental institutions. However, the mid-1800s saw a strong movement to abolish mechanical restraint in favour of seclusion. It is somewhat bizarre that, 150 years later, the reverse is occurring. There is a growing movement of opinion which sees the seclusion of patients as inhumane (the argument being that it is impossible to offer humane care to a person who is behind a locked door) and mechanical restraint is being heralded as a possible alternative!

This chapter provides an overview of the salient issues facing inpatient forensic mental health services and attempts to cover the uniqueness of delivering assessment, care and management in such circumstances.

Care and control

Forensic inpatient care involves the use of a specific set of knowledge and skills, the application of which aims to balance society's need for protection through risk management, security and containment with the client's need for care, treatment and intervention.

The issues of control via security and freedom have been captured recently in a number of reports (e.g. Department of Health 1994 (The Reed Report); Home Office and Department of Health and Social Services 1975 (The Butler Report); The Tilt Report 2000). The Reed Report laid down the principle that the level of control and security for an individual patient should be the least restrictive possible in order to best manage that individual's risks to themselves and others. The Tilt Report (2000) noted that the security of a forensic unit is not an end in itself but is one of the building blocks to ensuring a safe environment allowing the supportive and interventional work to occur. Recently the Forensic Mental

Health Services Managed Care Network in Scotland (2005: 33) reported on a review of security in forensic settings and proposed the following principle should be adopted when considering the issues of security in psychiatric care:

> The purpose of security in psychiatric care is to provide a safe and secure environment for patients, staff and visitors which facilitates appropriate treatment for patients and appropriately protects the wider community.

Some writers have termed this issue the 'care versus control' debate (e.g. Kitchiner 1999; Whyte 1997) (see Figure 21.1).

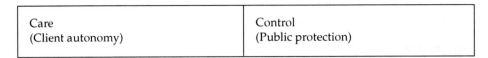

Care (Client autonomy)	Control (Public protection)

Figure 21.1 Conceptualisation of the 'care versus control' separation

Rae (1993) suggested that forensic services have been custodial in nature through environments where staff have placed too much emphasis on security, risk management and control. Rae argued that in such settings, education and training for inpatient staff, particularly nurses, was inadequate and that inpatient culture was ruled by a masculine standpoint, where care and sensitivity were seen as signs of weakness. Whittington and Balsalmo (1998) went further, suggesting that forensic environments can be brutal for both the staff and patient. Mason (2002) asked the question: 'What difficulties do psychiatric nurses, working in forensic settings, experience?' On the basis of 70 papers, Mason identified a series of major role issues, which were broadly categorised as negative and positive views, security vs. therapy, management of violence, therapeutic efficacy, training and cultural formation. Mason went on to offer six binary oppositions, or domains of practice, supposedly offered as a theoretical framework to develop further research. These were medical vs. lay knowledge, transference vs. counter-transference, win vs. lose, success vs. failure, use vs. abuse and confidence vs. fear. Further research is currently underway.

The tendency to separate care and control as two separate processes suggests that these processes are unrelated and do not interact (e.g. if staff do something that influences a person's care there is no effect on control and vice versa). Such a conceptualisation somehow views care and control as discrete 'things' that are 'done' to the client as opposed to incorporating the ethos of collaborative working.

It is more helpful to move away from such a dichotomous view of inpatient care to one which recognises the need to balance the individual's right for autonomy with the need for public protection. An alternative conceptualisation is that care and control are not two separate constructs but opposites, which lie on a continuum (the care–control continuum) (see Figure 21.2).

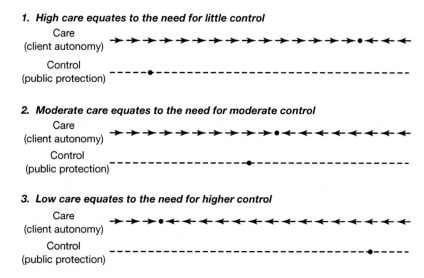

Figure 21.2 Conceptualisation of the care – control continuum

This conceptualisation suggests that the greater the level, intensity, quality and evidence base of care in collaboration with the client, the lower the need to externally exercise 'control'. Thus the more that staff and the client work together in partnership in order to address agreed goals, the less likely the need for external security measures.

Such a high-intensity approach of providing care, however, is dependent on the resources available to staff. This is a crucial issue for all clinicians and managers as the resources available within a service will, to a large degree, determine the options of care available to staff. If there is no time available to offer high-quality care then staff will be more likely to rely upon exercising measures of control as a means of managing the potential risks that a person poses.

Consequently, the care/control issue, while a dilemma for clinicians, needs to also be considered in terms of the service that clinicians work within. If staff are unable to offer patients time in order to collaborate and agree goals then the culture of the service will become restrictive and controlling where risks are undetermined or inadequately assessed and managed. The challenge for staff when exercising professional accountability for decision-making is to both consider and report how a range of external factors (e.g. pressure on bed occupancy) influences their day-to-day decisions and quality of care to individual patients and the milieu of the environment. The challenge for service managers is to understand that resources greatly affect culture and risk management.

Definition of inpatient forensic units

Recent developments in mental health services are being carried out in the context of the government's strategy for mental health as set out in *Modernising Mental Health Services* (Department of Health 1998). At that time, there was evidence that there were significant pressures on mental health beds.

Consequently, the National Beds Inquiry (Department of Health 2000) was commissioned. It found that there was a significant mismatch between mental health needs and the available services. The Inquiry also found that there were too few medium-secure and intensive-care beds, and a shortfall in supported accommodation in the community, including 24-hour staffed beds. One of the problems addressing the above findings was the lack of definition at that time as to what exactly constituted a medium-, low- or high-secure bed. Consequently, the following definitions were provided to the Health Committee (House of Commons 2000):

Low secure

Low secure or high dependency services are geared towards the client group who require long lengths of stay in a locked environment usually in excess of six months and many will require help and support for several years. Such facilities need to be lockable and focus on quality of life issues due to patients' long lengths of stay. A number of patients will have been admitted via the courts, often under a section of the Mental Health Act with restrictions, although it is deemed they do not need the higher levels of security offered in medium or high secure units. (House of Commons Select Committee on Health, Minutes of Evidence, para. A22)

This definition focuses on the length of stay required, although it fails to define 'long'. Additionally, and rather bizarrely, it defines low-secure patients as those who 'do not need the higher levels of security offered in medium or high secure units'. Therefore the definition is determined by what the patients do not need as opposed to what they do. Finally, there is no consideration as to the level of risk that the patient poses. As such, the above definition could be equally valuable to define patients with long-term treatment-resistant psychosis who have a significant number of negative symptoms.

Medium secure

Medium secure units or regional secure units are mainly geared towards forensic mental health, and although they will take patients who cannot be managed safely in local environments, they also take patients from prisons and other facilities. Medium secure facilities are intended as intensive rehabilitation units and generally therefore restrict admissions to patients who would not require a length of stay more than 18 months. They will also take people referred from the high secure hospitals, although many of these patients are assessed to require much longer lengths of stay. Many therefore remain for much longer periods than they need to in a high secure environment. (House of Commons Select Committee on Health Minutes of Evidence, para. A23)

This definition introduces the concept of 'forensic mental health' without offering any definition of what this means. Again the definition focuses on the length of admission (e.g. 18 months) but goes on to state that many high-secure patients need longer than this.

High secure

High security hospitals are intended to provide a high secure and safe environment for people regarded as a grave and immediate danger to the public. In physical security terms, the high security hospitals currently broadly equate to Category C prison standards. The average length of stay is in the region of seven to eight years, although some patients will require treatment in a high security environment for most, if not all, of their lives. (House of Commons Select Committee on Health, Minutes of Evidence, para. A24)

This definition provides reference to 'risk' by introducing the concept of a grave and immediate danger to the public. However, what constitutes 'grave' and 'immediate'? Some patients may pose a serious risk of violence to a named person in society (e.g. a family member) if they were in immediate contact with them, but the likelihood of that occurring may be near impossible and therefore pose a very low risk to everyone else. Should such patients be detained in high or medium security? Again, the length of stay is a predominant feature of the definition.

The above definitions do not provide sufficient information to assist clinicians or commissioners in truly determining which of the three types of available secure units should be chosen for a particular patient based upon their clinical presentation at that time. It could be argued that they would be of little help to a person who knows nothing about psychiatry or offending. The preoccupation with the length of stay in all three definitions without any consideration of the risks that the person poses is peculiar as it requires the clinician to somehow foresee a person's response to treatment interventions and rehabilitation.

This issue of length of detention deserves one final comment. It is apparent that it directs clinicians to 'fit' patients into one of the three types of unit as opposed to developing the appropriate security necessary to manage the risks around each individual. The question arises as to what happens to those patients who do not fit into any of these definitions or units easily, for example if they require longer than 18 months but less than seven years? Or they are a grave and immediate danger some of the time but not most of the time? Or that they require community rehabilitation but occasionally they need to be cared for in a more secure environment due to an exacerbation of acute symptoms? The probable answer is that patients are detained in higher conditions of security than necessary. The Forensic Mental Health Services Managed Care Network in Scotland (2005: 16) reviewed the research about security level and need and concluded that:

Much of the published literature illustrates the inappropriate placement of patients, usually in excessive security.

Interestingly, one would expect that decisions about which unit a person should go to are determined by their index offence and the nature of the level of security that a person needs. However, the review of the Forensic Mental Health Services Managed Care Network in Scotland (2005: 15) noted that:

A number of studies examining the patient characteristics in medium security reveal that patients with grave offences are frequently directly admitted (e.g. Murray *et al*. 1994; James *et al*. 1998; Coid *et al*. 2001). It would also be a mistake to assume that patients in England seamlessly travel down levels of security until final discharge to community care. Murray (1996) found that half of a sample of 555 patients in medium security were discharged straight into the community.

The conclusions of the review were that 'Security need is not necessarily the main factor influencing admission to medium security in England' and that 'Forensic needs assessment frameworks are in development'.

In summary, it is apparent that governmental definition is fraught with difficulties and that when examining clinical practices no clear consensus exists as to which patients should be admitted to which units.

The clinical team, multidisciplinary working and CPA

The ethos of multidisciplinary working in the care of people with mental health problems across a range of settings is now so well established that its importance is rarely if ever challenged. The acceptance of its benefits has not meant there have not been difficulties in achieving multidisciplinary working in practice. The literature reflects conflict over roles, responsibilities and accountability (Milne 1993; Diamond 1987; Margerison and McCann 1986). However, these are issues that are more related to problems in implementation rather than ideological opposition. While there is an acceptance that all healthcare professionals have a responsibility to work collaboratively the requirement has a particular resonance in forensic settings. The Confidential Inquiry into Suicides and Homicides by Psychiatric Patients (Department of Health 2001) has clearly documented the fatal consequences of a lack of effective multidisciplinary working. These dangers are apparent in general mental health services but are amplified in forensic services where the majority of the patient population have already engaged in 'risky' behaviours. Given the recognised link between previous violent behaviour and future risk the potential for these patients to re-engage in such behaviours requires careful assessment and management. In terms of the prevention of serious violence, effective multidisciplinary work within general mental health services plays a role in addressing the risk potential of a relatively small number of patients. In forensic inpatient services the base rate is higher with the risk of reoffending being significantly higher than that for a first offence for a patient under the care of general mental health services.

The effective treatment of mental disorder in any setting is clearly reliant on an effectively formulated package of multidisciplinary care. It is well established that the assessment and management of risk is a mandatory requirement of effective care in mental health services. This is reflected in it being a required component of the Care Programme Approach (CPA) in England, Scotland and Wales. CPA is a centrally devised framework for the planning, monitoring and review of the care provided by mental health services. Following its initial introduction in England in 1990, it has subsequently been adopted in slightly different versions in Wales and Scotland. The CPA framework emerged from the case management model developed in the USA to ensure that services were provided in a coordinated and effective manner (Warner 2005). The initial introduction of CPA was in response to concern about the level and consistency of aftercare and supervision provided to discharged patients. On its implementation CPA applied to inpatients at the point of discharge and to new referrals but it has subsequently been extended to everyone under the care of a mental health service. The key focus of CPA is to ensure the systematic assessment of a patient's health and social care needs, a care plan that addresses these needs, the appointment of a care coordinator and the regular review of the care plan. The CPA versions across England, Wales and Scotland all emphasise the need for the multidisciplinary team to work with the patient and other agencies to meet the identified needs.

The CPA within a forensic setting should provide a framework that facilitates an assessment and treatment approach that combines an understanding of both a patient's mental health and their potential risks. The care plan, which is at the core of the process, should be developed in partnership with the patient but also needs to take into account the views of family/carers and victim perspectives. The Home Office requires, in cases where a patient's care must involve agreement with the Home Secretary, that the victims' perspective must be given consideration. The multi-agency public protection arrangements (MAPPA) provide a framework for agencies to work collaboratively to protect the public through the appropriate sharing of information and agreeing risk management strategies (Home Office 2003). The CPA in a forensic environment should be the cornerstone on which the effective assessment and management of clinical need, including risks, is based.

Forensic nursing

Nurses working in forensic units are part of the only profession that has continuous 24-hour contact with the client group and along with medicine an overall responsibility for patients for 24-hours a day, 365 days per year. Therefore the contribution of nursing is paramount in managing both the immediate risks and care that a patient receives in inpatient settings. Additionally, nurses, by the nature of this responsibility, are likely to develop relationships with patients. This does not automatically mean that these relationships are therapeutic by their very nature, just that they exist. Furthermore, when considering that approximately half of the nursing workforce will be employed as healthcare assistants or nursing assistants and have no formal recordable qualification in nursing or any professional registration then it becomes obvious that nursing as a profession requires special consideration when considering inpatient care.

'Forensic nursing' is a relatively young concept compared to other branches of nursing. It is not recognised as a separate specialism within the wider remits of mental health/psychiatric nursing and there is no separate part of the Nursing and Midwifery Register maintained by the Nursing and Midwifery Council (NMC) which allows a nurse to register as a 'forensic nurse'.

However, forensic nurses have over the past 20 years attempted to establish a distinct specialism and define forensic nurses (as opposed to nursing) (Kettles and Robinson 2000). This is an important issue for the nursing profession and one that needs further discussion. Do forensic nurses require a separate body of knowledge, theory and skills that are separate from their colleagues in mental health nursing? Or do they merely extend pertinent areas of mental health nursing (e.g. risk assessment and risk management) in order to provide best care for their client group? Often forensic nursing is defined by the place a nurse works (e.g. high-secure hospitals, medium-secure hospitals) but not by the client group that nurses look after. This 'where you work' categorisation is somewhat misleading. For example, a person with mental health needs who has offended could be in an acute mental health unit one week, remanded in prison the next week and in medium security the following week. The person's needs, clinical presentation and risks may not have changed at all during this time. Thus it is important to delineate the difference between forensic nursing and forensic nurses. The former is a set of knowledge and skills that all nurses can be taught to apply in a variety of environments based upon the needs of the population. The latter is about nursing identity and all which that entails. This issue of identity is beyond the scope of this chapter. Furthermore, the concept of separate 'forensic nurses' only concentrates on those nurses registered with the NMC and with a recordable nursing qualification. It does not address the issue of unqualified nursing workers who make up approximately 50 per cent of the workforce which provides the management and care to patients.

The evidence base for inpatient forensic nursing

Nurses are repeatedly being challenged to be 'evidenced based'. The recent review of mental health nursing in England by the Chief Nursing Officer (Department of Health 2006a: 23) recommended that:

> All Mental Health Nurses will access, understand, and use evidence that can improve outcomes for service users.

Such an aspiration is laudable, if not rather obvious in today's climate. Surprisingly, the review did not consider any issue pertaining to forensic mental health care. Given the above recommendation, what, if any, evidence is available to support forensic nursing in inpatient settings to achieve the aim of accessing, understanding and using evidence that can improve outcomes for service users? In order to inform this chapter, an examination of the evidence base to support all mental health nurses working in inpatient settings was undertaken. Thus, irrespective of the 'forensic nursing label', an examination of the Cochrane Database of Systematic Reviews (CDSR) (Issue 2006/1) and the Database of Abstracts of Reviews of Effectiveness (DARE) (August 2006) for inpatient mental health nursing was conducted. Alarmingly, the findings were that there is no rigorous evidence base for anything that is done within inpatient settings by mental health nurses. A similar picture can be found when examining the evidence base for mental health services. A scoping review undertaken by the NHS CRD of the effectiveness of mental health services, linked to the recommendations from the English National Service Framework for Mental Health (Department of Health 1999a), found an absence of any evidence for the effectiveness of delivery of inpatient mental health services (Jepson *et al.* 2001).

Even, if we examine the evidence for mental health nursing outside of inpatient settings the findings are bleak. For example, the only available evidence that could be found of the effectiveness of nurses' contributions to patient care for those *possibly* in need of forensic services was by Woods and Richards (2003). The authors conducted a systematic review of nursing interventions for people with personality disorder (irrespective of setting) and found that of 18 studies of mental health care for people with personality disorders involving nurses, only five of these studies tested nursing-delivered interventions with wide variability in the actual interventions delivered by nurses. A range of professionals delivered the remaining eleven studies. This systematic review concluded that meta-analysis was untenable due to the heterogeneity of both interventions and outcome measures. The author's narrative analysis found that there was only a very weak evidence base for any effective nursing-delivered interventions for people with personality disorder.

Given these findings, it is questionable as to how nurses working in forensic settings can 'access, understand, and use evidence that can improve outcomes for service users' as recommended by the Chief Nursing Officer in England as there is no evidence to access. Consequently, there is a desperate need for nurses, services and research funders to recognise the limited evidence base that inpatient nurses have to determine the most effective way to care for and manage the most stigmatised and risky people for society. The need to develop an evidence base for inpatient nursing care and treatment within secondary and forensic inpatient settings must be seen as a high priority for the future.

Assessing and managing the environment

It is beyond the scope of this chapter to cover all the crucial aspects of the environment and their effects on patients' health and vice versa. The report of the Royal College of Psychiatrists (1998a) *Not Just Bricks and Mortar* provides detailed information on specific aspects of the environment. It is evident that the environment of care is crucial in all inpatient settings. It is possible and probable that poor environments not only reduce satisfaction, but also at the same time increase fear and maintain isolation. *The Mental Health Policy Implementation Guide: Adult Acute Inpatient Care Provision* recognises this and notes that:

> Poor standards of design, lack of space and access to basic amenities and comforts in much of our current inpatient provision have contributed to and reinforced service users' negative experiences of inpatient care as unsafe, uncomfortable and untherapeutic. (Department of Health 2004)

An under-reported but important aspect of inpatient management for services is the need to consider the effects that the environment has on the clinician's abilities to meet patients' needs. For example, a ward environment where violence and disturbance is high will only add to a new patient's already high levels of anxiety. Often, the effects that admitting a patient will have upon the patient are rarely considered. An example of where the environment was considered was through the results of a study examining the effectiveness of pre-admission nursing assessment in a medium secure unit (Watt *et al.* 2003a, 2003b). The authors reported on the use of their pre-admission assessment interview. Following the assessment, the nurse was asked to recommend in writing what current environmental considerations the clinical team needed to consider prior to admission (e.g. current patient mix in the proposed environment and its effect on the assessed patient; patient mix in the proposed environment and the effect of the patient on that environment). Patient mix included: gender mix in the proposed environment; religion/politics/culture/ethnicity mix in proposed environment and current resource drains in the proposed environment (e.g. observations, leave, staffing). Finally, and importantly, the nurse was asked to recommend and develop a contingency plan should the proposed admitting environment be later identified to not best match the patient's care and management needs. Although such detailed assessment of environmental effects and planning may not be possible on all referrals to forensic services (e.g. in times of emergencies), it is still necessary to carefully consider, prior to admission, the patient's potential effect on the ward environment and the ward environment's potential effect on the patient

Therapeutic environment

This chapter has covered a wide range of issues connected with the environment in which care and treatment takes place. As noted previously, *Not Just Bricks and Mortar* (Royal College of Psychiatrists 1998a) sets out some very important issues relating to the architecture of mental health units. While any planning of a new mental health unit will have factors such as ligature points and sightlines for observation as very important concerns, there is also a great need to attend to simple, but essential matters, such as the provision of access to fresh air and daylight. Unfortunately, many of the units planned in the post-deinstitutionalisation era failed to meet these basic requirements and patients are still housed in inpatient wards without easy access to either fresh air or daylight. Another obvious environmental issue is that of access to exercise. It seems particularly ironic that, despite the vulnerability of people with mental health problems to a range of physical disorders and with a notably higher than normal standardised mortality rate, there is often very restricted access to exercise. Providing a gymnasium and the correct equipment is only the first step in using exercise as a therapeutic tool. Furthermore, while those of us who exercise expect to go to a gym where we receive a detailed assessment from a fitness instructor and aspire to having supervised training from a personal trainer, the forensic patient is often provided with the facility without having access to this assessment, programme planning and ongoing supervision. The NICE guidelines for the treatment of depression (NICE 2004) recommend that exercise should be a first-line treatment for mild to moderate depression. However, mental health services do not offer this as a first-line treatment to inpatients, either in acute or forensic settings.

This chapter has also covered other issues that contribute to a 'therapeutic' environment, including providing wards that are sensitive to the patient's gender and ethnicity. If services do not provide environments that accommodate these needs, higher-level interventions (such as psychological therapies and medication) will not achieve their potential impact.

The final issue in providing a therapeutic environment is ensuring that all staff receive a reasonable level of training in matters such as observation, management of violence and aggression and assessment of mental state. All of these areas are deficient in respect of pre-registration training and the surveys carried out as background to the Standing Nursing Midwifery Advisory Committee Report on Inpatient Care (Department of Health 1999b) and the United Kingdom Central Council for Nursing, Midwifery and Health Visiting Report on the Prevention and Management of Violence (United Kingdom Central Council 2001) shows that a sizeable proportion of the inpatient workforce lack such training. Although there have been recent attempts to rectify this situation, it will be many years before all staff are appropriately trained.

Single-sex wards and gender issues

A systematic review undertaken by Lart *et al.* (1999) asked what are the needs of women in prison and secure services, and how effective are models of psychiatry currently employed for women in prisons in the UK and abroad? The review employed data from 62 papers, of which most described populations in England, Australia or the USA. The review found that less than 20 per cent of forensic service users were women, who are heterogeneous with regard to age and personal, psychiatric and forensic histories. Additionally, women were less likely to have committed serious offences and were more likely to have experienced a previous psychiatric admission. As commonly known, the review found that women were more likely to be diagnosed with a personality disorder and borderline personality disorder.

Since this review, there has been widespread recognition that women patients in mixed-sex inpatient mental health units are vulnerable to harassment and abuse by male patients (Mezey *et al.* 2005; Department of Health 2002). This concern led to government policy requiring the availability of women-only facilities for inpatient care with services needing to phase out any mixed sex units and direct direction that no new mixed sex units would be approved (Department of Health 2002, 2003b). It has been suggested by Mezey *et al.* (2005) that female forensic patients may be particularly vulnerable as inpatients given the higher incidence of histories of abuse within this population. However, the debate surrounding the segregation of sexes within forensic inpatient services has been limited by a shortage of empirical evidence. The assumption that female inpatients in forensic services feel safer if in a single-sex environment is partially supported by Mezey *et al.* (2005). Although the women in single-sex environments felt less vulnerable in relation to the threat of sexual assault or harassment, many would have preferred to be on a mixed-sex ward. An important finding was that women felt at no less risk of physical violence if on mixed wards, perhaps not that surprising given that women as well as men are liable to be detained in secure units because of their risk of violence (Mezey *et al.* 2005). The women patients tended to view single-sex wards as punitive and stigmatising. Additionally, it was perceived that the staff on the single-sex wards underestimated the extent of more subtle forms of abuse and bullying. On mixed sex wards there was the perception that staff minimised women's vulnerability to unwanted sexual approaches from male patients (Mezey *et al.* 2005). This study in many ways encapsulates the difficult issues involved with the development of single-sex wards. Although they may have the potential to provide women patients with a greater degree of protection from the risk of sexual harassment or assault they might subsequently be exposed to high levels of bullying and intimidation. It is possible that enforced separation may simply reinforce the stereotype of men as predatory without significantly reducing the risks that women are exposed to.

There are particular challenges in providing single-sex accommodation for women in secure services in a way that both recognises the homogeneity of clinical need and the requirement for a cost-effective service. The ratio of women to men found in secure inpatient units is approximately 1:5 (Coid *et al.* 2000; Hassell and Bartlett 2001). Consequently, there are practical difficulties in providing a locally delivered service that is able to offer women-only wards while also ensuring that wards do not have an inappropriate mix of patients based on diagnosis, dependency levels and security needs.

It has been pointed out by Parry-Cooke (2000) that there is a wide range of views from women in secure services about the perceived benefits of singe-sex wards. The question of how much weight should be attached to the views of women patients regarding this issue needs addressing. There is a broad consensus that patient choice should be a factor influencing the delivery of mental health services. However Mezey *et al.* (2005) point out that forensic mental health patients are rarely, if ever, given a choice on the place they are to be detained and go on to question whether women who are so vulnerable are always best placed to recognise and avoid the situations that may put them at most risk. What is clear from the limited evidence base available is that there is a need to assess women in forensic services for the risk both of perpetrating and being vulnerable to violence, harassment and bullying regardless of whether the ward is single-sex or not.

Black and minority ethnic groups

The issue of black and minority ethnic (BME) groups and health inequality in all mental health services has received increasing attention over recent years (Department of Health 2005). For example, a recent survey conducted by Sproston and Nazroo (2000) found that there are ethnic inequalities in physical health and a systematic review by Bhui (2003) found that there are significant differences between white and minority ethnic groups in experiences of mental health services and the outcome of such service interventions. Following the death of David Bennett in a medium-secure unit and the subsequent inquiry report, BME issues were given more attention. This inquiry report identified a number of issues arising from the death of David Bennett which occurred while he was being restrained in a forensic mental health inpatient unit (Cambridge, Norfolk, Suffolk and Cambridgeshire Strategic Health Authority 2004). The report set out 22 recommendations for the improvement of mental health services as experienced by BME communities.

In 2005, the first national mental health and ethnicity census of inpatients in mental health hospitals carried out by the Mental Health Act Commission found that the rates of admission to hospital were more than three times for black and white-black mixed groups compared with the average. Additional findings showed that black groups were up to 44 per cent more likely to be detained under the Mental Health Act and twice as likely to be referred by police. Furthermore, inpatient experiences differed with black men being 50 per cent more likely to have been secluded at least once during the three months prior to the census. In the same year *Delivering Race Equality in Mental Health* set out a clear action plan for achieving equality and eradicating unlawful discrimination in mental health services in England (Department of Health 2005). The vision is that by 2010 there will be services characterised by:

> ... less fear of mental health services among BME communities and service users; increased satisfaction with services; a reduction in the rate of admission of people from BME communities to psychiatric inpatient units; a reduction in the disproportionate rates of compulsory detention of BME service users in inpatient units; fewer violent incidents that are secondary to inadequate treatment of mental illness; a reduction in the use of seclusion in BME groups; the prevention of deaths in mental health services following physical intervention; more BME service users reaching self-reported states of recovery; a reduction in the ethnic disparities found in prison populations; a more balanced range of effective therapies, such as peer support services and psychotherapeutic and counselling treatments, as well as pharmacological interventions that are culturally appropriate and effective; a more active role for BME communities and BME service users in the training of professionals, in the development of mental health policy, and in the planning and provision of services; and a workforce and organisation capable of delivering appropriate and responsive mental health services to BME communities. (Department of Health 2005: 17)

The Forensic Mental Health Research and Development Programme published an expert paper in 2000 (Ndegwa 2000). This paper examines a number of important issues relating to the research evidence regarding the experiences of people from BME. However, little is known about the effects of the inpatient environment on health. Although the proportion of black and minority ethnic groups may be overrepresented in secure services, there may be situations that lead to patients from these communities feeling isolated. For example, the inquiry report into the death of David Bennett noted that the majority of patients were white and that there were very limited facilities for black and minority ethnic groups in the local area, particularly for African-Caribbeans. The Inquiry found that there were no clubs for black people, no local advocacy groups and no recreational activities specifically provided for black people.

Implications for professional practice, clinical practice and local policy are only gradually emerging and the impact on forensic services is yet to be fully determined. However, it is highly likely that black and minority ethnicity issues will become a key area that forensic services will be required to address. In addition, the need to embed the growing recommendations into undergraduate curricula has received little attention thus far but would appear to be an important consideration for the planners and deliverers of those curricula.

Overview of violence and aggression

Violence reduction and violence management have become key policy and practice workforce priorities for mental health and criminal justice agencies across the UK over the last ten years: Scottish Health Service Management Executive (1996); Royal College of Psychiatrists (RCP) (1998b); NHS Executive (2000); Nursing and Midwifery Council (NMC) (2001); NHS Security Management Service (NHS SMS) (2001); National Audit Office (NAO) (2003); Welsh Assembly Government (WAG) (2004); National Institute for Clinical Excellence (NICE) (2005a); National Institute for Mental Health England (NIMHE) (2005); and the Wales Audit Office (WAO) (2005). Although it has been well documented that violence is a major occupational hazard for mental health staff, it is only recently that the management of the issue through violence reduction measures has received the attention needed. However, recent interest in the approach continues to be hampered by a lack of high-quality research in order to inform policy and practice decision-making.

Interest in the issue of violence towards healthcare workers has grown dramatically over the past 20 years. In particular, attention has focused on violence and services for people with mental health problems or learning disabilities. There are many definitions of violence which makes public health initiatives relying on counting violent incidents and research fraught with difficulties. A number of reports outline the incidence of aggression and violence in services using different outcome measures. Consequently, in October 2005, NHS SMS published the first figures based on consistent definitions and this indicated that staff working in mental health and learning disability services faced a higher risk than nurses in other areas. The Department of Health (2003a) introduced a new national reporting system based on legal definitions of physical and non-physical assault. These clarified reporting procedures to ensure a consistent approach. The definition for physical assault, which replaced all previous definitions used in the NHS in England, was:

> The intentional application of force to the person of another, without lawful justification, resulting in physical injury or personal discomfort. (*Eisener v. Maxwell* (1951); *Kaye v. Robinson* (1991))

The NHS SMS (2001) stress that all incidents of physical assault must be reported. This applies whether they were committed intentionally or were linked to the patient's clinical condition. The nature and extent of an association between mental disorder and violence is highly controversial. There is no single model of violence causation. The risk factors for violence are multifaceted and triggers vary based on individual factors. Society or mental health professionals cannot therefore 'remove' such factors that are *causal* of violence as none have been identified. Consequently, a multifaceted approach to understanding violence, preventing violence and managing violence is needed. What may work for one person may not for another. Gaining an understanding of these factors and how they interact is the best way to prevent violence over the long term. The public health model advocated by the WHO to address workplace violence sees prevention as having three dimensions: primary, secondary and tertiary (WHO 2002). Each dimension is important, but the main emphasis is on primary prevention.

In terms of current evidence base, NICE published the Clinical Practice Guidelines for Violence, *The Short-term Management of Disturbed/Violent Behaviour in Psychiatric In-patient Settings and Emergency Departments* (NICE 2005a). Table 21.1 provides an overview of the findings of the NICE review in relation to the prevention of violence. The evidence base for prevention is somewhat limited and reflects the lack of high-quality research in this area. For example, the findings relating to antecedent and warning signs are based upon only one cohort study considered to be of sufficient design to enable generalisation (Whittington and Patterson 1996). However, given the epidemiological evidence that there is no single causal model of violence prevention then it is not surprising that a range of prevention strategies are indicated as no one model fits all problems. The NICE guidance concluded that disturbed/violent behaviour can never be predicted with 100 per cent accuracy. However, this does not mean that risk assessment should not be carried out.

Table 21.1 NICE findings on the evidence base for the prevention of violence

Question being addressed	Findings
What factors in the physical environment of adult psychiatric in-patient settings contribute to either the promotion or reduction of of disturbed/violent behaviour?	Evidence suggests that environmental factors; such as crowding, banning smoking, high staff turnover and limit-setting have an affect on the incidence of disturbed/violent incidents. Further research needed.
What are staff and service users' views about the role of the ward environment in promoting or reducing disturbed behaviour?	Evidence suggests that both staff and service users believe that environmental factors such as banning smoking, limit-setting, medication, seclusion, physical interventions and communication affect the incidence of disturbed/violent incidents. Further research needed.
What are the risk factors and antecedents for disturbed/ violent behaviour in psychiatric in-patient settings? Do they have good predictive validity?	Evidence suggests that the following may act as antecedents/warning: verbal abuse, aggressive/ agitated behaviour, threatening gestures, abnormal activity levels and staff limit-setting. Further research needed.
Which instruments most reliably predict disturbed/violent behaviour in psychiatric settings in the short term?	Evidence suggests that clinicians' judgment has a relatively low predictive validity, only slightly better than chance.

Table 21.1 (continued)

Question being addressed	Findings
Do they have good predictive validity?	Evidence suggests that the following may be risk factors: community violence, male gender, young age, younger age at first hospitalisation, not having own clothing, low level of self-care functioning, number and duration of admissions, coercive behaviour and lack of satisfaction of care, a diagnosis of organic psychotic condition, personality disorder, schizophrenia, and bipolar affective disorder. Further research needed. Evidence suggests greater predictive accuracy with actuarial tools than with clinical judgment alone. Insufficient evidence to determine a 'gold standard' predictive actuarial tool. Further research needed. Evidence suggests that there is greater predictive accuracy with structured clinical judgment tools than with clinical judgment. Insufficient evidence on which to determine a 'gold standard' structured clinical judgment instrument.
Are there any identifiable staff characteristics that act as risk factors for disturbed/violent behaviour?	Limited evidence suggests that the following staff characteristics may be associated with increased occurrence of incidents of disturbed/violent behaviour: younger age, level of experience, training and grade, gender and involvement in limit-setting activities. Further research is needed.
What factors do service users and staff report as increasing the risk of disturbed/violent behaviour?	Limited evidence suggests that service users regard external factors (such as limit-setting, verbal abuse by staff and other service users, lack of respect by staff and harassment) as likely reasons for assault rather than internal factors (that is, caused by illness). Limited evidence suggests that staff users regard internal factors (that is, caused by illness) and the interplay between internal and external factors (such as staff limit-setting) as contributing to disturbed/violent behaviour.

Table 21.2 provides an overview of the findings of the NICE review in relation to training. Again the evidence base for training is limited. For example, the findings relating to current training practices in the UK are based upon only four cross-sectional studies. The NICE review concluded that the limited scope of these studies limits the ability to generalise the findings.

Table 21.2 NICE findings on the evidence base for the effectiveness of training programmes

Question being addressed	Findings
What are the most effective and safe training programmes for the prevention of and the short-term management of disturbed/violent behaviour in adult psychiatric in-patient settings?	Limited evidence suggests that short-term improvements in knowledge, skills and reduction in stress occur after staff training. Evidence on current training practices in the UK indicates that there is a lack of standardisation in the way staff are targeted for courses, and in the range of interventions covered. In addition, the effectiveness of training has not been adequately evaluated in a clinical environment. The lack of evaluations of the effectiveness of training in a clinical environment means that a 'gold standard' training package cannot be determined.
What are the views of staff and service users about the various training programmes in adult psychiatric inpatient settings and their content?	Limited evidence suggests that training service users to respect themselves, peers and staff may reduce the occurrence of disturbed/violent incidents. Staff perceive that training in the short-term management of disturbed/violent behaviour is beneficial and that it also increases confidence. The evidence suggests that staff often feel that their need for training is not met. Insufficient evidence to determine service user perspectives on service user training to help them manage their disturbed/violent behaviour.

A more recent study (Rogers *et al.* 2006) which was published after the NICE guidance has questioned the effectiveness of current UK-based training. Recent policy guidance within the UK recommends that all mental health professionals who work in areas where they may be exposed to violence should have 'breakaway training' and that this should be refreshed yearly. This study evaluated the effectiveness of breakaway training in a sample of clinically based mental health nurses in a medium-secure forensic mental health unit. Participants were opportunistically recruited ward-based nursing staff.

Three registered mental health nurses randomly attended the wards, two of whom were breakaway instructors and one a ward manager. The participant was asked to select at random a breakaway technique to perform. Each participant was given five seconds to think about the scenario before given the instruction to commence. The scenario would then be enacted. Where ten seconds had elapsed, the scenario was stopped. The results found that of the 50 nurses asked to participate in the study, 47 agreed (94 per cent). All had had breakaway training. Eleven staff had received the full breakaway training more than once and 24 had at least one update since their original breakaway training course. None of the sample had used a breakaway technique in the preceding 12 months. Forty per cent (19/47) were unable to breakaway within the ten-second period. Of the entire sample, 60 per cent of staff did not employ the correct breakaway technique. Although replication is required, the results from this study question the efficacy of the current breakaway training in assisting staff to breakaway from an assailant.

In summary, therefore, the evidence base for prevention suggests that a range of issues need to be considered, while the evidence base for the effectiveness of training is limited. Given that any training programme should heavily rely upon the evidence base for prevention then it is difficult to determine what such training should include. Paradoxically, the NICE guidance provides hardly any guidance with which one can have confidence given the limitations of the studies which were included. Nonetheless it does provide some general 'point-ers' as to what may prevent violence and what may be effective in relation to training programmes. Given that practice change is dependent on training, this leads us to the question of how can those involved in mental health or criminal justice turn the policy imperative of violence reduction into practice? A two-pronged approach is obviously required. If the evidence base is weak then this must be strengthened. Funding is required to evaluate prevention strategies and training programmes, while at the same time a pragmatic approach which encompasses a range of strategies is required in violence reduction and training.

The evidence base for seclusion and restraint

A further example of the lack of evidence base to support forensic nursing can be found when considering seclusion and restraint, both of which are predomi-nantely procedures undertaken by nurses in inpatient settings. A Cochrane review undertaken by Salias and Fenton (2001) focused on the effectiveness of restraint and seclusion or strategies designed to reduce the need for restraint and seclusion in the treatment of mental illness. It found no trials that met the minimum criteria. The review (2001: 41) concluded:

> In the absence of any controlled trials in those with serious mental illness, no recommendation can be made about the effectiveness, benefit or harm-fulness of seclusion or restraint. In view of data from non-randomised studies, use should be minimised for ethical reasons.

A literature review undertaken for the United Kingdom Central Council for Nursing, Midwifery and Health Visiting report on the recognition, prevention and therapeutic management of violence in mental health care also found 'no high-quality studies that evaluated either the use of restraint or of seclusion in those with mental illness' (United Kingdom Central Council 2002). When considering that seclusion was advocated as an alternative to mechanical restraint in the 1840s, the fact that not one high-quality study examining its use can be reported must be considered alarming. Yet the Review of the Chief Nursing Officer for England rec-ommends that nurses should achieve something which is impossible – having access to, understanding and using evidence that can improve outcomes for serv-ice users. At present it is quite clear that this is not possible.

Observations

The observation of patients in all forensic and mental health inpatient facilities is one of the most important elements of inpatient care and observation is a core skill of mental health nurses. Although the section below will focus on the specific process of observing patients who are at risk of suicide/self-harm and violence, there is a need to emphasise that simple observation of all patients is an essential part of assessing the patient's condition and evaluating their progress. There are two specific elements to the observation process that need emphasis. The first is what to observe and the second is how such observations are recorded. The specifics of what needs to be observed are, in a sense, predefined in the initial clinical team assessments. Thus, for example, a depressed patient may well have a reduction in psychomotor activity, a preponderance of negative and self-defeating statements in their speech and a sad appearance. The nurse should therefore record their observations quite specifically and, rather than saying that the patient looks depressed, actually define the specific components of behaviour, speech and speech content.

The observation process of inpatients has recently been subject to scrutiny within the work of the Standing Nursing Midwifery Advisory Committee (Department of Health 1999b) and the development of NICE Guidance on the Management of Disturbed/Violent Behaviour in Mental Health Care (NICE 2005b). Both the Standing Nursing Midwifery Advisory Committee and NICE Guidelines emphasise the need to engage positively with the patient and the need to make the whole process as therapeutic as possible. The NICE Guidance states explicitly that every NHS trust must have a policy on observation and engagement and that the policies must include: who can instigate observation; who can increase or decrease observation levels; who must review the level of observation; when reviews must take place; how service user perspectives will be taken into account; and a process through which a review by the full clinical team will take place if observation above a general level is used for more than one week.

These guidelines define four levels of observation:

1 *General observation*. This is the minimum acceptable level for all inpatients. The location of all patients should be known to staff but not all patients need to be kept within sight. At least once per shift, the nurse should set aside a dedicated time to assess the mental state of the patient and engage positively with them. The aim should be to develop a positive, caring and therapeutic relationship and, at this time, there should be an evaluation of the patient's mood and behaviours associated with the risks they pose. These observations should be recorded in the patient's notes.
2 *Intermittent observation*. In this level of observation, the patient's whereabouts must be checked every 15 to 30 minutes (exact times should be specified in the notes following a multidisciplinary review). There is an emphasis on needing to ensure that at each observation there is positive engagement with the patient. This level is appropriate when patients are potentially, but not immediately, at risk of suicide/self-harm or disturbed/violent behaviour. Patients who have previously been at risk of harming themselves or others

but who are in the process of recovery require intermittent observation as a 'step down' from constant (within eyesight) observation.

3 *Within eyesight observation*. This is required when the patient could, at any time, make an attempt to harm themselves or others. The patient should be kept within eyesight and accessible at all times by day and by night and, if deemed necessary, any tools or instruments that could be used to harm themselves or others should be removed. It may be necessary to search the patient and their belongings, while having due regard to their legal rights, conducting the search in a sensitive way, which should be both reasonable and proportionate to the risks involved.

4 *Within arm's length observation*. This level of observation is used for patients who are at the highest risk of harming themselves or others and who need to be observed in close proximity. On rare occasions more than one member of staff may be necessary. While issues of privacy, dignity and consideration of gender in allocating staff are paramount, the overriding issue here is one of preserving safety.

There are a number of important issues that are essential in the management of patients at risk within all inpatient settings. Every patient needs to have their required observation level defined on admission and this process must be carried out by a qualified nurse and the responsible medical officer or their deputy. This is a minimum requirement, in terms of those making the decision, although obviously such decisions are best taken by as many people in the clinical team as possible. The decision to reduce the level of the patient's observations can only be taken as part of a joint process between nursing and medical staff. The decision to reduce observation levels should follow a joint risk assessment and should be recorded in the patient's clinical notes. With regard to increasing the level of observation, members of the nursing staff can make this decision unilaterally if the patient demonstrates an increased level of risk, but this decision should be followed as quickly as possible by a clinical team review. Similar to other clinical decisions, a careful note should be made in the patient's records, outlining the rationale for making the decision.

One issue that often crops up in the process of caring for patients at high levels of observation is the need to observe the patient on those occasions when they are attending to basic bodily functions or personal hygiene. Collaboration with the client should always take place on how best to manage the need for observation while also ensuring their safety. The team should discuss these matters very carefully and there should be clear decisions made about whether, for example, the patient is observed bathing, using the lavatory, etc. These decisions should be clearly recorded in the case record and there needs to be explicit mention made of each and every possible situation when observation may need to be continuous or indeed temporarily suspended.

Absconding

The term 'absconding' refers to a patient detained under the Mental Health Act 1983 who leaves a mental health inpatient unit without the agreement of their care team or who breaches the terms of an agreed leave (NPSA 2006). There has been recent focus on quantifying and reducing the levels of absconding from acute psychiatric wards (Bowers *et al.* 2002; NPSA 2006).

The latest report of the National Confidential Inquiry into Suicides and Homicides by People with a Mental Illness, published in 2006 (Department of Health 2006b) reported that 27 per cent of inpatient suicides occurred after the patient had left the ward without permission. These deaths mostly occurred in the first seven days after admission. The inquiry report emphasised that, while there was a great need to balance patient autonomy and safety, there was a need to provide solutions, because – as the report stated – 'the current situation in which patients admitted for their own protection can leave a ward within a few hours or days cannot continue'. The report recommended that wards can reduce absconding by understanding the factors that trigger it, such as a disturbed ward environment or an incident affecting the patient and making greater use of technology such as CCTV or a swipe card to observe and control ward entry and exit.

Given the self-evident link between the assessed need for a patient to be cared for in secure conditions and the perceived risk they pose, absconding is of particular importance in forensic inpatient settings. It is a guiding principle for mental health services that patients should be cared for in the least restrictive environment commensurate with their clinical needs and risk (Department of Health 1999a). Therefore, where a decision is made to detain a patient in a secure setting, it should be made as a result of either a risk assessment indicating its necessity or because of legal requirements. There should be a clear relationship between the level of security in which a patient is detained and the potential risk they pose.

As discussed earlier in this chapter, there has been criticism about the lack of clarity and consistency that exists in defining high-, medium- and low-security mental health units (Collins and Davies 2005). The lack of widely accepted definitions is referred to by Kennedy (2002) in describing the wide variation that exists in the levels of physical security provided by medium-secure units. A decision to admit a patient to a specified level of security based on an evidence-based risk assessment is not an end in itself. This should merely facilitate the appropriate care and treatment. The Forensic Mental Health Services Managed Care Network in Scotland (2005) identified the potential danger of judging the success of the clinical management of patients solely on security outcomes such as the number of patients absconding. A key component of any risk management plan should be the testing out of patients in a structured fashion. It may be possible to achieve a very low rate of absconding by not reducing levels of security but by doing so there is a failure to achieve wider treatment goals. It is the role of security to provide a basis in which clinical interventions can take place and from which patients can progress.

Managing and caring for suicidal/self-harming patients

The latest report of the National Confidential Inquiry into Suicides and Homicides by People with a Mental Illness, published in 2006 (Department of Health 2006b), reported on suicide by current or recent mental health patients occurring between April 2000 and December 2004. The Inquiry investigated

6,367 cases representing 27 per cent of all suicides in England and Wales during this period. This figure translates to over 1,300 patient suicides per year. Of the 6,367 cases, 856 were suicides by inpatients. Although the number of inpatient suicides reported for this particular period fell from the figure reported in the previous Inquiry (Department of Health 2001), there is little doubt that many of these tragedies were preventable. There are three major issues concerning the prevention of suicide or serious self-harm by inpatients: (1) absconding; (2) observation; and (3) the ward environment.

Suicide/self-harm and observation

The inquiry report stated that 22 per cent of inpatient deaths occurred in people who were (or were supposed to be) under observation. Eighteen (3 per cent) were said to be under 1:1 observation at the time of the suicide. As the report stated, the conclusions are clear. Firstly, intermittent observation regimes provide long gaps in observation and they are unsuitable for the care of high-risk patients unless additional measures are taken, such as the observation of ward exits. Secondly, close observation must be strictly carried out. There should be no gaps in 1:1 observation and, if the patient is to be observed every ten minutes, this time gap must be closely adhered to.

Observation is, too often, delegated to healthcare assistants and to bank and agency staff who have little knowledge of the individual patient or the ward. Obviously – and as both the Standing Nursing Midwifery Advisory Committee and NICE Guidance suggest – observation should be carried out by members of nursing staff who have been appropriately trained and who have good knowledge of the patient and the ward environment.

Suicide/self-harm and the ward environment

Most inpatient suicides still occur through self-strangulation and, while inpatient suicides have been reduced, partly because of the efforts made to remove non-collapsible curtain rails and other obvious ligature points, there is a need to think carefully about all aspects of the ward environment, including wardrobe doors, hooks and handles on windows and doors.

Inpatient suicide remains a major challenge for all mental health services and, at the time of writing this chapter, there is universal agreement that we need to do much more to reduce unnecessary deaths. While the primary responsibility for caring for suicidal patients rests with the nursing staff, there is a need to emphasise the role of the other professions involved in care and treatment and the need for mental health services to provide the necessary support in terms of managing risks in the environment, from ligature points to dealing with risks posed by doors and windows.

Service models

Evidence-based mental health care is the conscientious, explicit and judicious use of current best evidence in making decisions about the care of individual patients. There is a scarcity of evidence regarding the effectiveness of mental health service models and when compared to other fields of health research, this lack of evidence is alarming. As Lewis *et al.* pointed out in 1997, while, for example, there is a relatively complete effectiveness literature in obstetrics and gynaecology and this is being continually reviewed and updated, the task for the mental health profession is truly Herculean.

A recent scoping review of effective service models in (non-forensic) mental health based upon 36 completed systematic reviews and eight Cochrane protocols by the NHS Centre for Reviews and Dissemination (CRD) (CRD report 21 2001) found that there was only evidence for assertive outreach and community mental health teams, both of which are community-based models. There was no evidence of which service models are most effective in mental health inpatient settings or forensic inpatient settings. However, one of the problems with evaluating the effectiveness of these service models is that different organisations have different interpretations about what these terms mean and therefore fidelity to an assertive outreach or community mental health team 'model' is difficult to determine. What is assertive outreach in one trust may be a completely different thing in another.

In 1999, the CRD published a systematic review of the international literature on the epidemiology of mentally disordered offenders. Thirty-eight articles related to the British special hospitals were reviewed in this report. Much of the reviewed research concentrated on the characteristics of the patients, their diagnoses and behaviour. This review concluded that 'Few studies consider institutional factors like admission policies, staff attitudes and the physical design of the institution'. In the same year (1999b), CRD published a further scoping review which examined 'the health and care of mentally disordered offenders' (MDOs). The review examined 'pathways into and out of care', reporting:

> Very few studies have addressed pathways through the full range of provision; most take a small section only. Given the complexity, it was difficult to assess whether or not the system works. There is certainly a level of bias inherent in interactions between MDOs and various parts of the system based on a range of factors (which vary) but the overall effect of this is unclear.

In relation to service models, policy-based decision-making is the norm. However, the available systematic evidence is mainly relevant to community care models. There is little guidance on what constitutes an effective inpatient forensic unit. This is evidenced by the recent guidance from the National Institute of Mental Health England on Adult Acute Inpatient Care Provision (Department of Health 2004). The guidance within this document is based upon 'user and carer feedback, expert professional opinion and good practice'. This guidance offers some potential 'pointers' for inpatient service design.

The key recommendations from this guidance focus upon the following priority areas: integrating inpatient care within a whole-systems approach; care pathway arrangements; admission and reception; structuring inpatient ward arrangements to ensure patients are occupied therapeutically; leadership; staffing; education and training; the ward environment; and developing and sustaining improvement. It is uncertain how and whether these priorities for inpatient care are transferable to inpatient care in forensic settings; however, the need for integrating inpatient care within a whole-systems approach is increasingly becoming a priority in policy guidance. For example, the recent priorities identified in the Wanless review (2002) entitled *Securing Our Future Health: Taking a Long-term View* specified that in the future the public will expect an integrated, joined-up system, as well as a universal and fair service that contributes to social solidarity, fast access 'waiting, but only within reason', comfortable accommodation and services that are designed around patients' individual needs. Standards 4 and 5 of the National Service Framework for mental health relate to the 'effective services for people with severe mental illness'. Again, the need for integrated services is considered a priority:

> Better public and professional understanding, together with integrated mental health systems across primary and specialist services, will promote earlier intervention.

Finally, while considering service models, the Care Services Improvement Partnership & National Institute for Mental Health in England (CSIP & NIMHE) recently launched the 10 High Impact Changes for Mental Health Services programme (CSIP & NIMHE 2006). The high impact changes are the ten areas of service improvement in mental health that are considered to have the greatest positive impact on service user and carer experience, service delivery, outcomes, staff and organisations:

1 Treat home-based care and support as the norm for the delivery of mental health services.
2 Improve flow of service users and carers across health and social care by improving access to screening and assessment.
3 Manage variation in service user discharge processes.
4 Manage variation in access to all mental health services.
5 Avoid unnecessary contact for service users and provide necessary contact in the right setting.
6 Increase the reliability of interventions by designing care around what is known to work and that service users and carers inform and influence.
7 Apply a systematic approach to enable the recovery of people with long-term conditions.
8 Improve service user flow by removing queues.
9 Optimise service user and carer flow through the service using an integrated care pathway approach.
10 Redesign and extend roles in line with efficient service user and carer pathways to attract and retain an effective workforce.

The reason for a lack of evidence for forensic inpatient mental health services is difficult to determine. The lack of nurse-led research may have an impact on the questions that are being asked within forensic research generally. Amos *et al.* (2006) recently conducted a review of forensic reviews and examined the evidence base supporting inpatient care. The results were a damning indictment of how inpatient care and management have been grossly understudied:

There were no reviews which concentrated exclusively on the treatment and management of inpatients in forensic mental health services. One review found that mentally disordered offenders showed large gains in social skill acquisition compared to other groups (developmentally delayed, psychotic and non-psychotic populations) but retention was poor as was the effect on symptoms and social adjustment, possibly because the mentally disordered offenders were the only group coerced into treatment.

The other identified review in this area examined staff issues, particularly for nurses working in forensic settings. The main conclusions presented are that there is an encroachment of psychiatry and nursing traditions through surveillance and social control. It was suggested that nurses working in this field are aware of the power/knowledge equation that frames their practice, research and education. The penetration of forensic nursing into realms of society otherwise bereft of psychiatric intervention can be seen to have a darker dimension. (Amos *et al.* 2006: 89)

Summary

This chapter has highlighted a number of salient issues which need to be considered in relation to inpatient forensic mental health. There are undoubtedly many areas where further exploration and comment could have occurred and areas which have not been included. However, we have attempted to ensure those unique issues relevant to inpatient assessment, care and management have been discussed.

Undoubtedly, the theme running throughout the chapter has been the startling lack of evidence to support inpatient staff and services. In an era where clinicians and services are constantly being challenged to be evidence-based, it is alarming that traditional and opinion-led practice lead the way.

The need for high-quality outcome-based inpatient research is desperately needed if clinicians and services are to offer their clients a service which is modern, reliable and effective.

Selected further reading

Robinson, D. and Kettles, A. (2000) *Forensic Nursing and Multidisciplinary Care of the Mentally Disordered Offender*. London: Jessica Kingsley, provides a modern comprehensive account of forensic nursing within a multidisciplinary perspective by two respected nurses within the field.

The NICE Guidelines (2005), *The Short-term Management of Disturbed/Violent Behaviour in In-patient Psychiatric Settings and Emergency Departments*. London: NICE, provide the most recent account of the salient research and management of violence and aggression. Where lack of evidence exists, expert opinion is given. This publication is a pivotal guideline for inpatient staff.

Wix, S. and Humphreys, M. (2005) *Multidisciplinary Working in Forensic Mental Health Care*. London: Elsevier Churchill Livingstone, provide a practical guide to the establishment of effective multidisciplinary working methods in the care of mentally disordered offenders and others.

References

Amos, T., Frost, J., Lewis, G., Walker, J., Payne, S., Lart, R., Rogers, P., Lester, H. and Wall, M. (2006) Forensic Evidence 2006: Systematic Review of Reviews in Forensic Mental Health. Report submitted to the National Forensic Mental Health Research and Development Programme. Available to download from: http://www.nfmhp.org.uk/MRD%2012%2082%20Final%20Report.doc (last accessed 12 July 2007).

Bhui, K. (2003) 'Ethnic variations in pathways to specialist mental health services in the United Kingdom: a systematic review', British Journal of Psychiatry, 182: 105–16.

Bowers, L., Crowhurst, N., Alexander, J., Callaghan, P., Eales, S., Guy, S., McCann, E. and Ryan, C. (2002) 'Safety and security policies on psychiatric acute admission wards: results from a London-wide survey', Journal of Psychiatric and Mental Health Nursing, 9: 427–33.

Cambridge, Norfolk, Suffolk and Cambridgeshire Strategic Health Authority (2004) An Independent Inquiry set up under HSG (94)27 into the death of David 'Rocky' Bennett (The Blofeld Report). Available to download from: http://www.nscha.nhs.uk/scripts/default.asp?site_id=117andid=11516 (last accessed 12 December 2006).

Care Services Improvement Partnership & National Institute for Mental Health in England (2006) 10 High Impact Changes for Mental Health Services. CSIP & NIMHE. Available to download from: http://www.nimhe.csip.org.uk/silo/files/10-hics-full-publication.pdf (last accessed 28 May 2007).

Coid, J., Kahtan, N., Gault, S. and Jarman, B. (2000) 'Women admitted to secure forensic psychiatric services: comparison of men and women', Journal of Forensic Psychiatry, 11 (2): 275–95.

Coid, J., Kahtan, N., Gault, S., Cook, A. and Jarman, B. (2001) 'Medium secure forensic psychiatry services: comparison of seven English health regions', British Journal of Psychiatry, 178: 55–61. Cited in Forensic Mental Health Services Managed Care Network (2005) Definition of Security Levels in Psychiatric Inpatient Facilities in Scotland. Available to download from: http://www.forensicnetwork.scot.nhs.uk/documents/previous_reports/LevelsofSecurityReport.doc (last accessed 5 Jamuary 2007).

Collins, M. and Davies, S. (2005) 'The Security Needs Assessment Profile: a multidimensional approach to measuring security needs', International Journal of Forensic Mental Health, 4 (1): 39–52.

CRD Report 15 (1999a) Systematic Review of the International Literature on the Epidemiology of Mentally Disordered Offenders. Available to download from: http://www.york.ac.uk/inst/crd/report15.htm (last accessed 12 December 2006).

CRD Report 16 (1999b) Scoping Review of Literature on the Health and Care of Mentally Disordered Offenders. Available to download from: http://www.york.ac.uk/inst/crd/report16.htm (last accessed 12 December 2006).

CRD Report 21 (2001) Scoping Review of the Effectiveness of Mental Health Services 2001. Available to download from: http://www.york.ac.uk/inst/crd/report21.htm (last accessed 12 December 2006).

Department of Health (1994) Review of Health and Social Services for Mentally Disordered Offenders and Others Requiring Similar Services (The Reed Report). London: HMSO.

Department of Health (1998) Modernising Mental Health Services: Safe, Sound and Supportive. London: Department of Health.

Department of Health (1999a) National Service Framework for Mental Health: Modern Standards and Service Models, Executive Summary. London: Department of Health.

Department of Health (1999b) Standing Nursing Midwifery Advisory Committee Report: Assessing Acute Concerns. London: Department of Health.

Department of Health (2000) *Shaping the Future NHS: Long Term Planning for Hospitals and Related Services. Consultation Document on the Findings of the National Beds Inquiry.* London: Department of Health.

Department of Health (2001) *Safety First. Five-year Confidential Inquiry into Homicides and Suicides by People with a Mental Illness.* London: Department of Health.

Department of Health (2002) *Women's Mental Health: Into the Mainstream.* London: Department of Health.

Department of Health (2003a) *Secretary of State Directions on Work to Tackle Violence against Staff or Professionals Who Work in or Provide Services to the NHS.* London: Department of Health. Available to download from: http://www.cfsms.nhs.uk (last accessed 5 January 2007).

Department of Health (2003b) *Mainstreaming Gender and Mental Health. Implementation Guide.* London: Department of Health.

Department of Health (2004) *Mental Health Implementation Policy Guide: Adult Acute Inpatient Care Provision.* Available to download from: http://kc.nimhe.org.uk/upload/inpatientcp.pdf (last accessed 12 December 2006).

Department of Health (2005) *Delivering Race Equality in Mental Health.* Available to download from: http://www.dh.gov.uk/PublicationsAndStatistics/Publications/PublicationsPolicyAndGuidance/PublicationsPolicyAndGuidanceArticle/fs/en?CONTENT_ID=4100773andchk=grJd1N (last accessed 12 December 2006).

Department of Health (2006a) *From Values to Action: The Chief Nursing Officer's Review of Mental Health Nursing.* Available to download from: http://195.33.102.76/PublicationsAndStatistics/Publications/PublicationsPolicyAndGuidance/PublicationsPolicyAndGuidanceArticle/fs/en?CONTENT_ID=4133839andchk=RJV7mg (last accessed 5 May 2007).

Department of Health (2006b) *Avoidable Deaths: A Five Year Report of Suicides and Homicides by People with a Mental Illness.* London: Department of Health.

Diamond, D. (1987) 'Your disobedient servant', *Nursing Times*, 83 (4): 28–31.

Forensic Mental Health Services Managed Care Network (2005) *Definition of Security Levels in Psychiatric Inpatient Facilities in Scotland.* Available to download from: http://www.forensicnetwork.scot.nhs.uk/documents/previous_reports/LevelsofSecurityReport.doc (last accessed 5 May 2006).

Hassell, Y. and Bartlett, A. (2001) 'The changing climate for women patients in medium secure psychiatric units', *Psychiatric Bulletin*, 25: 340–2.

Home Office (2003) *MAPPA Guidance.* London: Home Office.

Home Office and Department of Health and Social Services (1975) *Report of the Committee on Mentally Abnormal Offenders* (Butler Report). London: HMSO.

House of Commons (2000) 'Minutes of evidence taken before the Health Committee – Thursday 23 March 2000'. Available to download from: http://www.parliament.thetationeryoffice.co.uk/pa/cm199900/cmselect/cmhealth/373/0032305.htm (last accessed 28 December 2006).

James, D., Cripps, J. and Gray, N. (1998) 'What demands do those admitted from the criminal justice system make on psychiatric beds? Expanding local secure services as a development strategy', *Journal of Forensic Psychiatry*, 9: 74–102. Cited in: Forensic Mental Health Services Managed Care Network (2005) *Definition of Security Levels in Psychiatric Inpatient Facilities in Scotland.* Available to download from: http://www.forensicnetwork.scot.nhs.uk/documents/previous_reports/LevelsofSecurityReport.doc (last accessed 5 January 2007).

Jepson, R., Di Blasi, Z., Wright, K. and Ter Riet, G. (2001) *Scoping Review of the Effectiveness of Mental Health Services*, NHS Centre for Reviews and Dissemination Report No. 21. York: NHS CRD, University of York.

Kennedy, H. (2002) 'Therapeutic uses of security: mapping forensic services by stratifying risk', *Advances in Psychiatric Treatment*, 8: 433–43.

Kettles, A. and Robinson, D. (2000) 'Overview and contemporary issues in the role of the forensic nurse in the UK', in D. Robinson and A. Kettles (eds), *Forensic Nursing and Multidisciplinary Care of the Mentally Disordered Offender*. London: Jessica Kingsley, pp. 25–38.

Kitchiner, N. (1999) 'Freeing the imprisoned mind: practice forensic care', *Mental Health Care*, 21 (12): 420–4.

Lart, R., Payne. S., Beaumont, B., MacDonald, G. and Mistry, T. (1999) *Women and Secure Services: A Literature Review*. York: Centre for Reviews and Dissemination.

Lewis, G., Churchill, R. and Hotopf, M. (1997) 'Editorial: systematic reviews and meta-analysis', *Psychological Medicine*, 27: 3–7.

Margerison, C. and McCann, D. (1986) 'High performance management teams', *Health Care Management*, 1 (1): 26–31.

Mason, T. (2002) 'Forensic psychiatric nursing: a literature review and thematic analysis of role tensions', *Journal of Psychiatric and Mental Health Nursing*, 9 (5): 11–520.

Mezey, G., Hassell, Y. and Bartlett, A. (2005) 'Safety of women in mixed sex and single sex medium secure units', *British Journal of Psychiatry*, 187: 579–82.

Milne, D. (1993) *Psychology and Mental Health Nursing*. London: Macmillan.

Murray, K. (1996) The use of beds in NHS medium secure units in England', *Journal of Forensic Psychiatry*, 7: 504–24.

Murray, K., Rudge, S., Lack, S. and Dolan, R. (1994) 'How many high security beds are needed? Implications from an audit of one region's Special Hospital patients', *Journal of Forensic Psychiatry*, 5: 487–99. Cited in Forensic Mental Health Services Managed Care Network (2005) *Definition of Security Levels in Psychiatric Inpatient Facilities in Scotland*. Available to download from: http://www.forensicnetwork.scot.nhs.uk/ documents/previous_reports/LevelsofSecurityReport.doc (last accessed 5 January 2007).

National Audit Office (2003) *A Safer Place to Work: Protecting NHS Hospital and Ambulance Staff from Violence and Aggression*. Report prepared by the Comptroller and Auditor General, HC 527. London: National Audit Office.

National Institute for Mental Health in England (2005) *Health Policy Implementation Guide: Developing Positive Practice to Support the Safe and Therapeutic Management of Aggression and Violence in Mental Health In-patient Settings*. Available to download from: http://www.nimhe.org.uk/downloads/78130-DoH-Viol%20Management.pdf (last accessed 5 January 2007).

Ndegwa, D. (2000) *Social Division and Difference: Black and Ethnic Minorities*. The Forensic Mental Health Research and Development Programme. Available to download from: http://www.nfmhp.org.uk/expertpaper.htm (last accessed 5 January 2007).

NHS Executive (2000) *Secure Futures for Women: Making a Difference*. London: Department of Health.

NHS Security Management Service (2001) *Promoting Safer and Therapeutic Services: Implementing the National Syllabus in Mental Health and Learning Disability Services*. Available to download from: http://www.sms.nhs.uk/doc/psts/psts. implementing.syllabus.pdf (last accessed 12 December 2006).

NICE (2004) *Depression: The Management of Depression in Primary and Secondary Care*. London: NICE.

NICE (2005a) *The Short-Term Management of Disturbed/Violent Behaviour in In-patient Psychiatric Settings and Emergency Departments*. London: NICE.

NICE (2005b) *The Short Term Management of Disturbed/Violent Behaviour in Adult Psychiatric Inpatient Settings and Accident and Emergency Settings*. London: NICE.

Nolan, P. (1993) *A History of Mental Health Nursing*. London: Chapman & Hall.

NPSA (2006) *With Safety in Mind: Mental Health Services and Patient Safety*. London: NPSA.

Nursing and Midwifery Council (NMC) (2001) *The Recognition, Prevention and Therapeutic Management of Violence in Mental Health Care*. Available to download from: http://www.nmc-uk.org/nmc/main/publications/TherapeuticManagement OfViolence.pdf (last accessed 12 December 2006).

Parry-Cooke, G. (2000) *Good Girls: Surviving the Secure System. A Consultation with Women in High and Medium Secure Settings*. London: University of North London.

Rae, M. (1993) *Freedom to Care: Achieving Change in Culture and Nursing Practice in a Mental Health Service*. Liverpool: Ashworth Hospital Graphics.

Rogers, P., Ghroum, P., Benson, R. and Forward, L. (2006) 'Is breakaway training effective? An audit of one medium secure unit', *Journal of Forensic Psychiatry and Psychology*, 17 (4): 593–602.

Royal College of Psychiatrists (1998a) *Not Just Bricks and Mortar, Council Report CR62: Report of the Royal College of Psychiatrists Working Party on the Size, Staffing, Structure, Siting and Security of New Acute Adult Psychiatric In-patient Units*. Available to download from: http://www.rcpsych.ac.uk/files/pdfversion/cr62.pdf (last accessed 5 January 2007).

Royal College of Psychiatrists (1998b) *Guidelines for the Management of Imminent Violence*. London: Royal College of Psychiatrists.

Salias, E. and Fenton, M. (2001) 'Seclusion and restraint for people with serious mental illness' (Cochrane Review), in *The Cochrane Library*, Issue 1 (2002). Chichester. John Wiley & Sons.

Scottish Health Service Management Executive – Clinical Resource Audit Group. (1996) *The Prevention and Management of Aggression: A Good Practice Statement*. Edinburgh: Clinical Resource Audit Group/Scottish Health Service Management Executive.

Sproston, K. and Nazroo, J. (eds) (2000) *Ethnic Minority Psychiatric Illness Rates Community (EMPIRIC): Quantitative Report*. London: Stationery Office.

Tilt Report (2000) *Report of the Review of Security at the High Security Hospitals*. London: NHS Executive.

United Kingdom Central Council for Nursing, Midwifery and Health Visiting (2001) *The Recognition, Prevention and Therapeutic Management of Violence in Mental Health Care*. London: UKCC.

Wales Audit Office (2005) *Protecting NHS Staff from Violence and Aggression, Report Prepared by the Auditor General for Wales*. Available to download from: http://www.wao.gov.uk/assets/englishdocuments/NHS_Violence_and_agression.pdf (last accessed 12 December 2006).

Wanless, D. (2002) *Securing Our Future Health: Taking a Long-term View, Final Report*. Available to download from: http://www.hm-treasury.gov.uk/wanless (last accessed 12 December 2006).

Warner, L. (2005) *Back on Track? CPA Care Planning for Service Users Who are Repeatedly Detained under the Mental Health Act*. London: Sainsbury Centre.

Watt, A., Topping-Morris, B., Mason, T. and Rogers, P. (2003a) 'Pre-admission nursing assessment in forensic mental health (1991–2000): Part 1 – A preliminary analysis of practice and cost', *International Journal of Nursing Studies*, 40: 645–55.

Watt, A., Topping-Morris, B., Rogers, P. and Mason, T. (2003b) 'Pre-admission nursing assessment in forensic mental health (1991–2000): Part 2 – Comparison of traditional assessment with the items contained within the HCR-20 structured risk assessment', *International Journal of Nursing Studies*, 40: 657–62.

Welsh Assembly Government (2004) *All Wales NHS Violence and Aggression Training Passport and Information Scheme*. Available to download from: http://www.wao.gov.uk/assets/englishdocuments/NHS_Violence_and_agression.pdf (last accessed 12 December 2006).

Whittington, R. and Balsalmo, D. (1998) 'Violence: fear and power', in T. Mason and D. Mercer (eds), *Critical Perspectives in Forensic Care Inside Out*. Basingstoke: Macmillan, pp. 64–84.

Whittington, R. and Patterson, P. (1996) 'Verbal and non-verbal behaviour immediately prior to aggression by mentally disordered people: enhancing the assessment of risk', *Journal of Psychiatric and Mental Health Nursing*, 3: 47–57.

WHO (2002) World Report on Violence and Health. Available to download from: http://www.who.int/violence_injury_prevention/violence/world_report/en/full_en.pdf (last accessed 12 December 2006).

Whyte, L. A. (1997) 'Forensic nursing: a review of concepts and definitions', *Nursing Standard*, 11: 46–7.

Woods, P. and Richards, D. (2003) 'Effectiveness of nursing interventions in people with personality disorders', *Journal of Advanced Nursing*, 44: 154–72.

Chapter 22

The crimes and pathologies of passion: love, jealousy and the pursuit of justice

Paul Mullen

Introduction

> What chance is there of the success of real passion ... [given] the unravel-
> ling of the web of human life into its various threads of meanness, spite,
> cowardice, want of feeling, and want of understanding ... and seeing
> custom prevail over all excellence. (William Hazlitt 2005: 119; orig. 1826)

Havelock Ellis (1890) considered crimes of passion to be responses to 'some
great unmerited wrong'. He thought that far from being the product of lawless-
ness and antisocial traits they often reflected noble and elevated sensitivities. In
nineteenth-century France under the influence of the Romantic movement,
crimes apparently evoked by love became matters of intense public interest. In
Paris, the author Alexander Dumas was permitted to stand behind the presid-
ing judge in cases involving crimes of passion to assert the rights of love (Zeldin
1977). Within the shores of the UK, crimes of passion were usually regarded
more prosaically as concerned only with the violence of jealousy (Mullen 1993).
Love, jealousy and the pursuit of justice have all been regarded as having the
potential to evoke criminal behaviour and each at different times and different
places have been viewed, if not with approval, at least with indulgence.

The tendency of these passions to predispose to violent and antisocial behaviours is even more marked in their pathological extensions. Pathologies of love
are associated with stalking, the pathologies of jealousy with assault and even
killing. The querulous plague the courts, agencies of accountability, politicians
and heads of state. Assessing those who offend while in the grips of such passions presents formidable problems which arise from:

- the difficulty of deciding where the limits of normality end and those of
  pathology begin;
- the almost total failure to incorporate the disorders of passion into the current diagnostic manuals;
- the reluctance of the courts to regard even the most exuberant manifestations
  as pathological;

- conversely the fashionable contempt for jealousy which encourages the pathologising of this passion even in its modest expressions;
- the construction of the mentally disordered offender as first and foremost an individual with a specifiable disorder of mental function, with behaviour being seen as either irrelevant or as secondary. This is particularly problematic in disorders of passion – how does one separate the state of mind associated with the madness of being in love from that in a mad form of loving? In practice, if you are to have any chance of separating the normal range from the pathological variants of these disorders you are thrown back on the behaviour itself;
- the low profile these disorders have had in general mental health;
- the absence of clinically relevant models for conceptualising emotions and disorders of emotion which leave assessors floundering when faced with jealousy, love or a passion for justice.

History

De Clérambault's (1942) category 'psychoses passionels' brought together erotomania, querulousness and morbid jealousy. He argued that these states are characterised by delusional systems and an all-absorbing sense of purpose which leads to a constant striving and to desires which bring the patient into direct conflict with others (Baruk 1959/1974). De Clérambault contrasted these disorders of passion with what he termed the interpretative delusions of paranoia, in which the patient is driven to seek explanations in a world experienced as hostile and constantly changing, a world which leaves the patient fearful and largely passive. Signer (1991), in an excellent account of the development of the ideas of de Clérambault, noted that de Clérambault viewed these disorders as precipitated by a shock or crisis which moved the patient from ordinary emotionality to a pathology of passion. The reactive element is present in the initiation of the disorder but once set in motion these disorders are prolonged, forceful and predisposed to action. It is important to note that although de Clérambault emphasised the continuity of disorders of passion with antecedent psychic life, and the reactive elements, he remained wedded to a fundamentally organic origin (Mullen 1997a). It was his followers and pupils who gave a strongly psychodynamic colouration to theories of the aetiology of disorders of passion (Lagache 1938).

The English meaning of 'passion' carried the implication of suffering and of something that is done to us or happens to us. Passions like all strong emotions are experienced as imposed rather than chosen. Passion is often regarded as the antithesis of reason and choice. This notion of being overcome by an external influence is expressed idiomatically when we say, 'infected by jealousy', 'bowled over by love', 'shot through with anger' and 'overtaken by rage'. The implications of 'sufferance' and the involuntary have over time added the connotations of being at the explosive end of the emotional spectrum. The notion of passions and their disorders as involving the wilful pursuit of desires accords with more recent conceptualisations which regard emotions as involving judgments, intentionality and motives (Solomon 1976, 1980; Gordon 1987; Greenspan 1988).

A broader view of the disorders of passion will be taken in this chapter than that of de Clérambault. Disorders of passion will be viewed not just as pure, or primary, syndromes, but also as secondary, or symptomatic (which only partly correspond to de Clérambault's associated syndromes). More importantly, the conceptualisation employed here will not be confined to disorders with clear-cut delusions.

The structure of emotions

Forensic mental health professionals are called upon to evaluate those in the grips of a passion, either after acts of violence or when an assessment of potential risk has been requested. The first question is usually to determine whether the passion is based on delusions and/or is part of a mental disorder. This approach works well enough when the patient has a major psychiatric disorder like schizophrenia and the passion manifests itself in bizarre delusions. For most cases, however, this approach is likely to leave the examiner floundering. Jealousy, love and the pursuit of justice, even in their mundane manifestations, can be associated with behaviours and beliefs which the outside observer may well be tempted to label mad. Equally even those in the grips of the pathological extensions of these passions may tell their tale with such facility, and with so much confirmatory detail, that all but the most sceptical and unsympathetic will be at risk of being drawn in. Asking questions about emotions in general and these passions in particular as if they were things, or seeking to label before adequately exploring, is a recipe for error. What is required is at least a basic model of the phenomenology of these experiences.

The phenomenology of emotion presents problems, particularly for those from medical or behaviour science backgrounds. Such professionals have usually acquired conceptual maps that view emotions as hard-wired, ingrained or even genetically determined responses to specific provocations. Emotions as the antithesis of reason, emotions as imposed, or at least unchosen and ultimately, emotions as a kind of black box are part of our professional and cultural baggage.

A description of an emotion should involve, as a minimum, what they are about, the judgments that constitute them, the feelings that accompany them, the fantasies they evoke, the desires which move them towards actions and the predispositions to behave which ultimately give them expression (see Figure 22.1).

Emotions, like most states of mind, are about something. Love is always love of someone or something. Jealousy is usually directed at one's partner. Querulousness fixes on that which has aroused the sense of injustice. Connected to the intentional object of the emotion is always a judgment which sets the passion in motion. Romantic jealousy is not possible unless you judge both that the other owes you some form of fidelity and that that fidelity is in question. Love is only possible when you judge some other to be a source of potential delight. Querulousness begins with a judgment that you have been mistreated. Without judgment there is no possibility of an emotional response let alone a state of mind as complex as a passion.

Emotions are formed in part by feelings – feelings of disquiet and pain, or of pleasure and satisfaction. For example, Bryson (1976) suggested that jealousy

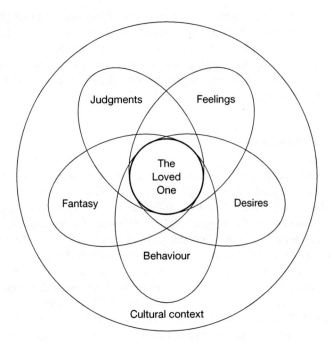

Figure 22.1 A simplified model of the elements which make up an emotion

involved feelings of devastation (perplexity, anxiety, depression), anger and the intropunitiveness of self-blame. The feelings evoked by love have been the staple diet of poets. Those of querulousness have rarely been articulated but seem often to involve fluctuating degrees of hopeful expectation, anger and inchoate distress. Emotions bring with them specific sets of desires. Love desires the intimacy of closeness and to be loved in return. Jealousy desires to know, or to be reassured. Querulousness desires vindication. Strong emotions are usually accompanied by fantasies, which may be particularly vivid, and either troubling or satisfying depending on context. Emotions produce dispositions to behave, such as to approach in love, to question in jealousy and to accuse in the querulous. Finally passion's dramas are given shape by the cultural context in which they emerge and are played out.

Whatever the deficiencies of this simple model it does provide a basis for an examiner to inquire into the nature of an emotional experience in something approaching a systematic manner. Those in the grips of a passion are often particularly sensitive to possible scepticism or criticism. In exploring their experiences, gentle prompting and genuine curiosity will serve better than more challenging demands for more information. The inquiries should be framed within the context of the examiner's desire to understand. It is best to start with what they hope for (the desires) and then move into the why (judgment), the expectations (fantasies) and what they intend to do. It is by politely seeking clarification, and clarifications of clarifications, that a picture may emerge of the world of the jealous, the lover and the dedicated pursuer of justice.

Primary (reactive) and secondary (symptomatic) disorders

The disorders of passion fall into two groups – the pure (primary) disorders of passion and the secondary (symptomatic) disorders.

The secondary (symptomatic) disorders occur as just one element in a more extensive disturbance, such as a schizophrenic syndrome. These are characterised by the following:

- The genesis and evolution are related to an underlying mental disorder which emerges prior to, or contemporaneously with, the pathology of passion.
- The clinical features of an underlying disorder are present alongside the pathology of passion.
- They usually resolve as the underlying disorder resolves.

Symptomatic disorders of passion are encountered as part of a wide range of mental disorders, including schizophrenic syndromes, organic psychoses, affective disorders, obsessional disorders as well as with disturbances of cerebral function, notably the dementias and multiple sclerosis. There is usually no problem clinically recognising the secondary nature of such disorders of passion. Those in association with dementias and other neurodegenerative disorders may, however, appear as the only manifestation of disturbed judgment and emotionality.

A number of authorities consider that the disorders of passion are always a symptom complex within some other mental disorder and never a discrete disorder (Hollender and Callahan 1975; Shepherd 1961). In forensic practice, however, patients are often encountered who have significant psychopathology revolving entirely around love, jealousy or querulousness. If these preoccupations are of delusional intensity the patient could be diagnosed as having a delusional disorder. If delusion is considered an inappropriate label for the beliefs at the core of the passion, then a diagnosis of paranoid personality might be entertained. The problem with this is it produces a circularity. Why are they abnormally jealous? Because they have a delusional disorder/paranoid personality disorder. What evidence is there of these disorders? Abnormal jealousy. It may be better just to accept that there are primary or pure disorders of passion, some of which will fit into the categories in the manuals for delusional disorders or personality disorders and some of which will be unclassifiable.

These pure or primary disorders of passion are often understood as emerging from an interaction between personality and a particular life situation, with or without the influence of additional mental or physical factors (Kretschmer 1918; Jaspers 1910, 1963; de Clérambault 1942; Retterstøl 1967; Retterstøl and Opjordsmoen 1991).

The features of pure (primary) disorders of passion are as follows:

1 The onset of the disorder occurs in a situation that can reasonably be related to evoking the particular passion (e.g. supposed infidelity or experienced injustice);
2 A state is present which renders the individual vulnerable to reacting passionately to the situation. This can involve any of the following:
   – a personality disorder (e.g. paranoid personality disorder or the sensitive

self-referential personality);
- past experiences (e.g. previous desertion or infidelity);
- chronic or recurrent confusion or intoxication (arising from, for example, cocaine abuse or alcoholism);
- a disturbance of mood, most frequently depressive, which may affect both the interpretation of events and the nature of the response. This is to be distinguished from passions emerging as a direct product of the symptomatology of the disorder. The sense of worthlessness and vulnerability of lowered mood is fertile ground for the self doubt which so easily becomes doubt of the other in jealousy. This is not to be confused with the jealousy which emerges from a schizophrenic process where the suspicion is a part of a psychotic restructuring of the patient's world;
- a mixture of the above (which is usually the case).
3 The response is extreme, being exaggerated psychologically and behaviourally (with respect to the norms for the individual and their culture).
4 The evolution of the morbid reaction may be influenced by factors in the provoking situation which tend to ameliorate or aggravate the evoked passion.

In practice, a vulnerability in their personality structure is the common ground from which these disorders spring. Such morbid reactions are usually understandable as an extension of the habitual way in which the individual elaborates and reacts to their lived experiences. For all their pathology these morbid reactions usually remain understandable as part of the unfolding of the individual's life. The problem is often where to draw the line between a reaction in the normal range and that which merits being regarded as a disorder, a matter of considerable moment when the passion has led to serious offending. To clarify the distinction which is often so problematic in practice, a general outline of the characteristics of a normal reaction is required.

Jealous and amorous responses together with reactions to perceived injustice or malfeasance remain within normal limits if:

- They are a response to events which can reasonably be related to evoking the particular passion (this may be difficult in love which is notoriously indiscriminate).
- The passion focuses on a plausible object or situation (e.g. one rival not a multitude, an understandable grievance not a constantly expanding litany of complaints and injuries).
- The feelings, desires and behaviours evoked broadly remain within the limits acceptable to the individual's self-concept and within the wider cultural norms (a particular problem with jealousy in today's multicultural world).
- The passion has a course and evolution that can understandably relate to the provoking events and subsequent developments.
- Perhaps most importantly, the subject either seeks (and eventually accepts) a reasonable resolution of their desires, or strives to extricate themselves from the situation if an irreconcilable conflict is generated.

Pathological reactions can give rise to delusional developments. The symptomatic forms of the pathologies of passion do not always involve delusions, as with those which arise on the basis of an obsessive-compulsive disorder or a neurodegenerative condition. The distinction between primary and symptomatic should not therefore be confused with a psychotic – non-psychotic dichotomy.

Jealousy

Those which are jealous proceed from suspicion to hatred; from hatred to frenzy; from frenzy to injury, murder and despair. (Burton [orig. 1621])

Jealousy is a complex emotion generated by a perceived threat to a valued relationship and though it can be evoked in a range of contexts it is in sexual and intimate relationships that it emerges most frequently. It is here that it creates the greatest distress and damage (White and Mullen 1989). Jealousy and envy are occasionally wrongly conflated. Envy is about what someone else possesses, either in its benign form of emulation or its malignant form of wishing to deprive or destroy the other's advantage. Jealousy is about the fear of losing what you believe you possess. Jealousy in intimate relationships may be evoked by the perception of a threat in the form of a rival but it is primarily a drama played out between the couple with the actual or supposed rival playing a bit part at best.

Jealousy is of particular importance in forensic mental health as it is a potent source of violence and intimidation in the domestic situation. Pathological forms of jealousy have a sinister, and entirely deserved, reputation for engendering violence (Mullen 1996).

Jealousy and the crime of passion

The crime of passion in the English-speaking world is virtually synonymous with violence in response to a perceived threat of infidelity

The manner in which jealousy is regarded is profoundly influenced by social and cultural contexts. Over the history of Western culture jealousy has been transformed from a socially sanctioned response to the threat of infidelity into a personal pathology which is the outward expression of immaturity, possessiveness and insecurity (Mullen 1991). Jealousy has changed from a passion grounded in the response to the flouting of moral and social imperatives, through an expression of distress at the threatened loss of a relationship, to its modern embodiment in the language of psychopathology. This changing cultural construction of jealousy has influenced the manner in which the violence engendered by jealousy has been viewed (Mullen 1993).

Legal systems also emerge from cultural contexts and, depending on the particular historical period, assume distinctive forms (Smith and Weisstub 1983). Shifts, for example, between legal procedures based on a patriarchal law of status to those based on law of contract or on mediation and arbitration profoundly affect how a particular act will be regarded (Northrop 1960). In societies where law of status is dominant the 'proper' relationship between a husband and wife rigidly defines the obligations of the wife. This includes fidelity and acquiescence in patriarchal dominance. An individual's position in such a society is intimately bound up with gender, kinship and temporal order of birth. Central to the power relationships of status societies is the enforcement of female fidelity and, through that, the reliability of kinship lines. It has been argued that in such cultures the condemnation of adultery does not arise primarily from emotional jealousy, as we now understand it, but from the necessity of the wife fulfilling her reproductive role in accordance with rules necessary to preserve the power relationships of the system (Gullerot 1971). In law-of-contract societies some people become more successful than others and form social and economic groups where prestige depends less on pedigree than on possessions. Marital relationships tend to be viewed as contractual obligations involving some romantic commitment, but are rooted in property relationships which are enforced ultimately through the courts. With the recent emergence of mediation and arbitration as the governing principles of consensus legal process, there is a move by the courts away from adjudicating the implicit and explicit contractual obligations involved in marriage towards the role of conciliating threatened unions and arbitrating rights over property and offspring in failed relationships.

Society's attitude to the violence of jealousy is profoundly influenced by both legal practice and the cultural construction of jealousy. In honour-based societies infidelity is not only a problem for the individual who is shamed in the eyes of others, but is also an affront to the values of the whole society. Infidelity threatens the social system by placing a question over paternity, which is the basis of the social order. Not surprisingly, honour-based societies, which usually have status-based legal systems, enforce fidelity and provide wide-ranging protections for those who avenge themselves against adulterers. Menelaus pursues Paris and Helen not out of individual pique, but from conformity to the duty he owes to his role as king and in consent to the values of his community.

The crime of passion manifests differently in societies where codes of honour and fear of public shame are displaced, in large part, by ethical and moral imperatives which have become matters of duty mediated by individual conscience. Moral duty becomes, in theory, the grounding which regulates interpersonal and sexual behaviour. In Renaissance Europe moral duty implied the existence of a debt to others; thus one owed one's partner fidelity just as one owed one's king fealty (Guth 1982). Infidelity remains a moral affront, but it becomes focused increasingly on the interpersonal, with less and less resonance in the wider social context: it is the obligation and debt owed to one personally which is flouted and it is one's righteous rage that is justified. Jealousy becomes grounded in a psychologically sensed wrong, independent of any threat to public prestige. The partner may still feel shamed by the infidelity and may still appeal to external authority, but the jealousy is now an internal, personal and isolating experience. The violence of jealousy is stripped of some of its legitimacy in terms of social duty, but acquires the new justification of personal provocation. Jealousy is now a passion embedded in the individual's psychological response to infidelity and the violence engendered, though no longer legitimised by the legal code, is still potentially cloaked in the defence of provocation. William Blackstone (1803, orig. 1783) noted that killing from the passions produced in response to infidelity 'is of the lowest degree of manslaughter … for there could not be a greater provocation'.

To understand crimes of passion arising from jealousy in the guise in which they now usually appear before the courts a further metamorphosis of jealousy needs to be considered. Sexual jealousy in the last 100 years has been viewed increasingly not only as damaging and potentially dangerous, but also as a symptom of immaturity or actual mental instability. Jealousy has been transformed from moral affront into a manifestation of personal pathology. Originally this expressed the notion that the blow of being exposed to infidelity was sufficient to derange the cuckold's mind, but subsequently the primary responsibility for the disordered state of mind was shifted from the blow occasioned by the infidelity to the jealous individual's own psychopathology. In the twentieth century the paradoxical situation emerged that as jealousy became less and less acceptable, and as it was stripped of its justification as a response to social and moral turpitude, the violence of jealousy acquired a powerful new claim to mitigate punishment. The less acceptable jealousy became within the culture, the more deviant its extreme manifestations became, the more akin those manifestations appeared to madness. If jealousy was the result of personal psychopathology, and if extreme manifestations of the passion were a form of madness, then it followed that the jealous killer could not be held responsible for his or her actions. In the courts of England and Wales diminished responsibility displaced provocation as the defence of the jealous killer. Abolishing the provocation defence, if it is intended to reduce the frequency with which men evade the full rigours of the law after killing their partners, is a reform too late. The horse has already bolted and is comfortably settled in the diminished stable.

Jealousy and domestic violence

Domestic violence and spousal homicide emerges from a complex concatenation of influences in which sexual jealousy may be prominent, though rarely sufficient. Jealousy is common, infidelity is common, but violence, though far too common, occurs in only a minority of such cases, and killing is an extreme rarity. Jealousy may well be the prime motivation for an act of violence but this still leaves open why this individual, on this particular occasion, resorted to force.

A community study of jealousy reported that 15 per cent of both men and women had, at some time, been subjected to physical violence at the hands of a jealous partner (Mullen and Martin 1994). In a study carried out in Scotland nearly half of the 109 battered women interviewed identified their partner's excessive possessiveness and sexual jealousy as the precipitant of violence (Dobash and Dobash 1980). Two-thirds of the women at a refuge for battered women in the London area reported that their partner's excessive jealousy was the primary cause of the violence and that in many cases the partner's suspicions were entirely without foundation (Gayford 1975, 1979). Studies from North America produced similar results with, for example, Hilberman and Manson (1977) reporting that extreme jealousy contributed to the violence in most of their group of 60 battered women. Rounsaville (1978) noted similar findings with 52 per cent of the battered women listing jealousy as the main problem and no less than 94 per cent naming it as a frequent cause. Interestingly, in one of the few studies to ask men why they battered their partners, they most frequently nominated anger at supposed infidelity as the cause (Brisson 1983). Whitehurst (1971) reported on 100 cases of spousal violence and noted in nearly every case that the husband appeared to be responding out of frustration at his ability to control his partner but that the overt justification, and accusation, was that the partner was sexually unfaithful. Jealousy would appear from such studies to be capable of both motivating domestic batterers and to offer an excuse, or rationalisation, for the violence.

The studies cited above do not distinguish between pathological and normal jealousy, though some might question whether jealousy that leads to battering your partner is ever normal. However grim the statistics on violence and jealousy in the general community and among victims of domestic violence are, the evidence from samples of the pathologically jealous are even more alarming. A UK study reported that more than half of the pathologically jealous who were referred to a general psychiatric service had physically assaulted their partners. This study excluded patients referred from the courts or specifically over violence issues (Mullen and Maack 1985). A smaller US study found similar results with the majority threatening and assaulting their partners (de Silva 2004).

Jealousy has emerged from a number of studies of homicide as one of the more frequently identified motivations (Gibbens 1958; Wolfgang 1958; West 1968). Daly and Wilson (1982) and Dally *et al.* (1988) concluded that male sexual jealousy is the commonest motivation for killing in domestic disputes. Jealous homicides are usually perpetrated by men, with the commonest victim being their female partner. Where domestic disputes generated by jealousy lead to women killing, it is claimed this is typically an act of self-defence to ward off the male partner's jealous rage (Daly and Wilson 1988).

Jealousy is evoked by the fear of the loss of what you regard as yours by right, or at least what you had hoped was about to become yours. A common theme in Western literature is the emergence of jealousy as the factor which reveals to the individual that they are in love. Jealousy does not precede or evoke the love but reveals that there had been a relationship in which hopes and expectations were invested albeit unacknowledged. The emotion of romantic jealousy is not just about a feared loss but about the twin objects, one who is unfaithful and the other who is the interloper. Using the simplified model of the phenomenology of emotion presented earlier in Figure 22.1 it is possible to more thoroughly explore the experience of jealousy. This provides a basis for more effectively evaluating the extent to which the individual's jealousy deviates from the usual. The phenomenology of jealousy within the normal range in our society today:

- is evoked in an actual intimate relationship by plausible threats to sexual exclusivity, or emotional commitment, or the future stability of the relationship, produced by a potential or actual rival;
- involves judgements which initiate and sustain jealousy that are to some extent connected to specific types of concomitant emotional states, desires and predispositions to behave;
- is accompanied by feelings of distress at apprehended loss and anger at betrayal;
- involves desires to clarify the situation, which may be by resolving the conflict, by reconciliation, by acceptance or by ending the relationship;
- predisposes to the behaviours to check whether the suspicions are well founded, primarily by questioning though occasionally by turning up

unexpectedly at home or work. In today's world checking the partner's SMS messages appears a commonplace accompaniment of jealousy;
- may be accompanied by painful fantasies of the actual or supposed infidelity with or without revenge fantasies.

The phenomenology of pathological extensions of jealousy are typically characterised by one or more of the following:

- Being evoked by events or occurrences which have no or little obvious connection to the behaviour of the partner.
- Emerging in the context of a fantasised or delusional relationship in which no prior commitment by the other existed, or even no actual contact.
- Focusing on an implausible rival or a multiplicity of unlikely rivals.
- Accompanied by intense arousal often involving anger and despair. A great sense of betrayal and injustice combined with self-righteousness is usually present. These feelings are out of keeping both with the jealous person's previous ways of responding to the world and with the expected responses in the culture. Angry, self-righteous entitled people who become jealous may appear more disordered than is the case.
- The behaviours accompanying pathological jealousies are almost always outside of normal and socially acceptable limits. The pathologically jealous take checking to extremes with following, spying, checking phone and bank records, opening mail, inspecting clothes and particularly underclothes for signs of illicit congress, lengthy cross questioning, repeated threats and frequent intimidation and violence. This violence in and of itself, even when it is homicidal, does not indicate the jealousy which motivated it was anything other than extreme or uncontrolled.
- The fantasies in pathological jealousy are often particularly vivid and extraordinary with the additional twist that they may be accorded the status of evidentiary proof by the sufferer.

A basic phenomenological examination lays the groundwork for deciding on whether the jealousy can reasonably be regarded as pathological. The next stage is to distinguish between secondary (symptomatic) and primary (reactive) pathologies.

Jealousy can emerge as a complication or symptom of a range of psychotic and non-psychotic mental disorders was well as in organic brain disorders and drug and alcohol use and abuse (for reviews see Enoch and Trethowan 1979; Langfeldt, 1961; Mullen 1990b; Kingham; Gordon 2004). The relationship between obsessional disorders and jealousy has been much debated (Cobb and Marks 1979; Bishay et al. 1989; Stein et al. 1994; Insel and Akiskal 1986; Kingham; Gordon 2004; Marazziti et al. 2003). Jealousy can present in the context of jealous rumination. Far more common is an obsessive concern over the fidelity of a partner which is regarded as reasonable, not resisted to any degree and fits in as part of the wider picture of jealous preoccupations. It could be argued that jealousy to any substantial degree will always be characterised by ruminations and intrusive thoughts about infidelity but unless they are regarded by the sufferer as absurd, or at least absurdly insistent, and also resisted, then there seems little point in trying to attribute them to an obsessional disorder. A similar reservation can be expressed to reformulating insistent suspicions of infidelity as overvalued ideas. Jealousy usually occurs in the context of a valued relationship being thought to be under threat. This almost inevitably means that the ideas are of intense personal concern. One of the many problems of jealousy is that you cannot prove a negative either in science or personal relationships. Once the notion of infidelity is entertained it may be possible to confirm but never to absolutely exclude. Trust is just that – replace trust with a question about infidelity and it's a one-way street to unresolvable doubt.

The primary (reactive) jealousies can be intractable in no small part because once fidelity is put in question it can never be entirely excluded, at least to the suspicious mind given to putting notions and observations together that were better kept apart. Intimate relationships depend on mixtures of trust and tolerance, and once either is destroyed or abandoned, restoring intimacy becomes problematic.

Assessing the probability of violence occurring or recurring in jealousy, particularly if pathological, is always important. In pathological jealousy the rates of violence toward the partner are so high you have to have very good reasons not to make the assumption that it is probable.

Careful and repeated questioning of the jealous individual and their partner is advisable. Specific inquiry should be made about:

- threats;
- damaging the partner's, or rival's, personal property;
- throwing objects;
- pushing, shoving or shaking;
- blows with hands, fists or feet;
- threatening with a potential weapon;
- throttling;
- the possession of firearms or other weapons;
- attacks with weapons;
- any other action which could have inflicted harm (e.g. driving at him/her with a vehicle or trying to produce an accident while partner was a passenger, poisoning, etc.).

The truth or falsity of an accusation of infidelity is difficult for a clinician to establish in the face of denials. It is also largely irrelevant to whether the jealousy is delusional and to assessment and treatment. Essentially correct suspicions about infidelity can still be delusional, as for example, when they are based on interpretations of totally unrelated events (e.g. the wife's infidelity revealed by the Christmas tree lights in her window going on and off in synchrony with those in a neighbour's window) (Mullen 1997b). When he followed up a large cohort of morbidly jealous men, Odegaard (1968) found a significant proportion of their ex-wives were now living with the objects of their previous husbands' delusional jealousy.

When violence has occurred the intent, the context and the nature of the damage inflicted should be noted. The level of the victim's fear is only a guide when it appears high in relation to acknowledged actions; it is not particularly reassuring if it is apparently low despite escalating aggression. In most cases, violence is preceded by clear indicators of mounting danger. These may be ignored or downplayed by the partner who cannot believe they are at risk from their loved one. A prudent clinician should not make the same mistake.

The features in a jealous individual which increase concern about violence include:

- escalating conflict between the couple;
- a history of violence, in the domestic context in particular;
- fantasies of violent retribution or strong impulses to attack (however reassuring they are about never 'really doing it');
- depression, even more so in the presence of suicidal preoccupations or behaviour;
- substance abuse;
- where the cultural and social background of the jealous individual is one which tends to condone the acceptability of violence in the face of infidelity.

Jealous preoccupations tend to be more intense in younger subjects and violence is resorted to more readily in youth. In pathological forms of jealousy, however, advancing years do less to ameliorate the risks of violence. Gender differences are mostly related to the seriousness of the damage inflicted rather than the frequency of assaultive behaviours.

Apprehending violence is one thing, preventing its realisation is another. In the pathological jealousies the option of admission (voluntary or compulsory) offers one protective route, but in those jealousies not clearly secondary to a severe mental illness this may be difficult. Mental health review commissioners and fellow clinicians on occasion give considerable latitude to sanity, particularly in the delusional disorders resulting in the patient rapidly returning to the community untreated and often even more convinced of the evil machinations of the partner. Negotiating separation with a couple embroiled in jealousy conflict is usually difficult and frustrating. Severe jealousy problems on occasion reflect a conflicted, but intensely involved, relationship. This relationship is usually not easily parted and even with less over-involved couples there may be, despite clear warnings, little appreciation of the risks. In those not labouring under frank delusions of infidelity it is sometimes possible to alter behaviour and de-escalate tensions simply by enumerating the risks and sharing one's anxieties about the future conduct. The management of jealousy is outside the scope of this chapter. For further discussion see White and Mullen (1989), Crow and Ridley (1990), Pines (1992), Mullen (1995), Dolan and Bishay (1996), Kingham and Gordon (2004), de Silva (2004).

Erotomania (The Pathologies of Love)

> All the motives for murder are covered by the four L's: Love, Lust, Lucre, and Loathing. They'll tell you, laddie, that the most dangerous is loathing. Don't you believe it. The most dangerous is love. (P. D. James 2003: 10)

The term erotomania has established itself as the term for pathological forms of love. This is unfortunate given the implications of both the erotic and the manic, neither of which are entirely appropriate. It is also unfortunate because of the historic baggage attached to the term. Alternative terms have been proposed including erotic paranoia (Krafft-Ebing 1879), erotic self-reference delusions (Kretschmer 1918), delusional loving (Seeman 1978) and pathological extensions of love (Mullen and Pathé 1994a). Erotomania, despite its drawbacks, remains the most commonly used term and will therefore be employed in this chapter.

History

Erotomania has been employed at various times to describe at least three putative disorders.

- The love melancholies, in which a wide range of symptoms, including those we would recognise as depression, were attributed to sentimental or erotic attractions which had either been unrequited or indulged in excessively (Burton 1621; Harvey 1672 (quoted in Hunter and McAlpine 1963)).
- Erotic manias (nymphomania, satyriasis), which were described vividly by Isaac Ray (1839: 192–3) as 'states of the most unbridled excitement, filling the mind with a crowd of voluptuous images, and ever hurrying its victim to acts of the grossest licentiousness'. This enviable form of erotomania was also on occasion extended to incorporate those sexual behaviours we now pusillanimously refer to as the paraphillias (Macpherson 1889).
- Erotomania, which Esquirol (1845/1965) included among his monomanias as a disorder characterised by an exaggerated and irrational sentimental attachment usually to someone who in reality has little or no relationship to the sufferer.

It is the latter use of the term erotomania which gave rise to our current concepts as it was redescribed and modified by authorities over the next century. Krafft-Ebing (1904/1879: 408) wrote 'the nucleus of the whole malady is the delusions of being distinguished and loved by a person of the opposite sex who regularly belongs to one of the higher classes of society [...] the love, as should be emphasised [is] romantic, enthusiastic, but absolutely platonic'. Kraepelin (1913: 245–9) gives the pre-eminent clinical description:

> ... the patient perceives that a person of the other sex distinguished really or presumedly by high position is kindly disposed to him [...] an intercepted glance, a chance meeting [...] let this hidden love become certainty to the patient [...] Very soon every chance occurrence, clothing meetings, reading, conversation acquire for the patient a relation to his imagined adventure [...] the whole colouring of the love is visionary and romantic [...] finally the patient resolves on further steps. He promenades before the window of the adored one, sends letters [...] but [if] things take an unfavourable turn the loved one can become the enemy and the persecutor of the patient.

Hart (1912) provided a very English construction of the disorder which he believed was entirely a female malady under the term 'Old Maid's Insanity'. He described this as characterised by 'an unmarried lady of considerable age, and blameless reputation, begins to complain of the undesirable attentions to which she is subjected by some male acquaintance [...] [who she explains] is obviously anxious to marry her and persistently follows her about' (p. 122). De Clérambault (1942), whose name has come to be attached specifically to this syndrome, added little to existing descriptions of erotomania but did, as described earlier, incorporate the state into the wider concept of disorders of passion.

Phenomenology

The nature of love has largely been the province of poets, novelists and artists. The psychiatric and psychological literature has tended to be reductionist, suggesting love is, if not frank self-deception, merely a cover for raw sexuality, or for such things as the mysterious forces of libido or a clinging form of object relationship (Buss 1994; Frijda 1986; Bowlby 1969; Harlow 1974). A scholarly literature, mainly from philosophers, has accorded love some respect as an emotional experience in and of itself (Scheler 1954, orig. 1912; Singer 1966, 1987; Scruton 1986; Solomon 1980). The infatuation of falling in love and being in love are suggested to be separable states of affairs (Fisher 1990). Infatuation does not necessarily require encouragement or even a response from the object of these affections. In normal individuals, however, if the love fails to elicit a favourable response the would-be lover usually eventually abandons the hope for a relationship and gradually detaches their affections from the lost cause. Some sense of sadness and residual longing for the failed romance may remain but the rejected suitor is left emotionally able to seek new attachments (Baumeister and Wotman 1992). Occasionally unrequited love in normal people may not wither but, by an act of self-abnegation, continue without the expectation, or demand, for a response (Fisher 1990). The borderline between the banalities of broken hearts and the realms of the pathological is approached when fantasy and self-deception begin to substitute for a lack of response from the beloved. Blocked from progress into the mutuality of attraction, desire and benevolent concern which constitutes being in love, the erotomanic turns to assertion and unfounded conviction. Theirs is not the sad acceptance of lost love but the strident claim that love is, or will be, theirs, irrespective of the apparent behaviour and stated feelings of the beloved. Love for the erotomanic is transformed from a communion with another into a lonely, idiopathic but utterly preoccupying erotic fixation. Love, like many complex emotional states, in part reflects the influence of cultural constructions which determine the meaning and to some extent the expression of the passion. As a result the way love is regarded and valued changes over historical periods (Singer 1966, 1987). Employing the model of the emotions set out previously, a simplified account of the phenomenology of love can be provided.

The loved one is endowed with those qualities by the lover that makes them an object of delight. In the erotomanic reality plays little part in constraining the process of endowing so an idealised other can be constructed. The judgments of the erotomanic, again unconstrained by reality, create the certainty of mutuality, or mutuality to come, or even the lover as infatuated pursuer. The erotomanic is secure in their constructed attachment so theirs is the enjoyment of the delights of being in love uncontaminated by the uncertainties evoked by real relationships. The desires of the erotomanic are often for an ethereal love abstracted from the challenges of the carnal, but not always so. Fantasy plays the major role in the world of the erotomanic. Exploring the fantasies is important as occasionally they can reveal unexpected and unpleasant possibilities. One of our intimacy-seeking stalkers who believed he was loved by a night-school teacher, despite her clear messages to the contrary, revealed detailed necrophilic fantasies at total variance with what had appeared until then as an almost puppy like devotion. The behaviours, or predispositions to behave, are essential to explore as they almost always reveal stalking activities or the plans for such action.

Prevalence

Erotomania is still regarded wrongly as a rarity (Enoch and Trethowan 1979; Retterstøl and Opjordsmoen 1991; Rudden *et al.* 1983, Menzies *et al.* 1995). This supposed rarity reflects a failure of recognition rather than a paucity of cases. The emergence of stalking as a category of offence in many jurisdictions has dramatically increased rates of ascertainment of erotomania (Mullen and Pathé 1994a; Leong 1994; Harmon *et al.* 1995; Menzies *et al.* 1995). Erotomania occurs in men and women, the homosexual and the heterosexual and in a variety of cultural contexts (Lovett Doust and Christie 1978; Taylor *et al.* 1983; Dunlop 1988; Eminson *et al.* 1988; El-Assra 1989). The gender ratio for erotomanic syndromes overall must still be considered uncertain though in the pure (reactive) forms females almost certainly predominate.

Love and infatuation

Esquirol (1845) and Kretschmer (1918/1930) considered erotomania to be based on an exaggeration of those dispositions to be found in normal lovers which could reflect both beliefs that one was loved as well as a morbidly enhanced infatuation. De Clérambault (1942) by contrast insisted cases should be confined to those who believe they are loved. De Clérambault's view has received the imprimatur of the DSM-IV which requires that erotomania be equated with 'a delusion that another person, usually of a higher status, is in love with the individual' (p. 765). The potential implications of such exclusivity was dramatically illustrated in the trial of John Hinkley Jr, who attempted to assassinate President Reagan. Hinkley had developed an intense and preoccupying infatuation with the actress Jodi Foster and had claimed that his desire to attract her attention lay behind the attack on the President. Evidence was given at the trial to indicate that Hinkley did not have erotomania because he at no time claimed that Jodi Foster loved him or even currently reciprocated his interest. The consuming infatuation with Jodi Foster, which had directly led, through a tortured reasoning process, to his trying to kill the President, was not considered capable of sustaining a diagnosis of delusional disorder because Hinkley made no claim that Jodi Foster had reciprocated his affections (Low *et al.*1986; Goldstein 1987; Meloy 1989). The question of a severe mental disorder based on a morbid infatuation, though important, was just one of the diagnostic issues in this trial where common sense and clinical experience confronted the word of the DSM-III, and the word won (Stone 1984).

The focus on a false belief of being loved in defining the psychopathology appears understandable, for a claim to be loved, and to have had that love revealed by specific actions and events, is usually open to falsification. In contrast, the assertion that one loves another is difficult to argue with, let alone declare to be false, particularly when no accompanying claim is made that the affection is returned (Mullen 1997a). In practice, however, it is not so much the falsifiability of the central belief which indicates a psychopathological process but the reasons advanced for the beliefs and the nature of the behaviour it evokes (Mullen *et al.* 2000).

The assumption of disorder in erotomania depends in large part on the grounds on which the patients base their unshakable convictions either of being loved or that their pursuit of love will eventually be blessed with a favourable response. They often have a remarkable capacity to reinterpret even the clearest of rejections as encouragement, if not as outright expressions of love. One of our morbidly infatuated patients, when the object of his relentless pursuit finally lost her temper and screamed at him to 'fuck off' and leave her alone, happily interpreted this as an indication of their developing intimacy. After all, he said, 'fucking was part of loving'. Pathology is also indicated by the extent of the pre-occupation with the supposed lover. In the erotomanias the days and nights are largely taken up with thinking and fantasising about the supposed love. Finally, it is the extent to which their behaviour disrupts their own lives and inflicts disturbance and distress on the object of their affection which distinguishes the pathological from the normal variants of love. The pathological infatuations share the same indicators of morbidity as the pathological beliefs in being loved with the sole exception of the convictions that they are the object of intense love from the victim of their unwanted attentions.

Erotomania can be characterised as involving:

- *either* a conviction of being loved despite the supposed lover having done nothing to encourage or sustain that belief, but on the contrary having either made clear their lack of interest or remained unaware of the claimed relationship;
  or an intense infatuation without necessarily any marked accompanying conviction that the affection is currently reciprocated;
- a propensity to reinterpret the words and actions of the object of their attentions to maintain the belief in their supposed romance;
- preoccupation with the supposed love which comes to form a central part of the subject's existence.

These three essential criteria are often accompanied by:

- a conviction that the claimed relationship will eventually be crowned by a permanent and loving union;
- repeated attempts to approach or communicate with the supposed lover.

In clinical practice the subject's conviction that the object of their affections loves them is usually accompanied with an acknowledged reciprocal affection. It is only the occasional patient who claims to be pursued by a lover to whom they remain indifferent (Mullen and Pathé 1994a).

Cases such as these have taken on a new prominence, with the emergence of stalking as a category of criminal offending and as a constellation of behaviours of concern to mental health professionals to whom police and the courts are turning for assessment and remedies.

In normal individuals periods of intense infatuation may occur (particularly in adolescents) but they fade when it is clear that no favourable response is to be expected from the beloved. The teenage 'crush' lacks the conviction of eventual fulfilment (though fantasies of such fulfilment are common) and acts as a pleasurable embellishment of their life not as a preoccupying and disruptive element. Teenage crushes are often social experiences which are shared with like-minded peers and pursued through groups and clubs, which is in stark contrast to the isolating nature of pathological infatuations.

In most erotomanics morbid infatuation coexists with a morbid conviction of being loved but there can be states which are virtually exclusively either morbid beliefs in being loved or morbid infatuations.

Symptomatic and pure (reactive) erotomanias

As discussed above the disorders of passion occur in symptomatic and pure or reactive forms.

Erotomania may occur as a symptom complex in association with the schizophrenic complex (Hayes and O'Shea 1985), affective disorders (Rudden *et al.* 1990; Raskin and Sullivan 1974), schizo-affective disorders (Gillett *et al.* 1990), a range of organic psychosyndromes including dementia (Lovett Doust and Christie 1978; Drevets and Rubin 1987; Signer and Cummings 1987; Gaddall 1989) and even as a side effect of pharmacotherapy (Adamou and Hale 2003). Rudden *et al.* (1990) reported 12 of their 28 cases had schizophrenia, Mullen and Pathé (1994a) reported that seven of their 16 cases had a primary diagnosis of schizophrenia and three of mania as part of a bipolar disorder; in the series of Menzies *et al.* (1995) nine of 13 cases had a primary diagnosis of schizophrenia and of Gillett *et al's* (1990) eleven cases, three had schizophrenia and four a bipolar illness.

The symptomatic erotomanias differ from the pure or reactive types not only by being accompanied by the other disturbances of mental state specific to the generating disorder but also by being more fickle in changing the object of their attentions over time and in tending to have more obviously carnal desires and intentions (Mullen and Pathé 1994a). One of our cases who had a schizophrenic syndrome had pursued six different women over a period of ten years and was convinced that they loved him. His victims were selected from health staff and on one occasion a young woman whom he saw in the street. Erotomanic symptoms associated with the schizophrenic syndrome were reported by Mullen and Pathé (1994b) to be associated with a greater frequency of sexual attacks but this was not found by Menzies *et al.* (1995) in their series.

The reactive or pure erotomanias have been suggested to emerge in response to a 'narcissistic wound' or loss (usually of a supportive relationship) (Enoch and Trethowan 1979; Hollender and Callahan 1975; Evans *et al.* 1982). These pure pathologies of love often appear to emerge from a context of emptiness to fill a vacuum in the patients' lives. Taylor *et al.* (1983) noted all their cases had led lonely and solitary existences with no sexual partners for many years prior to the emergence of the delusion. Segal (1989) pointed to the common themes of having socially empty lives, a lack of sexual contact and low socio-economic status. Mullen and Pathé (1994a) noted that all their five cases of pure erotomania when the disorder emerged were facing a life which appeared to them bleak, unrewarding and bereft of intimacy. The erotomanic fixation can be postulated to provide at least a semblance of an intimate relationship and a route to the engagement of the loving and erotic affections of the patients. Scheler (1912/1954) in his classic study of the phenomenology of love suggested that we do not love someone because they give us pleasure but we experience joy through loving. The act of love, even if unrequited, is itself still accompanied by a feeling of great happiness. For those whose life is empty of intimacy, the rewards of even a pathological love may be considerable (Mullen 1997a).

The pre-morbid personalities in pure cases of erotomania have variously been described as shy and awkward (Krafft-Ebing 1879/1904), hypersensitive and self-referential (Kretschmer 1918), proud and rebellious (de Clérambault 1942), narcissistic (Enoch and Trethowan 1979, Meloy 1989), schizoid (Munro *et al.* 1985), lacking in confidence, suspicious and socially avoidant (Retterstøl and Opjordsmoen 1991) and finally timid and withdrawn (Seeman 1978). The features common to these various formulations is of a socially inept individual isolated from others, be it by sensitivity, suspiciousness or assumed superiority (Mullen and Pathé 1994a).

Mullen and Pathé (1994a) in their series noted that within the pure syndromes, the pre-morbid personality was marked by considerable self-consciousness. Addionally, they had a tendency to refer the actions and utterances of others to themselves, usually endowing them with a denigratory or malevolent colouring. Such a tendency makes them susceptible to a pathology of love, given that all that may be required to set such a development in motion is seeing the actions and utterances of one particular person not as malevolent but as loving. These character traits may also provide some rationale for why apparently intelligent and attractive people are so handicapped in social and erotic relationships that they are driven into fantasy and delusion to satisfy their needs of intimacy.

The view advanced here of the pure or reactive forms of pathologies of passion being an extension of normal emotional reactions, leaves problems over the boundary between the pathological and the morbid. The boundary issues in erotomania are particularly acute in instances where there has been some form of real relationship, however fleeting, between the individual and the object of their affections, as portrayed in the film *Fatal Attraction*.

Stalking and other forms of violence

The erotomanias have long been known to be associated with violence and stalking. Esquirol (1845/1965) reported a case who both attempted to lift the skirts of the actress he stalked and assaulted the husband he believed stood between him and his beloved. Morrison wrote in 1848 'erotomania sometimes prompts those labouring under it to destroy themselves or others, for although in general tranquil and respectful, the patient sometimes becomes irritable, passionate and jealous' (quoted in Enoch and Trethowan 1979). De Clérambault (1942) believed that though erotomania began in pride, love and hope it all too easily degenerated into resentment and anger.

Stalking behaviours are an almost inevitable accompaniment of erotomanic disorders. Overt sexual approaches and attacks may also occur (Mullen and

Pathé 1994b; Menzies *et al.* 1995). Taylor *et al.* (1983) described four male erotomanics who as a result of their disorder acted violently. Menzies *et al.* (1995) also found significant levels of antisocial behaviour related to erotomania. Erotomanics can become violent in response to rejection or jealousy. Occasionally the assault may be an inadvertent by-product of the patient's clumsy attempts to approach the object of their attention (Mullen and Pathé 1994b). Those believed to impede access to the beloved may also fall victim to the violence of an erotomanic. Taylor *et al.* (1983) and Menzies *et al.* (1995) found the violence to be directed most frequently at someone other than the object of the patient's affections but in the series of Mullen and Pathé (1994b) and Harmon *et al.* (1995) the supposed beloved was the most common victim (see above).

The querulous

> We are ... almost ready to treat every death as chargeable to someone's account, every accident as caused by someone's criminal negligence, every sickness to someone's failure, whose fault is the first question ... then what damages? What compensation? What restitution? (Mary Douglas 1992)

Querulous (from the Latin for plaintive murmuring) describes a pattern of behaviour involving the unusually persistent pursuit of a personal grievance in a manner seriously damaging to the individual's economic, social and personal interests, and disruptive to the functioning of the courts and/or other agencies attempting to resolve the claims (Mullen and Lester 2006).

The mental health literature has traditionally focused on querulous behaviour as it manifests as part of paranoid or delusional disorders. This is reflected in the terms used for these disorders such as querulant paranoia (Kraepelin 1904), paranoia querulantium (Krafft-Ebbing 1879) and litigious paranoia (Goldstein 1995; Refsum 1983; Astrup 1984; Johanson 1964; Kolle 1931; Winokur 1977; Ungvari 1995; Pang *et al.* 1996; Munro 1999). The querulous are not necessarily psychotic, and these states can be part of a psychogenic reaction (Kraepelin 1904; Jaspers 1923). In the current diagnostic manuals the querulous are placed in the categories of paranoia querulants (ICD 10) or delusional disorder persecutory type (DSM IV-R).

Querulousness may, however, more usefully be regarded as a disorder of passion which can reflect a wide range of factors which may or may not include a psychosis. Pathology in this conceptualisation does not lie exclusively in the subject's mental state but also in their behaviour and its impact on themselves and others. This runs counter to a continuing tradition in psychiatry, but not in psychology, to source pathology primarily in abnormal states of mind and to avoid judgments about pathology based on behaviour alone (Lewis 1955; Clare 1997).

The law has long attempted to protect its courts from vexatious litigants by legislation, the earliest example being the Prussian Law of 1793 (Caduff 1995). Despite such a venerable tradition of declaring nuisances vexatious, such laws are rarely effective. Criminal laws once existed in England and Wales to protect the wider community from barrators, who were persistent complainers and fomenters of quarrels, but such laws have fallen into disuse (Freckelton 1988).

Not only have the laws aimed at curbing the querulous fallen into disuse but also the psychiatric categories once used to describe them. Caduff (1995) documented a threefold decrease in the use of the diagnosis of querulous paranoia over the last 80 years. In part the decline in interest was because of the distrust of the concept of paranoia (Post 1982). In part the decline reflected increased sensitivities among clinicians to issues of civil rights. This led to the rejection of judgmental labels, such as neurotic quarrellers or querulous psychopaths, for those who were over energetic in the pursuit of their vision of their rights (Kolle 1931; Schneider 1958; Stalstrom 1980).

The virtual disappearance of the querulous from the professional landscape occurred at a time when complaints and grievance procedures were emerging as a central mechanism for resolving conflict in Western societies (Mullen and Lester 2006). It also corresponded to the rise of the ideology of individual rights, rather than civil rights, as the touchstone of the new democratic liberalism. Ordinary citizens' capacity to seek justice and to claim redress came to depend on complaints departments and agencies of accountability such as ombudsmen's offices and commissions of, for example, equal opportunity. Few can now afford to go direct to the courts, so complaint resolution procedures have become the main defence against the power of private and public agencies. In this context it became problematic to discuss the pathologies of complaint which could potentially strip an individual's claims of legitimacy. Paradoxically then, at the very moment when vast numbers of people were being drawn, for the first time, into a multiplicity of new complaints resolution procedures there was an exclusion of knowledge of the problems such systems could create for a small, vulnerable, but increasingly salient group (Mullen and Lester 2006).

Complaining, litigating and petitioning

The querulous use three broad approaches to pursuing their campaigns for justice.

Complainants

Complaints organisations are often troubled by a small group of unusually persistent complainants who consume an inordinate amount of time and organisational resources in the pursuit of grievances. These in and of themselves seem, if not trivial, at least lacking in the complexity and import which might justify such lengthy and concentrated campaigns (Lester *et al.* 2004).

Vexatious litigants

Chronic litigators in the civil and family court have long been recognised as a problem (Rowlands 1988; Freckeleton 1988; Goldstein 1995). Vexatious litigants pursue their grievance predominantly within the courts, though they usually also access agencies of accountability and not infrequently petition politicians and royalty. They often appear as unrepresented litigants, sometimes because they have exhausted their funds or the patience of lawyers, but more often because they believe that nobody else can be trusted to adequately present their case. As unrepresented litigants they can be particularly challenging to the smooth functioning of the courts. This group also tend to find themselves charged with contempt of court when their passionate involvement in their case results in intemperate remarks to the judge. Attempts to exclude these dedicated litigators from the courts usually fail. Internet sites now provide information on how to circumvent orders declaring them vexatious, as well as mutual support from like-minded litigators (Mullen and Lester 2006).

Unusually persistent petitioners

A third type of querulous behaviour involves pursuing a quest for justice primarily through petitioning prominent people such as politicians and heads of state. This group typically send voluminous and repeated communications setting out their case and pleading for, or demanding, help. Like other querulous individuals they may gradually shift from requests to demands, from demands to recriminations and from recriminations to threats (Mullen and Lester 2006). They may make direct contact with the public figure, attempt to stalk them and on occasion launch attacks. This group have contributed many of the would-be assassins of British Royalty over the last 200 years and of politicians in more recent times (James *et al.* in submission; Poole 2000).

The clinical characteristics of the querulous

These querulous complainants suffer financially, professionally, socially and personally as a result of their persistence,. They often lose jobs, friends and partners as their lives are absorbed with the pursuit of their vision of justice.

Compared to the vast majority of complainants and claimants, the querulous pursue their complaints for longer, they produced far greater volumes of material in support of their case, and when their cases were closed there has rarely been anything approaching a mutually acceptable resolution (Lester *et al.* 2004). The querulous often show characteristic anomalies in the form and content of written statements of complaint (See Table 22.1). The querulous, in common with most claimants, seek reparation and compensation. In addition, they typically seek retribution and personal vindication. They want dismissed or criminally prosecuted those they believe responsible for the injustice or to have

Table 22.1 Jealousy: judgments and emotional concomitants

Judgment	Emotional and concomitant state	Associated desire	Behavioural predispositions
The relationship is in jeopardy	Apprehension, suspicion	To know for sure	Interrogating checking
There has been infidelity	Anger, self-righteousness	To punish	Threatening, attacking
Power and control is being lost	Helplessness, resentment	To reassert power To receive sympathy	Intimidation, appeals
The partner is lost to another	Despair Destructive envy	To deprive the other To hurt	Violence to self and partner
One's hopes and dreams for the future are lost	Pain	Vengeance	Violence to self and partner

obstructed their pursuit of redress. They may also demand organisations be closed down or made to pay punitive damages. In addition, the querulous often demand public recognition not only of the justice of their claims but of their struggle on behalf of the rights of all. They tend to regard themselves as champions of the common man whose grievances have transcended the personal to become of national or even international import. In short, the querulous seek retribution and personal vindication, aims which are incompatible with the objectives – and the powers – of the courts, the agencies of accountability and even the politicians and royalty to whom they present their petitions.

The querulous typically believe:

- Those who do not fully support their cause are enemies.
- Any lack of progress in their claim is the product of malevolent interference from someone.
- Any compromise is humiliating defeat.
- The grievance is the defining moment of their lives.
- Because they are in the right the outcomes they seek must not only be possible but necessary.

In assessing those showing querulous behaviour we have found it useful to assess changes that occur over time in seven domains: the behaviour, the nature of the grievance, the supposed agents of injustice, the psychological state, the social circumstances, the beliefs about the world and what is sought. A case history may assist.

Box 22.1 Case example

Mr X was in his late forties when his problems began. He made a complaint following the death of his mother about the manner in which she had been treated. There were some grounds for legitimate concern about the attitudes of some staff. His mother's death occurred at a time when Mr X was having problems at work and experiencing marital problems. He was treated in a peremptory manner by the hospital managers when he complained so he took the matter to the health commissioner. When this failed to produce the response he desired, he made official complaints to the medical board and nursing board. When he failed to obtain what he considered a satisfactory response from any of these agencies he attempted, without success, to initiate litigation against the hospital. When this failed to progress he petitioned his MP and later the Queen. Some two years into the process he began writing threatening letters to the staff members and repeatedly following one of the doctors. He picketed the hospital and the health board headquarters. He was convicted of stalking and naturally appealed. He made threats to kill a court official, was convicted and again appealed. When referred by the courts he presented as an energised and garrulous man totally preoccupied with the details of the perceived injustices and derelictions. He believed he was owed millions in punitive damages, and that when he inevitably prevailed, this would bring down not just the hospital and the doctors but the whole National Health Service. He regarded himself as a whistleblower who would be publicly recognised as one of the major social reformers of his generation. The changes over time in the grievance, the agents, his social situation, psychological state, beliefs abut the world and aims are presented schematically in Figure 22.2.

The case illustrates the typical devastating social decline, the way the grievance generalises to encompass wider and wider issues, together with the accretion of more and more agents supposedly responsible. The ultimate move into violent or otherwise threatening behaviours to draw attention to their grievances is far from unusual. The mental state of such individuals by the time we see them is dominated by apparently unshakeable beliefs around the justice and importance of their grievances and the extent of the opposition they face. Many provide detailed and plausible accounts with an infectious enthusiasm. Though they present their grievances in pedantic detail they often seem energised and almost manic. The superficial rationality with which they present their stories can distract the inexperienced from the extraordinary nature of their actual claims in which the manifestly minor has come to support a grand edifice of conjecture and accusation. It is not infrequent for such patients to insist on making notes of any interview or recording the interview. Inevitably they will request copies of your notes and, equally inevitably, one way or another they will eventually obtain them. Their speech may be marked by what Kraepelin (1904) referred to as 'a wearisome diffuseness of conversation' and often by the use of a multiplicity of technical terms, particularly from the legal discourse, employed idiosyncratically. They will often arrive dragging suitcases full of documents frequently graced with multiple marginalia and with words and phrases emphasised by underlining or highlighter pens.

The querulous have on occasion been considered to have an obsessional illness. The level of preoccupation, the ruminative quality of their thinking and the pedantic attention to the minutiae of their case do all suggest obsession. Certainly most, if not all, querulants have obsessional personality traits. But the querulant does not regard their core beliefs and the behaviour as absurd, or absurdly insistent, nor do they resist the urges to pursue their preoccupations. The querulous therefore may be regarded as obsessive or fixated but not as being obsessional. The querulous on occasion present with such enthusiasm and unbridled optimism that they can raise the question of an underlying manic disorder. When observed over time most will show fluctuations from energised engagement to hopelessness but this usually reflects the vicissitudes of their campaign for justice, not an underlying mood disorder.

The limits of normality

Querulous behaviour has to be separated from the over-enthusiastic, and even disruptive, pursuit of justice which remains within normal limits or is legitimised by the social agenda being pursued. Individuals can invest inordinate amounts of time in the pursuit of claims because of the inherent complexity and manifest importance of the complaint. These should not be regarded as querulous. There are difficult people who pursue claims filled with a sense of being victimised and distrustful of all except their own construction of the case, but who will ultimately settle for the best deal they can extract. This is difficult, but not querulous, behaviour. Querulousness involves not just persistence but a totally disproportionate investment of time and resources in grievances which grow steadily from the mundane to the grandiose, and whose settlement requires not just apology, reparation and/or compensation but retribution and personal vindication. Like other passions the pursuit of justice moves towards

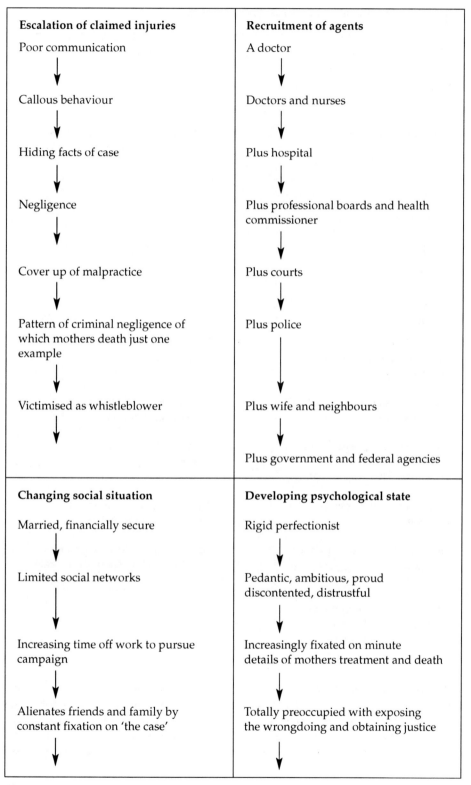

Figure 22.2   The unfolding of querulousness

Figure 22.2 The unfolding of querulousness (continued)

Changing social situation	Developing psychological state
Loses job ↓ Wife leave him ↓ Bankruptcy ↓ Living alone in hostel ↓ Destitute	 Mood fluctuating between elation and energetic engagement and fearful withdrawal and despondency
Relevant beliefs about world and himself	**What he seeks**
That chaos is kept in check by rules and agreements	Compensation for injuries (increasing constantly)
Things go wrong because others either fail in their responsibilities or deliberately cause damage	Reparation (for things to be as they were)
Others have not recognised his abilities	Retribution against those who failed their responsibilities
He is destined to some form of greatness	Vindication in the form of public recognition that through his struggle he is making the world a safer place
That he is more honourable, intelligent, honest, and persevering than others	

pathology when it ceases to seek resolution, or the best possible deal, and becomes self-sustaining, rejecting of all and every solution, and alters not in the hope of compromise, but conversely, only to maintain and extend the grievance.

Social reformers pursue issues of concern to groups of their fellow citizens, work with and through others, pursue objectives which are circumscribed and obviously related to the core issues driving the campaign, and will accept negotiated resolutions, even if these involve compromise. In contrast, the querulous claim wide social significance for idiosyncratic concerns while subordinating everything to personal issues, rarely work effectively with others, tend to repeatedly dismiss lawyers, or claims professionals who try to help them, and negotiation and compromise have no place in their quest for justice.

The clear theoretical dichotomy between social campaigning and querulous behaviour is not always so obvious in practice. Those whose behaviour is querulous can occasionally gather around them small groups of like-minded supporters, a process now assisted by the Internet. They can join social campaigns where their energies can compensate, for a time, for their self-absorption self-reference. Those who have shown querulous behaviour in the past may take on a role of lay advocate and use others to advance their own view of justice. Such individuals are recognised as a major problem for agencies of accountability. Campaigns over, for example, rights of victims can have immense personal import for all those involved and in these situations the risks of querulous behaviour emerging in some may be considerable. If there are doubts then the benefit of those doubts should go to the assumption of legitimate campaigning not to the presence of querulous behaviour. Whistleblowers, who usually claim to be exposing nefarious and corrupt practices in their place of work, are a particularly difficult group in which to separate altruistic from querulous behaviour. There is no doubt that errors occur.

Nosology

Jaspers (1923) regarded querulousness as similar to jealousy, being potentially the product of pathological reactions, developments or processes, with again normality being a further option. Van der Heydt (1952) attempted a typology of querulants incorporating: the opportunistic who were individuals with antisocial traits pursuing personal advantage; the paranoid justice seeker driven by delusional convictions specific to their particular grievances; the conjugal caught up in the passionate pursuit of property or parental rights following marital breakdown; the quarrelsome, who had personality traits conducive to protracted conflict with any and all; secondary to psychotic disorders notably the schizophrenias; and finally a normal group, the nature of which was left somewhat vague. Querulousness is destructive to the individual and their family as well as disruptive to agencies of accountability and the courts. This makes it difficult to regard querulousness as normal in either an ideal or statistical sense. It is, however, potentially possible for a relatively normal individual to be driven to querulousness by an experience of injustice as a result of insensitive complaint resolution procedures.

The division of querulous disorders into those secondary to some wider psychopathology like a schizophrenic syndrome and those emerging from an abnormal reaction to the perception of having been unjustly treated fits the clinical realities. The querulous encountered in clinical practice, unlike morbid jealousy and erotomanics, are only occasionally secondary to other mental disorders or impairments of mental function. This is perhaps because querulousness presupposes a persistence and a capacity for organisation incompatible with such states. It is the pure or reactive syndromes which predominate in the querulous states.

Clinically, the querulous prior to having become enmeshed in the pursuit of grievances, were usually functional individuals with families and without obvious antisocial traits. Their pre-morbid personalities are often marked by obsessional traits, self-absorption and more than the usual levels of sensitivity and self-reference. Many have had limited social networks and difficulties with intimate relationships. They tend to have been people disappointed in their expectations of life, short on trust and long on self-importance. The querulousness can be seen as imminent in these vulnerable individuals and all it took was the provocation of a perceived injury and subsequent injustice to set them on their pathological pursuit. A spectrum exists from, at one extreme, those with few propensities to become querulous who in response to some great unmerited wrong are forced down the path of chronic litigation and complaining, to at the other those so predisposed that the slightest of provocation will set them on this particular path to disaster.

Whether a querulous individual is, or is not, deluded often creates uncertainty. This distinction can be critical as it often determines whether or not the individual will be offered treatment or subjected to a court order mandating treatment. Given that few will accept treatment voluntarily, at least initially, what is at issue is, in effect, whether to treat. It can be a daunting task to try to concentrate on an unending stream of speech coupled with proffered documents, both of which when combined offer apparent plausibility, reasonableness, pedantic precision with rambling obscurantism. These factors can tempt the clinician to opt for some vague formulation in terms of overvalued ideas or paranoid personality disorder. It is remarkable how broad notions of non-delusional eccentricity become when confronted with the querulous. We have seen patients declared by mental health professionals to have 'no formal mental illness' and not requiring further intervention who, for example, entertained the absolute conviction that they are owed millions of dollars for an act of trespass. Another patient believed the government would fall when the truth of his dental mismanagement was finally acknowledged. Another patient assured us that the UN was keenly awaiting the results of his complaint against a local lawyer. Finally, another patient assured us that the Queen had joined herself to his quest for compensation from an insurance company. In each case the patient had a mass of documents to prove their case in which even the most imaginative would be hard pressed to find any connection to what they were claimed to prove. Attempts to avoid conferring on the querulous legitimacy as patients is also fed by the widespread, but incorrect, view of the untreatability of both delusional disorders and personality disorders. By normalising such extraordinary behaviour the clinician is in effect, dismissing the possibility of mandated treatment, which effectively removes the mental health treatment option. Evaluating the ideas that drive the querulous behaviour requires a careful history, a dispassionate examination of the documents and an active attempt to engage with the patient's ideas and claims. The extent to which the patient and those around them, are suffering as a result of their pursuit of justice should have some weight in making a decision about whether to recommend treatment.

Criminal behaviour and querulousness

The querulous are usually seen in our clinic on court orders following acts of violence or threats. Typically such individuals have been pursuing their campaigns for a number of years and have resorted to violence, or threats of violence, in a calculated attempt to further their causes. On occasion they move to stalking someone they blame for their predicament. Examples include an individual who arrived at an ombudsman office with dynamite strapped to himself, a patient who abducted a bank manager at gunpoint and several who were impolitic enough to make threats to judges. These people by the time they were referred by the courts were all living alone and destitute. Their lives revolved entirely around their quest for justice. The querulous in general, and those who resort to violence, are predominantly male (Kraepelin 1904; Kolle 1931; Heydt 1952; Caduff 1995).

Attacks by the querulous on court officials, claims officials and politicians are by no means uncommon. Health professionals may also fall victim to the querulous pursuing what they believe to have been malpractice or unfair personal injury reports. In such cases there has often been a course of conduct characterised by increasingly threatening and intrusive activities usually over many months which, with the benefit of hindsight, takes on a sinister import. In most cases of serious or fatal violence (of which we have knowledge) there had been clear and specific threats issued. In a study of unusually persistent complainants seen in agencies of accountability there were frequent overt, and covert, threats of violence made to claims professionals (Lester *et al.* 2004). The vast majority do not progress to assault but when they do serious injuries may be inflicted.

Conclusions

The disorders of jealousy, love and the pursuit of justice currently occupy a marginal status not only in general mental health but in forensic mental health. This virtual invisibility is difficult to justify. Jealousy plays a major role in domestic violence and what is (at least in the UK), still one of the most common types of homicide (or more strictly gynocide). The pathological extensions of love are almost always associated with stalking behaviours. Querulousness is fast becoming a significant drain on the resources of courts and agencies as well as an increasing risk to the safety of those who work in these organisations. Further, querulousness plays a major role in the harassment of and attacks on public figures. The low profile accorded the disorders of passion has more to do with the difficulties fitting these conditions into the worldview of most mental health professionals than it has to do with their actual significance in the offending of the mentally disordered.

Selected further reading

In Charles Dickens, *Bleak House* (multiple editions), Dickens's detestation of lawyers finds a focus in this novel as he traces the fate of three wards of court caught up in the interminable case of Jarndyce & Jarndyce. One of the wards, Richard Carstone, becomes increasing preoccupied with the case which eventually leads to his ruin.

The novel by Julian Barnes (2005) *Before She Met Me*. London: Picador Books, traces the disintegration of a man caught up in jealousy which is focused on his partner's prior relationships. In the process, a vivid portrayal of the state of mind in jealousy emerges.

Mullen, P. E., Pathe, M. and Purcell, R. (2000) *Stalkers and Their Victims*. Cambridge: Cambridge University Press (new edition 2008), is an account of the nature of stalking and its effects on victims. Included is an extended discussion of the erotomanic states.

Mullen, P. E. and Lester, G. (2006) 'Vexatious litigants and unusually persistent complainants and petitioners: from querulous paranoia to querulous behaviour', *Behavioural Sciences and the Law*, 24: 33–349, provide the only recent review of the literature on the querulous from a mental health perspective.

Mary Douglas (1992) *Risk and Blame, Essays in Cultural Theory*. London: Routledge, provides a thought-provoking account of our culture's changing attitudes to causality and how that underpins the radical shift towards current societal concerns with risk management and blame. Far removed from the usual trivial critiques of the culture of blame and victim consciousness, this book offers a series of essays with substantial analysis and insight.

One of the greatest phenomenologists, Max Scheler (1970) *The Nature of Sympathy*, trans. P. Heath. New York Archon Books, turns his attention to the experience of love. When he wrote this book his theological training was still very much in evidence but on the way to analysing the love of God he does a great job on the more bucolic forms of the emotion.

References

Adamou, M. and Hale, A. S. (2003) 'Erotomania induced by venlafaxine: a case study', *Acta Psychiatrica Scandinavica*, 107: 314–17.
Astrup, C. (1984) 'Querulent paranoia: a follow-up', *Neuropsychobiology*, 11: 149–54.
Baruk, H. (1974 [orig. 1959]) 'Delusions of passion', in M. Shepherd and S.R. Hirsch (eds), *Themes and Variations in European Psychiatry*. Bristol: Wright, pp. 375–84.
Baumeister, R.F. and Wotman, S.R. (1992) *Breaking Hearts: The Two Sides of Unrequited Loves*. New York: Guilford Press.
Bishay, N.R., Petersen, N. and Tarrier, N. (1989) 'An uncontrolled study of cognitive therapy for morbid jealousy', *British Journal of Psychiatry*, 154: 386–9.
Blackstone, E. (1803 [orig. 1783]) in St George Tucker (ed.), *Blackstone's Commentaries*. Philadelphia: Brich & Small.
Bowlby, J. (1969) *Attachment*. New York: Basic Books.
Brisson, N.J. (1983) 'Battering husbands: a survey of abusive men', *Victimology*, 338–44.
Bryson, J.B. (1976) *The Nature of Sexual Jealousy: An Exploratory Paper*. Paper presented at the annual meeting of the American Psychological Association, Washington, DC.
Burton, R. (1621) *The Anatomy of Melancholy*. Numerous reprints and editions.
Buss, D.M. (1994) *The Evolution of Desire: Strategies of Human Mating*. New York: Basic Books.
Caduff, F. (1995) 'Querulanz–ein verschwindendes psychopatholgisches Verhaltensmuster?', *Fortschr. Neurol. Psychiat.*, 63: 504–10.
Clare, A.W. (1997) 'The disease concept in psychiatry', in R. Murray, P. Hill, P. McGuffin (eds), *The Essentials of Postgraduate Psychiatry*. Cambridge: Cambridge University Press, pp. 41–52.
Cobb, J.P. and Marks, I.M. (1979) 'Morbid jealousy featuring as obsessive-compulsive neurosis: treatment by behavioural psychotherapy', *British Journal of Psychiatry*, 134: 301–5.
Crow, M.J. and Ridley, J. (1990) *Therapy with Couples*. Oxford: Basil Blackwell.
Daly, M. and Wilson, M. (1988) *Homicide*. New York: Aldine de Gruyter.

Daly, M., Wilson, M., Weghorst, S.J. (1982) 'Male sexual jealousy', *Ethology and Sociobiology*, 3: 11–27.

de Clérambault C.G. (1942) 'Les psychoses passionelles', in Oeuvres Psychiatriques. Paris: Presses Universitaires, pp. 315–22.

de Silva, P. (2004) 'Jealousy in couple relationships. Invited essay', *Behaviour Change*, 21: 1–13.

Dobash, R.E. and Dobash, R.P. (1980) *Violence against Wives: A Case against the Patriarchy*. London: Open Books.

Dolan, M. and Bishay, N. (1996) 'The effectiveness of cognitive therapy in the treatment of non-psychotic morbid jealousy', *British Journal of Psychiatry*, 168: 588–93.

Douglas, M. (1992) *Risk and Blame, Essays in Cultural Theory*. London: Routledge.

Drevets, W.C. and Rubin, E.H. (1987) 'Erotomania and senile dementia of Alzheimer type', *British Journal of Psychiatry*, 151: 400–2.

Dunlop, J.L. (1988) 'Does erotomania exist between women?', *British Journal of Psychiatry*, 153: 830–3.

El-Assra, A. (1989) 'Erotomania in a Saudi woman', *British Journal of Psychiatry*, 155: 553–5.

Ellis, H. (1890) *The Criminal*. London: Walter Scott.

Eminson, S., Gillett, T. and Hassanyeh, F. (1988) 'Homosexual erotomania', *British Journal of Psychiatry*, 154: 128–9.

Enoch M.D. and Trethowan W.H. (1979) *Uncommon Psychiatric Syndromes*. Bristol: John Wright.

Esquirol, J.E.D. (1965 [orig 1845]) *Mental Maladies: A Treatise on Insanity*, trans. R. de Saussure. New York: Hafner.

Evans, D.L., Jechel, L.L. and Slott, N.E. (1982) 'Erotomania: a variant of pathological mourning', *Bulletin of the Menninger Clinic*, 46: 507–20.

Fisher, M. (1990) *Personal Love*. London: Duckworth.

Freckelton, I. (1988) 'Querulent paranoia and the vexatious complainant', *International Journal of Law and Psychiatry*, 11: 127–43.

Frijda, N. H. (1986) *The Emotions*. Cambridge: Cambridge University Press.

Gaddall, Y.Y. (1989) 'De Clérambault's Syndrome (erotomania) in organic delusional syndrome', *British Journal of Psychiatry*, 154: 714–16.

Gayford, J.J. (1975) 'Wife battering: a preliminary survey of 100 cases', *British Medical Journal*, 1: 194–7.

Gayford, J.J. (1979) 'Battered wives', *British Journal of Hospital Medicine*, 22: 496–503

Gibbens, T.C.N. (1958) 'Sane and insane homicide', *Journal of Criminal Law*. Criminology and Police Science, 49: 110–15.

Gillett, T., Eminson, S.R. and Hassanyeh, F. (1990) 'Primary and secondary erotomania: clinical characteristics and follow up', *Acta Psychiatrica Scandinavica*, 82: 65–9.

Goldstein, R.L. (1987) 'More forensic romances: de Clérambault's syndrome in men', *Bulletin of American Academy Psychiatry Law*, 15: 267–74.

Goldstein, R.L. (1995) 'Paranoids in the legal system: the litigious paranoid and the paranoid criminal', *Psychiatric Clinics of North America*, 18: 303–15.

Gordon, R.M. (1987) *The Structure of Emotions*. Cambridge: Cambridge University Press.

Greenspan, P.S. (1988) *Emotions and Reasons*. New York: Routledge.

Gullerot, E. (1971) *Women, Society and Change*. New York: McGraw-Hill, pp. 19–28.

Guth, D.J. (1982) 'The age of debt, the Reformation and English law', in D.J. Guth and J.W. McKenna (eds), *Tudor Rule and Revolution*. Cambridge: Cambridge University Press, pp. 70–85.

Harlow, H.F. (1974) *Learning to Love*. New York: Aronson.

Harmon, R.B., Rosner, R. and Owens, H. (1995) 'Obsessional harrassment and erotomania in a criminal court population', *Journal of Forensic Sciences*, 40: 188–96.

Hart, B. (1912) *The Psychology of Insanity*. Cambridge: Cambridge University Press.

Harvey, G. (1672) quoted in R. Hunter and I. Macalpine (1963) *Three Hundred Years of Psychiatry 1535–1860*. Oxford: Oxford University Press, pp. 196–7.

Hayes, M. and O'Shea, B. (1985) 'Erotomania in Schneider positive schizophrenia', *British Journal of Psychiatry*, 146: 661–3.

Hazlitt, W. (2005 [orig. 1826]) *On the Pleasure of Hating*. London: Penguin Books.

Hilberman, E. and Manson, M. (1977) 'Sixty battered women', *Victimology*, 2: 460–71.

Hollender, M.H. and Callahan, A.S. (1975) 'Erotomania or de Clérambault's syndrome', *Archives of General Psychiatry*, 32: 1574–6.

Insel, T.R. and Akiskal, H.S. (1986) 'Obsessive-compulsive disorder with psychotic features: a phenomenologic analysis', *American Journal of Psychiatry*, 143: 1527–33.

James, D.V., Mullen, P.E., Meloy, J.R., Pathé, M.T., Farnham, F.R., Preston, L. and Darnley, B. (in press) 'The role of mental disorder in attacks on European politicians 1990–2004', *Acta Psychiatrica Scandinavica*.

James, P.D. (2003) *The Murder Room*. London: Faber & Faber.

Jaspers, K. (1910) 'Eifersuchtswahn', *Zeitschrift für die gesamte Neurologie und Psychiatrie*, 1: 567–637.

Jaspers, K. (1923) *General Psychopathology*, trans. J. Hoenig and M.W. Hamilton (1963). Manchester: Manchester University Press.

Jaspers, K. (1963) *General Psychopathology*, trans. J. Hoenig and M.W. Hamilton, 7th edn. Manchester: Manchester University Press.

Johanson, E. (1964) 'Mild paranoia', *Acta Psychiatrica Scandinavica*, Suppl. 177: 40.

Kingham, M. and Gordon, H. (2004) 'Aspects of morbid jealousy', *Advances in Psychiatric Treatment*, 10: 207–15.

Kolle, K. (1931) 'Über Querulanten', *Archiv für Psychiatrie und Nerven-Krankheiten*, 95: 24–102.

Kraepelin, E. (1904) *Lectures in Clinical Psychiatry*, trans. and ed. T. Johnstone. London: Baillière, Tindall & Cox.

Kraepelin, E. (1913) *Manic Depressive Insanity and Paranoia*, trans. M. Barclay (1921). Edinburgh: E.S. Livingstone.

Krafft-Ebing, R. von (1904 [orig 1879]) *Text Book of Insanity*, trans. C.G. Chaddock and F. A. Davis. Philadelphia: S. A. Davis.

Kretschmer, E. (1918) *Der sensitive Beziehungswahn*. Berlin: Springer. (Selection translated as 'The sensitive delusion of reference', in S. R. Hirsch and M. Shepherd (eds) (1974) *Themes and Variations in European Psychiatry*. Bristol: Wright.)

Lagache, D. (1938) 'Erotomanie et jalousie', *Journal de Psychologie Normale et Pathologique*, April–June: 127–60.

Langfeldt, G. (1961) 'The erotic jealousy syndrome: a clinical study', *Acta Psychiatrica Scandinavica*, 36 (Suppl. 151): 7–68.

Leong, G.B. (1994) 'De Clérambault syndrome (erotomania) in the criminal justice system: another look at this recurring problem', *Journal of Forensic Sciences*, 39: 378–85.

Lester, G., Wilson, B., Griffin, L. and Mullen, P.E. (2004) 'Unusually persistent complainants', *British Journal of Psychiatry*, 184: 352–6.

Lewis, A. (1955) 'Health as a social concept', *British Journal of Sociology*, 4: 109–24.

Lovett Doust, J.W. and Christie, E.H. (1978) 'The pathology of love: some clinical variants of de Clérambault's syndrome', *Social Science and Medicine*, 12: 99–106.

Low, P.W., Jeffries, J.C. and Bonnie, R.J. (1986). *The Trial of John W. Hinckley Jr: A Case Study in the Insanity Defence*. Mineola, NY: Foundation Press.

Macpherson, J. (1889) *An Introduction to the Study of Insanity*. London: Macmillan.

Marazziti, D., Di Nasso, E., Masala, I., Baroni S., Abelli, M., Mengali, F., Mungai, F. and Rucci, P. (2003) 'Normal and obsessional jealousy: a study of a population of young adults', *European Psychiatry*, 18: 106–11.

Meloy, R. J. (1989) 'Unrequited love and the wish to kill', *Bulletin of the Menninger Clinic*, 53: 477–92.

Menzies, R.P.D., Fedoroff, J.P., Green, C.M. and Isaacson, K. (1995) 'Prediction of danger-ous behaviour in male erotomanics', British Journal of Psychiatry, 166: 529–36.

Mullen, P.E. (1990a) 'A phenomenology of jealousy', Australian and New Zealand Journal of Psychiatry, 24: 17–28.

Mullen, P.E. (1990b) 'Morbid jealousy and the delusion of infidelity', in R. Bluglass and P. Bowden (eds), Principles and Practice of Forensic Psychiatry. London: Churchill Livingston, pp. 823–34.

Mullen, P.E. (1991) 'The fear of the mentally ill: is this public attitude justified?', New Zealand Medical Journal, 104: 90–2.

Mullen, P.E. (1993) 'The crime of passion and the changing cultural construction of jeal-ousy', Criminal Behaviour and Mental Health, 3: 1–11.

Mullen, P.E. (1995) 'The clinical management of jealousy', Directions in Psychiatry, 15, Lesson 20.

Mullen, P.E. (1996) 'Editorial: jealousy and the emergence of violent and intimidating behaviours', Criminal Behaviour and Mental Health, 6: 199–205.

Mullen, P.E. (1997a) 'Disorders of passion', in D. Bhugra and A. Munro (eds), Toublesome Disguises: Underdiagnosed Psychiatric Syndromes. Oxford: Blackwell Science, pp. 127–67.

Mullen, P.E. (1997b) 'Mental states and states of mind', in R. Murray, D. Hill and P. McGuffin (eds), Essentials of Postgraduate Psychiatry, 3rd edn. Cambridge: Cambridge University Press, pp. 3–40.

Mullen, P.E. and Lester, G. (2006) 'Vexatious litigants and unusually persistent com-plainants and petitioners: from querulous paranoia to querulous behaviour', Behavioural Sciences and the Law, 24: 333–49.

Mullen, P.E. and Maack, L.H. (1985) 'Jealousy, pathological jealousy, and aggression', in D.P. Farrington and J. Gunn (eds), Aggression and Dangerousness. Chichester: John Wiley & Sons, pp. 103–26.

Mullen, P.E. and Martin, J. L. (1994) 'Jealousy: a community study', British Journal of Psychiatry, 164: 35–43.

Mullen, P.E. and Pathé, M. (1994a) 'The pathological extensions of love', British Journal of Psychiatry, 165: 614–23.

Mullen, P.E. and Pathé, M. (1994b) 'Stalking and the pathologies of love', Australian and New Zealand Journal of Psychiatry, 28: 469–77.

Mullen, P.E., Pathé, M., Purcell, R. (2000) Stalkers and Their Victims. Cambridge: Cambridge University Press.

Munro, A. (1999) Delusional Disorder: Paranoia and Related Illnesses. Cambridge: Cambridge University Press.

Munro, A., Obrien, J.V. and Ross, D. (1985) 'Two cases of "pure" or "primary" erotoma-nia successfully treated with pimozide', Canadian Journal of Psychiatry, 30: 619–21.

Northrop, F.S.C. (1960) 'The comparative philosophy of comparative law', Cornell Law Quarterly, 45: 617–58.

Odegaard, J. (1968) 'Interaksjonen mellom partnerne ved de patologiske sjalusireak-sjoner', Nordisk Psykiatrisk Tidsskrift, 22: 314–19.

Pang, A., Ungvari, G., Lum, F., Lai, K., Leung, C. (1996) 'Querulous paranoia in Chinese patients: a cultural paradox', Australian and New Zealand Journal of Psychiatry, 30: 463–6.

Pines, A.M. (1992) Romantic Jealousy: Understanding and Conquering the Shadow of Love. New York: St. Martin's Press.

Poole, S. (2000) The Politics of Regicide in England, 1760–1850: Troublesome Subjects. Manchester and New York: Manchester University Press.

Post, F. (1982) 'Paranoid disorders', in J.K. Wing and L. Wing (eds), Psychoses of Uncertain Aetiology. Cambridge: Cambridge University Press, pp. 22–7.

Raskin, D.E. and Sullivan, K.E. (1974) 'Erotomania', American Journal of Psychiatry, 131: 1033–5.

Ray, I. (1839) Medical Jurisprudence of Insanity. Boston: Charles C. Little and J. Brown.

Refsum, H.E. (1983) 'Paranoiac psychoses: a follow up', Neuropsychobiology, 10: 75–82.

Retterstøl, N. (1967) 'Jealousy – paranoic psychosis', *Acta Psychiatrica Scandinavica*, 34: 75–107.

Retterstøl, N. and Opjordsmoen, S. (1991) 'Erotomania erotic self reference psychosis in old maids: a long term follow up', *Psychopathology*, 24: 388–97.

Rounsaville, B.J. (1978) 'Theories in marital violence: evidence from a study of battered women', *Victimology*, 3: 11–21

Rowlands, M.W.D. (1988) 'Psychiatric and legal aspects of persistent litigation', *British Journal of Psychiatry*, 153: 317–23.

Rudden, M., Sweeney, J. and Frances, A. (1983) 'A comparison of delusional disorders in women and men', *American Journal of Psychiatry*, 140: 1575–8.

Rudden, M., Sweeney, J. and Frances, A. (1990) 'Diagnosis and clinical course of erotomanic and other delusional patients', *American Journal of Psychiatry*, 147: 625–8.

Scheler, M. (1912) *The Nature of Sympathy*, trans. P. Heath (1954). London: Routledge & Kegan Paul.

Schneider, K. (1958) *Psychopathic Personalities*, 9th edn, trans. M.W. Hamilton. London: Cassell.

Scruton, R. (1986) *Sexual Desire: A Philosophical Investigation*. London: Weidenfeld & Nicholson.

Seeman, M.V. (1978) 'Delusional loving', *Archives of General Psychiatry*, 35: 1265–7.

Segal, J. (1989) 'Erotomania revisited: from Kraepelin to DSM-III-R', *American Journal of Psychiatry*, 146: 1261–6.

Shepherd, M. (1961) 'Morbid jealousy: some clinical and social aspects of a psychiatric symptom', *Journal of Mental Science*, 107: 607–753.

Signer, S.F. (1991) 'De Clérambault's concept of erotomania and its place in his thought', *History of Psychiatry*, 2: 409–17.

Signer, S.F. and Cummings, J.L. (1987) 'De Clérambault's syndrome in organic affective disorder', *British Journal of Psychiatry*, 151: 404–7.

Singer, I. (1966) *The Nature of Love*. Vol. 1. Plato to Luther. New York: Random House.

Singer, I. (1987) *The Nature of Love*. Vol. 2. Courtly and Romantic. Chicago: University of Chicago Press.

Smith, J. C. and Weisstub, D. M. (1983) *The Western Idea of Law*. London: Butterworth.

Solomon, R.C. (1976) *The Passions*. New York: Anchor Press.

Solomon, R.C. (1980) 'Emotions and choice', in A.O. Rorty (ed.), *Explaining Emotions*. California: University of California Press.

Stalstrom, O.H. (1980) 'Querulous paranoia: diagnosis and dissent', *Australian and New Zealand Journal of Psychiatry*, 14: 145–50.

Stein, D.J., Hollander, E. and Josephson, S. C. (1994) 'Serotonin update blockers for the treatment of obsessional jealousy', *Journal of Clinical Psychiatry*, 55: 30–3.

Stone, A.A. (1984) *Law, Psychiatry and Morality*. Washington, DC: American Psychiatric Press.

Taylor, P., Mahendra, B. and Gunn, J. (1983) 'Erotomania in males', *Psychological Medicine*, 13: 645–50.

Ungvari, G. (1995) 'Delusional disorder, litigious type', *Clinical Gerontologist*, 16: 271–3.

Van der Heydt, A. (1952) *Querulatoische Entwicklungen*. Marhold: Halle a. S.

West, D.J. (1968) 'A note on murders in Manhattan', *Medicine, Science and the Law*, 8: 249–55.

White, G.L. and Mullen, P.E. (1989) *Jealousy: Theory Research and Clinical Strategies*. New York: Guilford Press.

Whitehurst, R.N. (1971) 'Violently jealous husband', *Sexual Behaviour*, 1: 32–47.

Winokur, G. (1977) 'Delusional disorder (paranoia)', *Comprehensive Psychiatry*, 186: 511–21.

Wolfgang, M.E. (1958) *Patterns in Criminal Homicide*. Philadelphia: University of Pennsylvania Press

Zeldin, T. (1977) *France 1848–1945*, Vol. 2. London: Oxford University Press.

Glossary

actus rea
Derived from the principle stated by Edward Coke: *actus non facit reum nisi mens sit re*. This means that the act (*actus rea*) itself does not make a person guilty unless their mind is also guilty (*mens rea*).

Affect (affective)
Affect is a term used to describe a subject's externally displayed mood. Affective disorders are disorders of mood.

Anger management
Based upon cognitive behavioural principles, anger management is an intervention which aims to treat the underlying thoughts which cause anger or offer skills or alternative thoughts in order to reduce its expression.

Antisocial behaviour order (ASBO)
Antisocial behaviour orders were introduced by the Crime and Disorder Act 1998. Antisocial behaviour is defined as acting 'in a manner that caused or was likely to cause harassment, alarm or distress to one or more persons not of the same household as himself'. The breach of an ASBO is a criminal offence.

Antisocial personality disorder
A recognised disorder of personality which is characterised by a person's pervasive disregard for the law and the rights of others. Not to be confused with psychopathy.

Approved mental health professional (AMHP)
A new role to replace that of the 'approved social worker' (ASW). The ASW role will be extended to other mental health professions including nurses, chartered psychologists and occupational therapists. The AMHP's function will be the same as the role of the ASW under the 1983 Mental Health Act; however, they will be required to fulfil those additional functions relating to supervised community treatment (SCT).

Approved social worker
A qualified social worker who has undergone additional training and been approved by the local authority to carry out various designated functions within the Mental Health Act. An approved social worker has a role in mental health assessments undertaken jointly with medical professionals, which look at whether compulsory admission to hospital is necessary.

Assessment, Care in Custody and Teamwork (ACCT)
A process adopted by the Prison Service to help identify and care for prisoners at risk of suicide or self-harm which the majority of the Prison Service estate is now running. ACCT is the replacement for the old F2052SH system and is designed to be more flexible. ACCT aims to encourage staff and prisoners to work together to determine care plans.

Attention deficit hyperactivity disorder (ADHD)
One of the most common mental disorders that develop in children. Children with ADHD have impaired functioning in multiple settings, including the home and school, and in relationships with peers. If untreated, the disorder can have long-term adverse effects into adolescence and adulthood. The main symptoms are impulsiveness, hyperactivity and inattention.

Autism
Autism is a life-long developmental disability that affects the way a person communicates and relates to people around them. Symptoms include restricted interests and repetitive behaviour.

Automatism
A defence to a crime can be made if it was committed involuntarily. Where the involuntary act is beyond the control of the individual's mind, the term 'automatism' is applied.

Borderline personality disorder
A recognised disorder of personality which is characterised by pervasive instability in moods, interpersonal relationships, self-image and behaviour. This instability often disrupts family and work life, long-term planning and the individual's sense of self-identity.

Breach
Not conforming to the requirements of a criminal court order. Once a person has 'breached' an order, breach proceedings will be initiated and the person can be taken back to court or referred to the Parole Board. A 'breach' can result in a review of the original requirements of a criminal court order and resentencing or a return to prison.

Care Programme Approach
The CPA is a process which was introduced in England in 1990 to provide a framework for the effective care of mental health for people with severe mental health problems. It has four main elements: a systematic assessment of health and social needs; the care plan identifying health and social care required from providers; the appointment of a key worker (now care coordinator) as close contact to the service user and coordinator and monitor of care; and a regular review of the care plan.

Care Services Improvement Partnership
Launched in April 2005, CSIP took over the role of the NHS Modernisation Agency. CSIP's main objectives are to provide support for the improvement of services to achieve better outcomes for people; for people to live more independently by promoting more choice, control and equality; for community-based action to improve health and well-being and for system reform.

Cognitive-behavioural therapy
Cognitive-behavioural therapy (CBT) is a 'brief' psychological treatment usually taking no more than 20 sessions. It is a combination of cognitive therapy, which aims to modify or eliminate maladaptive thoughts and beliefs, and behavioural therapy, which aims to change or modify negative or maladaptive behaviours (e.g. avoidance and escape).

Community rehabilitation order
Previously known as a probation order, a community rehabilitation order specifies the conditions which an offender must abide by while in the community.

Community treatment order
Part of the revised Mental Health Act 2007 which received Royal Assent in July 2007. Community treatment orders have been established which aim to ensure that a patient continues to accept treatment while in the community. Should the patient not comply with treatment in the community then he/she can be recalled to hospital for such treatment.

Comorbid
Pertaining to two or more disorders which occur simultaneously.

Conduct disorder
A pattern of repetitive behaviour in children where the rights of others or the social norms are violated and in which the basic rights of others or major age-appropriate societal norms or rules are violated.

Court diversion scheme
The redirection of those deemed to be suffering from a mental disorder out of the immediate criminal justice system in order for mental health assessments to occur and to make representation to the police or courts on the most appropriate means of disposing of the case based on their mental health needs.

Dangerous and severe personality disorder (DSPD)
An assessment and treatment programme for individuals who satisfy three requirements: the individual has a severe disorder of personality; the individual presents a significant risk of causing serious physical or psychological harm from which the victim would find it difficult or impossible to recover; and the risk of offending is functionally linked to the personality disorder. Operational in England and Wales.

Delusion
A common symptom of psychosis, characterised by a belief system which is fixed (unamenable to reasoning) and false. An example is a delusion of persecution.

Dialectical behaviour therapy
A group-based psychological approach for the treatment of individuals with borderline personality disorder. It is based on a number of cognitive behavioural techniques but focuses on self-harming behaviours in particular.

Diagnostic and Statistical Manual of Mental Disorder (DSM)
A handbook published by the American Psychiatric Association which lists all the recognised American mental health disorders and the criteria for diagnoses.

Diminished responsibility
A legal doctrine that absolves an accused person of the liability for a criminal act if that person suffers from such abnormality of mind as to substantially impair his/her responsibility in committing the criminal act.

Director of Public Prosecutions (DPP)
The Director of Public Prosecutions is the head of the Crown Prosecution Service and is responsible for the conduct of all criminal proceedings.

Drug rehabilitation requirement
A sentence for problem drug users aged over 16. The requirement lasts between six months and three years and aims to: help offenders produce a relapse prevention plan;

help offenders understand the links between drug use and offending and how drugs affect their health; and help offenders identify realistic ways of changing their lives.

Epidemiology

Epidemiology is the study of factors affecting the health and illness of populations. It serves as the foundation of interventions made in the interest of public health and preventive medicine. The work of communicable and non-communicable disease epidemiologists ranges from outbreak investigation, to study design, data collection and analysis including the development of statistical models to test hypotheses.

European Convention on Human Rights (ECHR)

Rights which are guaranteed to protect fundamental freedoms. An individual can take a state party to the European Court of Human Rights if they believe their human rights have been violated. The Court has the power to award damages and the decisions of the Court are legally binding. The rights include: the right to life; the right to freedom from torture, inhumane and degrading treatment; the right to freedom from forced labour; the right to liberty; the right to a fair trial; the right not to receive retrospective penalties; the right to privacy; the right to freedom of conscience; the right of freedom of expression; the right of freedom of assembly; the right to marriage and family; and the right to freedom from discrimination.

Extended sentence for public protection (EPP)

Can be given to dangerous offenders convicted of sexual or violent offences that carry a maximum penalty of at least two but less than ten years' imprisonment. The sentence consists of a custodial period of at least 12 months and an extended licence period of up to eight years.

Forensic

Relates to the law, courts or legal process.

Forensic mental health

Specialism of mental health that involves the assessment, treatment and care of those who are both mentally disordered and whose behaviour has led, or could lead, to offending.

Forensic mental health nursing

Mental health nursing which takes place within all the areas of forensic mental health.

Forensic occupational therapy

Occupational therapy which takes place within all the areas of forensic mental health.

Forensic psychiatry

Branch of medicine which specialises in all aspects of forensic mental health.

Forensic psychology

Branch of psychology which specialises in all aspects of forensic mental health.

Forensic social work

Social work which takes place within all the areas of forensic mental health.

Guardianship order

Guardianship orders can be applied by a court to a person over the age of 16 years who is suffering from a mental disorder (as defined by the Mental Health Act) and requires 'guardianship' in the interests of the welfare of that person or for the protection of others. Guardianship can be applied initially for six months and is then renewable for a further six months and then for a year at a time.

Hallucination
Hallucinations are abnormal sensory perceptions that occur while a person is usually awake and conscious and are unrelated to outside events. An example is an auditory hallucination whereby a person can hear 'voices' talking about them or to them (auditory hallucination).

Her Majesty's Chief Inspector of Prisons (HMCIP)
Her Majesty's Inspectorate of Prisons for England and Wales (HMIP) is an independent inspectorate which reports on conditions for and treatment of those in prison, young offender institutions and immigration removal centres. HM Chief Inspector of Prisons is responsible for the inspectorate and is a five-year post.

High-secure hospital
There are four high-secure hospitals in the UK: the State hospital in Scotland and Broadmoor, Rampton and Ashworth Hospitals in England. A part of the NHS, high secure hospitals provide care, treatment and security for patients who pose a serious threat to others if living in the community. Most patients have a psychotic disorder (many have a comorbid personality disorder), and have been convicted (or found unfit to plead) of serious crimes.

Home Affairs Committee
The Committee is charged with examining the expenditure, policy and administration of the Home Office and its associated public bodies, and the administration and expenditure of the Attorney General's Office, the Treasury Solicitor's Department, the Crown Prosecution Service and the Serious Fraud Office.

Home detention curfew
Has been in force since 1999 and applies to prisoners who are serving sentences of between three months and under four years. It allows prisoners to live outside of prison providing they do not breach the rules of their curfew. Breach of the conditions can lead to a return to prison.

Home Office
The Home Office is the government department responsible for leading the national effort to protect the public from terrorism, crime and antisocial behaviour.

Imprisonment for public protection (IPP)
This indeterminate sentence applies to offenders who are convicted of a serious offence (that is a specified sexual or violent offence carrying a maximum penalty of ten years' imprisonment or more) and who are considered by the court to pose a significant risk of serious harm to members of the public.

Index offence
The current offence for which a person is detained in hospital or prison.

Insane
Historical term no longer in use meaning mentally ill.

Intellectual disability
Similar to the term learning disability (previously terms included 'mental retardation' or 'mental handicap'), intellectual disability is a significantly reduced ability to understand new or complex information or to learn new skills which started before adulthood, and is not the same as mental illness.

Intelligence quotient (IQ)
A score derived from one of a range of standardised tests designed to measure intelligence. The normal score is 100 but ranges from between 90 and 110 are considered normal.

International Classification of Diseases (ICD)
Similar to the DSM, the ICD was developed by the World Health Organisation and is used to classify diseases and other health problems recorded on many types of health (including mental health) and vital records including death certificates and hospital records.

Impulsivity
Acting or speaking too quickly (upon impulse) without first thinking of the consequences. Impulsivity can be subtyped into cognitive and motor impulsivity and non-planning.

Learning disability
A state of arrested or incomplete development of the mind which includes significant impairment of intelligence and social functioning.

Low-secure psychiatric care
Mental health units which are usually locked and geared towards the client group who require long lengths of stay, usually in excess of six months, many of whom will require help and support for several years. A number of patients will have been admitted via the courts, often under a section of the Mental Health Act with restrictions, although it is deemed they do not need the higher levels of security offered in medium- or high-secure units.

Manic depression
Correctly termed 'bipolar disorder', characterised by mood swings far beyond what most people experience in their lives. These can be (1) low, with feelings of intense depression and despair; (2) high (manic), with feelings of elation and excited behaviour; (3) mixed, where the person has both low and high episodes.

Medium Secure Unit (MSU)
Previously known as Regional Secure Units, MSUs take patients who cannot be managed safely in local hospitals and also take patients from prisons and high-secure hospitals. MSUs are intended as intensive rehabilitation units and generally therefore restrict admissions to patients who would not require a length of stay of more than 18–24 months.

mens rea
Derived from the principle stated by Edward Coke: *actus non facit reum nisi mens sit re.* This means that the act (*actus rea*) itself does not make a person guilty unless their mind is also guilty (*mens rea*).

Mentally disordered offender (MDO)

A person who is both mentally disordered and who has offended which is usually but not always as a result of the mental disorder.

Mental Health Act

Legislation which covers the care and protection of people who are mentally ill.

Mental Health Act Commission (MHAC)

Established in 1983 and consisting of over 100 members (Commissioners – including laypersons, lawyers, doctors, nurses, social workers and psychologists), the MHAC provides a safeguard for people who are detained in hospital under the powers of the Mental Health Act 1983. The MHAC is a monitoring body rather than an inspectorate or regulator. Its concern is primarily the legality of detention and the protection of individuals' human rights.

Mental Health Review Tribunal (MHRT)

The Mental Health Review Tribunal has the responsibility of hearing applications or references concerning people detained under the Mental Health Act 1983. The Tribunal members are appointed by the Department of Constitutional Affairs. The panel consists of a lay person and a psychiatrist and a legally qualified chairperson. In cases subjects to restriction orders the chairperson must be a judge.

Ministry of Justice

Created in May 2007 to deliver on the government's objectives of 'protecting the public, reducing re-offending and sense in sentencing'. The Ministry is responsible for the courts, prisons, probation, criminal law and sentencing.

Morbid

Can mean a condition which is related to or caused by disease. Can also mean a preoccupation with an idea or belief (e.g. morbid jealousy).

Multi-agency public protection arrangements (MAPPA)

Multi-agency public protection arrangements are the process in which the police, probation and prison services work together in order to carry out their statutory responsibilities to assess and manage the risk of harm posed by sexual and violent offenders in the community as a 'responsible authority'.

Multidisciplinary team (MDT)

A team, usually comprising a range of health professionals and can include the service user, who are responsible for the overall care and treatment that an individual receives. The MDT will meet regularly to coordinate and plan care and communicate progress to each other and, where appropriate, other parties.

Nacro

Nacro (formerly the National Association for the Care and Resettlement of Offenders) is a charity which focuses on crime reduction. Nacro is the largest voluntary agency working in the fields of crime reduction and offender resettlement in the UK.

National Confidential Inquiry into Homicides and Suicides

The National Confidential Inquiry is a national research project established at the University of Manchester in 1996. The Inquiry collects detailed clinical information on all suicides and homicides that occur under mental health services from England, Wales, Scotland and Northern Ireland and is funded by the National Patient Safety Agency.

National Institute for Clinical Excellence (NICE)
An independent organisation responsible for providing national guidance on the promotion of good health and the prevention and treatment of ill health. NICE produces guidance on public health, health technologies and clinical practice.

National Offender Management Service (NOMS)
The National Offender Management Service was established in 2004. NOMS is the system through which the government commissions and provides correctional services and interventions in order to protect the public and reduce reoffending.

National Patient Safety Agency (NPSA)
A special health authority that was established in July 2001 to coordinate the reporting of patient safety incidents and to learn from these incidents in order to improve patient safety in the NHS.

National Programme on Forensic Mental Health R&D (NPFMHR&D)
A strategic partnership between the Department of Health and the Home Office which provided research funding for forensic mental health academics. The Programme ended in June 2007.

National service framework
National service frameworks are policy documents which set out the longer-term strategic vision for a priority health area by describing national standards and service models for particular clinical specialties and care groups.

NHS Security Management Service
A special health authority which has responsibility for all policy and operational matters related to the management of security delivery within the NHS.

Offender Assessment System (OASys)
A risk assessment system jointly developed by the Prison and Probation Services. OASys was designed to help practitioners assess how likely an offender is to reoffend and the likely seriousness of any offence they might commit.

Order for life-long restriction (OLR)
A sentence introduced in Scotland in June 2006 which aims to ensure the life-long supervision of high-risk violent and sexual offenders.

Paranoia
An unfounded or disproportionate suspicion of others, sometimes becoming delusional.

Paraphilia
A collective term to describe the group of sexual fantasies, urges and behaviours that are considered deviant to societal norms. Some may be illegal (e.g. exhibitionism), whereas others are not (e.g. rubber fetish).

Parole Board
A non-departmental public body established in 1967 to advise the Home Secretary on the early release of prisoners. It has authority to decide applications for parole for those sentenced on or after 1 October 1992 to a determinate sentence of from four to less than 15 years. It also has the power to direct the release of life sentence prisoners (lifers) and those serving sentences for public protection. For other classes of prisoner, the Board makes recommendations to the Secretary of State.

Pathology
A branch of medicine which is concerned with the underlying structures and their functions underpinning a disease, illness or disorder.

Personality disorder
A severe, pervasive and enduring pattern of character, thoughts and behaviours which starts in early adulthood and which deviates markedly from the societal norms which usually leads to distress or impairment.

Police and Criminal Evidence Act 1984
The Act determines the manner and processes with which police and other investigative agencies deal with suspected offenders in respect of their arrest, detention, questioning and the obtaining of samples for forensic examination.

Posttraumatic stress disorder (PTSD)
A recognised mental disorder which occurs after experiencing or witnessing a death or life-threatening event characterised by symptoms of anxiety/arousal, avoidance and re-experiencing of events (e.g. nightmares, flashbacks).

Pre-morbid
A state prior to or preceding the development of a disease, illness or disorder.

Primary care trust
Locality-based statutory body which is responsible for delivering health care and health improvements to the local area as part of the wider National Health Service.

Prison Service Young Offender Institution (YOI)
Secure facilities or 'prisons' that detain 15–20-year-olds who have been either remanded or sentenced to custody by the courts.

Psychopath
Clinically, psychopath is a term commonly used in mental health to describe a person who has no concerns for the feelings of others and a complete disregard for any sense of social obligation. Psychopathy is characterised by lack of empathy and manipulative behaviours. It can be assessed using the Hare Psychopathy Checklist – Revised (PCL-R) or the screening version of this instrument (PCL: SV).

Legally, 'psychopathic disorder' is defined in the Mental Health Act as 'a persistent disorder or disability of mind (whether or not including significant impairment of intelligence) which results in abnormally aggressive or seriously irresponsible conduct on the part of the person concerned'.

Psychopathology
Often used as a descriptive term to describe signs and symptoms indicative of mental illness.

Psychosis
A term which describes a number of mental illnesses which are characterised by a lack of insight, hallucinations and delusions (e.g. schizophrenia, schizo-affective disorder or paranoid delusion disorder).

Randomised controlled trial (RCT)
A randomised controlled trial (RCT) is a scientific procedure most commonly used in testing medicines or psychological interventions. This is considered the most reliable

form of scientific evidence because it eliminates all forms of spurious causality. Subjects are allocated to to treatments at random to ensure that the different treatment groups are 'statistically equivalent'.

Trials are used to establish the efficacy of a treatment and the nature and frequency of side effects. Sometimes, one of the groups will be a 'no treatment group' in order to compare the effects of treatment with what would have happened if nothing was given – the placebo effect.

Recidivism
Refers to the reconviction of those who have previously been sentenced for committing a crime.

Resettlement and Aftercare Provision (Rap)
Covers a range of schemes aimed at young people who are vulnerable to substance misuse, mental health issues or dual diagnosis. Raps provide support to assist them rebuild relationships and find accommodation, employment or education.

Risk assessment
The process of an assessment of a given risk (e.g. violence, self-harm, suicide). This can range from clinical opinion alone to more evidence-based structured clinical judgment.

Royal College of Psychiatrists
The professional and educational body for psychiatrists in the United Kingdom and the Republic of Ireland.

Schizo-affective disorder
A recognised mental disorder characterised by both affective and schizophrenic symptoms within the same episode of illness, usually simultaneously. The boundary between this diagnosis and typical mood (affective) disorders and schizophrenic disorders is blurred.

Schizoid personality disorder
A recognised personality disorder which begins in early adulthood. It is characterised by a pervasive pattern of detachment from social relationships and a restricted range of expression of emotions in interpersonal settings.

Schizophrenia
A severe form of mental illness which usually develops in early adulthood and is characterised by delusions, hallucinations and disorganised thinking which can have a significant impact upon day-to-day functioning.

Secure training centre (STC)
Secure training centres (STCs) are purpose-built centres for child offenders up to the age of 17. STCs differ from Young Offender Institutions as they have higher staff to offender ratios, have fewer offenders and admit children as young as 12. Their focus is on providing education, vocational training and correction.

Sentencing Guidelines Council
The Council was set up under s. 167 of the Criminal Justice Act 2003. It receives reports from the Sentencing Advisory Panel and sets sentencing guidelines for judges and magistrates.

Service user
A person who makes use of mental health services.

Sex Offender Treatment Programme (SOTP)
The Sex Offender Treatment Programme (SOTP) began in 1991 as part of a national strategy for the integrated assessment and treatment of sex offenders. Based upon cognitive-behavioural treatment techniques, the central part of the SOTP is the Core Programme, the primary purpose of which is to increase the offender's motivation to avoid reoffending and to develop the self-management skills necessary to achieve this.

Symptom
A symptom is a sensation or change in health that is expressed by the patient and therefore 'subjective' as it cannot be observed, unlike a 'sign' which is observed by the clinician.

Syndrome
A set of symptoms that a person reports which occur together and indicate the possible presence of a certain illness or disorder (or an increased chance of developing the disease/disorder).

Systematic review
Systematic reviews are a method of undertaking a review of the evidence of an association between a treatment and an outcome or a risk factor for a disease and have superseded narrative reviews which introduce bias through personal preference. Systematic reviews aim to bring the same level of rigour to reviewing research evidence as should be used in producing that research evidence in the first place.

Therapeutic community
Therapeutic communities provide group-based therapeutic treatment. They work upon democratic doctrines where staff and patients work together to determine the community rules.

Threat/control-override (TCO)
Link and Stueve (1994) reported a number of symptoms called 'threat/control-override (TCO) symptoms' that were associated with an increase in violence. The three symptoms were feeling that others wished one harm, that one's mind was dominated by forces beyond one's control and that others' thoughts were being put into one's head. This association has been found in some but not all subsequent studies.

Youth Justice Board for England and Wales (YJB)
The Youth Justice Board (YJB) has been responsible for overseeing the youth justice system for England and Wales since 1998.

Youth Offending Teams (YOTs)
These are multi-agency, local authority-based teams which are made up of representatives from the police, probation, social services, health, education, drugs and alcohol misuse and housing officers. YOTs are responsible for the assessment and management of young offenders as well as the development and delivery of appropriate intervention programmes for individual offenders.

Index

Added to the page number 'f' denotes a figure, 'g' denotes the glossary and 't' denotes a table.

medium-secure CAMHS provision 105
offenders with health needs 105
substance misuse services 106
custody plus 145–6, 199t

D
dangerous and severe personality disorder
    programme *see* DSPD programme
dangerousness 64, 244, 246, 267
    assessing 238, 311
    implications 218, 219
    managing 8
    sentencing provisions 217–18, 291,
        311–13
DAST 367
Data Protection Act (1998) 213
David, Garry 519
DBT (dialectical behaviour therapy)
    390–1, 591g
Decision Chains 455, 458f
'deficit model' 509–10
    see also empathy deficits; intimacy
        deficits; problem-solving deficits
deinstitutionalisation 482
    and people with ID 328, 329–30
Delivering Race Equality in Mental Health
    537
delusional disorder 232–3
delusions 73–4, 591g
    and violence risk assessment 253
    see also persecutory delusions; sexual
        delusions
denial by sexual offenders 453–4
dependency 426
dependent personality disorder 377t, 383,
    386
    and substance abuse 427, 428
depression
    and exercise 534
    and substance abuse 428, 437
depression anxiety, in childhood and
    adolescence 99–100
detention
    convergence between legal frameworks
        of hospital and prison 291–2, 322–3
    length 529
    see also compulsory detention;
        indeterminate detention;
        preventative detention
developmental disabilities, intellectual
    and *see* ID
developmental psychology 110
deviancy

controlling 85
levels 465
deviant sexual arousal 467
deviant sexual scripts pathway 451–2
diagnosis 223, 227–40
    legal issues 237–8
    nature and purpose 228–30
    politics 232–3
    reliability, validity and utility 230–2
    stigmatic and dangerous use 233–6
    see also dual diagnosis
diagnostic manuals for mental disorder
    228
    and aggression problems 369
    legal issues 237–8
    and querulousness 574
    see also ICD
*Diagnostic and Statistical Manual of Mental
    Disorders see* DSM
dialectical behaviour therapy (DBT)
    390–1, 591g
diminished responsibility 48t, 50, 77–8,
    134, 302–6, 425, 503, 591g
Dingwall, Alexander 77
Director of Public Prosecutions (DPP)
    591g
Director of Public Prosecutions' Guidance
    on Charging 292
discharge
    from forensic psychiatric inpatient
        services 201–8
    see also release procedures; supervised
        discharge
disease
    definition 228
    identification of 228–9
'disease entity medical model' 229–30
disorders of passion 482, 555–84
    history 556–7
    pure (primary) and secondary
        (symptomatic) 558–60
distorted cognition pathway 452
diversion from the criminal justice system
    43, 46–7t, 268, 269, 273–88, 295, 322
    admission for assessment 29t, 31t, 224,
        279–80
    admission for treatment 280–83
        treatment in the community following
            283–7
    application for compulsory admission
        of those already inpatients 277–9
    case study 276, 277, 280, 288
    guardianship 287, 288, 318, 592g

interpersonal problem-solving, and ID
335–6
interventions *see* treatment interventions
interview schedules 384–5
intimacy deficits 451
and sexual offenders 468–9
intimate partner violence
alcohol and 425
situational factors 357
see also domestic violence
intoxication
description 426t
and legal defence 425
IPCUs (intensive psychiatric care units)
38
IPP (Imprisonment for Public Protection)
55, 198, 200, 217–18, 219, 238, 311,
312–13, 593g
IPT (Imaginal Provocation Test) 336

J
jealousy 482, 556, 557, 571
and crimes of passion 561–7
cultural construction 561
and domestic violence *see* domestic
violence, and jealousy
feelings evoked by 558
as a motivation for homicide 564
normal range 560, 564
pathologies *see* pathologies of jealousy
journals, specialist 10
'judgement after review' instruments
463–4
justice, pursuit of *see* pursuit of justice
Justice for all 197
juvenile delinquents
cognitive attributional bias 99
interventions 96–7
juvenile homicide 110–11
juvenile psychopathy 101–2
juvenile sexual offenders 111–13
assessment 111
treatment
outcome 112–13
process 111
juveniles and young persons 86, 89–116
adolescence *see* adolescence
autism spectrum disorders and learning
disability 100
and CAMHS *see* CAMHS
custodial places *see* custodial settings for
young people

depression anxiety and PTSD 99–100
early onset psychosis 100–1
needs
cost of unmet 97–8
responding to 103–7
offending 90
oppositional disorders, CDs and ADHD
99
pathways of care and the juvenile justice
system 94–5, 96f
'psychopathic personality' in 101
putting research into practice 97–9
relationship between callous-unemotional traits and CDs 101–2
screening and assessment instruments
in clinical (non-forensic) settings 92-3
in forensic settings *see* forensic assessment for juveniles and young
people
substance misuse 102
treatment and special crimes 110–15

K
Kansas v. Hendricks (1997) 518–19
knives, availability 357
knowledge base xxv, xxvi
constructing 10, 223–6
validity 11
see also research
Kraepelinian/categorical medical modelling 229–30

L
L v. Sweden (1988) 272
'late-starter' mental illness 433
learning disability 273, 594g
learning disabled offenders 80
and guardianship orders 317
'legal diagnoses' 237
legal insanity *see* insanity defence
legal responsibility 131
legal systems
cultural contexts 561–2
and medical diagnosis 237–8
in the UK 20, 21–3, 483, 485
see also courts
legislation 65–6, 224, 244
and querulousness 574–5
and the rights of patients 516–19, 520
on sentencing and release *see* release
procedures, legislation
and sexual offenders 470

in prisoners 182, 183
and sexual offending 446, 450, 452–3,
471
effect on interventions 465
substance-induced 426t, 432
psychotic symptoms 233
induced by drugs 432
and violent behaviour 412–15, 416t
psychotropic medications 177, 465
PTSD 237–8, 354, 597g
in childhood and adolescence 100
public asylums 69, 70, 71
public protection 269, 351
tension between treatment and 7–9, 381
see also MAPPA
public protection sentences 198, 200, 224,
291
see also Extended Sentence for Public
Protection (EPP); Imprisonment for
Public Protection (IPP)
punishment and rehabilitation orders 145
pure disorders of passion 559–60
pure erotomanias 572–3
'pure paedophiles' 452
pursuit of justice 557
normal limits 560
see also querulousness

Q
querulousness 555, 557, 574–83
case study 577–8, 579–80f
clinical characteristics 576–8
complaining, litigating and petitioning
575–6
criminal behaviour 583
feelings evoked by 558
limits of normality 578, 580–1
nosology 581–2
Questionnaire on Attitudes Consistent
with Sexual Offences (QACSO)
338–9

R
R&D Forensic Mental Health initiative see
National Programme on Forensic
Mental Health R&D
R (Anderson) v. HM Coroner for Inner North
Greater London (2004) 274–5
R (DR) v. Merseycare NHS Trust (2002) 284
R v. A (2005) 317
R v. Ahluwalia (1992) 303–4
R v. Birch (1989) 315, 316
R v. Byrne (1960) 50, 303, 305

R v. Cannons Park Mental Health Tribunal
515–16
R v. Dietschmann (2003) 304–5
R v. Drew (2003) 315
R v. Gardner (2005) 304
R v. Gittens (1984) 304
R v. Hallstrom ex parte W (1986) 281, 283
R v. Hobson 304
R v. Lloyd (1967) 305
R v. Mawditt (2005) 304
R v. Mental Health Review Tribunal for the
South Thames Region ex parte Smith
(1999) 281
R v. RMO Broadmoor Hospital and Others ex
parte Wilkinson (2002) 517
R v. Sullivan 300–1
R v. Vinagre 302–3
R v. Wragg (2006) 304
Rampton 36t, 80, 138, 381
randomised controlled trials (RCTs)
597–8g
RAOs (risk assessment orders) 42
RAP (Resettlement and Aftercare
Provision) 107, 598g
rape 449t
Rapid Risk Assessment for Sex Offender
Recidivism (RRASOR) 333
RCs (responsible clinicians) 270, 285, 324
reactive aggression 356
reactive erotomanias 569–70
recall to prison 198
recidivism 598g
by offenders with ID 329–31, 333, 343–4
and high-security hospitals 37
and personality disorders 382
self-esteem and victim empathy and
471
see also reoffending
Reducing Crime: Changing Lives 146
Reed Report (1994) 81, 525
Reforming the Mental Health Act (1983) 269
regional secure units 81
definition 528
see also medium-secure units
rehabilitative activities, traditional 359
Reid v. Secretary of State for Scotland (1999)
282, 516
release procedures 87–8, 196–219
controversies 208–19
current policy 196–8
from forensic psychiatric inpatient
services 201–8
legislation

Lightning Source UK Ltd.
Milton Keynes UK
UKOW020710230413

209615UK00005B/253/P